THE AFRICAN METHODIST

EPISCOPAL ZION CHURCH,

ORGANIZED - 1796

A BICENTENNIAL COMMEMORATIVE

HISTORY

1972 - 1996

African Methodist Episcopal Zion Church Board of Bishops, October, 1996

L-R Seated: Bishops Joseph Johnson; Samuel Chukakanne Ekemam, Sr., George Washington Carver Walker, Sr.; Cecil Bishop; Milton Alexander Williams, Sr., George Edward Battle, Jr.; and Richard Keith Thompson, Sr.

L-R Standing: Bishops James Clinton Hoggard, Sr., (Ret.); Nathaniel Jarrett; Enoch Benjamin Rochester; Marshall Hayward Strickland; Clarence Carr; Warren Matthew Brown; John Henry Miller, Sr.; (Ret.); Ruben Lee Speaks (Ret.)

Absent: Bishops William Alexander Hilliard (Ret.); Charles Herbert Foggie (Ret.); and Clinton Reuben Coleman, Sr. (Ret., Deceased Dec. 9, 1996)

THE

AFRICAN METHODIST EPISCOPAL ZION

CHURCH, 1972-1996

A BICENTENNIAL COMMEMORATIVE

HISTORY

by

Bishop James Clinton Hoggard

With a Foreword by Bishop Clarence Carr
And an Introduction by Bishop George Washington Carver Walker, Sr.

AFRICAN METHODIST EPISCOPAL ZION CHURCH
Bicentennial Historical Commission
1998

The African Methodist Episcopal Zion Church, 1972-1996: A Bicentennial Commemorative History

A. M. E. Zion Publishing House
1998

For information write A. M. E. Zion Publishing House
P. O. Box 30714, Charlotte, North Carolina 28230

Library of Congress Cataloging pending as of date of publication.

ISBN 0-966762-0-8 : $22.95

African Methodist Episcopal Zion Church

African Methodist Episcopal Zion Church

African Methodist Episcopal Zion Church

The Logo of the A. M. E. Zion Church

On August 2, 1984, at the 42nd General Conference held in St. Louis, Missouri, the A. M. E. Zion Church adopted an official denominational logo. The Rev. Dr. Percy Smith, Jr., formerly pastor of First A. M. E. Zion Church, San Francisco, and First A. M. E. Zion Church, San Jose, California, and currently a pastor in Salisbury, North Carolina in the Western North Carolina Conference, created the logo's design and interpretation

The Triangle: Representing the Godhead in this equilateral triangle is the Father, Son, and the Holy Spirit, or the Holy Trinity.

The Ecclesiastical Color:The colors of the logo suggest the mood of a church festival. Within recent years, the interpretation of black has changed to encompass a texture of the whole life. All colors blending and melting together signify joy, sadness, struggle, faith, hope, and, finally, eternal life.

V: The widely used symbol for victory represents a church born victoriously under the leadership of James Varick, our first Bishop. V also represents Varick.

LATIN CROSS: One of the most accepted symbols of Christianity, this plain and empty cross alerts the world to the reality that "He is not here, He is risen victoriously."

RED CROSS: It symbolizes power, love, glory,, and honor and is associated with our Lord's passion and suffering and the Christian's zeal.

A-AFRICAN: This refers to our African background. It is in black and suggests that Africa is the cradle of civilization from whence came all races and colors.

M-METHODIST: This refers to the doctrine about God and Christ to which we adhere. It is in green, the universal color of growth, progress, and hope.

E-EPISCOPAL: This means that we are a church overseen by Church Fathers called Bishops. Purple, so often worn by our Episcopate, denotes kingly authority in Godly judgment.

Z-ZION: God's Holy Hill stands for our branch of Methodism, which is a separate entity from the A. M. E., C. M. E., and M. E. Churches. The color blue is symbolic of heaven and sincerity.

African Methodist Episcopal Zion Church
The Forward

MODERN man is often the victim of what Sîren Kierkegåård refers to as "historical forgetfulness," a state of mind that entails a loss of history and contributes to a loss of identity. It is therefore imperative that we document and record past and present events, those fleeting moments in the life of our people and in the development of our institutions. Our historical perspective enhances our divine perspective. History is truly "His Story." It is a demonstrative record of a God who reveals himself by acting in human history.

Too often our history is fragmented or completely lost. Too often we allow others to interpret our history for us without our own input. This book documents our legacy, our contribution, and the achievements of those who made our denomination and all of its departments and institutions what they are today. We want future generations to love, respect, and appreciate that legacy.

With this is mind, the Board of Bishops of the A. M. E. Zion Church sought out one from among us in the personage of Bishop J. Clinton Hoggard, who, although retired, is yet active and steeped in the rich tradition of our beloved Zion. Author and compiler of this segment of our illustrious faith journey, Bishop Hoggard is a student of history with a keen intellect and insightful knowledge of the people and events that have brought us through to the twenty-first century.

This volume, which is in recognition of the Bicentennial Celebration of our African Methodist Episcopal Zion Church, held in October, 1996, in New York City, is our offering, our contribution to the next generation. It is our prayer that future generations will learn from history and chart an even greater future for our Zion.

Bishop Clarence Carr
Chair, Bicentennial Historical Commission Publication Committee

African Methodist Episcopal Zion Church

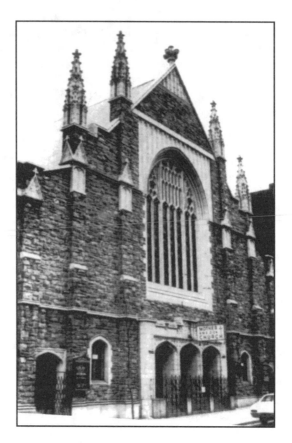

MOTHER ZION
AFRICAN METHODIST EPISCOPAL ZION CHURCH
140-6 WEST 137TH STREET
NEW YORK, NEW YORK 10030
Dr. Alvin T. Durant, Pastor
Officers & Members

On this our Bicentennial Celebration, we are thankful for God's steadfast blessings, grace and mercy. As we move rapidly toward the 21st Century, may the Lord grant us His spirit to empower us to do greater works for the kingdom.

African Methodist Episcopal Zion Church

Preface

THE *African Methodist Episcopal Zion Church, 1972-1996*: A Bicentennial Commemorative History is the fulfillment of a commission from the Board of Bishops of the African Methodist Episcopal Zion Church in February, 1995, to write a history in commemoration of the 200th Anniversary of the founding of Mother Zion African Methodist Episcopal Zion Church in October, 1796, in New York City . Mother Zion A. M. E. Zion Church, the first congregation from which the African Methodist Episcopal Zion Denomination in America grew, was incorporated on 9 March 1801, in New York City, N.Y. The first annual conference of the denomination was organized in 1821, and the first General Conference was held in 1822.

This volume continues the history of the church and builds on the works of its earlier historians: Christopher Rush, *The Rise and Progress of the African Methodist Episcopal [Zion] Church in America* (1843); John J. Moore, *History of the A. M. E. Zion Church in America* (1884); James W. Hood, *One Hundred Years of the African Methodist Episcopal Zion Church* (1895); David Henry Bradley, Sr., *A History of the A. M. E. Zion Church, 2 vols.* (1956 and 1971); and particularly William J. Walls, *The African Methodist Episcopal Zion Church: The Reality of the Black Church* (1974). As its immediate historical predecessor, Walls's volume was the chief reference for this historical account, which takes up the history of the church in 1972 where Walls's history ends.

The African Methodist Episcopal Zion Church, 1972-1996: A Bicentennial Commemorative History is divided into three parts. Part I: "Bicentennial Observances" provides accounts of the organized activities to commemorate the Bicentennial of the A. M. E. Zion Church at the general and episcopal district levels. The Bicentennial Celebration in New York City included an Ecumenical Worship Service, on October 10, 1996; an Exhibit on the A. M. E. Zion Church at the Schomburg Library and Research Center, a Freedom Heritage Gala Dinner, at the New York Hilton and Towers Hotel, followed by a late night Gospel Music Festival, on October 11, 1996; a Youth and Young Adult Oratorical Event at Mother A. M. E. Zion Church and a Bicentennial Mass Choir Concert at the Jacob Javitz Center, on Saturday, October 12, 1996. On Sunday, October13, 1996, the final day of the celebration, there was a Communion Worship Service at Mother Zion A. M. E. Zion Church..

During the 45th Quadrennial General Conference held in Washington, D. C., in July, 1996, under the supervision of Bishop and Mrs. Milton Alexander Williams and the Rev. John Cherry, pastor of Full Gospel A. M. E. Zion Church, Temple Hills, Maryland, the Fifth Episcopal District organized a Gala Evening, "Bishop James Varick

African Methodist Episcopal Zion Church

Quadrennial Salute to Service Celebrating From Africa to America'". This book contains accounts of bicentennial observances during the General Conference in Washington, D. C. and the bicentennial celebrations organized by each of the twelve episcopal districts. The latter reports are based on materials sent from the episcopal districts to the Bicentennial Historical Commission. Although the accounts of the episcopal district celebrations recorded here are not comprehensive, they do provide the reader with a spectrum of the activities organized throughout the A. M. E. Zion Church to mark this historical milestone. The reader is provided with reports of the manifold activities organized to commemorate the Bicentennial of the A. M. E. Zion Church.

With the growth and spread of Zion Methodism, an administrative structure has undergirded the development of the church. Part II: "The General Officers and Departments of the A. M. E. Zion Church" discusses administrative heads, their contributions, and ongoing and new developments in the departments of the A. M. E. Zion Church since the early 1970s. This section provides an overall survey of Records and Statistics; Finance; the A. M. E. Zion Publishing House; the Star of Zion; the A. M. E. Zion Quarterly Review and the Historical Society; Overseas Missions and the *Missionary Seer*; Brotherhood Pensions and Ministerial Relief; Christian Education; Church School Literature; Church Extension and Home Missions; Evangelism; Public Affairs and Convention Manager; and Health and Social Concerns. The Woman's Home and Overseas Missionary Society; the Commission on Pan-Methodist Cooperation; the Bicentennial Commission, the Connectional Lay Council, the Judicial Council; the Connectional Trustees; and Ecumenical Memberships of the A. M. E. Zion Church round off this section.

Part III: "The Bishops of the A. M. E. Zion Church" provides the reader with a profile and picture of each of the bishops of the A. M. E. Zion Church since its inception to the present day—a total of ninety-one bishops. This section affords the reader an opportunity to learn about the men who have provided overall spiritual and episcopal direction in the development of Zion Methodism. Through their episcopal leadership and supervision and with the support of the followers of the faith, the A. M. E. Zion Church has spread to all corners of the world.

Acknowledgments

An undertaking of this nature requires extensive cooperation. I am grateful to the Bicentennial Historical Commission who charged me with writing a volume covering the historic milestone of the Bicentennial of the A. M. E. Zion Church. Led by Bishop

African Methodist Episcopal Zion Church

Clarence Carr, chairperson of the Bicentennial Historical Commission Publication, the members of the commission, including Bishop George W. C. Walker, the general chairman, and all the members of the Board of Bishops, have taken time from their very busy schedules to visit the office while the work was underway and have offered valuable suggestions for shaping the content of the book and for its improvement after reading the draft manuscript. Bishop George E. Battle, Jr., has been a tower of strength in providing the episcopal stimulus for the budget related to this production. For this, I am eternally grateful.

My fellow bishops have responded to my requests for biographical data and accounts of episcopal bicentennial activities. The current general officers of the church who are responsible for the various departments that give flesh to the bones of the A. M. E. Zion Church have been prompt in responding to our request for information concerning the operation of their departments. Rev. Seth Moulton, associate, Dept. Of Ovearseas Missions, A. M. E. Zion Church; Mrs Abna Aggrey Lancaster, Salisbury, North Carolina (now of sainted memory); Bishop Alfred G. Dunston, Jr., (also of sainted memory); Dr. Armayne Dunston and the private library of Bishop Dunston were all helpful to me in my endeavor.

My research efforts to locate biographical information on episcopal leaders and sundry general information pertaining to the African Methodist Episcopal Zion Church have been facilitated by many people. They include members of the Board of Bishops of the A. M. E. Zion Church; Dr. Burnett Joiner, president of Livingstone College, Salisbury, North Carolina; the Rev. Mrs. Willie Aldrich, curator of Heritage Hall, Livingstone College; and Dean Albert J. D. Aymer and the staff of Hood Theological Seminary, Salisbury, North Carolina. Words of gratitude are due Dr. Howard Dodson, and Ms. Roberta Yancy, director and assistant director for public affairs and development, the Schomburg Center for Research in Black Culture, New York Public Library, for their assistance in mounting the exhibit at the Schomburg Center from 11 October to 31 December 1996 that publicized the Bicentennial of the African Methodist Episcopal Zion Church; Dr. Michael Winston, former vice president for academic affairs, Howard University, and currently president, Alfred Harcourt Foundation; Dr. Walter J. Leonard, formerly president, Fisk University and executive assistant to the president, Harvard University; the Howard University School of Divinity, of which Dr. Clarence Geno Newsome is dean, for making office space available to the Bicentennial Historical Commission; Dr. Henry Ferry, associate dean for academic affairs, Mrs. Carrie Hackney, librarian of the Howard University School of Divinity Library, Mr. Norman Bush and Mr. Eugene Waters, administrative staff of the library, Ms. Gail

African Methodist Episcopal Zion Church

Oliver, Ms. Cassandra Newsome, and Ms. Gail Reivas, administrative staff of the Divinity School; Mr. Martell Perry and Mrs. Kim Leathers, director and associate director, respectively, of Information and Sciences Clearinghouse; and Dr. Wardell Payne, formerly director, Research Center on African American Religious Bodies; and the Howard University Spingarn-Moorland Research Library staff led by its director, Dr. Thomas Battle. They have been of inestimable help in providing references and verifying information.

My wife, the late Eva Stanton Hoggard, provided the project with helpful material from her own records and helped to sustain me during this project as she had done throughout her lifetime in service to our family and the A. M. E. Zion Church. Our sons, James (Jay) Clinton Hoggard, Jr., and the Rev. Dr. Paul Stanton Hoggard, have given me support and encouragement throughout this project. Appreciation is due the Rev. Leon Watts, III, pastor of Jackson Memorial A. M. E. Zion Church, Hempstead, Long Island, N. Y., for his time, skill, and suggestions concerning the content and style of this volume. Dr. Lionel Barrow, Ms. June Slade Collins, and Ms. Ruby M. Essien have provided valuable editorial and secretarial assistance during the various stages of this undertaking. I am grateful for their contributions. Finally, I take full responsibility as its author for whatever strengths or limitations this volume may possess. I offer it to the faithful members of the A. M. E. Zion Church and to the general public in a spirit of thanksgiving and praise for what has been wrought by one denomination of the Black Church in its commitment to spread the universal teachings of Christianity during the last two hundred years—a period that gravely tested the mettle and faith of all black people in America. It is with utmost thanksgiving that we can look back with pride for what we have overcome and can look forward with hope and faith based on our past achievements and God's continuous blessings through Christ, the Great Head of the Church.

JAMES CLINTON HOGGARD
January, 1998

African Methodist Episcopal Zion Church

In Memoriam

Eva Stanton Hoggard

February 20, 1923-
February 12, 1997

With thanksgiving to God for her comfort,
inspiration and companionship, with love for God,
our family and the A. M. E. Zion Church, this work
is dedicated to the memory of my beloved wife, Eva.

May this book be an inspiration to people wanting
to learn about the birth, growth, and influence of
a branch of the Christian Church, namely, our
beloved African Methodist Episcopal Zion
Denomination.

INTRODUCTION

by

George Washington Carver Walker, Sr.
Chairperson, Bicentennial Commission
A. M. E. Zion Church, February, 1996-October, 1996

"Hallow the past—Consecrate the present—have
Faith in the future—and above all—Protect the Heritage."
(Walls, p. 552)

THE Bicentennial of the African Methodist Episcopal Zion Church in October, 1996 afforded once again, as had the Centennial and Sesquicentennial celebrations in 1896 and 1946, respectively, an auspicious occasion for the denomination to take stock of its historical journey and to project its future path. Of the many projects planned by the church to celebrate the 200th year of the A. M. E. Zion Church, the publication of *The African Methodist Episcopal Zion Church, 1972-1996: A Commemorative History*, written and compiled by Bishop James Clinton Hoggard, will prove of lasting value. Continuing the history of the church from *The African Methodist Episcopal Zion Church: The Reality of the Black Church*, by Bishop William Walls, the present volume records the various bicentennial celebrations of the episcopal districts and the national A. M. E. Zion Church, discusses development of the various departments of the A. M. E. Zion Church since 1972, and provides a profile of each bishop of the church since its establishment.

The African Methodist Episcopal Zion Church, 1972-1996: A Commemorative History provides detailed accounts of the panoply of activities that the membership devised to celebrate the bicentennial of the church. These various activities attest to the commitment to and pride in the A. M. E. Zion Church and its history felt by the members of the church. The accounts of the activities show that the membership engaged themselves joyfully and creatively in the episcopal district and in the national celebrations of this historic milestone in the development of the A. M. E. Zion Church. During 1996, the pre-bicentennial celebrations in the episcopal districts included a wide array of activities. There were compilations in journals and notebooks of the history of local

1

African Methodist Episcopal Zion Church

churches; dramatic presentations and pageants highlighting the founding and development of the A. M. E. Zion Church; talent shows, evangelical crusades, special worship
services; lunch and dinner banquets; appreciation banquets to honor outstanding service to the church by local church members; parades; beauty queen contests; and the
publication of souvenir journals. The Mid-Atlantic II Episcopal District, which hosted
the 45th General Conference in Washington, D. C. in July, 1996, presented a bicentennial musical gala, "The James Varick Quadrennial Salute to Service: Celebrating
From Africa to America'." The musical gala reflected the historical African American
experience in America. The program also included a James Varick Freedom Medal
Presentation to church members who had performed outstanding service to the A. M.
E. Zion Church. The A. M. E. Zion Church national bicentennial celebration comprised
an international reception; a worship service at Mother Zion A. M. E. Zion Church; a
banquet with special guest speakers; a special gospel choir service; an exhibition at the
Schomburg Center for Research in Black Culture, New York, N.Y., that highlighted the
development of the church; and a closing worship service. The quadrennial and national bicentennial celebrations were attended by thousands of A. M. E. Zion Church members and co-religious participants. Many of the events were recorded, photographed,
and filmed for posterity, some of which are displayed in the present volume. They provide a treasure trove for future generations to re-create their heritage.

The African Methodist Episcopal Zion Church, 1972-1996: A Commemorative
History reflects the steady course the church has followed over the years, with careful
amendments and changes made from time to time to improve the outcome of its efforts.
One of the major organizational changes effected during this period has been the implementation in 1996 of permanent and contiguous episcopal districts. The twelve episcopal districts have each been charged with the responsibility to purchase an episcopal
residence within its confines. A few of the official episcopal residences have already
been purchased.. Other important organizational changes were inclusion of the Lay
Connectional Council's report to the General Conference in 1984 and the reaffirmation
and implementation of equal lay representation in the administrative boards of the
church. The decision taken at the 44th General Conference, in Atlanta, Georgia, to separate Home Missions from Brotherhood Pensions and Ministerial Relief and merge it
with Church Extension in one department has also been implemented, and the successful establishment of the A. M. E. Zion Judicial Council as an appellate body in 1988
was yet another important organizational change in the structure of the church since
1972.

The departments of the A. M. E. Zion Church enable the church to function as an

Introduction

institution and to execute the various programs that minister to the spiritual, educational, and social needs of its members. A careful reading of the accounts of the various departments provided in this volume permits us to take some measure of the road we have trod during the last twenty-five years. The membership of the church has increased from 940,000 in 1972 to 1,230,842 in 1996. In 1996, there were 3,098 churches in the denomination with 2,257 pastors serving congregations and 2,767 clergy. There was an enrollment of 67,320 persons in 1,672 Sunday schools. As of May 31, 1997, the membership of the church had increased to 1,250,094. Of the fifteen new churches that were added between 1996 and 1997, nine were located in the Eastern West Africa Episcopal District. There has been significant membership growth in the overseas missions in both West Africa and South and Central Africa, such that the church will have to effect policies to accommodate and sustain the expansion.

Although financial constraints hobble the complete realization of the mission and vision of the A. M. E. Zion Church, there has nevertheless been a steady improvement in the economic profile of the church and its agencies. During 1972-76, the general assessment claims were $1,450,725. The comparable figure for the 1992-96 quadrennium was $5,044,721 with an additional sum of $353,130 earmarked for Livingstone College. There was significant improvement in the financial standing of the Department of Brotherhood Pensions and Ministerial Relief during the 1988-92 and 1992-96 quadrennia. The market value of the Brotherhood Pension Benefit Fund increased from $4,701,359.00 in 1988 to $7,334,384.00 as of May 31, 1992. When the funds were switched from equities to income producing securities, resources became available for increased pension benefits and other investments. The department has undertaken a plan for health insurance and is currently building a multipurpose Wellness Complex that will provide health care services, housing, and recreational facilities for Zion and the surrounding community. On May 30, 1997, a ground-breaking ceremony was held on the 86-acre site that is located in the Derita area of Charlotte, North Carolina.

In the publishing agencies, there has been a steady effort to utilize current technology to improve efficiency and cut costs of operation in the A. M. E. Zion Publishing House, *Star of Zion*, *A. M. E. Zion Quarterly Review*, and in the *Church School Herald* of the Church School Literature Department. The 1996 General Conference voted to make Vision Focus magazine, a quarterly publication established in support of the A. P. Morris Widows' Fund by the Department of Brotherhood Pensions and Ministerial Relief, an official denominational publication. The magazine, which costs $35.00 for an annual subscription, hopes to keep members of the A. M. E. Zion Church informed of

African Methodist Episcopal Zion Church

Brotherhood Pensions and Ministerial Relief programs, issues, and concerns. The A. M. E. Zion Publishing House and its bookstore have been refurbished, and the bookstore has been stocked with appropriate goods. The bookstore has shown increased revenue as a result.

The educational endeavor of the A. M. E. Zion Church during this period has been largely directed at strengthening Livingstone College and Hood Theological Seminary. In 1989, the Livingstone College administration successfully undertook a five-year capital improvement fund -raising campaign that achieved the target sum of $10 million in four years with a half-million dollars in excess. In 1992, the Southern Association of Schools and Colleges confirmed the accreditation of Livingstone College for ten years, and, for the first time in its 113-year history, Hood Theological Seminary also received full accreditation by this body. A more important milestone was achieved in May, 1998 when Hood Theological Seminary achieved full membership in the Association of Theological Schools. The new administration of Hood Theological Seminary undertook improvements in student numbers, curriculum, staff, and library holdings to meet the requirements of full accreditation by the Association of Theological Schools. During the 1992-96 quadrennium, each annual conference was assessed an additional 7 percent to benefit Livingstone College.

The A. M. E. Zion Church has been faithful to her commitment of "Winning The World for Christ," by supporting evangelical, ecumenical, and humanitarian organizations and projects, such as, the World Council of Churches, National Council of Churches of Christ in the U. S. A., Congress of National Black Churches, National Association for the Advancement of Colored People,National Urban League, World Methodist Conference and Council, Church Women United in the U. S. A., the Consultation on Church Union, and the Commission on Pan Methodist Cooperation. Our clergy and lay members have been elected or appointed to various offices of leadership and responsibility to make manifest the oneness in Christ with all believers. During the period of this review, the Rev. Dr. Staccato Powell, pastor of Washington Metropolitan A. M. E. Zion Church, St. Louis, Missouri, and a staff member of the National Council of Churches in the U. S. A., (NCCUSA) was elected Unit Director and Deputy-General Secretary of the National Ministries Unit by the Governing Board of NCCUSA.

The growth in church membership in the United States and in overseas missions is evidence of the deep commitment of the entire church and, particularly, the episcopal leadership and several of the mission agencies, namely, Evangelism, Home Missions, Church Extension, Overseas Missions, and the Woman's Home and Overseas

4

Introduction

Missionary Society to spread the gospel of Christianity. This volume gives detailed accounts of the work of each of these agencies in the pursuit of spreading the Good News. It also provides readers a historical spectrum of the A. M. E. Zion Church through its profiles of the bishops of the church from the beginning of its existence. *The African Methodist Episcopal Zion Church, 1972-1996: A Bicentennial Commemorative History* will affirm for readers Bishop William J. Wall's injunction to "hallow the past, consecrate the present, have faith in the future, and above all, protect the heritage."

We thank and congratulate Bishop J. Clinton Hoggard for writing and compiling this commemorative history of the Bicentennial of the African Methodist Episcopal Zion Church.

African Methodist Episcopal Zion Church

WHY A BICENTENNIAL CELEBRATION?

IN October, 1996, the African Methodist Episcopal Zion Church of America celebrated the 200th year of its first congregation, which was formed in New York City, in 1796, and was the seed from which this denomination grew. The African Methodist Episcopal Zion Church grew out of the dissatisfaction among the people of color with the treatment they received in the church services of the Methodist Episcopal (white) Church. In his *History of the A. M. E. Zion Church in America* (pp. 15-16), Bishop John Jamison Moore states that when the first Methodist Episcopal (M. E.) Society (white) was established in New York, among whom were several colored persons, the two races found no difficulty in the practice of religious fellowship and the equal enjoyment of religious rights and privileges, but as the Church grew popular and influential, prejudice of caste engendered Negro procription. As colored members increased, race friction and proscription increased, which finally exhausted the patience of the colored members of the M. E. Society. The Methodist Episcopal Church in New York licenced a number of colored men to preach but prohibited them from preaching independently, even to their own brethren, except occasionally, and never to white audiences. As they then stood connected with the white M.E. Church, the colored preachers were deprived of the opportunity of improving their gifts and graces and were prohibited from joining the (white) Annual M. E. Conference as itinerant preachers with their white brethren. Thus restricted in their church relations, the preachers were prompted to seek the privilege of holding meetings among themselves.

From the beginning of this independent movement, there were influential African American leaders who reacted to the unjust attitudes and practices of the John Street M. E. Church, lay and clergy. Among the church leaders were James Varick, Abraham Thompson, June Scott, and William Miller. The Rev. Christopher Rush (sometimes called *Father* Rush), the second Bishop elected and consecrated in the A. M. E. Zion Church movement, gives a detailed account of the events that led to the separation of African Americans from the M. E. Church in *The Rise and Progress of the African Methodist Episcopal [Zion] Church in America* (New York: The Author, 1843). Although much of Christopher Rush's account was related to him by others, he himself joined the A. M. E. Zion movement in 1803, eight years after its beginning. What had occurred in the previous eight years before his attendance is without a doubt one of

African Methodist Episcopal Zion Church

the most vivid and heroic stories of the formation of a Christian Church.

The fathers of the A. M. E. [Zion] Church agreed that they had no fault to find with the doctrines, form of government, and evangelistic and soul-saving emphases of Methodism, but they could not endure the constant humiliation and restrictions imposed by the people into whose hands American Methodism had fallen. The founders of Methodism were opposed to slavery and the inhumane treatment of slaves, so that they could logically remain Methodists because of the spirit of the orginators and the meaning of the original movement in England and America. The causes and the mission of this newly established church body are best expressed in the Founders' Address to the Members of the African Methodist Episcopal [Zion] Church in America [William J. Walls, *The African Methodist Episcopal Zion Church: Reality of the Black Church* (Charlotte, North Carolina: A.M.E. Zion Publishing House, 1974, pp. 49-50)]:

> BELOVED BRETHEN: We think it proper to state briefly that, after due consideration, the Offical Members of the African Methodist Episcopal Zion and Asbury Churches in the City of New York have been led to conclude that such was the relation in which we stood to the white Bishops and Conference, relative to the ecclesiastical government of the African Methodist Church or Society in America, so long as we remain in that situation our Preachers would never be able to enjoy these privileges which the Discipline of the white Church holds out to all its Members that are called to preach, in consequence of the limited access our brethren had to those privileges, and particularly in consequence of the difference of color. We have been led also to conclude that the usefulness of our Preachers has been very much hindered, and our brethren in general have been deprived of those blessings which Almighty God may have designed to grant them, through the means of those Preachers whom He has from time to time raised up from among them, because there has been no means adopted by the said Bishop and Conference for our Preachers to travel through the Connection and promulgate the Gospel of our Lord Jesus Christ; and they have had no access to the only source from whence they might have obtained a support, at least, while they traveled. Under these circumstances they believed that the formation of an itinerant plan and the establishment of a Conference for the African Methodist Preachers of the United States, who are not yet attached to any Conference of that nature, would be essential to the prosperity of the spiritual concerns of our colored brethren in general, and would be the means of advancing our Preachers (who are now in regular standing in connection with the white

African Methodist Episcopal Zion Church

Preachers of the Methodist Episcopal Church), whenever it should be found necessary for the advancement of the Redeemer's kingdom among our brethren, to bring forward for ordination those who are called of God to preach the Gospel of our Lord, which may be done from time to time, according to the best of our judgment of the necessity thereof, and not according to the method which is natural to suppose our white brethren would pursue, to determine upon the necessity of such ordination. We are under strong impression of mind that such measures would induce many of our brethren to attend divine worship, who are yet careless about their eternal welfare, and thereby prove effectual in the hands of God in the awakening and conversion of their souls to the knowledge of the truth.

And whereas, Almighty God in His all wise and gracious providence, has recently offered a favorable opportunity whereby these Societies may be regularly organized as an evangelical African Methodist Church, we have therefore resolved to embrace the said opportunity and have agreed that the title of the Connection shall be the African Methodist Episcopal [Zion] Church in America;* and we have selected a form of Discipline, with a little alteration from that of our Mother Church, which selection we recommend to you, for the Doctrines and Disciplines of our Church, hoping that the great Shepherd and Bishop of souls, the all wise and gracious God, will be pleased to approve of the above measures and grant that we may obtain and preserve those privileges which we have been heretofore deprived of; that thereby we may unite our mutual efforts for the prosperity of the Redeemer's kingdom among us, and for the encouragement of our colored brethren in the Ministry.

Earnestly soliciting your prayers and united endeavors for the same, we remain your affectionate brethren and servants in the kingdom of our ever-adorable Lord.

> Abraham Thompson,
> James Varick,
> William Miller.

*The word *Zion* was added to the title by the General Conference of 1848.

The Name
This first church organized in 1796 and built in 1800 was called Zion. The founders chose this name because "it is the name most frequently used in the

African Methodist Episcopal Zion Church

Bible to designate the Church of God." According to C. R.Harris, Zion Church was incorporated in 1801 by the name, *The African Methodist Episcopal Church in New York.* *"Methodist Episcopal* was always in the title to exhibit the retention of the doctrine and form of church government under which the denomination originated. African was prefixed to the rest of the title of this church because it was to be controlled by descendants of Africa, in the interest of humanity, regardless of race, color, sex, or condition." (Cicero R. Harris, *Zion's Historical Catechism: For Use in Families and Sunday Schools* [Charlotte, North Carolina: A. M. E. Zion Publishing House], pp. 8-9)

Therefore, these people of African descent, with an indubitable pride in the Fatherland and abiding love of kinship, desired to maintain their identity, their ancient cultures and background, for posterity. Because another organization came into existence around the same time, with the same title, and much confusion was brought about, the General Conference of 1848 voted to make Zion a part of the denominational name, henceforth to be known as the *African Methodist Episcopal Zion Church* (James Walker Hood, *One Hundred Years of the African Methodist Episcopal Zion Church* [New York: A. M. E. Zion Book Concern, 1895, p. 595]).

On this structure a denominational body has been built that currently comprises more than one and a quarter million communicants and members, almost three thousand preachers and clergy, and nearly three thousand churches. (Kenneth B. Bedell, ed., *Yearbook of American and Canadian Churches: 1997* (Nashville: Abingdon Press, 1997, p. 41). It therefore seems fitting and proper to direct the minds of each succeeding generation of adherents to the principles of human freedom, social justice, and evangelistic redemption of life as pronounced by the founding fathers of the A. M. E. Zion Church, whose sense of being and mission in life were rooted in the teachings of Jesus, the Christ. Therefore, our tradition justifiably observes jubilee years in the life of this church. This was done in 1896 when, four years previously, at the Pittsburgh General Conference of 1892, the fathers of the church decreed that 1896 would be observed as a year of Jubilee in the African Methodist Episcopal Zion Church, which had weathered the storms of slavery, emancipation, ignorance, poverty, and war since its birth in 1796. Glorious as that celebration was, the Church immortalized the Centennial Celebration by having national and international personalities of stature extend greetings and exhort the A.M.E. Zion Church to move onward and upward. The determination of the A. M. E. Zion Church was reflected in its assistance in the debt of

African Methodist Episcopal Zion Church

the Varick Memorial Publishing House in Charlotte, North Carolina and in providing additional support for the connectional schools. According to Bishop William J. Walls, "[T]he denomination salvaged enough to sponsor one project of note: The Centennial A. M. E. Zion Church of Mt. Vernon, N. Y., organized December 18, 1895 by Rev. William H. Eley, was placed on a firm foundation by the denomination as a memorial of the Centennial Celebration. Annual Conferences sponsored other mission projects within the bounds of their conferences." (*The African Methodist Episcopal Zion Church: The Reality of the Black Church* (p. 557).

Again in 1946, the denomination experienced great joy by participating in the Sesquicentennial Observance at the Mother A. M. E. Zion Church located now at 140-46 West 137th Street in New York City. Mother A. M. E. Zion Church was host to the Centennial Celebration in 1896 and was again host to the Sesquicentennial in 1946. The bishops issued a proclamation, which was publicized near and far, that recounted the pilgrimage of the denomination from 1796 to 1946. These celebrations are a time of renewal of our faith, our purpose, and our mission in this rapidly changing scientific and technological age. As we celebrate 1996, the 200th year of the birth of the Mother A. M. E. Zion Church congregation, the fountainhead of our denomination, we are challenged not to forget our past but to hallow it, not to desecrate the present but consecrate it, not to lose hope but to have faith in the future of our nation and our Church, and always to protect the heritage of the A. M. E. Zion Church as we continue to serve the present age.

PROCLAMATION
BICENTENNIAL OF THE AFRICAN METHODIST
EPISCOPAL ZION CHURCH
1796 - 1996

ALL praise and adoration to God, Whose Word is truth, Whose love is perfect, Whose presence is peace, and Whose faithfulness is forever, to His Son, Jesus Christ our Saviour, Who by His love has liberated and redeemed our lives; and to His Holy Spirit, Whose promptings have led us to a new reality of service and hope, by glory, honor, and enduring thanks. Amen.

WHEREAS: In the year of our Lord, one thousand nine hundred and ninety-six, the African Methodist Episcopal Zion Church will celebrate its Bicentennial Year, the fourth year of Jubilee; and

WHEREAS: Almighty God, in His all-wise and gracious providence, offered a favorable opportunity whereby societies may be regularly organized as an evangelical African Methodist Episcopal Zion Church; and

WHEREAS: James Varick, Peter Williams, Abraham Thompson, William Brown, William Hamilton, June Scott, Frances Jacobs, Thomas Miller and Samuel Pontier found it necessary to leave John Street Methodist Church in New York City, because people of color had been deprived of those blessings which Almighty God designed to grant them; and

WHEREAS: The African Methodist Episcopal Zion Church was established in order to provide the opportunity to give expression to their gifts and graces, and to experience their true humanity; and

WHEREAS: By God's Grace the African Methodist Episcopal Zion Church has remained in the vanguard of freedom and labored for the liberation of all people; and

WHEREAS: Divine Providence has provided the growth of institutions that have allowed for the freedom of expression, religious integrity, social responsibility, moral stability, and educational opportunities, and

WHEREAS: The Divine Spirit has kindled the missionary zeal of the African Methodist Episcopal Zion Church to extend its outreach beyond the continental United States to Bahamas, Jamaica, Barbados, Trinidad-Tobago, Liberia, Ghana, Cote d'Ivoire (Ivory Coast), Nigeria, South Africa, Virgin Islands, Guyana, England, and India, and created other independence movements which grew out of the impacting presence of the African Methodist Episcopal Zion Church; and

WHEREAS: The love of Christ Jesus, our Lord, has led the African Methodist Episcopal Zion Church to be a participant in the ecumenical movement of the world; and

African Methodist Episcopal Zion Church

WHEREAS: The Word of God and the fellowship of the Holy Spirit have nurtured the sons and daughters of the African Methodist Episcopal Zion Church and enabled them to make distinct worldwide contributions to humanity; Therefore

WE, THE BISHOPS OF THE AFRICAN METHODIST EPISCOPAL ZION CHURCH, DO HEREBY PROCLAIM A SEASON OF PREPARATION BEGINNING THIS, THE TWENTY-SIXTH DAY OF JULY, IN THE YEAR OF OUR LORD ONE THOUSAND NINE HUNDRED NINETY-TWO, AND A SEASON OF CELE-BRATION BEGINNING THE FIRST DAY OF OCTOBER IN THE YEAR OF OUR LORD ONE THOUSAND NINE HUNDRED NINETY-FIVE:

I. We call upon the African Methodist Episcopal Zion Church to turn to God with thankful hearts and reverential praise for the mercy and goodness that God has shown toward us and the heights to which God has lifted us in spite of horrendous barriers and deplorable circumstances that surround us.

II. We call upon all members of the African Methodist Episcopal Zion Church to commit themselves to a special day of fasting, prayer, and study each week during the Seasons of Preparation and Celebration.

III. We appeal to all souls in the African Methodist Episcopal Zion Church to dedicate their lives to Christ that they may be patient in tribulation, joyful in hope, and participants in the redeeming and liberating influence of Christ.

IV. We call upon all members of the African Methodist Episcopal Zion Church to reach out to one another in the perfect love of our Lord and Saviour Jesus Christ, that a new reality of peace may abide in our fellowship.

V. We appeal to all members of the African Methodist Episcopal Zion Church to act in this present world with merciful hearts, helping hands, and the liberating power of our Redeemer Christ Jesus to reclaim and restore those in our midst who are oppressed and without a Saviour.

VI. We call upon all members of the African Methodist Episcopal Zion Church to remember, with thankful hearts, the unselfish labors and extreme sacrifices which the founding fathers and those of successive generations have given, in order that we may appropriately and adequately prepare ourselves for the celebration of the Bicentennial.

VII. We hereby invite our friends of every Communion to share with us in this Season of Preparation as we glorify God, our Maker, and praise His Holy Name.

VIII. We hereby declare that the theme for our Celebration of 200 years with Jesus Christ shall be Reflecting, Reclaiming, Renewing, and Rejoicing.

GLORY BE TO THE FATHER, AND TO THE SON, AND TO THE HOLY GHOST: AS IT WAS IN THE BEGINNING, IS NOW AND EVER SHALL BE, WORLD WITHOUT END. Amen

PROCLAMATION

BICENTENNIAL OF THE AFRICAN METHODIST EPISCOPAL ZION CHURCH
1796 - 1996

All praise and adoration to God, Whose Word is truth, Whose love is perfect, Whose presence is peace, and Whose faithfulness is forever, to His Son, Jesus Christ our Saviour, who by His love has liberated and redeemed our lives; and to His Holy Spirit, Whose promptings have led us to a new reality of service and hope, be glory, honor, and enduring thanks. Amen.

WHEREAS: In the year of our Lord, one thousand nine hundred and ninety-six, the African Methodist Episcopal Zion Church will celebrate its Bicentennial Year, the fourth year of Jubilee; and

WHEREAS: Almighty God, in His all-wise and gracious providence, offered a favorable opportunity whereby societies may be regularly organized as an evangelical African Methodist Episcopal Zion Church; and

WHEREAS: James Varick, Peter Williams, Abraham Thompson, William Brown, William Hamilton, June Scott, Frances Jacobs, Thomas Miller and Samuel Pontier found it necessary to leave John Street Methodist Church in New York City, because people of color had been deprived of those blessings which Almighty God designed to grant them; and

WHEREAS: The African Methodist Episcopal Zion Church was established in order to provide the opportunity to give expression to their gifts and graces, and to experience their true humanity; and

WHEREAS: By God's Grace, the African Methodist Episcopal Zion Church has remained in the vanguard of freedom and labored for the liberation of all people; and

WHEREAS: Divine Providence has provided the growth of institutions that has allowed for the freedom of expression, religious integrity, social responsibility, moral stability, and educational opportunities; and

WHEREAS: The Divine Spirit has kindled the missionary zeal of the African Methodist Episcopal Zion Church to extend its outreach beyond the continental United States to Bahamas, Barbados, Trinidad-Tobago, Liberia, Ghana, Cote d'Ivoire (Ivory Coast), Nigeria South Africa, Virgin Islands, Guyana, England and India, and created other independence movements which grew out of the impacting presence of the African Methodist Episcopal Zion Church; and

WHEREAS: The love of Christ Jesus, our Lord, has led the African Methodist Episcopal Zion Church to be a participant in the ecumenical movement of the world; and

WHEREAS: The Word of God and the fellowship of the Holy Spirit have nurtured the sons and daughters of the African Methodist Episcopal Zion Church enabled them to make distinct worldwide contributions to humanity; Therefore

WE, THE BISHOPS OF THE AFRICAN METHODIST EPISCOPAL ZION CHURCH, DO HEREBY PROCLAIM A SEASON OF PREPARATION BEGINNING THIS THE TWENTY-SIXTH DAY OF JULY IN THE YEAR OF OUR LORD ONE THOUSAND NINE HUNDRED NINETY TWO, AND A SEASON OF CELEBRATION BEGINNING THE FIRST DAY OF OCTOBER IN THE YEAR OF OUR LORD ONE THOUSAND NINE HUNDRED NINETY FIVE;

I.   We call upon the African Methodist Episcopal Zion Church to turn to God with thankful hearts and reverential praise for the mercy and goodness that God has shown toward us and the heights to which God has lifted us in spite of horrendous barriers and deplorable circumstances that surround us.

II. We call upon all members of the African Methodist Episcopal Zion Church to commit themselves to a special day of fasting, prayer, and study each week during the Seasons of Preparation and Celebration.

III. We appeal to all souls in the African Methodist Episcopal Zion Church to dedicate their lives to Christ that they may be patient in tribulation, joyful in hope, and participants in the redeeming and liberating influence of Christ.

IV. We call upon all members of the African Methodist Episcopal Zion Church to reach out to one another in the perfect love for our Lord and Saviour Jesus Christ, that a new reality of peace may abide in our fellowship.

V.   We appeal to all members of the African Methodist Episcopal Zion Church to act in this present world with merciful hearts, helping hands, and the liberating power of our Redeemer Christ Jesus to reclaim and restore those in our midst who are oppressed and without a Saviour.

VI. We call upon all members of the African Methodist Episcopal Zion Church to remember, with thankful hearts, the unselfish labors and extreme sacrifices which the founding fathers and those of successive generations have given, in order that we may appropriately and adequately prepare ourselves for the celebration of the Bicentennial.

VII. We hereby invite our friends of every Communion to share with us in this Season of Preparation as we glorify God, our Maker, and praise His Holy Name.

VIII. We hereby declare that the theme for our Celebration of 200 years with Jesus Christ shall be Reflecting, Reclaiming, Renewing and Rejoicing.

GLORY BE TO THE FATHER, AND TO THE SON, AND TO THE HOLY GHOST: AS IT WAS IN THE BEGINNING, IS NOW AND EVER SHALL BE, WORLD WITHOUT END. Amen.

BISHOP RUBEN L. SPEAKS   BISHOP GEORGE E. BATTLE, JR.   BISHOP CHARLES H. FOGGIE

BISHOP HERMAN L. ANDERSON   BISHOP JOSEPH JOHNSON   BISHOP WILLIAM M. SMITH

BISHOP CECIL BISHOP   BISHOP RICHARD L. THOMPSON   BISHOP ALFRED G. DUNSTON, JR.

BISHOP GEORGE W. WALKER, SR.   BISHOP ENOCH B. ROCHESTER   BISHOP J. CLINTON HOGGARD

BISHOP MILTON A. WILLIAMS   BISHOP MARSHALL H. STRICKLAND   BISHOP CLINTON R. COLEMAN

BISHOP SAMUEL C. EKEMAM   BISHOP CLARENCE CARR   BISHOP JOHN H. MILLER, SR.

BISHOP WILLIAM ALEXANDER HILLIARD

13

BICENTENNIAL COMMISSION

Members appointed and approved by the General Conference

1988-92

Bishop Richard L. Fisher, chairperson, 1988-October 1991 (deceased)
Bishop Ruben L. Speaks, 1st vice chairperson (became chairperson October, 1991)
Bishop Cecil Bishop, 2nd vice chairperson, Budget and Finance
Rev. Dr. William C. Ardrey, executive director

BOARD OF BISHOPS

Bishop Herman L. Anderson
Bishop Cecil Bishop
Bishop Clinton R. Coleman
Bishop Alfred G. Dunston, Jr.
Bishop Samuel Chukukanne Ekemam, Sr.
Bishop Richard L. Fisher
Bishop Charles H. Foggie (retired)
Bishop Milton A. Williams

Bishop William Hilliard (retired)
Bishop J. Clinton Hoggard
Bishop John H. Miller, Sr.
Bishop William M. Smith
Bishop Ruben L. Speaks
Bishop George W. Walker, Sr.
Bishop Alfred E. White

CLERGY AND LAY MEMBERS

Rev. Vernon A. Shannon
Mr. Leonard Cooke
Rev. W. H. Thomas
Rev. O. R. Ellis
Rev. Robert Graham
Mrs. Dema Nappier
Rev. William C. Ardrey
Rev. Robert L. Clayton, Jr.
Rev. F. L. Rush
Rev. Gwendol F. McCaskill
Rev. Samuel L. Brown
Mrs. Janie A. Speaks

Mrs. Elizabeth Butler
Rev. J. W. Greene
Ms. Linda Cratic
Rev. George McKain
Ms. Joyce Lovett
Rev. H. T. Hutton
Mrs. Sadie Kirkwood
Rev. Dr. Godfred Zormelo
Ms. Cynthia Williams
Rev. Dr. Calvin Marshall
Dr. O. N. Ekemam, Atty.

1992-96

Bishop Ruben L. Speaks, chairperson (October 1991-February 1996 (resigned

Bicentennial Commision

because of health reasons)
Bishop George W. C. Walker, Sr., 1st vice chairperson (1992-February, 1996);
  chairperson (February -October, 1996)
Bishop Milton A. Williams, Sr., 1st vice chairperson
Bishop Marshall H. Strickland, 2nd vice chairperson
Bishop Cecil Bishop, chairperson, Budget and Finance
Rev. Dr. William C. Ardrey, executive director (1992-July 1994; resigned because of
  health reasons)
Mr. Andra' R. Ward, executive director (July 1994-   )

BOARD OF BISHOPS

Bishop Herman L. Anderson
Bishop George E. Battle, Sr.
Bishop Cecil Bishop
Bishop Clarence Carr
Bishop Clinton R. Coleman (retired)
Bishop Alfred G. Dunston, Jr., (retired)
Bishop Samuel Chukukanne Ekemam, Sr.
Bishop Charles H. Foggie (retired)
Bishop William A. Hilliard (retired)

Bishop J. Clinton Hoggard (retired)
Bishop Joseph Johnson
Bishop John H. Miller, Sr., (retired)
Bishop Enoch B. Rochester
Bishop William M. Smith (retired)
Bishop Marshall H. Strickland
Bishop Richard K. Thompson
Bishop George W. C. Walker, Sr.
Bishop Milton A. Williams

COMMITTEES

Administrative Operations and Management
Budget and Finance
Grants and Foundations
Evangelism and Church Growth

Theological Studies
Marketing and Public Relations
Music/ Hymn

Promotional Merchandise
Bishop Varick Bust Campaign
New York Logistics Planning
Corporate Solicitation and
  Partnerships
New York Program Planning
Bicentennial/Historical
Schomburg Center Archives and
  Collections

COMMITTEE CHAIRPERSONS

Rev. James D. Armstrong

Rev. Dr. Dennis V. Proctor, Sr.

African Methodist Episcopal Zion Church

Rev. Dr. Kermit J. DeGraffenreidt
Rev. Dr. Norman H. Hicklin
Mrs. Lula K. Howard
Rev. Raymon Hunt
Rev. Dr. Calvin B. Marshall

Mrs. Mary Hopkins-Runyon
Rev. Dr. Vernon A. Shannon
Mrs. Janie A. Speaks
Rev. Joan C. Speaks
Rev. Dr. Morgan W. Tann

CLERGY AND LAY MEMBERS

Rev. Johnson K. Asibuo
Rev. Joan C. Speaks
Mr. D. D. Garrett
Rev. Franklin L. Rush
Mrs. Corrie Winston
Rev. John G. Wyatt, Jr.
Ms. Marion Seay
Rev. Dr. Vernon A. Shannon
Rev. Robert L. Clayton (deceased)
Rev. G. Bernard Crawford
Mrs. Dema S. Nappier
Dr. O. N. Ekemam, Atty.
Rev. Dr. Calvin B. Marshall

Rev. George McKain, II
Mrs. Lillian T. Shelborne
Rev. William C. Bailey
Mrs. Dorothy S. Johnson
Mrs. Chiquita V. Lee
Rev. James H. Taylor, Jr.
Mr. Edgar E. Atkins
Rev. Earle E. Johnson
Ms. June Slade Collins
Rev. Dr. Kevin W. McGill, Sr.
Mr. Harold Croom
Rev. Dr. Percy Smith, Jr.

Rev. Dr. William C. Ardrey, director emeritus
Mr. Andra' R. Ward, executive director
Colleen Y. Butler, administrative assistant

("Bicentennial Commission of the A. M. E. Zion Church: Report to the 45th Quad. Sess. Gen. Conf.," pp. 1-16)

BICENTENNIAL HYMN
AFRICAN METHODIST EPISCOPAL ZION CHURCH
by Mrs. Dorothy S. Johnson

1. O God Our Rock and our Salvation.
Two hundred years you've heard our cries
Without your love, We would have faltered:
Thou art ever by our side.
Gracious Master, Zion doth praise Thee
For Thy great and steadfast love.
For Thy great and steadfast love.

2. Lift our minds to lofty places.
Give us visions of Thy will.
Lead us in Thy righteous pathways
Till our hearts with rapture thrill.
Blessed Saviour, Zion doth praise Thee
For Thy great and saving grace.
For Thy great and saving grace.

3. Guard our lives 'gainst evil forces.
Arm us with Thy power divine.
Spark our zeal to fight for freedom
Till sin's wars all be confined.
Strong deliverer, Zion doth praise Thee
For Thy mighty, sure defense.
For Thy mighty, sure defense.

4. O God, Our Rock and our Salvation.
Grant that Zion may ever be true.
Till her march on earth is ended.
Safe on high, in Zion with You.
King Eternal, Zion doth praise Thee
For Thine everlasting love.
For Thine everlasting love.
Amen.

African Methodist Episcopal Zion Church

Significance of Bicentennial Hymn Stanzas

Stanza 1:   Acknowledgment and praise to God for past blessings.

Stanza 2:   Prayer for vision and spiritual power to do God's Will.

Stanza 3:   Prayer for continued grace, spiritual power, and freedom in Christ Jesus.

Stanza 4:   Prayer for the opportunity to serve God till our earthly days are over, and we rest eternally with our God.

Two Hundred Years: The A. M. E. Zion Church
by Rev. Claude Christopher

God set them apart to serve in
Seventeen ninety-six,
To clear up a situation
They knew they had to fix.

So, the African Methodist
Episcopal Zion Church
Was founded in New York by men
Who chose to do God's work.

Varick, Miller, Scott and Brown
Were actors in the plan;
Peter Williams was also there
To lend a helping hand.

Hamilton, Jacobs and Pontier
Were also on the scene;
Little education they had;
But minds sharp and keen.

Two Hundred Years of the A. M. E. Zion Church

They built a chapel and declared
That they would separate
From others who controlled their lives,
And their religious fate.

The first chapel was called Zion,
The place where they could meet,
And feel the presence of their God,
As prayers they'd repeat.

This little movement spread abroad,
As others joined the band;
As congregations organized,
And spread throughout the land.

James Varick was elected
The first bishop of this church,
To be succeeded through the years
By others of great worth.

They were African Methodist
Episcopal by name;
Zion was added to the name
Of this great church of fame.

It's the church of Frederick Douglass,
An ex-slave, though he was,
Who was a strong voice of freedom,
As he upheld this cause.

It was the church of Sojourner Truth,
Whose strong voice could be heard
Speaking out for justice for all,
According to God's Word.

So, they call it the freedom church;

African Methodist Episcopal Zion Church

It always led the fight
For justice and equality,
And other human rights.

Two hundred years we've moved along,
Calling upon our God;
Trusting only in His mercy,
While troubled roads we've trod.

We know that God has been with us
Through every tearful day;
He's given us the inner strength
To make it, all the way.

Our preachers have preached the gospel
According to God's plan;
They've made disciples everywhere
And tried to improve man.

From Alaska to New England
We've spread across the land,
Constantly seeking souls to save,
And lend a helping hand

In South America and in
The Caribbean Sea;
In England and in India,
There will our presence be.

Across the African mainland
You'll find our presence yet;
Upon the A. M. E. Zion Church
The sun will never set.

In slavery we fought to free
The people from their bonds;
Then, to discrimination we

Two Hundred Years of the A. M. E. Zion Church

Found the need to respond.

Our schools were spread across the land,
Providing education;
An educated public is
Better for a nation.

In civil rights movements we've been
Forever in the fight.
For human rights and dignity;
Whatever is deemed right.

We've helped our people everywhere
To live a wholesome life;
Free from the chains of bondage and
Of misery and strife.

Two hundred years of work is done
And we pause now to say
We're thankful to Almighty God,
Who brought us to this day.

We've freed the minds and bodies of men
From sea to shining sea;
But our task will not be done
Until all souls are free.

CONNECTIONAL PRE-BICENTENNIAL OBSERVANCES

A CALENDAR of Special Events of Pre-Bicentennial Celebrations included:

A Faith and Practice Convocation was held April 20-22, 1995 at the Hyatt Regency, Inner Harbor, Baltimore, Maryland. The convocation featured Prof. Cornel West, Ph.D., scholar, lecturer, activist, and author of Race Matters as the keynote speaker. The convocation was organized by the Theological Committee of the Bicentennial Commission and included an in-depth review of the A. M. E. Zion Doctrine, workshops, and panel discussion on "Zion Methodism and Order of Worship," and various topics relevant to the A. M. E. Zion Church's role in the 21st century.

The Harriet Tubman Annual Pilgrimage to Auburn, New York, was held May 26-29, 1995. The pilgrimage was organized by the Western New York Conference and included a pre-Pilgrimage Banquet; a graveside memorial service at Fort Hill Cemetery; "The Freedom Fighter," a tribute and reflections on Harriet Tubman; a Harriet and John Tubman Youth Pageant; and tours of the historic Tubman Home and Library.

The Woman's Home and Overseas Missionary Society Salute to Zion's Bicentennial was held at the Westin Hotel, Detroit, Michigan, Sunday, July 30, 1995, at 8:00 p. m., during the W. H. & O. M. Society's 23rd Quadrennial Convention.

EPISCOPAL DISTRICT BICENTENNIAL OBSERVANCES

IN compliance with a 1992 General Conference mandate to the several episcopal districts of the A. M. E. Zion Church, all twelve districts observed Bicentennial Celebrations in local churches in the respective presiding elder's districts of the annual conferences. The celebration culminated with a grand finale presentation at the episcopal district level. This section of the book reports in words what was so magnificently presented in song, drama, pageant, and parade. Our gratitude is extended to the many persons who made the celebrations happen. Some very creative work was done in the form of dramatic presentations, historic displays, talent shows, worship services, and writing depicting the beginning and growth of the church. This record of "grassroots" involvement is presented in sequence beginning with the First Episcopal District through the Twelfth Episcopal District. It concludes with an account of the national Bicentennial Celebration in New York City.

The episcopal districts were renamed according to their geographical location by the General Conference meeting in Washington, D. C. in 1996. The former names of the twelve episcopal districts that applied during the 1992-96 quadrennium are shown in parenthesis. A full account of the sponsorship and participation of each episcopal district's bicentennial celebration activities is related in the following pages.

PIEDMONT (FIRST) EPISCOPAL DISTRICT

Bishop Ruben L. Speaks, Presiding Prelate
Mrs. Janie A. Speaks, Missionary Supervisor

PRESIDING ELDERS
Blue Ridge Conference: The Revs. James McDougald, Joan C. Speaks, and the late Dr. S. Benjamin Patterson; *West Central North Carolina Conference:* The Revs. Dr. James Robertson, Jr., Dr. O. C. Dumas, Sr., Dr. William L. Rush, Samuel Campbell, the late Dr. James W. Greene, and the late Dr. Charles H. Ewing; *Western North Carolina Conference:* The Revs. Dr. Smith Turner, III, Dr. A. C. Hunnicutt, Dr. Jerry T. White, Dr. Horace C. Walser, Henry L. Hall, and Wilford L. Bailey; *The Surrey (Jamaica) Conference*: The Revs. Vivien Gunter, Magnus McFarlane, Vernal Spencer and the late Lester Forrester; *Cornwall (Jamaica) Conference*: Revs. Dr. Andrew E. Whitted, Myra Samuels, and Astley Mullings; *Middlesex (Jamaica) Conference*: The Revs. Canute Clair, Vernal Surf, Herman Thomas, and Herman Long.

The Bicentennial Committee for the former First Episcopal District, now called the Piedmont District, included the Rev. Dr. Smith Turner, III, chair; Mrs. Annie Craig,

African Methodist Episcopal Zion Church

Mrs. Celesta Miller, Mrs. Alice S. Robinson, co-chairpersons; Mrs. Joyce Reid, Ms. Johnnie M. Tracey, Mrs. Deborah Johnson, Mrs. Pam Phillips, Mrs. Mary Jackson, Mrs. Carrie Warren, Mrs. Mary Griffin, Mrs. Mildred S. Harvey, Mrs. Jo L. Rusion, Mrs. Patricia Smoke, the Rev. Carlos Hinson, and Ms. Rosetta Ferguson, committee members.

The Bicentennial Special Recognition Planning Subcommittee included Mrs. Celesta Shropshire-Miller, chair-at-large; the Revs. Retoy Gaston, Walter Adams, Mr. Ulysses L. Sherard, Rev. Samuel Richardson, Mrs. Joyce Reid, Ms. Johnnie Mae Tracey, and Mrs. Annette Mason.

Media Coverage was provided by WPEG-FM and WBAV-M/FM.

The West Central North Carolina Conference of the former First Episcopal District celebrated the Bicentennial in four year-long celebrations: The first year, or the "Year of the Church," was entitled "Reflecting." The second and third years— the "Year of the Conference" and "Year of the Episcopal District"— were named "Renewing." The fourth year, or the "Year of the Denomination," was called "Rejoicing."

The first-year celebration highlighted the oldest church in each district. The churches so celebrated included Redding Springs A. M. E. Zion Church, Wadesboro-Monroe District, 1854; Zion Hill A. M. E. Zion Church, Concord District, 1859; Lee Thee A. M. E. Zion Church, 1865, Rockingham District; Trinity A. M. E. Zion Church, 1891, Greensboro District. The respective presenters of each program were the Rev. Myrtle Watkins; Mrs. Avis Steele Edmond and the Youth Department; Mrs. Doris McRae; and Mrs. Mary Griffin and the late Mrs. Mary Hopkins-Runyon.

During the celebration of the "Year of the District," each presiding elder distributed the Bicentennial Proclamation to each church member, held a district Bicentennial Revival, stressed the Bicentennial at district conferences, conventions, and mass meetings, and emphasized youth participation.

The celebration of the "Year of the Conference" was held November 26, 1994. The activities included a parade, a luncheon at Trinity A. M. E. Zion Church, and an African American Family Symposium with a Family Empowerment Series. Family and spiritual life, education and employment, finance and economics, and healthful living were discussed in the series. A heritage banquet and drama at the Joseph S. Koury Convention Center, Greensboro, North Carolina completed the day's activities.

The heritage drama, "Great Moments in Zion," was written and directed by the late Mrs. Mary Hopkins-Runyon. The play was written in two parts: "Zion Moves South" and "The Site," which dramatizes the founding of Livingstone College. The "Heritage Program" booklet features 115 salutes including one to James Varick, founder and first

Episcopal District Bicentennial Observances

bishop; Harriett Tubman, "The Moses of Her People"; the Rt. Rev. Ruben L. Speaks, senior bishop and Bicentennial Commission chairperson; and Mrs. Janie A. Griffin Speaks, missionary supervisor, international leader, and scholar, and others. Compiled by the Rev. Harold O. Robinson and Mrs. Alice Steele-Robinson, the booklet contains a chronology of events in the history of the A. M. E. Zion Church and the West Central North Carolina Conference.

The celebration of the "Year of the Episcopal District" was held September 22-24, 1995, in Charlotte, North Carolina. The events included a three-day Bicentennial Celebration. The celebration opened on Friday evening at Little Rock A. M. E. Zion Church, Charlotte, North Carolina, with the Rev. Dr. James Samuel, Sr., as host pastor. The celebration featured a "Youth Pageant" with the theme "Great Moments in Zion." Organized by Conference Youth Coordinator Ms. Sandra Williams, the pageant brought together talented youth from North Carolina, Tennessee, and the Virgin Islands. Part I focused on the "Origin of the A. M. E. Zion Church" and was written by Mrs. Margaret Hunnicutt. Part II: "The A. M. E. Zion Church Moves South" was written by the late Mrs. Mary Hopkins- Runyon, Ms. Harriette Ford, and Mrs. Doris M. Peay. Part III: "Immortalizing and Celebrating Personalities in the History of the A. M. E. Zion Church" was researched by Mrs. Margaret Hunnicutt. Ricky Jenkins, the Western North Carolina Christian Education Youth President, presided. The young adults and children made the history of the African Methodist Episcopal Zion Church come alive with drama and song. The activities were coordinated by Mrs. Alice Steele-Robinson.

On Saturday morning, floats, automobiles, marching bands, including the Livingstone College Band, and police escorts were participants in the Bicentennial Parade that proceeded to Clinton Chapel A. M. E. Zion Church, Charlotte, NC. Although it rained, the spirits of the enthusiastic participants were not dampened. The Saturday activities included storytelling for the children, food, and a tour of the Afro-American Cultural Center located at 7th and Myers Sts. Charlotte, NC, the former church building of the Little Rock A. M. E. Zion Church congregation. (Old Little Rock Church). Presiding Elder Dr. Smith Turner of the Charlotte District was the episcopal area coordinator; Mrs. Celesta Shropshire-Miller was the Western North Carolina Conference parade coordinator; and Ms. Annie Craig was the Blue Ridge Conference Coordinator.

A formal Freedom Banquet, held September 23, 1995, at the Adam's Mark Hotel in Charlotte, North Carolina, climaxed the Saturday events. Approximately 758 guests donated $200.00 or $100.00 per plate (with $50.00 for children) for the elegant affair. The overflow was accommodated at Appleby's Restaurant (in the Adam's Mark Hotel). Bishop Cecil Bishop, presiding prelate of the Third Episcopal District, was the speaker

African Methodist Episcopal Zion Church

for the evening. The Banquet Committee comprised hostesses Celesta Miller, Sharon Perkins, Brenda Owens, Cozzie Watkins, Jean Davis, Allegra Westbrooks, Octavia Woods, Pat Graham, Alice Steele Robinson, Myrtle Polk, Sherian Carr, and Joyce Reid; and representatives from the West Central North Carolina and the Blue Ridge Conferences. The Revs. Conrad and Woods of the Charlotte District Men's Booster Club were in charge of security. The proceeds will help to finish the $1.5 million Gymnatorium at Camp Dorothy Walls, Black Mountain, North Carolina. The facility will include a program for rehabilitation and youth retreats. It will be a permanent bicentennial memorial and will serve many generations to come.

EASTERN NORTH CAROLINA (SECOND) EPISCOPAL DISTRICT

The late Bishop Herman L. Anderson, Presiding Prelate
Mrs. Ruth R. Anderson, Missionary Supervisor

During the 1992-96 quadrennium, the Second Episcopal District, now called the *Eastern North Carolina Episcopal District*, was supervised by Bishop and Mrs. Anderson until his death in Charlotte, North Carolina, on January 26, 1995. He was funeralized from the Varick Auditorium on Livingstone College Campus, with interment at the U. S. Cemetery in Salisbury, North Carolina. Following this ceremony, the Board of Bishops of the A. M. E. Zion Church met and assigned Bishop George E. Battle, Jr. to the supervision of the Central North Carolina, North Carolina, and Virgin Islands Conferences; Bishop Clarence Carr to the Albemarle Conference; and Bishop Joseph Johnson to the supervision of the Cape Fear Conference until the convening of the 1996 General Conference in Washington, D. C. in August, 1996.

The Bicentennial Committee for the Eastern North Carolina Episcopal District, included Mr. D. D. Garrett, chairperson; Mrs. Jesse Riddick, secretary; Mrs. Brenda Overton, chairperson, Drama Committee; Mrs. Artelia M. Perry, chairperson, Documentary Committee; Mrs. Theresa Palmer-Walston, chairperson, Souvenir Journal Committee; the Rev. Gonzalez L. Harris, chairman, Worship Committee; and the Revs. Dr. S. J. Farrar and Larry Gordon, Facilities.

The then Second (now Eastern North Carolina) Episcopal District comprises the following conferences: *Albemarle Conference*: Edenton District—Presiding Elder Rev. J. A. Elliott; Elizabeth City District: Presiding Elder Rev. Dr. Clinton Brickhouse; *Cape Fear Conference*: Clarkton District, Presiding Elder Rev. Dr. Aaron Moore;

Episcopal District Bicentennial Observances

Goldsboro District, Presiding Elder Rev. A. D. Brown; Wilmington District, Presiding Elder Rev. T. D. Robinson; Wilson District, Presiding Elder Rev. Henry A. Gregory, Jr.; *Central North Carolina Conference*: Dunn-Lillington District—Presiding Elder Rev. Frederick K. Woods; Durham District— Presiding Elder Rev. Dr. S. J. Farrar; Fayetteville District— Presiding Elder Rev. Dr. William M. Freeman; Laurinburg District—Presiding Elder Rev. Dr. Milton H. Williams, Sr.; Raleigh District—Presiding Elder Rev. Dr. George F. Miller; Sanford District—Presiding Elder Rev. Dr. Ocie M. Brown. *North Carolina Conference*: Beaufort District—Presiding Elder Rev. Dr. Jeremiah Asbury; New Bern District—Presiding Elder Rev. W. L. Wainwright; Washington District: Presiding Elder Rev. Clyde L. Murphy. *Virgin Islands Conference*: Presiding Elder Rev. Dr. Lawrence A. Miller.

The then Second Episcopal District Bicentennial Observance was held at St. Peter's A. M. E. Zion Church, New Bern, North Carolina, on September 9, 1995, with Bishops George E. Battle, Sr., Joseph Johnson, and Clarence Carr all participating.

Other participants in the observance included: the Prelude—Mr. William Humphrey. Chief of Protocol Rev. W. L. Wainwright led the Procession; the Rev. Dr. Aaron Moore delivered the Invocation; the Rev. Dr. William M. Freeman lined the Hymn, "Zion Stands with Hills Surrounded"; the Rev. Dr. Ocie M. Brown led A Litany of Remembrance (written by the Rev. James A. French). Revs. J. A. Elliott and Dr. George F. Miller, respectively, read the Old Testament and New Testament lessons. Rev. H. A. Gregory, Jr., delivered the Prayer. The North Carolina Conference Choir, led by Director Mrs. Thelma Dillahunt, furnished music for the occasion. The Rev. Dr. Frederick K. Woods led the recitation of the Apostles' Creed; and Rev. Dr. Lawrence A. Miller read the Occasion. Bishop Joseph Johnson read the Bicentennial Proclamation. The Rev. Dr. Jeremiah Asbury received the Offering. Bishop Clarence Carr introduced the Preacher for the celebration—Bishop George E. Battle, Jr. Prior to Bishop Battle's sermon, the Rev. Dr. Milton H. Williams, Sr., lined the Bicentennial Hymn of the A. M. E. Zion Church (written by Mrs. Dorothy S. Johnson). Following the sermon, the Invitation to Christian Discipleship was extended by Rev. A. D. Brown. The Holy Communion was celebrated by Bishops Joseph Johnson, George E. Battle, Sr., Clarence Carr, and the Revs. Dr. Clinton Brickhouse, Dr. S. J. Farrar, Clyde L. Murphy, and T. D. Robinson.

The Bicentennial Celebration continued at St. Augustine's College, Raleigh, North Carolina, where the Bicentennial Dinner and Drama were held. Mrs. Leonia Farrar was drama director, and Mrs. Ruby S. Freeman was co-director. Participants in the drama included Dr. W. E. Beard as Bishop James Varick; Rev. Dr. L. A. Miller as the Rev. Henry Evans; Rev. Dr. F. K. Woods as the Rev. Dr. Joseph Charles Price; Rev.

African Methodist Episcopal Zion Church

Kenneth Brooks as Bishop James Walker Hood; Mrs. Mable White as Harriet Tubman; Rev. Leola Williams as Sojourner Truth; Rev. Naomi Douglas as Mary Talbert Jones; and the Rev. C. E. Willie, III, as Frederick Douglass.

Candle Bearers included Mrs. Gurtrude Johnson, Durham District; Ms. Annie McPherson, Fayetteville District; Mrs. Mary McLean, Sanford District; Mrs. Gurtrude Batcher, Laurinburg District; Mrs. Joyce Hawkins, Raleigh District; and Mrs. Cecil Lambert, Dunn-Lillington District.

Ushers included Mrs. Mattie Woods, Ms. Lecia Paschal, Ms. Cornelius Jones, Mrs. Laura Headen, Mrs. Debbie Lee, the Revs. B. C. Young and Maurice Little. The Decorating Committee included Mrs. Leonia B. Farrar, chairperson; Mrs. Joseph Smith, co-chairperson, and Mrs. Francie Slead, Mrs. Gladys B. Young, Mrs. Bellie Douglas, Mrs. Joyce Hawkins, and the Rev. Virginia Wyath, as members.

The Bicentennial Committee included Mrs. Artelia Perry, president; the Revs. S. J. Farrar, Ocie M. Brown, M. H. Williams, W. M. Freeman, G. F. Miller, F. K. Woods, William L. Burton, Jr., Henry Melvin, W. A. Eason, Maurice Little, G. W. Odoms, James Canty, B. C. Young, Jr., L. A. Miller, C. E. Willie, III, F. L. Rush, M. F. Ward, the late N. L. Stroud, Leola Williams, Naomi Douglas and France McLean. Also, Mrs. Elizabeth Edwards, Mrs. Helen Dorsy, Ms. Mable M. White, Mrs. Marthenia Miller, Mrs. Catherine D. McNeill, Mrs. Louise E. Davis, Mrs. Gladys B. Young, Mrs. Leonia Farrar, Mrs. Joyce Hawkins, Mr. John Sledge, Mr. Ruben Daniels, Ms. Kathi McNeill, Mrs. Mamie Jackson, Mrs. Eddie H. Ray, and Mr. Joseph Smith, Jr.

On December 16, 1995, the Eastern North Carolina Episcopal District sponsored a Drama and Dinner Presentation, "We're Marching to Zion!" at Raleigh Civic and Convention Center, Raleigh, North Carolina. This Bicentennial Celebration was presented with thanksgiving to God and was dedicated to the memory of the Rt. Rev. Herman Leroy Anderson, Sr. The drama was divided into four acts:

ACT I.- The Early Years, 1776-1828: Scene 1. From John Street Methodist to the African Chapel; Scene 2. The Church called Zion; Scene 3. The Long Road to Independence.

ACT II. The Freedom Church, 1828-1860.

ACT III. Growth and Expansion, 1860-1900: Scene 1. Mission to the South; Scene 2. North Carolina Looks for Zion; Scene 3. James Walker Hood Comes to North Carolina; Scene 4. Continental Expansion; Scene 5. Growth in Denominational Structure.

Episcopal District Bicentennial Observances

ACT. IV. The Twentieth Century, 1901- the present.

The cast included Mrs. Theresa Palmer-Walston, Ms. Clenora Austin, Rev. Joseph Perry, Rev. Jerry Jones, Rev. Otis Brothers, Mr. Kelly Jordan, Mr. Basheen Harr, Mr. Arthur Morris, Mr. Jesse Webb, Rev. Albert Spence, Mr. William Overton, Sr., Rev. Charlie Bowe, Rev. Clinton Brickhouse, Mrs. Cheryl Baker, Ms. Alicia Palmer, Mrs. Agnes Blount, Mrs. Judith Cooper, Mrs. Mary Stepney, Mrs. Jane Brickhouse, Mr. Zane Overton, Rev. Anthony Hathaway, Rev. Roger Greene, Mr. Melton Beasley, Mr. David Gramby, Rev. Robert Mullen, Mr. Roosevelt Wright, The Rev. Jerry Jones, Mrs. Doris Gramby, Mrs. Gloria G. Williams, Dr. Lawrence A. Miller, Rev. C. E. Willie, III, Rev. Mattie Walden, Ms. Mable White, Dr. W. E. Baird, Rev. Naomi Douglas, Mrs. Sherrill Ballard, Rev. Gonzalez L. Harris, Mrs. Helen Mapson, Mr. Clarence Tobias, Mr. Jermaine Artis, Mr. Oliver Dobson, Mr. Gerald Godette, Mrs. Joan Brown, Ms. Mary Hellen Carter, Mrs. Eloise Teel, Ms. Cynthia Evans, Mrs. Hester Patterson, Mrs. Bea Miller, Mr. Buddy Parker, Mr. Curtis Oden, Mrs. Barbara Jean Hobbs, Mrs. Evelyn Anthony, Mrs. Betty Tyson, Mrs. Nell Sauls, Rev. Ivan Morton, Rev. Paul Sewell, Mrs. Josephine Campbell, Brother Donald Mapson, Rev. Harry Hines, Breahn Powell, Jessica Adams, Myeshia Garner, Deedee Mozee, Michael Mozee, Codi Powell, Kendrick Evans, Mrs. Dora Dickerson, Mrs. Jeryl Anderson, Rev. Verlon Anderson, Rev. Linda Artis, Rev. Carolyn Bagley, Mrs. Ethel U. Baldwin, Ms. Lisa Davis, Ms. Nan Dawson, Mrs. Edrena Dixon, Mrs. JoAnne Durham, Dr. Joyce P. Edwards, Rev. Murray L. Edwards, Mrs. Willie S. Exum, Mrs. Mary G. Foy, Mrs. Gracie Golden, Mrs. Jacqueline Green, Mrs. Coleen Gregory, Mrs. Debbie Hall, Mrs. Joyce Hall, Mrs. Judy Herring, Mr. Michael Herring, Mrs. Bettie Hooker, Mrs. Bobbie Jones, Mrs. Jean Jones, Mrs. Jennie Lucas, Mrs. Louise Morton, Mrs. Joyce Paige, Rev. Michael Polk, Mrs. Gaynelle Poteat, Mrs. Marguerite Robinson, Mrs. Yvonne Swinson, Rev. Dorian Suggs, Mrs. Johnnie Suggs, Ms. Nevella Suggs, Mrs. Lisa Poteat Taylor, Rev. and Mrs. Johnas Freeman, Letisha Artis, Ms. Portia Suggs, Mrs. Ruby Stroud Freeman, and Dr. William M. Freeman.

The Eastern North Carolina (Second) Episcopal District Bicentennial Committee comprised the following: Mr. D. D. Garrett, chairman; Ms. Jessie M. Riddick, secretary; Mrs. Arnetha T. Robinson, treasurer; Dr. Jeremiah Asbury, chairman, Budget and Finance Committee; Dr. S. J. Farrar, chairman, Facilities & Banquet; Dr. William M. Freeman, chairman, Publicity; Rev. Gonzalez L. Harris, chairman, Worship Committee; Mrs. Brenda M. Overton, chairperson, Drama Committee; Mrs. Theresa Palmer-Walston, chairperson, Souvenir Journal Committee; Mrs. Artelia M. Perry, chairperson,

African Methodist Episcopal Zion Church

Documentary Committee; Dr. Clinton Brickhouse, Rev. Avery C. Brown, Rev. William Lloyd Burton, Dr. Joyce P. Edwards, Rev. Murray L. Edwards, Rev. Larry Gordon, Mrs. Lillar C. H. Hamilton, Rev. Godfrey Nelson, Mrs. Posey S. Johnson, and Rev. C. E. Willie, III.

Writers: Dr. Joyce P. Edwards, Mrs. Brenda M. Overton, Mrs. Posey S. Johnson, Mrs. Leona B. Farrar, and Rev. Avery C. Brown; Stage Production: Mrs. Brenda M. Overton & Mr. Leon Rouson, Albemarle Conference; Dr. William M. Freeman, Central North Carolina Conference; Dr. Joyce P. Edwards, Cape Fear Conference; and the Rev. Avery C. Brown, North Carolina Conference; Technical Production: Mr. Roy Swepson, Mr. Ayer Burgess, Mr. Herman Burgess, Mr. L. C. Burgess, Mr. Thurman Burgess, Mr. Charles Swepson, Mr. Otha Swepson, III, Mr. Victor Swepson, and Mr. Santi; Decorations: Mrs. Leonia B. Farrar and Mrs. Arnetha T. Robinson, Dr. B. Dexter Allgood, Mrs. Monnie F. Swepson, Dr. J. C. White; Musicians: Dr. B. Dexter Allgood, Mrs. Monnie F. Swepson, and Dr. J. C. White; Programs: Dr. Joyce P. Edwards; Hosts and Hostesses: Mrs. Lillar C. H. Hamilton, Mrs. Edith Boyd, Mrs. Laura Headen, Mr. Cornelius Jones, Ms. Anese Lee, Mrs. Patricia Lyles, Mrs. Nannie Mapson, Mr. William Riddick, Mrs. Arnetha Robinson, Ms. Sylvia Smith and Ms. Ericka Wright.

Cape Fear Conference
Bishop Joseph Johnson, Presiding Prelate
Mrs. Dorothy S. Johnson, Missionary Supervisor

The Cape Fear Conference of the Eastern North Carolina (Second) Episcopal District presented to its 82nd Session in October 1993 the "Historical Foundations of the African Methodist Episcopal Zion Church: A Study Guide for the Bicentennial Celebration of the African Methodist Episcopal Zion Church, 1796-1996." The Committee for the Development of the Study Guide included the Revs. Murray L. Edwards, chairman; James Canty; Alexander L. Jones, Sr., G. Curtis Newby, and Dr. Joyce P. Edwards.

The Bicentennial Historical Commission received the "History of Wactor Temple A. M. E. Zion Church, Hayes Street and Catherine Creek Road, Ahoskie, North Carolina" along with a photograph of the church from Mrs. Virginia A. Watson.

On Saturday, April 1, 1995, the Cape Fear Conference presented a pageant in observance of the forthcoming national Bicentennial Celebration. Entitled "Reviewing Our 200 Years," the pageant was performed at the Clinton Civic Center in Clinton,

Episcopal District Bicentennial Observances

North Carolina. The pageant was also held in thanksgiving to God, in honor of Missionary Supervisor Mrs. Ruth R. Anderson, and in memory of Bishop Herman L. Anderson, Sr., who was assigned the supervision of the entire former Second, now Eastern North Carolina, Episcopal District at the close of the 1992 General Conference.

Participants in the pageant included: Mr. Jimmy Lesane, Mrs. Sally Powell, Mrs. Suzette Lewis-Brooks, Brother William McDow, the Rev. Gonzalez Harris, the Rev. Jeremiah Beamon, Mr. Oliver Dobson, Mr. Donald Mapson, the Rev. J. W. Britt, Mr. Jermaine Artis, the Rev. Paul Sewell, the Rev. Melvin Ballard, the Rev. Eugene Shaw, Mrs. Marie Robinson, the Rev. O. Lacy Evans, Mrs. Mary Council, Mrs. Brenda Crumpler, Mr. Jonathan Deseraux, Mr. James Deseraux, Mrs. Brenda Evans, Miss Danita King, Miss Andrea Lacewell, Miss Jennifer Lacewell, the Rev. Marie .Lacewell, Mr. Ronald Mapson, Mrs. Frances Matthews, Mrs. Shirley Robinson, Ms Janine Ross, Mrs. Rebecca Wright, the Rev. Eddie Swindell, Brother William Peterson, the Rev. Harry Hines, Brother Johnnie Council, Brother John Mark Melvin, Ms. Cynthia Nichols, the Rev. James Robinson, Jr., the Rev. William L. Neill, Mrs. Delma Jones, Mrs. Helen Mapson, the Rev. Marvin Lee, Mrs. Anna Briggs Moore, the Rev. Frances Murray, the Rev. Murray L. Edwards, Mr. Michael Herring, the Rev. Dorian Suggs, Mr. Willie Exum, the Rev. Ivan Morton, Ms. Nan Dawson, Mrs. Jennie Lucas, Mr. Edward McCullen, Mrs. Stella McCullen, Miss Tracy Wellington, Master Ferronte Williams, Ms. Debbie Hall, Miss Charnell Green, Mrs. Joyce Paige, Ms. Portia Suggs, Mrs. Marguerite Robinson, the Rev. and Mrs. Johnas Freeman, Mrs. Bernice C. Jacobs, Mr. Obie Ellison, the Rev. G. Curtis Newby, the Rev. David Foy, the Rev. Eugene Shaw, the Rev. George Patrick, the Rev. F. W. Hough, Mr. Norris Ebron, Mr. Archie Brown, members of the Cape Fear Conference, members of the Wilson District, and members of the Clarkton District.

The Rev. A. D. Brown was responsible for Site Selection. Choral Music was rendered by the Cape Fear Conference Choir under the direction of Mr. Purcell Kelly and accompanied by Mrs. Veronica Kelly. Ushers were from the Goldsboro District, under the direction of Mrs. Phebie Moore.

Dr. Joyce P. Edwards and Mrs. Posey S. Johnson were Writers and Directors; Mrs. Connie B. Jacobs was Writer. The pageant coordinators were: Prologue— "From John Street to The African Chapel," the Rev. Gonzalez L. Harris and Mrs. Josephine Campbell; Part 1: "Conflicts and Solutions in the Formative Years, 1796-1822," Mrs. Lula B. White and Mrs. Marie Robinson; Part 2: "Struggle and Solidarity: 1823-1864," Mr. Donald Mapson and Mrs. Posey S. Johnson; Part 3: "Growth and Expansion, 1865-1900," Mrs. Coleen H. Gregory and Dr. Joyce P. Edwards; Part 4: Mrs. Connie B. Jacobs. The source for all material in this pageant was W. J. Walls, *The African*

African Methodist Episcopal Zion Church

Methodist Episcopal Zion Church: The Reality of the Black Church, published in 1974.

On April 2, 1995, the Cape Fear Conference held its Season of Preparation for the Celebration of the Bicentennial Worship Service at St. Luke A. M. E. Zion Church, Wilmington, North Carolina, with the Rev. Alexander L. Jones, host pastor, presiding. Bishop Joseph Johnson delivered the sermon. The Rev. Aaron Moore gave the Invocation. The Rev. Gonzalez L. Harris lined the hymn, "Zion Stands with Hills Surrounded." The Rev. Murray L. Edwards led the Litany of Remembrance. The Rev. A. D. Brown read the scripture followed by a prayer by the Rev. Henry A. Gregory, Jr. Music for the celebration was rendered by the St. Luke A. M. E. Zion Church Worship Choir. The Rev. Thomas Jacobs, Jr., led the recitation of the Apostles' Creed. The offering was received by the Rev. Joseph C. Brown, Sr. Announcements and notices were read by Dr. Joyce P. Edwards; the Rev. Harry D. Hines read the Bicentennial Proclamation, and Presiding Elder Rev. T. D. Robinson presented the presiding prelate, Bishop Johnson. Following Bishop Johnson's sermon, Rev. Terry L. Jones, Sr., extended the Invitation to Christian Discipleship.

The Cape Fear Conference Bicentennial Committee included the Rev. Gonzalez L. Harris, chairperson; the Rev. Alexander L. Jones, Sr., vice chairman; Dr. Joyce P. Edwards, secretary. The members of the committee were Mrs. Cassandra Bell-Morsey, Dr. Andrew A. Best, Mrs. Ella Brown, Mrs. Josephine S. Campbell, Mrs. Mary Council, Mrs. Obie S. Ellison, Mrs. Lottie D. Edwards-Clinton, Mrs. Coleen Gregory, the Rev. Harry Hines, Mrs. Connie B. Jacobs, Mrs. Posey Johnson, Mr. Donald Mapson, the Rev. Ivan Morton, the Rev. Michael Polk, Mrs. Alice Spicer, and Mrs. Lula B. White.

Central North Carolina Conference
Bishop George E. Battle, Jr., Presiding Prelate
Mrs. Iris Battle, Missionary Supervisor

The Central North Carolina Conference held its Bicentennial Celebration in Divine Worship at Simon Temple A. M. E. Zion Church, Fayetteville, North Carolina, on November 8, 1994. The Rev. Franklin L. Rush, host pastor; Rev. Dr. W. M. Freeman, presiding elder; Mrs. Artelia Perry, chairperson, and the Rev. Dr. Lawrence A. Miller, acting chairperson, were the leading participants.

The Organ Prelude and Postlude were played by Mr. George Currie. The Call to Worship was read responsively and led by Rev. Dr. Milton Williams, presiding elder of the Laurinburg District. The Invocation was delivered by Rev. Dr. F. K. Woods, presiding elder of the Dunn-Lillington District; the Scripture was read by the Rev. Dr. S.

Episcopal District Bicentennial Observances

J. Farrar, presiding elder of the Durham District, which was followed by a Prayer by Rev. Dr. Ocie M. Brown, presiding elder of the Sanford District. The occasion was read by Ms. Effie Woodard. Music was rendered by the Evans Metropolitan Choir (Fayetteville, North Carolina), the Maggie Lett Gospel Chorus, and Mr. Joseph Smith, Jr., soloist.

Denominational greetings were brought by the Rev. Lawrence Johnson, pastor, John Wesley United Methodist Church, Fayetteville, North Carolina; the Rev. Sheridan Knight, pastor, St. Luke A. M. E. Church, Fayetteville, North Carolina; Dr. George F. Miller, presiding elder, Raleigh District.

The speaker was introduced by the Rev. Dr. W. M. Freeman. The Bicentennial Address was delivered by Bishop Herman L. Anderson. The Benediction was given by the Rev. Dr. William Lloyd Burton, pastor, St. Mark A. M. E. Zion Church, Durham, North Carolina.

The Durham District of the Central North Carolina Conference Bicentennial Commission presented "The Old Fashion Way, 1800-1900 Fashions" on Saturday, August 21, 1993 at Chatham Middle School, Siler City, North Carolina. Mrs. Leonia B. Farrar, served as district president, Bicentennial Commission; Mrs. Artelia M. Perry, conference president, Bicentennial Commission; the Rev. Dr. S. J. Farrar, presiding elder. Mrs. Leonia B. Farrar and Mrs. Gladys B. Young were Mistresses of Ceremonies. The Old Time Prayer Meeting (Devotions) were led by the Class Leaders' Prayer Band of Jordan Grove A. M. E. Zion Church; the Scripture was read by Mrs. Elizabeth Edwards, with Prayer by Rev. L. J. Jeffries. Old Time Hymns were sung by Yesterday's Choir and led by Mr. Paul Farrar. Old Time Hymns were sung by Today's Choir and were led by the Rev. Berma Spinks. The Offering was lifted and accompanied by "The Old Time Way" by the Rev. Dr. M. F. Ward and the Rev. Dr. E. J. Alston, with Prayer by the Rev. W. E. Eason.

Fashions were presented in an Old Time Fashion Parade. Gifts were presented by the Revs. C. T. Farrar and J. C. Gray. Closing remarks were given and the Benediction pronounced by the Rev. Dr. S. J. Farrar.

The cast of characters included: Grandma, Mrs. Gertrude Johnson; Children: Oldest, Ms. Angie Alston, 2d, Ms. Crystal Tyson, 3d, Mr. Hubert Alston, 4th, Mr. Gene Alston, 5th, Ms. Stephanie Brewer; Great Grandma, the Rev. Chicanele Sada; Women around fireplace, Madames, Madeline Graves, Betty Farrar, Brenda Cheek, and Margie Foushee; Father, Mr. Walter Hatcher; Great Grandmama's Sister, Mrs. Minnie Jeffries; Woman washing clothes, Mrs. Gladys Matthews; Woman boiling clothes, Mrs. Betty Brooks; Woman making lye soap, Mrs. Virginia Horton; Woman churning butter, Mrs. Mary Fox; Grandpa at table, Mr. Sylvester Guthrie; Grandma at table, Mrs. Magnolia

African Methodist Episcopal Zion Church

Farrar; Man with corn, the Rev. B. C. Young; Man with potatoes, Mr. Ricky Allen; Quilters, Madames Dorothy McNeil, Willie Brewer, Estella Eubanks, and Claudia Powell; Members of Yesterday's Choir, Mr. Paul Farrar, Leader.

The Rev. Gloria Moore and Mrs. Vera Andrews were Marshals. At the autograph table were Mrs. Mary Odom, Mrs. Sandra K. Young, and Mrs. Gwendolyn Bobo. The Production Staff comprised Mrs. Leonia B. Farrar, director; Mrs. Artelia M. Perry and Mrs. Gertrude Johnson, co-directors; Dr. A. J. Farrar, stage coordinator; Mr. Leroy Farrar, stage manager; the Revs. Virginia Wyatt and Allen Moore and Mrs. Myrtie Powell were stage assistants.

MID-ATLANTIC I (THIRD) EPISCOPAL DISTRICT

Bishop Cecil Bishop, Presiding Prelate
Mrs. Marlene Y. Bishop, Missionary Supervisor

During the 1992-96 quadrennium the former Third Episcopal District, now called the *Mid-Atlantic I Episcopal District*, comprised the Ohio, Allegheny, New Jersey, Guyana, Trinidad-Tobago, and Barbados Conferences.

On June 12, 1996, the Ohio Annual Conference held a Welcome Night Service at the Wesley Temple A. M. E. Zion Church as part of its Bicentennial Celebration. Official participants included Bishop Cecil Bishop, Mrs. Marlene Y. Bishop, the Rev. Dr. Emmett D. Foster, presiding elder, Akron District, and the Rev. Dr. Curtis T. Walker, host pastor.

The service began at 7 p.m. with the Processional Hymn "Zion Will March On." Brother Odinga L. Maddox, II, gave the Invocation, which was followed by Host Pastor, Rev. Dr. Curtis T. Walker's Welcome Address. Passages from the Old and New Testaments were read. The Rev. Dr. Thaddeus Garrett, Jr., gave the Prayer for the Occasion. The Wesley Temple Gospel Choir then sang "We Give You The Praise Lord." Dr. Curtis Walker introduced Presiding Elder Emmett D. Foster who, in turn, introduced Bishop Cecil Bishop. A Presentation of Proclamations, a Presentation of Gifts, and a History of the A. M. E. Zion Church were each featured. The Congregation then sang the Bicentennial Hymn.

A history of Wesley Temple A. M. E. Zion Church, Akron, Ohio was narrated. A Historic Marker for Wesley Temple, indicating its inclusion in the National Register of Historic Places, was unveiled on this occasion. The Eugene E. Morgan, Jr. Ensemble sang "Make Us One Lord." This was followed by accounts of "Firsts from Wesley

Episcopal District Bicentennial Observances

Temple" and the Conference Offering. The Voices of Zion sang "Magnify the Lord" as Offertory Music.

A Parade of Banners accompanied by appropriate music ensued. For Advent, the Gospel Choir sang "The Lord Is My Light." The Chancel Choir sang "Do You Hear What I Hear?" to mark Christmastide. "Jubilee" was sung by the Voices of Zion in reference to Epiphany. The Combined Choirs of the Conference sang "Holy, Holy, Holy" to mark Lent. The Chancel Choir sang "Give Me Jesus" for the Eastertide banner. For Pentecost, the Gospel Choir sang "Holy Ghost, Don't Leave Me," and the Eugene E. Morgan, Jr. Ensemble sang "Order My Steps" for Kingdomtide. The Combined Choirs in attendance sang "O Ship of Zion" to celebrate the Bicentennial Theme: "Reflecting, Reclaiming, Renewing, Rejoicing: 200 Years with Jesus." Remarks by Bishop Cecil Bishop and the Benediction completed the program.

A Reception followed in the Lower Sanctuary of Wesley Temple.

NORTH EASTERN REGION (FOURTH) EPISCOPAL DISTRICT

Bishop George W. Walker, Sr., Presiding Prelate
Mrs. Geraldine J. Walker, Missionary Supervisor

During 1992-96 the former Fourth, now called the *North Eastern*, Episcopal District, comprised the New York, New England, Western New York, and Bahamas Conferences.

New England Conference

The presiding elders of the New England Conference were the Rev. Donald W. H. E. Ruffin, host; the Rev. James M. Hubert (deceased), and the Rev. Nathaniel K. Perry. The Rev. Lester A. McCorn was the host pastor.

The Bicentennial Program Committee included the Revs. Nathaniel Perry, Lester McCorn, Timothy Howard and Harrison Bonner; and Sisters Lillian Reason, Betty Lou Carthon, and Rosetta McKain.

A pre-Bicentennial Celebration hosted by the Varick Memorial A. M. E. Zion Church, 242 Dixwell Avenue, New Haven, Connecticut, was held at St. Paul's Union American Methodist Episcopal Church, 150 Dwight Street, New Haven, Connecticut, on Monday, May 15, 1995, at 7 p.m.

The distinguished Guest Preacher for the occasion was Bishop Thomas L. Hoyt, Jr., presiding bishop of the Fourth Episcopal District of the Christian Methodist Episcopal Church comprising Louisiana and Mississippi, chair of the Department of Lay Activities, and chair of the 125th C. M. E. Church Anniversary Celebration

African Methodist Episcopal Zion Church

Committee. Bishop Hoyt is author of over forty professional and scholarly articles and a contributor to *Stony the Road We Trod: An African American Biblical Interpretation*, edited by Dr. Cain Hope Felder.

Other active participants in the pre-Bicentennial Celebration of the New England Conference were the Revs. Nathaniel K. Perry and Lester A. McCorn who were the Worship Leaders; Sister Ingrid Fanuiel and Brother Jonathan Berryman, Musicians; Daniel Roberts who led the Processional Hymn "God of Our Fathers Whose Almighty Hand" in the Order of Service. The Conference Mass Choir led the Choral Response to the Invocation. The Hymn of Praise "O God, Our Rock and Our Salvation" was written by Ms. Dorothy S. Johnson. The Responsive Reading was led by the Rev. Dr. Elmer Brown, presiding elder/pastor of St. Paul's United African Methodist Episcopal Church. The New England Conference Mass Choir sang the Anthem "Let Mount Zion Rejoice." The Rev. Kevan Hitch, pastor, First and Summerfield United Methodist Church, New Haven, Connecticut, led in the recitation of the Apostles' Creed as the Affirmation of Faith. The Rev. Lester A. McCorn, host pastor, Varick Memorial A. M. E. Zion Church, gave the Welcome Address for the Occasion, to which the Rev. James Miller, executive director, Rhode Island Council of Churches, gave the Response.

Rabbi Herbert Brockman, Congregation Mishkan Israel, Hamden, Connecticut read the Old Testament Lesson, Psalm 33 in Hebrew. The Rev. J. Stanley Justice, pastor, Bethel A. M. E. Church, New Haven, read the Epistle from 1 Corinthians 12: 12-27, which was followed by a reading in Spanish from the Gospel by the Rev. Vernea Alford-Brown, pastor, Church of the Ascension Episcopal Church, New Haven, Connecticut. The Conference Mass Choir led the Choral Response—" God Be Merciful to Us."

Retired Bishop John H. Miller of the A. M. E. Zion Church and living in Raleigh, North Carolina gave the Evening Prayer, which was followed by Ecumenical Greetings from Bishop Michael S. Moulden, presiding prelate, Union American Methodist Episcopal Church; the Rev. Dr. Frederick J. Streets, chaplain, Yale University Battel Chapel Church of Christ; the Rev. Dianne Kessler, executive director, Massachusetts Council of Churches; and the Rev. Dr. Judy Fentress-Williams, director, Black Ministries Certificate Program, Hartford Seminary.

The Rev. Dr. Harrison D. Bonner, chair, New England Conference Finance Committee, made the Offering Appeal, followed by the Offertory "All Things Come of Thee." The Conference Mass Choir sang a Choral Selection, "Revival in the Land."

Additional Ecumenical Greetings were conveyed by the Most Rev. Daniel Cronin, archbishop of Hartford Archdiocese, Roman Catholic Church; Dr. Thomas

African Methodist Episcopal Zion Church

Ogletree, dean of Yale University Divinity School; Dr. Imani-Shelia McLaughlin, assistant dean, Boston University School of Theology; and the Rev. Stephen Sidorak, Jr., executive director, Christian Conference of Connecticut. The Conference Mass Choir then rendered a Choral Selection, "He's Been Faithful."

Presiding Elder Rev. Donald W. H. E. Ruffin, New Haven District, presented the presiding bishop, the Rt. Rev. George W. Walker, Sr., who in turn introduced the Preacher. This was followed by the Sermon Hymn, "Amazing Grace," written by John Newton.

Bishop Thomas L. Hoyt delivered the Sermon, after which the Rev. Dr. Anthony Campbell, professor of Preaching, Boston University School of Theology, made the Invitation to Christian Discipleship as the congregation sang the Invitational Hymn, "Just As I Am."

Remarks and Announcements were made by the Rev. Nathaniel K. Perry, presiding elder, Boston District, and by Bishop Walker, presiding prelate. Bishop Hoyt gave the Benediction, and the congregation sang the Recessional Hymn, "Mine Eyes Have Seen the Glory."

The special pre-Bicentennial Celebration Service was followed by a Reception held in the St. Paul's Fellowship Hall. Acknowledgments were made to Rev. Elmer Brown and Saint Paul's Church; Sister Ingrid Fanuiel and the Conference Mass Choir, all of the invited clergy of the New England area; the Varick Church office staff, Marcia Alexander and Jolene Augustine; Sister Gertrude Hood and the Connecticut State Ushers Association, and the hosts and hostesses of Walters and Varick A. M. E. Zion Churches.

New York Conference

The presiding elders of the New York Conference were the Rev. Belvie H. Jackson, host, the Rev. C. Guita McKinney, the Rev. George W. McMurrary. The Rev. W. Darin Moore was host pastor.

Program Participants included Bishop George Battle, Jr., A. M. E. Zion Church; Bishop James Clinton Hoggard, retired, A. M. E. Zion Church; Bishop James A. Mathews, area bishop, United Methodist Church; the Rev. George T. Johnson, district superintendent, United Methodist Church; the Rev. John Collins, United Methodist Church; the Rev. James Booker, African Methodist Episcopal Church; the Rev. James R. McGraw, John Street United Methodist Church; the Rev. John Carrington, Salem United Methodist Church; the Rev. Alvin T. Durant, pastor, Mother Zion A. M. E. Zion Church; Dr. Solomon Heriott, minister of music, Mother Zion A. M. E. Zion Church; and the Rev. Vernon A. Shannon, pastor, St. Catherine A. M. E. Zion Church,

African Methodist Episcopal Zion Church

New Rochelle, N.Y.

A pre-Bicentennial Celebration hosted by the Greater Centennial A. M. E. Zion Church, 312 South Eighth Ave., Mt. Vernon, New York, was held on Monday, June 19, 1995, at 7 p.m.

The distinguished Guest Preacher for the occasion was the Rev. Dr. Albert J. D. Aymer, dean, Hood Theological Seminary, Salisbury, North Carolina. Dean Aymer was the manager of eight primary schools and chair of the Ecumenical Council of Churches in Tobago, Trinidad & Tobago, West Indies; executive secretary in the World Division of the General Board of Global Ministries of the United Methodist Church; assistant dean of the Drew University Theological School and director of the Doctor of Ministry Program before assuming the deanship of Hood Theological Seminary. He is a member of the Society of Biblical Literature; the Consortium of United Methodist Theological Schools, and the Society for the Advancement of Continuing Education for Ministry. Dr. Aymer was a visiting lecturer in Homiletics at the United Theological College of the West Indies; and an instructor in personal relationships and ethical decision-making at the Nursing School of the University Hospital, Jamaica. He has taught courses in the New Testament, particularly Pauline theology and ethics, and in exegesis in both English and Greek texts of the New Testament, and courses in Deutero-Pauline letters and Hebrew.

Other active participants in the pre-Bicentennial Celebration Service were Dr. Solomon Heriott who rendered the Prelude to the Procession, "The Church's One Foundation," which was followed by the Call to Worship. Bishop J. Clinton Hoggard gave the Invocation, which was followed by the Choral Response "Hear Our Prayer, O Lord." The Hymn of Praise "O God, Our Rock and Our Salvation," written by Mrs. Dorothy S. Johnson, was sung. Bishop George Battle, Jr., led the Responsive Reading. The Mother Zion A. M. E. Zion Church Choir led by Director Solomon Heriott sang the Anthem, which was followed by the Affirmation of Faith.

The Rev. W. Darin Moore gave the Welcome Address, to which the Rev. George T. Johnson, district superintendent, United Methodist Church, gave the Response. The Scriptural Hymn, "Break Thou the Bread of Life" preceded the reading of the Old Testament Scripture, Psalm 116, by the Rev. John Collins. Presiding Elder Belvie H. Jackson read the New Testament Scripture, John 15: 1-13. The readings were followed by a Choral Response, "Hosanna in the Highest", and a Prayer Hymn, "From Every Stormy Wind That Blows."

Presiding Elder George W. McMurray gave the Evening Prayer, which was followed by a Mother Zion A. M. E. Zion Church Choir Selection.

Episcopal District Bicentennial Observances

Greetings were conveyed by representatives of other Methodist denominations: Bishop James Mathews of the United Methodist Church; the Rev. James Booker, African Methodist Episcopal Church; the Rev. James A. Jones, Christian Methodist Episcopal Church; the Rev. James R. McGraw, pastor of John Street United Methodist Church; and the Rev. John Carrington, Salem United Methodist Church.

The Rev. Alvin T. Durant, pastor, Mother Zion A. M. E Zion Church and chair, New York Conference Finance Committee, made the Offering Appeal after a Selection from the Mother Zion A. M. E. Zion Church Choir. Following the Offertory, Presiding Elder C. Guita McKinney introduced the Bishop, the Rt. Rev. George W. Walker, Sr., who in turn introduced the Preacher. This was followed by the Sermon Hymn "Zion Church Goes Marching Onward," written by The Rev. Claude Christopher for the Bicentennial.

Dean Albert J. D. Aymer's Sermon was followed by a Hymn of Dedication, "A Charge to Keep I Have"; the Benediction was given by Dean Aymer and followed by the Processional Hymn, "Mine Eyes Have Seen the Glory."

A reception was held in Fellowship Hall following the Service.

Western New York Conference
The Rev. Dr. Robert L. Graham, St. Luke A. M. E. Zion Church, 314 East Ferry Street, Buffalo, New York, was the host pastor.

As part of the pre-Bicentennial Celebration, the Western New York Conference enacted a pageant entitled "The Dawning of the Western New York Conference, African Methodist Episcopal Zion Church." Written by Marjorie Anderson, Roxie McMillian, the Rev. Dr. Vincent Howell, and Alean A. Rush, the pageant traces the historical development of the Western New York Conference within the African Methodist Episcopal Zion Church. Material for the two acts that comprise the pageant was based on *The History of the African Methodist Episcopal Zion Church: The Reality of the Black Church* by Bishop William J. Walls. Churches in the conference submitted data and special research data submitted by the Revs. Emory C. Proctor and Alphonso Whitfield were also important sources for references. Alfred R. Jarrett and Melvin Thompson contributed to the song arrangements.

Act I (scenes 1-3) was written by Marjorie Anderson, Roxie McMillan, the Rev. Dr. Vincent Howell, and Alean A. Rush. It incorporates the roles of historical persons in the establishment and development of the A. M. E. Zion Church. Characters depicted and participants in Act I: scene 1 of the play included: the Narrator: Sarah Lewis

African Methodist Episcopal Zion Church

and Julelalh E. Fuller; a Church Group: June Smith; Leora Davidson; William Bulow; the Rev. Maceo Freeman, Ruby Smith; and Evelyn Robinson; Bishop Varick: the Rev. Milton Lewis; Andrew Thompson: Clayton Wiley Sr.; Choir: Conference Mass/Choir Members; June Scott: the Rev. W. Moss; William Miller: Johnnie Searles; Betty (a slave): June Smith; Bishop Christopher Rush: the Rev. O. McLaughlin; Eliza Ann Galpin: Ann McCreg; Bishop William H. Bishop: the Rev. James Lewis; the Rev. Thomas James: the Rev. Paul G. Carter; Frederick Douglass: Clayton Wiley, Sr.; Harriet Tubman: Gwendolyn Clark; Susan B. Anthony: Sara Avant; the Rev. W. S. Sanford: the Rev. Maceo Freeman; Peter Webb: Willie Rudolph; the Rev. Jermain Wesley Loguen: the Rev. Terrance McKissick; and Ruby Smith and Gladys Hunter .

Characters and participants in Act I: scene 2 included: Mary Roberts: Phyliss Wright; William Hamilton: Clayton Wiley, Sr.; Ocie Derham: (not listed); Henry Gains: H. Robinson; Odessa Mitchell: June Smith; the Rev. John W. Jackson: the Rev. Melvin Brown; Albert Kelly: the Rev. Willie McCoy; James Lewis: Willie Lewis; the Rev. Parker: the Rev. Oscar McLaughlin; and Lula Taggart.

The characters and participants in Act I: scene 3 included four children: Stephanie Gillen, Leon Garner, Spankle Harris, and Shalese Garner; Bishop William J. Walls: John Ware; Bishop Herbert Bell Shaw and Mrs. Shaw: the Rev. Dr. Robert Graham and Mrs. Graham; Bishop James Clinton Hoggard and Mrs Eva Hoggard: the Rev. Cleveland Thornhill and Mrs. Thornhill.

Performing soloists included Leora Davidson who sang "God Has Promised to Provide for Me"; Robert Williams who sang "The Storm Is Passing Over"; and Anita Gambrell who sang "Stand By Me."

Act II, scene 4, which dramatizes events from 1985-95, was written by Presiding Elder Joseph D. Kerr, Curtis Rivers, Alean A. Rush, and Ada White Taylor.

Characters and participants in the performance of the last scene included Narrators: Sarah Lewis and Julelalh E. Fuller; First Adult Zionite: the Rev. M. Freeman; a Child: Rev. Freeman's son; Bishop Ruben L. Speaks: the Rev. Errol Hunt; Second Adult Zionite: William Bulow; Faith: Mary Williams; Hope: Sarlyn Tate; and Charity: Earlean Anderson; the Rev. Kenneth W. James: Played himself; Bishop George W. Walker, Sr., and Mrs. Geraldine J. Walker played themselves. Church Group 1: Delegates from Fifth Avenue, St. Mark, St. Paul, St. James, Harriet Tubman, and Walls Memorial congregations; Church Group 2: Delegates from Duryee Memorial, Dyer Phelps, St. James, and St. Luke congregations; Church Group 3: Delegates from Walls Memorial, St. Paul, Fifth Avenue, St. James, and Memorial congregations; Church Group 4: Delegates from Loguen Memorial, Bailey Avenue, Corn Hill, Blackwell Chapel, St. Matthew, and Thomas congregations; Church Group 5: Delegates from

Episcopal District Bicentennial Observances

People's (Syracuse) Centennial, Minnie L. Floyd, and Varick congregations; Church Group 6: Delegates from St. Luke, Walls Temple, and Thompson congregations; Church Group 7: Delegates from Centennial congregation; Church Group 8: Delegates from Logan and St. Luke congregations; Church Group 9: Delegates from People's (Gloversville), Sojourner Truth, People's (Syracuse), Memorial, Centennial, Durham, Corn Hill, Trinity, and Frederick Douglass congregations; Church Group 10: Delegates from Varick and Hope Chapel congregations; Church Group 11: Delegates from Memorial People's (Syracuse); Thompson Avenue, and Walls Temple congregations; Church Group 12: Delegates from Johnstown, Montrose, St. Paul, Frederick Douglass, Minnie L. Floyd, and Blackwell Chapel.

A reception followed the dramatization of the pageant.

MID-ATLANTIC II (FIFTH) EPISCOPAL DISTRICT
Bishop Milton Alexander Williams, Presiding Prelate
The Rev. Lula G. Williams, Missionary Supervisor

During the 1992-96 quadrennium, the former Fifth Episcopal District now called the Mid-Atlantic II, Episcopal District, comprised the Virginia, Philadelphia-Baltimore, East Tennessee-Virginia, India, London-Birmingham, and Manchester-Midland Conferences.

The former Fifth Episcopal District was the host district to the 45th General Conference, which was held at Full Gospel A. M. E. Zion Church, Temple Hills, Maryland, and the Renaissance Hotel, Washington, D. C., during July 24 - August 2, 1996. Bishop Milton Alexander Williams was host bishop, and the Rev. Dr. John A. Cherry was host pastor, the Rev. Joseph A. Davis, host Presiding Elder.

England Conferences
As a part of the pre-Bicentennial Celebrations, the England Conferences cele-brated their 25th Anniversary with a Sunday Worship Service and an Anniversary Banquet on November 12, 1995. Participants included: Bishop Milton A. Williams (USA), Bishop J. Clinton Hoggard (USA), the Rev. Lurleen Gooden, Mrs. Iolie Anguin, Miss Dorothy McFarland, Mrs. Bernice Higgins, Miss Joyce James, Miss Paulette Simpson, Rev. Carmel Jones, Rev. Dr. Kermit J. DeGraffenreidt (USA), the Rev. Assenath KcKenzie, the Rev. Cameron Jackson, Miss Patricia Neil, Mrs. Audrey Gilkes, Ms. June Higgins & Co., The YAMS Choir, the Rev. Horace Gordon, Rev. Dr. Kevin McGill (USA), the Rev. Gary W. Burns (USA), Manchester District Choir, the Rev. Louis B. Simpson, Evangelist Murdell Haughton, Mrs. Veronica Brown, Birmingham District Choir, Mr. Richard Hinds, Mrs. Joyce Lamb (USA), the Rev. Eric

African Methodist Episcopal Zion Church

Brown, London District Choir, the Rev. Noel Brown, the Rev. Lovel Bent, the Rev. Hewie Andrew, the Rev. Dorothy Hawkins,, the Rev. M. Luther Hill (USA), the Rev. Phillip Williams and the Rev. Thomas E. Tucker, Jr. (USA).

Virginia Conference

The Virginia Conference began the pre-Bicentennial Celebration on April 20, 1996, with a fifty-eight unit parade in Petersburg, Virginia. Bishop Milton A. Williams, Sr., Presiding Prelate, and Rev. Lula G. Williams, Missionary Supervisor, were Grand Marshals of the parade. Many churches from the Newport News, Norfolk, and Petersburg Districts were represented with church banners, floats, marching units, cars, and vans. Departments of the conference and districts were also represented. The Petersburg High School Marching Band and the Sussex Central High School Marching Band, Waverly, Virginia, participated in the parade. Ms. Della Woodruff served as Parade chairperson, and the Rev. T. Kenneth Venable was co-chairperson.

The celebration culminated with a dramatic presentation, "The Freedom Church Moves On: Reflecting, Reclaiming, Renewing, Rejoicing." The Rev. E. M. Wilson was conference chairperson. The presentation was held at the Petersburg High School. Mrs. Beverly Mason, Pageant chairperson, gave an overview of the three-act drama. Act I highlighted the beginning of the A. M. E. Zion Church. Act II emphasized the beginning of the Virginia Conference and the bishops that have served the conference since its beginning in 1868. Act III highlighted the Virginia Conference of today and chronicled the accomplishments of the conference under the episcopal guidance of Bishop Milton A. Williams, Sr. Participants included pastors, lay persons, and youth. The Youth Praise Dance groups were from Mt. Zion A. M. E. Zion Church, Dundas, and Gabriel Chapel A. M. E. Zion Church, Chesapeake, Virginia. Music was provided by choirs from St. Mark A. M. E. Zion Church, Suffolk, Virginia; Zion Chester A. M. E. Zion Church, Chester, Virginia; St. John A. M. E. Zion Church, Sunbury, North Carolina; and Gabriel Chapel A. M. E. Zion Church, Chesapeake, Virginia.

Governor George Allen of Virginia declared the date of the celebration "African Methodist Episcopal Zion Church Day." Mayor Rosalyn Dance of the City of Petersburg declared the day "African Methodist Episcopal Zion Church Day" in the City of Petersburg. Mrs. Marian Briley prepared the Souvenir Journal, which included written and pictorial histories of the denomination and the Virginia Conference.

The Bicentennial Committee members were the Revs. E. M. Wilson, Kenneth W. Crowder, Edmund H. Whitley, Lemuel Warren, T. Kenneth Venable, Leroy Blair, M. Luther Hill, Medis Cheek, Margery Glover, Sister Betty Logan, Mrs. Elaine Logan, Mrs. Sandra Crowder, Mrs. Catherine Whitley, and Mrs. Marian Briley.

Episcopal District Bicentennial Observances

Philadelphia-Baltimore Conference

The Philadelphia-Baltimore Conference held a pre-Bicentennial Celebration on Saturday, May 13, 1995, at John Wesley A. M. E. Zion Church, Washington, D. C. The Washington District East Christian Education Department published a Historic Journal, which included the Committee's Address on the Origin of the African Methodist Episcopal Zion Church; the definition of the A. M. E. Zion Church; "What Methodists Believe"; and the history of the eleven Washington District East churches. The Washington District East Bicentennial Observance Committee, which published the journal, comprised Sisters Betty A. Logan, coordinator, Mary Lee, Annette Morgan, Ruth Curry, and Helen S. Carter, district director of Christian Education.

The Philadelphia District, led by Presiding Elder Rev. Albert L. Kaiser, observed the Bicentennial by conducting several Crusades across the District. The theme was "200 New Souls for Christ." The Crusades were under the leadership and direction of the Rev. Charles Phillips, conference director of Evangelism.

Spot broadcasts containing historical information about the A. M. E. Zion Church were aired on radio stations within each area of the District. The churches in the City of Philadelphia also placed television spots.

A District Bicentennial Banquet featured a skit portraying several persons of historical significance in the life of the A. M. E. Zion Church.

Varick Memorial A. M. E. Zion Church, Philadelphia, Pennsylvania, pastored by the Rev. Clifford D. Barnett, Sr., prepared a Commemorative Bicentennial Souvenir Journal for the Philadelphia District. A Philadelphia District Bicentennial Concert was sponsored on Saturday, May 4, 1996 at Small Memorial A. M. E. Zion Church, York, Pennsylvania. The Mass Choir revisited Zion's musical history in song.

East Tennessee-Virginia Conference

The East Tennessee-Virginia Conference prepared a Notebook featuring the histories and pictures of the churches in the East Tennessee-Virginia Conference. The Notebook was presented at the District Conference in May, 1996. Included in the Notebook are the following churches:

St. Paul A. M. E. Zion Church, Johnson City, Tennessee, with photographs of the church and parsonage and its history written by Sister Viola Young. The Rev. James E. Yeary, Sr., is pastor.

Lyons Chapel A. M. E. Zion Church, New Canton, Tennessee, published a Bicentennial Edition Souvenir Journal in celebration of the 200th Birthday of the A. M. E. Zion Church and 118th Birthday of Lyons Chapel with a photograph of the church and parsonage. The Rev. W. R. W. Douglas, Sr., is pastor.

Goode Temple A. M. E. Zion Church, Lynch, Kentucky, prepared a very detailed history of its church with photographs of the church and parsonage. The Rev. Carlisle

African Methodist Episcopal Zion Church

Curry is pastor.

Mrs. Martha Faulkerson wrote a church history of Russell Chapel A. M. E. Zion Church, Rogersville, Tennessee. The history included photographs of the church and parsonage.

Using *The African Methodist Episcopal Zion Church: The Reality of the Black Church* by Bishop William J. Walls and the *Star of Zion* as basic references, White Memorial A. M. E. Zion Church, Middlesboro, Kentucky, compiled "Bits and Pieces: The Zion Family." The history includes photographs of the church and parsonage, of which the Rev. James Yeary is pastor.

Williams Chapel A. M. E. Zion Church, Big Stone Gap, Virginia, published a Homecoming Souvenir Journal with a brief history and a photograph of the church. The Rev. Shelton Lyons is pastor.

Blackman Chapel A. M. E. Zion Church, Norton, Virginia, included a copy of the original deed (1892) for the church property and photographs of the church and the Norton Community Choir. The Rev. Shelton Lyons is pastor.

Neal's Chapel A. M. E. Zion Church, Tazewell, Tennessee, of which the Rev. Hampton K. Turner is pastor, included a photograph of the church building.

Wells Chapel A. M. E. Zion Church, Pennington Gap, Virginia, of which the Rev. Hampton K. Turner is pastor, published "Precious Moments," a brief church history that is still being researched. Included were photographs of "Before Recon-struction" and "After Reconstruction," the interior of the church, and Livingstone-Wiggins Fellowship Hall.

Mrs. Nettie Leeper wrote a church history of Petersburg A. M. E. Zion Church, Rogersville, Tennessee, of which the Rev. Arlester Cartwright is pastor. The history included a photograph of the church.

Benham Chapel A. M. E. Zion Church, Benham, Kentucky, of which the Rev. Carlise Curry is pastor, included a photograph of the church.

Sanders Chapel A. M. E. Zion Church, Rogersville, Tennessee, where the Rev. Arlester Cartwright is pastor, included a photograph of the church.

St. Paul A. M. E. Zion Church, Stonega, Virginia; St. Paul A. M. E. Zion Church, Jenkins, Kentucky; and Zion Hill A. M. E. Zion Church, Surgoinsville, Tennessee, each submitted photographs of their respective churches, all of which are pastored by Presiding Elder Rev. Joseph P. Keaton.

Included in the Notebook was a page of statements: "I Am Proud to Be A Zionite." Statements were written by Mrs. Josephine Williams, Petersburg A. M. E. Zion Church; Ms. Sheba Keaton, Petersburg A. M. E. Zion Church, Mrs. Viola Young, St. Paul A. M. E. Zion Church; Mrs. Martha Faulkerson, Russell Chapel A. M. E. Zion Church; the Rev. James E. Yeary, Sr., St. Paul A. M. E. Zion Church; and Mrs. Mary

Episcopal District Bicentennial Observances

Looney, Russell Chapel A. M. E. Zion Church. Russell Chapel also presented photographs of the "Bicentennial Display."

The 74th District Conference of the Johnson City District celebrated with a Bicentennial Program on May 11, 1996 at Lyons Chapel A. M. E. Zion Church, New Canton, Tennessee. The Rev. Joseph P. Keaton, presiding elder, the Rev. W. R. W. Douglas, host pastor, Mr. T. D. Lassiter, Jr., chairperson, Bicentennial Committee, and Mrs. Norma Bowers, coordinator were leading participants. Mrs. Pam Hoard and Ms. Sheba Keaton played the Prelude. The Rev. Hampton Turner made the Call to Worship. The Rev. Arlester Cartwright read the Old Testament. Rev. W. R. W. Douglas read the New Testament. This was followed with a Prayer by the Rev. Carlisle C. Curry. The following Litany was read responsively:

LEADER: The need for independence, self-expression, and ecclesiastical freedom forced African Americans to leave John Street Methodist Episcopal Church in New York City to form the A. M. E. ZION CHURCH in 1796.

PEOPLE: *God, we are thankful for a denomination that has freedom as one of its principles and strives to share the Gospel without restrictions.*

LEADER: The A. M. E. ZION CHURCH has a rich heritage and is dedicated to the up building of God's Kingdom. It has also contributed greatly to the up building of people of color around the world.

PEOPLE: *O God, we give thanks for your sustaining power in the past and ask you to be with us in the present and future.*

LEADER: O God, we give thanks for the life of James Varick, a servant who exhibited prudence, humility, patience, firmness, forethought, and moderation. Because of his commitment, he became the first Bishop of the African Methodist Episcopal Zion Church.

PEOPLE: *For a life well spent and dedicated to God, we are thankful.*

LEADER: Just as James Varick fought slavery, prejudice, and discrimination among people so shall we continue that legacy and work for justice on all levels.

African Methodist Episcopal Zion Church

PEOPLE: *O God, help us to work to remove those feelings of dislike, jealousy, prejudice, and discrimination from the world so that we may practice your divine principle of love and peace.*

LEADER: James Varick found himself involved in meeting the needs of people by teaching school, providing leadership, and speaking out for justice for people of color.

PEOPLE: *Let us continue to keep the needs of persons before us as we minister, both as clergy and laity. Enable us to provide meaningful leadership, fellowship, and ministry for the furtherance of the Church Universal.*

LEADER: James Varick and other founders of the A. M. E. ZION CHURCH studied the Bible, possessed the Gospel in their hearts, and had an evangelistic zeal that has spanned the years.

PEOPLE: *Let us take up the task by first preparing ourselves through study of the Bible, the tenets of the faith, and the denominational doctrine so that we may be disciples, making and teaching other disciples.*

LEADER: We also offer thanks to God for John Wesley, The Founder of Methodism. It was the principles of Methodism which African Americans sought to incorporate into the new denomination.

PEOPLE: *We give thanks for the history and impetus of the World Methodist Movement.*

LEADER: Each member of the A. M. E. ZION CHURCH is challenged to study the history of the denomination and celebrate jubilantly its rich legacy. Not only should we celebrate, but we should assume responsibility to make the future accomplishments just as motivating.

ALL: *O God, we pledge to be faithful and follow the example given to us in Jesus, We are thankful for your grace, mercy, and sustaining power. Amen, Amen, Amen.*

Episcopal District Bicentennial Observances

Mrs. Vickie Crawford provided Bicentennial Thoughts. The singing of the Bicentennial Hymn followed. Reflections were given by representatives of the following A. M. E. Zion Churches: St. Paul, Goode Temple, Benham Chapel, Blackman Chapel, Wells Chapel, Williams Chapel, Neal's Chapel, White Memorial, Russell Chapel, Lyons Chapel, Sanders Chapel/Petersburg. Closing remarks were given by host Presiding Elder Rev. Joseph P. Keaton.

Russell Chapel A. M. E. Zion Church, Rogersville, Tennessee, compiled a history of the church that was written by Mrs. Martha A. Faulkerson, historian, who stated that it is not a complete history but includes a few facts and reflections.

EASTERN WEST AFRICA (SIXTH) EPISCOPAL DISTRICT

Bishop Samuel Chukukanne Ekemam, Sr., Presiding Prelate
Mrs. Faustina Ifechukwudinma Ekemam, Missionary Supervisor

During 1992-96 the former Sixth Episcopal District, now called the *Eastern West Africa Episcopal District*, comprised the Nigeria Conference (the Mother Conference), Central Nigeria, Rivers Nigeria, Lagos-West Nigeria, and Mainland Nigeria. Bishop Matthews A. M. E. Zion Church, the first A. M. E. Zion Church established in Nigeria, was organized in Iduassang, Oron, in 1932, by Bishop William W. Matthews. Several other churches followed. The Central Nigeria Conference was established in 1973 by Bishop Ruben L. Speaks; the Rivers Nigeria Conference was organized by Bishop Ruben L. Speaks and received into the A. M. E. Zion Church in 1980; the Lagos-West Nigeria Conference was organized in 1991 by Bishop S. C. Ekemam, Sr.; and the Mainland Nigeria Conference was set apart and organized in January, 1992 by Bishop S. C. Ekemam, Sr. There are currently twenty-eight presiding elder districts in Nigeria.

The Rev. Emmanuel J. Umoh is senior presiding elder in charge of the Oron District where the Mother Church is located. The Rev. Thomas D. Eshiet is presiding elder of the Ikono District; the Rev. Nnanna Offiong is the conference secretary and the presiding elder, Eastern District; the Rev. Isaac A. Ikono is the presiding elder of N.A. Odiong District; the Rev. Ituen H. Akpan is presiding elder of the Central District; while the Rev. (Barr.) Nya N. Ebito is the conference legal adviser, conference treasurer, and presiding elder of the Uyo District. Mrs. Ekanem U. D. Umoh serves as field worker; Chief E. S. Akpan is president of the Lay Council.

The Eastern West Africa Nigeria, former Sixth, Episcopal District Bicentennial Celebration was held October 12-15, 1995 at the Grasshopper International Handball Stadium in Owerri, Imo State, Nigeria, West Africa. The presiding bishop in his message said: "We are mindful of the unique history and religious circumstances that gave

African Methodist Episcopal Zion Church

rise to the birth of the Freedom Church then, and the purpose, meaning and raison d'e-tre of the Church now.

"The rich, evolving, and providential history of our Church and the great tradition which is ours, these 200 years, remain a forceful motivation for actualizing and claiming the biblical truism of the peculiarity and holy nationhood of the called-out people of Jesus Christ. "Look where he brought us!" That's where the future of our witness begins.

"The experience and the cumulative measureless success of our founders, Varick, Thompson, Williams, etc., and their followers must remind us that we, too, in our day, under any circumstances of religion, economy, and society, could be used of the God of Zion to bring hope, future, and rejoicing to many who in this day are oppressed, broken, and torn apart by poverty, racism, tribalism, and all that are ungodly. Zion is God's instrument for today and the future. We are partners in redemption, upliftment, and healing. . . .

"And let our celebration and reflection impact not only our faith and witness, but also all our organs and agencies, and the people of Zion. That in the end our gatherings would lead to true reclaiming, renewing, and rejoicing before, during and after our Bicentenary in 1996."

The Bicentennial Torch burned during the four-day celebration as five thousand Nigerians, representing the four conferences in Nigeria, celebrated "200 years with Jesus through the Freedom Church'." The Souvenir Journal and Program outlined the history of the A. M. E. Zion Church, both in America and Africa. The Rev. W. Robert Johnson, general secretary-auditor of the A. M. E. Zion Church, gave the Bicentennial Address at the official opening of the ceremony on October 13, 1995.

The three-hour Parade Extravaganza traveled along the major streets of Owerri. To commemorate the A. M. E. Zion Bicentennial, the Eastern West Africa Episcopal District designed a special bicentennial cloth depicting the image of Bishop James Varick, founder and first bishop of the A. M. E. Zion Church. Dr. Walter Carrington, U. S. Ambassador to Nigeria, addressed those gathered at the Zion-in-Celebration. On October 14, 1995, a Bicentennial Freedom Banquet was held at the Concorde Hotel, Owerri, Nigeria.

The Worship Service held on Sunday, October 15, 1995 was presided over by the Rev. Nya N. Ebito. In the Procession, the Clergy and Choir led the congregation in singing "All Hail the Power." The Rev. Nya E. E. Ebito invoked the Call to Worship. The Rev. E. J. Ekpo recited the communal Invocation. The Rev. I. William Isong led the

Episcopal District Bicentennial Observances

Responsive Reading which was followed by the Hymn of Praise "O God, Our Rock and Our Salvation." The Rev. I William Isong led the Responsive Reading which was followed by Praises led by the Rev. Ipeghan S. Eze. The Anthem was rendered by the A. M. E. Zion Mass Choir, led by Rev. F. C. Nkamiang. The Gospel Choir of the A. M. E. Zion Church sang Musical Selections. The Revs. Cheta Izogo and E. J. Ntukidem read the Scriptures, followed by a Prayer by Rev. Dr. J. J. Essien. The Affirmation of Faith was led by the Rev. B. N. Ndukwu. The Rev. Dr. J. J. Essien introduced Bishop S. Chuka Ekemam. This was followed by a Trumpet Solo "Amazing Grace! How Sweet the Sound." Bishop Ekemam delivered the Sermon, "On The Kingdom of God." The Rev. Ngozi Okwara offered the Invitation to Christian Discipleship which was followed by the Invitational Hymn "I Am Thine, O Lord." Bishop Ekemam recognized Special Guests. Chief Dr. Clement N. Isong, Commander of the Federal Republic of Nigeria, former governor of the Central Bank of Nigeria, and former governor of Cross River State, gave Words of Welcome. The Finance Committee then solicited Offerings, Donations, and Gifts while the Choirs sang Musical Selections. The Consecration of the Offering was followed by the Recessional Hymn "O God Our Help in Ages Past." The Benediction completed the Worship Service.

The members of the Bicentennial Committee included: A. CENTRAL WORKING COMMITTEE: Bro. Sam T. Anderson, chairperson; M. D. Udodong, first vice chairperson; and E. E. Udechukwu, second vice chairperson; Mrs. Ekanem U. D. Umoh, third vice chairperson; Bro. Tarkis E. J. Caiafas, fourth vice chairperson; S. A. Oghu, secretary; Rev. Nnana N. Offiong (deceased), first assistant secretary; Bro. D. J. Etti, second assistant secretary; Rev. Mrs. Umoh L. Udofa, treasurer; Rev. I. William Isong, financial secretary, I; Rev. Cheta Izogo, financial secretary, II; Bro. (Chief) R. C. Okorie, chairman, P. R. O.; Members: Rev. F. C. Nkamiang, Rev. I. E. Umoinyang, all presiding elders, all conference secretaries, all lay presidents, all field workers, all directors of ZEM, directors of Music, directors of Youth, and directors of Evangelism. B. Sub (Working) Committees: *Publicity:* Chief R. C. Okorie, chairman; Members: Bro. E. E. Udechukwu, Bro. (Chief) U. D. Umoh, Bro. (Chief) I. I. Inwang, Bro. Tarkis Caiafas, Rev. Imo E. Umoinyang, Bro. (Chief) Okon Udo-Aka, Rev. Itode Igbagri, Barr. O. V. Ekemam, Bro. Chris Nwosu. *Ceremonials and Program:* Rev. I. W. Isong, chairperson; Members: Sis. Ekanem U. Umoh, Revs. E. Iderima, Ngozi Okwara, and I. S. Eze, Bro. E. E. Udechukwu, Dr. R. S. U. Ebinyasi, and Imo E. Umoinyang. *Venue and Accommodations:* Bro. E. E. Udechukwu, Chairman; Members: Bro. K. Ebiyo, Rev. G. M. Ebinyasi, Dr. A. S. Iruka, Pastor O. J. J. Iwuji, Bro. N. Iheme, Bro. Alfios Ezewuike, Mrs. Nwachukwu, Bro. Ben Ndunji. *Transport:* Inspector D. Nwachukwu, chairperson; Members: Bro. I. I. Nwaehujor, Chief Agaebuonu, Bros. Cyril

African Methodist Episcopal Zion Church

Omouchuroba, Enoch Tashie, and Celestine Ejioafor. Journal: Rev. E. J. Umoh, chairman; Members: Revs. F. C. Nkamiang, and I. E. Umoinyang, Bro. M. D. Udodong, Rev. Dr. J. J. Essien, Sister Dorothy E. Anderson, Rev. E. J. Ekpo, Rev. Umoh L. Udofa, editor, Star of Zion, Bro. E. E. Udechukwu, the Rev. C. Izogo, Rev. I. William Isong. Protocol: Rev. F. C. Nkamiang, chairperson; Members: Chief R. C. Okorie, Sister Dorothy Anderson, Sister Bonye Finecountry, Bro. Nse Song, Bro. (Engr.) Japhet Nnaji-Iwualla, and Sis. Uduak Isong. Entertainment/Banquet: Mrs. P. N. Udechukwu, chairperson; Members: Sis. Eunice Isong, Ekanem Umoh, Arit Essien, and Dorothy Eze; Rev. Umoh L. Udofa, Sisters Rose Peace Iheonu, Comfort Nwadike, Patience Ejeofor, Margaret Caifas, and Winifred Ewang; Mrs. J. C. Ekemam, and Mrs. Ethel Igbadu. Budget/Finance:Bro. Sam T. Anderson, chairperson; Bro. S. A. Oghu, secretary; Rev. Umo Udofa, treasurer; Rev. I. William Isong, financial secretary; Bro. (Chief) R. C. Okorie, P. R. O. Members: Rev. I. Eze, Sister Bonye Finecountry, Bro. Ishmael Akpan, Bro. David J. Etti, Hon. Dr. Ita Udosun, Bro. Tarkis Caiafas, Barr. O. N. Ekemam, and sub-committee chairpersons and secretaries.

SOUTH ATLANTIC (SEVENTH) EPISCOPAL DISTRICT

Bishop George E. Battle, Jr., Presiding Prelate
Mrs. Iris M. Battle, Missionary Supervisor

During 1992-96, the former Seventh, now called the South Atlantic, Episcopal District comprised the Palmetto, Pee Dee, Georgia, South Georgia, South Carolina, Central North Carolina, North Carolina, and Virgin Islands. As part of its Bicentennial Celebration, in April 1995 and April 1996, the former Seventh Episcopal District published journals featuring the history of each local church in the various conferences of the episcopal district. Churches included in the historical journal of 1996 are:

SOUTH CAROLINA CONFERENCE (ROCK HILL DISTRICT)
Rev. W. O. Thompson, presiding elder
Catawba Chapel A. M. E. Zion Church, Catawba, South Carolina
Rev. Dr. W. R. Johnson, III, pastor
Cedar Grove A. M. E. Zion Church, Chester, South Carolina
Rev. Charles Smith, pastor
Center Emmanuel A. M. E. Zion Church, York, South Carolina

Episcopal District Bicentennial Observances

Rev. Loretta Adams, pastor
Chestnut Grove A. M. E. Zion Church, Rock Hill, South Carolina
Rev. Ralph Cunningham, pastor
China Grove A. M. E. Zion Church, Rock Hill, South Carolina
Rev. Timothy Graham, pastor
Foundation A. M. E. Zion Church, Rock Hill, South Carolina
Rev. Reginald Massey, pastor
Indian Hill A. M. E. Zion Church, Fort Mill, South Carolina
Rev. G. W. Smith, pastor (1995); Rev. Shawn Bell, pastor (1996)
Liberty Hill A. M. E. Zion Church, Clover, North Carolina
Rev. Terrence J. Jones, pastor
Mission Outreach A. M. E. Zion Church, York, South Carolina
Rev. Gloria Agurs, pastor
Mt. Calvary A. M. E. Zion Church, Rock Hill, South Carolina
Rev. Charles Agurs, pastor (1995); Rev. Michael Smith, pastor (1996)
Mt. Vernon A. M. E. Zion Church, Fort Lawn, South Carolina
Rev. J. E. Johnson, pastor
Mt. Zion A. M. E. Zion Church, Fort Mill, South Carolina
Rev. W. W. Choate, pastor
New Home A. M. E. Zion Church, York, South Carolina
Rev. Dr. C. J. Jenkins, pastor
New Loves Chapel A. M. E. Zion Church, Rock Hill, South Carolina
Rev. Paulette Littlejohn, pastor
New Mt. Olivet A. M. E. Zion Church, Rock Hill, South Carolina
Rev. Dr. Larry Crossland, pastor
O'Zion A. M. E. Zion Church, Charlotte, North Carolina
Rev. Frankie L. Smith, pastor
Pineville A. M. E. Zion Church, Rock Hill, South Carolina
Rev. Eugene Goodwin, pastor
Ramoth A. M. E. Zion Church, Charlotte, North Carolina
Rev. B. J. Davis, pastor
Red Oak A. M. E. Zion Church, Edgemoor, South Carolina
Rev. Gary Smith, pastor
Rock Grove A. M. E. Zion Church, Rock Hill, South Carolina
Rev. Ralph Washington, pastor
St. Matthew A. M. E. Zion Church, Rock Hill, South Carolina

African Methodist Episcopal Zion Church

Rev. S. Franklin Russell, II, pastor
Tabernacle A. M. E. Zion Church, Rock Hill, South Carolina
Rev. G. W. Thompson, pastor (1995); Rev. Herbert Crump, pastor (1996)
United A. M. E. Zion Church, Fort Mill, South Carolina
Rev. T. R. McBeth, pastor
White Hill A. M. E. Zion Church, York, South Carolina
Rev. W. O. Thompson, pastor

SOUTH CAROLINA CONFERENCE (YORK-CHESTER DISTRICT)
Rev. Dr. Carl A. Glenn, presiding elder
Brooklyn Tabernacle A. M. E. Zion Church, Chester, South Carolina
Rev. Sandra Sistare, pastor
Browns Chapel A. M. E. Zion Church, Lowrys, South Carolina
Rev. O. L. Smith, pastor
Clinton A. M. E. Zion Church, York, South Carolina
Rev. Rickey B. McCullough, pastor
Clover A. M. E. Zion Church, Clover, South Carolina
Rev. Michael E. Smith, pastor
Ebenezer A. M. E. Zion Church, Smyrna, South Carolina
Rev. Margaret Powell, pastor
Fairview A. M. E. Zion Church, Earl, North Carolina
Rev. Marion Jones, pastor
Gabriel A. M. E. Zion Church, Greenville, South Carolina
Rev. Lela Sullivan, pastor
Gower Street A. M. E. Zion Church
Greater Unity A. M. E. Zion Church, South Carolina
Rev. James Scott, Jr.
Jonesville Mission A. M. E. Zion Church
Metropolitan A. M. E. Zion Church, Chester, South Carolina
Rev. Grady Sharps, pastor (1995); Rev. Arthur Randolph, pastor (1996)
Metropolitan A. M. E. Zion Church, Gaffney, South Carolina
Rev. Hayward A. Boyd, Sr., pastor
Mt. Ararat A. M. E. Zion Church, Bauconville, South Carolina
Rev. Leroy Ellison, pastor (1996); Rev. D. B. Schultz (1996)
Mt. Hebron A. M. E. Zion Church, Chester, South Carolina
Rev. Dennis McCleave, pastor

Episcopal District Bicentennial Observances

Mt. Moriah A. M. E. Zion Church, Richburg, South Carolina
  The Rev. Dr. Carl A. Glenn, pastor (1995) Rev. Grady M. Sharps, pastor
  (1996)
Mt. Pleasant A. M. E. Zion Church, Gastonia, North Carolina
  Rev. Asa Wynn, pastor
Mt. Zion A. M. E. Zion Church, Hickory Grove, South Carolina
  Rev. Emmett Browning, pastor
Mt. Zion A. M. E. Zion Church, Catawba, South Carolina
  Rev. Alan Stewart, pastor
Shiloh A. M. E. Zion Church, Grover, South Carolina
  Rev. Franklin Kelly, pastor
Trinity A. M. E. Zion Church, Blacksburg, South Carolina
  Rev. William M. Long, pastor
Union Ezell A. M. E. Zion Church, Fort Lawn, South Carolina
  Rev. George Walker, pastor
Wilson Chapel A. M. E. Zion Church, Sharon, South Carolina
  Rev. W. E. Good, pastor
Zoar A. M. E. Zion Church, Clover, South Carolina
  Rev. Shirley S. Cullen, pastor

GEORGIA CONFERENCE (AUGUSTA DISTRICT)
  Rev. Dr. Robert Christian, presiding elder
Smith Chapel A. M. E. Zion Church, Girard, Georgia
  Rev. J. R. Williams
Mt. Zion A. M. E. Zion Church, Augusta, Georgia
  Rev. Clarence J. Shuford, Jr., pastor
Green Grove A. M. E. Zion Church, Gough, Georgia
  Rev. Samuel Grant, pastor
Jones Chapel A. M. E. Zion Church, Richmond County, Georgia
  Rev. Merritt Littlejohn, pastor

GEORGIA CONFERENCE (WINDER DISTRICT)
  Rev. Dr. M. C. Broughton, Sr., presiding elder
Bush Chapel A. M. E. Zion Church, Winder, Georgia
  Rev. Willie E. Campbell, Jr., pastor
Smith Memorial A. M. E. Zion Church, Monroe, Georgia

African Methodist Episcopal Zion Church

Rev. Ernest E. Lattimore, pastor
Prospect A. M. E. Zion Church, Monroe, Georgia
Rev. Anthony B. Sheats
Pleasant Hill A. M. E. Zion Church, Jersey, Georgia
Rev. G. Howard, pastor
Bethlehem A. M. E. Zion Church, Bethlehem, Georgia
Rev. G. W. Culpepper, Jr., pastor
Spring Hill A. M. E. Zion Church, Monroe, Georgia
Rev. Dr. M. C. Broughton, Sr., pastor
Simmons Chapel A. M. E. Zion Church, Lawrenceville, Georgia
Rev. John M. Clink, Sr., pastor
Mt. Zion A. M. E. Zion Church, Loganville, Georgia
Rev. John Paul Ruth, pastor
Carter Temple A. M. E. Zion Church, Monroe, Georgia
Rev. George Lee Howard, pastor
Union Temple A. M. E. Zion Church, Athens, Georgia
Rev. John M. Clink, Sr., pastor

GEORGIA CONFERENCE (SUMMERVILLE DISTRICT)
Rev. Dr. Talmadge Clark, presiding elder
Hemphill A. M. E. Zion Church, Summerville, Georgia
Rev. Forster R. Izi, pastor
Pond Spring A. M. E. Zion Church, Lyerly, Georgia
Rev. Dr. Talmadge Clark, pastor
Davenport Chapel A. M. E. Zion Church, Valleyhead, Alabama
Rev. Shawn, pastor
St. James A. M. E. Zion Church, Rome, Georgia
Rev. C. H. Rounsaville, pastor
Hilliard Temple A. M. E. Zion Church, Rossville, Georgia
Rev. C. H. Rounsaville, pastor
Napier Chapel A. M. E. Zion Church
The Rev. R. Johnson, pastor
Hilliard Temple A. M. E. Zion Church
Rev. C. H. Rounsaville, pastor
Mt. Zion A. M. E. Zion Church
Rev. W. Evans, pastor

Episcopal District Bicentennial Observances

Lawrence Temple A. M. E. Zion Church
Thomas Chapel A. M. E. Zion Church
Rev. W. Evans, pastor
Wood Station A. M. E. Zion Church

GEORGIA CONFERENCE (ATLANTA DISTRICT)
Rev. Dr. Louis Hunter, Sr., presiding elder
Shaw Temple A. M. E. Zion Church, Atlanta, Georgia
Rev. Dr. Louis Hunter, Sr., pastor
Decatur A. M. E. Zion Church, Lithonia, Georgia
Rev. Roe Nall, Jr., pastor
New Life A. M. E. Zion Church, College Park, Georgia
Rev. Charles H. Jackson, pastor
Emmanuel A. M. E. Zion Church, Stone Mountain, Georgia
Rev. Frederick A. Williamson, pastor

PEE DEE CONFERENCE (CHERAW-BENNETTSVILLE DISTRICT)
Rev. Dr. George D. Crenshaw, presiding elder
St. Peters A. M. E. Zion Church, Clio, South Carolina
Rev. Robert L. Gordon, Jr., pastor
Dyers Hill A. M. E. Zion Church, near Bennettsville, South Carolina
Rev. John L. York, pastor
Millers Chapel A. M. E. Zion Church, Little Rock, South Carolina
Rev. Charles Malloy, pastor
Angelus A. M. E. Zion Church, Jefferson, South Carolina
Rev. Lothell Boyd, pastor
Poplar Hill A. M. E. Zion Church, Pageland, South Carolina
Rev. James Herbert, pastor
Smithville A. M. E. Zion Church
Rev. Dyrrle G. Osborne, pastor
Greater Mt. Airy A. M. E. Zion Church, between Ruby and Chesterfield, South Carolina
Rev. Eugene Campbell, pastor
Piney Grove A. M. E. Zion Church, South Carolina
Rev. Leroy Feely, pastor
Greater Fair Plains A. M. E. Zion Church, McCall, South Carolina
Rev. Sandra Benton, pastor

African Methodist Episcopal Zion Church

Evans Metropolitan A. M. E. Zion Church, Bennettsville, South Carolina
  Rev. Kenneth Lee, pastor
Shiloh A. M. E. Zion Church, Robeson County, North Carolina
  Rev. Windford L. McMillian, pastor
New Zion A. M. E. Zion Church, Dillon County, South Carolina
  Rev. Roy H. Brice, pastor
St. James A. M. E. Zion Church
  Rev. Barbara O. Benjamin, pastor
Rhode Branch A. M. E. Zion Church, Mt. Croghan, South Carolina
  Rev. James McLean, pastor
Pleasant Grove A. M. E. Zion Church, between Cheraw and Chesterfield, South
Carolina Rev. Boyd Johnson, Jr., pastor
Robinson A. M. E. Zion Church, north of Cheraw, South Carolina
  Rev. George D. Crenshaw, pastor
Mt. Hebron A. M. E. Zion Church
  Rev. Albert Young, Jr., pastor
Drucilla A. M. E. Zion Church, near Chesterfield, South Carolina
  Rev. Otis C. Robinson, pastor
Rock Hill A. M. E. Zion Church, between Pageland and Jefferson, South Carolina
  Rev. Verlan Evans, pastor

PEE DEE CONFERENCE (LANCASTER DISTRICT)
  Rev. Dr. Lloyd Snipes, presiding elder
Mt. Zion A. M. E. Zion Church, Lancaster, South Carolina
  Rev. Dr. Jewett L. Walker, pastor
David Stand A. M. E. Zion Church, Lancaster, South Carolina
  Rev. Dr. Ernest White, Jr., pastor
Steele Hill A. M. E. Zion Church, Lancaster, South Carolina
  Rev. Marion Wilson, pastor
Mt. Tabor A. M. E. Zion Church, Lancaster, South Carolina
  Rev. Reid R. White, Jr., pastor
White Oak A. M. E. Zion Church, Van Wyck, South Carolina
  Rev. Lorinzer Johnson, pastor
Camp Creek A. M. E. Zion Church, Lancaster, South Carolina
  Rev. James Thomas, pastor
Mt. Carmel A. M. E. Zion Church, Heath Springs, South Carolina
  Rev. Arthur Howell, pastor

Episcopal District Bicentennial Observances

Elbethel A. M. E. Zion Church, Fort Mill, South Carolina
    Rev. C. J. Young, pastor
Mt. Calvary A. M. E. Zion Church, Lancaster, South Carolina
    Rev. Robert L. Davis, pastor
Mt. Moriah A. M. E. Zion Church, Lancaster, South Carolina
    Rev. Dr. M. F. Harrington, pastor
North Corner A. M. E. Zion Church, Lancaster, South Carolina
    Rev. Harold Jones, pastor
Gold Hill A. M. E. Zion Church, Lancaster, South Carolina
    Rev. Matthew Browning, pastor
St. Paul A. M. E. Zion Church, Lancaster, South Carolina
    Rev. Samuel Wright, pastor
Salem A. M. E. Zion Church, Heath Springs, South Carolina
    Rev. Robert A. Morrison, pastor
Centennial A. M. E. Zion Church, Lancaster, South Carolina
    Rev. Ira Benson, Sr., pastor
Clinton Chapel A. M. E. Zion Church, Lancaster, South Carolina
    Rev. Thomas Horray, pastor
New Hope A. M. E. Zion Church, Lancaster, South Carolina
    Rev. Doris Holmes, pastor
Cedar Creek A. M. E. Zion Church, Heath Springs, South Carolina
    Rev. Roosevelt Alexander, pastor
Mt. Nebo A. M. E. Zion Church, Lancaster, South Carolina
    Rev. Beatrice Jones, pastor
Pleasant Hill A. M. E. Zion Church, Heath Springs, South Carolina
    Rev. Deborah Waddell, pastor
Old Warner Chapel A. M. E. Zion Church, Lancaster, South Carolina
    Rev. Lena Clark, pastor
New Warner Chapel A. M. E. Zion Church, Lancaster, South Carolina
    Rev. Lena Clark, pastor
Palmetto Conference (Columbia-Camden District)
    Rev. Dr. Z. B. Wells, presiding elder
Jones Memorial A. M. E. Zion Church, Columbia, South Carolina
    Rev. Dr. Robert Christian, pastor
Antioch A. M. E. Zion Church, Eastover, South Carolina
    Rev. Sherman B. McBeth, Sr., pastor

African Methodist Episcopal Zion Church

Baum's Chapel A. M. E. Zion Church, Summerville, South Carolina
Rev. George E. McKain, II, pastor
Abundant Life Tabernacle A. M. E. Zion Church, Charleston, South Carolina
Rev. Brian D. Moore, pastor
Clinton Chapel A. M. E. Zion Church, Sumter, South Carolina
Rev. Daisy Fulton, pastor
Beaver Creek A. M. E. Zion Church, South Carolina
Rev. R. Billie, pastor
New A. M. E. Zion Church, Kingstree, South Carolina
Rev. Benjamin Miller, pastor
Trinity-Woodruff A. M. E. Zion Church, Woodruff, South Carolina
Rev. Jessee J. Peay, pastor
Pleasant Grove A. M. E. Zion Church, Fairfield, South Carolina
Rev. Dr. Z. B. Wells, pastor
Camp Welfare A. M. E. Zion Church, Fairfield County, South Carolina
Rev. Cordell A. Jenkins, pastor
Fairview A. M. E. Zion Church, Great Falls, South Carolina
Rev. W. H. Perry, pastor
Paradise A. M. E. Zion Church, South Carolina
Rev. John Long, pastor
Good News A. M. E. Zion Church, Orangeburg, South Carolina
Rev. Mary S. Tucker, pastor
Good Hope A. M. E. Zion Church, South Carolina
Rev. J. R. Williams, pastor
Mt. Nebo A. M. E. Zion Church, Bascomville, South Carolina
Rev. Sam Latta, pastor
Bethesda A. M. E. Zion Church, Winnsboro, South Carolina
Rev. E. L. Miller, pastor
Rossville A. M. E. Zion Church, Rossville, South Carolina
Rev. Rolly Dawkins, pastor

PALMETTO CONFERENCE (SPARTANBURG DISTRICT)
Rev. Dr. David L. Scott, presiding elder
Metropolitan A. M. E. Zion Church, Spartanburg, South Carolina
Rev. Dr. Robert L. Perry, pastor
New Hope A. M. E. Zion Church, Union, South Carolina
Rev. J. W. Boyd, Jr., pastor

Episcopal District Bicentennial Observances

Besides the compilation of a journal on the histories and development of churches in the episcopal district, the various conferences of the Seventh Episcopal District also had special events and programs as part of their pre-Bicentennial Celebrations.

South Carolina Conference

The South Carolina Conference held its pre-Bicentennial Celebration in conjunction with a Leadership Training Institute at New Mt. Olivet A. M. E. Zion Church with host Pastor Rev. Larry Crossland. The dramatic presentation, "200 Historical Years: A Legacy in Retrospective," written and directed by Mrs. Barbara S. Johns, was performed. The presentation highlighted the history of South Carolina and the contributions of its episcopal leaders since its organization on March 24, 1867, in Chester, South Carolina.

The Leadership Training Institute was taught by Dr. James David Armstrong, the editor of the *A. M. E. Zion Quarterly Review* and secretary of the A. M. E. Zion Historical Society.

On Saturday, April 29, 1995, the South Carolina Conference held a Gala Banquet at St. John United Methodist Convention Center, with Rev. Dr. Morgan W. Tann, editor of the *Star of Zion*, delivering the Keynote Address.

On Sunday afternoon, April 30, 1995, the Bicentennial Parade began with 109 floats, cars, and vans. The parade was led by Bishop and Mrs. George E. Battle, Jr., in the episcopal float, followed by district floats, church floats, organization floats, civic, fraternal, and business floats.

On Sunday evening, Bishop Clarence Carr was the speaker for the Ecumenical Program. His subject was "Now unto Him Who Is Able to Keep You from Falling." Music was rendered for the occasion by the South Carolina Mass Hymn Choir, the South Carolina Mass Youth Choir, and the Sanctuary Choir from New Mt. Olivet A. M. E. Zion Church. Other program participants included: The Revs. Asa Wynn, Loretta Adams, Larry Crossland, George Walker, Jr., Dr. Carl A. Glenn, Dr. W. O. Thompson, Rickey McCullough, S. Franklin Russell, and Paulette Littlejohn.

Rev. Dr. Marcus Hanna Boulware wrote "A History of the Metropolitan A. M. E. Zion Church, 1866-1979," Chester, South Carolina. Dr. Boulware was formerly a professor of speech communication at the Florida A. & M. University in Tallahassee, Florida and was a member of an outstanding, life-long A. M. E. Zion church family in Chester, South Carolina.

A significant church in the history of the Palmetto Conference is the Antioch A. M. E. Zion Church in Eastover, South Carolina. During the period of the denominational bicentennial celebration, one of their members, Dr. Juanita S. Scott, sent in a brief

African Methodist Episcopal Zion Church

summary of the history of this church. It seems appropriate to share some of this with those who are interested in the early development and later growth of specific A. M. E. Zion congregations.

Antioch African Methodist Episcopal Zion (A. M. E. Zion) Church was most likely organized between 1824 and 1838 by persons from Logue's Chapel Methodist Episcopal Church, which closed about 1824. Antioch was organized by white and colored members who first built a log house and worshipped together. The church was given to the blacks in 1866 after the Emancipation Proclamation.

Antioch became a part of the A. M. E. Church around 1866, and the A. M. E. Zion Church in the later 1800s. Though the exact date and reasons for the changeover are not recorded, "story" has it that members of the church were dissatisfied because they could not always get a preacher through the head church (St. Phillips) because Antioch was a mission church. Consequently, when an A. M. E. Zion presiding elder, who was "walking through," promised that he could get preachers for them, Antioch joined the A. M. E. Zion Church. Antioch has since been an integral part of the connectional work of the A.M. E. Zion Church and has hosted district and annual conferences and Sunday School Conventions over the years. Antioch has gone through the phases of being a mission, a circuit, and now a station church.

Antioch Church has always been in the same location as far as can be determined. The land on which the church currently stands was owned by the Crooms family in the early 1900s and was officially deeded to the church in 1955 by Alvin L. Bostic. The first church building was a log house that was torn down in 1874, after which another log house was built. It is possible that a bush harbor was used between the second log house and the wood frame church, which was built about 1900. This building, 30 x 40 feet with a fireplace for heating was renovated, remodeled, enlarged, redesigned, etc., over the years. It was covered by imitation brick siding and then cinder blocks. The fireplace was replaced by wood burning heaters in the early 1940s and gas heaters in the 1960s. Electricity was added to the church in 1940 and indoor toilets were added along with Sunday School rooms in the early 1960s.

In May and June of 1984, the entire church building was dismantled to make way for the current modern and much larger brick sided facility with stained glass windows. The new facility included a 50 x 70 foot sanctuary with stands for four choirs, and a 40 x 50 foot fellowship hall with three classrooms, a pastor's study, two lounges, finance room, kitchen, and spacious hallways. The front porch opens into a foyer with rest rooms and choir rooms on each side. The church is highlighted by two steeples.

Episcopal District Bicentennial Observances

The Bicentennial Celebration Committee comprised Rev. Dr. Larry Crossland, Rock Hill District, director of the Bicentennial Celebration and chairman of the Program Committee; Mrs. Lillian T. Shelborne, Seventh Episcopal Area Committee director; Ms. Mary Archie, South Carolina Conference director; Mrs. Rose McCullough, chairman of Banquet Committee; Mrs. Frances Glenn, secretary and chairperson for the Souvenir Journal Committee; Mrs. Barbara S. Johns, director and presenter of the Bicentennial Drama Committee; Rev. Grady Sharps, treasurer; Mrs. Sharon Kirk, director of Youth Mass Choir; and Mrs. Lois Parker, bicentennial consultant.

Georgia-South Georgia Conference

The Georgia-South Georgia Conference celebrated the pre-Bicentennial at a special service held on Wednesday, November 1, 1995, at New Life A. M. E. Zion Church, College Park, Georgia. The host pastor and host presiding elder, Rev. Charles Herbert Jackson and Rev. Dr. Louis Hunter, Sr., Atlanta District, respectively, were the Worship Leaders. The Prelude was played by Mrs. Sandy Johnson, pianist; Rev. Louis Hunter, Sr., gave the Call to Worship. Rev. Dr. M. C. Broughton, presiding elder, Winder District, gave the Invocation. The Scripture was read by Rev. Dr. Robert Christian, presiding elder, Augusta District, followed by a Prayer by Rev. Talmadge Clark, presiding elder, Summerville District. The choral selection "We've Come This Far by Faith" was sung by the Bicentennial Choir, with Dr. Montina Golphin Jackson as director. Mrs. Merchuria Chase Williams introduced the vignette "From New York to Georgia and Beyond." The vignette, "A History of the A. M. E. Zion Church," was written by Mrs. Stephanie Brown, Mrs. Vivian Brown, Mrs. Cathy Monroe, and Mrs. Merchuria Chase Williams. Remarks were given by Mrs. Mayfred Nall, bicentennial director, Georgia-South Georgia Conferences, Mrs. Lillian T. Shelborne, bicentennial director, Seventh Episcopal District, and Bishop George E. Battle, Jr., presiding prelate, Seventh Episcopal District.

The cast of "From New York to Georgia and Beyond" included Mrs. Vivian Brown, as Narrator; Ms. Cathy Monroe, as Reporter; Ms. Rosanna Brandon, as Praise Dancer; Mr. Elliott Valez, as Preacher; Mr. Henry Brown, as Man #1; Mr. Fred Burks, as Man #2; Mrs. Mayfred Nall, as Woman; Rev. John Paul Ruth, as James Varick; Mrs. Betty Ruth, as Historian #1; Mr. Julian Parker, as Historian #2; Ms. Linda Cratic, as Historian #3; Mrs. Mollie Lewis, as Historian #4; Mrs. Mendi Lewis-Reed, as Historian #5; and Rev. Claude J. Shuford, as Historian #6.

The following committees were responsible for the success of the celebration: Bicentennial Directors: Mrs. Lillian T. Shelborne, Seventh Episcopal District; Mrs.

African Methodist Episcopal Zion Church

Mayfred Nall, Georgia-South Georgia Conferences; Ms. Sadye Potter, Atlanta-Summerville Districts; Mrs. Mollie Lewis, Winder-Augusta Districts. Bicentennial Steering Committee: Dr. Louis Hunter, Sr., Rev. Charles H. Jackson, Rev. Roe Nall, Jr., Rev. Frederick Williamson, Mrs. Ingrid Hunter, Dr. Montina G. Jackson, Mrs. Mayfred Nall, Ms. Sadye Potter, Mrs. Rosemary Williamson. Bicentennial Program Committee: Mrs. Ingrid Hunter, Chairperson, Mrs. Mayfred Nall, Ms. Sadye Potter, Mrs. Carolyn Huff, Mrs. Mollie Lewis, Mr. Timothy Watkins. Bicentennial Exhibition: Ms. Sadye Potter and Mrs. Ingrid Hunter. Props and Costumes: Mrs. Carolyn Huff and Ms. Lesa Hamlett. Bicentennial Music Committee: Dr. Montina G. Jackson and Mrs. Sandy Johnson. Historical Journal and Souvenirs: Mrs. Ingrid Hunter.

SOUTH WESTERN DELTA (EIGHTH) EPISCOPAL DISTRICT

Bishop Joseph Johnson, Presiding Prelate
Mrs. Dorothy Johnson, Missionary Supervisor

During the 1992-96 quadrennium, the former Eighth, now called the South Western Delta, Episcopal District comprised the Arkansas, West Tennessee-Mississippi, South Mississippi, Louisiana, Texas, and Oklahoma Conferences.

Arkansas Conference

Ms. Carrie B. Evans, a member of Cherry Street Memorial A. M. E. Zion Church, Pinebluff, Arkansas, gave the Bicentennial Historical Commission a scrapbook containing extensive materials on the history of Cherry Street Memorial A. M. E. Zion Church, which was organized in 1892, on the corner of 8th Avenue and Cherry Street, in a blacksmith shop, by a group of loyal Zionites led by the Revs. E. B. Wall and S. Parker, the presiding elder.

The Pine Bluff/Wilmot Districts of the Arkansas Conference presented a District Black History Celebration on Saturday, February 17, 1996 at Zion Temple A. M. E. Zion Church, Crossett, Arkansas. The program highlighted the history of the A. M. E. Zion Church, the theme of which was "Two Hundred Years: The A. M. E. Zion Church Preparing All God's People, Ephesians 4: 11-13." Rev. Leonard Scott was the host pastor, Rev. James A. Vault, presiding elder.

Participants in the celebration included Mrs. Doris Wimberly, Christian Education director; Mrs. Joyce Block, director of Youth; and Mrs. Sadie Darden, direc-

Episcopal District Bicentennial Observances

tor of Children. Each church in the Pine Bluff/Wilmot District was represented with at least one contestant in the Oratorical Contest on the theme "Called to Be Disciples at the Dawn of the 21st Century."

Louisiana Conference
Dr. Clara Robertson of the Louisiana Conference sent a brief account of the Bicentennial Celebration in the Louisiana Annual Conference, which was sponsored by the Christian Education Department during Education Night at the Annual Conference. Dr. Clara Robertson was conference director. Participants included Brother Hollis Bush from Trinity A. M. E. Zion Church; Brother Jarvis McRae of Petty A. M. E. Zion Church; Sister Leona Morris, district director of the Roseland District; and Sister Beverly Littlejohn, district director of the New Orleans District. Music was rendered by Petty and Butler A. M. E. Zion Church Choirs. Solos were rendered by the following: Rev. John Mabry, Rev. Frank Garrett, and Dr. Shirley Robertson Glover. Rev. Willie G. Johnson, presiding elder of the New Orleans District of the Louisiana Conference, delivered the Message.

Oklahoma Conference
Ms. Priscilla F. Workman, director, of the former Eighth Episcopal District Christian Education Department, supplied each of the district's churches with information culled from *The African Methodist Episcopal Zion Church: Reality of the Black Church*, by Bishop William J. Walls. Varick Chapel A. M. E. Zion Church observed "Black History Month" on successive Sundays for a month during the 11:00 am service. Each Sunday several youth reported what they had learned about a particular black person. On the fourth Sunday, during an afternoon program, they recounted the history of Varick Chapel and the A. M. E. Zion Church. In this way, they highlighted their heritage in Zion Methodism during the pre-Bicentennial Celebration.

ALABAMA/FLORIDA (NINTH) EPISCOPAL DISTRICT

Bishop Richard K. Thompson, Presiding Prelate
Mrs. Georgia McNair Thompson, Missionary Supervisor

The former Ninth, now the Alabama/Florida, Episcopal District during the 1992-96 quadrennium comprised the Alabama, Cahaba, Central Alabama, North Alabama, South Alabama, West Alabama, Florida, and South Florida Conferences.
Rev. Dr. Erskine R. Faush was the host presiding elder, Birmingham District.
Rev. Darryl B. Starnes, Sr., was host pastor and chairperson of the 1995 Alabama-

African Methodist Episcopal Zion Church

Florida Episcopal District Bicentennial Celebration Committee.
The Alabama-Florida Episcopal District of the A. M. E. Zion Church sponsored an "Evangelistic Crusade and Training Institute" at the Metropolitan A. M. E. Zion Church, Birmingham, Alabama, May 25-27, 1995, as part of the official program of the 1995 Bicentennial Celebration. The theme of the crusade and training institute was "Celebrating Our Bicentennial By Observing, Renewing, and Rejoicing Through Evangelism."

Program Participants
Thursday, May 25, 1995. The Welcome Program was led by the Metropolitan A. M. E. Zion Church, Birmingham. The Revs. Fred and Barbara Rogers led the Praise Service. Rev. Ezekiel Washington was Worship Leader for the Evangelistic Service. The Metropolitan Mass Choir, Birmingham, St. Peters Mass Choir, Tuscaloosa, and Sister Robin Tiggs, as Featured Soloist, provided music. The Fayette-Jasper District supplied the Ushers for the occasion. Bishop George E. Battle, Jr., presiding prelate, Seventh Episcopal District, A. M. E. Zion Church, was the Evangelist for the occasion.

Friday, May 26, 1995. After breakfast, a Praise Service was led by the directors of Evangelism, with the Meditation given by Rev. Claude J. Shuford. Rev. Dr. Lewis Drummond, director of the Institute of Church Growth and Evangelism, Beeson Divinity School, Samford University, Birmingham, Alabama, delivered a lecture on "The Ministry of Evangelism in the Local Church." In the noonday Evangelistic Service, the Praise Service was led by the Praise Team with Sister Vera Kolb featured as soloist. Dr. Norman H. Hicklin, director, Bureau of Evangelism, A. M. E. Zion Church, was the noonday Evangelist. The afternoon Praise Service was led by directors of Evangelism, A. M. E. Zion Church. A panel discussion concerning "Critical Issues in Evangelism," was moderated by Rev. James French. Panelists included Rev. George Washington, Alabama Conference; Dr. William Scott, Cahaba Conference; Dr. Atheal Pierce, Central Alabama Conference; Rev. Lester Jacobs, Florida Conference; Dr. Donnell Williams, North Alabama Conference; Rev. Richard Dockery, South Alabama Conference; Dr. Mozella G. Mitchell, South Florida Conference; and Dr. Richard Chapple, West Alabama Conference. Bishop Richard K. Thompson, presiding prelate of the former Ninth Episcopal District, shared "Episcopal Insights on Evangelism" with the audience. The evening Praise Service was led by the Revs. Fred and Barbara Rogers. Rev. Robert Perry was the Worship Leader in the evening Evangelistic Service. The Weeping Mary Youth Choir, Tuscaloosa, and the Mt. Zion Mass Choir, Montgomery, with Tandra Jones as Featured Soloist supplied the music.

Episcopal District Bicentennial Observances

The Tuscaloosa District supplied Ushers for the occasion. Bishop George E. Battle, Jr., was the Evangelist for the evening service.

Saturday, May 27, 1995. A Breakfast and Forum for Christian Education Directors was held at the Holiday Inn, Redmont City Centre, Birmingham, Alabama. The morning Praise Service was led by directors of Evangelism. Rev. David Richardson delivered the Meditation. Training Forums for Youth and Adults were held. The Youth Forum was led by the Revs. Symanksi Fields and Roosevelt Acoff, assisted by youth leaders, Brother Douglas McKensie and Sister Francilla Allen. The Adult Forum (for Ministers and Laity) was led by Dr. Norman H. Hicklin, as Facilitator.

Rev. Darryl B. Starnes was the Worship Leader of the Bicentennial Service at Noon. The Alabama-Florida Episcopal District Choir supplied music and the Birmingham District supplied Ushers for the occasion. Bishop George E. Battle, Jr., was the Evangelist for the occasion.

"We're Marching to Zion" was the Processional Hymn, which was followed by the Call to Worship and the Introit. Presiding Elder Dr. R. M. Richmond gave the Invocation. This was followed by a Choral Response. The Hymn of Praise was "I Love Thy Kingdom, Lord." Presiding Elder Rev. James Jackson gave the Responsive Reading: "The Spirit of Missions," Acts 13:2-3; 44-47. The Gloria Patri followed.. Presiding Elder Dr. Leo Meriweather gave the Scripture Lesson. Presiding Elder Dr. A. L. Wilson gave the Prayer. Presiding Elder and Director of the Alabama-Florida District Choir Dr. Erskine R. Faush led the Choral Selection. Presiding Elder Dr. J. E. Fields led the recitation of the Apostles' Creed, which was followed by the Offertory and Announcements and Notices. After a choral selection by the Alabama-Florida District Choir, Presiding Elder Rev. James E. Hendrix introduced Bishop Richard K. Thompson, who subsequently introduced the Evangelist for the Celebration—Bishop George E. Battle, Jr., presiding prelate, Seventh Episcopal District. The Hymn of Preparation was "Amazing Grace." After the Sermon, the Invitation to Christian Discipleship was extended. "Just As I Am" was the Invitational Hymn for the service. This was followed by the Recession and the Benediction.

After the Bicentennial Celebration Service a dinner was held.

The 1995 pre-Bicentennial Celebration Committee Organization comprised the following committees:

African Methodist Episcopal Zion Church

Program Committee
Rev. Darryl Starnes, Chairperson
Dr. E. R. Faush
Dr. Leo Meriweather
Dr. James E. Hendrix
Dr. Donnell D. Williams
Rev. Roosevelt Acoff
Rev. T. S. Felder
Rev. Robert Anderson

Sister Francilla Allen
Sister Farris A. Williams
Sister Dollie Hendrix
Sister Erma Patton
Bishop Richard K. Thompson, ex-officio

Publicity Committee
Rev. Homer Jackson, chairperson
Sister Doris W. Adams
Sister Marjorie Lawson
Sister Tawanna Burton
Sister Patricia S. McAdory
Sister Mary Metcalfe

Evangelistic Canvass Committee
Rev. T. S. Felder, chairperson
Rev. Roosevelt Acoff
Rev. Robert Anderson
All pastors and directors of Evangelism

Lodging Committee
Sister Faye White, chairperson
Sister Atrie B. Robinson

Literature Committee
Sister Thelma Richardson, co-chairperson
Rev. Jeffrey Cammon, co-chairperson
Sister Ella Pruitt
Sister Ethel Evans
Brother James Wright
Rev. Doris Rogers
Sister Lillie B. King
Rev. Robert Anderson

Transportation Committee
Brother Willie Hale, chairperson
Sister Nettie Clayton
Brother Robert McKinney
Brother Kenneth Turner
Rev. James L. Bufford
Rev. J. L. Allen

Food and Catering Committee
Sister Irma Patton, chairperson
Sister Dovie H. Ward
Sister Bama Wilson
Food and Catering

Souvenir Booklet Committee
Sister Carolyn Washington, chairperson
Dr. Robert Carter
Sister Myra Wright
Souvenir Booklet Committee (cont'd)

Episcopal District Bicentennial Observances

Sister Cherry Lewis
Sister Mary Speed
Sister Gertrude Skates
Sister Christine Lanster
Sister Melissa Parrish
Sister Patricia McAdory
Rev. Lucille Y. Latham

Sister Ethel Evans
Sister Edith Hill
Sister Carrie Cook
Sister Ola S. Rogers
Sister Therolene W. Hardy
Sister Dollie Hendrix, Booster

During the pre-Bicentennial Celebration, On Saturday, May 4, 1996, at the Birmingham Jefferson Civic Center, the North Alabama Conference had an "Appreciation Celebration" for Mrs. Farris A. Williams for her many years of dedicated service to the A. M. E. Zion Church. Participating in the celebration were Rev. Dr. Erskine R. Faush, Master of Ceremony; Rev. Dr. Fred D. Mayweather, presiding elder, emeritus, delivered the Invocation; and Rev. Darryl B. Starnes said the Grace. Other participants included Bishop J. Clinton and Mrs. Eva S. Hoggard, Bishop Richard K. and Mrs. Georgia M. Thompson, and Bishop Cecil Bishop. The honoree was introduced by her son, Rev. Dr. Donnell Williams, pastor of Hunter Chapel, Tuscaloosa, Alabama.

MID-WEST (TENTH) EPISCOPAL DISTRICT
Bishop Enoch B. Rochester, Presiding Prelate
Dr. Mattilyn T. Rochester, Missionary Supervisor

The former Tenth Episcopal District during the 1992-96 quadrennium, now called the *Mid-West Episcopal District*, comprised the Indiana, Michigan, Kentucky, Missouri, Tennessee, and South Africa Conferences.

Tennessee Conference
The pre-Bicentennial Celebration, "A Taste of the Past," was held on Saturday, April 13, 1996, at Greater Warner Tabernacle A. M. E. Zion Church, Knoxville, Tennessee. The Rev. Eric L. Leake was host pastor, and the Rev. Dr. George C. Sanders, Sr., presiding elder, Chattanooga District, was host presiding elder.

Tennessee Conference Bicentennial Celebration Committee
The celebration committee included: Bishop Enoch B. Rochester, Presiding Elder George C. Sanders, Sr., Presiding Elder Vincent M. Jones, Sr., Rev. J. R. Bridgeman, Dr. Marcia Donaldson, Mrs. Beulah Gillespie, Ms. Barbara A. Haigler, Mr. James H.

African Methodist Episcopal Zion Church

Harper, Mrs. Daisy Henson, Rev. Dr. J. D. Howell, Rev. Eric L. Leake, Mrs. LaFonde McGee, Rev. Michael J. McNair, Mr. Monroe Powers, Mr. Nelson Stephens, Rev. Arthur Tuggle, Mr. Leonard E. Wallace, and Mr. Larry Woods.

Participating in the program, which included a well-written skit and an opportunity to taste the foods of late eighteenth-century America, were: Mr. Leonard E. Wallace, Mrs. E. Babington-Johnson, Mrs. Kathleen Stephens, Mr. Robert Boyd, Rev. Dr. George C. Sanders, Sr., Rev. Eric Leake, Rev. Dr. Gloria Moore, Mr. James Blair, Rev. Dr. Vincent M. Jones, Sr., First A. M. E. Zion Church Sanctuary Choir, Mrs. Martha Blanton, Rev. R. E. Sharp, Mrs. Ronnie Chandler, First A. M. E. Zion Male Choir, and the St. Paul A. M. E. Zion Church Choir.

The program included "A Walk Through A. M. E. Zion History": "Establishment of the Church"; " Moving South: 1st and 2nd Half of the 20th Century"; "Lay Council"; "Christian Education Department"; and "Missionary Department." The skit was written by Mrs. LaFonde W. McGee, Mr. Nelson Stephens, and Ms. Rose Weaver.

The Knoxville-Maryville District celebrated the Bicentennial with a Leadership Training Workshop, Theater Dinner, and a Praise Service held on November 12 and 13, 1994. The Souvenir Journal for the two-day observance contains a Proclamation from Mayor Edmund A. Nephew, City of Oak Ridge, Tennessee (home of Spurgeon Chapel A. M. E. Zion Church), designating November 13, 1994 as A. M. E. Zion Day in Oak Ridge; a letter from Presiding Elder Vincent M. Jones, Sr., a Historical Sketch of the African Methodist Episcopal Zion Church, and the Founders' Address of the A. M. E. Zion Church.

The Leadership Training Workshop was held at Greater Warner Tabernacle A. M. E. Zion Church. Knoxville, Tennessee. The Workshop theme was "Equipping The Membership to Serve." Rev. Dr. Dennis V. Proctor led Plenary Session I, "Prerequisite for Lay Leadership in Local Church: What God Requires." Rev. Darryl B. Starnes, Sr., led Plenary Session II, "Problems of Lay Leadership in the Local Church: What Happens When Churches Break Down?" The following Workshops were presented: "Trustees and Stewards: Who's in Charge?" by Rev. Dr. Dennis V. Proctor; "Missionary Societies/Deaconesses: Staying in or Reaching Out?" by Dr. Grace L. Holmes; "Evangelism, and Community Outreach: Church Gathered vs. Church Scattered" by Rev. Kenneth Yverlton; "Class Leaders: Collecting Dues vs. Seeking the Lost" by Rev. Darryl B. Starnes, Sr.; "Christian Education/Sunday School/ Starting and Maintaining a Children's Church Ministry: Developing Ministries That Build Strong Families" by Ms. Jacqui Hart, Ms. Marian Walls, Mrs. Pam Perkins; and

Episcopal District Bicentennial Observances

"Building a Brotherhood Ministry: Reaching The Black Male" by Rev. W. Darin Moore.

The Praise and Worship Service was held on Sunday, November 13, 1994 at Greater Warner Tabernacle A. M. E. Zion Church, Knoxville, Tennessee, with Rev. Daniel Webb serving as the Announcer. Rev. Dr. Vincent M. Jones declared the Call to Worship. Rev. Eric L. Leake delivered the Invocation. The congregation sang the hymn "Work of Our Founders We Extol," which was written for the Sesquicentennial Celebration of the A. M. E. Zion Church by Mrs. Bettye Lee Roberts Alleyne. Rev. Eric L. Leake read the Scripture from the Old Testament. The New Testament Scripture was read by the Rev. Arthur Tuggle. The Rev. L. C. Dillingham gave the Prayer. The United Fellowship Mass Choir provided Music. Rev. Dr. Vincent M. Jones introduced Bishop Enoch B. Rochester, the Speaker.

Mr. Leonard E. Wallace compiled the "A. M. E. Zion Church Tennessee Annual Conference History," which included material sent by Mr. James H. Harper to the episcopal district from *The French Broad Holston Country: A History of Knox County, Tennessee* on the founding of the African Methodist Episcopal Zion Church in Knoxville, Tennessee. The roster below shows the dates when churches were established in the respective presiding elder districts of the Tennessee Conference:

KNOXVILLE DISTRICT	DATE
1. Greater Warner Tabernacle	1845
2. Logan Temple	1865
3. Oakgrove	1868
4. Concord Chapel	1872
5. Lomax Temple	1876
6. Edgewood Chapel	1890
7. Stanford Chapel	1898
8. Grady Chapel	1906
9. Wallace Chapel	1930
10. Spurgeon Chapel	1945
11. First A. M. E. Zion	1958

MARYVILLE DISTRICT	
1. Saint Paul	1867
2. Clinton Chapel	1875
3. Mount Pleasant	1880

African Methodist Episcopal Zion Church

4. Craig Chapel	1896
5. Rice Chapel	1898
6. Mount Zion	1904

CHATTANOOGA DISTRICT	Date
1. St. Mark	1867
2. Pikeville Chapel	1869
3. Braxton Chapel	1874
4. Tompkin Chapel	1875
5. Pleasant Hill	1880
6. Price Memorial	1882
7. Brakebill Chapel	1886
8. Mt. Olive	1886
9. Patten Memorial	1886
10. Watson Chapel	1886
11. Mount Morriah	1891
12. Cleages Chapel	1896
13. Speights Chapel	1896
14. Uchee Chapel	1900
15. Fields Chapel	1900
16. Williams Chapel	1909
17. Harwell Chapel	1909
18. Gillespie Chapel	1910
19. Alleyne Memorial	1937
20. Cox Chapel	1946
21. Harris Chapel	1950
22. Lane Chapel	1954

The Bicentennial Celebration Committees: *Theatre Dinner*: Mr. Nelson Stephens, Rev. Dr. Gloria Moore, Dr. Grace L. Holmes; *Exhibit*: Ms. Barbara A. Haigler and Mr. E. Wallace; *Reception*: Mrs. H. Harper, *Souvenir Journal*: Mr. James H. Harper and Rev. Dr. Vincent M. Jones; *Praise and Worship*: Mrs. Kathleen Stephens, Mrs. K. Thompson, Rev. B. Thomas, Rev. H. Poindexter, and Rev. L. Brinson; *Budget:* The Revs. Arthur Tuggle, A. Petway, B. Thomas, and Michael J. McNair; Musicians:Mrs. E. Babington-Johnson and Mr. E. Wallace; *Ushers*: Knoxville-Maryville District Churches; Publicity: Mrs. A. McNair, Mrs. W. Meriweather, and Ms. Rose Weaver.

Episcopal District Bicentennial Observances

Missouri Conference
"Reflecting! Reclaiming! Renewing! Rejoicing ! Zion Methodism: 1796-1996" was the title of the dramatic presentation by the Missouri Conference on June 11, 1996. The historic presentation told the story of the A. M. E. Zion Church, its leaders, and their contributions during the church's 200 years.

WESTERN WEST AFRICA (ELEVENTH) EPISCOPAL DISTRICT

Bishop Marshall Hayward Strickland, Presiding Bishop
Dr. Dorothy J. Brunson, Missionary Supervisor

During the 1992-96 quadrennium the former Eleventh Episcopal District, now called the Western West Africa Episcopal District, comprised the Liberia, East Ghana, West Ghana, Mid-Ghana, and Cote d'Ivoire Annual Conferences. The former Eleventh Episcopal District sponsored its pre-Bicentennial Celebrations from March 28, 1996 to April 28, 1996. The celebrations included a tour from America to Ghana, West Africa.

West Ghana Conference
The West Ghana Conference hosted the Episcopal District's Woman's Home and Overseas Missionary Society Bicentennial Convention April 2-7, 1996 at Price Memorial A. M. E. Zion Church, Winneba, Ghana. Presiding Elders in the conference included the Revs. Dr. Godfred N. Zormelo, Winneba District; Anna Quansah, Cape Coast District; Kofi Simmons, Sekondi District; S. K. Ghartey, Akim Manso District; Sir George Zormelo, Akim Akroso District; and Ben Ackon Effum, Assim District.

East Ghana Conference
The East Ghana Conference hosted the Episcopal District's "Zion Men United in Celebration" under the auspices of the Sons of Varick and the Men's Fellowship during April 11-14, 1996 at the Aggrey Memorial A. M. E. Zion Church, Mamprobi and Big Zion A. M. E. Zion Church, La. Presiding Elders included the Revs. P. E. T. Sefogah, Accra District; A. K. Nyavedzie, Ho District; E. K. Pomeyie, Tema District; J. B. C. Adjavor, Agbozume District; C. K. Gbabo, Penyie District; and F. F. Logah, Keta District.

Coordinators for the celebration included Bro. Chris Y. Torkornoo, East Ghana; Mr. Nana Barima Oduro, I, West Ghana; Mr. Torgbui Tsagli, II, Mid Ghana; Bro.

African Methodist Episcopal Zion Church

Gabriel Akpallo, Cote d'Ivoire; and Rev. Isaac Gibson, Liberia.

The celebration began with Zion's "Thousand Men March" through the city and included preaching by Rev. John Comme, pastor, Cole Memorial A. M. E. Zion Church, Sekondi, and Rev. P. E. T. Sefogah, presiding elder, Accra District. Music was furnished by the Men's Fellowship Choirs of the East Ghana, Mid-Ghana, and West Ghana Conferences, the Bicentennial Men's Mass Choir, and the Men's Fellowship Mass Choir. The Warriors for Christ from each conference led the devotions.

Lectures included: 1. "The Saga of the Black Church: Myth or Reality: Sustaining the Twin Pillars of the Black Church: Black Liberation and Christian Evangelism in the Face of Economic Exploitation, Spiritual, Psychological Subjugation, Political and Social Marginalization of Africans and African Americans" by Attorney F. K. Korley, executive secretary, Legal Aid Board; 2. "Outstanding Fathers in America and Ghana: Contributions to the Genesis, Growth, and the Development of the A. M. E. Zion Church," by Rev. Dr. Joseph Aggrey-Smith, presiding elder, Kumasi District, Mid-Ghana Conference; 3. "Saving The Male Seed: Confronting Satanic Harassment and the Systematic, Calculated Destruction of the Male Gender," by Mr. R. E. Dennis, managing director, Dunkwa Continental Gold Fields; "Wanted: A Role Model Head of Family," by Dr. Jimmy Heymann, medical practitioner and consultant, and 4. "Polity, Practices and Procedures."

Mid-Ghana Conference

The Mid-Ghana Conference hosted an Episcopal Youth Bicentennial Fellowship on April 24-28, 1996, at Bishop Small Memorial A. M. E. Zion Church, Kumasi, Ghana. Official participants included Rev. Dr. Joseph Aggrey-Smith, presiding elder of the conference, and conference directors: the Revs. F. Logah, East Ghana Conference; Francis Badu Agyare, West Ghana Conference; and John Jude Mensah, Mid-Ghana Conference, who was the host director.

The Youth Celebration began with a Prelude of Praise to the Bicentennial Eucharistic Celebration by affiliated Youth Groups. The Special Bicentennial Holy Communion Service was celebrated by Bishop Marshall H. Strickland and Bishop J. Clinton Hoggard. Music was rendered by the Mass Youth Choirs of the West Ghana, East Ghana, and Mid-Ghana Conferences.

Preaching during this celebration was led by Rev. Emmanuel K. B. Essilfie, Good Shepherd A. M. E. Zion Church, Agona Odoben, Winneba District; Rev. Emmanuel Nti Asumadu, regional manager of schools, A. M. E. Zion Educational Unit and pastor A. M. E. Zion Church, Sunyani. Speakers included: Rev. Wireko

Episcopal District Bicentennial Observances

Wilberforce, chaplain, Aggrey Memorial Zion Secondary School Cape Coast, who delivered the Keynote Address; Brother Henry Baye, graduate student, University of Ghana, Legon, who spoke on "Youth and Moral Discipline: Implications for Spiritual and Physical Growth—Bicentennial and Beyond."

A featured event of the celebration was the final winner of the Bicentennial Oratorical Contest. Finalists of all age groups addressed the theme: "200 Years: The Vision, the Goals, the Reality, the Celebration." This was followed by a Cultural Display and Bicentennial Musical Fiesta.

WESTERN (TWELFTH) EPISCOPAL DISTRICT

Bishop Clarence Carr, Presiding Prelate
Mrs. Barbara S. Carr, Missionary Supervisor

During 1992-96, the former Twelfth Episcopal District, now called the *Western Episcopal District*, comprised the Alaska, Oregon-Washington, Southwest Rocky Mountain, Arizona, Colorado, and California Conferences. The then Twelfth District held a grand pre-Bicentennial Celebration on Saturday, May 18, 1996, at the Cathedral Hill Hotel in San Francisco, California. The theme of the celebration was "Reasons for Rejoicing." The special celebration was the culmination of a series of Bicentennial Celebrations held in each annual conference of the then Twelfth Episcopal District, in which a queen was selected to represent the annual conference at the grand Twelfth Episcopal District pre-Bicentennial Celebration. The highlight of the episcopal program was the coronation of the Queen of the Twelfth Episcopal District from among the winners selected in each annual conference.

The conferences within the former Twelfth District sent representatives to the celebration:

California Conference: Rev. Keith I. Harris, host pastor, First A. M. E. Zion Church, San Francisco, California; Rev. Dr. Percy Smith, Jr., presiding elder, Bay Cities District, and pastor, First A. M. E. Zion, San Jose; Rev. John A. Harrison, pastor, Greater Cooper, Oakland; Rev. John E. Watts, pastor, Kyles Temple, Vallejo; Rev. Edwin Harris, pastor, University, Palo Alto; Rev. James A. Davis, pastor, St. James, San Mateo; Rev. John Fomby, pastor, Stewart Chapel, Redwood City; Rev. Lyrtee B. Gulley, pastor, St. Mark, East Palo Alto; Rev. Eugene S. Watkins, presiding elder, Central Valley District; Rev. James R. McMillan, pastor, Kyles Temple, Sacramento; Rev. Billy Bunts, pastor, Mt. Pisgah , Merced; Rev. Richard Brent, Stewart Tabernacle,

African Methodist Episcopal Zion Church

Fresno; Rev. Greylin Young, pastor, Knox Chapel, Madera; Rev. Michael Henderson, pastor, Clinton Chapel, Modesto; Rev. Veronica Buckner, pastor, Hilliard Chapel, Stockton; Rev. Dr. John Randle, pastor, St. Stephens A. M. E. Zion, Sacramento; Rev. Dr. Betty Jo Smith, pastor, Varick Center, Oakland.

Arizona Conference: Rev.Windel Tucker, presiding elder, Rev. Gina Casey, pastor, Fisher Chapel, Phoenix, Arizona; Marshall Memorial, Arizona.

Colorado Conference: Rev. Kay Blunt, presiding elder; Rev. Jerry Patton, Jr., pastor; Spottswood Memorial, Denver; Rev. Willie Long, Jr., pastor, Miracle Mountain, Aurora.

Alaska Conference: Rev. Dr. Theodore A. Moore, presiding elder and pastor, Leake Temple, Anchorage (Mountain View); Rev. Charles I. Brown, pastor, St. James, Fairbanks.

Oregon-Washington Conference: Rev. L. J. Thompson, presiding elder, Cascade District, and pastor, Ebenezer, Seattle; Rev. Dr. Osofo L.H. McDonald, First A. M. E. Zion, Portland; Rev. Robert N. Probasco, Pastor, People's, Portland; Rev. Robert F. Kemp, pastor, Community , Vancouver; Rev. Curtis R. Barnes, Sr., pastor, Catherine Memorial, Seattle; Rev. Melba O. Thomas, pastor, New Life Mission, Seattle; Rev. Joyce M. Smith, pastor, Pauline Memorial; Brother Herman Smith, pastor, Daily Bread, Seattle.

Southwest Rocky Mountain Conference: Rev. Eugene Harvey, presiding elder, Los Angeles District, and pastor, St. James, San Diego; Rev. Windle Tucker, First A. M. E. Zion, Los Angeles; Rev. George E. Kent, pastor, Second A. M. E. Zion, Inglewood; Rev. Robert Peyton, pastor, First A. M. E. Zion, Pasadena; Rev. Roy Swann, pastor, Metropolitan, Los Angeles; Dr. Harriet O. Hooks, pastor, Martin Temple, Compton; Rev. Helen McCall, pastor, Shiloh, Monrovia; Rev. Charles Bebelle, pastor, Howard Chapel; Hanford; Rev. Rodney Bonwell, pastor, St. Mark, Los Angeles; Rev. Walter Jones, pastor, New Life, Los Angeles; Dr. Mildred Gilmore, pastor, People's A. M. E. Zion, Los Angeles; Rev. Quinton P. Jordon, Pastor, Living Word, Los Angeles; Rev. Elvira Miles, pastor, Faith, Los Angeles; Rev. Dr. Howard Hagler, Sr., presiding elder, San Diego District, and pastor, Logan Temple, San Diego; Rev. Henrietta Parks, pastor, Marion Memorial, San Diego; Rev. William Brown, pastor, Winston Chapel, San Diego.

Program and Participants

A Musical Interlude was provided by Rev. Dr. John Randle. Presiding Elder Rev. Dr. Eugene Harvey, Los Angeles District, gave the Invocation. This was followed by

Episcopal District Bicentennial Observances

Mrs. Christine Brown singing the Lord's Prayer. Rev. Dr. Percy Smith, Jr., presiding elder, Bay Cities District, California Conference, gave the Welcome Address, to which Rev. Dr. Theodore A. Moore, presiding elder, Alaska Conference, responded. Mrs. Amelia Ashley-Ward, editor, Sun Reporter newspaper, San Francisco, was the Mistress of Ceremonies for the occasion.

During the Luncheon, there were representations from each of the six conferences in the Twelfth Episcopal District. Mrs. Michelle Harris gave a dramatization of James Weldon Johnson's Sermon "The Judgment Day." Rev. Keith I. Harris, host pastor, presented the Bishop. Ms. Pat Blunt presented the winning queens of the six respective conferences who were vying to become Queen of the Twelfth Episcopal District. Ms. Blunt read a biographical sketch of each and the contestant's reflections on the Bicentennial of the A. M. E. Zion Church. Bishop Carr announced luncheon receipts of over $67,000 and the outcome of the contest. Mrs. Alberta G. Tucker, of First A. M. E. Zion, Los Angeles, of the Southwest Rocky Mountain Conference, was declared Queen. Ms. Armonia F. Williams, of the California Conference was first runner up. The other four conference queens were Mrs. Kathy Meadows, Arizona Conference; Mrs. Willene Long Collins, Colorado Conference; Mrs. Mary Epperson, Alaska Conference; and Mrs. Doris Ann Smith, Oregon-Washington Conference. After Mrs. Tucker's acceptance speech and coronation, Bishop Carr spoke about the significance of two hundred years of the African Methodist Episcopal Zion Church for black people and humanity. Mrs. Brenda Lowe sang two gospel solos for the occasion: "Have I Ever Told You, You're My Hero (Jesus)" and "He's Working It Out For You." Mrs. Sheila Robinson, the Keynote Speaker, spoke on the day's theme: "Reasons for Rejoicing." She praised the A. M. E. Zion Church for its 200 years in the service of Christ and mankind. Mr. Patrice Alexander commended the arrangements, order, and Souvenir Program to commemorate the occasion. He also gave the Benediction.

California Conference Pre-Bicentennial Celebration

Official participants in the pre-Bicentennial Celebration of the California Conference included the Rt. Rev. Clarence Carr, presiding prelate, and Mrs. Barbara S. Carr; missionary supervisor; Rev. Sherman G. Dunmore, chairman, 1995 Bicentennial Committee, and Mrs. Sharon Dunmore.

On July 22, 1995, after its annual conference, the California Conference celebrated its pre-Bicentennial Celebration with an evening banquet and pageant held at the Parc Oakland Hotel, Oakland. During the ceremony, the royal African queen contestants of the California Conference were presented. Ms. Ricki Stevenson, a media personality, was the mistress of ceremonies. Bishop Clarence Carr crowned Armonia F.

African Methodist Episcopal Zion Church

Williams, one of fourteen contestants and a member of Varick Center A. M. E. Zion Church, Oakland, California, Queen of the California Conference.

Southwest Rocky Mountain Conference Pre-Bicentennial Celebration

Official participants in the pre-Bicentennial Celebration included: Bishop Clarence Carr, presiding prelate, and Mrs. Barbara S. Carr, missionary supervisor; Dr. H. Dwight Bolton, host pastor; Presiding Elder Rev. Dr. Eugene Harvey, Los Angeles District; Presiding Elder Rev. Richard Campbell, San Diego District; Presiding Elder Rev. Windel Tucker, Phoenix District, Arizona.

The Southwest Rocky Mountain Conference held its pre-Bicentennial Celebration during its annual conference, July 11-16, at the First A. M. E. Zion Church, 1440 W. Adams Blvd., Los Angeles, California. A parade and banquet were organized on July 15, 1995 to highlight the approaching Bicentennial of the A.M. E. Zion Church. Program participants included Bishop Clarence and Mrs. Barbara S. Carr, who rode in the parade; contestants vying for Queen; Los Angeles Councilman Mark Ridley Thomas, and representatives from the L.A. Sheriff Youth Athletic League; Coyal C. Cooper, a lay officer from Tutsin; Rev. George E. Kent, pastor, and the Drill Team of Second A. M. E. Zion, Inglewood; the Buds of Promise, Shiloh A. M. E. Zion, Monrovia; Rev. Helen McCall, pastor, the Living Word A. M. E. Zion, Las Vegas; and Rev. Quintin Jordan, pastor; Little Angels Choir and Christian Cadets, with Walter Brownley, commanding officer; Queen contestants included: Mrs. Hortense Lee of Second A. M. E Zion; Mrs. Geraldine Croom, Martin Temple, Compton; and Mrs. Alberta Tucker of First A. M. E. Zion, Los Angeles. Mrs. Tucker was chosen queen to represent the Southwest Rocky Mountain Conference at the Twelfth Episcopal District Bicentennial Celebration.

Oregon-Washington Conference Pre-Bicentennial Celebration

Official participants of the pre-Bicentennial Celebration included Presiding Elder Rev. L. J. Thompson, Rev. Robert F. Kemp, host pastor, Community A. M. E. Zion Church, Vancouver, Washington, and Mrs. Jennie T. Kemp.

The Oregon-Washington Conference sponsored a public parade and a barbecue on the church grounds of Community A. M. E. Zion Church. They completed the celebration with a grand banquet, a program, and the crowning of the Oregon- Washington Queen. Mrs. Doris Ann Smith, a twenty-year member of the Community A. M. E. Zion Church, was crowned queen of the Oregon-Washington Conference.

Episcopal District Bicentennial Observances

Arizona Conference Pre-Bicentennial Celebration

The Rev. Gina Casey, pastor, Fisher A. M. E. Zion Church, Phoenix, Arizona, was the host pastor. As part of their celebration, they chose Mrs. Kathy Meadows, queen, to represent the Arizona Conference at the Twelfth (Western) Episcopal District celebration.

Colorado Conference Pre-Bicentennial Celebration

Rev. Willie Long, Jr., pastor of Miracle Mountain A. M. E. Zion Church, Aurora, Colorado, was the host pastor of the Colorado pre-Bicentennial Celebration. As part of the celebration, the conference selected Mrs. Willene Long Collins, Queen of the Colorado Conference. Mrs. Collins is the daughter of Rev. and Mrs. Willie Long, Jr. Mrs. Willene Long Collins was born into the church and serves as the choir director and key board` player.

Alaska Conference Pre-Bicentennial Celebration

The Alaska Pre-Bicentennial Celebration was celebrated during the Alaska Annual Conference, August 15-18, 1996. Mrs. Mary Epperson, a member of Leake Temple A. M. E. Zion Church, Anchorage, Alaska, was chosen Queen to represent the Alaska Conference at the Twelfth Episcopal District Bicentennial Celebration. Mrs. Epperson is a church leader. She is president of the District and the Local Lay Council, president of the Mission Choir, and a member of the Home Mission Board and the Missionary Society. The Rev. Dr. Theodore A. Moore, pastor of Leake Temple, Anchorage, Alaska, was the host pastor.

GENERAL CONFERENCE BICENTENNIAL OBSERVANCES

As a fitting climax to the denominational observances of the bicentennial year of the Mother Zion A. M. E. Zion Church congregation in New York City and the development of the African Methodist Episcopal Zion Church as a denomination, the Fifth Episcopal District presented a magnificent pageant, "Bishop James Varick Salute to Service: From Africa to America," on Saturday, July 27, 1996, at 7:30 p.m., at the Washington, D. C. Convention Center. The General Conference observance and this memorable and historic pageant were directed by the episcopal leadership of Bishop and Mrs. Milton A. Williams, who were supported by the clergy and laity of the Philadelphia-Baltimore, the East Tennessee-Virginia, the Virginia, the London-Birmingham, the Manchester-Midlands (England), and India Conferences. The pageant was videotaped for posterity, and copies of it can be purchased from the Events Coordinator, Full Gospel A. M. E. Zion Church, 4207 Norcross Street, Temple Hills, MD 20748.

This gala celebration highlighted the rich history of the A. M. E. Zion Church as the 200th anniversary of her birth was celebrated. A quadrennial award program to honor those who had given exemplary service to the community and the church was inaugurated. Recipients of the Bishop James Varick Freedom Medal Award included Bishop Ruben Lee Speaks, Bishop Herman Leroy Anderson (posthumously), Bishop Cecil Bishop, Bishop George Washington Carver Walker, Sr., Bishop Milton Alexander Williams, Sr., Bishop Samuel Chukakanne Ekemam, Sr., Bishop George Edward Battle, Jr., Bishop Joseph Johnson, Bishop Richard Keith Thompson, Bishop Enoch Benjamin Rochester, Bishop Marshall Hayward Strickland, Bishop Clarence Carr, Bishop William Alexander Hilliard, Bishop Charles Herbert Foggie, Bishop James Clinton Hoggard, Bishop Clinton Reuben Coleman, Bishop John Henry Miller, Sr., Hon. Louis Stokes, member, U. S. House of Representatives, and Dr. Josephine H. Kyles. Presenting the awards were the Rev. Dr. Bernard L. Richardson, dean of the Howard University Andrew Rankin Memorial Chapel and Mrs. Joanne M. Collins, executive director of Community Leaders Network for Urban Energy and Transportation Corporation and former president, City Council of Kansas City, Missouri, both members of the A. M. E. Zion Church. The Souvenir Journal highlighted the recipients of the Bishop James Varick Medal and the artists who performed during the evening.

Performing Artists included Evelyn Simpson Curenton, artistic and music director; Eric Torain, vocalist; Sandra Reaves, actress/singer; Jay Hoggard, vibra-phonist; Twinkie Clark-Terrell, gospel vocalist; William E. Becton, Jr., gospel vocalist; Curtis King, theatrical director; Fabian Barnes, artistic director of the Dance Institute of Washington, D. C.; and the South Carolina Conference Mass Hymn Choir. Actors Ossie Davis and Ruby Dee narrated the occasion.

General Conference Bicentennial Observances

Social Expressions

During the General Conference, on Thursday, July 25, 1996 at 8:00 a.m., the Woman's Home and Overseas Missionary Society was invited to join the Rev. Mrs. Lula G. Williams, missionary supervisor of the Fifth Episcopal District at a breakfast at the Sam Rayburn House (U. S. House of Representatives) Office Building. The theme of the occasion was "Priorities for Christian Women Moving into The Twenty-First Century." Special Guests included the Hon. Rep. Maxine Waters, U. S. Congress, (D.-Calif.); the Hon. Delegate. Eleanor Holmes Norton, U. S. Congress (D.-Wash. D. C.); and Dr. Sarah Moten, special assistant to the president, National Council of Negro Women.

On July 25, 1996, the National Council of Negro Women, Inc., founded by Mary McLeod Bethune and led in 1996 by Dr. Dorothy I. Height as president and chief executive officer, honored the leadership of the African Methodist Episcopal Zion Church. The bishops were each presented with an autographed picture of the new headquarters building of the National Council of Negro Women, which is located at 633 Pennsylvania Avenue, N. W., Washington, D. C.

MOTHER A. M. E. ZION CHURCH CONGREGATION OBSERVES 200 YEARS OF CHRISTIAN SERVICE

THE LEGEND

HISTORIC Mother Zion A. M. E. Zion Church, the mother church of the African Methodist Episcopal Zion Church denomination, celebrated the 200th anniversary of her founding in New York City, October, 1796, with a banquet on Saturday, September 21, 1996 at the InterChurch Center, 475 Riverside Drive, New York, N. Y. This was followed by a week of revival services beginning on Monday, September 30 and concluding on Friday, October 4, 1996. The 200th anniversary Worship Service was conducted in the Sanctuary of Mother Zion A. M. E. Zion Church, which is located at 140-6 W. 137th Street, New York, N. Y. 10030, on Sunday, October 6, 1996, at 11:00 a. m. In the afternoon, Dr. Solomon Heriott, Jr., the long-time serving choir master and organist of the church, gave an Organ Concert supplemented by timpani and brass.

The Rev. Dr. Alvin T. Durant, the current pastor of Mother Zion A. M. E. Zion Church congregation, is the 36th pastor in succession since 1820 when the Rev. Abraham Thompson served as the first African-American pastor after the arrangement with the white Methodist Episcopal Church to supply preachers for the Zion constituency was terminated. The current serving presiding elder of Mother Zion A. M. E. Zion Church is the Rev. Dr. C. Guita McKinney. Under the present conference organization structure, Mother Zion A. M. E. Zion is in the Hudson River District of the New York Conference. The New York Conference is presided over by Bishop George W. C. Walker, Sr., who has served as the presiding bishop of the Mother Conference of Zion Methodism since 1992.

The Anniversary Banquet, previously referred to, was popularly identified as an African Banquet. The chairperson for this observance was Bro. Dabney N. Montgomery, a long-time lay member of the Mother Zion Church congregation. He gave the Welcome Remarks for this occasion. Other participants included: The Rev. Cecil G. M. Muschett, assistant pastor of Mother Zion, who delivered the Invocation; Karen O. Krieger, program chairperson, introduced the master and mistress of Ceremonies, James Welch and Yvonne Singleton-Davis, respectively, who in turn introduced the dais guests. Elizabeth D. Chappelle of Mother Zion A. M. E. Zion Junior Church delivered the Bicentennial Moment. Carolyn Sebron (mezzo soprano) rendered a solo. Following dinner, Lynnard Williams, accompanied by Karen O. Krieger, performed a dance selection. This was followed by another solo by Carolyn Sebron. The guest speaker, Mrs. Myrlie Evers-Williams, chairperson of the National Board of Directors

Mother Zion A. M. E. Zion Church Bicentennial Observances

of the National Association for the Advancement of Colored People, was introduced by Theodore W. Daniels, Jr. The program concluded with remarks by Dabney N. Montgomery, the Rev. Dr. Alvin T. Durant, Rev. Dr. Calvin Butts, pastor of Abyssinian Baptist Church, Bishop J. Clinton Hoggard, historiographer for the Bicentennial Commission of the A. M. E. Zion Church, and Bishop George W. C. Walker, Sr., chairperson of the Bicentennial Commission for the denomination. The Benediction was pronounced by the Rev. Mrs. Nina M. Neely, minister of Means and Grace at the Mother Zion Church.

The week-long revival was distinguished by dynamic preaching of several pastors in the New York area: On Monday, September 30, 1996, the Rev. James McCoy, pastor of First A. M. E. Zion Church, Brooklyn, New York, delivered the opening revival sermon, which was followed on Tuesday, October 1, by the Rev. Wyatt T. Walker, pastor of Canaan Baptist Church, Harlem, New York. On Wednesday, October 2, Father Howard Blunt, pastor of St. Phillip Episcopal Church, Harlem, New York, and on Thursday, October 3, the Rev. W. Darin Moore, pastor of Greater Centennial A. M. E. Zion Church, Mt. Vernon, New York delivered sermons. The closing revival sermon was delivered by the Rev. James McGraw, pastor of John Street United Methodist Church, New York City, from which the A. M. E. Zion Church denomination originated.

The 200th Anniversary Worship Service was held on Sunday, October 6, at 11:00 a. m. The program of worship included: Greetings by Dabney Montgomery, the Scripture Lessons by the Revs. Dawn Hardy and Lester Canty, the Prayer by the Rev. Cecil G. M. Muschett; and Announcements by Cynthia Ehigie. A special Bicentennial Award was presented to Dr. Solomon Heriott, Jr., organist of Mother Zion. The Message of Christian Stewardship was delivered by the Rev. Nina M. Neely. The Speaker for this historical occasion, Bishop George W. C. Walker, Sr., presiding prelate of the North Eastern Region Episcopal District, was introduced by Dr. Alvin T. Durant. Music was rendered by the Cathedral Choir, the Living in Faith Ensemble, Dianne Chappelle, the Odell Ricks Combined Gospel Chorus, the Inspirational Choir, and Delma and Monica Marshall.

On Sunday afternoon, the Concert featured Dr. Solomon Heriott, Jr., on organ with timpani and brass. His selections included: Psalms XIX, "The Heavens Declare the Glory of God" by Benedetto Marcello; "Festival Prelude" by Marc-antoine Charpentier; "Jesu, Joy of Man's Desiring"; "Toccata and Fugue"; "If Thou Be Near"; and "Passaceglia and Fugue in C Minor," all written by Johann Sebastian Bach; "Praise The Lord with Timpani and Cymbals" composed by Sigfrid Karg-Elert; "Grand Choeur

African Methodist Episcopal Zion Church

Dialogue" written by Eugene Gigout; "Romanza" by Edvard Griegg; and "March Triumphal" by Louis Vierne.

Organist Dr. Solomon Heriott, Jr., who died in November, 1996, had Graduate and Postgraduate Diplomas from the Guilmant Organ School. He continued his musical studies at Mannes College of Music and at the Julliard School of Music. He had the great fortune of having studied organ with Virgil Fox and choral directing with Richard Weagly. In 1985, he received a Doctor of Humane Letters from the Clinton Junior College in Rock Hill, South Carolina. For thirty-five years he served as minister of music at Mother Zion.

THE NATIONAL A. M. E. ZION CHURCH BICENTENNIAL OBSERVANCES

October 10-13, 1996

THE following pages record the variety of events in the national A. M. E. Zion Church observance of the Bicentennial Celebration. The climax of the observance occurred in Rye, New York and New York City. An International Welcome Reception was enthusiastically attended and particpated in by members and friends of the A. M. E. Zion Church from the United States, the Caribbean, South America, Africa, Asia, and Europe.

An Ecumenical Worship Service was observed on Thursday, October 10th, 1996, in the Mother Zion A. M. E. Zion Church, at 7:30 p.m. Many representatives of churches and theological seminaries were in attendance when Bishop McKinley Young, president and ecumenical officer of the African Methodist Episcopal Church, preached the Bicentennial Ecumenical Sermon.

A Bicentennial Forum and Panel Discussions were held in the Rye Town Hilton Hotel, Rye Brook, New York, on Friday morning, October 11, 1996.

A Freedom Heritage Gala Dinner was shared in by representatives of city, state, national government, and church agencies on Friday, October 11, 1996, in the New York Hilton and Towers Hotel, New York City, at 6:30 p. m. The Honorable Kweisi Mfume, president and chief executive officer, National Association for the Advancement of Colored People, gave the Bicentennial Address. Mrs. Marva M. Robinson, mezzo-soprano from Wilmington, North Carolina, and Mrs. Karen O. Krieger, soprano, Brooklyn, New York, provided vocal solos. Mr. Jay Hoggard, vibraphonist, and his Ensemble provided musical selections throughout the evening. Mrs. Jylla Moore Foster, vice president for the Northeastern Area Marketing Operations, IBM Corporation, was Toastperson/Mistress of Ceremonies.

A Twilight Gospel Concert was held at Mother Zion A. M. E. Zion Church, on Friday, October 11, 1996, featuring Cece Winans, William E. Becton, Jr., Hezekiah Walker, and James Hall with the Praise & Worship Choir, and the Men of Standard Choir.

On Saturday, October 12, 1996, at the Mother Zion A. M. E. Zion Church, at 10 a.m., a very meaningful Youth & Young Adults Essay & Oratorical Exposition were presented under the auspices of the Christian Education Department of the A. M. E. Zion Church, led by the Rev. Raymon E. Hunt, secretary-treasurer.

At 1:00 p.m., on October 12, 1996, a Pilgrimage to the old John Street United Methodist Church, New York, N. Y., pastored by the Rev. James R. McGraw, where a significant and memorable experience was had by all who attended and reflected on

African Methodist Episcopal Zion Church

the history of the Church, beginning before 1796, at which time the break occurred that led to the creation of the A. M. E. Zion congregation and later A. M. E. Zion denomination.

A Bicentennial Mass Choir Concert was held on Saturday evening, October 12, 1996, at 7:00 p.m., at Mother Zion Church. The program included Special Selections from the A. M. E. Zion South Carolina Hymn Choir.

A triumphant, hallelujah-like climax to the glorious week of reflection, jubilation, and challenge was manifest in the Bicentennial Morning Worship Service, observed Sunday, October 12, 1996, in the Mother Zion Church. The Organ Music was provided by Dr. Solomon Heriott, Jr., the organist and choir master for thirty-five years at Mother Zion Church. Although manifestly in fading health, Dr. Herriot manipulated the keys of the great organ with dexterity and great mastery. He told others that he was living to accomplish his particpation in this denominational Bicetennial Celebration. Very briefly after our gathering, he fell on eternal sleep. Bishop George W. C. Walker, Sr., was the presiding officer for this Worship Service, and rightly so, because he is the presiding bishop of the New York Conference, host bishop of the Bicentennial Celebration, and chairperson of the Bicentennial Commission.

PART II: DEPARTMENTS OF THE A. M. E. ZION CHURCH, 1972-1996

OFFICE OF THE GENERAL SECRETARY-AUDITOR
1972-1996

THE account of the formation and early history of the Office of the Secretary-Auditor of the A. M. E. Zion Church is adequately presented by William J. Walls, *The African Methodist Episcopal Zion Church: The Reality of the Black Church.* The department is directed by the general-secretary auditor, who is elected by the General Conference and is not appointed unless the office is declared vacant by the Board of Bishops during the interim of the General Conference. In such an event, the Board of Bishops appoints an interim office holder until the next General Conference elects a general secretary-auditor.

The following officeholders were responsible for the report of this office as submitted to the several General Conferences since 1972 through 1996:

Rev. Dr. R. H. Collins Lee	July 1967- May 1976
Rev. Herman L. Anderson	May 1976-May 1980
Rev. Earle E. Johnson	May 1980-July 1988;
Rev. Dr. W. Robert Johnson, III	July 1988-

These officers reported on the state of the church: the numerical strength of the denomination; the growth in general claims assessment; the necrology of the general church; and the organization of new congregations in the several conferences of the A. M. E. Zion Church. At the beginning of this period in 1972, church membership in the denomination was 940,000. Rev. Dr. R. H. Collins Lee reported in 1976 that the full membership of the church was 1,024, 974; number of local churches 5,994; number of ordained clergy 6,873; number of Sunday School pupils 111,790; number of teachers and officers in Sunday Schools 48,210, all of which represented the state of the church as reported in *The Yearbook of American and Canadian Churches, 1976*, published by the National Council of Churches of Christ in the U. S. A. (Nashville: Abingdon Press, 1976; see also *Official Journal, 40th Quad. Sess. Gen. Conf.*, p. 334)

For the 1972-76 quadrennium, the national church general claims assessment was $6,035,103.59. Additional denominational askings for the 1972-76 quadrennium were:

African Methodist Episcopal Zion Church

General Conference Expense Fund	$375, 742.01
Capital Reserve Fund	46, 053.99
Contingent Fund	40,957.73
Tri-College Fund	963,578.47
TOTAL	$7,461,435.79

After serving with distinction as a U. S. Army Chaplain during World War II, Rev. Dr. R. H. Collins Lee pastored the Metropolitan Wesley A. M. E. Zion Church in Washington, D. C., when he returned to civilian life. He was appointed general secretary-auditor from this pulpit by the Board of Bishops at the Connectional Council meeting in Brooklyn, New York, in July 1967. He served in this office until the 1976 General Conference. Rev. Lee did not stand for reelection at this General Conference because of his declining health. He was succeeded in this office by the Rev. Herman L. Anderson, pastor of Broadway Temple A. M. E. Zion Church, Louisville, Kentucky, who was elected general secretary-auditor by the denomination.

Rev. Anderson served in this office for one quadrennium. He was elected and consecrated a bishop in May, 1980, at the General Conference meeting at Greensboro, North Carolina. He was succeeded in the office of general-secretary-auditor by Rev. Earle E. Johnson who filled the office responsibly from 1980 to the 1988 General Conference. Rev. Anderson, with the consent of the Board of Publications, moved the office during the summer of 1976 from the headquarters building in Washington, D. C. to the A. M. E. Zion Publishing House in Charlotte, North Carolina. He reported that membership changes in the denomination showed a gain of 45,210 members and a loss of 13,035, or a net gain of 32,175 persons during the 1976-80 quadrennium. He strenuously urged strengthening the evangelistic program for recruiting and converting more of the 30 million blacks in America to membership in the A.M.E. Zion Church, which, according to the *Yearbook of American and Canadian Churches*, had 1,093,001 members in 1980. Rev. Anderson urged the General Conference to improve the record-keeping methods of the church: "It is our hope that we will begin to use statistics in developing our strategy for kingdom building." Rev. Anderson noted the expansion of the denomination through the organization of new congregations in both American and overseas conferences. This general secretary-auditor carefully reported the participation of the A. M. E. Zion Church in the ecumenical agencies supported by the denominational budget: the World Council of Churches, the World Methodist Council, the National Association for the Advancement of Colored People (NAACP), the Consultation on Church Union, and the National Council of Churches. *(Official Journal, 40th Quad. Sess. Gen. Conf., p. 337; Yearbook of American and Canadian Churches, 1980, p. 23)*

General Secretary -Auditor

New societies reported during the 1976-80 quadrennium were as follows: *1976*: New England Conference: St. Luke Christian, Boston, Mass.; Philadelphia-Baltimore Conference: S. G. Spottswood, Landover, Maryland; Indiana Conference: Varick, Kokomo, Indiana; *1977*: New England Conference: New Life, Brockton, Mass.; Sojourner Truth, Framingham, Mass., Shaw Memorial, Providence, Rhode Island; Warren M. Brown Chapel, North Adams, Mass.; Bahama Island Conference: Holy Trinity; New York Conference: St. Peters Independent, Felix Street, Bklyn., N. Y.; Philadelphia-Baltimore Conference: Turner, Baltimore, Maryland; South Florida Conference: Brown Temple, Haynes City, Florida; *1978*: New York Conference: Thirteen missions; Michigan Conference: Hilliard Chapel, Grand Rapids, Michigan; Ohio Conference: Calvary Mission, Columbus, Ohio; Philadelphia-Baltimore Conference: Beth Shalom, Washington, D. C.; Virginia Conference: First Hampton, Hampton, Virginia; *1979*: New York Conference: E. S. Purvis Community; Warren's Consecrated, Ossining; New Britain Connecticut; London-Birmingham Conference: New Triumphant, Birmingham, England; Jamaica-Surrey Conference: Shiloh, Winchester; Mt. Calvary , York District; Ground of Truth, Rio Grand; Ebenezer, Kingston; Jamaica-Cornwall Conference: Mt. Olivet, Clarkes Town; Jamaica-Middlesex Conference: Mt. Faith, Contrivance; Mt. Olive, Treadlight; Mt. Olivet, Mike Town, St. Peter, Clarksonville, Mt. Zion, Rock; North Alabama Conference: Thomas Chapel Mission; East Tennessee & Virginia Conference: A. M. E. Zion, Covington, Virginia; Albemarle Conference: Anchor Person; Palmetto Conference: Arch Street, Spartanburg, South Carolina; Southwest Rocky Mountain Conference: St. James, San Diego, California; California Conference: Hanford Community, Hanford, California. (*Official Journal, 41th Quad. Sess. Gen. Conf.*, pp. 330-51)

During the 1980-84 quadrennium, Rev. Earle E. Johnson emphasized "the need for accurate statistical records and the apportionment of the budget based on current demographic patterns within the church." He reported an increase in membership of 47,146, and a loss of 14,277, with a net gain of 32,869 persons. In 1984, total membership was recorded as 1,134,179. The administrative mission of the A. M. E. Zion Armed Services Ministry and Veterans Administration Chaplaincy was transferred in February, 1983 to the Office of the General Secretary-Auditor. A list of the A. M. E. Zion pastors who have served as chaplains in the various U. S. Armed Services, Veteran Affairs Hospitals, and Prisons during the period 1972-97 are listed at the end of this report. (*Official Journal, 42nd Quad. Sess. Gen. Conf.* pp. 350-51)

New societies added during the 1980-84 quadrennium were recorded as follows: 1981: New York Conference: Smith Chapel, Wappinger Falls, and Dixon Mission,

African Methodist Episcopal Zion Church

Yonkers, New York; West Central North Carolina Conference: Turner Grove; New England Conference: Mother Storms Chapel, Dunston Chapel, and Good Samaritan Rescue; California Conference: Second Church; Washington-Oregon Conference: Esperance and Sojourner Truth; West Ghana Conference: Tsintsimhwe, Ebenezer, Goaso, Akatachiwa, and Ola; Central Nigeria Conference: Abraham and St. James; East Ghana Conference: Klikor and Sukula; *1982*: New England Conference: Harriet Tubman; Philadelphia-Baltimore Conference: Full Gospel, Temple Hills, Mary-land; Alabama-North Alabama Conference: St. James, Birmingham; Central North Carolina Conference: Christ Missionary; Virginia Conference: Greater Faith; Texas Conference: Eagle Rock; East Ghana Conference: Asiama Bethel; *1983*: New England Conference: Alfred E. White, New Britain, Connecticut; Bloomfield Mission, Bloomfield, Connecticut; North Alabama Conference: A. O. H., Tuscaloosa; Virginia Conference: Virginia Beach and Trinity; Michigan Conference: Resurrection and New Zion; South Carolina Conference: Grover Street; and California Conference: Leake Temple. (Ibid.., pp. 355-56)

During the 1984-88 quadrennium, Rev. Earle Johnson recorded a net gain in church membership of 50,371. Total membership was recorded as 1.20 million in 1988. New societies were listed as follows: *1984*: New England Conference: St. John and Samuel; Ohio Conference: Bethesda; Michigan Conference: Faith Temple; South Carolina Conference: Rock Hill; Georgia Conference: Decatur; and Cape Fear Conference: A. M. E. Zion Church Mission; *1985*: Philadelphia-Baltimore Conference: Heritage, Manassas, Virginia; Central North Carolina Conference: Grace Tabernacle; 1986: New York Conference: Eglise du Nouveau Commandement; Barbados Conference: Mission; Philadelphia-Baltimore Conference: Charles H. Foggie, Bridgeville, Delaware; Michigan Conference: Coleman Chapel; California Conference: North Highland; *1987*: New Jersey Conference: Mission; Western New York Conference: Bailey Avenue, Buffalo, N. Y.; South Mississippi Conference: Sims/Speaks, Jackson, Mississippi; and Southwest Rocky Mt. Conference: Winston Chapel. (*Official Journal, 43rd Quad. Sess. Gen. Conf.*, pp. 379-80; *Yearbook of American and Canadian Churches*, 1992, p. 270)

Rev. Earle Johnson did not stand for re-election to this office at the 1988 General Conference. Rev. Dr. W. Robert Johnson, III (no relation to his predecessor), was elected to the office of general secretary-auditor in 1988. For the 1988-92 quadrennium, he reported 51,703 new members; 21,142 baptisms; the ordination of 190 local preachers as deacons and 211 deacons as elders; the admission of 352 ministers on trial; 246 ministers were received into full connection; and 462 ministers retired. Total membership for the year 1991 was 1,200, 000.

General Secretary -Auditor

New societies founded during the 1988-92 quadrennium were recorded as follows: *1989*: Philadelphia-Baltimore Conference: John Paul Scott, Harrisburg, Pennsylvania; Kentucky Conference: 34th Street, Louisville; Georgia Conference: New Life, Atlanta; West Ghana Conference: Breman Agikuma; Agona Nsasa; Agona Kivanyarko; Ofoase; Sunyani; and Tabitha; East Ghana Conference: Nkonya Ahenkro, Denu St. James, Tema Calvary, Accra Faith; *1990*: New York Conference: Smith Chapel; Philadelphia-Baltimore Conference: First, Silver Spring, Maryland; New Life, Cambridge, Maryland; and The Lord's, Oxon Hill, Maryland; Palmetto Conference: Abundant Life, Charleston, South Carolina; South Carolina Conference: First, Pendleton, South Carolina; St. James, Easley, South Carolina; Central Nigeria Conference: Umuachia; *1991*: Western North Carolina Conference: Faith Tabernacle; Ohio Conference: Gospel; Jamaica Conference: St. Peter's, Bruntie, Jamaica, and Mt. Refuge, Chevoil Hill, Jamaica; Georgia Conference: Emmanuel, Stone Mountain; Nigeria Conference: Ikot Akpa Ekop, and Ikrine.

The general secretary-auditor reported that fifteen chaplains of the A.M. E. Zion denomination served in active duty with the U.S. Armed Forces and the Veterans Affairs Hospital Service. The general secretary-auditor represents the A.M. E. Zion Church on the Board of Endorsers at the National Conference on Ministry to the Armed Forces. (*Official Journal, 44th Quad. Sess. Gen. Conf.*, pp. 474-76; *Yearbook of American and Canadian Churches*, 1992, p. 270)

For the period 1992-96, ten pastors of the denomination were in active duty with the U. S. Armed Forces. Rev. Robert Johnson served as chair of the Endorsers Conference for Veterans Affairs Chaplaincy (ECVAC) in December 1996. The following church statistics were reported for the 45th quadrennium: 86,637 new members; 33,724 baptisms; 395 local preachers were ordained as deacons; 501 ministers were received on trial; 266 ministers were received into full connection; and 604 ministers were retired. Total membership for the year 1996 was 1,230, 842 as reported in the 1997 edition of the *Yearbook of American and Canadian Churches* (p. 252). There were a total of 3,098 churches in the denomination with 2,571 pastors serving congregations and 2,767 clergy. The general secretary reported a total enrollment of 67,320 persons in 1,672 Sunday schools.

New societies were recorded as follows: *1992*: New England Conference: Mount Calvary; South Carolina Conference: Gabriel; *1993*: New Jersey Conference: Christ Temple; Philadelphia-Baltimore Conference: Liberty Temple; Virginia Conference: All Saints, and New Hope; Nigeria Conference: Eyo Abasi; Kentucky Conference: Hope Chapel; Liberia Conference: Faith Temple, and Full Gospel; West Ghana Conference:

African Methodist Episcopal Zion Church

Assin Aksopong; East Ghana Conference: Hodzoga, and Amutinu, Mid-Ghana Conference: Nakpanduri, and St. Mark; Cote d'Ivoire Conference: New Hope; *1994*: Virginia Conference: Full Gospel, and New Hope; Mainland Nigeria Conference: James Varick, and A.M.E. Zion; Rivers Nigeria Conference: Obrany, and Adada II; West Nigeria Conference: Holy Hill, Lagos; Central Nigeria Conference: Full Gospel (Amakohia), Full Gospel (Umiba Amagigbo), Wesley, and All Saints; Nigeria Conference: St. Paul, All Saints, Full Gospel, and Calvary; South Carolina Conference: Mission Outreach; Texas Conference: Holy Ghost; Arkansas Conference: St. Paul Temple: South Mississippi Conference: Neal Street; Louisiana Conference: Faith; South Florida Conference: Love of Christ Tabernacle; Florida Conference: Joy Chapel Mission; Central Alabama Conference: Varick Chapel; South Africa Conference: Mwamadi, Khumunye, Chimadzi, Mulambe, Chinsuwi, Mpobvu, Jali, Chimanda, Mati-Mati, Nthobwa, Sozola, Magreta, Mabala, Bwanali, M'balakasi, Nkhundi, Ntira, Mchacha, Katunga, Kaputeni, Nota, Makuwa, Nakhulukute, Marka, Namitonga, Mbodi, Namwea, Laisi, Kachingwe, Phirikeya, Chiweni, Tizola, Mare, Kamoto, Mulima, Murumbala, Chifunga (Nkondesi), Mohakomango, Makwasa, Nselema, Lirangwe I, Lirangwe II, Nkatkhiwa, Nyambilo, Chitsitu; Indiana Conference: Liberation, Indianapolis; West Ghana Conference: Gomoa Fete, and Kasonia; *1995-96*: Western North Carolina Conference: New Life, Lindsey Memorial and Price Tabernacle; Ohio Conference: Word of Truth; Allegheny Conference: Ralph N. Reynolds Memorial; New England Conference: New Life; Philadelphia-Baltimore Conference: Abba; Mainland Nigeria Conference: A. M. E. Zion, Ikot Obong, Ikot Abasi L.G.A.; Central Nigeria Conference: Amaoku Alayi; Nigeria Conference: Mt. Carmel, Our Redeemer, Bethel, Victory; Rivers Nigeria Conference: Ogbele, Aboada, Bughma; South Carolina Conference: Shepherds Fold; Alabama Conference: James Varick Christian Center; North Alabama Conference: Varick Memorial; South Florida Conference: Holy Trinity; South Africa and Central Africa Conferences: Kaliati, Thapo, Chakhomango, Namagawa, Kangankundi, Nyajidu, Tchinga, Mwenye, Namaka, Mphura, Khuzupa, Chaweza, Majimbi; Nyangu, Namatapa, Njerwa, Sitivini, Mpilisi, Zamasiya, Bwanali, Mulambe, Rivirivi, Komehela, Nalingula, Alawe, Likangaliya, Shaibu, Muhowa, Liwonde, Kangankundi, Makwinja, Edward, Mnyumwa, Ntira, Chirimba, Kapalamula, Nangu; Michigan Conference: Brown Hutcherson, and Full Gospel; Mid-Ghana Conference: St. Paul (Bekwuian), and A. M. E. Zion (Ayanfwi), Kibi (Kibi), Grace (Tuswk), Tatara No. I, Bunkura, Dabare, Nakpanbuan, Nambigo, Yamburi, Yagonia Ashan, Prasu, Kade, Akomadan, Teciman, Bi-Centennial, New Century, and Sambukpon; Liberia Conference: New Century, Hope, Effort, Faith; East

90

General Secretary Auditor

Ghana Conference: Bi-Centennial, New Century, Peace, Hope, and Charity; West Ghana Conference: Agonia, Bawjuase, Akroso-St. Michael, Assin Foso-Assin Daaman, New Century and Bi-Centennial; Southwest Rocky Mountain Conference: People's A.M. E. Zion, Carson Community, Marshall Memorial, and Living Word; Oregon-Washington Conference: Daily Bread. ("Quadrennial Report, Department of Records and Research, 45th Quad. Sess. Gen. Conf.," pp. 3-10; *Yearbook of American and Canadian Churches*, 1997, p. 252)

At the Connectional Council meeting in Louisville, Kentucky, in August, 1997. Rev. Dr. W. Robert Johnson, III, general-secretary, reported that from June 1, 1996 to May 31, 1997, 15 new societies (churches) were organized and 19,252 members were added to the church. This brings the total official membership to 1,250,094, according to Rev. Johnson's report and statistics. Rev. Johnson also reported that 68 ministers were received into full connection; 101 aspiring ministers were received on trial; 83 deacons were ordained as elders; 60 local preachers were ordained as deacons; 24 ministers were received on credentials; 35 ministers died during the year; 9 ministers withdrew; and 23 ministers were dropped from the A. M. E. Zion rolls. Nine of the fifteen new churches were located in the Eastern West Africa Episcopal District. ("Annual Report of the Dept. of Statistics and Records to the Board of Bishops and Connectional Council, July 29-August 2, 1997," pp. 4-5)

A. M. E. Zion Armed Services Ministry

According to the records of the department, the following A. M. E. Zion pastors have served either as Active Duty or Reserve Chaplains with the U. S. Armed Forces during the period 1972-97: Blake Bennett, Jr., Joseph K. Blay, James M. Clark, Richard C. Jackson, Donald L. Jones, Phillip D. Kalyanapu, Perry W. Medley, Charles E. Moss, William H. Pender, III, Edward H. Saxon, Kevin B. Weston, Benjamin L. Morrow, Orlando R. Dowdy, Walter E. Beamon, Andrew O. Gwinn, James Brown, Alvin Tyrone, Raymond C. Hart, John W. Haynes, Alexander L. Jones, Virgil L. Lattimore, III, Ricky Lett, Lorenza R. Meekins, Alexander Person, Jr., Louis E. Sanders, Eli D. Smith, Gary M. Tydus, Floyd A. Walker, George R. Washington, Marion R. Wilson, Raymond Helms, Charles E. Quick, Jerry A. Quick, Kathy A. Thomas, Edward Hart, Hezekiah Lawson, Juanita Elizabeth Carroll, Johnnie Henderson, Wilbert Gambel, Gary W. Burns, Charles J. Burt, Michael E. Ellis, William C. Gibson, Paul S. Hoggard, Dorothy King, Malinda Moore, Edgar S. Bankhead, James Jackson, James McArthur Sloan, and Albert Downing.

The following A. M. E. Zion pastors served as Veterans Affairs (Hospital) Chaplains during the period 1972-97: James N. Brown, III, Juanita Elizabeth Carroll,

African Methodist Episcopal Zion Church

Reginald Massey, Willie A. Mcdaniels, William H. Pender, III, Silas E. Redd, Andrew O. Gwinn, Clarence Cross, Floyd Parker, and Charles E. Quick.

The following A. M. E. Zion pastors served as Institutional Chaplains during the period 1972-97: Sherman B. McBeth, Sr., Ernest H. White, Jr., Reid R. White, Jr., and Cassandra M. Tate.

Ministers of the A. M. E. Zion Church who were serving in the various U. S. Armed Services Chaplaincy in 1997 are as listed: *U. S. Army*: Phillip D. Kalyanapu (Philadelphia-Baltimore Conference); Joseph K. Blay (East Tennessee-Virginia Conference); Kevin Weston (Virginia Conference); *U. S. Air Force (Active)*: Walter E. Beamon (Georgia Conference); Raymond C. Hart (Philadelphia-Baltimore Conference); Lorenza Meekins (Virginia Conference); Alexander Person (South Carolina Confer-ence), Ernest H. White, Jr. (Pee Dee Conference), Reid R. White, Jr. (Pee Dee Conference); and Rose Sharon Bryan; *U. S. Navy (Active)*: Charles J. Burt (New England Conference); Wilbert Gambel; *U. S. Air Force (Reserves)*: Virgil L. Lattimore, III; (Western New York Conference); Gary M. Tydus, Juanita Elizabeth Carroll, Alexander Jones (Cape Fear Conference); Johnnie Henderson (West Central North Carolina); *U. S. Navy (Reserves)*: James McArthur Sloan (Western North Carolina Conference); and Linda S. Moore (North Carolina Conference); *Veterans Affairs [Hospital] Chaplains:* Clarence Cross (Philadelphia-Baltimore Conference); Reginald Massey (South Carolina Conference) Floyd Parker, Silas Redd (Arkansas Conference); *Prison Chaplains*: Sherman B. McBeth, Sr. (South Carolina Conference).

The office of the general secretary-auditor of the denomination has expanded appreciably from the days of its inception in 1872 when Elder James A. Jones of Philadelphia was elected the first general secretary of the A. M. E. Zion Church. This office is the main link to the Board of Bishops, to the several annual conferences, and to the entire ministry of the church. The present officeholder, Rev. W. Robert Johnson, III, envisions a larger appropriation from the general church to adequately staff the Office of the General Secretary-Auditor. This would facilitiate improved communications, reporting, and statistics to meet the manifold demands made by our growing denomination as we begin the third century of the A. M. E. Zion Church and approach the twenty-first century.

The Board for Statistics and Records for 1972-2000 has been as follows:

General Secretary -Auditor

BOARD FOR STATISTICS AND RECORDS
1972-2000

1972-76
Bishop J. W. Wactor, chairperson
Bishop F. S. Anderson, 1st vice chairperson
Bishop W. A. Stewart, 2nd vice chairperson
Members:

1. Rev. W. D. Hogans
2. Rev. R. L. Perry
3. Mr. G. Thomas Price
4. Rev. C. Mifflin Smith
5. Mrs. Lizzie Sykes
6. Mrs. Lucille Weatherton

7. Rev. George Tharrington
8. Rev. A. F. Johnson
9. Rev. G. E. Battle
10. Rev. D. A. Parker
11. Rev. Fred Hubbard
12. Mrs. Hettie Daniels

1976-80
Bishop J. W. Wactor, chairperson
Bishop J. Clinton Hoggard, 1st vice chairperson
Bishop John H. Miller, 2nd vice chairperson
Members:

1. Rev. L. R. Blair
2. Mr. Albert E. Stout
3. Mr. George E. Ziegler
4. Rev. C. Mifflin Smith
5. Rev. J. A. Stringfield
6. Mrs. Kathleen Dunn

7. Rev. O. S McMurren
8. Rev. Curtis Brown
9. Rev. Eugene Goodwin
10. Ms. Barbara Metcalf
11. Mr. Raymon Hunt
12. Mr. A. U. Ekpo

1980-84
Bishop Herman L. Anderson, chairperson
Bishop J. C. Hoggard, 1st vice chairperson
Bishop John H. Miller, 2nd vice chairperson
Members:

1. Rev. William J. Jiles
2. Mr. Daniel Murrell, Jr.
3. Mrs. Marjorie B. Walton

4. Rev. Alphonso P. Petway
5. Mr. James F. Sparks
6. Rev. S. Paul Spottswood

African Methodist Episcopal Zion Church

7. Mrs. Clara V. Robertson
8. Mrs. Cora L. Johnson
9. Mrs. Josephine Spaulding

10. Rev. Bennie Luckett
11. Mr. Theodore Shaw
12. Mr. A. U. Ekpo

1984-88
Bishop H. L. Anderson, chairperson
Bishop J. H. Miller, 1st vice chairperson
Bishop Arthur Marshall, Jr., 2nd vice chairperson
Members:
1. Mr. Reed Thompson
2. Mr. Daniel W. Murrell, Jr.
3. Rev. Louis Hunter
4. Rev. Roe Nall
5. Rev. Kenneth Arrington
6. Rev. Carl A. Glenn

7. Mrs. Friedia Moss
8. Rev. I. K. Anderson
9. Mrs. Gladys Pettus
10. Mrs. Arthur M. Norris
11. Rev. C. H. Little
12. Rev. A. V. Ekpo

1988-92
Bishop H. L. Anderson, chairperson
Bishop J. H. Miller, 1st vice chairperson
Bishop A. E. White, 2nd vice chairperson
Members:
1. Rev. Belvie H. Jackson
2. Rev. Errol Hunt
3. Mr. James Stamper
4. Mrs. Avonne Scott
5. Mrs. Peggy Miller
6. Rev. Ollieway Byers

7. Rev. C. H. Little
8. Rev. Roe Nall
9. Ms. Frances Glenn
10. Mrs. Arthur M. Norris
11. Miss Barbara Durante
12. Miss Roxanne D. Hannon
13. Mr. U. Thomas

1992-96
Bishop Enoch B. Rochester, chairperson
Bishop Milton A. Williams, 1st vice chairperson
Bishop Herman L. Anderson, 2nd vice chairperson
Members:
1. Rev. Sheldon Shipman
2. Rev. Errol E. Hunt
3. Rev. D. D. Harrield, Jr.

4. Mrs. Lillian Reason
5. Ms. Allean Brown
6. Mr. Monday D. Udodong

General Secretary -Auditor

7. Rev. George Crenshaw
8. Rev. Mamie M. Wilkins
9. Mrs. Arthur Mae Norris

10. Mrs. Kathleen Stephens
11. Ms. Carmen Maxwell
12. Rev. Charles I. Brown

1996-2000
Bishop Warren M. Brown, chairperson
Bishop Milton A. Williams, 1st vice chairperson
Bishop Ruben L. Speaks, 2nd vice chairperson
Members:
1. Rev. W. L. Rush
2. Mrs. Lillian Reason
3. Ms. Allean A. Brown
4. Mrs. Rosetta Dunham
5. Ms. Brenda McCormick
6. Rev. George Crenshaw

7. Mrs. Martina Parker-Sobers
8. Ms. Martha Edmundson
9. Rev. D. D. Harrield, Jr.
10. Mr. George Perkins
11. Rev. Mamie M. Cooper
12. Rev. Joseph Walton

DEPARTMENT OF FINANCE
1972 - 1996

THE Department of Finance of the A. M. E. Zion Church has been directed throughout the years by the Financial Secretary, an officer elected by General Conference. From 1952-76, this office was held by Mr. Richard Wadsworth Sherrill, Sr., a distinguished layman and a long-time servant of the A. M. E. Zion Church. Mr. Sherrill had served as manager of the A. M. E. Zion Publishing House from 1928-48. He took a respite from denominational duties and then stood for election to the office of financial secretary of the church in 1952. He was elected and served through 1976. During these twenty-four years, he distinguished himself as a dedicated layperson in the A. M. E. Zion Church. He was a native of Rowan County, North Carolina, the son of Rosa and James Sherrill and the son-in-law of Dr. Joseph Charles Price, first president of Livingstone College, Salisbury, North Carolina. He was a successful businessman as an insurance company agent and officer prior to his managerial and financial services to the A. M. E. Zion Church.

During the 1972-76 quadrennium, Mr. Sherrill reported the denominational asking budget was $5,261,367.48 per annum. This represented more than twice the sum previously received and disbursed by the Finance Department for the denominational budget. An achievement in denominational financing was recognized when a surplus of $61,635.34 was recorded in the departmental fund at the end of that quadrennium. The competent staff employed in Mr. Sherrill's office contributed significantly to his effective management of denominational financial affairs. At the 1976 General Conference meeting in Chicago, Illinois, for the 40th Quadrennial Session, Mr. Sherrill did not stand for reelection. He encouraged, supported, and was delighted to see Ms. Madie L. Simpson elected as his successor. Ms. Simpson had been the office manager for many years during Mr. Sherrill's service. (Official Journal, 39th Quad. Sess. Gen. Conf., p. 260; 40th Quad. Sess. Gen. Conf., p. 68)

Speaking to the 41st General Conference in Greensboro, North Carolina, in May 1980, Ms. Simpson said among other things:

"Four years ago, in Chicago, the 40th Quadrennial Session of the General Conference elected your humble servant to the office of Financial Secretary of our Church: A first for Zion—the first female Connectional General Officer.Entrusted to my hands were the General Funds of the Connection. Though my tenure in the Department has been long and steady, it was still a giant step for the church to place me in this position. From that day in 1976 until this present day, I have sought to give of my best to the Master,' and

96

Finance

efforts toward effective, and affective services rendered Zion. "It has been a short four years for me, but I sincerely feel that much has been accomplished. The Lord has blessed us, and our prayer is, He will continue to spread his mercies upon us all.

"Words of appreciation may seem futile, as well as, inadequate, but expressions of deep gratitude are due so many. Permit me to say: Thank you over and over again, for the excellent cooperation and words of encouragement received from the entire official and supporting family of Zion.'" *(Official Journal, 41st Quad. Sess. Gen. Conf.*, p. 352)

Since the 1980 General Conference, Ms. Simpson has been reelected each successive General Conference, and she continues to serve as the able custodian of the multimillion dollar denominational budget, which exceeded thirty-one million dollars for the 1992-96 quadrennium. Her tenure of office has enabled the bishops and the Connectional Budget Board to implement modern financial methods for receiving, accounting for, disbursing, and investing the funds of the denomination for salaries, pensions, education, program development, mission services, health services, and ecumenical representation on a world-wide basis, the likes of which had not been previously known in the financial annals of Zion.

All Finance Department reports have been audited and verified by certified public accountants, as has been the custom and the law of the A. M. E. Zion Church from time immemorial. The Connectional Budget Board has oversight responsibility for the Department of Finance. The following bishops have been chairpersons and vice chairpersons of this board from 1972-96:

Quadrennium	Chairperson	Vice Chairpersons
1972-76	Bishop H. B. Shaw	Bishop S. G. Spottswood
		Bishop C. R. Coleman
1976-80	Bishop H. B. Shaw	Bishop C. R. Coleman
		Bishop G. J. Leake,III
3 Jan. 1980-84	Bishop C. R. Coleman	Bishop G. J. Leake, III
		Bishop W. M. Smith
1984-88	Bishop C. R. Coleman	Bishop W. M. Smith
		Bishop H. L. Anderson
1988-92	Bishop C. R. Coleman	Bishop W. M. Smith

African Methodist Episcopal Zion Church

		Bishop H. L. Anderson
1992-95	Bishop H. L. Anderson	Bishop R. L. Speaks
		Bishop G. E. Battle, Jr.
1995-96	Bishop R. L. Speaks	Bishop G. E. Battle, Jr.
		Bishop E. B. Rochester
1996-2000	Bishop G. E. Battle, Jr.	Bishop E. B. Rochester
		Bishop Cecil Bishop

Chief Finance Officer Madie L. Simpson reported progress in the new budget in her account to the Connectional Council in Louisville, Kentucky, August, 1997. Because some conferences reported increases for the 1996 and 1997 conference years, the Connectional Budget Office was able to meet the allocations and salary payments for the fiscal year that ended May 31, 1997. For the period ending May 31, 1997, receipts totalled $8,272,485.82 with disbursements of $7,853,239.55. Mrs. Simpson compared the cash balance of $362,811.99 with the cash balance of $782,058.26 on May 31, 1997. ("Annual Report of Financial Department to the Connectional Council, July 29-August 1, 1997," p. 2)

Ms. Simpson reported the death of Mr. Spencer Williams who served devotedly as the secretary of the Connectional Budget Board for many years. (Ibid., p. 1)

As executive secretary until his death in 1991, Rev. Dr. Eugene E. Morgan worked assiduously for the development of the present form and structure of the Connectional Budget Board in association with the executive committee of the board. He was a successor to the late Rev. Dr. E. Franklin Jackson who initiated the idea of a Connectional Budget Board. Mr. Spencer Williams of Tuskegee, Alabama, succeeded Rev. Morgan as executive secretary and served faithfully until his death on April 9, 1997.

The offices of the Finance Department are housed in the A. M. E. Zion Church Publishing House, at 2nd and Brevard Streets, Charlotte, North Carolina. The A. M. E. Zion Church budget allocations and assessments for each year from 1972 to 1996 were as follows:

Finance

A. M. E. Zion Church Connectional Budget Allocations, 1972-76

CONNECTIONAL CLAIMANTS

Bishop's Salary	(12 @ 12,500)	$150,000
Administrative Expense	(12 @ 3,600)	43,200
Retired Bishops	(6 @ 6,250)	37,500
General Officers	(10 1/2 @ 8,000)	84,000
		$ 314,700

ADMINISTRATION

Connectional Budget Office	$ 15,000
General Conference Expense Fund	25,000
Travel and Sustentation	20,000
Annual Conference Expense	20,000
Public Relations Office	6,000
General Secretary's Office	6,000
	$ 92,000

DEPARTMENTAL SUPPORT

Church Extension	$ 95,000
Christian Education	40,000
Home Missions	40,000
Foreign Missions	65,000
Evangelism	3,600
Laymen's Council	2,400
Health Department	1,200
	$ 247,200

EDUCATIONAL INSTITUTIONS

Livingstone College	$ 350,000
Hood Theological Seminary	35,000
Clinton Jr. College	70,000
Lomax-Hannon Jr. College	70,000
Inoperative Schools	10,000
	$ 535,000

African Methodist Episcopal Zion Church

MINISTERIAL RELIEF
Superannuated Ministers	1,000
Bishops' Widows	7,000
Ministers' Widows	75,000
Pension Supplement	10,000
Minimum Salary	<u>30,000</u>
	$ 123,000

PUBLICATIONS/PERIODICALS
Historical Society	1,200
Quarterly Review	1,800
Publications House	60,000
Historical Section	5,200
Star of Zion Expense	<u>2,400</u>
	$ 70,600

ECUMENICAL/SOCIAL CONCERNS
Membership	20,000
Capital Reserve	10,000
Contingency	$ 36,000

Summary
Connectional Claimants	$ 314,700
Administration	92,000
Departmental Support	247,200
Educational Institutions	535,000
Ministerial Relief	123,000
Publication House & Periodicals	70,600
Ecumenical and Social Concerns	<u>36,000</u>
	$1,418,500

A. M. E. ZION CHURCH CONFERENCE ASSESSMENTS, 1972-76

CONFERENCE	ASSESSMENT
Alabama	$ 20,000
Albemarle	25,000
Allegheny	30,500
Arkansas	4,000

Finance

CONFERENCE	ASSESSMENT
Blue Ridge	22,000
Cahaba	12,000
California	18,500
Cape Fear	50,000
Central Alabama	26,125
Central North Carolina	80,250
Colorado	1,000
East Tennesee & Virginia	11,000
Florida	6,000
Georgia	3,500
Indiana	10,000
Kentucky	26,125
Louisiana	10,000
Michigan	90,250
Missouri	20,000
New England	44,000
New Jersey	78,500
New York	100,250
North Alabama	35,000
North Arkansas	3,500
North Carolina	33,125
Ohio	79,250
Oklahoma	1,500
Oregon-Washington	1,500
Palmetto	22,500
Pee Dee	28,500
Philadelphia-Baltimore	120,500
South Alabama	15,000
South Carolina	27,250
South Florida	6,500
South Georgia	4,500
South Mississippi	6,000
South West Rocky Mountain	13,000
Tennessee	35,000
Texas	2,200

African Methodist Episcopal Zion Church

CONFERENCE	ASSESSMENT
Virginia	46,500
Virgin Islands	200
West Alabama	33,000
West Central North Carolina	84,000
Western New York	32,000
Western North Carolina	115,000
West Tennessee and Mississippi	6,500

OVERSEAS MISSIONS CONFERENCES	
Bahama Islands	1,000
East Ghana	500
Liberia	1,200
London-Birmingham	1,000
Nigeria	1,000
Guyana	1,000
West Ghana	3,000
Jamaica	1,000
Total	**$1,450,725**

A. M. E. ZION CHURCH CONNECTIONAL BUDGET ALLOCATIONS, 1976-80

CONNECTIONAL CLAIMANTS

Bishops' Salary	(12 @ $12,000)	$144,000
Administrative Expense	(12 @ $3,000)	36,000
Parsonage Allusion	(12 @ $3,000)	36,000
Retired Bishops	(2 @ 6,000)	12,000
General Officers	(11 1/2 @ 10,000)	115,000
Health Director (Stipend)		1,200
		$ 344,200

ADMINISTRATION

Connectional Budget Office	$ 20,000
General Conference Expense Office Fund	75,000
Travel and Sustenance	20,000
Annual Conference Expense (Developing Conferences)	15,000
General-Secretary-Auditor's Office	7,000

Finance

Public Relations Office	4,000
Office Expense—Secretary Board of Bishops	1,200
	$ 142,200

DEPARTMENTAL SUPPORT

Church Extension	90,000
Christian Education	40,000
Home Missions	38,000
Foreign Missions	55,000
Evangelism	5,000
Laymen's Office	5,000
	$ 233,000

EDUCATIONAL INSTITUTIONS

Livingstone College	485,000
Hood Theological Seminary	100,000
Clinton Jr. College	75,000
Lomax-Hannon Jr. College	75,000
Tri-College:	
Livingstone College	115,000
Clinton Junior College	50,000
Lomax-Hannon Junior College	50,000
Institute for Black Ministries	15,000
Inoperative Schools	5,000
	$970,000

MINISTERIAL RELIEF

Superannuated Ministers	1,000
Bishops' Widows	10,000
Ministers' Widows	75,000
Ministers' Minimum Salary	30,000
	$116,000

BROTHERHOOD PENSION	**$378,600**

PUBLISHING HOUSE PERIODICALS

Historical Society and Quarterly Review	$ 4,000
Publication House	90,000
Church School Editorial Section	6,000
Star of Zion (Editor's Office)	2,400
	$102,400

African Methodist Episcopal Zion Church

(Connectional Budget Allocations, 1976-80, cont'd.)
ECUMENICAL AND SOCIAL CONCERNS
Ecumenical Membership	$ 20,000
Harriet Tubman Home	10,000
Camp Barber	10,000
Zion's Office (Inter-Church Center)	5,000
Representation	<u>10,000</u>
	$ 55,000

RESERVE FUND	
Capital Reserve	6,157.50
Contingent Fund	<u>3,000.00</u>
	$ 9,157.50
Total	**$2,355,557.50**

A. M. E. ZION CHURCH CONFERENCE ASSESSMENTS, 1976-80

CONFERENCE	ASSESSMENT
Alabama	$ 31,000.00
Albemarle	38,000.00
Allegheny	42,000.00
Arkansas	5,600.00
Blue Ridge	34,100.00
Cahaba	18, 600.00
California	29,600.00
Cape Fear	77,500.00
Central Alabama	40,493.75
Colorado	1,400.00
Central North Carolina	136,425.00
East Tennessee & Virginia	17,050.00
Florida	10,070.00
Georgia	5,425.00
Indiana	15,500.00
Kentucky	38,943.75
Louisiana	15,500.00
Michigan	162,450.00
Missouri	31,000.00

Finance

CONFERENCE	ASSESSMENT
New England	70,400.00
New Jersey	124,000.00
New York	190,475.00
North Alabama	54,250.00
North Arkansas	5,025.00
North Carolina	53,000.00
Ohio	133,725.00
Oklahoma	2,325.00
Oregon-Washington	2,325.00
Palmetto	34,875.00
Pee Dee	44,175.00
Philadelphia-Baltimore	186,775.00
South Alabama	23,250.00
South Carolina	42,625.00
South Florida	9,300.00
South Georgia	6,975.00
South Mississippi	9,685.00
South West Rocky Mountain	20,150.00
Tennessee	56,800.00
Texas	3,410.00
Virginia	79,050.00
West Alabama	52,800.00
West Central North Carolina	120,400.00
Western New York	50,200.00
Western North Carolina	207,000.00
West Tennessee & Mississippi	9,685.00

Overseas Missions

Alaska	50.00
Bahamas	1,150.00
Central Nigeria	50.00
East Ghana	575.00
Guyana	1,150.00
Jamaica	1,150.00

African Methodist Episcopal Zion Church

CONFERENCE	ASSESSMENT
Liberia	1,380.00
London-Birmingham	1,150.00
Nigeria	1,150.00
Trinidad	50.00
Virgin Islands	315.00
West Ghana	3,450.00
Total	$2,355,557.50

(Official Journal, 40th Quad. Sess. Gen. Conf., pp. 495-98)

A. M. E. ZION CHURCH CONNECTIONAL BUDGET ALLOCATIONS, 1980-84

CONNECTIONAL CLAIMANTS

Bishops' Salary	(12 @ $ 16,000)	$ 192,000
Administrative Expense	(12 @ $3,600)	43,200
Parsonage Allusion	(12 @ $6,000)	72,000
Retired Bishops	(3 @ $9,000)	27,000
Retired Bishops' Parsonage Allusion	(3 @ $1,000)	3,000
General Officers	(11 1/2 @ $15,600)	179,400
Health Director's Stipend		1,200
		$ 517,800

ADMINISTRATION

Connectional Budget Office	30,000
General Conference Expense Fund	75,000
Travel and Sustentation Annual	20,000
Annual Conference Expense (Develop Confs)	15,000
General Secretary-Auditor's Office	7,000
Public Relations Office	5,000
Office Expense - Secretary Board of Bishops	1,200
	$ 153,200

DEPARTMENTAL SUPPORT

Church Extension	$ 80,000
Christian Education	55,000
Home Missions	35,000
Overseas Missions	65,000
Evangelism	10,000
Laymen's Office	10,000
	$ 255,000

Finance

EDUCATIONAL INSTITUTIONS

Livingstone College	$ 700,000
Hood Theological Seminary	145,223
Clinton Jr. College	193,723
Lomax-Hannon Jr. College	193,723
Institute for Black Ministries	15,000
Inoperative Schools	5,000
	$ 1,252,669

MINISTERIAL RELIEF

Superannuated Ministers	1,000
Bishops' Widows	10,000
Ministers' Widows	75,000
Ministers' Minimum Salary	30,000
	$ 116,000

BROTHERHOOD PENSION	**$ 378,600**

PUBLICATIONS/PERIODICALS

Historical Society & Quarterly Review	4,000
Publication House	80,000
Church School Editorial Section	6,000
Star of Zion (Editor's Office)	2,400
	$ 92,400

ECUMENICAL AND SOCIAL CONCERNS

Ecumenical Membership	20,000
Harriet Tubman Home	10,000
Camp Barber	10,000
Zion's Office (Inter-Church Center)	5,000
Representation	10,000
Camp Dorothy Walls	1,000
	$ 56,000

African Methodist Episcopal Zion Church

RESERVE FUND
Capital Reserve	$ 3,300
Contingent Fund	2,000
	5,300

GRAND TOTAL   **$ 2,826,969**

A. M. E. ZION CHURCH CONFERENCE ASSESSMENTS, 1980-84

CONFERENCE	ASSESSMENT
Bahama Islands	$ 1,380.00
Cape Fear	93,000.00
Jamaica	1,380.00
London-Birmingham	1,380.00
New England	84,480.00
New York	228,570.00
Trinidad	60.00
Western New York	60,240.00
New Jersey	149,520.00
West Albama	63,360.00
Western North Carolina	248,400.00
Central North Carolina	163,710.00
Guyana	1,380.00
Michigan	194,940.00
Ohio	160,470.00
Virgin Islands	678.00
Central Alabama	48,592.50
North Carolina	63,600.00
South Alabama	27,900.00
West Central North Carolina	144.480.00
Allegheny	50,400.00
Philadelphia/Baltimore	224,130.00
Virginia	94,860.00
East Tenn./Virginia	19,460.00
Indiana	18,600.00
Kentucky	46,731.50

Finance

Conference	Assessment
North Alabama	65,100.00
Albemarle	45,600.00
Blue Ridge	40,920.00
Florida	12,084.00
South Florida	11,160.00
Georgia	6,510.00
South Georgia	3,370.00
South Mississippi	11,622.00
Tennessee	68,160.00
West Tennessee/Mississippi	11,622.00
Alabama	37,200.00
Louisiana	18,600.00
Palmetto	41,850.00
Pee Dee	53,010.00
South Carolina	51,150.00
Arkansas	6,720.00
Cahaba	22,320.00
North Arkansas	6,030.00
Oklahoma	2,590.00
Texas	4,092.00
Alaska	60.00
California	35,520.00
Colorado	1,680.00
Missouri	37,200.00
Oregon/Washington	2,790.00
South West Rocky Mt.	24,180.00
Central Nigeria	60.00
East Ghana	725.00
Liberia	1,656.00
Nigeria	1,380.00
West Ghana	4,140.00
Rivers	150.00
Barbados	150.00

(Official Journal, 41st Quad. Sess. Gen. Conf., pp. 589-91)

African Methodist Episcopal Zion Church

A.M.E. ZION CHURCH CONNECTIONAL BUDGET ALLOCATIONS, 1984-88

CONNECTIONAL CLAIMANTS

Bishops' Support	(12 @ $18,000)	$ 216,000
Admin. Expenses	(12 @ $3,600)	43,200
Parsonage Exclusion	(12 @ $6,000)	72,000
Retired Bishops	(3 @ $9,000)	27,000
Retired Bishops' parsonage	(3 @ $3,000)	9,000
General Officers	(11 @ $ 16,600)	182,600
General Officers' rent excl.	(11 @ $1,000)	11,000
Manager, Publishing House	16,600	**$ 577,400**

ADMINISTRATION

Connectional Budget Office	60,000
General Conference Expense Fund	100,000
Travel and Sustentation Annual	35,000
Annual Conference Expense (Developing Confs.)	15,000
General Secretary-Auditor's Office	12,000
Office Expense - Secretary, Board of Bishops	1,200
	$223,200

DEPARTMENTAL SUPPORT

Church Extension	95,000
Christian Education	65,000
Home Missions	35,000
Overseas Missions	75,000
Evangelism	20,000
Laymen's Office	11,000
Public Relations Office	10,000
	311,000

EDUCATIONAL INSTITUTIONS

Livingstone College	900,000
Hood Theological Seminary	215,897
Clinton Jr. College	250,000
Lomax-Hannon Jr. College	250,000
Institute for Black Ministries	15,000
Inoperative Schools	5,000
	$ 1,635,897

Finance

MINISTERIAL RELIEF
Superannuated Ministers	1,000
Bishops' Widows	10,000
Ministers' Widows	100,000
Ministers' Minimum Salary	30,000
$	**141,000**

PUBLICATION/PERIODICALS
Historical Society/ Quarterly Review	6,500
Publications House	50,000
Church School Editorial Section	11,000
Star of Zion (Editor's Office)	4,900
$	**72,400**

BROTHERHOOD PENSION	$ **378,600**

ECUMENICAL/SOCIAL CONCERNS
Ecumenical Membership	$ 20,000
Harriet Tubman Home	20,000
Camp Barber	10,000
Zion's Office (Inter-Church Center)	6,000
Representation	15,000
Camp Dorothy Walls	2,500
$	**73,500**

RESERVE FUND
Capital Reserve	$ 44,000
Contingent Fund	5,910
$	**49,910**

Grand Total	**$ 3,462,907**

African Methodist Episcopal Zion Church

A.M.E. ZION CHURCH ANNUAL BUDGET APPORTIONMENT, 1984-88*

EPISCOPAL DISTRICT	CONNECTIONAL BUDGET	TOTAL
BISHOP WILLIAM M. SMITH		
First District:		
Bahama Islands	$ 1,691.00	
India	74.00	
New York	279,998.00	
Western North Carolina	304,290.00	**$586,053.00**
BISHOP A.G. DUNSTON, JR.		
Second District:		
Albemarle	$ 55,860.00	
New England	103,488.00	
New Jersey	183,162.00	
North Carolina	77,910.00	
Virgin Islands	463.00	**$420,883.00**
BISHOP C. H. FOGGIE		
Third District:		
Allegheny	$ 61,740.00	
Barbados	184.00	
Guyana	1,691.00	
Ohio	196,576.00	
Philadelphia-Baltimore	274,559.00	**$534,750.00**
BISHOP J. C. HOGGARD		
Fourth District:		
East Tennessee-Virginia	$ 25,063.00	
Indiana	22,785.00	
Jamaica (Cornwall, Middlesex, Surrey)	1,691.00	
Kentucky	57,245.00	
London-Birmingham	1,691.00	
North Alabama	79,747.00	
Western New York	73,794.00	**$262,016.00**

Finance

BISHOP C. R. COLEMAN
Fifth District:

Michigan	$238,802.00	
Tennessee	83,496.00	
Trinidad-Tobago	74.00	
Virginia	116,203.00	**$438,575.00**

BISHOP ARTHUR MARSHALL, JR.
Sixth District:

Georgia	$ 7,975.00	
Palmetto	51,266.00	
Pee Dee	64,937.00	
South Carolina	62.659.00	
South Georgia	10,253.00	
West Central North Carolina	176,988.00	**$374,078.00**

BISHOP J. H. MILLER
Seventh District:

Blue Ridge	$50,127.00	
Central North Carolina	200,545.00	
Colorado	2,058.00	
Missouri	45,570.00	**$298.300.00**

BISHOP R. L. SPEAKS
Eighth District:

Cape Fear	$113,925.00	
Louisiana	22,785.00	
South Mississippi	14,237.00	
West Tennessee-Mississippi	14,237.00	**$165,184.00**

African Methodist Episcopal Zion Church

BISHOP L. ANDERSON
Ninth District:

Alaska	$ 74.00	
California	43,512.00	
Oregon-Washington	3,418.00	
Southwest Rocky Mountain	29,621.00	
West Alabama	77,616,000	**$154,241.00**

BISHOP CECIL BISHOP
Tenth District:

Alabama	$ 45,570.00	
Cahaba	27,342.00	
Central Alabama	59,525.00	
South Alabama	34,178.00	**$166,615.00**

BISHOP R. L. FISHER
Eleventh District:

Arkansas	$ 8,232.00	
Florida	14,803.00	
North Arkansas	7,387.00	
Oklahoma	3,173.00	
South Florida	13,671.00	
Texas	5,013.00	**$52,279.00**

BISHOP A. E. WHITE
Twelfth District:

Central Nigeria	$ 74.00	
East Ghana	889.00	
Liberia	2,028.00	
Nigeria	1,690.00	
Rivers	184.00	
West Ghana	5,068.00	**$9,933.00**

Total-Connectional Budget	**$3,462,907.00**	**$3,462,907.00**

(Official Journal, 42nd Quad. Sess. Gen. Conf., pp. 626-26)
*The report of the Budget Committee to the 42nd Quadrennial Session of General Conference, meeting July 25-August 3, 1984, in St. Louis, Missouri, did not report the budget askings of the annual conferences in alphabetical order as is customarily done.

Finance

A. M. E ZION CHURCH CONNECTIONAL BUDGET ALLOCATIONS, 1988-92

CONNECTIONAL CLAIMANTS

Bishops' Support	(13 @ $40,000)	$ 520,000
Episcopal Assistance	(13 @ $10,000)	130,000
Episcopal Travel	(13 @ $10,000)	130,000
Parsonage Exclusion	(13 @ $10,000)	130,000
Retired Bishops' Salaries	(2 @ $20,000)	40,000
Retired Bishops parsonage	(2 @ $ 5,000)	10,000
		$ **960,000**

GENERAL OFFICERS

Salaries	(11 @ $24,000)	$ 264,000
Travel	(11 @ $ 3,500)	38,500
Administration	(11 @ $ 2,500)	27,500
Rent Exclusion	(11 @ $ 5,000)	55,000
Total — General Officers		$ **385,000**
Manager Publishing House		$ **24,000**

ADMINISTRATION

Connectional Budget Office	$ 76,940
General Conference Expense Fund	175,000
Travel and Sustentation	50,000
Annual Conference Expense	16,000
General Secretary's Office Expense	17,760
Office Expense - Secretary Board of Bishops	1,200
Judicial Council	$ 10,000
	$ **346,900**

DEPARTMENTAL SUPPORT

Church Extension	$ 112,100
Christian Education	76,700
Home Missions	41,300
Overseas Missions	88,500
Evangelism	20,000
Laymen's Office	12,980
Public Relations Office	11,800
	363,380

African Methodist Episcopal Zion Church

EDUCATIONAL INSTITUTIONS
Livingstone College	$ 1,095,242
Hood Theological Seminary	254,758
Clinton Jr. College	295,000
Lomax-Hannon Jr. College	250,000
Inoperative Schools	5,000
	$ 1,900,000

MINISTERIAL RELIEF
Superannuated Ministers	1,180
Bishops' Widows	11,800
Ministers' Widows	118,000
Ministers' Minimum Salary	35,400
	$ 166,380

PUBLICATIONS/PERIODICALS
Historical Society &Quarterly Review	$ 7,670
Publication House	50,000
Church School Editorial Section	22,000
Star of Zion (Editor's Office)	6,000
	$ 85,670

BROTHERHOOD PENSION	**$ 378,600**

ECUMENICAL/SOCIAL CONCERNS
Harriet Tubman Home	$ 20,000
Ecumenical Membership	34,000
Ecumenical Representation	50,000
Zion's Office (Inter-Church Center)	6,000
Camp Barber	10,000
Camp Dorothy Walls	3,000
	$ 123,000

RESERVE FUND
Capital Reserve	$ 50,000*
Contingent Fund	39,571**
Connectional Endowment	222,220***
	$ 311,791
Total	**$ 5,044,721**

Finance

Notes: For the fiscal year of the quadrennium the following adjustments are necessary: $255,000.
* Special stipend to Clinton Junior College. (This reduces Capital Reserve to $33,610)
** This will reduce Contingency Fund to $23,181.
*** Adjustment in General Officers Salaries: $177,780.
(This reduces the Connectional Endowment to $222,220 for the 2nd-4th years of the Quadrennium.)

A.M.E. ZION ANNUAL CONFERENCE ASSESSMENTS, 1988-92

CONFERENCE	ASSESSMENT
Alabama	$66,410
Albemarle	81,405
Allegheny	89,973
Alaska	107
Arkansas	107
Arizona	107
Bahama Islands	2,042
Barbados	268
Blue Ridg	73,050
Cahaba	39,846
Cape Fear	166,022
California	63,410
Central Alabama	86,746
Central Nigeria	107
Central North Carolina	292,254
Colorado	2,999
East Ghana	1,296
East Tenn.-Virginia	36,524
Florida	21,753
Georgia	11,621
Guyana	2,042
India	107
Indiana	33,131
Jamaica	2,042
Kentucky	83,423

African Methodist Episcopal Zion Church

CONFERENCE	ASSESSMENT
Liberia	2,955
London-Birmingham	2,045
Louisiana	33,204
Missouri	66,410
Michigan	348,006
New England	150,813
New Jersey	266,921
New York	408,042
North Alabama	116,216
North Arkansas	10,764
North Carolina	113,538
Nigeria	2,463
Ohio	286,471
Oklahoma	4,624
Oregon-Washington	4,981
Palmetto	74,710
Pee Dee	94,633
Philadelphia-Baltimore	400,115
Rivers	268
South Alabama	49,808
South Carolina	91,313
South Florida	19,923
South Georgia	14,942
Tennessee	121,678
Texas	7,305
Trinidad-Tobago	107
Virginia	169,343
Virgin Islands	559
West Alabama	113,110
West Central North Carolina	257,924
West Ghana	7,385
Western New York	107,504
Western North Carolina	443,444
West Tennessee-Mississippi	20,748
Total:	**$5,044,721**

Finance

A. M. E. ZION CHURCH CONNECTIONAL BUDGET, 1992-96

CONNECTIONAL CLAIMANTS
Bishops

Salaries	(12 @ $40,000)	$ 480,000.00
Episcopal Assistance	(12 @ $10,000)	120,000.00
Parsonage Exclusion	(12 @ $10,000)	120,000.00
Episcopal Travel	(12 @ $10,000)	120,000.00
Retired Bishops' Salaries	(7 @ $16,000)	112,000.00
Retired Bishops' Rent Exclusion	(7 @ $4,000)	28,000.00

GENERAL OFFICERS
Salaries

	(11 @ $24,000)	$ 264,000.00
Health & Social Concerns		12,000.00
Rent Exclusion	(11 @ $5000)	55,000.00
Travel	(12 @ $3,500)	41,500.00
Administration	(12 @ $5,000)	60,000.00
		$1,412,500.00

ADMINISTRATION

Connectional Budget Office	$ 76,940.00
General Conference Expenses	225,000.00
Travel/Sustentation	50,000.00
Annual Conference Expenses	- - - -
General Secretary-Auditor (Off.)	27,600.00
Secretary, Board of Bishops	1,200.00
FICA	25,000.00
	$ 405,740.00

DEPARTMENTAL SUPPORT

Church Extension	$ 100,100.00
Home Mission	31,300.00
Christian Education	76,700.00
Overseas Missions	88,500.00
Evangelism	40,000.00
Connectional Lay Council	12,980.00
Public Affairs/Convention Manager	11,800.00
Health and Social Concerns	5,000.00
	$ 366,380.00

African Methodist Episcopal Zion Church

(CONNECTIONAL BUDGET, 1992-96)

EDUCATIONAL INSTITUTIONS

Livingstone College	$1,095,242.00
Hood Theological Seminary	254,758.00
Clinton Junior College	295,000.00
Clinton Junior College Loan	25,000.00
Inoperative Schools	5,000.00
Zion Community College	20,000.00
Lomax-Hannon Junior College	75,000.00
	$1,770,000.00

MINISTERIAL RELIEF

Superannuated Ministers	1,180.00
Bishops' Widows	15,800.00
Ministers' Widows	118,000.00
Ministers' Minimum Salary	0.00
Total Ministerial Relief	**$134,980.00**

PUBLICATIONS/PERIODICALS

Historical Society and Quarterly Review	12,670.00
Publishing House	74,000.00
Church School Editorial	32,000.00
Star of Zion	16,000.00
	$ 134,670.00

BROTHERHOOD PENSION	**$ 200,000.00**

ECUMENICAL/SOCIAL CONCERNS

Harriet Tubman	25,000.00
Ecumenical Membership	55,000.00
Ecumenical Representation	50,000.00
Zion Office (Inter-Church Center)	6,000.00
Camp Barber	10,000.00
Camp Dorothy Walls	3,000.00
	$ 149,000.00

Finance

RESERVE FUND

Capital Reserve	50,000.00
Contingency Fund	51,451.00
Connectional Endowment	<u>200,000.00</u>
	$ 301,451.00

JUDICIAL COUNCIL	**$ 20,000.00**
BICENTENNIAL COMMISSION	**$ 150,000.00**
GRAND TOTAL	**$ 5,044,721.00**

*LIVINGSTONE COLLEGE 7%	**$ 353,130.47**

*This was a one-time asking for liquidating the debt of Livingstone College and was not included in the quadrennial appropriations.

A.M.E. ZION CHURCH ANNUAL CONFERENCE ASSESSMENTS, 1992-1996

	ACTUAL	LIVINGSTONE COLLEGE (7%)
Alabama	$ 66,410.00	$ 4,648.70
Alaska	107.00	7.49
Albemarle	81,405.00	5,698.35
Allegheny	89,973.00	6,298.11
Arkansas	10,764.00	753.48
Arizona	107.00	7.49
Bahama Islands	2,042.00	142.94
Barbados	268.00	18.76
Blue Ridge	73,050.00	5,113.50
Cahaba	39,846.00	2,789.22
California	63,410.00	4,438.70
Cape Fear	166,022.00	11,621.54
Central Alabama	86,746.00	6,072.22
Central Nigeria	107.00	7.49
Central North Carolina	292,254.00	20,457.78
Colorado	2,999.00	209.93
Cote d'Ivoire	0.00	0.00
East Ghana	1,296.00	90.72

African Methodist Episcopal Zion Church

Conference	Actual	Livingstone College—7%
East Tennessee-Virginia	36,524.00	2,556.68
Florida	24,699.00	1,728.93
Georgia	11,621.00	813.47
Guyana	2,042.00	142.94
India	107.00	7.49
Indiana	33,131.00	2,319.17
Jamaica	2,042.00	142.94
Kentucky	83,423.00	5,839.61
Lagos-West Nigeria	0.00	0.00
Liberia	2,955.00	206.85
London-Birmingham	2,042.00	142.94
Louisiana	33,204.00	2,324.28
Mainland-West Nigeria	0.00	0.00
Manchester-Midlands	0.00	0.00
Mid-Ghana	0.00	0.00
Michigan	348,006.00	24,360.42
Missouri	66,410.00	4,648.70
New England	150,813.00	10,556.91
New Jersey	266,921.00	18,684.47
New York	408,042.00	28,562.94
Nigeria	2,463.00	172.41
North Alabama	116,216.00	8, 135.12
North Arkansas	11,997.00	839.79
North Carolina	113,538.00	7,947.66
Ohio	286,507.00	20,055.49
Oklahoma	4,624.00	323.68
Oregon-Washington	4,981.00	348.67
Palmetto	74,710.00	5,229.70
Pee Dee	94,633.00	6,624.31
Philadelphia-Baltimore	400,115.00	28,008.05
Rivers	268.00	18.76
South Alabama	49,808.00	3,486.56
South Carolina	91,313.00	6,391.91
South Florida	16,797.00	1,175.79
South Georgia	14,942.00	1,045.94

Finance

CONFERENCE	ACTUAL	LIVINGSTONE COLLEGE—7%
South Mississippi	20,748.00	1,452.36
Southwest Rocky Mountain	43,167.00	3, 021.69
Tennessee	121,678.00	8,517.46
Texas	7,305.00	511.35
Trinidad-Tobago	107.00	7.49
Virgin Islands	559.00	39.13
Virginia	169,343.00	11,854.01
West Alabama	113,110.00	7,917.70
West Central North Carolina	257,924.00	18,054.68
West Ghana	7,385.00	516.95
West Tennessee-Mississippi	20,748.00	1,452.36
Western New York	107,504.00	7,525.28
Western North Carolina	443,443.00	31,041.01

TOTAL CONNECTIONAL BUDGET
(REVENUE) $5,044,721.00 $ 353,130.47
(Official Journal, 44th Quad. Sess. Gen. Conf., pp. 843-46)

A.M.E. ZION CHURCH CONNECTIONAL BUDGET, 1996-2000

CONNECTIONAL CLAIMANTS	1992-96 Actual	1996-2000 Budget
BISHOPS' Salaries (12 @ $40,000)	$ 480,000.00	$480,000.00
Episcopal Assistance (12 @ $15,000)	120,000.00	180,000.00
Episcopal Travel (12 @ $15,000	120,000.00	180,000.00
Parsonage Exclusion (12 @ $10,000)	120,000.00	120,000.00
Retired Bishops' Salaries (6 @ $16,000)	112,000.00	96,000.00
Rent Exclusion (6 @ $7,000)	28,000.00	42,000.00
Total	**980,000.00**	**1,098,000.00**
GENERAL OFFICERS		
Salaries (11 @ $29,000)	264,000.00	319,000.00
Health & Social Concerns (1 @ $14,500)	12,000.00	14,500.00
Travel (12 @ $5000)	42,000.00	60,000.00

African Methodist Episcopal Zion Church

Administration (12 @ $7,000)	60,000.00	84,000.00
Rent Exclusion (11 @ $7,000)*	55,000.00	77,000.00
Total	**433,000.00**	**554,500.00**
Total Connectional Claimants	**1,413,000.00**	**1,652,500.00**
*None for Health/Social Concerns		
ADMINISTRATION		
FICA**	25,000.00	30,000.00
Connectional Budget Office	76,940.00	125,000.00
General Conference Expenses	225,000.00	250,000.00
Travel/Sustentation	50,000.00	60,000.00
General Secretary's Office Expense	27,600.00	40,000.00
Secretary, Board of Bishops	1,200.00	0.00
Judicial Council	20,000.00	20,000.00
Bicentennial Commission	150,000.00	0.00
Total Administration	**575,740.00**	**525,000.00**

** Paid by Financial Dept.
  for all General Officers

DEPARTMENTAL SUPPORT		
Church Extension	100,100.00	100,100.00
Christian Education	76,700.00	100,000.00
Home Missions	31,300.00	80,000.00
Overseas Missions	88,500.00	100,000.00
Evangelism	40,000.00	75,000.00
Connectional Lay Council	12,980.00	13,000.00
Public Relations Office	11,800.00	12,000.00
Health and Social Concerns	5,000.00	5,000.00
East & West Africa	0.00	50,000.00
Total Departmental Support	366,380.00	535,100.00
EDUCATIONAL INSTITUTIONS		
Livingstone College	1,095,242.00	1,095,242.00
Hood Theological Seminary	254,758.00	400,000.00
Clinton Junior College	295,000.00	450,000.00

Finance

Clinton Junior College Loan	25,000.00	25,000.00
Lomax-Hannon Junior College	75,000.00	75,000.00
Inoperative Schools	5,000.00	0.00
Zion Community College	20,000.00	50,000.00
Hood-Speaks Seminary—Nigeria	0.00	50,000.00
Total Educational Institutions	**1,770,000.00**	**2,145,242.00**

MINISTERIAL RELIEF		
Superannuated Ministers	1,180.00	10,000.00
Bishops' Widows	15,800.00	20,000.00
Ministers' Widows	118,000.00	150,000.00
Total Ministerial Relief	**134,980.00**	**180,000.00**

PUBLICATIONS/PERIODICALS		
Historical Society Quarterly Review	12,670.00	15,000.00
Publication House	74,000.00	74,000.00
Church School Editorial	32,000.00	50,000.00
Star of Zion (Editor's Office)	16,000.00	30,000.00
Total Publications/Periodicals	**134,670.00**	**169,000.00**

BROTHERHOOD PENSION	**200,000.00**	**200,000.00**

ECUMENICAL/SOCIAL CONCERNS		
Harriet Tubman	25,000.00	30,000.00
Ecumenical Memberships	55,000.00*	50,000.00
Ecumenical Representation	50,000.00*	55,000.00
Zion's Office (Inter-Church Center)	6,000.00	12,000.00
Camp Barber	10,000.00	10,000.00
Camp Dorothy Walls	3,000.00	3,000.00
Total Ecumenical/Social Concern	**149,000.00**	**160,000.00**

RESERVE FUND		
Capital Reserve	50,000.00*	65,000.00
Contingency Fund***	51,451.00*	65,394.00
Connectional Endowment	200,000.00*	100,000.00
Total Reserve Funds	**301,451.00**	**230,394.00**

African Methodist Episcopal Zion Church

Connectional Education Fund****	353,130.00	866,000.00
Total Connectional Claimants	1,413,000.00	1,652,500.00
Total Administration	575,740.00	525,000.00
Total Department Support	366,380.00	535,100.00
Total Educational Institutions	1,770,000.00	2,145,242.00
Total Ministerial Relief	134,980.00	180,000.00
Total Publications/Periodicals	134,670.00	169,000.00
Total Brotherhood Pension	200,000.00	200,000.00
Total Ecumenical/Social Concerns	149,000.00	160,000.00
Total Reserve Funds	301,451.00	230,394.00
Total Connectional Education Fund	353,130.00	866,000.00
GRAND TOTAL	$ 5,398,351.00	$6,663,236.00

*from Ecumenical Memberships	5,000.00
*from Ecumenical Representation	5,000.00
*from Capital Reserve Fund	10,000.00
* from Contingency Fund	9,606.00
* from Connectional Endowment Fund	100,000.00
	$129,606.00

A. M. E. ZION CHURCH ANNUAL CONFERENCE ASSESSMENTS, 1996-2000

CONFERENCE	1992-1996 OLD ASSESSMENT	32% INCREASE	1996-2000 NEW ASSESSMENT
Alabama	$66,410.00	21,251.00	87,661.00
Alaska	107.00	693.00	800.00
Albemarle	81,405.00	26,050.00	107,455.00
Allegheny	89,973.00	28,791.00	118,764.00
Ark. & N. Ark.	22,761.00	7, 823.00	30,584.00
Arizona	107.00	293.00	400.00
Bahama Islands	2,042.00	653.00	2,695.00
Barbados	268.00	86.00	354.00

Finance

Annual Conference	1992-1996 Assessment	32 % Increase	1996-2000 Assessment
Blue Ridge	73,050.00	23,376.00	96,426.00
Cahaba	39,846.00	12,751.00	52,597.00
California	64,410.00	22,486.00	85,896.00
Cape Fear	166,022.00	53,127.00	219,140.00
Central Alabama	86,746.00	7,759.00	14,505.00
Central Nigeria	268,00	86.00	354.00
Central N. C.	292,254.00	93,521.00	385,775.00
Colorado	2,999.00	-1,748.00	1,251.00
Cote d'Ivoire	107.00	34.00	141.00
East Ghana	1,189.00	380.00	1,569.00
E. Tenn.-Vir.	36,524.00	11,688.00	48,212.00
Florida	24,699.00	7,904.00	32,603.00
Georgia	11,621.00	3,719.00	15,340.00
Guyana	2,042.00	653.00	2,695.00
India	107.00	34.00	141.00
Indiana	33,131.00	10,602.00	43,733.00
Jamaica	2,042.00	653.00	2,695.00
Kentucky	83,423.00	26,696.00	110,119.00
Lagos-W. Nigeria	107.00	34.00	141.00
Liberia	2,955.00	946.00	3,901.00
London-Birm.	1,935.00	619.00	2,554.00
Louisiana	33,204.00	10,625.00	43,829.00
Main. W. Nigeria	107.00	34.00	141.00
Manchester-Midlnds	107.00	34.00	141.00
Mid Ghana	107.00	34.00	141.00
Michigan	348,006.00	11,362.00	459,368.00
Missouri	66,410.00	21,251.00	87,661.00
New England	150,813.00	48,260.00	199,073.00
New Jersey	266,921.00	85,415.00	352,336.00
New York	408,042.00	130,573.00	538,615.00
Nigeria	2,463.00	788.00	3,251.00
North Alabama	116,216.00	37,189.00	153,405.00

African Methodist Episcopal Zion Church

Conference	1992-1996 Old Asseessment	32% Increasee	1996-2000 New Assessment
North Carolina	113,538.00	36,332.00	149,870.00
Northern Nigeria	0.00	0.00	0.00
Ohio	286,507.00	91,682.00	378,189.00
Oklahoma	4,624.00	1,480.00	6,104.00
Oregon-Washington	4,981.00	2,766.00	7,747.00
Palmetto	74,710.00	23,907.00	98,617.00
Pee Dee	94,633.00	30,283.00	124,916.00
Phila.-Baltimore	400,115.00	128,037.00	528,152.00
Rivers Nigeria	107.00	34.00	141.00
South Africa	0.00	0.00	0.00
South Alabama	49,808.00	15,939.00	65,747.00
South Carolina	91,313.00	29,220.00	120,533.00
South Florida	16,797.00	5,375.00	22,172.00
South Georgia	14,942.00	4,781.00	19,723.00
South Mississippi	20,748.00	6,639.00	27,387.00
SW Rocky Mountain	43,167.00	15,480.00	58,647.00
Tennessee	121,678.00	38,937.00	160,615.00
Texas	7,305.00	2,338.00	9,643.00
Trinidad-Tobago	107.00	34.00	141.00
Virgin Islands	559.00	179.00	738.00
Virginia	169,343.00	54,190.00	223,533.00
West Alabama	113,110.00	36,195.00	149,305.00
W. Cntrl. N. Carolina	257,924.00	82,536.00	340,460.00
West Ghana	7,385.00	2,363.00	9,748.00
W. Tenn.-Mississippi	20,748.00	6,639.00	27,387.00
Western New York	107,504.00	34,401.00	141,905.00
Western N. Carolina	443,443.00	141,902.00	585,345.00
Total Assessments	**$5,045,042.00**	**$1,618,194.00**	**$ 6,663,236.00**

CONNECTIONAL BUDGET BOARD
1972-96

1972-76
Bishop Herbert Bell Shaw, chairperson
Bishop S. G. Spottswood, 1st vice chairperson

Finance

Bishop Clinton R. Coleman, 2nd vice chairperson
Members:

1. Rev. M. A. Williams
2. Rev. A. W. Mapp
3. Rev. E. Eugene Morgan
4. Mr. D. D. Garrett
5. Rev. E. Franklin Jackson
6. Rev. M. C. Williams
7. Rev. M. B. Robinson
8. Rev. O. R. Hayes
9. Rev. George Sanders
10. Rev. Raymond Hart
11. Rev. O. D. Carson
12. Rev. W. H. Coleman
13. Rev. C. G. McKinney
14. Rev.James E. McCoy
15. Rev. D. L. Blakey
16. Rev. S. S. Seay
17. Rev. G. W. Kendall
18. Mrs. Abbie C. Jackson
19. Rev. R. L. Lee
20. Rev. C. B. Howell
21. Rev. W. J. Neal
22. Rev. James G. Crowder
23. Rev. S. L. Hopkins
24. Mrs. Betty V. Stith

1976-80
Bishop Herbert B. Shaw, chairperson
Bishop Clinton R. Coleman, 1st vice chairperson
Bishop George L. Leake, III, 2nd vice chairperson
Members:

1. Rev. Milton A. Williams
2. Rev.C. G. McKinney
3. Dr. A. W. Mapp
4. Rev.James E. McCoy
5. Dr. Eugene E. Morgan
6. Rev. D. L. Blakey
7. Mr. D. D. Garrett
8. Rev. G. Ray Coleman
9. Rev. Cecil Bishop
10. Rev. George Kendall
11. Rev. M. C. Williams
12. Mr. Woodford R. Porter
13. Rev. W. A. Eason
14. Rev. R. L. Lee
15. Rev. O. R. Hayes
16. Rev. Bennie Luckett
17. Rev. B. W. Moncur
18. Rev. A. L. Wilson
19. Rev. Silas Redd
20. Rev. Harvest T. Wilkins
21. Rev. William Coleman
22. Dr. Gossie Hudson
23. Mrs. Betty Stith
24. Rev. Clarence Carr

1980-84
Bishop C. R. Coleman, chairperson
Bishop George J. Leake, III, 1st vice chairperson
Bishop W. M. Smith, 2nd vice chairperson

African Methodist Episcopal Zion Church

Members:
1. Rev. James E. McCoy
   Mrs. Betty V. Stith
2. Dr. A. W. Mapp
   Mr. W. D. Blount
3. Dr. E. E. Morgan, Jr.
   Mrs. Elnora H. Askey
4. Rev.M. C. Williams
   Mr. Chester Moran
5. Rev. R. L. Lee
   Mr. Arthur Jones
6. Dr. George W. Walker
   Mrs. Grace L. Holmes

7. Dr. A. L. Wilson
   Mr. Spencer Williams
8. Rev. W. A. Eason
   Mrs.Arthur M. Norris
9. Dr. William H. Coleman
   Mr. Eugene Atkins
10. Rev. Silas Redd
    Mrs. Odell Fleming
11. Mr. J. R. Broughton

12. Rev. Clarence Carr
    Mr. James F. Roseman

1984-88
Bishop Clinton R. Coleman, chairperson
Bishop W. M. Smith, 1st vice chairperson
Bishop H. L. Anderson, 2nd vice chairperson
Members:
1. Rev. James McCoy
2. Mrs. Betty Stith
3. Mrs. Bertha M. Perry
4. Rev. Andrew M. Mapp
5. Rev. E. E. Morgan
6. Mrs. June Slade Collins
7. Rev. Brownell D. Pagan
8. Mr. Chester Moran
9. Rev. George Walker
10. Mrs. Grace Holmes
11. Rev. David L. Scott
12. Mr. W. E. Staten

13. Rev. L. A. Miller
14. Mr. Vernon Stevens
15. Rev. J. M. Sloan
16. Mrs. Clara Robertson
17. Rev. Milton Williams
18. Ms. Mary Moore
19. Rev. A. L. Wilson
20. Mr. Spencer Williams
21. Rev. Harvest T. Wilkins
22. Mr. Merritt Thomas
23. Rev. Harrison D. Bonner
24. Mr. James F. Roseman

1988-92
Bishop Clinton R. Coleman, chairperson
Bishop W. M. Smith, 1st vice chairperson

Finance

Bishop Herman L. Anderson, 2nd vice chairperson
Members:

1. Dr. James E. McCoy
2. Dr. Betty V. Stith
3. Mrs. Bertha G. Perry
4. Dr. Harrison D. Bonner
5. Rev. G. Ray Coleman
6. Mr. Ward DeWitt
7. Rev. General L. Scott
8. Mr. James H. Harper
9. Rev.Lawrence A. Miller
10. Mr. Chester Moran
11. Dr. Dennis V. Proctor
12. Mrs. Lessie Polk
13. Dr. E. E. Morgan
14. Mr. Sanford Davis
15. Rev. Michael A. Frencher
16. Mr. H. W. Robinson
17. Rev. David L. Scott
18. Dr. Clara V. Robertson
19. Rev. A. L. Wilson
20. Mr. Spencer Williams
21. Rev. Percy Smith
22. Mrs. Emma Barnes
23. Rev. S. O. Greene
24. Mrs. Lonia M. Gill
25. Rev. James Samuel
26. Chief U. D. Umoha

1992-96
Bishop Herman L. Anderson, chairperson
Bishop J. Clinton Hoggard, 1st vice chairperson
Bishop Cecil Bishop, 2nd vice chairperson
Members:

1. Rev. Smith Turner
2. Mr. Albert Stout
3. Rev. L. A. Miller
4. Mrs. Bertha Perry
5. Rev. Lawton Nelson
6. Mrs. Mary Taylor
7. Rev. James E. McCoy
8. Mr. Ward DeWitt
9. Rev. G. Ray Coleman
10. Mrs. Lessie Polk
11. Rev. James R. Samuel
12. Dr. Betty Stith
13. Rev. David L. Scott
14. Ms. Vera Jeter-Jones
15. Rev. Silas W. Redd
16. Dr. Clara V. Robertson
17. Rev. Malone Smith, Jr.
18. Mr. Spencer Williams
19. Rev. Roy Holmes
20. Ms. Jacqueline Hart
21. Rev. Gregory R. Smith
22. Mr. Raleigh Singletary
23. Rev. Percy Smith
24. Mr. James Hewitt

1996-2000
Bishop George E. Battle, Jr., chairperson
Bishop Enoch B. Rochester, 1st vice chairperson

African Methodist Episcopal Zion Church

Bishop Cecil Bishop, 2nd vice chairperson
Members:

1. Dr. Smith Turner, III
2. Mr. Albert Stout
3. Dr. James E. McCoy
4. Mr. Ward DeWitt
5. Rev. Cameron W. Jackson
6. Mrs. Alma Coles Charles
7. Dr. Thaddeus Garrett, Jr.
8. Mr. Ward DeWitt
9. Rev. Lawrence Miller
10. Mr. D. D. Garrett
11. Rev. Dr. David Scott
12. Ms. Vera Jeter-Jones
13. Rev. Malone Smith, Jr.
14. Mr. Spencer Williams
15. Rev. Roy A. Holmes

A. M. E. ZION PUBLISHING HOUSE
1972-1996

The A. M. E. Zion Church Publishing House has been a venture of economic development. Its history is traced by W. J. Walls in *The History of the African Methodist Episcopal Zion Church: Reality of the Black Church*. This story depicts the creative activities of all the predecessors of the Rev. Durocher L. Blakey who became general manager in 1963. During Rev. Blakey's administration, the present Publishing House, known as the New Varick Memorial Publishing House, was constructed at a cost of $550,000 and was formally opened on October 30, 1966. The building is located at the corner of Brevard and 2nd Streets, Charlotte, North Carolina, in the midst of a very affluent commercial and industrial area of the city . Rev. Blakey served until the General Conference of 1972, when he was succeeded by Mr. Lem Long. Bishop William Andrew Stewart was chairperson of the Publishing House Board until 1972, when he was succeeded by Bishop Arthur Marshall, Jr. (Walls, pp. 336-46).

It should be noted that a revised policy in the appointment of the manager of the Publishing House was effected during the 1960s. The General Conference of 1960, on recommendation of the Board of Bishops through its Episcopal Address and the Publishing House Board, made major revisions in the law affecting the operation of the Publishing House. One of the chief revisions was that the manager of the Publishing House be nominated by the Publishing House Board and that his nomination be confirmed by the Board of Bishops. This revision made possible a direct relationship between the Publishing House Board and the manager of the Publishing House. During the period 1972-96, the manager was directly accountable to the Publishing House Board. (*Official Journal, 36th Quad. Sess. Gen. Conf.*, p. 345)

Mr. Lem Long served as interim manager of the Publishing House while he was the elected secretary-treasurer of the Church Extension Department. Mr. Long successfully managed the affairs of the Publishing House through the General Conference of 1992. At that time, Bishop George W. Walker, Sr., succeeded the late Bishop Alfred G. Dunston, Jr., as chairperson of the Publishing House Board. Rev. Dr. Milton B. Robinson and Rev. Louis J. Baptiste were editor, respectively, of the *Star of Zion* and of Church School Literature. The Star of Zion was published and distributed from the Publishing House. (*Official Journal, 44th Quad. Sess. Gen. Conf.*, pp. 519-20)

African Methodist Episcopal Zion Church

Ministerial Relief Department with offices in the Publishing House at Charlotte, North Carolina. After four months of managerial responsibility, Rev. Miller had transformed the physical appearance of the Publishing House. The James Varick Bookstore has been modernized and stocked with updated publications, worship materials, church furnishings, and vestments. (*44th Quad. Sess.*, pp. 519-20)

At the Connectional Council meeting in July, 1997 at the Broadway Temple A. M. E. Zion Church in Louisville, Kentucky, Rev. Dr. David Miller, general manager of the Publishing House, reported progress in its operation. The James Varick Christian Bookstore has sustained sales between $10,000 and $13,000 per month. Unfortunately, A. M. E. Zion churches are not patronizing the book store as they should. Only five tenants are paying rent; the others are occupying the building rent free. The Publishing House depends on the Finance Department to pay its mortgage obligations. Dr. Miller thought that the Publishing House should require rent at a fair market rate, or it would need an additional subsidy of $116,048.40 per year. He recommended a rental rate of $8.65 per square foot for each tenant. The market rate in downtown Charlotte with parking was $22.00 per sq. ft. The Publishing House Board recommended that the Department of Church School Literature be responsible for full preparation and printing of each of its books before delivering them to the Publishing House for distribution. The financial operation of the Publishing House at this time gives the denomination high hope that before the end of the twentieth century, the A. M. E. Zion Publishing House would be a financially solvent, self-operating, and economically productive enterprise of the church. Thus it would fulfill its mandated mission to provide profits from the operation of the Publishing House "to the relief of supernumerary and superannuated Ministers, their Widows and Orphans." ("Report of the A. M. E. Zion Publishing House, to the Board of Bishops and the Connectional Council, July 30-August 2, 1997," pp. 23-24; *The Book of Discipline*, 1992, p. 218)

For the period 1972-2000, the Publishing House Board members have been:

PUBLISHING HOUSE BOARD

1972-76
Bishop Arthur Marshall, Jr., chairperson
Bishop William M. Smith, 1st vice chairperson
Bishop William A. Stewart, 2nd vice chairperson
Members:
1. Rev. Leon W. Watts, II   2. Rev. Leon W. Watts, I

Publishing House

3. Rufus M. Jones
4. Rev. W. J. W. Turner
5. Rev. J. D. McArthur
6. Rev. F. M. Webb
7. Rev. W. A. Eason

8. Rev. J. A. Arnold
9. Rev. Ollie Graves
10. Rev. J. W. Jingles
11. Rev. G. W. Whisonant
12. Rev. James A. Brown

1976-80
Bishop Arthur Marshall, Jr., chairperson
Bishop William M. Smith, 1st vice chairperson
Bishop Clinton R. Coleman, 2nd vice chairperson
Members
1. Rev. H. D. Bonner
2. Rev. Dr. Frank M. Allen
3. Rev. William Cunningham
4. Rev. W. J. W. Turner
5. Rev. William M. Patterson
6. Rev. J. L. Walton

7. Rev. E. J. Henry
8. Mrs. Grace L. Holmes
9. Rev. S. W. Schultz
10. Rev. Raymond E. Price
11. Rev. William Seals
12. Rev. Dr. Godfred N. Zormelo

1980-84
Bishop Arthur Marshall, Jr., chairperson
Bishop Herman L. Anderson, 1st vice chairperson
Bishop William Milton Smith, 2nd vice chairperson
Members:
1. Dr. V. Loma St. Clair
2. Rev. Andrew Mackey
3. Dr. Willa Mae Rice
4. Rev. F. D. Mayweather
5. Mr. George Zeigler
6. Rev. O. R. Hayes

7. Rev. Dr. C. C. Tyson
8. Rev. J. H. Williams
9. Rev. Leroy Blair
10. Rev. Harvest T. Wilkins
11. Mrs. Catherine Whitley
12. Rev. Vernon Shannon

1984-88
Bishop Arthur Marshall, Jr., chairpersonn
Bishop J. H. Miller, 1st vice chairperson
Bishop H. L. Anderson, 2nd vice chairperson
Members:

African Methodist Episcopal Zion Church

1. Rev. Calvin B. Marshall
2. Rev. Donald Ruffin
3. Mr. Lynwood Lewis
4. Rev. F. D. Mayweather
5. Mrs. Daisy Henson
6. Rev. Clarence C. Tyson
7. Rev. J. F. Wills
8. Rev. John Evans
9. Rev. B. Leon Carson
10. Rev. Joshua Bettis
11. Rev. Mozella Mitchell
12. Mrs.Willa M. Rice

1988-92
Bishop A. G. Dunston, Jr., chairperson
Bishop J. H. Miller, Sr., 1st vice chairperson
Bishop R. L. Fisher, 2nd vice chairperson
Members:

1. Mr. Edward O. Tracy
2. Rev. Donald W. H. E. Ruffin
3. Rev. Louis Hunter
4. Rev. Richard A. Council
5. Dr. F. George Shipman
6. Rev. Kenneth Monroe
7. Rev. Odinga L. Maddox
8. Rev. F. D. Mayweather
9. Rev. C. C. Tyson
10. Rev. Joshua Bettis
11. Mrs. Willa Mae Rice
12. Mrs. Margie Bonner

1992-96
Bishop George W. C. Walker, Sr., chairperson
Bishop George E. Batttle, Jr., 1st vice chairperson
Bishop J. Clinton Hoggard, 2nd vice chairperson
Members

1. Rev. David R. Baker
2. Rev. W. L. Wainwright
3. Rev. Emmett Foster
4. Rev. Robert L. Graham
5. Rev. Raymond Dickerson
6. Mrs. F. I. Ekemam
7. Rev. Louis Hunter
8. Rev. John Evans
9. Rev. James French
10. Rev. Kenneth Moore
11. Rev. Robert L. Perry, Sr.
12. Rev. Theodore Moore

1996-2000
Bishop George W. C. Walker, Sr., chairperson
Bishop George E. Battle, Jr., 1st vice chairperson
Bishop J. Clinton Hoggard, 2nd vice chairperson
Members

Publishing House

1. Rev. David R. Baker
2. Rev. Dr. Robert L. Graham
3. Rev. Raymond M. Dickerson
4. Dr. Clara Robertson
5. Rev. Claude Willie
6. Rev. Dr. Louis Hunter
7. Rev. James French
8. Rev. Staccato Powell
9. Rev. Emmett Foster
10. Rev. Dr. Theodore Moore
11. Rev. John C. Evans, Jr.
12. Rev. Edmond Whitley

THE STAR OF ZION
1972-1996

During the years 1972-96, the *Star of Zion* was edited by the Revs. M. B. Robinson and Morgan W. Tann. Rev. Robinson was initially appointed in 1970 by the Board of Bishops to complete the term of the Rev. Walter R. Lovell who had died in 1968. Rev. Robinson was elected editor in 1972 and was reelected in 1976. He was succeeded by Rev. Morgan W. Tann who was elected in 1980 and continues as editor. (*Official Journal, 39th Quad. Sess. Gen. Conf.*, pp. 258, 262-63)

During the 39th quadrennial session of General Conference meeting in Mobile, Alabama, in 1972, Rev. Robinson reported that the *Star of Zion* had increased its circulation from 4,700 copies in January 1969 to 6,650 as of March 31, 1972. He noted that although the *Star of Zion* was not established as a commercial enterprise, it could offset some of its costs through advertisements. He reported that the *Star of Zion* had become a member of the Associated Church Press. Various libraries and organizations subscribed to the journal, and many well-known journals had placed the *Star* on their exchange list. The accounts for the four years showed receipts of $27,245.40, with disbursements of $25,573.91, as of March 31, 1972. (Ibid., p. 263)

A report by Rev. M. B. Robinson in May, 1976 at the 40th quadrennial session of General Conference showed receipts of $30,273.33 and disbursements of $29,545.49 as of November 1, 1975. Accounts for the four-years 1976-80 recorded receipts of $31,078.40 and expenditures of $31,078.40. Rev. Robinson noted that the *Star of Zion* was celebrating its 100th anniversary in May , 1976 and was among the oldest religious publications in the nation. The Lincoln University School of Journalism had awarded the Star of Zion a plaque for winning first place in community affairs in competition with eighty other applicants. He also reported that classified advertising revenue was growing.

In May, 1980, the circulation of the *Star of Zion* had increased to 7,500 copies. Rev. Robinson attributed the increase to the active support of Bishops Herbert Bell Shaw and William Milton Smith and other members of Zion. There was a concerted effort by the Star of Zion to promote *The African Methodist Episcopal Zion Church: Reality of the Black Church* by Bishop William Jacob Walls and the two volumes of *A History of the A.M.E. Zion Church* by Dr. David Henry Bradley, Sr. (Official Journal, *40th Quad. Sess. Gen. Conf.*, p. 343; 41st Quad. Sess., pp. 373; 378-79)

Rev. Morgan W. Tann was elected in 1980 to succeed Rev. Robinson as editor of the *Star of Zion*. Among the goals established for the organ by Rev. Tann were the binding of back issues of the journal; control of circulation through the *Star of Zion* office

Star of Zion

with remuneration and reports submitted to the Publishing House; capacity for camera-ready copy; establishment of circulation and advertising functions within the department with the purpose of becoming self-supporting, and organizing an active editorial staff. The Publishing House manager purchased an electronic typesetting machine that enabled the *Star of Zion* to originate camera-ready copy, thus saving both time and money. Dr. Tann observed that a better educated and a more affluent membership within the denomination should be reflected in the number of subscribers and in the commitment to develop writers among the young people of the church. The financial statement for the 1980-84 quadrennium showed total receipts of $43,338.13 (including a balance brought forward of $712.61); total disbursements of $42,324.62; and a balance carried forward of $1,013.51. (*Official Journal, 42nd Quad. Sess. Gen. Conf.*, pp. 388-93)

At the 43rd General Conference in July, 1988, Rev. Tann reported an increase in the church subsidy of $2,500, bringing the total annual subsidy to $19,580. *The Star of Zion*, Rev. Tann reported, had receipts of $78,220.51 and expenditures of $74,071.57 during the 1984-88 quadrennium. Improvements included the hiring of a full-time secretary, the achievement of printing facilities, including the capacity to print in color within the *Star of Zion* office, and the acquisition of additional machinery, including an IBM workstation, made possible through advertising revenues, and a duplicating machine, purchased for use in conjunction with other sections of the Publishing House. The editor spoke of the need to include the *Star of Zion* in denominational activities. He represented the Church press at the Consultation on Church Union (COCU) talks with the Christian Methodist Episcopal Church, participated in the North Carolina Council of Churches Committee of Church Newspapers, and attended the Annual Conferences of the Virgin Islands and the Bahama Islands through the courtesy of Bishops Dunston and Smith, respectively. He also noted that the late Bishop Marshall and Rev. George. L. Blackwell had each provided him an opportunity to address their respective annual conference and general education convention. These opportunities enhanced his effort to develop young writers for the *Star of Zion*. (Official Journal, *43rd Quad. Sess. Gen. Conf.*, pp. 458-62)

At the 44th General Conference held in Atlanta, Georgia, Rev. Dr. Tann reiterated many of his concerns, namely, the relatively small increase in *Star of Zion* subscriptions, the inadequacy of the annual subsidy to the *Star of Zion* office, and his lack of access to the subscription records. Rev. Tann reported receipts of $109,673.87 and disbursements of $109,498.84 for the 1988-92 quadrennium. These receipts included a bank loan of $4,017.00 obtained by the editor to pay for office operations. Rev. Tann pointed out the need for the denomination to comply with the law in the payment of

African Methodist Episcopal Zion Church

Social Security taxes for full-time employees. He recommended that bishops allow him to promote subscriptions for the *Star of Zion* during their annual conferences. The editor attended the three-day Associated Church Press convention held in Alexandria, Virginia, where he submitted the *Star of Zion* for critical assessment by a committee of the association. Both favorable comments and recommendations for improvement were received. He also represented the church at the World Methodist Conference in Singapore during the quadrennium. He expressed gratitude to the church for including the editor of the *Star of Zion* in the Bicentennial Commission, designating him Publicity Committee chairperson, and for making him a member of the Restructuring Commission. He thanked Livingstone College and Hood Theological Seminary for bestowing an` honorary doctorate degree on him. (*Official Journal , 44th Quad. Sess. Gen. Conf.*, pp. 531-34)

At the 45th General Conference held in Washington, D. C., in July, 1996, the editor stated that Bishop Walker, chairperson of the A. M. E. Zion Publishing House, had reviewed the financial status of the Publishing House and the impact of the *Star of Zion* on its finances. This review prompted an increase in the subscription price of the *Star of Zion* and a change to a bimonthly publication with 16-24 pages. The current circulation stands at 6,500 copies. A subscription drive was projected for the period immediately following the General Conference. The editor noted the improvement in the production of the paper, which is now being produced electronically by desktop publishing. Rev. Dr. Tann represents the denomination at the National Council of Churches of Christ Communications Commission and its Inclusiveness and Justice Committee. He was a participant in the Congress of National Black Churches Press Corp and is chairperson of the Western North Carolina Conference Public Relations Committee. Bishop Ruben Speaks awarded Dr. Tann the Walter R. Lovell Memorial Award for creative service in the promotion of pre-bicentennial activities in the Western North Carolina Conference. ("Report of the Star of Zion at the 45th Quad. Sess. Gen. Conf.," pp. 3-8)

A. M. E. ZION QUARTERLY REVIEW
AND HISTORICAL SOCIETY
1972-1996

In The *African Methodist Episcopal Zion Church: The Reality of the Black Church*, William J. Walls discusses the founding of the *Quarterly Review* by Dr. George W. Clinton in 1890 and its acceptance as an official publication of the denomination by the General Conference in 1892. It has continued as such ever since. Since its inception in 1892 the editors of the *A. M. E. Zion Quarterly Review* have been Dr. (later Bishop) George W. Clinton, Dr. J. C. Dancy, Dr. (later Bishop) C. C. Alleyne, Dr. P. K. Fonville, Dr. W. O. Carrington, Dr. (later Bishop) James Clair Taylor, Dr. David H. Bradley, Dr. John H. Satterwhite, and the current editor, the Rev. James David Armstrong. (pp. 356-58)

In 1972, Rev. Dr. David H. Bradley was the erudite editor-manager of the *A. M. E. Zion Quarterly Review*. Dr. Bradley served as the distinguished editor-manager from 1948 until his death on September 24, 1979, at the Presbyterian Hospital in Pittsburgh, Pennsylvania. Thus, he served for thirty-one continuous years. During those years the periodical underwent changes in format, number of subscriptions, and subscription rates. Through the Quarterly Review, Dr. Bradley "sought to encourage study and preparation on the part of the ministry [so that] through its pages the contributions of many of our outstanding leaders [could be] preserved for posterity. Its editors, from the days of the founder, Dr. George W. Clinton, later Bishop, have kept this in mind as one of the magazine's major functions." (*Official Journal, 40th Quad. Sess. Gen. Conf.*, p. 344)

The *A. M. E. Zion Quarterly Review* has served the A. M. E. Zion Church and beyond, for its readership has included the United Presbyterians, United Methodists, Baptists, A. M. E., C. M. E., and clergy and lay persons of interdenominational and interfaith persuasions. This periodical is found in the libraries of major theological institutions throughout the United States. (Ibid., pp. 344-45)

Following the demise of Editor Bradley, his wife-widow, Mrs. Harriett M. Bradley, completed his term of office until the May, 1980 General Conference when Rev. Dr. John H. Satterwhite (former dean of Hood Theological Seminary, Salisbury, North Carolina) was elected to succeed Dr. Bradley. Dr. Satterwhite was editor from 1980 to May, 1989. [The A. M. E. Zion Church will long remember the passionate concerns that Rev. Dr. Satterwhite had throughout his entire professional ministry for the worldwide Church and her ecumenical concerns, and his absolute devotion to the high ideals of a trained ministry as necessary for all persons actively engaged in the preaching or teaching ministry of the Christian faith.] His death in May, 1989 caused the

African Methodist Episcopal Zion Church

Board of Bishops to appoint the Rev. James David Armstrong, pastor of Spottswood A. M. E. Zion Church, New Britain, Connecticut, interim editor. Rev. Armstrong was elected editor of the *Quarterly Review* in his own right at the 1992 General Conference and was reelected in 1996.

The Quarterly Review has been printed over the years at places convenient to the respective editor's arrangements. During the editorship of Rev. Dr. John H. Satterwhite, the Quarterly Review was published by the A. M. E. Zion Publishing House in Charlotte, North Carolina. This arrangment has continued during the administration of Rev. Armstrong, who moved the administrative offices of the Quarterly Review and the Historical Society to Charlotte, North Carolina. The joint offices of the *Quarterly Review* and the Historical Society are currently housed in the A. M. E. Zion Publishing House building.

Rev. Armstrong has provided the church with scholarly contributions on current religious, social, literary, and ecumenical issues by both denominational and interdenominational scholars, pastors, teachers, and lay persons. The circulation throughout the United States, Alaska, Canada, South America, Great Britain, Europe, and Africa now exceeds 5,000 copies per quarterly publication. This publication is regarded by the denomination as the literary and scholarly production of the church. The hope is that it will develop a broader appeal to the lay membership of the church and that a larger number of the 1,250,000 members of the denomination would show more interest in what the clergy read and write about. ("Report of the A. M. E. Zion Quarterly Review and Historical Society, 45th Quad. Sess. Gen. Conf.," pp. 1, 3, 5).

During the period under review, the current dean of Hood Theological Seminary, Rev. Dr. Albert J. D. Aymer, and his immediate predecessor and former interim dean, Rev. Dr. James E. Samuel, were contributors to the *Quarterly Review*, in addition to the bishops, presiding elders, pastors, and laity of the church, who contributed sermons, addresses, and articles, thus fulfilling the purposes of founder Bishop George Wylie Clinton. Faculty members of Hood Theological Seminary and Livingstone College who were not members of the A. M. E. Zion Church have also greatly enriched the thought and motivation of readers of the *Quarterly Review*.

In December 1992, the *Quarterly Review* secured an International Standard Serial Number (ISSN), which is an international identifier for serial publications. The journal has also created an innovative service in the publication of a single copy of each issue in Braille. The Braille copy is deposited at Heritage Hall, Livingstone College, Salisbury, North Carolina, for the benefit of the blind. The Rev. Willie Aldrich is currently the director of Heritage Hall. (Ibid., p. 2)

A. M. E. Zion Quarterly Review & Historical Society

As a contribution to the literature of the A. M. E. Zion bicentennial observance, current editor Rev. Armstrong produced a dramatic presentation, "Meet James Varick," which is an addition to the material now available about the founder and first bishop of the A. M. E. Zion Church.

A. M. E. Zion Historical Society

The A. M. E. Zion Historical Society was established in 1944, at the 32nd General Conference, meeting in Detroit, Michigan, with Dr. Rufus E. Clement, then president of Atlanta University, serving as the first officer. Lacking funds, the society remained somewhat dormant until it was reactivated through the leadership of Dr. David H. Bradley and the Ministers' and Laymen's Association at the May, 1956 General Conference meeting in Pittsburgh, Pennsylvania. The General Conference combined the part-time offices of the *Quarterly Review* and the Historical Society and elected Dr. Bradley editor of the *Quarterly Review* and secretary of the A. M. E. Zion Historical Society. (Walls, *The African Methodist Episcopal Zion Church*, p. 453)

The Connectional Council's approval in 1993 of Heritage Hall at Livingstone College, Salisbury, North Carolina, as the official archival depository for the A. M. E. Zion Church was a positive response to the resolution by the Board of the Historical Society proposing a church policy for the preservation of official records by serving officials of the A. M. E. Zion Church:

> Connectional, Episcopal, Annual Conference, District and Local Church officials are stewards of the records they create and accumulate while acting in their official capacities, and that such records are not their personal property, but rather belong to the Connectional, Annual Conference, District or Local Church bodies which they serve. The officials are hereby advised that they have the responsibilities for ensuring systematic preservation of all valuable records with which they are entrusted for the duration of their service in their official capacities. ("Report of the A. M. E. Zion Church Quarterly Review and Historical Society," 45th Quad. Sess. Gen. Conf., p. 4)

The Historical Society office published a *Handbook for the Local Historical Society of the African Methodist Episcopal Zion Church* in September 1995. The handbook provides guidelines for organizing local historical societies and preserving historical records.(Ibid., p. 5)

African Methodist Episcopal Zion Church

Under the structure of the Administrative Boards of the A. M. E. Zion Church, there is a lack of clarity as to the duties and function of the officer charged with responsibility for the Public Relations Board and the Historical Society. Currently, the officer of the Public Relations Department is charged with different responsibilities from that of the Historical Society. A clarification of this problem needs to be made at a forth-coming General Conference. At the present time, the editor of the *Quarterly Review* is accountable to the Board of Publication, which is interchangeably identified as the Publishing House Board. The Public Relations Board does not relate to the Historical Society Board. This "in-house" lack of clarity makes for unclear lines of accountability for the officer elected to handle Historical Society matters.

PUBLISHING HOUSE BOARD
1972-76
Bishop Arthur Marshall, Jr., chairperson
Bishop William M. Smith, 1st vice chairperson
Bishop William A. Stewart, 2nd vice chairperson
Members:

1. Rev. Leon W. Watts, II	7. Rev. W. A. Eason
2. Rev. Leon W. Watts, I	8. Rev. J. A. Arnold
3. Rev. Rufus M. Jones	9. Rev. Ollie Graves
4. Rev. W. J. W. Turner	10. Rev. J. W. Jingles
5. Rev. J. D. McArthur	11. Rev. G. W. Whisonant
6. Rev. F. M. Webb	12. Rev. James A. Brown

1976-80
Bishop Arthur Marshall, Jr., chairperson
Bishop William M. Smith, 1st vice chairperson
Biship Clinton R. Coleman, 2nd vice chairperson
Members:

1. Rev. H. D. Bonner	7. Rev. E. J. Henry
2. Rev. Dr. Frank M. Allen	8. Mrs. Grace L. Holmes
3. Rev. William Cunningham	9. Rev. S. W. Schultz
4. Rev. W. J. W. Turner	10. Rev. Raymond E. Price
5. Rev. William M. Patterson	11. Rev. William Seals
6. Rev. J. L. Walton	12. Rev. Dr. Godfred N. Zormelo

A. M. E. Zion Quarterly Review & Historical Society

1980-84
Bishop Arthur Marshall, Jr., chairperson
Bishop Herman L. Anderson, 1st vice chairperson
Bishop William Milton Smith, 2nd vice chairperson
Members:
1. Dr. V. Loma St. Clair
2. Rev. Andrew Mackey
3. Dr. Willa Mae Rice
4. Rev. F. D. Mayweather
5. Mr. George Zeigler
6. Rev. O. R. Hayes
7. Rev. Dr. C. C. Tyson
8. Rev. J. H. Williams
9. Rev. Leroy Blair
10. Rev. Harvest T. Wilkins
11. Mrs. Catherine Whitley
12. Rev. Vernon Shannon

1984-88
Bishop Arthur Marshall, Jr., chairperson
Bishop J. H. Miller, Sr., 1st vice chairperson
Bishop H. L. Anderson, 2nd vice chairperson
Members:
1. Rev. Calvin B. Marshall
2. Rev. Donald Ruffin
3. Mr. Lynwood Lewis
4. Rev. F. D. Mayweather
5. Mrs. Daisy Henson
6. Rev. Clarence C. Tyson
7. Rev. J. F. Wills
8. Rev. John Evans
9. Rev. B. Leon Carson
10. Rev. Joshua Bettis
11. Rev. Mozella Mitchell
12. Mrs. Willa M. Rice

1988-92
Bishop A. G. Dunston, Jr., chairperson
Bishop J. H. Miller, Sr., 1st vice chairperson
Bishop R. L. Fisher, 2nd vice chairperson
Members:
1. Mr. Edward O. Tracy
2. Rev. Donald W. H. E. Ruffin
3. Rev. Louis Hunter
4. Rev. Richard A. Council
5. Dr. F. George Shipman
6. Rev. Kenneth Monroe
7. Rev. Odinga L. Maddox
8. Rev. F. D. Mayweather
9. Rev. C. C. Tyson
10. Rev. Joshua Bettis
11. Rev. Theodore Moore
12. Mrs. Willa Mae Rice
13. Mrs. Margie Bonner

African Methodist Episcopal Zion Church

1992-96
Bishop George W. C. Walker, Sr., chairperson
Bishop George E. Battle, Jr., 1st vice chairperson
Bishop J. Clinton Hoggard, 2nd vice chairperson
Members:
1. Rev. David R. Baker
2. Rev. W. L. Wainwright
3. Rev. Emmett Foster
4. Rev. Robert L. Graham
5. Rev. Raymond Dickerson
6. Mrs. F. I. Ekemam
7. Rev. Louis Hunter
8. Rev. John Evans
9. Rev. James French
10. Rev. Kenneth Monroe
11. Rev. Robert L. Perry, Sr.
12. Rev. Theodore Moore

1996-2000
Bishop George W. C. Walker, Sr., chairperson
Bishop George E. Battle, Jr., 1st vice chairperson
Bishop J. Clinton Hoggard, 2nd vice chairperson
Members:
1. Rev. David R. Baker
2. Rev. Robert L. Graham
3. Rev. Raymond M. Dickerson
4. Dr. Clara Robertson
5. Rev. Claude Willie
6. Rev. Louis Hunter
7. Rev. James French
8. Rev. Staccato Powell
9. Rev. Emmett Foster
10. Rev. Theodore Moore
11. Rev. John C. Evans, Jr.
12. Rev. Edmond Whitley

BOARD OF PUBLIC RELATIONS AND HISTORICAL SOCIETY
1972-76
Bishop G. J. Leake, II, chairperson
Bishop J. H. Miller, vice chairperson
Members:
1. Rev. J. W. Findley
2. Mrs. Lonia M. Gill
3. Rev. John T. Frazier
4. Rev. R. L. Lyons
5. Rev. George A. Fitch
6. Rev. C. E. Edge
7. Rev. D. R. Curry
8. Rev. J. W. Smith
9. Rev. David L. Scott
10. Mrs. Annie L. Miles
11. Rev. L. J. Johnson
12. Rev. E. K. Aidou (Mrs. Rosemarie R. Holmes)

A. M. E. Zion Quarterly Review & Historical Society

1976-80
Bishop G. J. Leake, II, chairperson
Bishop J. Clinton Hoggard, 1st vice chairperson
Bishop Herbert Bell Shaw, 2nd vice chairperson
Members:

1. Mr. Gregory Smith
2. Rev. Alfred E. Garnette
3. Mrs. Josephine Riggins
4. Rev. R. L. Lyons
5. Rev. G. A. Fitch
6. Rev. Raymond Dickerson
7. Miss Esther Carson
8. Rev. Calvin Smith
9. Rev. W. O. Thompson
10. Mrs. A. R. Hunter
11. Mr. Vernon Stevenson
12. Mr. B. K. Wobil

1980-84
Bishop G. J. Leake, II, chairperson
Bishop J. Clinton Hoggard, 1st vice chairperson
Bishop Cecil Bishop, 2nd vice chairperson
Members:

1. Mr. Albert Stout
2. Rev. Alfred E. Garnette
3. Mrs. Irene Simpson
4. The Rev. A. N. Gibson
5. Mrs. Artelia M. Perry
6. Rev. R. R. Purnell
7. Mrs. Algenia Thomas
8. Mr. W. J. Longmire
9. Mr. Vernon Stevens
10. Rev. Curtis Brown
11. Miss Della Woodruff
12. Mr. B. K. Wobil

1984-88
Bishop R. L. Fisher, chairperson
Bishop J. Clinton Hoggard, 1st vice chairperson
Bishop Charles H. Foggie, 2nd vice chairperson
Members:

1. Mr. Oscar McLaughlin
2. Mr. D. D. Garrett
3. Mr. Gossie Hudson
4. Rev. Sherwin O. Greene
5. Mr. Theodore Shaw
6. Mrs. Odessa Tyson
7. Rev. Osofo McDonald
8. Mrs. Josephine Spaulding
9. Mr. Claudie Price
10. Mrs. Estelle Longmire
11. Rev. R. L. Lee
12. Rev. B. K. Wobil

African Methodist Episcopal Zion Church

1988-92
Bishop R. L. Fisher, chairperson
Bishop J. Clinton Hoggard, 1st vice chairperson
Bishop Charles H. Foggie, 2nd vice chairperson
Members:
1. Mrs. Mildred Neely
2. Mr. D. D. Garrett
3. Rev. Frederick W. Barnes
4. Mr. Theodore Shaw
5. Rev. Gwendol Fay McCaskill
6. Rev. Harvest T. Wilkins

7. Rev. Ronald Butler
8. Mr. J. R. Broughton
9. Rev. George McKain, III
10. Mrs. Estelle Longmire
11. Mrs. Ida M. Francis
12. Rev. Audie V. Simon
13. Ms. Randi Stith

1992-96
Bishop Richard K. Thompson, chairperson
Bishop George W. C. Walker, Sr., 1st vice chairperson
Bishop Charles H. Foggie, 2nd vice chairperson
Members:
1. Rev. James R. Stanley
2. Mr. Roosevelt Wright
3. Ms. Cheryl Y. Stone
4. Miss Sarah Lewis
5. Rev. Joseph L. Walton
6. Chief U. D. Umoh

7. Rev. C. J. Jenkins
8. Mrs. Dora Mae Ricks
9. Rev. Leon Henderson
10. Mr. Benjamin Howard
11. Dr. Gossie H. Hudson
12. Mr. Anthony Brown

1996-2000
Bishop Richard K. Thompson, chairperson
Bishop George W. Walker, Sr., 1st vice chairperson
Bishop Charles H. Foggie, 2nd vice chairperson
Members:
1. Dr. Marie Tann
2. Mr. William A. Bulow
3. Rev. Thomas Sweatt
4. Mr. Takis E. J. Caiafas
5. Rev. Ronald Butler
6. Rev. George W. C. Walker, Jr.

7. Dr. John Winston
8. Mr. Michael Lisby
9. Mr. Andra' Ward
10. Mrs. Winifred Sharper
11. Ms. Dora Mae Ricks
12. Mr. Daniel Brown

OVERSEAS (FOREIGN) MISSIONS
1972-1996

The contributions of the A. M. E. Zion Church to the propagation and development of world Christianity have been effected through the Department of Overseas Missions, which was formerly called the *Department of Foreign Missions*. Supported by the vitalizing enthusiasm of its chief auxiliary, the Woman's Home and Overseas (Foreign) Missionary Society, the Department of Overseas Missions has been a strong witness for evangelization of the continent of Africa, the isles of the sea, and parts of the world hitherto unknown to African American missionaries.

During the period under review there were three administrative officers who handled the day-to-day activities of budget, personnel, and program for the denomination. The Rev. J. Clinton Hoggard, whose twenty years of service as secretary-treasurer to the department ended at the 1972 General Conference, was the connecting link to previous administrations that had carried on the A. M. E. Zion Church mission cause from 1876 through 1972. The persons who gave of themselves in this capacity are discussed in *The African Methodist Episcopal Zion Church: Reality of the Black Church* by Bishop Walls. In May, 1972, at the 39th General Conference of the A. M. E. Zion Church, meeting in Mobile, Alabama, the Rev. Hoggard was elected and consecrated the 70th Bishop of the A. M. E. Zion Church. He was succeeded as secretary-treasurer by the Rev. H. A. L. Clement who served the denomination for two quadrennia, 1972-76 and 1976-80. In 1980, the General Conference elected the Rev. Kermit J. DeGraffenreidt secretary-treasurer. He has effectively served in this office up to the present time (1997).

Enthusiasm for the ongoing work in the overseas missions was reflected in visits by church members and officials of the A. M. E. Zion Church to West Africa, to the Caribbean, and to Britain in 1971. In fulfillment of the late Bishop Solomon Dorme Lartey's dream of an All-Africa Conference meeting in West Africa, a contingent of Zionites traveled to West Africa on March 9, 1971, under the leadership of Bishop William A. Hilliard, of the Board of Foreign Missions and episcopal supervisor of the East and West Ghana Conferences, and Bishop Alfred G. Dunston, Jr., episcopal supervisor of the Liberia and Nigeria Conferences from December 1969 until the General Conference meeting in 1972. Following the death of Bishop Lartey on August 3, 1969, the Board of Bishops appointed Bishops Hilliard and Dunston to these respective. Those who traveled to West Africa on March 9, 1971, journeyed from the John F. Kennedy Airport in New York City to the Fatherland of Africa, landing first at Dakar, Senegal and later at the Roberts Airfield in Monrovia, Liberia. The journey was to conduct memorial services for Bishop Lartey. The seventeen persons traveling in this entourage included Bishop and Mrs. W. A. Hilliard; Bishop A. G. Dunston, Jr.; Ms. E. Loujean Lovett, missionary supervisor, Mrs. Emma B. Watson, general president, Woman's Home & Foreign Missionary Society (WH&FM); Mrs. Minnie D. Hurley, general treasurer, WH&FM Society; Prof. and Mrs. B. M. Montgomery, president, Lomax-Hannon Junior College, Greenville, Alabama; Dr. John H. Winston, Jr., president, Laymen's Association, Central Alabama Conference, Montgomery, Alabama; the Rev. James E. Cook, pastor, Butler Chapel A. M. E. Zion Church, Greenville, Alabama; the Rev. George Kendall, pastor, Wesley Center A. M. E. Zion Church, Pittsburgh, Pennsylvania; the Rev. Solomon Snowden Seay, pastor, Clinton Chapel A. M. E. Zion Church, Selma, Alabama; Ms. Evelyn Harris, New York City; Ms. Sarah Lipscomb, Washington, D. C.; Ms. Viola Smith, Philadelphia, Pennsylvania; and the Rev. J. Clinton Hoggard, then secretary-treasurer of Foreign Missions. The Foreign Missions office arranged and executed all the travel details for this "first" visit to Africa by a contingent of A. M. E. Zion members.

Jamaica

In the 1960s and early 1970s, much of the growth in overseas missions was sparked by the remarkable accomplishments of Bishop Herbert Bell Shaw. He organized the Jamaica Annual Conference on January 19, 1967 at the Shaw Temple A. M. E. Zion Church, Black River, Jamaica. As a consequence of this conference, Bishop Shaw cultivated association and friendship with Jamaican clergy and laity who had connections with Jamaicans in England. Through such contacts, Bishop Shaw developed the London-Birmingham Conference. This conference was organized at the Ransom-Pentecostal A. M. E. Zion Church, at 2A Mallison Road, S. W. Battersea, London, England, during May 13-24, 1971. By 1972, there were nine churches, nine pastors, and 400 members in the London-Birmingham Conference, with A. M. E. Zion societies in London, Birmingham, Bristol, and Manchester. (*Official Journal, 39th Quad. Sess. Gen. Conf.*, pp. 284-85)

By 1972, the Jamaica Conference was one of the fastest growing conferences within the denomination. There were 177 churches, 107 pastors, and an active membership of 25,750 people. Attached to Jamaica A. M. E. Zion churches, there were nine primary schools, 1,195 pupils, and 34 day school teachers. Some government support was provided for the schools.. During the 1968-1972 quadrennium, the Jamaica Annual Conference sessions were held in different cities and in newly-erected church edifices, one of which was the Shaw Temple A. M. E. Zion Church in Black River. Such phenomenal growth stimulated other congregations of evangelistic and pentecostal persuasion in Jamaica to join succeeding annual conferences until each of the three divisions of the original conference became as large as the organizing conference. The

Overseas Missions

three conferences include the Cornwall Conference in the west; the Middlesex Conference in central Jamaica; and the Surrey Conference in the east. St. Elizabeth Parish at Black River is the Mother Congregation in Jamaica. A Jamaica Evangelistic Center was established at 22 Penn Street, Kingston, Jamaica. Presiding Elder Samuel Hart Williams of the Brooklyn District, New York Conference, a native Jamaican, and his counterparts, the Revs. Charles DeCosta and Arnold DeCosta Wright of the former Holy United Church in Jamaica, were   prominent in initiating the Jamaican missionary endeavor so effectively developed by Bishop Shaw. *(Official Journal, 39th Quad. Sess. Gen. Conf., pp. 285-86; 42nd Quad Sess. Gen. Conf.,* p. 430)

In 1976, a delegation of thirty-five Zionites traveled to Jamaica to celebrate the Decade of Progress engendered by Bishop Herbert Bell Shaw's missionary effort in Jamaica from 1966. Outstanding achievements in Jamaica and the First Episcopal District during the 1972-76 quadrennium included dedication of a nine-room episcopal residence in Kingston, Jamaica in January 1976, the erection of several churches, and land reclamation for a housing development in Spanish Town. In Trinidad and Tobago, the government permitted the A. M. E. Zion Church to establish as a corporation with the right to hold land and other property for the establishment of a church. In the Bahamas Conference, Rev. John Hensfield and his wife built a new church with seating for 250 people in Nichols Town on Andros Bay. In England, a priority was established to house each congregation in its own edifice. Bishop Shaw's outstanding missions work from 1960-72 brought in 119 new pastors, 189 new congregations, and 26,655 new communicants from the Bahama Islands, Jamaica, the West Indies, and England. *(Official Journal, 40th Quad. Sess. Gen Conf.,* p. 285, p. 353)

After Bishop Shaw's death, he was succeeded as supervising prelate of the First District, which included Jamaica and England, by Bishop J. Clinton Hoggard. By 1984, the Jamaica Conference had three divisions—one in each of the three counties of Surrey, Cornwall, and Middlesex. Surrey Division had 53 churches and 40 pastors; Cornwall Division had 56 congregations with 34 pastors; and Middlesex reported 62 congregations and 40 pastors. By the end of the 1984-88 quadrennium under Bishop J. Clinton Hoggard's episcopal supervision, there were 171 congregations, 114 pastors, and 654 home mission workers in the Jamaica Conference. Friendly competition among the annual conferences stimulated the raising of money to develop mission work and support the conferences. Secretary-treasurer DeGraffenreidt thought that the Jamaica mission would benefit from fund-generating projects and trained pastors so that the fifty-seven circuit churches could have their own ministers. Although pastors received stipends in U. S. dollars instead of Jamaican dollars, as they formerly had, the stipends

African Methodist Episcopal Zion Church

were not adequate for the pastors and missionary workers. Funds were also needed to renovate some of the churches. (*Official Journal, 42nd Quad. Sess. Gen. Conf., p. 430; 43rd Quad. Sess. Gen. Conf.*, pp.486-87)

Early on in the 1988-92 quadrennium, Jamaica was devastated by Hurricane Gilbert. Zionites contributed more than $19,446 to repair the damage done to church property. The Rev. Dr. and Mrs. Andrew E. Whitted significantly enhanced the mission work by their presence in the field as missionaries. Workshops and leadership training were conducted throughout the conference. Monthly stipends were sent from the Depart-ment of Overseas Missions to the pastors to assist in the work. (*Official Journal, 44th Quad. Sess. Gen. Conf.*, p. 549)

England

In May, 1971, Bishop Shaw led a contingent of sixty-three persons to England for the first London-Birmingham Annual Conference, meeting May 13-24, 1971 at Ransom-Pentecostal A. M. E. Zion Church at 2A Mallison Road, Battersea S. W. 11, England. This was the largest delegation of A. M. E. Zion Church members to leave America at one time for the purpose of spreading the borders of Zion. (*Official Journal, 39th Quad Sess. Gen. Conf.*, pp. 128-30)

The London-Birmingham Conference received four new churches into the conference during the 1976-80 quadrennium; one in Wolverhampton, one in Birming-ham, and two in Manchester, England. Expansion of this conference was notable by the purchase of a property for use by the Shaw Temple A. M. E. Zion Church, located at Brownley Road, Whithenshawe, Manchester, and the purchase of a property for a congregation located in the Birmingham, England area. These property transactions were in process at the time of Bishop Shaw's unexpected death on January 3, 1980, in Indianapolis, Indiana, the night prior to the opening of the Winter Meeting of the Board of Bishops. Such property expansion proved to be an incentive to the members of the A. M. E. Zion Church in the United Kingdom. There was marked improvement in their financial report at the 1979-80 London-Birmingham Annual Conference. (*Official Journal, 41st Quad. Sess Gen. Conf.*, pp. 390-91)

After the death of Bishop Herbert Bell Shaw, Bishop J. Clinton Hoggard and then Bishop Milton A. Williams effectively supervised the mission work in the England Conferences. The Revs. Vincent G. Fagan and Horace G. Gordon had helped Bishop Shaw to pioneer the mission work in England and were instrumental in the growth of church membership. Despite financial constraints, there were about four hundred members in nine churches altogether in London, Birmingham, Bristol, and Manchester by 1984. During the 1984-88 quadrennium, in the London/Birmingham Conference in

Overseas Missions

England, the annual conference sought to win converts by distributing tracts in the community. As earlier indicated, the A. M. E. Zion Church had bought some property, but most congregations were still in rented buildings paid for from the allocation by the Department of Overseas Missions . There was also a serious threat of losing property unless a hundred thousand dollars ($100,000) was found to renovate properties to meet government standards. Bishop Hoggard reported that the Shaw Temple A. M. E. Zion Church property in Manchester, which was purchased by the denomination under Bishop Shaw's supervision, was in litigation in the British courts because the pastor Rev. R. L. Blake who openly withdrew from the A. M. E. Zion Church at the annual conference in 1982 had kept control of the church property. The Rev. L. B. Simpson, the presiding elder of the Birmingham-Manchester District attended the 42nd General Conference as a delegate of the London-Birmingham Conference. (*Official Journals, 42nd Quad. Sess.Gen. Conf.,* pp. 183, 431; *43rd Quad.* Sess., p. 487)

During the 1988-92 quadrennium, the London-Birmingham Conference was supervised by Bishop Milton A. Williams. In July, 1990, the London-Birmingham Conference celebrated its twentieth anniversary. The celebration was held at Ransom Pentecostal A. M. E. Zion. The Revs. Assenath McKenzie, Horace G. Gordon, and L. B. Simpson, charter members of the conference, participated in the celebration. Two newly purchased churches were dedicated in May, 1992—Mt. Bethel and Tabernacle. Bishop Williams was ably assisted in his mission by Administrative Assistant Rev. Horace G. Gordon , the zealous work of Presiding Elders Rev. L. B. Simpson and Rev. Philip Williams, and the outstanding leadership of Rev. Assenath McKenzie as field-worker. Two new congregations were added to the conference during the quadrennium, which brought the total number of pastors to twelve. (*Official Journal, 44th Quad. Sess. Gen. Conf.,* p. 443)

Bishop Williams reported the organization of the Manchester-Midland Conference in 1990, which came about as a means of settling the legal action in the courts over the ownership of Shaw Temple in Manchester. After prolonged discussion and prayer, Rev. Blake was persuaded, along with the six congregations he had organized, to return to the A. M. E. Zion Church. During the interim, Rev. Blake had built a new Christian Education Building as an annex to the Shaw Temple. Bishop Williams noted that the addition was "a very lovely facility." The Manchester-Midlands Conference had representatives at the 44th General Conference in Atlanta, Georgia, in 1992. (*Official Journal, 44th Quad. Sess. Gen. Conf.,* p. 444)

African Methodist Episcopal Zion Church

Barbados

Bishops Shaw and Spottswood planned to expand Zion in Barbados, where lots had been purchased in Christ Church parish with the intention of erecting a church building to the memory of Bishops John Bryan Small and Cameron Chesterfield Alleyne, both Barbadians by birth, of whom the Rev. Hoggard remarked, "Each served the cause of missions in Zion in a memorable and unforgettable manner." (*Official Journal, 39th Quad. Sess. Gen. Conf.*, pp. 285-86)

Bishop William Alexander Hilliard was assigned by the Board of Bishops to supervise the Barbados Conference following Bishop Shaw's death. After several pre-conference consultations, the Barbados Conference was organized on Thursday, March 20, 1980, by Bishop William Alexander Hilliard. The official name given to the A. M. E. Zion's first society in Barbados was the Alleyne-Hilliard-Babb A. M. E. Zion Church. On March 20, 1980, Bishop Hilliard held the first organizing conference in Barbados—the 1978 and 1979 sessions of conference were consultative and explorative. The 1980 session was held at the Alleyne-Hilliard-Babb A. M. E. Zion Church with the Rev. George H. Grimes, a native of Barbados, serving as pastor.(*Official Journal, 41st Quad. Sess. Gen. Conf.*, pp. 162-63; 391)

In his 1984 General Conference Report, Bishop Charles H. Foggie reported two churches, three ministers, and a presiding elder in Barbados— the Rev. Ralph King, the Rev. Bertram Green, the Rev. Horace Cave, and Presiding Elder Rev. Dr. William T. Kennedy. The Barbados Conference is very much mission work. In 1988, the secretary-treasurer felt there was need for a plan to put missionaries in the field to grow the work. The churches in the conference had had numerous problems: withdrawals, property damage by storms, and there was a threat of property loss of $8,000.00. There was also a crucial need to salvage the situation in the face of Bishop Foggie's retirement. Presiding Elder William T. Kennedy supervised the work. By 1992, there were three churches in this conference. Bridgetown Mission, the oldest and the largest work, was pastored by the Rev. Ralph King. The membership was small and most of the members knew little about how the A. M. E. Zion Church operated. In the Jackson section of the island is Hoggard A.M.E. Zion Church, a lovely church built under the episcopal administration of Bishop J. Clinton Hoggard during the 1988-92 quadrennium, which was pastored by the Rev. Martin L. Holligan. Rev. Holligan, in addition to being a minister, had musical skills that meant much in developing congregational singing. His wife, Mrs. Izalene Holligan, served as the field worker for the WH & OM Society. Three presiding elders had served this conference by 1992: Rev. Dr. William T.

Overseas Missions

Kennedy, Rev. Brownell D. Pagan, and the Rev. Dr. Richard K. Thompson.(*Official Journal, 43rd Quad. Sess.*, p. 486; 44th *Quad. Sess. Conf.*, pp. 180-81)

A new church was near completion at the end of the 1988-92 quadrennium. The Rev. Martin L. Holligan was the pastor. The Third Episcopal District Mission Fund was the source of funds. Early in 1995, the Rev. Pedro Cox, who was a member of Hoggard Church, was asked to start a new congregation and was directed to name the new church Alleyne Memorial A.M.E. Zion Church in memory of Bishop Cameron C. Alleyne who was a native of the island. Rev. Cox held services in a tent until such time as he could secure a meeting place. (*Official Journal, 44th Quad. Sess.*, p. 548; "Report of the Third Epis. Dist. to the 45th Quad. Sess. Gen. Conf.," p. 33)

Virgin Islands

Under the episcopal supervision of Bishop Alfred G. Dunston, Jr., in the Second Episcopal District, the Rev. and Mrs. Stanley Dennison were missionaries in the field in the Virgin Islands during the 1984-88 quadrennium. A nursery school was established in the church. Ministers and lay persons in the Second District traveled with Bishop Dunston to conduct workshops to assist the Christian Education Department. The district distributes Church School Literature regularly. (*Official Journal, 43rd Quad. Sess. Gen. Conf.*, p. 486)

In 1989, destructive Hurricane Hugo hit the islands. Bishop Dunston reported that two churches—the Beulah and Medford A. M. E. Zion Churches in St. Croix— had been restored but that "the nucleus on St. Thomas had not experienced progress." The work of the Rev. George Lewis was supported by missionaries throughout the Second Episcopal District. In the Third Episcopal District, Full Gospel A. M. E. Zion Church, led by the Rev. John A. Cherry, in Temple Hills, Maryland, was very supportive in the construction of a new school. (*Official Journal, 44th Quad. Sess.Gen. Conf.*, pp. 141-42)

Trinidad and Tobago

In June 1979, on the death of Rev. Edward Pierre, the Rev. Gilda Carrington was assigned to lead the Trinidad-Tobago Conference. There were three churches in the conference at the end of the quadrennium. (*Official Journals, 41st Quad. Sess. Gen. Conf.*, p. 390)

During the 1984-88 quadrennium, a new Smith-Coleman Annex was completed and put into use in the Trinidad and Tobago mission in the Fifth Episcopal District, which was supervised by Bishop Clinton R. Coleman. The supply department sponsored a feeding program for needy families. Because of high unemployment, the congregation helped families with financial aid from $70-$100 for rent, utility bills, and

African Methodist Episcopal Zion Church

food. Emergency medical services were provided by trained persons through the Red Cross Grays at the A. M. E. Zion Church. Bishop Coleman supported ministerial training in the U. S. Mrs. Grace Holmes, president of WH&OMS, and other Zionites attended the 1988 Annual Conference. (Official Journal, 43rd Quad. Sess. Gen. Conf., p. 487)

In 1992, as reported by the Rev. DeGraffenreidt, Presiding Elder Gilda Carrington was still leading the mission work in Trinidad and Tobago. She was assisted in her endeavor by local preachers and evangelists. The youth were active and parti-cipated in the educational programs, including the memorization of scripture that developed into a healthy competition among themselves. A new society was organized outside of Port of Spain. Land was offered by one of the members of the congregation, and a temporary shelter was constructed on the site. (*Official Journal, 44th Quad. Sess. Gen. Conf.*, p. 548)

Guyana

The Guyana Conference was founded in 1911 in Hague, Demerara, Guyana, by the noble soul, Dr. W. A. Deane. In 1972, the Guyana Conference had been under the episcopal supervision of Bishop Spottswood since 1964 and had been led by Presiding Elder Rev. R. C. Rodney until he passed away in June 1971. Rev. Rodney's service to Zion was characterized by the Rev. Hoggard, then secretary of the Department of Foreign Missions, as "long, distinguished and significant." Rev. Rodney was succeeded by the Rev. Dr. Benjamin O. Berry, a Guyanese, who had served Zion in South Bend, Indiana. Through the Foreign Missions Board, the Guyana Conference operated the Alleyne High School and Domestic Science Center at 150 Regent Street, Georgetown. There were thirteen clergy and eleven pastoral appointments in the conference. The Rev. Dr. B. O. Berry and Mr. Cyril Eastman attended the 39th Quadrennial Session of General Conference in 1972 as "first time" delegates. (Walls, T*he African Methodist Episcopal Zion Church: Reality of the Black Church*, p. 246; *Official Journal, 39th Quad. Sess. Gen. Conf.*, pp. 285-86)

The Third District, encompassing the Guyana Conference, was under the episcopal supervision of Bishop Hilliard, who led the Guyana Conference in purchasing St. Stevens Church property in Campbelleville, Georgetown, during the 1972-76 quadrennium. This was the second A. M. E. Zion Church established in the capital city. Prime Minister Linden Forbes Sampson Burnham also granted a plot of land for church development and a proposed school in Carifesta, Georgetown. In March, 1975, during the

Overseas Missions

annual conference, a ceremony was held on the proposed site and a sign was raised, "PROPOSED SITE FOR THE HILLIARD A. M. E. ZION CHAPEL." During the 1976-1980 quadrennium, Bishop Hilliard reported fourteen churches in Guyana with the Rev. Dr. Benjamin O. Berry serving as presiding elder and principal of the Alleyne High School in Georgetown. (*Official Journal, 40th Quad. Sess. Gen. Conf.*, p. 354; 41st Quad. Sess., pp. 158-59)

During the 1980-84 quadrennium, as reported by Dr. DeGraffenreidt in his first report to General Conference, in Guyana, South America, then under the episcopal supervision of Bishop Charles H. Foggie, the Rev. Benjamin O. Berry, whose work had contributed to significant numerical growth of the mission, retired on grounds of poor health at the 67th Annual Session of the Guyana Conference in 1981. He was succeeded as resident missionary by the Rev. Cynthia Willis, who had graduated from Hood Theological Seminary that same year. She was appointed the Bishop's administrative assistant and presiding elder. By 1984, there were three presiding elders, one of whom was Rev. Cynthia Willis, and more than twenty-five elders, deacons, lay preachers, and exhorters, with a total membership close to six hundred. Rev. Willis started a training school for ministers, and Mr. Michael Murray, an excellent student and considered a great future leader in Guyana, was sent to Livingstone College on scholarship. The Alleyne High School was still in operation, but its administration had become the responsibility of government. (*Official Journal, 42nd Quad. Sess. Gen. Conf.*, pp.179-80; p. 429)

The then Third Episcopal District was supervised by Bishop Charles H. Foggie during the 1984-88 quadrennium. In the Guyana, South America Conference, Presiding Elder Cynthia Willis returned to the U. S. for medical attention. The Rev. and Mrs. Vaughn Adams spent nine months in the missionary field. They started a feeding program for the elderly. Rev. and Mrs. Adams were succeeded in the field by the Rev. Dr. and Mrs. Andrew Whitted. During their stay, two secondhand vans were purchased with funds from Bishop Foggie for $10,600.00. The new transportation project, managed by a Conference Transportation Commission, showed potential. The Alleyne A. M. E. Zion Church was renovated for hosting the 1987 Annual Conference. (*Official Journal, 43rd Quad. Sess. Gen. Conf.*, p. 486)

During 1988-92, the Guyana Conference dedicated a new church building that had been under construction for several years. The Hilliard A. M. E. Zion Church had been constructed, completely furnished, and equipped, and was dedicated on Sunday, March 22, 1992, with the first service being held on Thursday, March 19, 1992. The Rev. Joseph Jordan was pastor of the new church. The A. M. E. Zion Third District outreach ministry, which donated $(U.S.) 25,000.00, was the main source of funds to

African Methodist Episcopal Zion Church

finance the cost. The Guyana Conference mourned the loss of two ministers during the quadrennium, the Rev. George McDonald and the Rev. Harold McDonald. (*Official Journal, 44th Quad. Sess. Gen. Conf.*, p. 181-82)

Bishop Cecil Bishop reported to the 45th Quadrennial Session of General Conference in July, 1996 that the Guyana Conference comprised fifteen churches and two presiding elder districts, with the Rev. Stanley Eastman serving both districts. (*"Report of the Third Epis. Dist. to the 45th Quad. Sess. Gen. Conf.,"* p. 33)

Bahama Islands

As episcopal supervisor of the then Second Episcopal District, Bishop Shaw had also resurrected the Bahama Islands Conference in 1959. By 1972, the conference had three churches, three pastors, and 505 members of the A. M. E. Zion Church in the Bahama Islands. In May, 1978, Bishop Shaw purchased land and an unfinished building to house the Holy Trinity A. M. E. Zion Church in Nassau, Bahama Islands. The Rev. Wilbert Rolle was appointed presiding elder to succeed the recently deceased Rev. A. C. Rolle. The Rev. Artemis Rolle, son of the latter, was appointed pastor of Shaw Temple Church in Nassau. (Official Journals, 39th Quad. Sess. Gen. Conf., p. 283; 41st Quad. Sess. Gen. Conf., p. 391)

WEST AFRICA

Altogether, by 1976, there were over 800 churches in West Africa with 21 presiding elder districts, over 200 pastors and religious workers, 62,000 members, and nearly 150 schools and 22,500 students.(*Official Journal, 40th Quad. Sess. Gen. Conf.*, p. 356)

Ghana

In 1972, the then Ninth Episcopal District comprised the Liberia, Nigeria, and Ghana Conferences. On Bishop Solomon Dorme Lartey's death in August 1969, Bishop Alfred G. Dunston, Jr., was assigned the Liberia and the Nigeria Conferences until the end of the quadrennium. Bishop W. A. Hilliard was assigned the East Ghana and West Ghana Conferences. Mrs. Alicia Lartey continued as missionary supervisor at the request of each bishop. The East Ghana And West Ghana Conferences presided over by Bishop Hilliard continued to grow and thrive. In 1972, the East Ghana Conference had 38 schools, 5,859 pupils, 79 churches, 25 pastors, and 9,000 members. The West Ghana Conference had 80 schools, 13,085 pupils, 147 churches, 30,000 members, and 70 catechists and pastors. (*Official Journal, 39th Quad. Sess. Gen. Conf.*, p. 286)

Overseas Missions

In the then Twelfth Episcopal District, comprising East Ghana, West Ghana, Liberia, and Nigeria, under supervising prelate Bishop Ruben L. Speaks, significant developments included the relocation of health facilities from New Tafo to Osina in Kumasi, Ghana. On August 19, 1974, Bishop and Mrs. Speaks dedicated a new 100-bed hospital complex. Medical instruments and supplies valued at more than $39,000 were donated by friends of Bishop Speaks in New York. Property owned by the late Bishop Lartey was offered to the church by the Lartey family and was purchased by the A. M. E. Zion Church in Ghana for episcopal development. In East Ghana and West Ghana, the A. M. E. Zion Church educational effort was facilitated by the government's universal, compulsory education policy. At the end of 1976, the East Ghana Conference had about 42 schools, 6000 students, 83 churches, 27 pastors, and 10,000 members. In the West Ghana Conference, there were approximately 154 churches, with 35,000 members, some 80 schools, and 14,000 students (*Official Journal, 40th Quad. Sess. Gen. Conf.*, pp. 355-56)

In the Ghana Conferences, through a loan of $164,000 in 1980, work on 47 acres of land at Chattan near Abeka and Achimota was progressing. Agricultural and fish-rearing ventures were underway as revenue-generating projects. Members of Aggrey Memorial A. M. E. Zion Church were organized for cooperative farming and had realized significant revenue from the sale of produce. The Ghana mission work had shown extraordinary progress. By 1984, there were ninety churches in the East Ghana Conference. (*Official Journal, 42nd Quad. Sess. Gen. Conf.*, pp. 433-34)

In the West Ghana Conference, where missionary work in Ghana had been financially enhanced by the African Memorial Bank Fund established by the New York, Western New York, New England, and Western North Carolina Conferences under the leadership of Bishop William J. Walls in 1954, the episcopal residence in Accra, Ghana had already been built and had been paid for in full, and the Varick Memorial Chapel , Cape Coast, Ghana, West Africa, was nearing completion. A committee was appointed to manage the episcopal residence building. In January, 1983 during Bishop Cecil Bishop's administration, Bishop and Mrs. R. L. Speaks were among a tour group of sixteen persons who attended the official opening of the episcopal residence. Included among the group were Woman's Home and Overseas Missionary Society President Mrs. Alcestis Coleman; Connectional Lay Council President Mrs. Betty V. Stith; Public Relations Officer Mr. Gregory R. Smith; and WH & OM Society Treasurer Mrs. Josephine Spaulding. By 1984, the number of churches had grown to 147, with approximately thirty thousand communicants, and seventy-five catechists. (*Official Journal, 42nd Quad. Sess., pp. 287-88; 43rd Quad. Sess.*, p. 418,)

African Methodist Episcopal Zion Church

During the 1984-88 quadrennium in the Twelfth Episcopal District, led by Bishop Alfred E. White, in the West Ghana Conference, which was then over eighty-nine years old, the Woman's Home and Overseas Missionary Society's donation of $25,000 was used to purchase property to house the Janie A. Speaks Hospital. The Rev. Dr. G. N. Zormelo, the Bishop's deputy, reported the new hospital was under construction. Presiding Elder J. Aggrey-Smith sought election as bishop during the 1988 General Conference but was not successful. Financial support given to the conference had been used for construction and property development. The secretary-treasurer expressed the hope of establishing a seminary in the future to train ministers for the West and East Ghana Conferences, both of which now rely on Trinity College at Legon. The East Ghana Conference had four presiding elder districts, and Field Worker Mrs. Theresa Acolatse visited other conferences in West Africa to foster a spirit of oneness and cooperation. Bishop White responded to the Department of Overseas Missions' appeal to save property at Keta from sea erosion. Trinity College, where the denomination had pastors in training, received help to purchase a van. The A. M. E. Zion properties in the conference included schools, hospitals, and churches. There was still hope of establishing a seminary in the future. The unoccupied episcopal residence was then under the management of a housing committee. The structure had been paid for but required adequate furnishing. (*Official Journal, 43rd Quad. Sess. Gen. Conf.*, p. 487)

During the 1988-92 quadrennium, there was substantial evidence of continuing growth in Ghana, in the existence of three conferences, the West Ghana, East Ghana, and Mid-Ghana Conferences. At the 83rd session of the West Ghana Annual Conference meeting, July 17-22, 1990, at the Bishop Small Memorial Church in Kumasi, Ghana, the Mid-Ghana Conference was set aside by Bishop Milton Alexander Williams, Sr., who was quoted in the Ghanian Times, August 1, 1990: "[T]o enhance the administration and implementation of development projects, the A. M. E. Zion Church in Ghana has been demarcated into three zones—the West Ghana Conference, the East Ghana Conference and the Mid Ghana Conference." During the 84th session of the West Ghana Conference held in 1992, at Sekondi, Ghana, it was reported that the conference had eighty pastors and five presiding elder districts: the Winneba District, led by Rev. G. N. Zormelo; Cape Coast District led by Rev. A. K. Zormelo; the Sekondi District led by Rev. Sir George Zormelo; Akim Manso District led by Rev. S. K. Ghartey; Akim Akroso District led by Rev. Kofi Simmons; and assisted by Mrs. Elizabeth Hutchful, the field worker for the Woman's Home and Overseas Missionary Society. The Aggrey Memorial Secondary School is located at Cape Coast in this conference. It had an enrollment of 1,200 students in 1992. (*Official Journal, 44th Quad. Sess. Gen. Conf.*, p. 443).

Overseas Missions

The Mother Conference of the A. M. E. Zion Church in Ghana is the East Ghana Conference, which observed its 93rd Annual Conference in June, 1992 at the Mother Church, St. John A. M. E. Zion, in Keta. As of 1992, this conference had fifty-three pastors and five presiding elder districts: the Accra District led by Rev. E. D. Dogbe-Gakpetor; the Keta District, led by Rev. Capt. Seth Pomeyie; the Ho District led by Rev. A. K. Nyavedeze; and the Tema District led by Rev. A. K. Zormelo. Mrs. Theresa Acolatse continued as the field worker for the Woman's Home and Overseas Missionary Society in this conference. (Ibid., p. 443)

For the Mid-Ghana Conference, the six presiding elder districts were the Kumasi District led by Rev. Dr. J. Aggrey-Smith, the Tafo District led by Rev. Johnson K. Asibuo; the Osenase District led by Rev. O. K. Quansah; the Twifu District led by Rev. J. F. Coleman; the Afrancho-Sunyani District led by Rev. C. N. Oppong; and the Tamale District led by Rev. J. K. Walker. The Rev. Felicia Amoah was the field worker for the Woman's Home and Overseas Missionary Society. This conference is blessed to have Brother W. Enningful-Eghan as the Lay Council president. He has served the conferences without remuneration as the architect for many of the buildings constructed by the A. M. E. Zion Church in Ghana during this period. At the 1991 annual conference session, Brother Enningful-Eghan donated a public address system to be used throughout the conference for evangelistic work. (Ibid., pp. 443-44)

During the 1992-96 quadrennium. Bishop Marshall H. Strickland served as presiding prelate of the Eleventh Episcopal District, which comprised Ghana, Liberia and Cote d'Ivoire. Sixty-eight new congregations of converts were started. Over one hundred churches needed their infrastructures fortified, but the work of the A. M. E. Zion Church in Ghana continued to grow. Varick A. M. E. Zion Church in Cape Coast and Bishop Small Memorial A. M. E. Zion Church in Kumasi were completely renovated during the 1992-96 quadrennium. The three conferences in Ghana made a special effort to form a National Hospital Board, with Presiding Elder Rev. Anna Quansah appointed as its chairperson. The Janie Speaks Clinic-Hospital in Afrancho-Sunyani was closed down for renovation. By the end of the 1992-96 quadrennium, with the exception of running water, which requires government approval for the drainage system to be connected to the facility, this structure was renovated and in operation. From the profits of the hospital, a new long-term care facility is to be built adjoining the hospital. The first wing will be used for long-term care, and the new wing will be used for stomach and intestinal care. A new clinic at Gomoa Akwamu A. M. E. Zion Church, which is waiting to be commissioned by the government, will serve twenty-five villages. Disputes are to be settled by the chiefs at the Fasina and Tanyibe Clinics. ("Report to the 45th

African Methodist Episcopal Zion Church

Quad. Sess. Gen. Conf. of the 11th Epis. District," pp. 13; 16-17)

Cote d'Ivoire

Supporting Bishop Williams in the expansion of the A. M. E. Zion mission work in Cote d'Ivoire (Ivory Coast) were the Rev. Dr. Godfred N. Zormelo, administrative assistant to the Bishop; Rev. E. D. Dogbe-Gakpetor and Rev. Sir George Zormelo, presiding elders; and Mrs. Theresa Acolatse and Mrs. Elizabeth Hutchful, field workers. The Rev. Pauline Kummadey, Rev. A. K. Zormelo, the Bishop's deputy, other pastors, and directors of evangelism traveled from Ghana to the Ivory Coast at their own expense to conduct training sessions, conference study sessions, and to keep the new conference engaged. (*Official Journal 44th Quad. Sess. Gen. Conf.*, p. 442)

In his report to the General Conference in 1992, Bishop Milton A. Williams recounted how history had been made on Sunday, November 24, 1991, when the Cote d'Ivoire Conference was organized: "Since the establishment [of the A. M. E. Zion Church] on African soil, it has been the wish of the church fathers to establish the A. M. E. Zion Church beyond the borders of English-speaking West Africa to the French-speaking countries located in that geographical area. On the day of organization, the church was filled to capacity. The Holy Spirit took absolute control over the Divine Worship Service, and we felt [that] Heaven had opened its doors and windows with angels descending and ascending with messages of joy from heaven to earth and earth to heaven. New appointments for the conference were made and seven missionary pastors were appointed to take charge of the new churches. The first annual session of the Cote d'Ivoire Conference was held June 11-13 1992, at Jean Folley, Abidjan." The Cote d'Ivoire Conference comprised six churches. *(44th Quad. Sess.*, p. 442)

At the 1996 General Conference, Bishop Marshall Strickland, who succeeded Bishop Williams as the supervising prelate of this conference, reported that in Cote d'Ivoire, the prime concern of the episcopal leaders was to become a recognized legal religious body, which was necessary before property could be bought for church building. It was decided that Zion should create a presence in Abidjan to attract converts. Property was paid for, and plans were made to build a clinic and school in Grand Bassam, Abidjan. (*"Report of the 11th Epis. Dist to the 45th Quad. Sess. Gen. Conf.,"* pp. 14, 17)

Overseas Missions

Liberia

In Liberia, West Africa, the Rev. Andrew Cartwright established the first mission of the A. M. E. Zion Church on African soil, in Brewerville, Liberia, in 1876. It is the oldest overseas work of the church. Bishop John Bryan Small was the first bishop to visit Africa. The Liberia Conference was organized on March 3, 1910, by Bishop Alexander Walters who was assisted by Revs. Joseph Drybauld Taylor and J. J. Pearce. (Walls, *The African Methodist Episcopal Zion Church*, p. 239)

Although this history of the life, development, and work of the A. M. E. Zion Church covers the years 1972-96, the linkage for updating the overseas missions work must begin with the quadrennium 1968-72. At the 38th General Conference, which met in Detroit, Michigan, in May, 1968, the Episcopal Committee assigned the supervision of the then Ninth Episcopal District to Bishop Solomon Dorme Lartey. This district comprised the Liberia, East Ghana, West Ghana, and Nigeria Conferences. Hale and hearty, Bishop Lartey returned to West Africa and laid out plans to execute during the 1968-72 quadrennium. Like a thunderbolt jolting Mother Earth, while a clear sky was overhead, the sudden news flashed round the continents, "Bishop Lartey is dead." The Bishop passed to his eternal resting place on August 3, 1969. He was the first African elected to the episcopacy of the A. M. E. Zion Church. The suddenness of his death caused a tremor among the believers in the A. M. E. Zion Church in Liberia, Ghana, and Nigeria. The Board of Bishops designated Bishop William Alexander Hilliard, chairman of the Board of Foreign Missions, and Secretary-treasurer of Foreign Missions Rev. J. Clinton Hoggard to proceed to West Africa to convey the sorrow and sympathy of the church to Mrs. Lartey, her family, and the conferences over which Bishop Lartey presided. Bishop Hilliard and Dr. Hoggard left the U. S. A. on September 4, 1969 and returned on September 19th. A full report of their travels and discoveries of the business of the conferences was made to the Board of Bishops and approved by them in December, 1969. The Board of Bishops assigned Bishop Alfred G. Dunston, Jr., to supervise the Liberia and Nigeria Conferences until the end of the 1968-72 quadrennium. Bishop W. A. Hilliard was assigned supervision of the East Ghana and West Ghana Conferences. Each of these bishops requested that Mrs. Alicia Lartey, widow of the bishop, would continue her service as the beloved missionary supervisor of the Ninth Episcopal District until the 1972 General Conference.

Bishop Dunston conducted the 1970, 1971, and 1972 sessions of the Liberia Annual Conference. During the 1971 annual conference, Bishop Dunston participated in the memorial service planned by the American Ambassador, the Hon. Samuel Z. Westerfield, for Whitney Moore Young who died suddenly on March 11, 1971, in

African Methodist Episcopal Zion Church

Lagos, Nigeria, while the A M. E. Zion delegation was in Liberia. Although the death of President Tubman caused a gap in the relationship of the A. M. E. Zion Church with the government of Liberia, it was significant that President Tolbert, successor to the late President Tubman, continued relationships with church bodies having missions in Liberia. During this period, the Liberia Conference claimed approximately 20 schools; 29 day school teachers; 1,000 pupils, 42 churches, 42 pastors and approximately 5,000 members. This conference had three presiding elder districts—the Brewerville District, led by Rev. B. R. Williams; the Greenville District, led by Rev. Edwin M. Flowers, Sr.; and the Barfowin District, led by Rev. Richard C. Barkue. (*39th Quad. Sess. Gen. Conf.*, pp. 286-87)

Delegates from Liberia to the 1971 WH&OM Society Convention included the Rev. Mrs. Regina Davis, who attended as a field worker at the W. H. &. F. M. Society training sessions at Livingstone College, July, 1971, Mrs. Alicia Lartey, and Mrs. Nora Williams. The latter two were additional delegates to the general convention, in August, 1971, at Buffalo, New York. General Conference delegates in attendance at the 39th General Conference, in Mobile, Alabama, May, 1972, were Rev. Richard C. Barkue, Mr. John T. A. Jabbah, Mrs. Alicia Lartey, and the Rev. Edwin Flowers. It was at this time that Rev. Mrs. B. Margheretta Jones, pastor of St. John A. M. E. Zion Church, Bethlehem, Pennsylvania, made a gift of $1000, in memory of her late beloved sister, Edna Earl Jones Wright, to the A. M. E. Zion mission work in Liberia. Her gift was to aid in the establishment of a school in Liberia. Mrs. Wright had been a missionary of the A. M. E. Zion Church in Liberia, West Africa, from 1904-08, when she died and was buried in Liberia. She was the wife of the late Rev. H. T. Wright.

As the 1968-72 quadrennium drew to a close, there was much speculation concerning the episcopal successor to Bishop W. A. Hilliard and Bishop A. G. Dunston, Jr., each of whom completed the unexpired term of the late Bishop S. Dorme Lartey. The 1972 General Conference was held in Mobile, Alabama, with Big Zion A. M. E. Zion Church serving as the host congregation. Seven new bishops were elected at this conference, namely, Revs. J. Clinton Hoggard, James W. Wactor, Clinton R. Coleman, Arthur Marshall, Jr., John H. Miller, Sr., George J. Leake, and Ruben L. Speaks. The Episcopal Committee assigned Bishop Ruben L. Speaks to the supervision of all of the West African Conferences—Liberia, East Ghana, West Ghana, Nigeria, and Central Nigeria. Undergirded with strong faith in Almighty God through our Lord Jesus Christ and surrounded with the loving, understanding and knowledgeable faculties of his good wife, Mrs. Janie Griffin Speaks, Bishop Speaks went forward to serve Christ and the A. M. E. Zion Church in West Africa. The record shows that he was substantially encouraged by the support given to him and the West African Conferences by then Secretary-

Overseas Missions

treasurer of the Foreign Missions Department, the Rev. Dr. Harold A. L. Clement; the Executive Board of the Woman's Home and Foreign Missionary Society, with Mrs. Willa M. Rice, as president; Mrs. Grace L. Holmes immediate past executive secretary, and Mrs. Lonia M. Gill, the newly-elected executive secretary, and members of the Board of Bishops, a multitude of pastors, and many lay people throughout the A. M. E. Zion Church. In 1972, the Liberia Conference had about 20 schools; 29 day-school teachers, 1,000 pupils, 42 churches, 42 pastors; and about 5,000 church members. The major problem confronting the Liberian Conference was support for church schools that were not government assisted. This review of the Liberia Conference up to 1972 provides the bridge for relating the rest of the story of Liberia and the vicissitudes of the mission work of the A. M. E. Zion Church in that country through 1996. (*Official Journal, 39th Quad. Sess. Gen. Conf.*, pp. 286-87)

At the 1976 General Conference, Bishop Speaks stated that the A. M. E. Zion Church was determined to serve the new Africa. He proposed a new thrust in African missions that would entail a seven-fold ministry and a six-point program. The seven-fold ministry comprised: (A) Ministry of Christian Evangelism; (B) Ministry of Reconciliation; (C) Ministry of Health and Social Welfare; (D) A. M. E. Zion Church Hospital Ministry; and (E) Educational Ministry; (F) Agriculture Ministry, and (G) an Artistic and Recreational Ministry. The six-point program of the West African conferences for the 1972-76 quadrennium was delineated as follows: 1. careful planning and episcopal supervision; 2. leadership training; 3. Christian evangelism; 4. involvement of the A. M. E. Zion Church in America with the new thrust of African development in the areas of economics; agriculture, and health services; 5. solicitation of funds from philanthropic persons, agencies, and business institutions interested in supplementing funds from local, national, and international church budgets; 6. a quest to establish an A. M. E. Zion Church sponsored four-year college and theological seminary in West Africa. During this quadrennium Bishop Speaks reminded the church that "the African nations represent a staggering diversity of people, languages, and cultures." He urged "every Black American to take peculiar pride in the existence of the Republic of Liberia." He contended that this country represents a dream of Black Americans seeking to develop a democracy in place of autocratic, colonial governments. He held to the premise that has been enunciated for more than one hundred years by the forebears in the A. M. E. Zion Church that many African-Americans "returned to the Fatherland to establish a great experiment in democracy and to produce a new nation that would become a citadel of liberty and a paragon of freedom." Bishop Speaks also reminded the church of the need to make provision for the educational development of young people in Liberia. (*Official Journal, 40th Quad. Sess. Gen. Conf.*, pp. 328-29)

African Methodist Episcopal Zion Church

In 1973, the Rev. Kermit and Mrs. Guytanna DeGraffenreidt and their daughter Keisha, caught up in the spirit of missions, began serving as overseas missionaries in Liberia; the first missionaries on the continent since 1937. Their service overseas would last for six years, during which Rev. DeGraffenreidt served as presiding elder in the Brewerville District; pastor of Brown Memorial A. M. E. Zion Church in Sinoe County; Bishop's administrative assistant; and principal of Zion Academy mission school. Rev. Kermit DeGraffenreid was appointed to Brown Memorial Church after the building had been condemned and ordered for demolition. During his three-years of leadership, a new church was erected, the membership increased, and the church was revitalized. Another important development was Rev. DeGraffenreidt's leadership of A. M. E. Zion Academy. This institution was well on its way to first-class standing among the high schools in the city of Monrovia prior to the outbreak of the Civil War. An effort was also made to make the Annie W. Blackwell School located in Mt. Coffee and relocated to the Po River area operative. (*Official Journal, 40th Quad. Sess.Gen. Conf.*, pp. 328-29)

The observance of the Centennial Celebrations, representing over one hundred years of Zion Methodism through the Board of Missions of the A. M. E. Zion Church in Africa, was suitably observed with President William R. Tolbert of Liberia and His Excellency Col. I. Acheampong of Ghana in attendance at respective ceremonies in Liberia and Ghana. The A. M. E. Zion Liberia Annual Conference was able to raise $10,000, which was matched by a $10,000 gift from the Friends of African Missions based in the U. S. A. President Tolbert was a closing speaker at the ceremony in Liberia. He made a commitment of $1,000 per year for ten years for the new Commercial High School under the auspices of the church. While visitors from the United States were made welcome many times during their visit to Liberia, the most memorable occasion was when President William R. Tolbert bestowed upon the presiding bishop, the Right Rev. Ruben L. Speaks, in association with the missionary supervisor, Mrs. Janie Speaks, and the four associate bishops in attendance at the celebration, namely, Bishops William Alexander Hilliard, Charles Herbert Foggie, Clinton Reuben Coleman, Arthur Marshall, Jr., the highest honor of the country, KNIGHT GREAT BAND, HUMAN ORDER OF AFRICAN REDEMPTION. One should remember while reading this passage on the development of schools, churches, and health centers that the expectation of growth of the A. M. E. Zion Church in Liberia was to be blunted by the advent and prosecution of a Civil War in Liberia. At the close of the 1976-80 quadrennium, the Liberia Conference reported approximately 20 schools, a farm training center, 30 teach-

Overseas Missions

ers in day schools, 1,050 registered students, 55 churches, 48 pastors, and almost 6,500 members. *(40th Quad. Sess. Gen. Conf.,* pp. 329-30; .355; 432)

Bishop Cecil Bishop succeeded Bishop Ruben L. Speaks as supervising prelate in the Twelfth District, in 1980. In Liberia, there were five presiding elder districts: Greenville, Brewerville, Plahn, Barfowin, and Rivercess. Brewerville District alone had eight churches: Cartwright Memorial, Brown Memorial, Prayer and Deliverance, St. Paul, and St. Mathias. The total membership of the five presiding elder districts was nearly five thousand, with over forty pastors. In 1878, when Rev. Andrew Cartwright established the first church in Brewerville, there were forty-nine members; in 1984, Brewerville District comprised eight stations. Liberia had an A. M. E. Zion school system comprising seven schools: A. M. E. Zion Academy, Annie W. Blackwell School, DeGraffenreidt School, S. D. Lartey School, Wactor School, Speaks Institute, Grand Gedeh, and Rivercess School, but the schools lacked sufficient financial resources to provide quality education. *(Official Journal, 41st Quad. Sess. Gen. Conf.,* p. 433)

In his report to the 42nd General Conference, meeting in July, 1984, in St. Louis, Missouri, Bishop Cecil Bishop reported five presiding elder districts; 28 churches, with 1,400 members, six primary schools, and one secondary school in Liberia. A. M. E. Zion Academy, the secondary school, had an enrollment of 366 students. The school ranked with the top three secondary schools in Liberia. The Rev. Frederick Umoja, an American missionary, was president of Zion Academy, the Rev. Dr. Edwin M. Flowers served as the field superintendent, and the Rev. Frances Johnson served as field worker. *(Official Journal 42nd Quad. Sess. Gen Conf.,* p. 344)

At the 43rd General Conference held in Charlotte, North Carolina in July, 1988, Bishop Alfred E. White reported growth in the Liberia Conference. In 1988, the conference comprised five presiding elder districts: Brewerville, Plahn, Greenville, Barfowin and Rivercess. The educational institutions included Zion Community College, Zion Academy, and the Dorothy Walls Elementary School. The A. M. E. Zion Church was commended for "its efforts to provide the best possible educational services, management systems, personnel and leadership for the children of Liberia." The mission of the A. M. E. Zion Church School System in Liberia was "to promote excellence by providing a viable and comprehensive instructional program, leading to the attainment of knowledge, competency, and skills which, upon completion, will enable each student to function as a useful citizen." *(43rd Quad. Sess. Gen. Conf.,* p. 371)

Since 1990, the A. M. E. Zion Church in Liberia, as the country itself, has been besieged by civil wars. However, church membership in Liberia grew to almost six thousand converts during the 1992-96 quadrennium. At the annual conference of 1995, the membership in Full Gospel A. M. E. Zion Church (Liberia) grew to 495 members. The congregation purchased an old burned out building that was previously occupied by a dry cleaning plant to house the church, which seats 800 worshippers. Property was also purchased in Rivercess where a new church and day care center were started, and assistance was given to the Woman's Home and Overseas Missionary Society to refurbish new sites for new churches. (*"Report to 45th Quad. Sess. Gen. Conf.* of the 11th Epis Dist.," p. 45)

In March, 1996, civil war broke out again in Liberia. Brown Memorial A. M. E. Zion Church in Monrovia and Full Gospel A. M. E. Zion Church in Congotown, Liberia were destroyed in the 1996 war. A search was made through enemy lines to discover churches and persons lost in the war. Funds to build a House of Hope, which will address the needs of the whole person, were established. Basic needs of the people are being addressed by the Brewerville District, which distributed food, clothing, and other essential items behind enemy lines and in the city. Before the 1996 civil war, the Brewerville District had been the only full functioning district in Liberia. (Ibid., pp. 14, 17)

Nigeria

In Nigeria, despite the government takeover of schools in the early 1970s, Zion continued to operate the A. M. E. Zion Secondary Commercial College and the A. M. E. Zion Interdenominational Theological Seminary under the supervision of Rev. J. J. Essien.

In 1972, Nigeria was still smarting from the ravages of civil war. Bishop Dunston, with the assistance of field superintendent Rev. Young E. O. Eta, had previously established ten congregations during 1964-68. Despite the civil war and postwar challenges, Bishop Dunston supervised the annual conference of 1972 in Owerri, East Central State, Nigeria. Because of the great size of the conference and for political reasons, two conferences were later thought necessary. (*Official Journal, 39th Quad. Sess. Gen. Conf.*, p. 287)

In 1984 in Nigeria, there were three annual conferences: the Nigeria, Central Nigeria, and Rivers Conferences with about 126,000 members collectively. The former Teacher Training College was converted to a secondary commercial school in 1972 when the Federal Government decided to take over public schools. It had an enrollment of 1,123 students with more than seventy-five academic and non-academic staff. (*39th Quad. Sess., Gen. Conf.* p. 434)

Overseas Missions

During the 1984-88 quadrennium, the Nigeria Conferences included the Nigeria, Central Nigeria, and Rivers. The Nigeria Conference organized a befitting retirement program for its field superintendent the Rev. Young E. O. Eta in January, 1988. He was succeeded as field superintendent by the Rev. J. J. Essien. The Nigeria Conference was well organized, and the ministers received a stipend from a central fund. The Missionary Department under the guidance of Mrs. Elizabeth Eta had a visitation program for orphans and the mental hospital. Clothing, food, and other items were provided by the society. There was a Service Center for training the women and youth, and Mrs. Eta traveled to other conferences to encourage missionary workers. There were eight presiding elder districts to facilitate close supervision and growth. The secretary-treasurer observed, "The Nigeria Conference is worthy of emulation by all other Conferences." The field superintendent and field worker were on stipends to encourage them., and financial assistance was given to the Lagos building project. (*Official Journal, 43rd Quad. Sess. Gen.Conf.*, p. 488)

The Rivers Conference was under the presiding elder leadership of the Rev. E. J. Ekpo. Earlier property loss in Port Harcourt had been regained through the leadership of the Rev. J. K. Asibuo, Jr., from Ghana who is a missionary in the field. The Alfred E. White A. M. E. Zion Church was completed and played host to the annual conference in January, 1988. Although the youngest conference in West Africa, the Rivers Conference had shown itself competitive with the others. Six new churches were established during the 1984-88 quadrennium. (Ibid., p. 488)

During 1984-88, the Central Nigeria Conference was led by the Rev. S. C. Ekemam, who was a successful candidate for bishop at the General Conference in 1988. The Rev. Ekemam's effort had made the A. M. E. Zion Church visible in Nigeria. His participation in the Nigerian ecumenical movement had placed the A. M. E. Zion Church in the forefront of the Christian Association of Nigeria (CAN). The conference grew considerably. The Missionary Society under Mrs. Faustina I. Ekemam's leadership was moving to "Win the World for Christ." Rev. DeGraffenreidt pronounced Mrs. Ekemam "a blessing to the African Missionary Field." (Ibid., p. 489)

For the 1984-88 quadrennium, the secretary-treasurer identified several practical as well as theoretical issues confronting the A. M. E. Zion Church in its missionary efforts. He expressed the "need for a resident bishop." There were also other related concerns: "The question now is, what are we doing about our overseas missions to prevent them breaking away in Africa? How are we going to get the missions overseas properly equipped for the work? How are we going to get the A. M. E. Zion Hymn Books, Christian Education Literature, publications like the *Star of Zion, Missionary Seer*, and *Church School Herald* to them on a consistent schedule knowing the high cost of postage? Our ability to supply our overseas constituency with periodicals was less than satisfactory. What is our relationship going to be in the next decade and century? In short what is our philosophy of Missions?" (*43rd Quad. Sess. Gen Conf.*, p. 488)

The General Conference of 1988 elected a person who was born, raised, and trained in his home country of Nigeria with the exception of the years he spent in the United States as a student at the Clinton Junior College, Rock Hill, South Carolina; Livingstone College, Salisbury, North Carolina; Columbia University, New York City, and Yale University in New Haven, Connecticut. This person distinguished himself within the boundaries of the A. M. E. Zion Church after his presiding bishop, the late Bishop Alfred Gilbert Dunston, Jr., found ways to bring him and other Nigerian students to America for training in the teaching and preaching ministry of the A. M. E. Zion Church and the larger Christian community. The Rev. Samuel Chuka Ekemam, Sr., was elected and consecrated the 83rd Bishop in line of succession in the A. M. E. Zion Church at the 43rd Quadrennial Session of General Conference meeting in Charlotte, North Carolina, during July 27 - August 5, 1988. Following his election and consecration he was assigned by the Episcopal Committee to the 13th District of the A. M. E. Zion Church, which comprised at that time the Liberia, Nigeria, Central Nigeria, and Rivers Conferences, all in West Africa. (Ibid., pp. 54, 64, 65)

Bishop Ekemam's report to the 1992 General Conference justified the opinion of the Episcopal Committee that a person indigenous to the culture and climate of West Africa would be a stimulus to the mission work of the A. M. E. Zion Church in that territory and a blessing for the Church in West Africa. Bishop Ekemam became the second person in the denominational history who was born in West Africa to become a bishop in the A. M. E. Zion Church. The late Bishop Lartey, born in Ghana, West Africa, was the first person born on African soil elected a bishop in the A. M. E. Zion Church in May, 1960. Following Bishop Lartey's consecration, he was assigned to the Liberia and West Ghana Conferences in his first term and ultimately in 1968 was assigned the supervision of Liberia, East Ghana, West Ghana, and the Nigeria Conferences, until his death occurred on August 3, 1969 in Liberia. From 1969 to 1988, all of the West African conferences of the A. M. E. Zion Church had been under the supervision of American-born Bishops. Bishop Ekemam, in his first quadrennium, justified the thinking of those who believed that his ministry would be a blessing wherever he served, but there would be greater satisfaction if his service in his first quadrennium was in the territory most familiar to him. By the 1992 General Conference, there had been such phenomenal growth in the Nigeria conferences that the American church was surprised, thankful, and challenged by his ministry. Although the Nigeria Conference was organized in 1932 by Bishop William Walter Matthews, it was not until the 1988-92 quadrennium that the A. M. E. Zion Church in Nigeria became incorporated and was registered as a religious body. This process enabled the church to buy and own landed property legally in the cities of Nigeria. Heretofore, the mission work flourished in villages where, according to Bishop Ekemam, "a majority of the people or their chief were either illiterate or Zionites or both. And when there arose disagreement or quarrel the church or school property so acquired bolted away unhindered and many did, lost to Zion." (*Official Journal, 44th Quad. Sess. Gen. Conf.*, p. 447)

Bishop Ekemam continued: "To God be the glory, that kind of scenario and such stories have become a thing of the past. For within the first six months of our episcopacy, having known the sad situation, we embarked upon, and vigorously and expeditiously, pursued the idea of registering the church in Nigeria. This was singlehandedly accomplished within a record time. We are now registered in Nigeria like other major denominations. A copy of the certificate of incorporation issued by the Nigeria Internal Affairs Ministries was promptly deposited with the Department of Overseas Missions in New York." Resulting from this action there is great joy in the hearts and minds of the Nigerian Zionites who know the value of being able to purchase property in the name of the A. M. E. Zion Church. Following this act the various conferences have purchased several pieces of property in Lagos, in West Nigeria, Nigeria, Mainland Nigeria, Central and Rivers Nigeria Conferences. All of which have been deeded properly to the A. M. E. Zion Church perpetually and irrevocably.

As of 1992 the following statistics show the ever-growing position of the A. M. E. Zion Church in Nigeria:

The Nigeria Conference: Organized in 1932 (the Mother of all the conferences in Nigeria), has five presiding elder districts: the Oron District reported 11 ministers, 10 churches; the Central District reported 7 ministers, 9 churches; the Ikono District reported 9 ministers, 9 churches; the Nya District reported 7 ministers, 8 churches; and the Eastern District reported 10 ministers, 17 churches.

The Central Nigeria Conference was organized by Bishop Ruben L. Speaks in his first quadrennium as presiding prelate from 1972-76. In 1988, there were four presiding elder districts. In 1992, there were six presiding elder districts: Aba District reported 7 ministers, 10 churches; Ogwa East District reported 5 ministers, 5 churches; Ogwa West District reported 6 ministers, 6 churches; Mbieri District reported 3 ministers, 4 churches; Owerri District reported 8 ministers, 8 churches; and Umuahia District reported 6 ministers, 8 churches.

African Methodist Episcopal Zion Church

The Rivers Nigeria Conference, which was created out of the Nigeria Conference by Bishop Ruben L. Speaks and organized by Bishop Cecil Bishop had four presiding elder districts: Port Harcourt District reported 8 ministers, 15 churches; Abua East District reported 9 ministers, 13 churches; and the Degema/Ahoada District reported 9 ministers, 14 churches; and the Abua West District reported 5 ministers, 7 churches.

The Lagos-West Nigeria Conference was organized in 1990. The conference was originally a part of the Nigeria Conference and grew out of the work of the Rev. Emmanuel J. Ekpo under the auspices of Bishop A. G. Dunston, Jr., in 1965. There are two presiding districts: Surulere District reported 2 ministers, 2 churches; Apapa District reported 3 ministers, 5 churches.

The Mainland Nigeria Conference was created out of the Nigeria Conference in 1992. The conference comprises six presiding elder districts: Ndiya District with 13 ministers, 13 churches; Eket District with 9 ministers, 9 churches; Effoi District with 1 minister, 1 church; Ikot Ntot reported 11 ministers, 11 churches; Ikot Abia District reported 8 ministers, 8 churches; and Ikot Edim District reported 6 ministers, 6 churches. (*Official Journal, 44th Quad. Sess Gen. Conf.*, pp. 457-69)

India

In 1988, in the Episcopal District One, under Bishop William Milton Smith's supervision, the India Mission, led by its founder, Rev. P. James Herbert, was rapidly growing with nearly five hundred members and with six new branches, the latest being Arilova. A convent school had been started, and a sewing center was in the planning stage. Money for sewing machines was donated by Rev. Dr. Warren Brown of the Second Episcopal District. A typing institute was also planned contingent on receipt of typewriters. Other needs included medical aid, clothing, Bibles and tracts, musical instruments, a van for transportation, and a projector. A motorbike was purchased for the minister who sold his own car to develop the church work in its early beginnings. (*Official Journal, 43rd Quad Sess. Gen. Conf.*, pp. 485-86)

In the report to General Conference in the 1988-92 quadrennium, the secretary-treasurer reported continued growth of the India Conference. The A. M. E. Zion's Mission for India group was very active and sought to be more involved. Responses for adopting a congregation came from St. Catherine A. M. E. Zion Church, New Rochelle, New York; and the New York Conference Mission Education Committee, which donated hymn books and Bibles. The North Charlotte District donated clothing and medical supplies, and Mrs. Alcestis Coleman provided support to the ministry. The

Overseas Missions

Rev. and Mrs. Herbert's efforts in India have engendered nine congregations and over twelve hundred members. (*Official Journal, 44th Quad. Sess. Gen. Conf.*, p. 548)

South Africa

In 1972, a South African preacher, the Rev. Maruping Samuel Macarvy Phasumane, sought association with the A. M. E. Zion Church. The Rev. Christopher W. B. Deane, son of the founder of the A. M. E. Zion Church in Guyana, contacted Bishop Spottswood, his episcopal prelate, to initiate discussion with Rev. Phasumane. Bishop Stephen Gill Spottswood acknowledged the efforts of the two churchmen on separate continents and created a provisional South Africa Conference attached to the Guyana Conference during the 1968-1972 quadrennium, with the Rev. Phasumane as presiding elder. Personal funds were sent and appointments were made in the South Africa Republic A. M. E. Zion Church Conference. This initial action by Bishop Spottswood eventually led to the present successful mission in South Africa. (*Official Journal 39th Quad. Sess. Gen. Conf.*, p. 148)

Adverse political circumstances of apartheid, lack of direct communications, the absence of fiscal resources, and the ongoing political rebellion threatened to destroy our struggling South African ministry, yet it survived. In the early 1980s, the Rev. Phasumane re-established the link. He requested the A. M. E. Zion to send a delegation to South Africa. The emissaries of the church—Bishop Hilliard and Rev. Clement—visited South Africa and felt optimistic about Rev. Phasumane's efforts. The Board of Bishops assigned Bishop Rochester to the South Africa Conference until the 1996 General Conference. The Rev. Harold O. Robinson was recruited, trained, and spent two years in missionary service in South Africa. A four-bedroom parsonage was purchased with adequate facilities for meetings and meals. Spottswood A. M. E. Zion Church in Seshego, an impressive worship center that accommodates 450 people, was built and paid for with significant help from Bishops Milton A. Williams, George W. C. Walker, Cecil Bishop, George E. Battle, Ruben L. Speaks, and Clarence Carr. In January, 1994, death claimed Rev. Phasumane. He was funeralized at the new church and buried in the church grounds. The Tenth Episcopal District placed a memorial marker to identify his grave. (*"Report of the Tenth Epis. Dist. to the 45th Quad. Sess. Gen. Conf.,"* pp. 6-8)

Central Africa Conference

At the 45th General Conference, a recommendation was made by Bishop Enoch B. Rochester, presiding prelate of the Tenth Episcopal District to admit forty-six churches from Malawi and Mozambique with a membership of four thousand two hundred thirty-three (4,233) souls. By the first annual conference in December 1995, the Central African Conference had sixty-three (63) churches and a total membership of five thousand seventeen (5,017) "saints." There are nine (9) congregations that have started and were scheduled to be received in May, 1996. Lack of a budget and financial constraints led to the cancellation of Rochester's trip. (*"Report of the Tenth Episcopal District to the 45th Quad. Sess. Gen. Conf.,"* pp. 7-8)

Korea

In 1969, the secretary-treasurer of the Overseas Missions Department, the Rev. J. C. Hoggard, received a letter from the Korea Methodist Church of Jesus expressing an interest in uniting with the A. M. E. Zion Church. A reply was sent and the last communication from Korea was received on April 2, 1969. The letter expressed an interest in visiting the U. S. or receiving a delegation in Korea. The Korea Methodist Church of Jesus reported 70 churches, 9,500 members, 42 ministers, one orphanage with 150 orphans, and a Bible school with 40 students. However, there was no further communication with the Korea Methodist Church. (*Official Journal, 39th Quad. Sess. Gen. Conf.*, p. 288)

Department of Overseas Missions

The Rev. Dr. H. A. L. Clement was re-elected secretary-treasurer of this department at the 1976 General Conference, having served since 1972. His report for the 1976-80 quadrennium paid tribute to the visionary missionary achievements of the recently deceased Bishop Herbert Bell Shaw who presided over the then First Episcopal District comprising Jamaica, the Bahama Islands, Trinidad-Tobago, and England: "We knew Bishop Shaw as a Man of God. He will ever be remembered as the glowing example of commitment to his task as reflected in Kingdom extension." Rev. Clement asked: "Who can measure the vision once possessed by Bishop Herbert Bell Shaw?

He went down

As a lordly cedar, green with boughs

Goes down with a great shout upon the hills,

and leaves a lonesome place against the sky.

—Edwin Markham'" (*Official Journal, 41st Quad Sess. Gen. Conf.*, p. 390)

The Rev. Dr. Kermit DeGraffenreidt was elected to succeed the Rev. Harold A. L. Clement as secretary-treasurer of the Foreign Missions Board and Department at the 41st General Conference in 1980. Rev. DeGraffenreidt has been secretary-treasurer since then throughout the period of this history.

Overseas Missions

The *Missionary Seer*, the official organ of the Department of Overseas Missions of the A. M. E. Zion Church, was first established in 1901 by Bishop J. B. Small to stimulate the work in foreign territory. During the 1972-76, quadrennium, the Missionary Seer appeared regularly, but increased production costs led the secretary-treasurer to advise that the subsidy be reassessed. In the 1988-92 quadrennium, the Department of Overseas Missions developed and published meaningful services based on the quadrennial theme in the *Missionary Seer* for Mission Sunday service observance. During the 1992-96 quadrennium, the Department of Overseas Missions modified the appearance of the Missionary Seer, which is published bi-monthly in a 5,000 edition. The journal added a new column, "Encounter with Truth," written by Craig Keener, author of numerous books and a lecturer at Hood Theological Seminary, Salisbury, North Carolina. It also added "The President's Forum," which is a regular feature in the Woman's section. (Walls, *The African Methodist Episcopal Zion Church: Reality of the Black Church*," p. 238; *Official Journal, 40th Quad. Sess. Gen. Conf.*, p. 357; *44th Quad. Sess Gen. Conf.*, p. 550; *"The Dept. of Overseas Missions, Quad. Report,"* 45th Quad. Sess. Gen. Conf.*, p. 1)

The secretary-treasurer's ecumenical representation at both national and international levels included attendance as a U. S. fraternal delegate of Black Churchmen at the 1974 Assembly of All Africa Conference of Churches, Lusaka, Zambia; NCCCUSA Triennium in Dallas and New York; Divisions of Overseas Ministries, World Council of Churches; the National Conference of Black Churchmen, the Church World Service Committee, the Africa Committee, Technoserve; Black Executives in Denominations, Related Organizations and Communions (BEDROC); American Bible Society Advisory Committee; and the NCC Administration and Finance Committee. (*Official Journal, 39th Quad. Sess. Gen. Conf.*, p. 357)

Ecumenical and relief activities of the A. M. E. Zion Church included a contribution of $23,700.00 for world hunger relief. This contribution was for Ghana, West Africa, which was sent through the Church World Service Agency. Foodstuff for Ghana was distributed through the Ghana Christian Council, where the Rev. Anselm Zormelo, an A. M. E. Zion minister, was the new secretary general of the council. The A. M. E. Zion Church benefitted from the services of Church World Service in purchasing and shipping two new generators destined for the Janie A. Speaks and Wilhelma Bishop Clinics in Ghana. The savings were so great by using the Church World Service Agency that two machines were purchased instead of one.

Bishop Philip Cousin, president of the National Council of Churches of the USA, convened a meeting to increase Black Church involvement with Church World Service

(CWS). Recommended actions included: Improve channels of information into black churches; improve CWS recruitment procedures to include people from black churches; utilize PIE network to advertise jobs or as a source of names of potential candidates; groom people for anticipated openings through internships and on-the-job training; CWS to develop ways to assist black churches with delivery of goods to mission sites utilizing the ocean freight reimbursement by U. S. government; CWS to list services to denominations that could be utilized by black denominations; development of ecumenical projects by black churches that CWS could seek funds for; CWS and black churches might develop models of how to work together in the Caribbean and Africa; black churches provide CWS lists of their best communications channels; establish a nationwide dialogue between black churches and NCCCUSA focused on mutual needs and benefits of working together. (*Official Journal 42nd Quad. Sess. Gen. Conf.*, pp. 416-17)

Rev. DeGraffenreidt reported the installation of a computer in the department that would improve the overall mailing and accounting practice of the office. He reported that the department had developed useful services for Mission Sunday, the fourth Sunday in September. The services were developed around the Missionary Society's quadrennial theme with emphasis on a different segment of the theme each year. The services are printed in the Missionary Seer so that they can be copied and used during the Mission Sunday observance. (*Official Journal, 44th Quad. Sess. Gen. Conf.*, p. 550)

In his report to General Conference for the 1992-96 quadrennium, the Secretary-treasurer Rev. DeGraffenreidt outlined the objectives of his newly introduced Mission Advocate Project (MAP). Mission advocates would support, promote involvement, motivate, and develop awareness of mission issues at home and overseas. They are charged with promoting the "Mission Trinity: Mission Education, Mission Exposure, and Mission Empowerment." During the 1992-96 quadrennium, MAP assisted in the planning and implementation of outreach efforts in Guyana, Jamaica, the Bahama Islands, and South Africa. Over 125 short-term and three full-time missionaries were assisted in preparing for missionary service. As director of MAP, the secretary-treasurer represented the A. M. E. Zion Church at the Ecumenical Monitoring Programme on South Africa (EMPSA) and witnessed the first democratic elections held in South Africa that brought Nelson Mandela to power. A Mission Resource Center was established with maps, slides, books, charts, etc., for use in mission education from the local level up. Mission Advocate volunteers were invited to participate in Disaster Response Training in the fall, 1996 so that Zion might have trained persons who can be sent out

Overseas Missions

to assist people when disasters strike. (*"Department of Overseas Missions Report to the 45th Gen. Conf.,"* pp. 2-3)

Ecumenical Involvement

Ecumenical activity during 1968-72 quadrennium included representation in the World Council of Churches units, the Division and the Commission on World Mission and Evangelism, and at the National Council of Churches of Christ, U. S. A. (NCC-CUSA). The secretary-treasurer also participated in discussions, annual meetings, and programs of the National Committee of Black Churchmen, American Committee on South Africa, Concerned Clergy and Laity about Viet Nam, and Technoserve, a technical group interested in scientific and economic development of underdeveloped countries. Important ecumenical events during the quadrennium included the All Africa Conference of Churches meeting in Lusaka, Zambia, which the secretary-treasurer and the Revs. Carroll Felton and George B. Thomas attended. Rev. Hoggard noted the much discussed desire for independence among African Christians.(*Official Journal, 39th Quad. Sess. Gen. Conf.*, pp. 289-91)

During the 40th General Conference, the Rev. H. A. L. Clement, elected secretary-treasurer in Mobile, Alabama, in 1972, reported for the Department of Foreign Missions. He highlighted the celebration of the Centennial of the Board of Missions of the A. M. E. Zion Church in Liberia and Ghana. In January, 1976, a delegation led by Bishop and Mrs. Ruben Speaks visited West Africa, where President William R. Tolbert of Liberia, and His Excellency Colonel Ignatius K. Acheampong participated respectively in the closing programs of the Centennial celebrations of the Board of Foreign Missions held in Liberia and Ghana. President Tolbert was a closing speaker at the ceremony in Liberia. He was awarded the A. M. E. Zion Church Rev. Andrew W. Cartwright Memorial Award. In Ghana, Col. Acheampong participated in the morning worship. He was presented with the Dr. J. E. K. Aggrey Memorial Award of the A. M. E. Zion Church. Representatives of the A. M. E. Zion Church at these celebrations included: Bishops W. A. Hilliard, chairman of the Board of Foreign Missions, C. H. Foggie, secretary of the Board of Bishops, C. R. Coleman, retiring president of the Board of Bishops. A. Marshall, president of the Board of Bishops, and Ruben L. Speaks, prelate of the Twelfth Episcopal District; two General Officers; the General President and Secretary of Supplies of the Woman's Home and Foreign Missionary Society; and three Missionary supervisors and a former supervisor. (*Official Journal, 40th Quad. Sess. Gen. Conf.*, pp. 350-52)

In July, 1974, the Board of Bishops directed that 5 percent of the general claims be raised for the African Centenary Fund to establish an episcopal residence and center in Africa. The Foreign Missions Department received $69,755 and there was on deposit in New York $47,650, of which $22,500 was used to repay the loan for the purchase of land and the pews. During the Sahel famine, $8,177.65 was contributed to aid those affected. The A. M. E. Zion Church was the first denomination in the National Council of Churches to give a $1,000 cash contribution through the Church World Service to build a silo in Mali. (*Official Journal, 40th Quad. Sess.*, pp. 356-57)

Despite financial and manpower constraints, there were significant achievements in the field during the 1984-88 quadrennium. These accomplishments included two buses for Guyana, South America, a junior business college in Liberia; electrical appliances to the Virgin Islands; medical supplies to South America and Rivers, Nigeria; a motorbike for India; generators to Ghana; computers and typewriters to Liberia; financial assistance to needy areas, contributions to the Ethiopia Hunger Crisis ($102,000.00), leadership training for sixty ministers, missionaries and lay persons, and eighteen ministers at Hood Theological Seminary and Livingstone College and other schools. (*Official Journal, 43rd Quad. Sess. Gen. Conf.*, pp. 488-89)

The A. M. E. Zion Church is a Charter Member and is represented in the World Council of Churches; National Council of Churches of Christ in the USA; Church World Service, the Africa Office of the Division of Overseas Ministries of the NCC-CUSA, and ecumenical agencies that are interdenominational, interfaith, and interracial by membership and witness.

Through a grant from Church World Service and Witness, the Board of Overseas Missions and Mission Advocates participated in two days of mission consultation-training and information during the 1992-96 quadrennium. The goal of the meeting was to strengthen ties and create a better relationship with the historic Black Church. The training session provided an opportunity for the Board of Overseas Missions and MAP to develop a mission statement for each organization. ("Report of Dept. of Overseas Missions to the 45th Quad. Sess. Gen. Conf.," p. 2)

The secretary-treasurer highlighted missionaries in the field overseas and those from overseas who are serving in important positions in the U.S. Missionaries who served overseas during the 1992-96 quadrennium include the following:

The Rev. Paul Whiteurs served in St. Croix, Virgin Islands. The hurricane season was a challenge for him.

The Rev. Harold O. Robinson completed his tour of duty and service to the people of Northern Transvaal of South Africa. A cornerstone, a gift from the local funeral homes, was dedicated at the last annual conference.

Overseas Missions

The Rev. Dr. and Mrs. Andrew Whitted served Jamaica faithfully by enhancing leadership development among church officers—pastors, field workers, Christian Education workers, and missionaries.

The Rev. Frederick Umoja completed sixteen years as a missionary in Liberia. Most of those years were during the civil war, yet he has remained there. He survived many attempts on his life and property.

Overseas missionaries in the United States during the 1992-96 quadrennium included:

The Revs. Johnson and Evelyn Asibuo, from Ghana and Nigeria, serve as ministers at Soldiers Memorial A. M. E. Zion Church, Salisbury, North Carolina. They have been involved in counseling and prison ministry.

The Rev. Seth Martin Moulton, from Liberia, served as managing editor of the *Missionary Seer*. He was also pastor of Naomi Temple A. M. E. Zion Church, Roosevelt, New York. The Rev. and Mrs. Moulton were active in a teaching ministry and church development.

The Rev. Michael L. Murray, from Guyana, served as presiding elder in the Missouri Conference. He was pastor of Kyles A. M. E. Zion Church, Des Moines, Iowa.

The Rev. Paul Sewell from Jamaica was pastor of Invitation A. M. E. Zion Church, Snow Hill, North Carolina. Rev. Sewell and his family contributed to the Wilson District, Cape Fear Conference.

The Rev. Dr. Cynthia Willis Stewart was administrative assistant to Bishop Cecil Bishop, Presiding Bishop of the Guyana Conference. Dr. Stewart was pastor of Westbury A. M. E. Zion Church, Westbury, New York.

The Rev. Herolin Aikens from Jamaica was pastor of Warner Temple A. M. E. Zion Church, Wilmington, North Carolina and of St. Matthew A. M. E. Zion Church, Kansas City, Missouri. A popular evangelist, he is now the pastor of St. Paul A. M. E. Zion Church, Toledo, Ohio..

The Rev. Seth O. Lartey, grandson of the late Bishop S. D. Lartey and a Liberian citizen, was pastor of Goler Memorial A. M. E. Zion Church, Winston-Salem, North Carolina. He was a Christian Education resource person.

The Rev. Amelia Quist, also Liberian, was a Mission Advocate at Alleyne A. M. E. Zion Church, Arlington, Virginia.

Others from overseas included Mr. James Obeng, Albany, New York; Mr. Alexander Marshall, Department of Overseas Missions, New York; and the Rev. D. Bestman, Salisbury, North Carolina. ("Report of the Dept. of Overseas Missions to the 45th Quad. Sess., Gen. Conf.," pp. 3-4)

African Methodist Episcopal Zion Church

BOARD OF OVERSEAS (FOREIGN) MISSIONS

1972-76

Bishop William A. Hilliard, chairperson
Bishop J. Clinton Hoggard, vice chairperson
Members:

1. Rev. Warren M. Brown
2. Rev. O. R. Lyons
3. Rev. L. A. Miller
4. Rev. J. C. Sawyer
5. Rev. S. P. Spottswood
6. Rev. R. S. Terry
7. Rev. H. F. Simons
8. Rev. J. C. Goode
9. Rev. B. W. Moncur
10. Rev. Sherman Lewis
11. Rev. K. Melvin Taylor
12. Rev. Paul Thurston

1976-80

Bishop Bishop William A. Hilliard, chairperson
Bishop J. Clinton Hoggard, vice chairperson
Members:

1. Rev. Warren M. Brown
2. Rev. O. R. Lyons
3. Rev. J. A. Brown
4. Rev. Arthaniel E. Harris
5. Rev. S. P. Spottswood
6. Mrs. Abbie C. Jackson
7. Rev. H. F. Simons
8. Rev. J. C. Goode
9. Rev. W. M. Bryson
10. Rev. W. J. Lewis
11. Rev. K. M. Taylor
12. Rev. Joseph Johnson

1980-84

Bishop R. L. Speaks, chairperson
Bishop H. Foggie, vice chairperson
Members:

1. Rev. George E. Battle
2. Rev. Warren Brown
3. Miss Susie M. Moore
4. Rev. Milton A. Williams
5. Mrs. Bertha Perry
6. Rev. J. C. Goode
7. Rev. B. W. Moncur
8. Rev. W. J. Lewis
9. Mr. William Doughthit
10. Rev. W. J. Neal
11. Mrs. Lorene Bird Jones
12. Rev. Richard K. Thompson

1984-88

Bishop R. L . Speaks, chairperson

Overseas Missions

Bishop C. H. Foggie, 1st vice chairperson
Bishop J. Clinton Hoggard, 2nd vice chairperson
Members:

1. Rev. George Battle
2. Rev. Warren Brown
3. Mrs. Marjorie Walton
4. Rev. Joseph Walton
5. Rev. Gloria S. Moore
6. Rev. Robert L. Postell
7. Mrs. Helen Watts
8. Rev. W. A. Eason
9. Rev. W. J. Neal
10. Mrs. Vivian Williams
11. Rev. Willie Lewis
12. Mrs. Margie Bonner

1988-92

Bishop R. L. Speaks, chairperson
Bishop A. G. Dunston, Jr., 1st vice chairperson
Bishop J. C. Hoggard, 2nd vice chairperson
Members:

1. Dr. George E. Battle, Jr.
2. Dr. Warren M. Brown
3. Rev. Joseph T. Kerr
4. Rev. Gloria S. Moore
5. Rev. Joseph L. Walton
6. Rev. Henry A. Gregory
7. Ms. Vivian Williams
8. Mrs. Marjorie Walton
9. Rev. W. O. Thompson
10. Rev. Bennie Luckett
11. Rev. Richard G. Stewart
12. Rev. Gary M. Tydus
13. Rev. Vernon Shannon

1992-96

Bishop George Battle, chairperson
Bishop Clarence Carr, 1st vice chairperson
Bishop John H. Miller, 2nd vice chairperson
Members:

1. Mr. Edward O. Tracey
2. Rev. Henry Gregory
3. Mrs. Marjorie Walton
4. Rev. Raymond Price
5. Rev. Dennis V. Proctor
6. Rev. Vernon Shannon
7. Rev. W. O. Thompson
8. Rev. Bennie Luckett
9. Mrs. Vivian Williams
10. Rev. Gloria Moore
11. Rev. Melvin L. Tate
12. Rev. Windle Tucker

African Methodist Episcopal Zion Church

1996-2000
Bishop Enoch B. Rochester, chairperson
Bishop Clarence Carr, 1st vice chairperson
Bishop John H. Miller, Sr., 2nd vice chairperson
All Bishops are Members
Members:

1. Mr. Edward Tracey
2. Rev. Nathaniel K. Perry
3. Rev. Dr. Dennis V. Proctor
4. Rev. Vernon Shannon
5. Rev. Henry A. Gregory
6. Rev. W. O. Thompson
7. Rev. Lester A. Jacobs
8. Rev. Michael Murray
9. Mrs. Marjorie Walton
10. Rev. Windle Tucker
11. Rev. Bennie Luckett
12. Rev. Harrison Bonner

HOME MISSIONS, BROTHERHOOD PENSIONS AND MINISTERIAL RELIEF 1972-1996

AS the title of this department would suggest, there were three distinct concerns for the executive secretary-treasurer who administered these agencies. Prior to 1972, the executive officer and the administrative board, which was restructured every four years at the General Conference, varied the emphasis of this department. The Home Missions Board had the responsibility, through the administrative officer, to develop maps and charts specifying areas of potential growth within the United States. The Connectional Budget allocated funds to this department. These funds were distributed to each episcopal district of the A. M. E. Zion Church by the respective administrative boards. However, the funds allocated were inadequate for the development of proposed new congregations and the support of pastors assigned to Home Missions territories and churches. Consequently, many of the forty-eight American annual conferences sponsored and promoted Home Mission projects within their own boundaries. During the period under review there was agitation for a general policy to prohibit funds allocated to Home Missions from being used in reasonably affluent areas. Many of the clergy and lay delegates to the General Conferences advocated that funds be spent in a designated "Home Mission area" for a full quadrennium to reinforce the work of the Church Extension Department, which was concerned with acquisition of properties needed to establish new congregations within given annual conference boundaries, while the Home Missions Department would undergird the project with salary and support for persons assigned to implement the Home Missions effort. In support of this approach, the Woman's Home and Overseas Missionary Society provided $170,000.00 from their quadrennial budget for implementation of Home Missions activities. (*Official Journal, 40th Quad. Sess., Gen. Conf.*, p. 361)

The Discipline of the A. M. E. Zion Church states that the purpose of the Ministerial Relief department is "to see that proper relief is given to our Bishops' Widows, Widows and orphans of our deceased Ministers." The Department of Brotherhood Pension Service has the duty of the "supervision of the funds for the Brotherhood Pension Service." The Department of Ministerial Relief has custody of the Harriet Tubman Home property located in Auburn, New York, and is charged with the authority to develop this property for indigent Ministers, Widows, and Old Folk Relief along with the Harriett Tubman Home Association. An additional source of revenue for the widows, retired ministers, and minor children of ministers' families was established and named the *Christmas Cheer Fund*, which is now called the *A. P.*

African Methodist Episcopal Zion Church

Morris Memorial Christmas Cheer Fund. These funds are collected from congregations and pastors across the church who are sensitive to the purpose of the Christmas Cheer Fund. Each year showed a considerable increase in participants and revenue derived from voluntary contributions to the Ministerial Relief Department. Realizing that the existing pension benefits program was inadequate for attracting young ministers to serve the church as pastors, teachers or seminary professors, each secretary-treasurer of this department from 1972-96 made a concerted effort to increase the funds available. (Ibid.)

During the 1972-76 quadrennium, Rev. Austin Paul Morris was secretary-treasurer for the Department of Home Missions, Brotherhood Pension Service and Ministerial Relief. Dr. Morris served creatively and faithfully until his death in 1974. The Board of Bishops appointed the Rev. Dr. Jewett L. Walker, pastor of Metropolitan A. M. E. Zion Church, Los Angeles, California, to complete the unexpired term of Dr. Morris. At the 40th General Conference, in May, 1976, held at the Greater Walters A. M. E. Zion Church and McCormick Inn, Chicago, Illinois, the Brotherhood Pension Service Board, under the chairmanship of Bishop J. Clinton Hoggard, offered a resolution to the General Conference "to upgrade and establish security for ministers of Zion." The resolution was approved by the General Conference and an appropriation of $378,600.00 from the Connectional Budget to the Pension Plan was initially provided to fund the plan intended to service 1,254 ministers. The proposed plan would offer the following benefits: retirement income, insurance benefits, life insurance coverage for spouses, spousal income, and disability income. The Woman's Home and Overseas Missionary Society donated $189,230.00 for Home Missions responsibilities to the department during the 1972-76 quadrennium. The A. P. Morris Memorial Christmas Cheer Fund received $2,742.00 in 1974 and $2,458.43 in 1975 for distribution to widows. The Rev. Dr. Jewett L. Walker was elected secretary-treasurer in his own right at this conference. (*Official Journal, 40th Quad. Sess. Gen. Conf.*, pp. 360-61)

During the 1976-80 quadrennium, there was a controversy between the secretary-treasurer and the Brotherhood Pension Service Board as to whether the 40th General Conference had passed the enabling resolution for the new budget plan. Secretary Walker reported at the 41st General Conference that he had implemented the new pension plan but had been constrained by members of the Board who insisted that the 40th General Conference had not approved the resolution. In April, 1980, the Board voted that nothing was binding in the 1976 General Conference and offered another plan that the secretary-treasurer rejected because it neglected spousal benefits as granted by the 1976 General Conference. The controversy was carried forward to the 41st General Conference and became manifest when a resolution to abolish the office of secretary-treasurer was put forward but failed. Nevertheless, Rev. Walker reported that there had been a 33 percent increase in the number of ministers covered under the Pension and Benefit Plan. The secretary reported that the $378,600 provided during the previous quadrennium was insufficient to cover additional ministers and that an increase of $158,645 was needed to strengthen the plan. During the quadrennium, death claims for ministers totaled $169,350.00 and $31,000.00 was paid to spouses. Rev. Walker had worked hard to establish a viable pension plan for ministers within the A. M. E. Zion Church. His effort was appreciated, and he was reelected to head the department. (Official Journal, 41st Quad. Sess. Gen. Conf., pp. 401-9)

Rev. Walker reported that four important A. M. E. Zion Churches had burned down or had major insurance claims during the last six months of the 1980-84 quadrennium. Consequently, Bishops Foggie and Wactor, chairpersons of the Home Missions Board and Ministerial Relief, respectively, authorized Rev. Walker at the Connectional Council meeting held in Tuscaloosa, Alabama to do a study on a Group Fire and Casualty Insurance Plan. Data were gathered and presented to the Board of Bishops in Detroit, Michigan, who strongly approved the study. The study was authorized and ordered to be presented to the Connectional Council held in Charlotte, North Carolina. The Council found it feasible for the A. M. E. Zion Church to establish a Group Fire and Casualty Insurance Plan and approved a resolution to be presented to the General Conference. A minimum salary proposal recommended by the Ministerial Relief Board was also approved by the Connectional Council in Charlotte, North Carolina. The fire and casualty insurance resolution was approved. The Brotherhood and Pension Department has arranged for "all risks" fire and casualty insurance coverage for the building, contents, and parsonage of individual A. M. E. Zion churches. (*Official Journal, 42nd Quad. Sess., Gen. Conf.*, pp. 435-36; Brotherhood Pensions and Ministerial Relief, "A Comprehensive Look At Our Products and Services.")

During the 1980-84 quadrennium, the number of ministers in the New Pension Plan increased from 1,254 to 1,474. Home Missions received annually $65,000.00 from the Woman's Home and Overseas Missionary Society and $35,000.00 from the Finance Department for the support of missions. However, to operate the department effectively, Rev. Walker said an annual budget of $300,000.00 was needed. The quadrennium allocation of $378,600.00 for pensions and benefits was not adequate to provide benefits at the current rate of inflation. More money was required to strengthen the insurance plan. Under the pension plan, 108 ministers received benefits totaling $383,978.00 and death claims were $256,023.00. There were eighty-three ministers who had joined the pension plan in 1944 who were still in active pastorates. Spouse benefits paid out during the quadrennium came to $22,270.00. The Old Pension Plan paid $25.00 a month each to thirty-three retired ministers and $50.00 monthly to four ministers. Seventeen widows received benefits. During this quadrennium, Old Pension Plan payments totaled $75,106.00, and $4,450.00 was paid out for death claims. Rev. Walker thought that the $86,000.00 allocated to widows under the old system—a payment of $12.00 per month—was inadequate and needed to be increased to $25.00 a month. Rev. Walker was reelected secretary of Home Missions, Brotherhood Pensions and Ministerial Relief at this conference. (Ibid., pp. 435-36, 56)

In his report to the 43rd General Conference, the secretary-treasurer reported that the allocation of $378,600.00 for pensions had provided enough money to fund the present benefit structure and provide increased benefits across the board by 10 percent. This gave the A. M. E. Zion Church Plan the distinction of having the leading pension plan of the historic black denominations. During the 1988-92 quadrennium, Home Missions received $165,200.00 from the Finance Department and $517,107.00 from the Woman's Home and Overseas Society. Interest, endowment, and other income brought total receipts to $762,602. Disbursements came to $664,682. The Finance Department allocated $378,600 annually for the Old Pension Program. Under the New Pension, death claims came to $289,701.00; pension payments were $744, 799.00; and widows' payments came to $142,523.00 during the quadrennium. Under the Old Pension Plan, $18,000, which was paid out of the allocation from the Financial Department, was paid in pension dues. Rev. Walker, as secretary of the Department of Home Missions, Brotherhood Pensions and Ministerial Relief, indicated that Camp Barber Memorial, West Granville, Massachusetts, was under the direction of his department. The camp comprises 350 acres and has two lakes. It is a suitable recreation site for children, young people, and adults. The New England Conference directed its use at the time. Rev. Walker was reelected secretary-treasurer of the department. (*Official Journal, 43rd Quad. Sess. Gen. Conf.*, pp. 505-6; 517)

At the 44th General Conference, which met in Atlanta, Georgia, the Restructuring Commission recommended that Home Missions be separated from Brotherhood Pensions and Ministerial Relief and be merged with Church Extension in one department, although each agency would retain its identity and function. The Restructuring Commission also recommended that the funds for Ministerial Relief be held by the Finance Office, from which checks for ministerial relief could be distributed directly. By removing the tasks connected with Ministerial Relief and Home Missions from the secretary treasurer, it was felt that the secretary of Brotherhood Pensions would be able to concentrate his efforts on improving the pension system and bringing it closer to current economic reality. Rev. Walker reported a significant increase in net assets in the Brotherhood Pension Benefit Fund during the 1988-92 quadrennium. The market value of the fund increased from $4,701,359.00 in 1988 to $7,334,384.00 as of May 31, 1992. Benefits of $887,322.00 were paid to retirees and surviving spouses of retirees. Death benefits during the quadrennium came to $289,701.00 and a total of $1,177,023.00 was paid to ministers and beneficiaries for retirement, disability, widows' benefits and lump sum death benefits. The Rev. David Miller was elected to serve as secretary-treasurer of the Department of Brotherhood Pensions and Ministerial Relief. (*Official Journal, 44th Quad. Sess. Gen. Conf.*, pp. 561-609; 811-12; 62)

At the 45th General Conference, held in Washington, D. C., Rev. David Miller, the new secretary-treasurer reported total receipts of $424,332.00 and total disbursements of $32,141.00 during the 1992-96 quadrennium for the Brotherhood Pension Service. The Pension Service paid out $9,096.00 in pension payments, and $100.00 in death claims. There was an excess of receipts over disbursements of $552,372.00. Ministerial Relief had a total income of $573,270.00, of which $539,920.00 was allocated from the Finance Department, with disbursements of $447,364.00. Payments to widows, superannuated ministers' allowances, and orphans were $443,103.00, $1,400.00, and $191.00, respectively, for the 1992-96 quadrennium. The 1996 General Conference voted to make *Vision Focus* magazine, a publication established in support of the A. P. Morris Widows' Fund by the Department of Brotherhood Pensions and Ministerial Relief, an official denominational publication. Vision Focus is a quarterly publication with a $35.00 annual subscription cost. Besides assisting financially in the support of widows, the magazine hopes to keep members of the A. M. E. Zion Church informed of Brotherhood Pensions and Ministerial Relief programs, issues, and concerns. Besides its oversight of the A. M. E. Zion Pension Plan, the Casualty and Insurance plan for churches, and Ministerial Relief, the department has undertaken a plan for health insurance and is currently building a multipurpose Wellness Complex that will provide health care services, housing, and recreational facilities for Zion and the surrounding community. On May 30, 1997, a groundbreaking ceremony was held on the 86-acre site located in the Derita area of Charlotte, North Carolina. Phase I of the development will include a 17,000 sq. ft. administrative retreat center, walking trail, amphitheater and 10-acre park area. Later phases will include senior assisted living housing, a family life center, day care, and a free standing medical center. The Wellness Center seeks to foster preventive health care measures. It has also joined in the effort to fight against drug and substance abuse by holding classes on "Counseling the Substance Abusing Member." The classes are held during a five-week period and are

African Methodist Episcopal Zion Church

intended to assist drug team trainers in dealing with members of the congregation who have drug and alcohol addictions. ("Brotherhood Pension and Ministerial Relief Report, 45th Quad. Sess. Gen. Conf.," pp. 3-4, 12; *Star of Zion*, September 5-12, 1996, p. 7; July 10-17, 1997, pp. 1-3; correspondance with Rev. David Miller, June, 1998.)

BOARD OF BROTHERHOOD PENSION SERVICE

1972-76
Bishop J. Clinton Hoggard, chairperson
Bishop Arthur Marshall, Jr., 1st vice chairperson
Bishop Herbert Bell Shaw, 2nd vice chairperson
Members:

1. Rev. J. C. Ruffin
2. Rev. Frank M. Allen
3. Rev. W. M. Cunningham
4. Rev. L. C. Asbury
5. Rev. J. Oliver Hart
6. Rev. W. F. Owens
7. Rev. J. A. Lipsey
8. Rev. W. A. Potter
9. Rev. R. L. Graham
10. Rev. William Seals
11. Rev. Jewett Walker
12. Rev. E. L. Whitley

1976-80
Bishop J. Clinton Hoggard, chairperson
Bishop Herbert Bell Shaw, 1st vice chairperson
Bishop Arthur Marshall, Jr., 2nd vice chairperson
Bishop William M. Smith, 3rd vice chairperson
Members:

1. Rev. L. W. Watts, II
2. Rev. E. B. Rochester
3. Rev. M. F. Ward
4. Rev. L. C. Asbury
5. Rev. W. W. Bowden
6. Rev. W. F. Owens
7. Rev. J. A. Lipsey
8. Rev. W. A. Potter
9. Rev. Francis Williams
10. Rev. L. W. Raspberry
11. Rev. Ronald Rogers
12. Rev. James Milton

1980-84
Bishop J. Clinton Hoggard, chairperson
Bishop Arthur Marshall, Jr., 1st vice chairperson

Home Missions, Brotherhood Pensions & Ministerial Relief

Bishops William M. Smith and Herman L. Anderson, 2nd vice chairpersons
Members:
1. Rev. Leon W. Watts, II
2. Rev. Vaughn T. Eason
3. Rev. W. W. Bowden
4. Mr. H. C. Duncan
5. Rev. M. F. Ward
6. Mr. Alonzo Dargon
7. Rev. Francis Williams
8. Rev. J. E. Fields
9. Rev. Ronald Rogers
10. Mrs. Corine Hart
11. Rev. W. A. Potter
12. Rev. Cameron Jackson

1984-88
Bishop J. Clinton Hoggard, chairperson
Bishop Alfred E. White, 1st vice chairperson
Bishop Arthur Marshall, Jr., 2nd vice chairperson
Members:
1. Rev. Robert L. Perry
2. Rev. C. L. Murphy
3. Rev. W. W. Bowden
4. Rev. James E. Powell
5. Mrs. Lizzie Sykes
6. Rev. William A. Potter
7. Rev. Robert Graham
8. Rev. Jimmie Hicks
9. Rev. Ronald Rogers
10. Rev. J. E. Fields
11. Rev. M. D. Nathan
12. Rev. Cameron Jackson

1988-92
Bishop J. Clinton Hoggard, chairperson
Bishop Alfred E. White, 1st vice chairperson
Bishop William M. Smith, 2nd vice chairperson
Members:
1. Rev. Robert L. Perry, Sr.
2. Rev. W. L. Wainwright
3. Rev. W. W. Bowden
4. Mrs. Lizzie Sykes
5. Rev. George F. Miller
6. Rev. M. D. Nathan
7. Rev. James E. Powell
8. Rev. Carl Glenn
9. Rev. J. E. Fields
10. Rev. Charles Shakespeare
11. Rev. George Buie
12. Rev. Jimmie Hicks

1992-96
Bishop Ruben L. Speaks, chairperson
Bishop Marshall H. Strickland, 1st vice chairperson
Bishop Enoch B. Rochester, 2nd vice chairperson

African Methodist Episcopal Zion Church

Members:
1. Rev. James Robertson, Jr.
2. Rev. George Miller
3. Rev. William Kelly
4. Rev. Leon W. Watts, II
5. Rev. Wesley W. Bowden
6. Rev. A. C. Hunnicutt

7. Mrs. Theodora Smith
8. Rev. Jimmie Hicks
9. Rev. Joanthan E. Fields
10. Rev. W. Darin Moore
11. Rev. Kevin W. McGill
12. Rev. Eugene Harvey

During the 1992 General Conference, the Departments of Brotherhood Pension and Ministerial Relief were combined, but they retained separate boards.

BROTHERHOOD PENSION BOARD

1992-96
Bishop Ruben L. Speaks, chairperson
Bishop Marshall H. Strickland, 1st vice chairperson
Bishop Enoch B. Rochester, 2nd vice chairperson
Members:
1. Rev. James Robertson, Jr.
2. Rev. George Miller
3. Rev. William Kelly
4. Rev. Leon W. Watts, II
5. Rev. W. W. Bowden
6. Rev. A. C. Hunnicutt

7. Mrs. Theodora S. Smith
8. Rev. Jimmie Hicks
9. Rev. Jonathan E. Fields
10. Rev. W. Darin Moore
11. Rev. Kevin W. McGill
12. Rev. Eugene Harvey

1996-2000
Bishop Marshall H. Stickland, chairperson
Bishop Enoch B. Rochester, 1st vice chairperson
Bishop J. Clinton Hoggard, 2nd vice chairperson
Members:
1. Rev. A. C. Hunnicutt
2. Rev. Leon W. Watts, II
3. Rev. Wesley W. Bowden
4. Rev. Nya E. Ebito
5. Rev. W. L. Wainwright
6. Mrs. Theodora S. Smith

7. Rev. Jonathan E. Fields
8. Rev. Kenneth Arrington
9. Rev. Lawton Nelson
10. Rev. Eugene Harvey
11. Rev. Jimmie C. Hicks
12. Rev. Gary Burns

Home Missions, Brotherhood Pensions & Ministerial Relief

MINISTERIAL RELIEF BOARD

1972-76

Bishop J. W. Wactor, chairperson
Bishop Joseph D. Cauthen, vice chairperson
Members:

1. Rev. A. E. Whitted
2. Rev. W J. Powell
3. Rev. James A. Brown
4. Rev. E. A. Blanks
5. Rev. W. C. Sapp
6. Rev. S. H. Hairston
7. Rev. Charles Ford
8. Rev. Walter E. Beamon
9. Rev. A. L. Wilson
10. Rev. T. G. Gilliam
11. Rev. J. Mayo Roberts
12. Rev. Joseph Johnson

1976-80

Bishop James W. Wactor, chairperson
Bishop Ruben L. Speaks, 1st vice chairperson
Bishop Charles H. Foggie, 2nd vice chairperson
Members:

1. Rev. Vernon Shannon
2. Rev. Thomas C. Gill
3. Rev. George W. Walker
4. Rev. Joseph E. Holt
5. Rev. G. L. Scott
6. Rev. F. D. Mayweather
7. Rev. Charles Ford
8. Rev. Raymond L. Hart
9. Rev. R. L. Pyant
10. Rev. T. G. Gilliam
11. Rev. Fred Hubbard
12. Rev. B. Leon Carson

1980-84

Bishop James W. Wactor, chairperson
Bishop William A. Hilliard, 1st vice chairperson
Bishop Alfred G. Dunston, Jr., 2nd vice chairperson
Members:

1. Rev. Thomas C. Gill
2. Rev. A. E. Harris
3. Rev. Carroll M. Felton
4. Mr. Willie King
5. Rev. F. I. Lowe
6. Mrs. Lizzie Sykes
7. Rev. R. P. Pyant
8. Mrs. Esther Carson
9. Rev. Percy Smith
10. Rev. Jimmy Hicks
11. Rev. B. Leon Carson
12. Mr. Melvin Stevens

African Methodist Episcopal Zion Church

1984-88

Bishop Herman L. Anderson, chairperson
Bishop Alfred G. Dunston, Jr., 1st vice chairperson
Bishop James W. Wactor, 2nd vice chairperson
Members:

1. Rev. Alexander L. Jones
2. Rev. Audie V. Simon
3. Rev. Roy Holmes
4. Rev. James Hendrix
5. Mrs. Alberta Hicks
6. Rev. R. L. Pyant
7. Rev. Osofo L. H. McDonald
8. Rev. Francis WIlliams
9. Rev. Percy Smith
10. Rev. H. K. Matthews
11. Rev. M. S. Chatman
12. Rev. George C. Sanders

1988-92

Bishop John H. Miller, Sr., chairperson
Bishop Alfred E. White, 1st vice chairperson
Bishop S. Chuka Ekemam, 2nd vice chairperson
Members:

1. Rev. Oscar McLaughlin
2. Rev. Clyde L. Murphy
3. Rev. Marshall Strickland
4. Rev. Kenneth Arrington
5. Rev. James H. Dunlap
6. Rev. A. D. Brown
7. Rev. David R. Baker
8. Rev. Francis Williams
9. Rev. H. K. Matthews
10. Rev. Reginald Broadnax
11. Rev. Alexander Jones
12. Ms. Julia Murphy

1992-96

Bishop S. Chuka Ekemam, chairperson
Bishop Enoch B. Rochester, 1st vice chairperson
Bishop John H. Miller, Sr., 2nd vice chairperson
Members:

1. Rev. S. Benjamin Patterson
2. Rev. A. D. Brown
3. Rev. Audie Simon
4. Rev. Donald W. H. E. Ruffin
5. Rev. Kenneth Arrington
6. Rev. Jerrod Brumfield
7. Rev. Carl Glenn
8. Rev. Francis Williams
9. Rev. James E. Powell
10. Rev. James H. Dunlap
11. Rev. Gloria N. Snipes
12. Rev. Eugene Parker

Home Missions, Brotherhood Pensions & Ministerial Relief

1996-2000
Bishop Samuel Chuka Ekemam, chairperson
Bishop Enoch B. Rochester, 1st vice chairperson
Bishop Joseph Johnson, 2nd vice chairperson
Members:

1. Rev. James Robertson, Jr.
2. Rev. W. H. E. Ruffin
3. Rev. Kevin W. McGill, Sr.
4. Rev. Arthur Randolph, Jr.
5. Rev. Andrew D. Brown
6. Rev. Carl Glenn
7. Rev. Leon Henderson
8. Rev. James H. Dunlap
9. Rev. Audie V. Simon
10. Rev. James R. McMillian, Sr.
11. Rev. Francis Williams
12. Rev. Kenneth Crowder

HOME MISSIONS BOARD

1972-76
Bishop Charles H. Foggie, chairperson
Bishop Joseph D. Cauthen, vice chairperson
Members:

1. Rev. James C. Brown
2. Rev. James T. Goode, Sr.
3. Rev. Novie S. Chaney
4. Rev. Cecil Bishop
5. Rev. G. L. Smith
6. Rev. H. T. Harvest
7. Rev. M. S. Chatman
8. Rev. Robert L. Postell
9. Rev. C. J. Jenkins
10. Rev. T. H. Hibbler
11. Rev. Paree Porter
12. Rev. M. F. Ward

1976-80
Bishop Charles H. Foggie, chairperson
Bishop John H. Miller, Sr., vice chairperson
Members:

1. Rev. Ralph W. Gullette
2. Rev. Alton C. Hunnicutt
3. Rev. W. C. Ardrey
4. Rev. Harlee H. Little
5. Rev. George L. Smith
6. Rev. A. J. Blake
7. Rev. M. S. Chatman
8. Rev. Robert L. Postell
9. Rev. C. J. Jenkins
10. Rev. D. A. Parker
11. Rev. Richard Fisher
12. Rev. Paul F. Thurston

African Methodist Episcopal Zion Church

1980-84
Bishop Charles H. Foggie, chairperson
Bishop Richard L. Fisher, vice chairperson
Members:

1. Rev. Alton Hunnicutt
2. Rev. R. C. Price
3. Mrs. Loretta Sutton
4. Rev. E. R. Faush
5. Mrs. Callie V. Harris
6. Rev. William C. Ardrey
7. Rev. C. J. Jenkins
8. Rev. S. S. Seay
9. Mr. Howard Crooms
10. Rev. C. R. Thompson
11. Mrs. Piccola Jones
12. Rev. R. L. Postell

1984-88
Bishop C. H. Foggie, chairperson
Bishop R. L. Fisher, vice chairperson
Members:

1. Rev. Alton Hunnicutt
2. Rev. Raymond E. Price
3. Mrs. Loretta Sutton
4. Rev. E. R. Faush
5. Rev. General L. Scott
6. Rev. C. J. Jenkins
7. Rev. Ocie M. Brown
8. Rev. Stacatto Powell
9. Mr. Howard E. Croom
10. Rev. James E. Milton
11. Rev. C. R. Thompson
12. Rev. Dennis V. Proctor

1988-92
Bishop Richard L. Fisher, chairperson
Bishop Charles H. Foggie, 1st vice chairperson
Bishop George W. Walker, Sr., 2nd vice chairperson
Members:

1. Rev. Alton C. Hunnicutt
2. Rev. Raymond E. Price
3. Rev. Robert T. Graham
4. Rev. William C. Ardrey
5. Rev. Ocie M. Brown
6. Rev. C. R. Thompson
7. Mrs. Anna Richardson
8. Rev. Erskine R. Faush
9. Rev. C. J. Jenkins
10. Rev. Vincent T. Frosh
11. Mr. Howard Croom
12. Rev. Freddie Massie

CHRISTIAN EDUCATION
1972-1996

IN fulfilling her mission to the world through service to those who are of the "household of faith," the African Methodist Episcopal Zion Church has developed and supported several agencies to enable the church to achieve her goals. One of these agencies is the Department of Christian Education, which was directed by the Rev. Dr. George Lincoln Blackwell, II, from 1967-92, with offices in Chicago, Illinois, at 128 E. 58th Street. He was appointed by the Board of Bishops in February, 1967 to complete the unexpired term of Dr. James W. Eichelberger who served this church in several capacities in the Department of Christian Education and its antecedent agencies for more than fifty years. (Walls, *The African Methodist Episcopal Zion Church*, pp. 290-94)

Rev. Blackwell was elected in his own right as Secretary-Treasurer of the Department of Christian Education of the A. M. E. Zion Church at the 1968 General Conference held in Detroit, Michigan. He brought to this office a wealth of experience accrued from his earlier ministry as a Youth Director in the Christian Education Department. He told the 1972 General Conference that he was addressing the issues of the early 1970's after having "labored through the '60's with its assassinations, riots, moon landings, civil rights protests, the Viet Nam War; and its new morality, Hippies, Yippies, Black Panthers, White Hats, Black P. Stone Rangers; and its communal living, mini-skirts, maxi-coats, long hair, wigs, pot and LSD; and its campus unrest, heart transplants and Boeing 747's." He further observed:

> We are now together in the '70's. May the experiences of the '60's better enable us to comprehend the gigantic responsibilities that are ours as we move forward in Christian Education in this decade. May God help us not only to comprehend, but also to have the will to solve our many problems—problems that certainly have to do with ethical issues involving religion and theology; world diplomatic and political issues; issues of economics; issues relating to our social, political and ecological environments; and issues concerning how we will govern ourselves as children of liberation and how we will be governed." (*Official Journal, 39th Quad. Sess. Gen. Conf.*, p. 304)

Dr. Blackwell reminded the denomination:
"I am but one, but I am one,
I cannot do everything, but I can do something,

African Methodist Episcopal Zion Church

What I can do I ought to do,
What I ought to do,
By the grace of God, I will do." (*39th Quad. Sess.*, p. 304)
This office and this department thrived on having a continuing leadership for several quadrennia. In 1972, at the 39th General Conference meeting at Mobile, Alabama, Rev. Blackwell was reelected to this office as spokesman for the development of programs, ministries and the standards for the more than 5,994 churches of the African Methodist Episcopal Zion denomination. These ministries are the means by which the 1,024,974 confirmed members, 6,873 ordained clergy, 111,790 Sunday School students and the 48,210 Sunday school teachers and officers were enabled to possess the religious heritage that is rightfully theirs. They provide the nurture essential for development as Christians, as responsible churchmen and churchwomen, and as members and leaders in the communities and societies for which the church has concern. (*Yearbook of American and Canadian Churches*, 1975)

Dr. Blackwell implemented the extensive program of this department with the help of a very small staff at the Christian Education Department headquarters. Included among the staff were Ms. Rowena Turk, Mrs. Bernice Trice, the late Mrs. Evelyn Wilcher, and Mrs. Geraldine Blackwell (whom Dr. Blackwell called "My Girl Friday.") He said of her, "She is always available to tackle most any job. Without her tremendous dedication, we would find difficulty in operation." (Mrs. Blackwell died suddenly in February, 1996, in Williamston, North Carolina where she and her husband were living in retirement with his mother, Mrs. Clayvonne Andrews Blackwell. (*Official Journal, 39th Quad. Sess. Gen. Conf.*, pp. 304-5)

Within the system of the A. M. E. Zion Church, the Christian Education Department has the strong undergirding of all the bishops, presiding elders, pastors, general officers, the General Convention and the National Youth Council Executives, Annual Conference Boards of Christian Education, directors of Christian Education, Sunday School superintendents and teachers who provide leadership on the national and local church level. During the 1972-76 quadrennium, the Board Chairpersons were Bishop Alfred G. Dunston, Jr., (Home and Church) and Bishop John H. Miller, Sr., (School and College). The Vice Chairpersons of the Board were Bishops Herbert Bell Shaw, William M. Smith, George J. Leake, III, and William Jacob Walls, who died in April 1975. (*Official Journal, 39th Quad. Sess. Gen. Conf.*, pp. 304-8; 40th Quad. Sess., pp. 366-99)

Christian Education

During 1976-80, Bishop John H. Miller was chairperson, and Bishops George J. Leake, III, and William A. Hilliard were co-chairpersons of the Home and Church Division. In the School and College Division, Bishop Alfred G. Dunston, Jr., was board chairperson and president of the corporation; Bishops William M. Smith and Herbert Bell Shaw were vice chairpersons. Bishop Shaw died in January, 1980, while attending the Board of Bishops meeting in Indianapolis, Indiana. The staff of the Christian Education Department included administrative assistants Rev. C. R. Thompson, Dr. Josephine H. Kyles, and Rev. Enoch B. Rochester. The Rev. Nathaniel Jarrett was chairperson of the Commission on Youth Ministry. Dr. David H. Bradley was also an administrative assistant and director of Leadership Education. He passed away on September 24, 1979. Other officers were Dr. John H. Satterwhite, coordinator of Ministerial and Lay Institutes; Dr. Senora B. Lawson, president of the General Convention Executive Committee; Mr. James E. Boger, chairperson of the Commission on Boy Scouting; and Mrs. Gertrude Kelley, chairperson of the Commission on Girl Scouting. (*Official Journal, 41st Quad. Sess. Gen. Conf.*, pp. 422-39)

During the 1980-84 quadrennium, Bishops John H. Miller and Clinton R. Coleman were co-chairpersons of the Home and Church Board. Bishop Alfred G. Dunston, Jr., and Bishop Cecil Bishop were co-chairpersons of the School and College Board. Staff of the Christian Education Department included Administrative Assistants Dr. Enoch B. Rochester, Dr. C. R. Thompson, and Dr. Josephine Kyles; Dr. John H. Satterwhite, coordinator of Ministerial and Lay Institutes; Rev. Nathaniel Jarrett, director of the Commission on Youth Ministry; Rev. (Mrs.) Willie L. Aldrich, chairperson of the Commission on Children's Ministry; Mr. James E. Boger, chairperson of the Commission on Boy Scouting; and Mrs. Gertrude Kelley, chairperson of the Commission on Girl Scouting. The department was saddened at the sudden passing on December 27, 1982 of Dr. (Mrs.) Senora B. Lawson, who was president of the General Convention Executive Committee. Dr. Lawson passed away while attending the National Christian Youth Council Meeting in Arlington, Virginia. (*Official Journal, 42nd Quad. Sess. Gen. Conf.*, pp. 471-90)

During the years 1984-88, the Department of Christian Education Home and Church Board chairperson was Bishop John H. Miller. Bishop Clinton R. Coleman was the co-chairperson. Bishop Alfred G. Dunston, Jr., was chairperson and president of the School and College Board Corporation, and Bishop Cecil Bishop was vice chairperson. The office staff of the Christian Education Department included Mrs. Rowena Turk, who had been with the department since 1972, and Mrs. Geraldine Blackwell, who had worked beside Dr. Blackwell for many years. The various heads of commissions included Dr. John H. Satterwhite, coordinator of Ministerial and Lay Institutes; Dr.

African Methodist Episcopal Zion Church

Enoch B. Rochester, administrative assistant for Adult Ministries; Dr. Nathaniel Jarrett, director of the Commission on Youth Ministry; Dr. Josephine H. Kyles, administrative assistant and chairperson of the Commission on Social Education and Action; Rev. (Mrs.) Willie Aldrich, chairperson of the Commission on Children's Ministry; Mr. James E. Boger, chairperson of the Commission on Boy Scouting; and Mrs. Gertrude Kelley, chairperson of the Commission on Girl Scouting. (*Official Journal, 43rd Quad. Sess. Gen. Conf.*, pp. 570-91)

The report of Rev. Blackwell, general secretary of the Christian Education Department, for the years 1988-92, was his seventh and final report to the General Conference. During this quadrennium, Bishop Cecil Bishop was chairperson of the Home and Church Board; Bishop Clinton R. Coleman was its vice chairperson. Bishop Herman L. Anderson was chairperson of the School and College Board; and Bishop George W. Walker, Sr. was the vice chairperson. The office staff comprised Mrs. Rowena Turk and Mrs. Geraldine Blackwell. The staff of the department included Dr. Josephine H. Kyles, administrative assistant and chairperson of the Commission on Social Education and Action; Dr. Enoch B. Rochester, administrative assistant and chairperson of the Commission on Adult Ministries; Rev. Thaddeus Steele, chairperson of the Commission on Youth Ministry; Rev. (Mrs.) Willie L. Aldrich, chairperson of the Commission on Children's Ministry; Rev. Raymon E. Hunt, staff associate and convention coordinator; Mr. James E. Boger, chairperson of the Commission on Boy Scouting; and Mrs. Nellie M. Dudley, chairperson of the commission on Girl Scouting. After serving the Christian Education Department for thirty-eight years, twenty-five years as general secretary and in other capacities, Rev. Blackwell did not seek reelection. (*Official Journal, 44th Quad. Sess. Gen. Conf.*, pp. 609-29)

An appropriate recognition of Dr. Blackwell's service to God through the A. M. E. Zion Church for forty years was observed on February 27, 1992 at the Trinity A. M. E. Zion Church, Washington, D. C. This was at the Winter Meeting of the Board of Bishops, just prior to his last report to General Conference. Representatives of denominational and ecumenical agencies with which Dr. Blackwell had been associated through the years were represented and participated in the celebration. The steering committee for the occasion comprised: Dr. Enoch B. Rochester, chairperson, Bishop Cecil Bishop, Bishop Herman L. Anderson, Ms. June Slade Collins, the Rev. William Kelly, Ms. Brenda McCormick, Dr. Curtis T. Walker, Dr. Joseph Johnson, Ms. Mary A. Love, and the Revs. W. Darin Moore and George W. Walker, Jr.

The Rev. Raymon Hunt was elected general secretary of the Christian Education

Christian Education

Department at the 1992 General Conference. The headquarters of the department, located for many years in Chicago, Illinois, was moved to the A. M. E. Zion Publishing House in Charlotte, North Carolina. Bishop Joseph Johnson was chairperson, and Bishop Marshall H. Strickland and Bishop Richard K. Thompson were vice chairpersons of the Board of School and College during the 1992-96 quadrennium. The chairperson of Board of Home and Church was Bishop Milton A. Williams; Bishops Clarence Carr and Enoch B. Rochester were vice chairpersons. The Christian Education Department staff included Dr. Joanne Barnett, administrative assistant to the department; Dr. Nathaniel Jarrett, senior administrative assistant; Rev. W. Darin Moore, administrative assistant, Young Adults in Christian Ministries (YACM); Dr. Helen C. Scott-Carter, director of Children's Ministry; Rev. Clifford D. Barnett, Sr., director of Youth Ministry; and Rev. Harold O. Robinson, director of Boy Scouts; Dr. Ndugu GBT'Ofori-Atta, director of Family Ministries; and Ms. Jennifer Andrews, administrative assistant to the General Secretary. ("The Department of Christian Education, A. M. E. Zion Church, 45th Quad. Sess. Gen. Conf. Report, 1992-96," p. 5)

As secretary of the Department of Christian Education, Rev. Raymon E. Hunt served with distinction during the 1992-96 quadrennium. When the General Conference met in 1996 during the Bicentennial Year of the A. M. E. Zion Church, Rev. Hunt was reelected for another quadrennium. His sensitivity to the programmatic needs of the department was revealed in the presentation of audio visuals and photographic displays of the several age-group levels under the supervision of the Christian Education Department. He reminded the general church that "the primary purpose of the Department of Christian Education is to give overhead guidance and direction in the Christian nurture, training and development of children, youth, young adults, and adults in their homes, churches, camps, conventions, conferences, and other assemblies; and in the Church related schools, colleges and seminaries. The Department must cultivate and develop Christian attitudes and skills; and through the grace of God, lead them [all] to the supreme decision, conversion, and commitment to Christ and the Church. The Church's Christian Education program should impart to its membership knowledge of biblical truth, words and tunes to meaningful tunes and songs, and moral and spiritual values." It is believed that with the vision expressed by Rev. Hunt the cause of Christian education and its implementation in the A. M. E. Zion Church will continue to be a high priority in its development, nurture, and budgetary considerations for years to come. (Ibid., p. 12)

African Methodist Episcopal Zion Church

General Convention on Christian Education

One of the most effective means for nurturing Christian development among all age groups of the denomination is the General Convention on Christian Education, which meets quadrennially. The 1974 session of the General Convention on Christian Education met on the campus of Livingstone College at Salisbury, North Carolina, August 4-9, 1974 , and registered 1,484 children, youth and adults. There were also nearly six hundred unregistered attendees. The convention observed the 50th anniversary of the Home and Church Board, one of the two divisions of the Christian Education Department that dates back to a resolution in 1924 sponsored by Bishop William J. Walls and Dr. James W. Eichelberger that proposed its creation at the General Conference held in Indianapolis, Indiana. In his report to the 1976 General Conference, Rev. Blackwell recalled one of the highlights of the convention:

"It was befitting to include in the 1974 General Convention program proper recognition of the founding of the Home and Church Board. It was most fortunate that Bishop Walls was present to relate to the assembly the story of the formation of this Board, and to also give a sweeping and masterful, historical account of the growth and development of the Christian Education Department. The delegates, both youth and adults, were amazed by the 90 year old prelate's ability to recall. They were also impressed by learning that he had recently completed a 669-page history of the A. M. E. Zion Church at age 89, and that he had served as an active Bishop of the Church for 50 years. Tributes on the occasion were made by Dr. David H. Bradley, Dr. Daniel H. Hughlet, Mr. Arthur E. Brooks and the Rev. C. R. Thompson. Mrs. Dorothy Walls gave expressions of appreciation for the recognition given to her husband and pledged her continued support to the work of Christian Education." (*Official Journal, 40th Quad. Sess. Gen. Conf.*, p. 365)

A plaque was presented to Bishop Walls on behalf of the Board of Christian Education and its chairpersons, Bishop John H. Miller and Bishop Alfred G. Dunston, Jr. The plaque was inscribed as follows:

BISHOP WILLIAM JACOB WALLS
in recognition of faithful and untiring service
in Christian Education — A. M. E. Zion Church
and Chairman of the Home and Church Board
1924-1968
General Convention on Christian Education
Salisbury, N. C.
August 1974 (Ibid.., p. 365)

Christian Education

Dr. Blackwell further observed that it was "the genius of Bishop Walls and Dr. Eichelberger" that led the church to the first General Convention on Christian Education in Asheville, North Carolina in 1922, under the theme, "The Child in Our Midst." During the period 1970-94, conventions were held quadrennially as follows: Livingstone College in 1970, with the theme "The Black Man's Contribution to World Culture"; Livingstone College in 1974, with the theme: "The Church's Opportunity: Discovering in Crisis—Acting in Faith"; Livingstone College in 1978 with the theme:"A Power System: Equipment for the Present—Resource for the Future"; Livingstone College in 1982 with the theme: "The Challenge of Christian Education: From Limited Resources to Unlimited Possibilities"; Livingstone College in 1986 with the theme: "Christ's Message—The Church's Mission—Zion's Direction"; Livingstone College in 1990 with the theme: "Building Ministries that Change Lives, Alter Conditions, Enhance Relationships and Create New Communities"; Livingstone College in 1994 with the theme: "Called to Be Committed Disciples at the Dawn of the 21st Century: Envisioning the Future, Elevating Our Stewardship, Equipping for Ministry, and Empowering by the Spirit." (*40th Quad. Sess. Gen. Conf.*, pp. 365, 368)

The 1978 General Convention on Christian Education held at Livingstone College, Salisbury, North Carolina, on August 6-11, was well received by delegates in the workshops and in public sessions. Over two thousand persons attended the convention, of whom there were 550 registered adults and 886 registered youth. Jamaica and Liberia were represented by one youth, and one adult and three youths, respectively. (*Official Journal, 41st Quad. Sess. Gen. Conf.*, p. 425)

The establishment of the Assembly of Christian Educators (ACE) by Rev. Blackwell, with the approval of the Home and Church Board, was one of the significant achievements during his tenure. A forum for educators during the interval of conventions, ACE would also be responsible for continued planning of the General Convention of Christian Education. At the 1982 General Convention, members voted affirmatively for the new structure. Mr. D. D. Garrett of Greenville, North Carolina and Mrs. Ola W. Crawley of Madisonville, Kentucky, were elected president and vice president, respectively. The executive committee of the Assembly of Christian Educators was to meet annually at the same time and place as the National Christian Youth Council. The General Convention on Christian Education was held at Livingstone College on August 1-6, 1982. Dr. Benjamin Ruffin, special assistant to the governor of North Carolina, and Dr. Thaddeus Garrett, assistant to then U. S. Vice President George Bush, enriched the discourse of the convention in separate addresses. Over two thousand persons attended the convention, including four registered conferees from the

African Methodist Episcopal Zion Church

Virgin Islands Conference, two from the West Ghana Conference, and one from the Nigeria Conference. (*Official Journal, 42nd Quad. Sess. Gen. Conf.*, pp. 472-73)

The 1986 General Convention on Christian Education met at Livingstone College, Salisbury, North Carolina, August 10-15. Guest participants included Dr. Don Steger, assistant city manager of Charlotte, North Carolina, and Dr. George E. Riddick, pastor of Blackwell Memorial A. M. E. Zion Church, Chicago, and vice president at-large of OPERATION PUSH. Dr. Riddick delivered the civil rights message. The General Convention adopted a new constitution on August 12, 1986. The Assembly of Christian Educators (ACE) was institutionalized during this convention. The following officers were elected to serve for four years: Mr. D. D. Garrett of Greenville, North Carolina was re-elected president of ACE. The Rev. E. B. Rochester, administrative assistant of the Christian Education Department, served as advisor to ACE. (*Official Journal, 42nd Quad. Sess. Gen. Conf., p. 474; 43rd Quad. Sess. Gen. Conf.*, pp. 573-74)

At the General Convention of Christian Education, August 5-10, 1990, Dr. Josephine Kyles, who had served as the director of Social Education and Action since 1938, was awarded the first Dr. James W. Eichelberger Meritorious Service Award. Young Adults in Christian Ministries (YACM) became a unit of the Christian Education Department when its officers were elected. The Rev. W. Darin Moore became its first chairperson. The Rev. C. R. Thompson, YACM advisor, was instrumental in helping the group become organized. The president of the National Christian Youth Council was Rev. George W. Walker, Jr. The Rev. Thaddeus Steele was advisor. Ms. Brenda McCormick was president of ACE, and the Rev. Enoch B. Rochester continued as advisor to the new body. (*Official Journal, 44th Quad. Sess. Gen. Conf.*, p. 611)

The General Convention on Christian Education met at Livingstone College, Salisbury, North Carolina, August 1-5, 1994. An outstanding event of the convention was the performance of the C. R. Thompson Mass Choir. Comprising over three hundred youths, young adults, and adults, the choir generated much excitement as it appeared for the first time in a live recording concert at Coppal Auditorium on the campus of Catawba College in Salisbury, North Carolina. ("Department of Christian Education, A. M. E. Zion Church, 45th Quad. Sess. Gen. Conf. Report, 1992-96," pp. 12-13)

National Christian Youth Council

One of the achievements of the Christian Education Department during the 1972-76 quadrennium was the development of a vital National Christian Youth Council. In addressing the General Conference, Dr. Blackwell made the following observation on

Christian Education

the important role of the NCYC:

> One cannot completely assess the value of the National Christian Youth Council to Zion's youth and to Zion. It can be said, however, that this organization has provided an opportunity for many young people to learn some of the history and mechanics of the denomination, how to perform in a deliberative body, and to learn what it is to be an active churchman or churchwoman. Youth who have had such exposure have also had the opportunity to travel across our Zion during the quadrennium—to Compton, Calif., Trenton, N.J., Greensboro, N. C., and Dallas, Tex.—and visit our churches and meet other Zion members. These young people, and those youth who will be influenced by them, should provide another generation of loyal Zionites. (*Official Journal, 40th Quad. Sess. Gen. Conf.*, p. 368)

The Rev. (now Bishop) Nathaniel Jarrett, was approved by the Home and Church Board in July, 1974 to serve as national chairperson of the Commission on Youth Ministry. He succeeded Rev. C. R. Thompson who had served with distinction as director of youth since 1965 and had been approved by the board to serve as administrative assistant to the Secretary of Christian Education. Rev. Jarrett reported for the National Christian Youth Council (NCYC) at the General Conference. The Rev. Blackwell expressed gratitude to the Revs. Nathaniel Jarrett, C. R. Thompson, (now Bishop) Enoch B. Rochester, Dr. Josephine H. Kyles, Mrs. Willie L. Aldrich, and Mrs. Geraldine Blackwell for their invaluable contributions to youth concerns. He especially congratulated Mr. Raymon Hunt for his capable leadership as president of the National Christian Youth Council (*40th Quad. Sess.*, pp. 367-68)

During the 1976-80 quadrennium, the Rev. Raymon Hunt of Vallejo, California, elected national president in 1974, was succeeded by Mr. Thaddeus Steele of Tuscaloosa, Alabama, at the 1978 General Convention. The NCYC met annually each December during the quadrennium at various locations and with the following themes: "Christian Principles and Social Choices," in 1976, Jackson Memorial A. M. E. Zion Church, Hempstead, Long Island, with Rev. Clarence Carr and Bishop Herbert Bell Shaw as host pastor and bishop, respectively; "Who Am I? (Biologically, Sociologically, Religiously)," in 1977, Kyles Temple A. M. E. Zion Church, Sacramento, California, with Dr. Oscar M. Peavy and Bishop George J. Leake, as host pastor and bishop; "The Bible: All the Truth You'll Ever Really Need," in 1978, Wesley Center A. M. E. Zion Church, Pittsburgh, Pennsylvania, with Dr. Carroll M. Felton and Bishop Charles H. Foggie as host pastor and bishop; "Broadening Denominational

African Methodist Episcopal Zion Church

Understanding," in 1979, Butler Chapel A. M. E. Zion Church, Tuskegee, Alabama, with Rev..H. T. Hutton and Bishop Arthur Marshall as host pastor and bishop. (*Official Journal, 41st Quad. Sess.Gen. Conf.*, p. 425)

During the 1982 General Convention on Christian Education, Brother George McKain, II, of Ridgewood, New Jersey, succeeded Mr. Thaddeus Steele as president of the NCYC. The National Christian Youth Council and the Executive Committee of the Assembly of Christian Educators agreed that the December 27-30, 1984 meeting be held jointly at Big Zion A. M. E. Zion Church, Mobile, Alabama, where Rev. (now Bishop) Milton A. Williams and Bishop William M. Smith were host pastor and presiding prelate. (*Official Journal, 42nd Quad. Sess. Gen. Conf.*, pp. 473-74)

Rev. Eric Leake of Mt. Gilead, North Carolina was elected president of the NCYC during the 1986 General Convention on Christian Education. Dr. Nathaniel Jarrett continued as chairperson of the NCYC Commission. The locations and themes of NCYC and ACE annual meetings were: 1986—St. Catherine A. M. E. Zion Church, New Rochelle, N. Y. and LaGuardia Marriott Hotel, East Elmhurst, N.Y.: "Christ's Message." Rev. Vernon A. Shannon and Bishop W. M. Smith were host pastor and bishop, respectively. 1987—Metropolitan A. M. E. Zion Church, Kansas City, Missouri and the Adam's Mark Hotel: "The Church's Mission," Rev. Kenneth Monroe and Bishop John H. Miller were host pastor and bishop. 1988—Baum's Temple, Summerville, South Carolina, and Omni Hotel, Charleston, South Carolina: "Zion's Direction," with Rev. George McKain, II, and Bishop Richard L. Fisher, as host pastor and bishop, respectively. 1989— Community A. M. E. Zion Church, Vancouver, Washington, and the Portland Hilton Hotel, Portland, Oregon: "Zion's Direction: Charting the Course," with the Rev. Robert S. Kemp and Bishop George W. Walker, as host pastor and host bishop, respectively. 1990—St. Luke, Buffalo, New York and Hyatt Regency Hotel: "Building Ministries That Change Lives," with Rev. Robert L. Graham and Bishop J. Clinton Hoggard as host pastor and bishop, respectively. 1991— Livingstone College, Salisbury, North Carolina: "Building Ministries That Alter Conditions, " with Bishop William M. Smith as host bishop. (*Official Journal, 43rd Quad. Sess.Gen. Conf.*, p. 574; *44th Quad. Sess*, pp. 611-12)

During the 1992-96 quadrennium, the National Christian Youth Council changed its name to the more inclusive Varick International Christian Youth Council (VICYC). The new president of the VICYC is Mrs. Dana Miggins-Rice. Mrs. Autry K. Richmond serves as president of the Assembly of Christian Educators (ACE). ACE has been assigned the GRACE project—an acronym for Growing Roots Academically in Christian Education, which is designed to motivate, teach, nurture, equip, and elevate

Christian Education

church school superintendents and teachers. Mrs. Bobby D. Floyd is a major contributor to this project. The Young Adults in Christian Ministry unit is directed by the Rev. W. Darin Moore, administrative assistant. ("Dept. of Christian Education, Quad. Conf. Report, 1992-96," pp. 13-14)

Ecumenical Activities

The Department of Christian Education of the A. M. E. Zion Church manifests its commitment to work for the unity of the faith through its memberships and participation in the following interdenominational organizations and social agencies: the National Council of Churches of Christ in America: Division of Education and Ministry and Inter-Unit Projects, Division of Church and Society and Inter-Unit Projects; Related Consortia: World Council of Churches; International Society of Christian Endeavor; Religious Education Association; Black Christian Education Administrative and Coordinating Committee; National Interfaith Coalition on Aging; General Commission on Chaplains and Armed Forces Personnel; National Committee of Black Churchmen; American Council on Education ; American Academy of Political Science; National Civil Liberties Clearing House; National Interreligious Service Board for Conscientious Objectors; John Milton Society; American Bible Society; National Association for the Advancement of Colored People; Southern Christian Leadership Conference; and OPERATION PUSH. (*Official Journal, 40th Quad. Sess. Gen. Conf.*, pp. 375-76)

The International Society of Christian Endeavor has been one of the dominant ecumenical youth organizations officially developed by the Christian Education Department under the umbrella of the Varick Christian Endeavor Society. The Rev. C. R. Thompson, now of sainted memory, and the Rev. (now Bishop) Nathaniel Jarrett served with the secretary of Christian Education on the International Board of Trustees of Christian Endeavor. Mr. Thaddeus Steele of Tuscaloosa, Alabama, was a member of the National Christian Youth Council and was elected to the Youth Assembly of Christian Endeavor in 1973. Bishops Charles H. Foggie and J. Clinton Hoggard were long-time members of the International Society and during the 1972-76 quadrennium provided leadership and participation. During the 1976-80 quadrennium, the Revs. Blackwell and Nathaniel Jarrett attended the 54th Convention of the International Society of Christian Endeavor at Albright College in Reading, Pennsylvania, in 1977, as representatives of the A. M. E. Zion Church. Rev. Blackwell delivered the Holy Communion Sermon, and Rev. Jarrett was honored at the convention by being elected a vice president of the society. During the 1980-84 quadrennium, Dr. Nathaniel Jarrett

African Methodist Episcopal Zion Church

was the liaison with the national and international body as a vice president and member of its executive committee. He traveled for the society and shared in its decision making. The 58th International Christian Endeavor Convention was held at Hope College in Holland, Michigan, on July 1-5, 1985. In 1988, the secretary and Dr. Jarrett were both members of the board of trustees of the international body, and Dr. Jarrett served on its executive committee as well. The 60th International Christian Endeavor Convention was held in Harlingen, Texas, July 3-7, 1989. The Christian Education Department prepared and mailed promotional materials to various churches with Christian Endeavor societies during Christian Endeavor Week. In 1991, the board of trustees of the society changed the name of the society to Christian Endeavor International, and the motto is "For Christ and His Church." The 62nd Convention of Christian Endeavor International was held in Honolulu, Hawaii in 1993. (*Official Journal, 40th Quad. Sess. Gen. Conf.*, pp. 372-73; *41st Quad. Sess.*, p. 428; *42nd Quad. Sess.*, p. 475; *43rd Quad. Sess.*, p. 575; *44th Quad. Sess.*, p. 613)

The Christian Education Department was also active in the National Council of Churches of Christ in the U. S. A. Division of Education and Ministry. The secretary was a member of the Unit Committee of the Division of Education and Ministry and the Program Committee on Education for Christian Life and Mission. In June 24-26, 1980, member churches of the National Council celebrated the 200th Anniversary of the founding of the Sunday School. Topics discussed during the conference examining the future of the Sunday School included: (1) historical and philosophical issues that shaped the development of the Sunday School as a movement and institution in our society; (2) current educational policies and practices of the Sunday School; and (3) future direction of the Sunday School. Dr. David H. Bradley was nominated by Rev. Blackwell as a principal speaker, but his death on September 24, 1979 precluded the fulfillment of this task. A. M. E. Zion participants included Rev. George Blackwell, Ms. Mary A. Love, Mrs. Dorothy Johnson, Dr. Josephine H. Kyles, Dr. and Mrs. George B. Thomas, Rev. (Mrs.) Willie Aldrich, Rev. Morgan W. Tann, Mr. Calvin Callahan, and Rev. Dr. John H. Satterwhite. The Christian Education Department also participated in the Indiana Council of Churches (also related to the National Council of Churches of Christ) yearlong celebration of the 200th Anniversary of the Sunday School in Indianapolis. The secretary served on the leadership team on September 19-21, 1980. Rev. Nathaniel Jarrett and Mr. Thaddeus Steele represented the A. M. E. Zion Church at the North American Youth Coalition for Global Interdependence and the Youth Age Group Forum that met in Toronto, Canada on October 12-14, 1979, as part of activities arising from the National Council of Churches (NCCC). The NCCC co-sponsored a literacy conference with the Johnson Foundation in Racine, Wisconsin, on September 14-

Christian Education

16, 1987. The Rev. Harry Spigner, pastor of John Wesley A. M. E. Zion Church, Muskegon, Michigan, was the A. M. E. Zion Church representative and one of sixty participants that included national and international literacy and church leaders. The conference was a reflection of the need to address growing illiteracy in America and its social consequences. Recurring themes in the conference were "Literacy is one way to help poor people become self-determining and responsible members of their communities." "The Church's Involvement in North American Literacy" was the conference report. Dr. D. C. Thompson was the Christian Education Department's representative on the Ecumenical Young Adult Ministries Staff Team (EYAMST), a sub-agency concerned with providing inspired leadership to young adults. The Secretary of Christian Education and Mrs. Brenda Smith attended an awards dinner and the celebration of the United Nations International Literacy Year at the NCCC Interchurch Center in September, 1990. From December 28, 1990-January 1, 1991, 2,100 Christian college students, including thirty-five international students, gathered for worship, Bible study, workshops, and fun at the Gault House, Louisville, Kentucky, guided by the theme "Celebrate 90 . . . Many Gifts, One Spirit." In 1991, two major ecumenical conferences were held at the Congress Hotel in Chicago, Illinois. The Black Family Ministries Conference, organized to equip Black Church leaders for their role as change agents in the wider society and as support system leaders for black families, was held April 9-10, 1991. The provision of *trained* consultants to black congregations was a specific goal of the conference. Rev. Darryl B. Starnes, Ms. Vertell Govan , Dr. Ndugu GB T'Ofori-Atta, Rev. Raymon Hunt, Mr. Theodore Shaw, and Ms. Evelyn Holden were Zionites recruited as consultants. The Families 2000 Conference was held April 10-14, 1991. Ms. Mary A. Love and Dr. Morgan W. Tann joined the aforementioned consultants as leaders engaged in family education, advocacy, and pastoral support in church and public policy. Both conferences were linked to NCCC through its Commission on Family Ministries and Human Sexuality. The 16th World Methodist Council and Conference were held in Singapore, July 24-31, 1991, at the Westin Stamford Hotel. About fifty-five Zionites attended the conference. Bishop Herman L. Anderson presided during the opening Communion Service; Bishop Ruben L. Speaks delivered the Sunday Morning Worship Service sermon. Bishops J. Clinton Hoggard and Cecil Bishop served on the Conference Program Committee and on the World Executive Committee, respectively.

During the 1992-96 quadrennium, Secretary Raymon Hunt served as secretary for the National Ministries Unit and as treasurer of the Ministries in Christian Education, an umbrella group for a number of ecumenical committees. The Ministries Unit in Christian Education has long served as a cooperative agency for curriculum develop-

African Methodist Episcopal Zion Church

ment, often jointly preparing materials, such as uniform lessons and resources for vacation and camping ministries, and distributing them to denominations. (*Official Journals, 41st Quad. Sess. Gen. Conf.*, pp. 427-28; *42nd Quad. Sess.*, pp. 489-90; *43rd Quad. Sess.*, pp. 575-76; "*45th Quad. Sess.*," p. 14)

Consultation on Church Union (COCU)

In 1974, the A. M. E. Zion Church jointly published a fifty thousand edition of Liberation and Unity, a Lenten booklet, in cooperation with the Theological Commission of the National Council of Black Churchmen and the Consultation on Church Union (COCU), which includes the A. M. E. and C. M. E. denominations. Members of each denomination contributed articles for meditation and reflection during the Lenten season. The project was inspired by Dr. John H. Satterwhite, associate general secretary of the Commission on Church Union, and has continued as a cooperative effort. A. M. E. Zion has been well represented in contributions to the Lenten booklet over the years. During 1976-80, Bishop Marshall was president of COCU, and Bishop Hoggard was vice chairperson of its Church Order Commission and leader of Zion's delegation at COCU meetings. He held both offices throughout the decade. During 1984-88, Rev. Blackwell was chairperson of the editorial board. (*Official Journal, 40th Quad. Sess. Gen. Conf.*, p. 375; *41st Quad. Sess.*, p. 427; *42nd Quad. Sess.*, p. 477; *43rd Quad. Sess.*, p. 576)

CHRISTIAN EDUCATION
HOME AND CHURCH DIVISION

THE Christian Education Department has two distinct divisions: the Division of Home and Church and the Division of Schools and Colleges. Each is an incorporated unit with a separate administrative board appointed at General Conference. The members of the boards are representatives of the twelve episcopal districts of the A. M. E. Zion Church. The following material relates to the Home and Church Division.

Leadership Education
The execution of Christian Education Department programs is reported to the General Conference by administrative assistants and chairpersons of various commissions. During the 1972-76 quadrennium, Dr. David H. Bradley was administrative assistant and director of Leadership Education, which is charged with training lay and clergy persons, through the study of Christian Education manuals, for leadership roles in schools and annual conferences. First A. M. E. Zion Church, Brooklyn, New York, provided one such leadership education training program. In 1976, the Rev. Dr. V. Loma St. Clair, minister at First Church, Brooklyn, enrolled over one hundred students and encouraged the in-service training program. Ms. Willie M. Stone of the Central Alabama Conference also had success with leadership development. Seven district schools, with encouragement from presiding elders, were conducted in the Central North Carolina Conference. Dr. Josephine Kyles headed another district project at Dinwiddie Institute, Dinwiddie, Virginia. In December 1975, over two hundred youth leaders attended the National Christian Youth Council meeting in Dallas, Texas. At that meeting, Dr. Bradley's service was recognized when he was presented the Distinguished Service Award by Secretary Blackwell on behalf of the youth and leadership of the church. (*Official Journal, 40th Quad. Sess. Gen. Conf.*, p. 376)

Ministers and Lay Institutes
The Rev. Dr. John H. Satterwhite, coordinator of institutes, was responsible for organizing the preparation and distribution of the Conference Courses of Study Work Book by the faculty of Hood Theological Seminary and staff of the Christian Education Department. The purpose of this program has been to involve Clinton Jr. College, Rock Hill, South Carolina; Lomax-Hannon Jr. College, Greenville, Alabama; Johnson Rural Institute, Batesville, Mississippi; Dinwiddie Institute, Dinwiddie, Virginia; and the (now defunct) Institute for Black Ministries, Philadelphia, Pennsylvania in the continuing education program of Hood Theological Seminary, Salisbury, North Carolina. As

noted above, Dr. Satterwhite was also actively involved in the communications work-shop organized by the Consultation on Church Union (COCU), the outcome of which was the joint publication of *Liberation and Unity*, initially planned as a three-year pro-ject involving the Christian Education Departments of the three historically and pre-dominantly black Methodist denominations. This project has continued since the first publication of *Liberation and Unity* in 1974. A pre-Lenten Retreat of Zion ministers was also successfully completed during March 8-12, 1976. Dr. Satterwhite died in May, 1989. The Rev. George Blackwell, secretary of the Department of Christian Education, paid tribute to the "exceptional leadership" Dr. Satterwhite had given as coordinator of the ministers and lay institutes and for his concept of the institute as training agencies for developing leaders in this area. *(Official Journals, 40th Quad. Sess. Gen. Conf.*, p. 429; *42nd Quad. Sess.*, pp. 476-77; *43rd Quad. Sess.*, pp. 574-76)

Commission on Social Education and Action
Dr. Josephine Kyles served as administrative assistant and chairperson of the Commission on Social Education and Action from 1938-92. Her position allowed her to participate in hearings, testimony, and other legislative matters through agencies and corporate councils. She was included in commissions in the National Health Education and Human Resources Department. She served on the following boards and organiza-tions: The Robert Woods Johnson Board and Network on Care Giving to the Frail Elderly; the Commonwealth Organization; and the National Gerontological Department for Minority Elderly in the A. M. E. Zion Church through the AARP (American Association of Retired Persons); Board of Directors of Arthritis Association, National Capital Area; Board of Directors of the National Capital Area, YWCA; Chairperson of the Board of Directors of the National Interfaith Coalition on Aging; and the Leadership Council of Aging Organizations (comprising thirty-seven agencies dealing with leg-islative and other problems of aging). As a member of the Society for International Development, she traveled to the 14th World Conference at Abidjan, West Africa, in August 1974, where cooperation and sharing emerged as major themes. She also visit-ed drought-stricken Upper Volta in West Africa (now Burkina Faso) through the aegis of the United Nations International Children's Emergency Fund (UNICEF). She was a member of the Association of Professors and Researchers in Religious Education; the Society for the Scientific Study of Religion; the Religious Education Association of the U. S. and Canada; and the National Council of Religion and Public Education. *(Official Journals, 40th Quad. Sess. Gen. Conf.*, pp. 377-79; *43rd Quad. Sess.*, pp. 578-79)

Christian Education: Home and Church

During 1976-80, Dr. Kyles worked with the Washington Office on Africa, publisher of *Washington Notes on Africa*, a journal that provides information on legislative, social, and economic matters concerning the governments and peoples of Africa; was a member of the World Future Society, which analyzes current trends for future living; cooperated with the National Senior Citizens Council Law Center to assist older people through free legal counsel and information; participated in the Older Americans Health Fair Program and in hearings sponsored by the Select Committee on Aging of the U. S. House of Representatives, in April 23-24, 1979. On October 22-23, 1979, she participated in the National Council of Churches and the District of Columbia Health and Welfare Organization's Planning Conference on Social Welfare Policy Issues Affecting Families. She was chairperson of the District of Columbia Chapter of the Retired Senior Volunteer Program (RSVP), which placed over four hundred people in voluntary service each year. She participated in the Methodist Commission on Social Action; conducted workshops and conferences at Dinwiddie Institute; served on staff at the winter meeting of the NCYC; was Exhibit Director at each General Convention on Christian Education; and participated in the annual sessions of the Religious Education Association. (*Official Journal, 41st Quad. Sess. Gen. Conf.*, p. 431)

In the 1980-84 quadrennium, Dr. Kyles testified before the U. S. Senate and House Committees on behalf of the aging and national health care. She was a staff member on the Public Program Committee for the 1980 White House Conference on the Aging; and a member of the National Leadership Council comprising thirty organizations concerned with life aspects of the elderly (housing, welfare, legal matters, etc.); and a member of the Advisory Board of the Robert Wood Johnson Foundation on the Interfaith Volunteer Caregivers Program that awarded three-year grants of $125,000 each to twenty-five coalitions of churches and synagogues for model projects that demonstrated effective development and coordination of volunteer services in local communities to assist the frail and elderly and disabled to remain in their homes, rather than be institutionalized. She also published a research paper "The Black Church and the Elderly" in the 1983 fall issue of the *Journal of the Western Gerontological Society.* (*Official Journal, 42nd Quad. Sess. Gen. Conf.*, pp. 480-81)

Dr. Kyles had an audience with Dr. Fish, commissioner of aging, during the 1984-88 quadrennium. She served as director of the Exhibits at the General Convention on Christian Education; was conference director of Christian Education of the Philadelphia/Baltimore Conference; conducted four education leadership institutes; and was writer of the *Junior Quarterly* of the School Church Literature Department. She

African Methodist Episcopal Zion Church

was honored for dedicated, outstanding leadership and work in public service with the following awards: the 1986 Living Legacy Award by the National Caucus and Center on Black Aged; the first Josephine H. Kyles Award by the YWCA of the National Capital Area; a Certificate of Appreciation from Galbraith A. M. E. Zion Church, Washington, D. C.; and an Award of Appreciation from John Wesley A. M. E. Zion Church, Washington, D. C. She was also honored by the Retired Senior Volunteer Program (RSVP) for a decade of outstanding service as a volunteer. (*Official Journal, 43rd Quad. Sess. Gen. Conf.*, pp. 578-79)

As earlier indicated, Dr. Kyles was awarded the first Dr. James W. Eichelberger Meritorious Service Award at the General Convention of Christian Education, April 5-10, 1990. She continued her work with the Christian Education Department as a member of the Home and Church Board, the General Convention Exhibit Coordinator, and director of Christian Education of the Philadelphia and Baltimore Conference. Mrs. Kyles, widow of the late Bishop Lynwood Westinghouse Kyles, is now director emerita in her official capacity as a professional servant of the church. During the 1996 session of General Conference at the Bicentennial Gala Celebration, Dr. Kyles was among the recipients of the James Varick Freedom Medal Award. (*Official Journal, 44th Quad. Sess., Gen., Conf.*, p. 611; "Department of Christian Education, A. M. E. Zion Church, 45th Quad. Report, 1992-96," p. 5)

General Convention Executive Committee

In her first report to General Conference in 1976, Dr. Senora B. Lawson, president of the General Convention Executive Committee, reported that she had traveled during the quadrennium to workshops in Los Angeles, California; Dallas, Texas; Wilmington, North Carolina; Norfolk, Virginia and its environs; and Chicago, Illinois. She served as Adult Instructor in her local church, Girl Scout Leader, and Trainer and Teacher of a Mission Class in the Virginia Conference. Members of her staff included Mrs. Ola M. Crawley, Mr. D. D. Garrett, and Mr. Arthur Brooks. During the 1976-80 quadrennium, Dr. Lawson, president of the General Convention Executive Committee, reported that she had attended most of the workshops in the Virginia Conference, the NCYC winter meeting in Pittsburgh, Pennsylvania, the Albemarle Conference in North Carolina, and the 14th Plenary Session of COCU in Cincinnati, Ohio. She served as a guest instructor of thirty or more adults in California at a Baptist Institute with the theme "Helping Adults to Sharpen and Improve Their Skills in Adult Work." Dr. Lawson died suddenly while attending the National Christian Youth Council meeting on December 27, 1982 at Lomax A. M. E. Zion Church in Arlington, Virginia. The General Convention Executive Committee was replaced by the Executive Committee of the Assembly of

Christian Education: Home and Church

Christian Educators (ACE), the new agency established to plan General Conventions of the Christian Education Department on an ongoing basis. *(Official Journals, 40th Quad. Sess. Gen. Conf.,* pp. 388-89; *41st Quad. Sess.,* pp. 431-32; *42nd Quad. Sess.,* p. 473)

Commission on Youth Ministry

During the years 1972-74, the Rev. C. R. Thompson, administrative assistant to the secretary of the Christian Education Department, was chairperson of the Commission on Youth Ministry, an agency responsible for "ministry to, by, and with youth." He was involved in developing and coordinating the plans and program for the General Convention on Christian Education and General Youth Assembly held at Livingstone College, Salisbury, North Carolina, August 4-9, 1974, which brought together two thousand youths and laid the foundation for the National Christian Youth Council. *(Official Journal, 40th Quad. Sess.,* Gen. Conf., pp. 380-81)

The Rev. (now Bishop) Nathaniel Jarrett participated in the following activities during the 1976-80 quadrennium: NCYC Convention, at Jackson Memorial A. M. E. Zion Church, Hempstead, Long Island, N. Y., December 26-29, 1976; 54th International Christian Endeavor Convention, Albright College, Reading, Pennsylvania, July 11-15, 1977; NCYC Convention, Kyles Temple A. M. E. Zion Church, Sacramento, California, December 27-30, 1977; Christian Education Workshop, Second A. M. E. Zion Church, Los Angeles, California, December 31, 1977; General Convention on Christian Education, Livingstone College, Salisbury, North Carolina, August 6-11, 1978; NCYC Convention, Wesley Center A. M. E. Zion Church, Pittsburgh, Pennsylvania, December 27-30, 1978; North American Youth Coalition for Global Interdependence, Bolton, Ontario, Canada, October 12-14, 1979; NCYC Convention, Butler Chapel A. M. E. Zion Church, Tuskegee, Alabama, December 27-30, 1979; Christian Education Workshop, St. Peter's A. M. E. Zion Church, Cleveland, Ohio; and the annual Fall and Spring Trustee Board meetings of the International Christian Endeavor. *(Official Journal, 41st Quad. Sess., Gen. Conf.,* pp. 432-33)

During the years 1980-84, among his many activities on behalf of Christian youth education, Dr. Jarrett was featured speaker at the World Christian Endeavor Union, in Guatemala City, Guatemala, in July 1980; at the Christian Education Convention, in Portland, Maine, in August 1981; at the Second Century Conference, International Society of Christian Endeavor, in Edinburgh, Scotland, in August 1982; at the Christian Endeavor Convention, in Seattle, Washington, in July 1983; and was a member of the Executive and Program Committee, International Society of Christian Endeavor, in Holland, Michigan in 1984. Dr. Jarrett worked on the outline of a series of lectures to enhance Christian education during the 1984-88 quadrennium. The lectures centered on the three stages of human development and appropriate Christian education programming for each stage. (*Official Journals, 43rd Quad. Sess. Gen. Conf.*, pp. 582-83; *42nd Quad. Sess.*, pp. 483-84)

The Rev. Nathaniel Jarrett resigned as chairperson of the Commission on Youth Ministry because of his election to the Judicial Council of the denomination at the 1988 General Conference. Rev. Thaddeus Steele succeeded him as chairperson of the Commission on Youth Ministry during the 1988-92 quadrennium. With establishment of the Young Adults in Christian Ministry (YACM) in 1990, the age focus was shifted slightly to address the needs of young persons between 22-40 years of age. At the 1990 General Convention on Christian Education, the charter Steering Committee elected the Rev. W. Darin Moore chairperson. In 1994, he was replaced by Ms. Nora Kathy McNeill as YACM chairperson. Rev. Moore is currently serving as advisor for Young Adults, with Rev. Kathi Brown as assistant advisor. ("Dept. of Christian Education, A. M. E. Zion Church, Quad. Report, 1992-96," pp. 15-16)

Adult Ministry
At the 39th General Conference meeting in 1976, Ms. Willie M. Stone, chairperson of the Commission on Adult Ministry, expressed gratitude for the certificate awarded her for five years of service to the Christian Education Department. She proposed basic guidelines for the Adult Education Program. The chairperson of the Commission on Audio-Visual Education, Ms. Mamie E. Gordon, who was also a staff member of Livingstone College and taught the course on audio-visuals during the 1974 General Convention on Christian Education, urged all departments of Christian Education to enhance the content of lessons through greater use of audio-visuals. (*Official Journal, 39th Quad. Sess. Gen. Conf.*, p. 389)

There were no subsequent reports for adult ministry until 1988, when the Rev. (now Bishop) Enoch B. Rochester was responsible for this ministry during 1984-88. In his report to the 43rd General Conference, he stressed the need to fund the Board of Christian Education adequately for staff and support staff to assist congregations, districts, conferences, and episcopal areas. (*Official Journal, 43rd Quad. Sess. Gen. Conf.*, p. 619).

Commission on Children's Ministry
The chairperson of the Commission on Children's Ministry during 1972-76 was the Rev. Mrs. Willie Aldrich who stressed the importance of Christian Education to the life

214

of the church. Rev. Aldrich was involved in the planning and attended National Christian Education meetings; NCYC meetings; and the General Convention on Education. She also conducted workshops for various presiding elder districts, served on the summer planning committee and staff for the Ministers and Lay Institute at the W. J. Walls Center at Hood Theological Seminary, and was director of Christian Education for the Salisbury District of the Western North Carolina Conference. Rev. Aldrich proposed that a task force comprising Christian educators study Christian education in the A. M. E. Zion Church and make recommendations to the Connectional Council for its improvement. (*Official Journal, 40th Quad. Sess. Gen Conf.*, pp. 382-83)

Rev. Aldrich planned, directed, supervised, and/or participated in workshops and scheduled mass meetings/conferences during 1980-84 in the Winston-Salem District; West Central North Carolina Conference; Western North Carolina Conference; and the National Christian Youth Council (NCYC) at the national, conference, district, and local levels. She organized a Festival of Choirs, including children, youth, and adults in the Salisbury District, Western North Carolina Conference. She served as conference secretary of the Western North Carolina Conference and as vice chairperson of the Christian Education Board at Soldiers Memorial A. M. E. Zion Church. She initiated the Children's and Youth Revival at the district level. Rev. Aldrich was also chairperson of Children's Ministry during 1988-92. She complained that her vision had not been realized over the years because of inadequate financing of the agency. Rev. Aldrich is curator at the Heritage Hall facility at Livingstone College in Salisbury, North Carolina. (*Official Journal, 42nd Quad. Sess. Gen. Conf.*, p. 481-82; *44th Quad. Sess.*, pp. 620-21)

In 1994, Dr. Helen C. Scott-Carter, a retired school teacher and administrator in the District of Columbia school system as well as the wife of the senior pastor of Contee A. M. E. Zion Church, Washington, D. C., the Rev. Manford Carter, was appointed director of Children's Ministry. She organized one-day workshops at the General Convention on Christian Education in 1994 on the theme "Called to Be Committed Disciples at the Dawn of the 21st Century." More than forty children participated in the workshops. Her other activities during 1994-96 included participation in annual conferences; workshops for children; writing a history of the A. M. E. Zion Church; study guides, and activity packages for young children. Her husband, the Rev. Manford Carter, supports and assists his wife in her office as director of Children's Ministry. ("The Department of Christian Education, A. M. E. Zion Church, Quad. Report, 1992-1996," pp. 17-20)

African Methodist Episcopal Zion Church

Commission on Boy Scouting

Another agency nurtured by the Christian Education Department for all of the A. M. E. Zion Church is the Boy Scouts of America (BSA). During 1972-92, the national chairman of Boy Scouting was Mr. James E. Boger of the Philadelphia and Baltimore Conference, a long-time member of Lomax A. M. E. Zion Church, Arlington, Virginia, Mr. Boger succeeded Mr. Simon Lowrey, also a member of the Philadelphia and Baltimore Conference and a long-time member at John Wesley A. M. E. Zion Church in Washington, D. C. According to Information Services Report, No.557, Boy Scouts of America, New Brunswick, N. J., there were 179 Boy Scout units and 2,576 Boy Scouts registered in the A. M. E. Zion Church in 1975.

During 1976-80, a conference on scouting involving six black denominations was held in 1978 at the St. Paul School of Theology in Kansas City, Missouri. It was attended by fifty representatives from the A. M. E. Zion, A. M. E., C. M. E., National Baptist Convention, U. S. A., Progressive National Baptist Convention, and the National Baptist Convention of America. These black denominations had decided to make the program of the Boy Scouts a significant part of their youth ministry. A. M. E. Zion representatives included Bishop John H. Miller, Sr., Rev. George L. Blackwell, Mr. James E. Boger, Mr. Grady Moss, Mr. T. W. Campbell, the Revs., W. A. Potter, W. H. Seals, and Mr. P. Smith. Mr. James E. Boger also attended two training conferences at Philmont Training Center, Cimmaroon, New Mexico, 1976-77 and the United Methodist Workshop, Lake Junaluska, North Carolina in 1979. Mr. Boger emphasized the need to "recruit, train, inspire and encourage" Scout Coordinators who would work with the local organization, the District BSA Council and/or his Conference Scout Coordinating Committee in order to achieve the youth objectives of the organization. Mr. Boger received ten certificates or awards from the national and regional councils of the BSA as well as three from national churches. He was also cited at Philmont, New Mexico. The A. M. E. Zion Boy Scouts in the Washington, D. C. area in 1977 and 1979 presented the colors when the Livingstone College Band played during a Redskins football game in Washington, D. C. (*Official Journal, 41st Quad. Sess., Gen. Conf.*, pp. 433-34)

During the 1980-84 quadrennium, Mr. Boger participated in the joint publication of the brochure Exploring and Your Youth Ministry, which was published by the A. M. E., A. M. E. Zion, C. M. E. Churches and the Boy Scouts. During the next two quadrennia, Mr. Boger continued to emphasize the critical need to recruit Scout Coordinators to train Boy Scouts. He saw the agency as a powerful instrument for revitalizing our culture, customs and traditions. In his final report to the 1992 General Conference, he cited Boy Scouts membership in the A. M. E. Zion Church: 97 Scout

Christian Education: Home and Church

units; 1,300 youth members; and 530 adult members. (*Official Journal, 42nd Quad. Sess. Gen. Conf.*, pp. 583-84; 43rd Quad. Sess., pp. 584-85; *44th Quad. Sess.*, pp. 622-23)

The Rev. Harold O. Robinson was appointed director of the Boy Scouts Ministry in 1994. Rev. Robinson's activities during 1994-96 included organizing the first African Boy Scout troop in Seshego, South Africa and delivery of the BAden-Powell Founder's Day Lecture at Pietersburg for the Boy Scouts of South Africa; organizing workshops; presenting the goals and objectives of the Boy Scouts; compilation of a directory of A. M. E. Zion Boy Scouts; and representing the A. M. E. Zion and A. M. E. Churches at the South African Centennial Celebration in Johannesburg, South Africa, where President Nelson Mandela was the banquet speaker. Rev. Robinson has proposed using the renovated campgrounds at Camp Dorothy Walls at Black Mountain, North Carolina for overnight camping for Boy Scouts. ("The Dept. of Christian Education, A. M. E. Zion Church, Quad. Report, 1992-1996," pp. 23-25)

Commission on Girl Scouting

From 1972-88, Mrs. Gertrude Kelley was commissioner of the Girl Scout Ministry. In this capacity, she attended the quadrennial General Conventions on Christian Education. At these conventions, Mrs. Kelley conducted classes and mounted exhibits on scouting. She was also a regular participant at the National Girl Scout Conventions and at the annual meetings of the Girl Scout Council of Washington, D. C. Other significant events in which she was a participant included her attendance on March 17, 1975, at the 25th Anniversary of the Girl Scouts of Mother Zion A. M. E. Zion Church, New York City. Mrs. Kelley's service to the Girl Scouts and to the A. M. E. Zion Church were acknowledged as follows: on March 6, 1976, she received the 30-year pin of the Girl Scouts of America; on February 23, 1980, Mrs. Kelley received the 35-year pin and awards and plaques from the Christian Education Department, Girl Scouts, and the Woman's Home and Overseas Missionary Society of Washington, D. C.; on February 11, 1984, she was the recipient of a 40-year pin and numeral from the Girl Scout Council of the Nation's Capital. At the 43rd General Conference Mrs. Kelley retired as chairperson of Girl Scouting after forty-one years of Girl Scout service. On November 2, 1985, a special tribute was held in her honor: "Stroll Down Memory Lane: 41 Years of Girl Scout Service," at her home church, Galbraith A. M. E. Zion Church, Washington, D. C. Mrs. Kelley was replaced by Mrs. Nellie M. Dudley, a member of her staff, who reported for the first time at the 44th General Conference. Mrs. Kelley was assisted by the following directors/leaders: Mrs. Nellie M. Dudley, Washington, D. C., Girl Scout director, Mrs. Mary H. McGhee, Salisbury,

African Methodist Episcopal Zion Church

Maryland; Mrs. Brunhilda M. Simmons, Girl Scout Leader at Mother Zion, New York City; and Ms. Evelyn Hodge, Philadelphia, Pennsylvania. (*Official Journal, 40th Quad. Sess. Gen. Conf.*, p. 371; *41st Quad. Sess.*, 387-88; *42nd Quad. Sess.*, pp. 434-35; *43rd Quad. Sess.*, pp. 586-87; *44th Quad. Sess.*, pp. 624-25)

General Commission on Chaplains and Armed Forces

The A. M. E. Zion Church retained membership in the General Commission on Chaplains and Armed Forces personnel through the chairperson of the Board of Christian Education until the demise of the organization in October 1981. The General Commission had its headquarters in Washington, D. C. during the years of its existence from 1917-81. Bishops Stephen Gill Spottswood, Herbert Bell Shaw, and Alfred Gilbert Dunston, Jr., served respectively as the A. M. E. Zion representative and member of the General Commission for the terms of their active episcopacy. During the 1972-76 quadrennium, Chaplain Col. Raymond E. Tinsley served as chairperson of the A. M. E. Zion Church Commission on Overseas Ministry. Rev. W. Robert Johnson, III, general secretary-auditor of the denomination, is now the official certifying officer of the A. M. E. Zion Church to the current National Conference on Ministry to the Armed Forces and is accountable to the Board of Bishops and the General Conference. (*Official Journals, 40th Quad. Sess. Gen. Conf.*, pp. 371-72; *42nd Quad. Sess.*, p. 476)

The general secretary met annually during the 1976-80 quadrennium with the former commission, which was represented by thirty-three member communions and several consultative and contributing bodies. Bishops Alfred G. Dunston, Jr., and Herbert Bell Shaw were members of the commission, with Bishop Dunston serving as the endorsing agent of the denomination. (*Official Journal, 41st Quad. Sess. Gen. Conf.*, p. 427)

The final business meeting of the general Commission on Chaplains and Armed Forces Personnel, which was established as a broad Protestant liaison agency with the federal government in policy matters that affected the Chaplaincy of the Armed Forces and other agencies, was held October 26, 1981. The Commission was ended on December 31st and was replaced by the new National Conference on Ministry to the Armed Forces. (*Official Journal, 42nd Quad. Sess. Gen. Conf.*, p. 476)

Members of the Christian Education Home and Church Division Board from 1972-2000 have been :

Christian Education: Home and Church

1972-76
Bishop John H. Miller, chairperson
Bishop George J. Leake, 1st vice chairperson
Bishop Herbert B. Shaw, 2nd vice chairperson
Members:
1. Rev. George J. Hill
2. Rev. Ruben L. Drew
3. Rev. Cameron Jackson
4. Rev. J. E. Cook
5. Rev. W. T. Kennedy
6. Rev. Herman Anderson
7. Mrs. Mattie Eagan
8. Rev. G. Sims Rivers
9. Rev. J. B. Bennett
10. Rev. James M. Sloan
11. Rev. L. Roy Bennett
12. Mrs. Annette Whitted

1976-80
Bishop John H. Miller, chairperson
Bishop W. A. Hilliard, 1st vice chairperson
Bishop G. J. Leake, 2nd vice chairperson
Members:
1. Rev. A. E. Whitted
2. Rev. W. R. Johnson
3. Rev. Nathaniel Jarrett
4. Rev. James E. Cook
5. Rev. Marshall Strickland
6. Rev. Arthur W. Walls, Sr.
7. Rev. S. L. Brown
8. Rev. R. M. Richmond
9. Rev. David L. Scott
10. Rev. Dennis Bradley
11. Rev. Parree Porter
12. Rev. R. L. Dawson

1980-84
Bishop John H. Miller, Sr., chairperson
Bishop George J. Leake, III, 1st vice chairperson
Bishop C. R. Coleman, 2nd vice chairperson
Members:
1. Dr. C. D. Rippy
2. Rev. Enoch B. Rochester
3. Dr. Josephine H. Kyles
4. Miss Georgia Jones
5. Mrs. Louise Davis
6. Rev. G. L. Scott
7. Mr. M. M. Sittons
8. Rev. J. A. Farnsworth
9. Mrs. Gwen Johnson
10. Rev. G. Sims Rivers
11. Mrs. Minnie K. Harvey
12. Rev. G. Ray Coleman

African Methodist Episcopal Zion Church

1984-88

Bishop J. H. Miller, chairperson
Bishop C. R. Coleman, 1st vice chairperson
Bishop W. A. Hilliard, 2nd vice chairperson
Members:

1. Mr. Albert S. Stout
2. Rev. Enoch B. Rochester
3. Mrs. Josephine Kyles
4. Rev. R. M. Dickerson
5. Ms. Della Woodruff
6. Rev. Joseph Johnson
7. Mr. Carson Bethea
8. Rev. W. M. Bryson
9. Mrs. Gwendolyn Johnson
10. Rev. R. M. Richmond
11. Mrs. Minnie K. Harvey
12. Mr. Jasper J. McCormick

1988-92

Bishop Cecil Bishop, chairperson
Bishop C. R. Coleman, 1st vice chairperson
Bishop W. A. Hilliard, 2nd vice chairperson
Members:

1. Dr. C. Guita McKinney
2. Rev. Enoch B. Rochester
3. Mrs. Josephine H. Kyles
4. Rev. Otis R. Hayes
5. Mr. Carson Bethea
6. Rev. Staccato Powell
7. Rev. James H. Taylor, Sr.
8. Rev. Joseph Johnson
9. Rev. W. M. Bryson
10. Rev. R. M. Richmond
11. Mrs. Minnie K. Harvey
12. Mr. Isiah O. Pinkney
13. Ms. Ella Moore

1992-96

Bishop Milton A. Williams, chairperson
Bishop Clarence Carr, 1st vice chairperson
Bishop Enoch B. Rochester, 2nd vice chairperson
Members:

1. Rev. Joan C. Speaks
2. Rev. C. R. Thompson
3. Rev. Curtis Walker
4. Rev. C. Guita McKinney
5. Rev. Warren M. Brown
6. Ms. Ella Moore
7. Rev. Cynthia Russell
8. Rev. W. M. Bryson
9. Rev. Claude Shufford
10. Rev. Nathaniel Jarrett
11. Rev. Gary W. Burns
12. Rev. Mary Helen Moore

Christian Education: Home and Church

1996-2000
Bishop Milton A. Williams, chairperson
Bishop Clarence Carr, 1st vice chairperson
Bishop Enoch B. Rochester, 2nd vice chairperson
Members:

1. Rev. Andrew Smoke
2. Rev. Alvin T. Durant
3. Rev. Gloria M. Snipes
4. Rev. Melinda Moore
5. Rev. Charlie O. Caldwell
6. Rev. George Crenshaw
7. Rev. Claude A. Shufford
8. Rev. Gloria Moore
9. Rev. Curtis Walker
10. Rev. Mary Helen Moore
11. Rev. William M. Bryson
12. Ms. Ruth Gough

Schools and Colleges

The reports of the individual schools and colleges of the Christian Education Department School and College Division are examined separately because the heads of these institutions report directly to General Conference and are under the supervision of Boards of Trustees separate from the National Board of Christian Education.

CHRISTIAN EDUCATION
SCHOOL AND COLLEGE DIVISION

SECRETARY George L. Blackwell emphasized the significance of A. M. E. Zion's schools and colleges when he addressed the 41st General Conference:

> The church has no treasure more valuable than the institutions of higher learning founded and nurtured by it. . . .The A. M. E. Zion Church has always counted on the marriage of liberal learning and vital piety as being the most profound form of faithfulness in the gospel. It has been founded on the simple notion that all proper judgements, actions, political gestures, acts of love and trust, and acts of moral heroism ultimately are grounded in the integrated life of faith and reason. At no time in the history of the A. M. E. Zion Church has the need for our schools been more urgent than now. . . .We need, today, a renewed sense of reason and responsibility, under God and through faith, that will again emanate from our senior and junior colleges . . . that once provided the only education for Black children in those areas. (*Official Journal, 41st Sess. Gen. Conf.*, p. 423)

The Christian Education Department School and College Division has responsibility for overall administration and supervision of secondary schools and junior colleges under the auspices of the A. M. E. Zion Church. It approves budgets, campus building plans, elects trustees based on the nomination of the respective chairperson of the board of each institution; requires accurate records and audits; and plans for educational institutes. The institutions in this division include: Clinton Junior College, Rock Hill, South Carolina; Lomax-Hannon Junior College, Greenville, Alabama; Johnson Memorial Institute, Batesville, Mississippi; Walters Institute, Warren, Arkansas; Atkinson College, Madisonville, Kentucky, and Dinwiddie Normal and Industrial School, Dinwiddie, Virginia.

Lomax—Hannon Junior College
Lomax-Hannon Junior College was first established in 1893 as Greenville High School by Bishop Thomas H. Lomax, leading elders in the East Alabama Conference, and members of Butler A. M. E. Zion Chapel, Greenville, Alabama. The Rev. Allen Hannon, then a former presiding elder of the Montgomery District, helped to acquire the land for what was the first high school, for either blacks or whites, in Butler County, Alabama. The mission envisioned in establishing Lomax-Hannon was to produce edu-

Christian Education: School and College

cated ministers for the black community. (Walls, *The African Methodist Episcopal Zion Church*, pp. 322-23)

This junior college is located on one of three parcels of land of a 250-acre campus in Greenville, Alabama. It is the only junior college of either race in Butler County or Greenville, Alabama. The property currently comprises fourteen buildings — five rental dwellings, the president's residence, teacher's cottage, Founder's Dormitory, J. W. Alstork Memorial Building, Montgomery Hall, Dunston Hall, Zion Hall, and C. Mifflin Smith Memorial Building. This last edifice was dedicated on March 4, 1980. (*Official Journal, 41st Quad. Sess. Gen. Conf.*, p. 436)

On July 26, 1972, Dr. B. M. Montgomery who had served with distinction as president of Lomax-Hannon College Junior College since 1968 resigned. Dr. Montgomery's ambition was not to make Lomax-Hannon a great big school but one of the best small schools in the state. Lomax Hannon's story was one of insufficient funds, but it was a school that put forth every effort to do the best with what they were given. (*Official Journal, 39th Quad. Sess. Gen. Conf.*, pp. 346-47; *40th Quad. Sess.*, p. 459)

The Rev. C. Mifflin Smith was appointed on August 15, 1972 to succeed Dr. Montgomery as president. He remained in office until his death on November 1, 1977. However, Dr. Smith did live to see and achieve many of his objectives. During his administration, the college met the eligibility requirements for participation in the following federal aid to education programs: the Higher Education Act of 1965 (as amended); the Title IV Student Assistant Programs: A. Educational Opportunity Grants (1)Basic (2) Supplemental (3) Talent Search, Upward Bound, and Special Student Services B. Guaranteed Student Loan Program C. College Work-Study Program D. National Direct Student Loan Program. The college was listed in the Higher Education Directory and received the following grants in 1973: (1) The United States Department of Agriculture (USDA) School Lunch Program ,which was phased out in 1975; (2) the EAA, Title II Library Program (for library books); (3) Department of Health, Education, and Welfare (HEW) "Help Communities Help Themselves Grant"; (4) Alabama State Council on the Art and Humanities, and the National Endowment of the Arts Grant (for two summers); (5) Alabama State University Graduate Extension Courses at Lomax-Hannon. (*Official Journal, 40th Quad. Sess. Gen. Conf.*, p. 393)

The college also received certification by the Alabama State Department of Veteran Affairs to provide training for persons who served in the Armed Forces and was also approved in 1974 as a junior college eligible to issue the AA Degree by the Alabama State Department of Education. It was admitted on first-year probation to the Alabama Junior College Athletic Conference. The junior college added an addition to the Dunston Gymnasium at a cost of $27,000 in addition to other physical improvements. It was also involved in the development of a Comprehensive Community Services Complex for the elderly and handicapped to serve rural citizens in counties in the vicinity of the school through a cooperative venture by the A. M. E. Zion and Baptist Churches and the participation of Selma University. (Ibid.)

The student body increased from seven in the 1972-73 school year to 151 in the 1975-76 school year. The administrative staff and faculty included Ms. Dorinda Hurst, secretary to the president; Rev. James E. Cook, dean of the college and part-time instructor; Mrs. Theodora Shippy Smith, administrative assistant and part-time instructor; Mr. Frank Lewis, dean of Evening School and instructor; Ms. Barbara Maye, secretary to the dean; Mr. W. J. Longmire, treasurer, superintendent of buildings and grounds, and athletic director; Ms. Ruby Love, fiscal officer; Ms. Brenda Miller, financial director; Mr. Gerald Ferguson, English and Spanish instructor; Ms. Jacqueland Hemphill, music and social science instructor; Mrs. Lula P. Seay, librarian, and instructor; Ms. Ruby H. Shambray, social science and education instructor; and Mr. Willie Watkins, coach and physical education instructor. In 1976, Lomax-Hannon graduated thirty-nine students, the largest graduating class in its history. At the May 1976 commencement at Livingstone College, an honorary Doctor of Humane Letters was conferred on President C. Mifflin Smith, and Hood Theological Seminary conferred a honorary Doctor of Divinity on Dean James E. Cook. In March 1977, the Alabama Historical Commission designated Lomax-Hannon a significant landmark and added the school to the Alabama Register of Landmarks and Heritage. (*Official Journal, 41st Quad. Sess. Gen. Conf.*, pp, 511-12)

When President C. Mifflin Smith passed away, Bishop Alfred G. Dunston, Jr., chairperson of the Board of Trustees, approved an Interim Committee to guide the college until a new president was appointed. The members of the committee were Mr. W. J. Longmire, Mrs. Theodora S. Smith, Dr. James E. Cook, Rev. Morgan McCampbell, and Mr. Jerome Harris. Notable achievements during the 1976-80 quadrennium included beginning construction of a new male hall residence and cafeteria in 1976; the implementation of a Senior Citizens Day Care Center; a National Science Foundation Grant for two years to improve physical science and the mathematics laboratory; the creation of a biological science laboratory and a media center; for upgrading the faculty and the library. In August, 1977, CETA (Comprehensive Employment Training Act) was implemented for employment and training in respect of the library, cafeteria, senior citizen, and recreational aide. In 1978, a Special Services Program was implemented to provide remedial reading and mathematics; academic, career, and personal counselling; and cultural enrichment and tutorial programs. A hardwood floor was laid

Christian Education: School and College

in the main area of the Dunston Gymnatorium. The College Work Study Fund was increased, and the Business Education Department was upgraded in 1979.On March 4, 1980, the C. Mifflin Smith Memorial Building was dedicated. (*Official Journal, 41st Quad. Sess. Gen. Conf.*, pp. 436-37)

Lomax-Hannon fell on hard times during the 1980-84 period. The Interim Committee reported to the 41st General Conference, meeting in Greensboro, North Carolina in May, 1980 that there was an immediate need for $100,000 to pay debts to the Internal Revenue Service and other agencies. An appeal in 1983 to the Connectional Council yielded $100,200, but it did not fully cover the shortfall. The Connectional Council established a Task Force: to insure that the funds would be disbursed as intended; to review the operation of the college; and to make corrective recommendations. The following persons were named to the Task Force: Rev. Richard L. Fisher; Rev. A. E. White, Dr. Novie S. Chaney, Dr. T. X. Graham, Dr. C. DuPont Rippy, Mrs. Josephine Riggins, Dr. Clara Robertson, Dr. Frank Jones, Rev. Dennis Proctor, Rev. William M. White, Sr., Interim President James E. Cook and Secretary George L. Blackwell of the Christian Education Department served as consultants. The Connectional Council also approved a mechanism for raising this amount. Bishop John H. Miller was the chairperson of the Board of Trustees. (*Official Journal, 42nd Quad. Sess., Gen. Conf.*, p. 561)

As the result of an audit, it was determined that Lomax-Hannon Junior College was in debt for approximately $661,170.68 to the Internal Revenue Service, the U. S. Office of Education, the State of Alabama Department of Revenue, and the Department of Christian Education of the A. M. E. Zion Church. In addition, salaries, utility bills, state withholding taxes, State Unemployment Insurance, liability insurance, loans, general bills and a mortgage were also in arrears. Recommendations were made to the General Conference by the Task Force to discontinue all academic pursuits until the college was free from indebtedness and to restructure the curriculum, staff, and capital improvements. At the 1984 General Conference, the Christian Education Department was given the responsibility of eliminating the financial debt on Lomax-Hannon. During the quadrennium, the U. S. Department of Education and others informed the school of additional financial responsibility. (Ibid., pp. 561-562)

The Task Force recommended that (1) the Lomax-Hannon Commission be continued until the future of the school could be determined; (2) that the institution be provided $45,000.00 annually for normal operational costs; (3) that a feasibility study be made to determine the best use of this facility; and (4) that the remaining $205,000.00 of the Lomax-Hannon annual $250,000.00 allocation be placed in escrow to be used to care for any additional liabilities to the federal and state governments, to finance the cost of a feasibility study, and to provide the necessary funds for programs that could best be carried out at the institution. Bishop Cecil Bishop was added to the commission, and Dr. John H. Winston was appointed as consultant. (*Official Journal, 43rd Quad. Sess., Gen. Conf.*, p. 706)

The Report of the Task Force to the 44th General Conference indicated that all debts on the Lomax-Hannon Junior College had been paid, but, in order for the property to be used, major improvements had to be made to the Montgomery Building, the Alstork Building, the Smith Building, the Boy's Dormitory, and the Dunston Gymnatorium for which $386,506.94 was paid. The property was used for leadership training institutes, retreats, a senior care center and other related functions. The overseas delegates to the Quadrennial Convention of the W. H. &. O. M. Society were housed at the college prior to and after the convention. (*Official Journal, 44th Quad. Sess., Gen. Conf.*, pp. 736-37)

On January 24, 1996, Bishop Richard K. Thompson recommended that Rev. David L. Knight serve as interim president of Lomax-Hannon Junior College. He was approved by the Board of Trustees of the college and given responsibility for developing Lomax-Hannon as an Alternative School for At-Risk Students within the Ninth Episcopal District and throughout Zion. ("Report to the Board of Bishops, 27 Feb.- 1 Mar 1996.")

The Lomax-Hannon Alternative School for At-Risk Students has developed the following Mission Statement: "The mission of Lomax-Hannon Alternative School is to produce a literate and disciplined life-long learner, who can live, interact and be productive in our diverse society. We will accomplish this by providing a well-balanced, relevant and challenging curriculum, which will be taught by a professional, dedicated and spirited staff. The teaching will be done in an environment that is conducive to learning and supported by the A. M. E. Zion Church, parents, and the residential and businesses communities." The primary focus of the school is to provide at-risk students with the opportunity to earn a high school diploma and to develop life-long skills in a non-traditional school setting. (Ibid., pp. 1-2)

At the 45th General Conference, President Knight reported numerous physical improvements made on campus. Zion Hall was demolished; some buildings were air conditioned; landscaping, sidewalks, bathrooms, new plumbing, lighting, new or repaired flooring, fire alarm systems, new furniture, and a portable communion rail were some of the many improvements. In addition to the Senior Adult Day Care Program, the facility is used for annual conferences, convocations, check-up meetings,

Christian Education: School and College

Founders' Day, retreats, banquets, institutes, and workshops. The "only goal for the quadrennium was to breathe life back into Lomax-Hannon, and generate a resurgence of a sense of ownership and responsibility for our institution." The approaching quadrennium (1996-2000) is the season for Lomax-Hannon Junior College to fulfill its destiny, and open its doors once again to educate young black men and women. ("Report of the Interim President of Lomax-Hannon to the 45th Quad. Sess., Gen. Conf." pp. 2-4)

Clinton Junior College

Clinton Junior College was founded as Clinton Institute in Rock Hill, South Carolina, in 1894, by Presiding Elder Nero A. Crockett of the Yorkville District and the Rev. W. M. Robinson. It was named in honor of the presiding bishop of the episcopal district, Rt. Rev. Isom Caleb Clinton. Clinton College offers two years of high school (college preparation) and two years of college work. (Walls, *The African Methodist Episcopal Zion Church*, pp. 320-21)

For years Clinton College has struggled to survive without adequate funding in a changing educational environment. Under the dedicated leadership of Chairperson Bishop Arthur Marshall, Jr., and President Sallie V. Moreland, Clinton Junior College made significant strides during the 1972-76 quadrennium. With the completion of the Arthur Marshall, Jr. Hall for male students and faculty, the campus comprised six buildings: Walter William Slade Hall, John William Martin Gymnasium, which houses the administrative offices and class and conference rooms; Herbert Bell Shaw Student Union Building for dining, conference, and recreation; Joseph Dixon Cauthen Hall for female students and faculty; and a library that had been recently renovated for temporary use. (*Official Journal, 40th Quad. Sess. Gen. Conf.*, pp. 393-94; *41st Quad. Sess. Gen. Conf.*, p. 436)

An important development in 1973 was the settlement, to the satisfaction of the college, of the litigation with the City of Rock Hill, South Carolina pertaining to the condemnation of college property for a highway right-of-way by the city. Clinton Junior College received Work Study and Supplemental Educational Opportunity Grants, and was in compliance with the various laws of the Veterans Administration Act that enabled enrollment of a sizeable number of veterans. President Moreland emphasized the need for additional qualified teachers, improved salaries, and enrichment opportunities for teachers, and improved library, science laboratory, and other facilities in Business Education to facilitate the offering of the AA degree in Business Education. There were 207 students and twenty-one faculty and staff members in 1976. (*Official Journal, 40th Quad. Sess. Gen. Conf.*, p. 394; 456-57)

African Methodist Episcopal Zion Church

In the following quadrennium, the college qualified for the Science and National Direct Student Loan Grants, Work Study and Supplemental Educational Opportunity Grants. President Moreland stressed the importance "of the acquisition of an adequate library with approved facilities." Three additional parcels of land adjoining the college were purchased in 1978 and 1979. Bishop Arthur Marshall, Jr., was chairperson of the Board of Trustees. (*Official Journal, 41st Quad. Sess. Gen. Conf.*, p. 436)

Clinton College acquired additional land, erected a men's dormitory, and purchased a bus during 1980-84. The college was engaged in a Self-Study Evaluation Program in preparation for full accreditation by the Commission on Colleges of the Southern Association of Colleges and Schools. Committees examined the governing board, administration, finances, faculty, instructional program, library, and student activities. (*Official Journal, 42nd Quad. Sess. Gen. Conf.*, p. 488)

A financial drive was launched to obtain emergency funding for the college at the beginning of the 1984-88 quadrennium. A little more than $59,187 was received. The physical facilities required upgrading to meet accreditation standards. A new library, redesigned curriculum, and better qualified academic staff were needed. Bishop Richard L. Fisher replaced the late Bishop Arthur Marshall, Jr., as chairperson of the Board of Trustees. (*Official Journal, 43rd Quad. Sess. Gen. Conf.*, p. 589)

Following the death of Bishop Marshall in April 1987, the College continued the effort to upgrade the curriculum and staff under the guidance of Bishop Richard L. Fisher, chairperson of the Board of Trustees and President Sallie V. Moreland during 1988-92. Bishop Fisher died in 1991. Happily, the mortgage for Clinton Junior College was retired, which freed up some funds for capital improvements. However, in the fall of 1992, the college suffered a severe setback when Congress cut off all federal aid eligibility to institutions that were not fully accredited. The loss of federal assistance also included federal student financial aid. Since then Clinton has had to survive wholly on its A. M. E. Zion Church allocation, funds raised by the Georgia, South Georgia, Palmetto, Pee Dee, and South Carolina Conferences, and gifts. Following Bishop Fisher's death, Bishop Charles H. Foggie was appointed interim chairperson of the Board of Trustees.(*Official Journal, 44th Quad. Sess., Gen. Conf.*, pp. 627-28)

After serving as president of Clinton Junior College for forty-eight years, Dr. Sallie V. Moreland retired in June 1994. The Board of Trustees voted to name the administration building in her honor, and at the Commencement Exercise in May 1995, the Slade-Moreland Academic and Administration Building was dedicated. Later that year, Dr. Cynthia McCullough-Russell was appointed president of Clinton Junior College. The curriculum was expanded to include the Associate in Divinity program, a four-year, part-time course designed to give non-seminary clergy and laity an opportu-

Christian Education: School and College

nity to gain knowledge and competence in biblical studies, pastoral care, theology, church history, Christian education, and practical ministry. ("Report of President, Clinton Jr. College to 45th Quad. Sess. Gen. Conf.," pp. 2-3)

In order to expand library capabilities during the 1996-97 school year, Clinton Junior College purchased CD-ROM resources and an Internet hookup. Buildings were spruced up and an unused garage was converted into the "Thomas Wilkes Memorial Bookstore" in honor of a deceased alumnus and member of the Board of Trustees. Clinton Junior College still labors to achieve accreditation and challenges the A. M. E. Zion Church to make resources available to this end. (Ibid., p. 5)

A. M. E. Zion Community College, Monrovia, Liberia

The A. M. E. Zion Community College, located in Monrovia, Liberia, was founded in 1987 in Congo Town, a suburb of Monrovia. The Rev. Frederick Umoja, an American missionary, served as president. The college received funds annually from the A. M. E. Zion Church and the Woman's Home and Overseas Missionary Society from Life Members Council funds.

Liberia had been involved in a civil war since 1990, but in support of the nation's educational effort, the A. M. E. Zion Community College was the first institution of higher learning to reopen in 1992. Since then, the number of students attending the institution annually have been 1,250. The number of graduates during the years 1993-96 were as follows:

School Year	Graduates
1993-94	87
1994-95	442
1995-96	415
Total	944

("Report of the President to the 45th Quad. Sess. Gen. Conf.," pp. 5-6)

In 1989, the A. M. E. Zion College Board of Trustees requested the Liberia legislature to grant a charter of incorporation to the A. M. E. Zion Community College to upgrade it to university status. This request was eventually approved, and the school was renamed the *African Methodist Episcopal Zion University*. (Ibid., p. 6)

The A. M. E. Zion University comprises seven colleges: Business and Public Administration; Liberal Arts; Criminal Justice and Law Enforcement Administration; Science and Technology; Allied Health Sciences; Education; and Engineering. (Ibid.)

African Methodist Episcopal Zion Church

Despite the Civil War in Liberia, thirty-seven employees returned to work following the cease fire. The university resumed and graduated students during each successive graduation. However, during 1996, as a consequence of renewed fighting, the school lost over $250 thousand worth of equipment—vehicles, computers, diesel generators, photocopying machines, and other office equipment. Nevertheless, the university was committed to reopen. Thankfully, basic furniture was spared, and the library records were intact. The university's major task during this period was to make modifications that would enable them to reopen fully in September, 1996. (Ibid.)

Hood-Speaks Theological Seminary, Uruan, Akwa Ibom, Nigeria

In June, 1990, Bishop S. Chuka Ekemam, Sr., Bishop of the then 13th Episcopal District, convened a consultative meeting of ministers and leaders of the entire Episcopal District at Bishop Walls Memorial A. M. E. Zion Church, Aba, Nigeria, to improve the ministry of the 13th Episcopal District (Nigeria). The Bishop made known his desire to establish a theological seminary and presented a program for the project to the body. Bishop Ekemam assigned a task force for immediate implementation of the project. The Rev. Dr. J. J. Essien was appointed chairperson, and Rev. T. W. Mbaeri was appointed the secretary. ("Report of the Dean to the 45th Quad. Sess. Gen. Conf.," p. 2)

The Hood-Speaks Seminary was established on October 21, 1991 to provide theological education for the ministry and develop leadership in West Africa. Rev. Essien was appointed dean of the seminary. At the 44th General Conference meeting in Atlanta, Georgia in July, 1992, the school was recognized as a connectional school of the A. M. E. Zion Church, although without budget allocation. Volunteer contributions were given at the connectional meeting in Alabama, by the W. H. &. O. M. Society, Bishop and Mrs. Speaks, Dr. Betty Stith, the Ministers and Lay Association, and by the Connectional Lay Council.(*Official Journal, 44th Quad. Sess. Gen. Conf.*, p. 449; "Report of Bishop Ekemam, 45th Quad. Sess. Gen. Conf.," p. 7) Hood-Speaks Seminary is located in Ndon Ebom, Uruan Local Government Area, Uyo, Akwa Ibom, Nigeria and comprises two dormitories, an office complex that includes a library, a two-classroom block, and a three-bedroom house for the dean. It was declared open on September 21, 1992 with thirty-six students. The first graduation ceremony was held on February 12, 1994. Ten young men and one young woman received the Diploma in Theology.The faculty currently has eight teachers. The student enrollment for the 1992-1993 school year was 61; for 1993-94, 24; for 1994-95, 21; and for 1995-96, 60. The Rev. Reginald Broadnax of Chicago, Illinois, volunteered his services to lecture for three weeks in Nigeria. ("Report of Dean, 45th Quad. Sess. Gen. Conf.," pp. 4-6; pp. 10, 12)

Christian Education: School and College

At the 45th General Conference held in Washington, D. C., in July, 1996, the administration of the school appealed to have Hood-Speaks Theological Seminary included in the 1996-2000 budget. In 1996, the Governing Council of Hood-Speaks included Bishop S. Chuka Ekemam, Sr., chairperson; Chief Emmanuel Iwuanyanwu; His Excellency, Dr. Clement Isong; Chief E. E. Dike; Dr. M. P. Okonny; H. R. H., Edidem I. E. Nyong; Chief E. S. Akpan; Chief O. U. Ekpo; Mrs. F. I. Ekemam; the Rev. Umoh L. Udofa; Mrs. B. A. Fine-Country; Mr. T. Caiafas; the late Chief Jenkins E. Akpan; Chief Ndem Effiong; the Rev. E. J. Umoh; Mr. Samuel T. Anderson; the Rev. Dr. Thad Garrett; and the Rev. Dr. Greg Smith. (Ibid., p. 14 , 16)

Dinwiddie Institute, Dinwiddie, Virginia

The land on which Dinwiddie Institute is built came to the A. M. E. Zion Church as a gift from Mr. Alexander Van Rensaler of Philadelphia. This facility was originally established as Dinwiddie Agricultural and Industrial School and was opened on January 1, 1910, with Prof. T. C. Irwin as its first principal. The main administration building of this institution was completed in 1972 and was named the *Woodyard Memorial Building* in 1975 in honor of educator and statesman Professor W. E. Woodyard who had served the school as principal for thirty years from 1912-44. In 1944, the school was discontinued after a county training school had been established nearby. The Woodyard Memorial Building is an imposing two-storey structure, containing a dining room with capacity for seating 200, a kitchen, four class-rooms, modern bath and toilet facilities, seventeen bedrooms, matron's quarters, a dispensary room, and two lounges, on land of 177.31 acres, located 15 miles north of Petersburg, Virginia. The new building was rebuilt from an existing structure. The property was improved for camping, and a swimming pool was added during the 1960s under the direction of Bishop W. A. Stewart and the Virginia Conference. There are also two other buildings on the campus. The Philadelphia-Baltimore and Virginia Conferences donated much of the equipment for the building. (Walls, *The African Methodist Episcopal Zion Church*, p. 330, 549; *Official Journal, 40th Quad. Sess. Gen. Conf.*, p. 393)

The Rev. John A. Stringfield was supervisor, and Rev. Raymond E. Tinsley was treasurer of this facility during 1976-80. The institute is used for ministerial and lay institutes, district conferences, check-up meetings, retreats, and the WH&OM Society Summer Conferences. Timber on the property was sold to make improvements to the facility. Maintenance support is supplied by area annual conferences and receipts from various activities. Bishop Clinton Coleman was the chairperson of the Board of Trustees during 1984-88. Negotiations between the Dinwiddie County Water Authority,

African Methodist Episcopal Zion Church

the School and College Board of the Christian Education Department, and the local Dinwiddie Institute Board took place regarding the use of a portion of the Dinwiddie property during 1988-92. The land is some distance from the institute building and would not affect its current use. (*Official Journals, 40th Quad. Sess. Gen. Conf.*, p. 393; *41st Quad. Sess.*, p. 437; *43rd Quad. Sess.*, p. 589; *44th Quad. Sess.*, p. 627)

Atkinson Property
The Christian Education Department also supervises other properties, including the Atkinson Property in Madisonville, Kentucky, which comprises 34 acres of land and two buildings. This facility was originally established as Madisonville High School in 1889 by Bishop Thomas H. Lomax and the Revs. E. H. Curry, James B. Johnson, and George B. Weaver. In 1894, John B. Atkinson, a wealthy white citizen interested in the elevation of the black race, helped to ease the financial burden of the school. In January 26, 1896, the school was incorporated as Atkinson Literary and Industrial College, with the Rev. E. H. Curry as its first president. It functioned successfully until 1936 and was thereafter used as a summer religious training institute. (Walls, *The African Methodist Episcopal Zion Church*, p. 325-26)

Bishop J. Clinton Hoggard was chairperson of the Board of Trustees that governed this property during 1972-88. The Kentucky Conference hoped to use this facility for leadership training institutes and possibly a day-care center. Presiding Elder Joseph P. Keaton was supervisor of the Atkinson property. The former academic administration building was unused. During 1980-84, the local treasurer of the Board of Trustees reported a financial balance, which was earmarked for improvements. During 1988-92, Bishop John Miller was the chairperson of the Board of Trustees for this property. (*Official Journals, 40th Quad. Sess. Gen. Conf.*, p. 394; *41st Quad. Sess.* , pp. 437-38; *42nd Quad. Sess.*, pp. 488-89; *44th Quad. Sess.*, p. 627)

Johnson Memorial Institute
The Johnson Memorial Institute had its beginning as Johnson Rural High School, in Batesville, Mississippi. Named after the wealthy black plantation owner Albert J. Johnson who donated the land and advanced money for the erection of two modern buildings, the school was a realization of Johnson's vision to provide post-primary education for rural blacks in the vicinity of Batesville, Mississippi. The school was established in 1919. (Walls, *The African Methodist Episcopal Zion Church*, p. 330)

The present facility comprises about 12 acres of land, on which there is a modern school building, a cottage, and a small A. M. E. Zion Church. The building is used for

Christian Education: School and College

leadership education institutes, district and missionary conferences, and retreats sponsored by annual conferences. Bishop Clinton R. Coleman was chairperson of the board that supervised this property during the years 1972-80. During 1976-80, the property was also used for a Head Start program. A Conference Committee, with Rev. C. C. Goodloe as chairperson, Rev. G. Sims Rivers as secretary, and Mrs. Sadie Kirkwood, who succeeded the late Mr. Tom Cooper, as treasurer and overseer, provides custodial care. The property serves the needs of the episcopal district as well as the community. During 1980-84, the building housed a day-care center and was used for ministerial and lay institutes. Bishop Ruben L. Speaks, chairperson of the Board of Trustees, and local annual conferences envisioned a continuing education program at this school that could include a pre-school program for children; a pre-employment program for adults; and quarterly workshops for ministers and laity. A district-wide finance drive was undertaken to raise funds for building repairs. The building was leased to the Institute of Community Services (ICS) for its Head Start program. The agency installed and equipped a modern kitchen and also provides maintenance care. A new roof was installed by Johnson Memorial during the 1984-88 quadrennium and was paid for by September, 1988. The unleased part of the property is used for ministerial and lay institutes for the presiding elder and episcopal districts. Ms. Sadie Kirkwood was treasurer of Johnson Memorial, and Bishop Speaks was chairperson of the board. During the 1988-92 quadrennium, Bishop Alfred E. White replaced Bishop Speaks as chairperson. (*Official Journals, 40th Quad. Sess. Gen. Conf.*, p. 394; *41st Quad Sess. Gen. Conf.*, p. 437; *42nd Quad. Sess.*, p. 489; *43rd Quad. Sess.*, p. 589)

Walters Institute

Most of the Walters Institute property in Bradley County, Arkansas, comprising 123.11 acres of land, of which 49.10 acres were owned by the City of Warren but was deeded to Walters so long as it was used for educational purposes, was sold to the Warren Industrial Development Corporation of Warren, Arkansas. Children's Colony (for the mentally retarded), an Arkansas state project built on the sold Walters property, was dedicated during the 1976-80 quadrennium. The new facility serves a humanitarian need in Bradley County, Arkansas and provides job opportunities for blacks in Warren, Arkansas. Bishop John H. Miller was chairperson of the Walters Board of Trustees during 1972-80. He supervised the sale and negotiated the new project. During 1988-92, the remaining property was exchanged for clear title to property owned by the family of James W. Hargis in Warren, Arkansas. The new land is adjacent to New Zion A. M. E. Zion Church and has two houses suitable for rehabilitation. Bishop George W.

African Methodist Episcopal Zion Church

Walker was chairperson of the board of trustees during this transaction. (*Official Journals, 40th Quad. Sess. Gen. Conf., 41st Quad. Sess. Gen. Conf.*, p. 395; *44th Quad. Sess.*, p. 627)

Institute for Black Ministries

The Institute for Black Ministries, founded in 1970 to provide theological education from a Black Church perspective, was located in Philadelphia, Pennsylvania. In 1972, at President Vaughn T. Eason's suggestion, the General Conference voted to make the institute a denominational school and referred the matter to the Board of Bishops "for guardianship, development and direction." In 1976, the General Conference appropriated an allocation to the institute, but unfavorable conditions following the retirement of President Eason led to its closing in December 1977. In February 1978, the $15,000 allocation for the institute was transferred to the Department of Christian Education and, although inadequate, was used toward mortgage payments on the property. In 1979, Bishop Herbert Bell Shaw was appointed as a permanent chairperson to manage the situation. On the death of Bishop Shaw, Bishop Charles H. Foggie assumed the chair. During 1980-84, the building was destroyed by fire, and litigation was initiated. The appropriation from the Financial Department continued throughout the quadrennium. The balance of these funds was held in escrow for meeting financial obligations. (*Official Journals, 40th Quad. Sess. Gen. Conf.*, p. 395; *41st Quad. Sess.*, p. 438; *42nd Quad. Sess.*, p. 479)

NCCCUSA Agencies for Higher Education

In 1965, the National Council of Churches of Christ in the U. S. A (NCCCUSA) organized a major conference involving college presidents, trustees, and college board secretaries to organize support for historically black colleges. The United Board for College Development was an outgrowth of this meeting. With headquarters in Atlanta, Georgia, the agency was established by the Division of Higher Education of NCCCUSA. Representatives from church denominations with a particular interest in black higher education and other agencies that support historically black colleges comprised the United Board. Membership also included civil leaders, persons from educational agencies, area consortia involving historically black colleges, and the staff of the National Council of Churches. The secretary of the Christian Education Department of the A. M. E. Zion Church was a member from 1968. The United Board was funded by the participating denominations and the Ford and other foundations. Lomax-Hannon and Clinton Junior Colleges and Livingstone College were institutions on the United Board's roster. Livingstone College benefited from an initial grant of $25,000 from the

Christian Education: School and College

United Board's Student Services Institute, which sought to improve student services in the various institutions. Consultants, workshops, and conferences provided enrichment for student services personnel, chief student administrators, residence hall personnel, guidance and activity counselors, administrative assistants, and student leaders to improve their professional and leadership skills. In April 1975, Dr. Joseph Settle was the chief student services officer of the Student Services Institute at Livingstone College. In 1979, Dr. F. George Shipman was nominated to serve on the United Board. Unfortunately, because of inadequate funding by member denominations, the United Board for College Development closed down on December 21, 1983. The demise of this agency was a lost opportunity for HBCUs to pool their resources for upgrading personnel and student services. (*Official Journals, 40th Quad. Sess. Gen. Conf.*, p. 396; *41st Quad. Sess.*, p. 439; *42nd Quad. Sess.*, p. 476)

The Program Committee for Education in the Society is also part of the National Council of Churches of Christ Division of Higher Education. It comprises denominational executives in the areas of higher education and elementary and secondary public education. Professional and lay persons who are knowledgeable and concerned about issues of contemporary education and the mission of the church are also members. Mrs. Joanne Barnet, a public school teacher and then a student at Boston School of Theology, was appointed by the A. M. E. Zion School and College Board to serve on the Program Committee for Education in Society for the 1979-81 National Council triennium. (*Official Journal, 41st Quad. Sess. Gen. Conf.*, p. 439)

Members of the Department of Christian Education Board of School and College Division from 1972-2000 have been as listed:

1972-76
Bishop Alfred G. Dunston, Jr., chairperson
Bishop Felix S. Anderson, 1st vice chairperson
Bishop C. Eubank Tucker, 2nd vice chairperson
Bishop W. M. Smith, 3rd vice chairperson
Members:

1. Rev. A. E. White	7. Rev. S. M. Taylor
2. Rev. C. E. Bourne	8. Rev. Amanda D. Ballard
3. Rev. William M. Poe	9. Dr. Sallie V. Moreland
4. Rev. E. N. French	10. Rev. C. R. Thompson
5. Rev. J. A. Browne	11. Rev. Richard Fisher
6. Mrs. Ola Crawley	12. Rev. Sidney Waddell

African Methodist Episcopal Zion Church

1976-80

Bishop A. G. Dunston, Jr., chairperson
Bishop W. M. Smith, vice chairperson
Members:

1. Rev. A. E. White
2. Dr. James T. Goode, Sr.
3. Rev. Cameron W. Jackson
4. Rev. Edgar N. French
5. Rev. Jackson A. Browne
6. Rev. J. P. Keaton
7. Rev. J. F. Wills
8. Rev. Amanda D. Ballard
9. Dr. Sallie V. Moreland
10. Rev. C. R. Thompson
11. Mr. Howard Croom
12. Rev. W. M. White

1980-84

Bishop A. G. Dunston, chairperson
Bishop Cecil Bishop, vice chairperson
Members:

1. Rev. J. Thomas Goode, Sr.
2. Dr. Alfred White
3. Rev. Novie Chaney
4. Rev. T. X. Graham
5. Rev. G. Curtis Newby
6. Mrs. Josephine Riggins
7. Dr. Sallie V. Moreland
8. Dr. James E. Cooke
9. Dr. Richard L. Fisher
10. Rev. Bennie Luckette
11. Rev. R. L. Graham
12. Mr. Willie Dowdy

1984-88

Bishop A. G. Dunston, Jr., chairperson
Bishop Cecil Bishop, vice chairperson
Members:

1. Rev. William M. White
2. Rev. William E. Kelly
3. Rev. G. Ray Coleman
4. Rev. T. X. Graham
5. Mrs. Josephine Riggins
6. Mrs. Sallie Moreland
7. Rev. Howard E. Haggler
8. Rev. Bennie Luckett
9. Rev. T. C. Gill
10. Rev. James E. Cooke
11. Rev. Mamie Wilkins
12. Rev. Novie S. Chaney

1988-92

Bishop H. L. Anderson, chairperson
Bishop George W. Walker, vice chairperson

Livingstone College and Hood Theological Seminary

Members:
1. Rev. William M. White
2. Rev. William E. Kelly
3. Mrs. June Slade Collins
4. Ms. E. Loujean Lovett
5. Rev. T. X. Graham
6. Rev. Clarence Carr
7. Rev. Malone Smith
8. Mrs. Loretta Sutton
9. Dr. Sallie V. Moreland
10. Rev. Curtis T. Walker
11. Mr. Melvin Stevens
12. Mr. Jasper McCormick
13. Rev. David Moore

1992-96
Bishop Joseph Johnson, chairperson
Bishop Marshall Strickland, 1st vice chairperson
Bishop Richard K. Thompson, 2nd vice chairperson
Members:
1. Rev. Michael Frencher
2. Rev. David L. Moore
3. Ms. Loretta Sutton
4. Rev. Michael E. Ellis
5. Rev. Cameron W. Jackson
6. Mrs. Brenda Smith
7. Dr. Sallie V. Moreland
8. Rev. Dennis Haggray
9. Rev. A. L. Wilson
10. Rev. William M. White
11. Mrs. Lillian Shelborne
12. Dr. Osofo L. H. McDonald

1996-2000
Bishop Joseph Johnson, chairperson
Bishop Marshall H. Strickland, 1st vice chairperson
Bishop Richard K. Thompson, 2nd vice chairperson
Members:
1. Dr. Michael A. Frencher
2. Rev. Kenneth Monroe
3. Rev. Doretha Hawkins
4. Rev. Ronald E. Miller
5. Rev. David L. Moore
6. Rev. Dr. Cynthia Russell
7. Rev. James H. Taylor
8. Rev. Earle E. Johnson
9. Mrs. Loretta Sutton
10. Rev. Roy A. Swann
11. Rev. Willie G. Johnson
12. Rev. Felix Ofosu

LIVINGSTONE COLLEGE AND HOOD THEOLOGICAL SEMINARY
1972-1996

LIVINGSTONE COLLEGE, nestled among "the maples and oaks" on a campus with imposing structures in Salisbury, North Carolina, was founded by the African Methodist Episcopal Zion Church as Zion Wesley Institute in 1879. Livingstone College is the four-year liberal arts institution of the A. M. E. Zion Church. Hood Theological Seminary, the denomination's school for training Christian ministers, is located on the Livingstone College campus. (Walls, *African Methodist Episcopal Zion Church*, pp. 305-19)

At the 40th Quadrennial Session of General Conference, in Chicago, Illinois, in May 1972, Dr. F. George Shipman, president of Livingstone College and Hood Theological Seminary from 1969-82, urged that attention be given to competitive salaries for faculty and staff of black institutions of higher learning. The quadrennium of 1972-76 was a challenging period in the life of the college. As Livingstone College looked toward its 100th year in 1979 as a vital institution of higher learning for African American students, grave financial challenges confronted the school. The college had a faculty and staff of 150 persons with student enrollment of 926, 938, 962, and 927, respectively, for each school year of the quadrennium. The land, buildings, and physical plant of Livingstone College were valued in excess of $15 million. The college was, however, running a deficit. The deficit increased from $421,859 in 1972-73 to $793,346 in 1974-75. To achieve and sustain accreditation, Livingstone College would have to increase the number of faculty with the doctorate degree, increase staff in student services, and provide fringe benefits for faculty and staff. These were requirements of the Southern Association of Colleges and Schools (SACS)— the accrediting agency— that Livingstone College would have to satisfy. In the late 1970s and early 1980s, the school initiated a $5 million centennial campaign, which was facilitated by a historical film about Livingstone College called *The Coming of Morning*. Dr. F. George Shipman presided during the campaign and this period of austerity. (*Official Journal, 40th Quad. Sess. Gen. Conf.*, p. 435)

During the 1980-84 quadrennium, the Livingstone College family mourned the deaths of Bishop Herbert Bell Shaw, chairperson of the Board of Trustees, and the Rev. Harlee Little, who had faithfully served the college and church for many years. Bishop William Milton Smith assumed the chair of the Board of Trustees after the death of Bishop Shaw. The other active Bishops included: William Alexander Hilliard, Alfred Gilbert Dunston, Jr., Charles Herbert Foggie, James Clinton Hoggard, James Wesley

Livingstone College and Hood Theological Seminary

Wactor, Clinton Ruben Coleman, Arthur Marshall, Jr., John Henry Miller, Sr., George Julius Leakes, III, Ruben Lee Speaks, Mr. Leslie Stokes, alumni representative; Dr. Wiley Lash, mayor of the City of Salisbury; Dr. Wilbert Greenfield, president of Virginia State University; Mr. Henry Brown, vice president, Anheuser-Busch; Mr. William English, vice president, Control Data Corporation, and Mr. Preston Edwards, editor, Black Collegian Magazine. Other leaders at Livingstone College during this period included: Dr. F. George Shipman, president; Dr. Olivia T. Spaulding, academic dean; Dr. Walter L. Yates, dean of Hood Theological Seminary; Dr. Joseph C. Settles, director of Student Affairs; Dr. Larry R. Shannon, director of Planning and Advancement Affairs; Mr. Bobby E. Aldrich, business manager; and Mr. Edward I. Clemmons, registrar and director of Admissions. There were sixty-seven faculty members with a student enrollment of 938 in twenty-five subject areas. In 1982, the college's accreditation by the Southern Association of Colleges and Schools was reaffirmed. Professor J. W. Younge, Jr., served as interim president of Livingstone College before Dr. William H. Greene was appointed president of Livingstone College in 1983. The profile of the school was significantly raised during the 1980-84 quadrennium by the designation of thirteen buildings on campus as historical sites. The buildings included the Tomb of Joseph C. Price, Price Memorial Building, the Old Hood Building, Goler Hall, Carnegie Library, Dodge Hall, Ballard Hall, the apartment building at 427 South West Street, John C. Dancy House, Wallace Hall House, Trent House, Hannum House, and Crittenden House. The entire administration of the college supported a recruitment of students' program. (*Official Journal, 41st Quad. Sess. Gen. Conf.*, p. 436; *42nd Quad. Sess.*, p. 488; p. 543)

Dr William H. Greene had to guide the college through a period of financial crisis during 1984-88. The college launched a three-phase financial campaign to deal with the crisis. The last phase of the campaign culminated on Founder's Day, 1989. New programs were instituted at the college, including remedial programs to strengthen academic performance. Rooms were set aside in the dorms for meditation. The effort to increase student enrollment from 650 to 900 continued. A photographic display called "Image of Success," which featured the pictures and achievements of successful graduates, was mounted. Dr. Ozell K. Beatty was appointed interim president in succession to Dr. William H. Greene. He served in this capacity from January 1988 - July 1988. He then served as president until July 1989, when Dr. Bernard W. Franklin was elected president. Bishop William M. Smith presided as chairperson of the Board of Trustees. (*Official Journal, 43rd Quad. Sess. Gen. Conf.*, p. 588)

On July 1, 1989, Dr. Franklin became the ninth president of Livingstone College. He initiated a $10 million capital campaign fund that generated $7 million in the first two years. The accreditation of Livingstone College was confirmed by the Southern

African Methodist Episcopal Zion Church

Association of Colleges and Schools. The Social Work program was also accredited by the Council on Social Work Education. A Joseph Charles Price Honors Program was established with the opening of an honors residence hall for young women. The second phase will establish an honors hall residence for male students. Dr. Bernard Franklin served as president of Livingstone College until January, 1995. During his administration the school made significant progress. The physical plant was improved; buildings were painted, and new landscaping was done. A community outreach program led to the establishment of a Boy Scout Troop. The five-year capital campaign launched in 1990 to raise $10 million was completed in four years with some half-million dollars in excess of the goal. Bishop William Smith was chairperson of the Board of Trustees during the 1988-92 quadrennium. (*Official Journal, 44th Quad. Sess. Gen. Conf.*, p. 626)

Dr. Roy D. Hudson, a 1955 graduate of Livingstone College, was named interim president of Livingstone College on February 9, 1995. His term began on March 1, 1995. He served for fifteen months and was succeeded by Dr. Burnett Joiner who was elected July 1, 1996. Dr. Joiner, formerly president of LeMoyne-Owens College in Memphis, Tennessee, became the tenth president of Livingstone College. His vision for the college includes a program to cut costs and increase income. One of his priorities is to increase the number of students who are members of the A. M. E. Zion Church. There are plans to add an evening and a weekend college to accommodate students who might wish to enroll in continuing education or alternative studies. (*The Maples and Oaks*, vol. 1 [Summer 1995], p. 9; *Star of Zion*, vol. 120, No. 37-38, pp. 1, 6)

Hood Theological Seminary

Located on the campus of Livingstone College, Hood Theological Seminary was established in 1903 by Dr. William Harvey Goler, the second president of Livingstone College. The seminary was named after Bishop James W. Hood, the first chairperson of the Livingstone College Board of Trustees. Established to educate and train men and women for leadership in the Christian church, the seminary currently offers the Master of Divinity and the Master of Religious Education degrees. (Walls, *The African Methodist Episcopal Zion Church*, pp. 316-19)

During the years 1970-84, Dr. Walter L. Yates was dean of Hood Theological Seminary. The seminary was seeking accreditation and faced similar pressures as Livingstone College during the 1972-76 quadrennium. Hood needed to improve and enlarge its faculty; upgrade its curriculum, increase the number of candidates for the Master of Divinity Degree, and enlarge its budget. At that time, the seminary offered

Livingstone College and Hood Theological Seminary

two degrees—the Bachelor of Theology and the Master of Divinity—and a limited number of Certificates in Christian Education. Student enrollment had increased from 37 in 1972-73 to 73 in 1975-76. Thirty-five degrees were conferred during the period. Forty percent of the students and 34 percent of the graduates were enrolled in the undergraduate degree program. However, the Association of Theological Schools (ATS) required that only 20 percent of the students be enrolled in the undergraduate degree program. "Hood," the report said, "is moving in that direction but this must be a gradual phasing out in order to meet the needs of the Black Church."

To meet the requirements for accreditation, the administration continued the effort to increase student enrollment and improve faculty credentials and program offerings during 1976-80. Hood Theological Seminary undertook a three-year self-study analysis and evaluation of its program, based on which a report was submitted to the Association of Theological Schools (ATS) on May 1, 1980. An outcome of this self-evaluation was the introduction of a new degree program leading to a Master of Religious Education. This program was designed to provide a basic knowledge of religious education that would permit students to interpret and integrate other aspects of theological study with religious education. Sixty hours of course work were required for the degree. Two candidates enrolled for the degree in May, 1980. After the accreditation team of the Association of Theological Schools visited Hood Theological Seminary in 1980, the committee decided in January, 1981 to defer its decision for one year. The seminary was asked to submit a written report on how it would address the following deficiencies: Undergraduates still exceeded 10 percent of its student enrollment; inadequate supervision of field education; inadequate library holdings; insufficient student enrollment in one or more programs of studies. Hood Seminary was not successful in achieving accreditation in 1982 and had to wait until 1985 for reassessment. After fourteen years of devoted service to Hood Theological Seminary, Dean Walter L. Yates passed away in 1984 and was replaced as dean by Dr. William F. Lawrence, Jr. (*Official Journals, 41st Quad. Sess. Gen. Conf.*, pp. 436, 480; *42nd Quad. Sess.*, pp. 549-50)

In January, 1988, the ATS reported to Hood Seminary that the ATS Commission on Accrediting, which met January 13-15, 1988, had retained its notation regarding inadequate expenditure on books and periodicals and indicated that 50 percent of the median expenditure for a nonaccredited institution would be required of Hood, which then had an associate membership with the Association of Theological Schools. Dean William Lawrence put a cost-cutting policy into effect and reported appreciable savings in student food, utility, and energy costs annually. A milestone occurred during the

African Methodist Episcopal Zion Church

1984-88 quadrennium with the election of Ms. Rose Sharon Bryan, president of the Hood Student Union, the first woman so elected. Ms. Bryan was a graduate of the class of 1988. (*Official Journal, 43rd Quad. Sess. Gen. Conf.*, pp. 588, 689)

The devotion of time and energy and the use of financial resources to sustain and improve Livingstone College and Hood Theological Seminary during the previous twenty years were rewarded with the reaccreditation of Livingstone College for a period of ten years and the first full accreditation of Hood Theological Seminary in its 113-year history by the Southern Association of Colleges and Schools in 1992. Hood Theological Seminary had made a significant transition. There were other achievements that reflected the strengthened foundation of the institution. Ninety percent of the faculty held doctoral degrees, the highest doctoral rating in the history of the school at that time. Four academic departments were established to reflect faculty specialization: Biblical Studies, Theological Studies, Historical Studies, and Practical Studies. New courses were offered: the History and Polity of the A. M. E. Zion Church; the Psalms in Worship, Preaching and Devotion; and Clinical Pastoral Education, which was offered in partnership with the North Carolina School of Pastoral Care. An evening program offering the Master of Divinity and the Master of Religious Education was established. The first annual Hood Theological Seminary Achievement and Awards program was held to recognize outstanding faculty in April, 1991. A sister institution, the Hood-Speaks Theological Seminary, was founded in Nigeria, West Africa, in 1992. During the 1988-92 quad-rennium, Dr. James R. Samuel was interim dean of the Hood seminary and continued in office until the fall semester 1993, when he was reassigned by his bishop. (*Official Journal, 44th Quad. Sess. Gen. Conf.*, p. 703)

Hood Theological Seminary was administered from the office of the president of Livingstone College during the spring semester 1994. In August, 1994, the Rev. Dr. Albert J. D. Aymer was appointed dean. He was tasked with the responsibility of advancing the seminary to full accreditation in the Association of Theological Schools (ATS). Dr. Aymer assumed office in 1995 and has worked devotedly to meet the challenge of accreditation. To this end, he initiated changes in the curriculum, grading system, and academic standards in the masters' program to raise them to the standard of the ATS. The catalogue was rewritten to reflect changes in the curriculum and academic standards. A two-year certificate program for uncolleged pastors was introduced to provide them theological education. In 1995, Hood achieved the status of Candidate for Accreditation in the ATS. This put the seminary in the second category of relationship with ATS. The candidature term is for two years, during which time, the school must undertake a self-evaluation in preparation for full accreditation. The full accreditation visit was scheduled for September, 1997. In the interval, Dean Aymer had to address issues of academic quality and quantity; adequate library holdings; size of the student population and its diversity; and a substantial endowment to meet ATS standards. Innovations and improvements included the establishment of the Ruben L. Speaks Annual Lectureship Series; the full functioning of the students' computer center; the inclusion of Hood Theological Seminary among African American seminaries; access free of charge to Institute of Church Administration and Management seminars to theological students at the Interdenominational Theological Center in Atlanta; and a projected joint doctoral degree program (D. Min.) with United Theological Seminary in Dayton, Ohio. At the end of May, 1998, a jubilant Dean Aymer announced that Hood Theological Seminary had achieved full membership in the Association of Theological Schools (ATS). ("Official Report, President, Livingstone College, to the 45th Quad. Sess. Gen. Conf."; *Star of Zion*, June 4-11, 1998)

Student Enrollment at Hood Seminary
1992/93 to 1995/96

Masters	*1992-93*	*1993-94*	*1994-95*	*1995-96*
Male	35	54	41	38
Female	13	18	17	20
Total	48	72	58	58
Graduates				
M. DIV.	7	5	10	13
M.R.E.	1	6	2	2
Total	8	11	12	15
Certificate Program				
Male	—	—	7	
Female	—	—	5	
Total			12	

CHURCH SCHOOL LITERATURE
1972-1996

Bishop Walls reminds us in *The African Methodist Episcopal Zion Church: The Reality of the Black Church* that the Black Church was the cornerstone of education for many freedmen. "In the beginning, our race church was an education center for children and adults who were denied this privilege during slavery. Catechizing was the primary teaching method of reading, writing, and religious training in the African Methodist Episcopal Zion Church." Walls traces the development of the Church School Literature Department in the A. M. E. Zion Church from the early efforts of Rev. Robert Russell Morris, who was appointed the first general superintendent of Sunday Schools by the Board of Bishops in 1888, and Rev. Titus Atticus Weathington, the first elected financial secretary of the department. Their efforts were continued by successive Christian educators: Rev. George Lincoln Blackwell, who was assisted and later succeeded by Rev. Robert Blair Bruce, Rev. Francis Lee, Prof. James W. Eichelberger, Jr., Rev. Buford F. Gordon, Rev. Dr. J. S. Nathaniel Tross, and Rev. Dr. John Van Catledge, Jr. All of these churchmen were well educated and served with distinction. At the beginning of the period under review, Rev. Dr. Louis J. Baptiste was editor of Church School Literature. He had been elected initially in June, 1962 to fill a vacancy and was re-elected at three successive General Conferences through 1972. (Walls, pp. 353-56)

Rev. Dr. Louis J. Baptiste was re-elected at the 1972 General Conference and reported for Church School Literature at the 40th General Conference in 1976. He recommended that the budget for the Department of Church School Literature be increased to provide adequate remuneration for writers, salaries for a secretary and office help, and monies for travel, promotion, and representation. He contended that the department's budget should allow staff writers to attend at least one writing seminar during the quadrennium. He thought that church school literature publications would be improved by printing some of the visual aids in color. He requested an annual budget of $30,000 for the department. (*Official Journal, 40th Quad. Sess. Gen. Conf.*, pp. 404-5)

Dr. Baptiste retired in 1980 at the 41st General Conference meeting in Greensboro, North Carolina. Ms. Mary A. Love was elected to succeed him as editor of Church School Literature. During her first quadrennium in office, the Home and Church Division of the Board of Christian Education recommended changes in the format of the *Church School-Herald Journal*. The space formerly used for printing the Sunday School lesson was used to provide additional information in the hope of stimulating educational inquiry. In 1982, a survey conducted to determine reaction to the new format and elicit suggestions for improvement resulted in mixed reactions from the

Church School Literature

rather limited number of respondents—some wished to restore the old format, others were favorable to the changes. However, subscriptions to the journal increased, and Christian educators of other major denominations—the C. M. E., A. M. E., Baptists, and Presbyterians—used the *Herald-Journal*. It was also purchased by various seminaries and libraries for their periodical collections: Hood Theological Seminary, Carnegie Library, Drew University, Interdenominational Theological Center, Wesley Theological Seminary, the Black Resource Center, NCC (New York), and Allen Weisson Research Department. Distribution of the journal to overseas conferences presented problems. Although expensive, the Woman's Home and Overseas Missionary Society Supply Department, some episcopal and lay districts, and various churches assisted with the cost of postage to Caribbean and African conferences, or with actual delivery. In some cases, because of mail tampering in overseas countries, individual travelers volunteered to deliver packages containing issues of the journal. Writers for the various grade levels during the 1980-84 quadrennium included Dr. Mozella G. Mitchell, Dr. William Freeman, Rev. O. Lawrence Maddox, Mrs. Dorothy S. Johnson who began writing under Dr. Baptiste in 1974, Dr. Josephine H. Kyles, and Mrs. Geraldine Blackwell. Staff and contributors included Ms. Cynthia McCullough, Mrs. Mattie T. Lakin, the Revs. Douglas L. Maven, Larry Crossland, Roderick Lewis, Cynthia Willis, Ms. Irma L. Sadler, Mrs. Diana Flournoy, and Ms. Francina Ferguson. (*Official Journal, 42nd Quad. Sess. Gen. Conf.*, pp. 495-96)

As mentioned previously, Robert Russell Morris was elected the first general superintendent of Sunday Schools and editor of Sunday School Literature in the A. M. E. Zion Church by the Board of Bishops, in Asheville, North Carolina, in September, 1888. In 1988, Ms. Mary A. Love, the editor of Church School Literature, highlighted the centennial of the Sunday School movement in the A. M. E. Zion Church in her report to the 43rd General Conference, held in Charlotte, North Carolina. A commemorative issue of the *Church School Herald-Journal* was published to celebrate this milestone. During this quadrennium, the department produced the first coloring book designed for use with lessons. Mr. Harry Hines, a gifted Sunday School teacher in Bladenboro, North Carolina, was the artist responsible for this achievement. The staff of writers during 1984-88 included: Mrs. Geraldine G. Blackwell, Mrs. Dorothy S. Johnson, Dr. Mozella G. Mitchell, Rev. William Freeman, II, Dr. Josephine H. Kyles, Miss Raymona Jones, Rev. Larry Crossland, Rev. Cynthia E. Willis, Mrs. Helen Scott-Allen, and Mr. Horace Huston. Mrs. Barbara Summey-Marshall and Ms. Cynthia McCullough developed a section "Tips for Teachers." Secretarial services were provided by Ms. Joyce Hood, Rev. Larry Crossland, Ms. LaDorsa Warren, and Ms. Robin

African Methodist Episcopal Zion Church

Massey. Besides her duties as editor, Ms. Love gave service to various ecumenical organizations: the Governing Board of the National Council of Churches of Christ, the Constituent Membership Committee of the Governing Board (NCC), the Division of Education and Ministry Program Unit Committee (NCC), Research and Evaluation Committee (NCC), the Commission on Pan Methodist Cooperation, and the Black Family Conference sponsored by Joint Educational Development (JED). She also served as quarterly subcommittee chairperson for the Committee on Uniform Series for the Fourth Quarter of 1992. (*Official Journal, 43rd Quad. Sess. Gen. Conf.*, pp. 596-99) Various changes were effected in the Church School-Herald Journal quarterlies during the 1988-92 quadrennium. The number of pages was increased in all the journals as well as the print runs. The use of graphic illustrations was increased, and the illustrations were carefully linked with quarterly biblical themes and African American culture. Ms. Love reported at the 44th General Conference in 1992, in Atlanta, Georgia, that the Department of Church School Literature suffered from both financial and physical constraints. The resources made available were inadequate for realizing the goals established, and the office was too small to absorb the growth that had occurred in the department. During 1988-92, the staff included: Mrs. Lisa Barkley, Rev. Dwight Cannon and Mrs. Delores Mitchem. The writers included Dr. Josephine H. Kyles, who had served for twenty-five years as a writer for the *Junior Quarterly*, and Mrs. Geraldine G. Blackwell, who had served for forty-seven years with the Beginner Quarterly. Ms. Love contributed the essays "The Black Experience and Religious Education," in *Harper's Dictionary on Christian Education*, ed. Iris V. and Kendig Brubaker Cully; and "The A. M. E. Zion Church," in *An Encyclopedia of Religions in the United States: 100 Religious Groups Speak for Themselves*, ed. William B. Williamson; and wrote *Stones of Promise Leader's Guide: Resources for Black Family Ministry.* She was elected secretary of the Governing Board of the NCCC USA National Council of Churches and continued to work with the Commission on Pan-Methodist Cooperation in a new capacity as administrative secretary. She delivered addresses and conducted a large number of workshops at various institutes organized by the denomination and occasionally by other bodies. (*Official Journal, 44th Quad. Sess. Gen. Conf.*, p. 634-37)

The Department of Church School Literature mourned the passing of two curriculum writers, Mrs. Geraldine G. Blackwell, who had resigned in 1990, and Dr. Frank Brown, who wrote parts of the Adult People-Adult lessons in the 1980s. An important development occurred in the distribution of Sunday School literature to overseas conferences during the 1992-96 quadrennium. The delivery overseas of electronic stencils significantly reduced postal costs because the literature could be duplicated locally

Church School Literature

instead of being mailed. In this endeavor, the department was assisted by contributors to the "Called to Care" Fund, which was established to provide financial assistance for overseas distribution. The denomination also responded to critical needs of the department. In 1995, the Connectional Council provided $4,250.00 that enabled the department to upgrade its computer equipment; and individual churches made additional donations that made possible the purchase of a second workstation and a laser printer. The move by the department to a larger space within the Publishing House eased the problem of cramped working conditions. ("Report of Dept. of Church School Literature, 45th Quad. Sess. Gen. Conf.," pp. 1-4)

During the 1992-96 quadrennium, the staff included Mrs. Lisa Barkley and Mrs. Charlotte Perry. Writers of the Church School Herald-Journal quarterlies during the quadrennium were: *Young People-Adult Quarterly*—Dr. Mozella G. Mitchell, Rev. Carolyn Moore, Rev. Curtis T. Walker, Ms. Mary A. Love, Rev. Larry Crossland, Dr. Cynthia E. Willis-Stewart, Ms. Carroll A. Belt, and Ms. Amanda Coke; *Intermediate-Senior Quarterly and Primary Quarterly*—Mrs. Dorothy S. Johnson; *Junior Quarterly*—Dr. Helen Scott-Carter; *Beginner Quarterly*—Mrs. Annie Posey; and the Quarterly Worship Programs— Rev. Larry Crossland. (Ibid., pp. 2-4)

Ms. Love continued to serve as a member of the General Board of the National Council of the Churches of Christ in the U. S. A; as secretary of the General Board from November, 1991 to November, 1995; as administrative secretary of the Commission on Pan-Methodist Cooperation; and as chair of the 125th Anniversary Committee of the 2000-2001 December-February quarterly sub-committee of the Committee on the Uniform Series. In recognition of her devoted commitment and outstanding service to the Church School Literature Department and the A. M. E. Zion Church, Ms. Mary A. Love was awarded an honorary Doctor of Humane Letters Degree by Livingstone College at its 1996 Commencement Exercises. Ms. Love continues in her quest for the development of useful and relevant curriculum materials. She believes that the denomination must seriously reexamine its commitment to the curriculum development process if the A. M. E. Zion Church is to stay abreast of current demands and those of the approaching century. (Ibid., pp. 1-11)

CHURCH EXTENSION AND HOME MISSIONS
1972-1996

IN *The African Methodist Episcopal Zion Church, Reality of the Black Church*, Bishop Walls discusses the interrelated functions of Church Extension and Home Missions, traces the historical development of these two agencies and the eventual joining of them into one department within the A. M. E. Zion Church, and examines whether these two agencies should continue as a single department. Although Church Extension and Home Missions are closely connected in their objectives, which is the spread of Zion Methodist Christianity, Walls notes the difference in emphasis between Home Missions and Church Extension. "The primary function of the Department of Home Missions is to help mission churches support their ministers and presiding elders." Church Extension, on the other hand, was more directly concerned with "assisting the conferences in building and buying churches in new and expanded territories." Although church extension and home missions activities were intrinsic to the development of the A. M. E. Zion Church, the Department of Church Extension was formally established as a connectional department in 1892; Home Missions became a department and was placed with the Department of Church Extension in 1916. The Hon. John C. Dancy, Sr., who was corresponding secretary of Church Extension, was re-elected to lead both Church Extension and Home Missions in 1916 and 1920. Dr. Dancy died on July 15, 1920, and Dr. Simon Green Atkins was appointed by the Board of Bishops at the Connectional Council in August, 1920 to succeed Dancy as corresponding secretary. He served until 1924. Others who led the combined units include Samuel Madison Dudley; Esq., (1924-32); Mr. Oscar W. Adams, Sr., (1936-46); the Rev. C. W. Lawrence (1946-48); and Mr. Daniel Webster Andrews (1948-68). In 1968, the General Conference elected Mr. Lem Long, Jr., corresponding secretary. (Walls, pp. 362-71)

In 1972, after the Home Missions Department was separated from the Department of Church Extension, Mr. Long administered the latter as a separate department. He was re-elected to this office in 1972 and in each subsequent General Conference, including the 1996 General Conference. When he was elected, Mr. Long relocated the office of the Department of Church Extension from Winston Salem, North Carolina, where Mr. Andrews lived, to the Varick Memorial Publishing House Building, in Charlotte, North Carolina, where he lived.

During the years 1972-92, the Home Missions Department was administered in a tri-department arrangement of the Brotherhood Pension Department, the Ministerial Relief Department, and the Home Missions Department under one administrator. Dr.

Church Extension and Home Missions

Austin Paul Morris served as secretary-treasurer of these three departments from May 1956 until his death on December 17, 1973. The Board of Bishops then appointed the Rev. Dr. Jewett L. Walker, a pastor at Metropolitan A. M. E. Zion Church, Los Angeles, California, of the Southwest Rocky Mountain Conference, to fill the vacancy for administering these three departments in 1974. He served until 1992 when the Department of Home Missions was removed from this three-agency arrangement and was again joined with the Department of Church Extension.

The reorganization was in response to concerns expressed by church members and their pressure for separation of Home Missions from the Brotherhood Pension Service and Ministerial Relief Departments. At the 44th General Conference, held July 22-31, 1992, in Atlanta, Georgia, the Restructuring Commission of the A. M. E. Zion Church recommended that the Home Missions Office be removed from the Department of Brotherhood Pension Service and Ministerial Relief and be merged again with the Department of Church Extension. However, each department would retain its separate identity and function, but they would be supervised by a single board. The commission justified its recommendation as follows: " . . . there seems to be a reciprocal relation between the two departments which could be better served under the administration of one department." The re-established department, the Church Extension and Home Missions Department, is administered by veteran administrator and lay leader Dr. Lem Long, Jr. (*Official Journal, 44th Quad. Sess. Gen. Conf.*, pp. 811-12)

The current arrangement benefits from the common objectives of the Church Extension and Home Missions Department, a single administrator, and a program centered on providing money to establish new churches (Church Extension) and salaries for pastors of newly established congregations; or for pastors of long-established churches with declining populations (Home Missions). Appropriations are made through the department on the recommendation of the secretary-treasurer in consultation with the bishops of the respective episcopal districts and the approval of the governing board of the department.

The Board of Church Extension has had dedicated and creative leadership in its respective chairpersons and members. The following have served as chairpersons and members:

1972-76
Bishop William M. Smith, chairperson
Bishop Arthur Marshall, Jr., vice chairperson
Mr. Lem Long, Jr., secretary-treasurer

African Methodist Episcopal Zion Church

Members:

1. Rev. G. W. McMurray	7. Rev. L. A. Williams
2. Rev. Alton C. Hunnicutt	8. Rev. R. M. Richmond
3. Rev. W. C. Ardrey	9. Rev. George E. Battle
4. Rev. S. A. Speight	10. Rev. Dennis Bradley
5. Rev. H. H. Sink	11. Rev. Roger Willis
6. Rev. E. R. Faush	12. Rev. T. C. Gill

1976-80
Bishop William M. Smith, chairperson
Bishop Arthur Marshall, Jr., vice chairperson
Members:

1. Rev. George W. McMurray	7. Rev. S. L. Brown
2. Rev. George E. Battle	8. Rev. R. M. Richmond
3. Rev. C. M. Felton	9. Rev. David L. Scott
4. Rev. Stephen A. Speight	10. Rev. Dennis Bradley
5. Rev. J. O. Hart	11. Rev. Parree Porter
6. Rev. E. R. Faush	12. Rev. R. L. Dawson

1980-1984
Bishop William M. Smith, chairperson
Bishop Arthur Marshall, Jr., vice chairperson
Members:

1. Rev. George W. McMurray	7. Rev. David L. Scott
2. Mr. D. D. Garrett	8. Rev. W. L. Burton, Jr.
3. Rev. George L. Smith	9. Rev. Parree Porter
4. Mr. James Stamper	10. Rev. Amanda P. Ballard
5. Rev. M. S. Chatman	11. Rev. Dennis Bradley
6. Mrs. Alberta Hicks	12. Mrs. T. P. Rivers

1984-1988
Bishop William M. Smith, chairperson
Bishop Ruben L. Speaks, vice chairperson
Members:

1. Rev. George W. McMurray	3. Rev. Richard K. Thompson
2. Rev. O. L. Lyons	4. Rev. Joseph D. Kerr

Church Extension and Home Missions

5. Rev. Parree Porter
6. Rev. G. G. Johnson
7. Rev. Charles Ford Bradley
8. Rev. Amanda Ballard

9. Rev. W. L. Burton
10. Rev. Curtis Walker
11. Rev. Dennis
12. Ms. Lou Jean Lovett

1988-1992

Bishop William M. Smith, chairperson
Bishop Ruben L. Speaks, 1st vice chairperson
Bishop Milton A. Williams, 2nd vice chairperson
Members:

1. Rev. George W. McMurray
2. Rev. Lawton Nelson
3. Rev. Richard K. Thompson
4. Rev. Parree Porter
5. Rev. M. F. Ward
6. Rev. T. D. Robinson
7. Rev. W. L. Burton

8. Rev. John W. Smith
9. Rev. G. G. Johnson
10. Rev. James E. Cook
11. Rev. Morgan McCampbell
12. Mr. Albert Stout
13. Rev. Raymon Hunt

The following members served on the Board of Church Extension and Home Missions:

BOARD OF CHURCH EXTENSION AND HOME MISSIONS

1992-96

Bishop Cecil Bishop, chairperson
Bishop Richard K. Thompson, 1st vice chairperson
Bishop Clarence Carr, 2nd vice chairperson
Members:

1. Dr. Vilma D. Leake
2. Rev. T. D. Robinson
3. Rev. John Wesley Smith
4. Rev. George W. McMurray
5. Rev. General L. Scott
6. Mr. Jasper J. McCormick

7. Rev. Z. B. Wells
8. Rev. Willie G. Johnson
9. Rev. Erskine R. Faush
10. Rev. Gwendol F. McCaskill
11. Ms. June Slade Collins
12. Rev. Keith I. Harris

1996-2000

Bishop Cecil Bishop, chairperson

African Methodist Episcopal Zion Church

Bishop Richard K. Thompson, 1st vice chairperson
Bishop Clarence Carr, 2nd vice chairperson
Members:

1. Dr. Vilma D. Leake
2. Rev. W. Darin Moore
3. Rev. General L. Scott
4. Rev. George McNeely
5. Rev. Jeremiah Asbury
6. Rev. Z. B. Wells
7. Rev. James Cook
8. Rev. Gwendol F. McCaskill
9. Rev. John Wesley Smith
10. Rev. Keith I. Harris
11. Rev. Silas E. Redd
12. Rev. Donald Jones

EVANGELISM
1972-1996

IN *The African Methodist Episcopal Zion Church: Reality of the Black Church*, Bishop Walls tells how a felt need to rekindle and spread the faith in accordance with Zion Methodism led to the establishment of the Bureau of Evangelism in 1920 by the General Conference. Walls traces the development of this agency into a separate department directed by a full-time salaried general officer and reviews the contributions of its early leaders. Founded by the Rev. (later Bishop) Benjamin Garland Shaw, who directed it from 1921-28, the department was led successively by the Rev. (later Bishop) Walter William Slade, 1928-36; Rev. William S. Dacons, 1936-60; Rev. Elias S. Hardge, Sr., 1960-68; and at the beginning of this current history by the Rev. J. Dallas Jenkins, who was elected director in 1968, at the 38th General Conference in Detroit, Michigan. (Walls, pp. 445-48; *Official Journal, 38th Quad. Sess. Gen. Conf.*, p. 84)

In May, 1972, at the 39th General Conference meeting in Mobile, Alabama, the Rev. J. Dallas Jenkins made his first quadrennial report as director of the the Bureau of Evangelism. He had effected a reorganization with twelve divisions: Preaching Ministry, Teaching Ministry, Lay Evangelism, Music, Research and Records, Armed Forces, Mission Uplift, Child Evangelism, Special Ministries, Overseas Concerns, Social Concerns and Publications. The above divisions were each led by a divisional leader assisted by other subordinates. The divisional leaders comprised the national staff—an organization of volunteers committed to execute the program of the department. Rev. Jenkins had also requested each bishop to appoint area, district, and annual conference directors and for local pastors to appoint directors of evangelism for the local church. This plan had been approved by the Board of Evangelism and was recommended to the Board of Bishops for implementation during the 1968-72 quadrennium. (*Official Journal, 39th Quad. Sess. Gen. Conf.*, pp. 325-27)

Rev. Jenkins was re-elected director of the Bureau of Evangelism by the General Conference in 1972. During the 1972-76 quadrennium, the Bureau participated in several ecumenical meetings, denominational and international evangelical convocations, and various local evangelical crusades. Ecumenical activities included: informal talks on organic union with Bishop David E. Hackett, presiding prelate of the First and Fourth Episcopal Districts of the Union American Methodist Episcopal (UAME) Church. (Rev. Jenkins urged the A. M. E. Zion General Conference to appoint a commission to pursue the issue formally with the UAME Church.); representing the A. M. E. Zion Church in the meeting at Westminster Central Hall, London, England in preparation for Mission 75, a project of the World Methodist Conference; attending from May 1-4, 1973 the World Methodist Committee on Evangelism in St. Louis, Missouri, where a formula of twenty-cents per member to meet the budget needs of the triennial meeting was established. (Based on national per capita income, the United Methodist Church was assessed a goal of two million dollars, and the A. M. E. Zion Church was assessed $51,700); attending two meetings of the North American Regional Congress, one of seven regional congresses on evangelism that Wesleyan Methodist Churches held that involved all fifty-nine constituent churches of the World Methodist Council and the eighty-seven countries where Methodism is established, from January 7-11, 1974, in Dallas, Texas, and from February 27-28, 1974, in Atlanta, Georgia (Rev. Jenkins was elected vice chairperson of the North American Region of World Methodism's Evangelistic Section); and attending The World Consultation and Convocation on Evangelism of the World Methodist Council in Jerusalem, November 16-23, 1974, along with Bishop Ruben L. Speaks who presented a paper written by Rev. Jenkins on the Black Church in America, were Bishop James E. Wactor, Dr. Walter Yates, and thirty-two A. M. E. Zionites who were members of the World Methodist Convocation. (*Official Journal, 40th Quad. Sess. Gen. Conf.*, pp. 410-16)

Significant denominational evangelistic activities also occurred during the 1972-76 quadrennium. The General Evangelistic Convocation took place at East Stonewall A. M. E. Zion Church, Charlotte, North Carolina in 1973. Bishop William Milton Smith and the Rev. James E. McCoy were host bishop and pastor, respectively. Bishop Speaks, chairperson of the Board of Evangelism, delivered the keynote sermon. Other participating bishops included Bishops William Alexander Hilliard, George J. Leake, Arthur Marshall, Jr., and Alfred G. Dunston, Jr. Outstanding service awards were presented to Presiding Elder C. V. Flack, Pastor Walter Beamon, Bishop William Milton Smith, Dr. Walter Yates, Mrs. Wilhelma Bishop, and the Trinity Gospel Singers of Greensboro, North Carolina. A special award was also presented to Mrs. Marian E. Jenkins, wife of the director.

An Evangelistic Clinic held in the Kansas City District of the Missouri Conference in cooperation with the Tri-Council, comprising the A. M. E., the C. M. E. and the A. M. E. Zion Churches, was spearheaded by Bishop George J. Leake and was ably directed by the late Rev. S. L. Hopkins, a presiding elder and his wife, Dr. Mary

Evangelism

Hopkins. A similar Evangelistic Clinic was held in Waterbury, Connecticut, in the Hartford District, New England Conference in February, 1974. Bishop Charles H. Foggie, vice chairperson of the Board of Evangelism, presided, and the outstanding Rev. H. D. Bonner, pastor-evangelist of the Mt. Olive Church and director of evangelism in the conference, provided dedicated leadership. Rev. Jenkins also participated in the annual "Back to God Campaign" instituted by the late Bishop R. L. Jones in the Salisbury District of the Central North Carolina Conference. Presiding Elder Rev. N. K. Byers and the Rev. Jerry Quick, district director of evangelism, were hosts of the annual campaign. The crusade was based at White Rock and Soldiers Memorial A. M. E. Zion Churches. In early 1974, participation in the Southwest Regional Evangelistic Convocation, held at Smith Metropolitan, Anniston, Alabama, included taping the choir of Smith Metropolitan and other artists by the Department of Evangelism for use by the local television station. Gilmore Broadcasting Corporation provided access to its widely viewed television show "Perspective Black" for a series of talk shows and lectures on the Black Church. Based on these successful uses of the mass media, Rev. Jenkins urged the General Conference to use the media to spread the Good News of the Gospel.

Rev. Jenkins preached the Sunday morning sermon during a special high worship service at Ransom Pentecostal A.M.E. Zion Church, Battersea, London, England, during the 1973 London-Birmingham Annual Conference. This visit afforded him an opportunity to witness the mission work Bishop Herbert Bell Shaw was undertaking in England. In January, 1976, the director visited the Jamaica (West Indies) Annual Conference. Despite political upheavals, Bishop Shaw directed the business of the annual conference and dedicated the newly renovated episcopal residence. (*40th Quad. Sess. Gen. Conf.*, p. 410)

The department participated in various institutes and lecture series during the 1972-76 quadrennium. Dr. Charles Mack, member, and the director participated in the Laymen's Institute of the 5th Episcopal Institute at Dinwiddie Normal and Industrial Institute, Dinwiddie, Virginia, July 2-3, 1975. The institute was led by Rev. J. A. Stringfield under the guidance of Bishop Charles H. Foggie. The director also took part in the Raleigh District's "Preaching-Teaching Mission" held at the Rush Metropolitan A. M. E. Zion Church from April 18-May 2, 1975 and conducted by Presiding Elder E. H. Beebe. Rev. Jenkins delivered a series of lectures for the Black Studies Program on "The Black Church and Evangelism" at the Duke University School of Divinity. The series was proposed by the Rev. (later Bishop) Joseph Johnson, then a student at the School of Divinity. Members of the Central North Carolina Conference of the A. M. E. Zion Church jointly sponsored the series under the guidance of Bishop William Alexander Hilliard and Dr. Howard E. Haggler, the conference director of evangelism. Rev. Jenkins also gave lectures on evangelism at the Hood Theological Seminary, where the response of faculty and students was encouraging. Among the many revivals conducted during the quadrennium, the crusade organized at Clinton Chapel, Knoxville, Tennessee, on May 5-12, 1974, was particularly effective. The outstanding Rev. Ollie Graves was the evangelist for this crusade as well as an earlier crusade in the Knoxville District. During Holy Week, 1975, a revival was held in Harlem, New York City, at Hood Memorial A. M. E. Zion Church pastored by the Rev. David Pharr. *(40th Quad. Sess.,* pp. 416-23)

During the 1976-80 quadrennium, Dr. Jenkins participated in a broad array of ecumenical, denominational, and revival activities. In 1976, the 13th World Methodist Council met in Dublin, Ireland and adopted a five-year plan for evangelism that emphasized personal experience of God, private integrity of living, and a radical challenge to the unjust structures of society. The director was elected to continue as a member of the Committee on Evangelism that was responsible for keeping the entire church informed of the liberation struggle. The A. M. E. Zion Church Department of Evangelism sponsored a youth to the World Methodist Youth Conference at the Dublin meeting. *(Official Journal, 41st Quad. Sess. Gen. Conf.,* p. 453)

In January, 1977, Rev. Jenkins met with the Evangelism Committee of the World Methodist Council in Chicago. The resolutions of the Dublin, Ireland Conference were refined and set in motion. In 1978, Rev. Jenkins was one of the A. M. E. Zion delegates to Stage Two of the World Mission in Evangelism in London, England. Dr. David H. Bradley was a member of the Planning Committee for this celebration and Senior Bishop Herbert Bell Shaw, who led the A. M. E. Zion delegation, was one of the scheduled speakers. Rev. Jenkins also served as instructor of the class on the Holy Spirit during the General Congress of Evangelism of the C. M. E. Church, which met in Charlotte, North Carolina, in 1978. *(41st Quad. Sess.,* pp. 455, 460-61)

In early 1980, the World Methodist Council Evangelism Committee launched the "Mission to the Eighties," which started with a world-wide prayer mission on January 1, 1980. This was followed by a launching in Washington, D. C., on February 14, 1980, at the 4-H Center,where thirty Methodist missionaries from all over the world met.

Evangelism

Representatives of Zion included Bishop Charles Herbert Foggie, Dr. Fred W. Barnes, Rev. J. H. Arrington, Dr. Cecil Bishop. Dr. Charles H. Mack, Rev. J. D. McArthur, Rev. M. J. McRae, Rev. Frank Randall, Dr. John H. Satterwhite, Dr. George L. Smith, Dr. Marshall Strickland, and the Rev. Richard K. Thompson. The Evangelism and Youth Committees of the World Methodist Council jointly sponsored an International Christian Youth Conference in England from July 22-29, 1980, the purpose of which was to call all young people of ages 15-30 to a personal commitment to Jesus Christ and to equip them to share in the evangelization of the world. (*41st Quad. Sess.*, p. 466)

On February 26-March 9, 1980, the director flew to the Holy Lands for the Galilean Covenant Experience. This was an event "to renew world covenant with God through Christ; a covenant beginning at the Sea of Galilee where the first call came; to Jerusalem where He sealed it; and then to Athens and Corinth for the sending out." Rev. Jenkins presided over the climactic session at the base of Mars Hill where the final Act of Dedication took place. (Ibid., p. 467)

Rev. Jenkins's speaking and preaching engagements during 1976-80 included the Annual Revival in 1976 at Small Memorial A.M. E. Zion Church, York, Pennsylvania, where the Rev. Leslie G. Lawson was pastor; the Week of Prayer Speaker during the annual revival in 1976 of Trinity A. M. E. Zion Church, Washington, D.C., with the Rev. Richard K. Thompson as pastor; Oak Street A. M. E. Zion Church, Petersburg, Virginia, pastored by the Rev. E. H. Whitley during the Petersburg District Conference; the District Revival for the Petersburg District of the Virginia Conference at the invitation of the Rev. John H. Stringfield; at Soldiers Memorial A. M. E. Zion Church, Salisbury, North Carolina, of the Salisbury District of the Western North Carolina Conference, the Rev. Joseph Johnson, a member of the Board of Evangelism and pastor where the Rev. Jerry Quick served as the District Director of Evangelism; an Annual Revival in the New Hope A. M. E. Zion Church, East Spencer, North Carolina, where the Rev. W. E. Blalock, pastor, was assisted by lay leaders of the District, namely, Brothers Harvey Robinson and Albert Stout. Rev. Jenkins was the Chaplain Preacher for the annual revival held at the Hood Theological Seminary and Livingstone College, Salisbury, North Carolina, where the Rev. Dean Walter Yates was host. Rev. Jenkins was also the guest speaker at the College Vesper Services at the invitation of the Rev. Andrew M. Spaulding, College Minister of Livingstone College, and his wife, Mrs. Olivia Spaulding, the Dean of the College. (*41st Quad. Sess. Gen. Conf.*, pp. 464-65)

The director participated in the October, 1976 revival organized by the East Tennessee-Virginia Conference at Bethel A. M. E. Zion Church, Kingsport, Tennessee,

African Methodist Episcopal Zion Church

where the Rev. J. L. Walton was the pastor. The following week, he was in Bluefield, West Virginia as guest of Presiding Elder S. H. Hairston. Services were held at Clinton Chapel, Jenkinjones, West Virginia. They were joined by communicants from Mt. Bethel, Zion Temple, Conly's Chapel, Porter's Memorial, First Church of the A. M. E. Zion Church and First Baptist Church. Bishop J. Clinton Hoggard was the presiding prelate of this conference. In 1977, the department also took part in revivals held at Scott A. M. E. Zion Church, Wilmington, Delaware, where the Rev. Madison J. McRae was pastor, and in Statesville District, Hickory, North Carolina, led by Rev. Thomas M. Powe, presiding elder. Under the leadership of Bishop William A. Hilliard, a three-day evangelistic clinic was launched by the Central North Carolina Conference with the theme "From Hood to Hilliard and Beyond." The Department of Evangelism also conducted a Fall Revival at Hood A. M. E. Zion Church, Bristol, Tennessee, in November, 1978, under the supervision of Bishop J. Clinton Hoggard, with the Rev. William R. W. Douglas as pastor. (Ibid., pp. 456-57, 462-63)

Other places where the Director of Evangelism served as guest preacher were: Slade's Chapel A. M.E. Zion Church, Morganton, North Carolina, pastored by Rev. William Green; First A. M. E. Zion Church, Brooklyn, New York, pastored by the Rev. Dr. V. Loma St. Clair; Warner Temple A. M. E. Zion Church, Wilmington, North Carolina, pastored by Rev. Leroy Blair; and the Evangelism and Communication Project of the Disciples of Christ in Ohio, which expanded into an ecumenical program in communications with its meeting in New Orleans, Louisiana. Rev. Jenkins taught a class in Evangelism in 1976 at Johnson Memorial Institute, Batesville, Mississippi, during the leadership training institutes held by the West-Tennessee and Mississippi Conference, under the guidance of Bishop Clinton Coleman. In 1977, Rev. Jenkins served as supply pastor to St. John A. M. E. Zion Church, Cincinnati, Ohio, during the interim of the appointment of a new pastor by Bishop William A. Hilliard, and he filled the pulpit of St. Paul A. M. E. Zion Church at the request of Bishop Hilliard. The pulpit had been left vacant by the death of its pastor, the Rev. E. Nathaniel Jackson. (*41st Quad. Sess.*, pp. 453-59)

In the East Ghana Conference, under the leadership of Bishop Ruben L. Speaks, an intensive program of evangelism was launched during the 1976-80 quadrennium. Campaigns led to the conversion of over sixty people, and new stations were planned for Denu, Klikor, Norliwotagbor, and other districts in Ghana. In the Accra District, Aggrey Memorial Church, Mamprobi, was the leading church in raising money for evangelism. The Rev. E. G. Fiawoo and Dr. J. K. O. Lavie, pastor and presiding elder, respectively, were honored among others for their work. The Rev. Emmanuel J. Ekpo was appointed director of Evangelism in the Nigeria Conference. (Ibid., pp. .455-56)

The director led a pilgrimage to the Harriet Tubman Home in Auburn, New York. Inspired by Mrs. Alice Austin, a busload of people from Dayton joined the director on the trip to the historic site. They shared this experience with the First Episcopal District's Pilgrimage. Bishop Herbert Bell Shaw, then presiding prelate of the First Episcopal District, dedicated the new library of the home. The director expressed the hope that the general church would "come to realize the tremendous aid to Evangelism it possesses in this historic property and will begin to share more fully with the First District in developing this national shrine." (Ibid., pp. 467-68)

During the 1980-84 quadrennium, the director continued his involvement in evangelism at the global and national levels. Rev. Jenkins was a member of the launching committee of the Institute for World Evangelism that opened at the Emory University Candler School of Theology, Atlanta, Georgia, with Dr. George Morris as director. This institute was established to train ministers and laity in evangelism from around the world. Rev. Jenkins also taught a course on the History of Methodism during the World Camp-Meeting Planning sessions held in Ocean Grove, New Jersey, the week after the 42nd General Conference of the A. M. E. Zion Church. (*Official Journal, 42nd Quad. Sess. Gen. Conf.*, p. 515)

At the national level, during 1980-84, Aldersgate A. M. E. Zion Church in Dayton, Ohio became the second mission established by the Department of Evangelism to become a full-scale church. Begun as an apartment mission in a housing project of Dayton, after one year it had grown sufficiently to warrant its establishment as a church in its own edifice. The director's activities, as usual, included teaching and training in evangelism and participation in revivals. He took part in the Fourth General Evangelistic Convocation organized by the then Tenth Episcopal District presided over by Bishop Ruben L. Speaks with the Rev. Harold Chandler as presiding elder. This convocation was held at the Sheraton Convention Center, in Memphis, Tennessee in September 1981. Other noteworthy activities during this quadrennium included the publication of *The Flame and Zion's Evangel*. *The Flame* was distributed free to pastors three times a year. Subscriptions to *Zion's Evangel* did not meet expectations, but the director hoped that increased financial assistance from the church would permit continued publication to give the journal time to increase its circulation. (*42nd Quad. Sess.*, pp. 515-18)

African Methodist Episcopal Zion Church

In his report to the 43rd General Conference held in Charlotte, North Carolina, in 1988, Rev. Jenkins said that Zion would need to establish three thousand new churches by 1998 to achieve its proportionate share of the U.S. church population. The director contended that new churches would help renew the church because they attract more new converts than older established churches. Two significant events for the Department of Evangelism during the 1984-88 quadrennium were its participation in a march against South African apartheid policies and the launching of a church-wide celebration of Pentecost '87. At the Board of Bishops meeting in February, 1986, at Trinity A. M. E. Zion Church, Washington, DC, the entire church hierarchy—the Board of Bishops, general officers, clergy and lay leadership—highlighted "the social dimension of the Gospel" by marching against South African apartheid policies. Rev. (now Bishop) Richard K. Thompson was the pastor of Trinity at that time. The church-wide Pentecost '87 celebration was approved by the Board of Bishops at its winter, 1985 meeting. It was launched at Old Ship A. M. E. Zion Church in Montgomery, Alabama on June 7, 1987, with concurrent services at presiding elder districts throughout Zion in the afternoon or evening. The Department of Evangelism provided literature, orders of service, offering envelopes, and report forms to presiding elders or bishops to ensure that distribution to pastors was efficient. At Old Ship, then pastored by the Rev. Curtis Walker, Bishop Herman Anderson delivered the keynote sermon. Bishops Clinton Coleman, Cecil Bishop and John H. Miller followed with challenges. The Rev. George Maize, III, the Metropolitan A. M. E. Zion Church, Jersey City, New Jersey and local choirs from Montgomery provided music for the occasion. (*Official Journal, 43rd Quad. Sess. Gen. Conf.*, pp. 620-21)

The Department of Evangelism participated in several ecumenical events during the 1984-88 quadrennium. Rev. Jenkins was a member of the task force on evangelism at the Congress of National Black Churches, which met in December, 1984. The Congress focused on the problems facing the Black Church in America and throughout the world. The A. M. E. Zion representatives were led by Bishops Herman Anderson and Cecil Bishop. Rev. Jenkins attended a meeting in April, 1984 of the Institute for World Evangelism, which had been established in 1982 by the World Methodist Council Committee on Evangelism. At the 1984 meeting, successive world seminars on evangelism were planned as follows: South American Regional Seminar, Lima, Peru, December 30, 1985 - January 10, 1986; Caribbean Regional Seminar, June 16, 1986 - July 3, 1986; West African Regional Seminar, December 29, 1986 - January 16, 1987; Third International Seminar, Atlanta, Georgia, June 15, 1987 - July 3, 1987.

Evangelism

In December, 1985, Rev. Jenkins participated in the third summit meeting of Black Church leaders, together with the Church World Service, at the Interchurch Center in New York City. Mr. Gregory Smith, A. M. E. Zion's director of public relations, helped put the meeting together. A. M. E. Zion church leaders at that meeting included Bishops J. Clinton Hoggard, Ruben L. Speaks, Herman Anderson, Richard L. Fisher, and Alfred E. White. General officers in attendance included Drs. Jewett Walker, George L. Blackwell, Morgan Tann, John H. Satterwhite, and Kermit DeGraffenreidt. Mrs. Alcestis Coleman, president of the Woman's Home and Overseas Missionary Society, and Ms. Betty Stith, president of the Connectional Lay Council, also attended. (Ibid.,pp.618-19)

Rev. Jenkins conducted the School of the Prophets at the West Alabama Conference in October, 1986 and attended in December, 1986 the Annual Fellowship of American Directors of Evangelism, held at the National 4-H Conference Center, Chevy Chase, Maryland. The denomination's Fifth General Evangelistic Convocation was held at Lomax-Hannon College, Greenville, Alabama, in July , 1985. The event was hosted by the Tenth Episcopal District, with Bishop Cecil Bishop as host bishop and the Rev. James Cook, pastor of Butler Chapel, as host pastor. Bishop J. Clinton Hoggard was the keynote speaker, and Bishop Ruben L. Speaks delivered the lecture "One People Under God." The Fourth Episcopal District's convocation was held in April, 1986, at Broadway Temple A. M. E. Zion Church, Louisville, Kentucky. It was convened by Bishop J. Clinton Hoggard, and the Rev. Tecumseh Graham was host pastor. (Ibid., pp. 619-20)

At the 43rd General Conference meeting at Little Rock A. M. E. Zion Church, Charlotte, North Carolina, after twenty years of devoted service, Dr. Jenkins was succeeded in office as director of the Department of Evangelism by the Rev. Norman H. Hicklin who served the department from 1988-96. As a new director, Rev. Hicklin and the Board of Evangelism spent the first four years assessing and evaluating the development of projects, programs, and resources for evangelism. On October 4, 1988, the director outlined eight goals that would direct his effort: "Goal 1: To reach the masses of people through spiritual, powerful and convincing preaching for God and Zion, through a developed evangelistic preaching team. . . . Goal 2: To develop and implement a training program for Annual Conference, District Directors of Evangelism, and other appropriate individuals. The appointed Board of Evangelism would serve as resource persons both at the development and implementation stages. . . .Goal 3: To communicate regularly to all departments of the Church information that is [relevant] to evangelistic work. . . .Goal 4: To increase the memberships of the Church through varying forms of evangelism ministry such as revivals and crusades. . . .Goal 5: To develop evangelistic workshops in cooperation with Directors of Evangelism throughout Zion for their use . . . Goal 6: To actively participate in all church-related activities upon request—convocations, workshops, etc. . . . Goal 7: To develop and implement a tract ministry with lay involvement (adults and youth) designed to witness for God. . . . Goal 8: To establish a television and radio ministry." (*Official Journal, 44th Quad. Sess. Gen. Conf.*, pp. 621-22)

Rev. Hicklin reported in 1992 that many of the above goals had been implemented. Several pastors throughout Zion volunteered to serve on a preaching team. The Connectional Board had developed and implemented a training program for all annual conference, district, and local directors of evangelism and other appropriate individuals. The training program was put into effect at the 1990 Connectional Congress on Evangelism. "The Connectional Comprehensive Program on Evangelism" was accepted and approved by the Board of Bishops in February, 1992, at a special session in Washington, D. C. Although the goals to establish a tract and a television and radio ministry are still on the drawing board, all the others were in the process of being implemented. (Ibid., pp. 658-60)

The director reported on his first revival, which was held at Mt. Zion A. M. E. Zion Church, Wetumpka, Alabama, then presided over by Bishop Alfred E. White, chairperson of the Connectional Board, and pastored by the Rev. George T. Britt. The revival was held August 9-12, 1988. The various boards, clubs, choirs, and the local church were all responsive. The Central Conference and the City of Wetumpka attended and led the worship. The director's second revival was held at York Memorial A. M. E. Zion Church, Greenville, North Carolina, where the late Rev. Luther Brown was pastor. This church was in the North Carolina Conference and was presided over by Bishop Alfred G. Dunston, Jr. Capacity crowds came each evening, and "souls were saved, revived, and added to the church." During the quadrennium, Rev. Hicklin conducted ten district evangelistic revivals; twenty-two local church revivals; four Connectional Board retreats; and four regional workshops and seminars. (Ibid.., pp. 660-61)

During the 1992-96 quadrennium, the director and the Board of Evangelism assessed and evaluated the fiscal and programmatic concerns of the department. They planned and organized the first Quadrennial Connectional Congress on Evangelism to

Evangelism

equip the leadership in the fields of evangelistic ministries of the A. M. E. Zion Church. The Department of Evangelism completed and published *The Model Comprehensive Resource of Evangelism and Its How-To-Manual.* In his report to General Conference, Rev. Hicklin recommended that the Quadrennial Connectional Congress be observed during May following each General Conference and that the Connectional Church observe "Decision Day Sunday" each October as stated in the Discipline. ("Report of the Dept. of Evangelism to the 45th Quad. Sess. Gen. Conf.," pp. 3-4)

The Rev. Hicklin served the church as director of the Department of Evangelism in a creative manner during his eight years in that office. He made the denomination aware of the necessity for winning new persons as converts for the Kingdom of God on Earth by going into the hedges, highways, byways, and streets among the lonely, the downtrodden, and the outcasts of our society as well as preaching to the more privileged persons in our several communities.

At the 45th General Conference held in Washington, D. C., in July, 1996, strong contestants competed to serve as director of the Department of Evangelism. Of the five candidates seeking this office, the Rev. Darryl B. Starnes, Sr., was elected for the 1996-2000 term. Rev. Starnes was pastor of Metropolitan A. M. E. Zion Church in Birmingham, Alabama. He is a graduate of Livingstone College and Hood Theological Seminary. He also pastored Spottswood, New Britain, Connecticut; Thompkins Chapel, Chattanooga, Tennessee; Greater Warner Tabernacle, Knoxville, Tennessee, and Mount Moriah/Mount Ararat Circuit, Richburg and Bascomville, South Carolina. He was the director of evangelism for the Alabama/Florida Episcopal District and for the Knoxville District and Tennessee Conference. ("Profile of Candidate for General Officer, 45th Quad. Sess., Gen. Conf.," p. 34)

In a semi-annual report to the Connectional Council Meeting held in Mount Vernon, New York, in October, 1996, Rev. Starnes announced the following five objectives for the department: (1) to exercise general supervision over the field of evangelism; (2) to promote the evangelization of the lost within and without the church; (3) To promote revivals of religion throughout the territory occupied by the church to vitalize and restore the waste places in our Zion; (4) to promote expansion of the denomination through the planting of new churches; (5) to promote evangelistic training and education at all levels for ministers and laity. ("Semi-Annual Report of the Director of the Bureau of Evangelism to the Connectional Council Meeting, October, 1996," p. 7)

African Methodist Episcopal Zion Church

Rev. Starnes also set goals that included expanding the director's immediate staff by adding a part-time financial officer and a part-time assistant by September 1, 1997; mobilizing and utilizing the official structure of the department so that every episcopal district, annual conference, presiding elder's district, and local church would have an active director by September 1, 1997; promoting Decision Day (the fourth Sunday in October) throughout the connection; and developing mass media initiatives, institutional ministries, child evangelism initiatives, and street ministries; promoting the revitalization of prayer ministries, conducting solemn assemblies, and revival services; in key areas. (Ibid., pp. 8-10)

Under the dynamic leadership of the Rev. Darryl Starnes, Sr., the Bureau of Evangelism sponsored the Fourth Quadrennial Evangelistic Convocation April 15-18, 1997, at the Radisson Grand Resort Hotel in Fort Mill, South Carolina. Among the featured presenters were Rev. Dr. Dennis Proctor, pastor of Pennsylvania Avenue Church, Baltimore, Maryland, who taught daily Bible Studies; Dr. Lewis Drummond of Beeson Divinity School, Birmingham, Alabama, who delivered two lectures on Biblical Revival; Dr. John Cherry , pastor of Full Gospel, Temple Hills, Maryland, who preached and taught on Church Growth; Dr. Carlyle Fielding Stewart, pastor of Hope United Methodist Church, Detroit, Michigan, who preached and taught on Church Revitalization. Convocation highlights included evangelistic workshops led by sixteen facilitators, music ministries led by the Rev. Charles Phillips, Rev. Cheryl Phillips, Rev. Scot Moore, the T. J. Max Band of Blair Metropolitan, Jackson, Mississippi, outstanding choirs from North and South Carolina, and the Friday Youth Extravaganza and Late-night Concert. Bishops Clarence Carr, chairperson of the Board of Evangelism, Milton A. Williams and George E. Battle, first and second vice chairpersons, respectively, contributed significantly to the success of the convocation. During the previous six-month period, Dr. Starnes trained and taught in nine of the twelve episcopal districts of the A. M. E. Zion Church. ("Bureau of Evangelism, Annual Report to the Board of Bishops and the Connectional Council, July 30- August 2, 1997," p. 8)

Because of the spark provided by the leadership of the Rev. Starnes and the Board of Evangelism, the A. M. E. Zion Church expects a revitalization of the Department of Evangelism so that by the dawn of the twenty-first century the community will feel a vital renewal of faith and witness in the total life of the A. M. E. Zion Church.

During the period under review, the following members of the Board of the Bureau of Evangelism were responsible for guiding the department:

Evangelism

BOARD OF EVANGELISM

1972-76
Bishop Ruben L. Speaks, chairperson
Bishop Charles H. Foggie, vice chairperson
Members:

1. Rev. A. F. Hooper
2. Rev. William A. Blackwell
3. Mrs. Ethel V. McIver
4. Rev. S. R. Lomax
5. Rev. C. H. Mack
6. Rev. G. W. Bolden
7. Rev. J. D. Armstrong
8. Rev. C. L. Jones
9. Rev. C. O. Newton
10. Rev. Raymond Hart
11. Rev. B. Leon Carson
12. Rev. Lillian Brunner

1976-80
Bishop Ruben L. Speaks , chairperson
Bishop Charles H. Foggie, vice chairperson
Members:

1. Rev. G. J. Hill
2. Rev. Hera B. Lovell
3. Rev. S. J. Farrar
7. Rev. F. I. Lowe
8. Rev. Idonia Anderson
9. Rev. Hollis Calahan
4. Rev. C. L. Winslow
5. Rev. Charles H. Mack
6. Rev. C. E. Edge
10. Mrs. Cora L. Johnson
11. Rev. George W. Maize, Sr.
12. Rev. Joseph Johnson

1980-84
Bishop Cecil Bishop, chairperson
Bishop John H. Miller, Sr., 1st vice chairperson
Bishop Clinton R. Coleman, 2nd vice chairperson
Members:

1. Rev. John E. Durham
2. Mr. Miller
3. Rev. Charles H. Mack
4. Ms. Mary E. Jackson
5. Rev. S. J. Farrar
6. Mrs. Medis G. Warren
7. Rev. W. O. Thompson
8. Rev. N. H. Hicklin
9. Rev. P. D. McKinney
10. Mrs. Maggie Patterson
11. Rev. E. H. Whitley
12. Mr. Jasper McCormick

African Methodist Episcopal Zion Church

1984-88
Bishop Cecil Bishop, chairperson
Bishop Alfred E. White, 1st vice chairperson
Bishop John H. Miller, Sr., 2nd vice chairperson
Members:

1. Rev. J. E. Durham
2. Rev. Jeremiah Asbury
3. Rev. Charles Mack
4. Rev. J. H. Dunlap
5. Rev. George W. Maize, III
6. Rev. W. O. Thompson
7. Mr. George S. Ziegler
8. Mrs. Alice Spicer
9. Rev. E. E. Parker
10. Rev. Eddie Hicklin
11. Rev. Mozella Mitchell
12. Rev. Odinga L. Maddox

1988-92
Bishop Alfred E. White, chairperson
Bishop George W. Walker, 1st vice chairperson
Bishop John H. Miller, Sr., 2nd vice chairperson
Members:

1. Rev. John E. Durham
2. Rev. George W. Maize, II
3. Rev. Dr. William T. Kennedy
4. Rev. Claude Christopher
5. Rev. C. E. Willie
6. Rev. Herolin Aiken
7. Mrs. Helena Zacharias
8. Rev. James Robertson, Jr.
9. Rev. Z. B. Wells
10. Rev. Eddie Hicklin
11. Rev. John W. Forbes
12. Rev. James L. Allen
13. Rev. Kenneth James
Rev. Harrison D. Bonner, consultant

1992-96
Bishop Clarence Carr, chairperson
Bishop Milton A. Williams, 1st vice chairperson
Bishop George E. Battle, Jr., 2nd vice chairperson
Members:

1. Rev. J. A. McDougal
2. Rev. Clinton Brickhouse
3. Rev. George Maize
4. Rev. John E. Durham
5. Rev. Lewis M. Anthony
6. Rev. H. D. Bonner
7. Rev. R. L. Pyant
8. Rev. John W. Forbes, III
9. Rev. Paul Whiteurs
10. Rev. James E. Tutt
11. Mrs. Florence Hudson
12. Rev. H. Dwight Bolton

Evangelism

1996-2000
Bishop Clarence Carr, chairperson
Bishop Milton A. Williams, 1st vice chairperson
Bishop George E. Battle, Jr., 2nd vice chairperson

1. Rev. James McDougal
2. Rev. Michael E. Ellis
3. Rev. Rita J. Colbert
4. Rev. J. Wardell Henderson
5. Rev. Terry L. Jones, Sr.
6. Rev. Charles Jackson
7. Rev. James Cooke
8. Rev. Harvest T. Wilkins
9. Rev. George Maize
10. Rev. John Harrison
11. Rev. John W. Forbes, III
12. Rev. G. Michael Tydus

PUBLIC AFFAIRS AND CONVENTION MANAGER
1972-1996

In *The African Methodist Episcopal Zion Church: Reality of the Black Church,* William J. Walls traces the beginning and development of the Department of Public Affairs and Convention Manager (formerly called the *Public Relations and Social Service Department*) from the establishment of a part-time office and the election of the first director— the Rev. J. W. Findley—by the Board of Bishops in August 1952 to the first election of Alexander Barnes of North Carolina by the General Conference in 1956 and his re-election thereafter in 1960, 1964, 1968, and 1972. (Walls, p. 274)

Thus, at the beginning of this account, Mr. Alexander Barnes had already served as director of the then Public Relations and Social Service Department for sixteen years and was beginning his last quadrennium in this office. During his tenure, he traveled extensively to represent the A. M. E. Zion Church and wrote the column "The Moving Finger" for the *Star of Zion.* In his reports to General Conference during this period, Mr. Barnes emphasized the benefits that would accrue to the A. M. E. Zion Church from a larger allocation of money and better strategic use of his office, particularly in the arrangements made for national conventions and the possibilities of attracting public grants to Zion's educational efforts. (*Official Journal, 39th Quad. Sess. Gen. Conf., p. 328; 40th Quad. Sess. Gen. Conf.,* pp. 427-28)

At the 40th Quadrennial Session of General Conference in Chicago, Illinois, in 1976, Mr. Gregory R. Smith was elected to succeed Mr. Barnes as the Director of Public Relations. Among the accomplishments Mr. Smith cited in his first quadrennial report were the publication of a public relations handbook for general church use; the compilation of a comprehensive press kit to enable the press to provide better coverage of the church; and a featured article in *Ebony Magazine* on the A. M. E. Zion Church. The Public Relations Department was also instrumental in commissioning an oil portrait based on a drawing of Bishop James Varick. The painting was presented to the World Methodist Council in August 1978 and now hangs in its headquarters building at Lake Junaluska, North Carolina. Mr. Smith was re-elected director during the 41st General Conference held at Greensboro, North Carolina, May 7-16, 1980. (*Official Journal, 41st Quad. Sess. Gen. Conf.,* pp. 473, 62)

Following the 1980 General Conference, the officer elected to this responsibility

Public Affairs and Convention Manager

was also charged with the duties of convention manager for the denomination. This meant that one person would be responsible for all details of travel to and from the site of connectional meetings. The recommendations of this officer must be approved and finalized by the board which governs this office and ultimately by the Board of Bishops. During the 1984 General Conference, Mr. Smith emphasized the discounts that could redound to the church if its convention manager were given adequate responsibility to coordinate and manage A. M.. E. Zion conventions. He discussed the significance of media ownership, the role of the mass media in today's society, and how the A. M. E. Zion Church could effectively utilize these communication tools for her own religious and social objectives. Mr. Smith was re-elected director of this department at this session of General Conference. (*Official Journal, 42nd Quad. Sess. Gen. Conf.*, pp. 524-27, 52)

During the 1984-88 quadrennium, the renamed department, now the *Office of Public Affairs and Convention Manager*, compiled a handbook of operational guidelines for connectional meetings. Mr. Smith stressed the necessity for advance planning of all meetings to reap the benefits derived from convention expertise. He cited savings of over $21,000 achieved by this office in arranging the WH&OM Society's July 1987 Convention, which met in Boston, Massachusetts, as an example of what could be realized. (*Official Journal, 43rd Quad. Sess. Gen. Conf.*, pp. 644-46)

The director reviewed the participation of the A. M. E. Zion Church in the ongoing struggles and crises in Africa and in the United States of America. The A. M. E. Zion Church raised over a hundred thousand dollars for African relief and hunger in response to the Ethiopian famine of 1985. A. M. E. Zion bishops, general officers, and over a hundred Zionites meeting in Washington, D. C., in February 1986, participated in anti-apartheid demonstrations in front of the South African Embassy. Officers of the A. M. E. Zion Church attended a summit called by the National Council of Churches of Christ in the U. S. A. and raised $7,500 of the $50,000 pledged by black churches to pay church administrative costs for the anti-apartheid campaign, church support for disinvestment, and the boycott of companies doing business with apartheid South Africa. Mr. Smith stressed the need for the A. M. E. Zion Church to address the issues of homelessness and rising poverty among children in the U. S. He advised the church community to harness the efficiencies of the computer age by establishing a centralized computer system for the A. M. E. Zion Church. Mr. Smith was re-elected for a fifth quadrennium at the 43rd General Conference meeting in Charlotte, North Carolina, July 27- August 5, 1988. (Ibid., pp. 57; 646-48; 649-50)

African Methodist Episcopal Zion Church

Before completing the 1988-92 quadrennium, Mr. Smith resigned as director in 1991 to accept an appointment as president of the African Development Foundation in Washington, D. C. The Board of Bishops filled this office by appointing the Rev. Dr. Thaddeus Garrett, Jr., as director of Public Affairs and Convention Manager on August 14, 1991. As an experienced public relations businessman and a person with religious, political, educational, and international links, Dr. Garrett skillfully negotiated and renegotiated, when necessary, contracts for the sites of connectional meetings. He also used his network to publicize the A. M. E. Zion Church. His appointment was confirmed by the 44th General Conference meeting in Atlanta, Georgia, which elected him director of this department. *(Official Journal, 44th Quad. Sess. Gen. Conf.*, pp. 63, 667)

In his report to the 45th General Conference meeting in Washington, D. C., Dr. Garrett spoke of the need for the A. M. E. Zion Church to enlarge her profile and involvement in the issues that affect black Americans. He prepared a brochure on the A. M. E. Zion Church that was widely circulated. He emphasized the need for additional resource materials for circulation. Dr. Garrett proposed guidelines for planning the sites of connectional meetings. He did not stand for reelection. The Rev. George E. McKain was elected as director of Public Affairs and Convention Manager at the 45th General Conference meeting in Washington D. C. at the Renaissance Hotel and Full Gospel A. M. E. Zion Church, July- August 1996. ("Report of the Department of Public Affairs and Convention Manager of the A. M. E. Zion Church Made to the General Conference, July 24-August 2, 1996," pp. 1, 3, 5-6)

Rev. McKain is a graduate of Livingstone College and Hood Theological Seminary. He is pastor of Baum's Temple A. M. E. Zion Church, Summerville, South Carolina. He has served the church in several capacities: president, Jersey City District, New Jersey Conference National Christian Youth Council; vice president and president, Eastern Regional National Christian Youth Council. He represented the church at the National Council of Churches of Christ; Young Christians for Global Justice; International Christian Youth Council; World Methodist Evangelism Youth Conference; World Methodist Council; and at other ecumenical youth organizations. ("Profile of Candidate for General Officer, 45th Quad. Sess. Gen. Conf.," p. 36)

Public Affairs and Convention Manager

PUBLIC AFFAIRS AND CONVENTION MANAGER BOARD
1972-76

Bishop George J. Leake, chairperson
Bishop John H. Miller, vice chairperson
Members

1. Rev. J. W. Findley
2. Mrs. Lona M. Gill
3. Rev. John T. Frazier
4. Rev. R. L. Lyons
5. Rev. George A. Fitch
6. Rev. C. E. Edge
7. Rev. D. R. Curry
8. Rev. J. W. Smith
9. Rev. David L. Scott
10. Mrs. Annie L. Miles
11. Rev. L. J. Johnson
12. Rev. E. K. Aidou—
(Mrs. Rosemarie R. Holmes)

1976-80

Bishop G. J. Leake, chairperson
Bishop J. Clinton Hoggard, 1st vice chairperson
Bishop H. B. Shaw, 2nd vice chairperson
Members

1. Mr. Gregory Smith
2. Rev. Alfred E. Garnette
3. Mrs. Josephine Riggins
4. Rev. R. L. Lyons
5. Rev. G. A. Fitch
6. Rev. Raymond Dickerson
7. Ms. Esther Carson
8. Rev. Calvin Smith
9. Rev. W. O. Thompson
10. Mrs. A. R. Hunter
11. Mr. Vernon Stevenson
12. Mr. B. K. Wobil

1980-84

Bishop George J. Leake, II, chairperson
Bishop J. Clinton Hoggard, 1st vice chairperson
Bishop Cecil Bishop, 2nd vice chairperson
Members

1. Mr. Albert Stout
2. Rev. Alfred E. Garrnette
3. Mrs. Irene Simpson
4. Rev. A. N. Gibson
5. Mrs. Artelia M. Perry
6. Rev. R. R. Purnell
7. Mrs. Algenia Thomas
8. Mr. W. J. Longmire
9. Mr. Vernon Stevens
10. Rev. Curtis Brown
11. Ms. Della Woodruff
12. Mr. B. K. Wobil

271

African Methodist Episcopal Zion Church

1984-88
Bishop R. L. Fisher, chairperson
Bishop J. Clinton Hoggard, 1st vice chairperson
Bishop Charles H. Foggie, 2nd vice chairperson
Members

1. Mr. Oscar McLaughlin
2. Mr. D. D. Garrett
3. Mr. Gossie Hudson
4. Rev. Sherwin O. Greene
5. Mr. Theodore Shaw
6. Mrs. Odessa Tyson
7. Rev. Osofa McDonald
8. Mrs. Josephine Spaulding
9. Mr. Claudie Price
10. Mrs. Estelle Longmire
11. Rev. R. L. Lee
12. Rev. B. K. Wobil

1988-92
Bishop Richard L. Fisher, chairperson
Bishop J. Clinton Hoggard, 1st vice chairperson
Bishop Charles H. Foggie, 2nd vice chairperson
Members

1. Mrs. Mildred Neely
2. Mr. D. D. Garrett
3. Rev. Frederick W. Barnes
4. Mr. Theodore Shaw
5. Rev. Gwendol Fay McCaskill
6. Rev. Harvest T. Wilkins
7. Rev. Ronald Butler
8. Mr. J. R. Broughton
9. Rev. George McKain
10. Mrs. Estelle Longmire
11. Mrs. Ida M. Francis
12. Ms. Rhandi Stith

1992-96
Bishop Richard K. Thompson, chairperson
Bishop George W. Walker, Sr., 1st vice chairperson
Bishop Charles H. Foggie, 2nd vice chairperson
Members

1. Rev. James R. Stanley
2. Mr. Roosevelt Wright
3. Ms. Cheryl Y. Stone
4. Ms. Sarah Lewis
5. Rev. Joseph L. Walton
6. Chief U. D. Umoh
7. Rev. C. J. Jenkins
8. Mrs. Dora Mae Ricks
9. Rev. Leon Henderson
10. Mr. Benjamin Howard
11. Dr. Gossie H. Hudson
12. Mr. Anthony Brown

Public Affairs and Convention Manager

1996-2000
Bishop Richard K. Thompson, chairperson
Bishop George W. Walker, Sr., 1st vice chairperson
Bishop Charles H. Foggie, 2nd vice chairperson
Members

1. Dr. Marie Tann
2. Mr. William A. Bulow
3. Rev. Thomas Sweatt
4. Mr. Takis E. J. Caiafas
5. Rev. Ronald Butler
6. Rev. George W. C. Walker, Jr.

7. Dr. John Winston
8. Mr. Michael Lisby
9. Mr. Andra' Ward
10. Mrs. Winifred Sharper
11. Ms. Dora Mae Ricks
12. Mr. Daniel Brown

HEALTH AND SOCIAL CONCERNS
1972-1996

IN *The African Methodist Episcopal Zion Church: Reality of the Black Church,* William J. Walls tells how the Rev. Dr. Samuel C. Coleman, a minister, medical doctor, and presiding elder of the A. M. E. Zion Church of the Crossett District of Arkansas, built a health clinic at Hot Springs, Arkansas and offered to operate it for the denomination. On August 25, 1956, the Board of Bishops approved the project and issued a certificate of appointment to Dr. Coleman as health director. This was the beginning of the Department of Health.. (Walls, *A. M. E. Zion Church,* p. 449; *Official Journal, 39th Quad. Sess. Gen. Conf.,* p. 398)

In 1972, the General Conference allocated a small stipend for the Health Department to supplement Dr. Coleman's program at Hot Springs. The department functioned in a limited way until Dr. Coleman's death, which occurred during the 1984-88 quadrennium. The Board of Bishops did not fill the vacancy immediately. At the 1988 General Conference, a resolution to reestablish and rename the department was passed by the General Conference with the provision that it be implemented in 1992 and that an interim director, the Rev. Dr. James E. Milton, pastor of Butler Chapel, Tuskegee, Alabama, be appointed. He was subsequently elected by the General Conference to serve as a General Officer with the title "Director of the Department of Health and Social Concerns." (*Official Journal 43rd Quad. Sess. Gen. Conf.,* pp. 733-36.)

Dr. Milton enunciated his goals in his first quadrennial report to General Conference in 1992 . He hoped to sensitize the church membership to medical and social problems, provide information on treatment, and offer assistance, when possible, through referrals, and solicitations from foundations or other agencies. The social concerns function would focus attention on problems of the elderly, the handicapped, single parenthood, AIDS victims, and the homeless. He envisioned the department serving as an information agency on VA benefits, the construction of personal care facilities, and/or 202 housing. (*Official Journal 44th Quad. Sess. Gen. Conf.,* p. 675)

Among his accomplishments during the 1988-92 quadrennium, Dr. Milton listed a KIDSAVER program and a Ministerial Education and Training Proposal. The KIDSAVER program entailed matching an adult with an at-risk child for at least four hours a week. Partial funding for the KIDSAVER program came from the Alabama Substance Abuse Policy Board. Dr. Milton thought the KIDSAVER program could be effectively meshed with evangelical outreach. The second proposal was intended as a training program in detection, intervention, and counseling in substance abuse for ministers. A third proposal centered on establishing a sub-acute detoxification center if funding could be obtained. These were all Alabama-based programs that could have been duplicated in other areas, but they would have required similar funding. Dr. Milton also envisioned a first-aid station at all General Conferences to provide emergency care, assisting in securing hospitalization, or other required medical treatment beyond first-aid care. Dr. Milton's appointment was confirmed by the General Conference when he was elected director of Health and Social Concerns. (Ibid., pp. 675, 63)

Dr. Milton's quadrennial report to the 45th General Conference for the 1992-96 quadrennium stated that programs had been developed for substance use and abuse; mentoring at-risk youth; teen pregnancy; comprehensive day-care; and a domicilary program for the elderly. Dr. Milton said that although these programs were developed in Alabama, they could be used in any locale with some adjustments. The department had made proposals for the health director's major focus, which was on alcoholism and substance abuse. ("Quadrennial Report to the 45th General Conference of the African Methodist Episcopal Zion Church," pp. 3-4)

Dr. Milton represented the A. M. E. Zion Church at the White House Task force for Welfare Reform and Health Care Reform and at "Healing Communities 96" sponsored by the Emergency Medical Services for Children, an agency of Public Health Services. Such meetings afforded the director an opportunity to network in grant writing and proposals. The department also wrote the health-care policy statement of the A. M. E. Zion Church; a special statement on HIV/AIDS; Zion's position on HIV/AIDS; and a statement on the role of the church in substance abuse. Dr. Milton wrote a primer on cocaine and established Zion Health/Social Service, Inc., a 501(C)3 organization that can operate nationwide. (Ibid., pp. 3-5)

The director noted that the Department of Health and Social Concerns was offering health education and screening for the first time at the General Conference and that emergency medical service would be in effect round the clock. A questionnaire that would facilitate emergency care was circulated to all Zionites in attendance. Dr. Milton highlighted the Red Cross blood drive and marrow donor recruitment. He noted that greater genetic diversity among African Americans made donor matches more difficult and stressed the need for African Americans to get tested for marrow typing. The health director urged the A. M. E. Zion community to support a denominational health survey. Information derived therefrom could be used for church based programs to overcome inadequate health care access and delayed detection of disease that lead to over one million preventable deaths annually. Dr. Milton served faithfully until the 1996 session of General Conference, which elected the Rev. Dr. Bernard H. Sullivan, Jr., as successor to Dr. Milton. (Ibid., pp. 3-5)

African Methodist Episcopal Zion Church

Dr. Sullivan has a Ph.D. in clinical community psychology from the University of South Carolina and a Master of Divinity in pastoral counseling from Livingstone College. He has been a teacher, community and health consultant, and pastor. He has pastored five A. M. E. Zion Churches: Snow Hill, Newton, North Carolina; Clement Memorial, Charlotte, North Carolina; St. Peter's, Gastonia, North Carolina; East Stonewall, Charlotte, North Carolina; and St. Stephen's, Gastonia, North Carolina. He developed the St. Stephen's After Care Program with a staff of sixteen that serves about one hundred children. Dr. Sullivan continues to serve as pastor of St. Stephen's Church in Gastonia and director of the Department of Health and Social Concerns with offices in Gastonia, North Carolina. ("Profile of Candidate for General Officer, 45th Quad. Sess. Gen. Conf.," p. 42)

WOMAN'S HOME AND OVERSEAS MISSIONARY SOCIETY, 1972-1996

THE Woman's Home and Overseas Missionary (WH&OM) Society was not officially organized as a national organization until 1880, but there were local and regional women's organizations in the African Methodist Episcopal Zion Church that antedated the present organization. From the beginning of the African Methodist Episcopal Zion Church, the women of the church have shared the vision of spreading the Gospel of Christianity. They have used their energies and resources to support the church in this effort. In *The African Methodist Episcopal Zion Church: Reality of the Black Church*, Bishop Walls traces the historical development of the WH&OM Society before 1972. (pp. 388-424)

During the period 1972-96, the Woman's Home and Overseas Missionary Society continued to fulfill its objectives: to assist the denomination in its mission to spread the Gospel by raising money to meet both home and overseas mission needs. At the beginning of this current history, the WH&OM Society comprised the parent body, including women aged 26 on; the Young Women's Department, including women from age 13-26; the Buds of Promise, with four age groups: Readiness 1-3; Beginner 4-6; Primary 7-9; and Junior 10-12; the Bureau of Overseas Supply; and the Life Members' Council.*

In the effort to utilize its own membership more fully, the WH&OM Society established new departments. In 1975, a proposal for a Young Adult Missionary Society (YAMS) for women between the ages of 27 and 40 to harness the energy of the young women of the denomination was initiated by then president, Dr. Willa Mae Rice, who presented the idea to the General Convention. This idea was approved, and YAMS groups were organized throughout the church within the parent body. In 1983, the 20th Quadrennial Convention approved the establishment of YAMS as a separate department, with the second vice president as its department head. This decision was ratified by the 1984 General Conference which directed "that district and general offices be established; and that all rights and privileges stated in the Constitution be granted, including delegate representation at General Conventions, District assessments, A District Day, and a purpose and theme song adopted." (Cited in "Historical Highlights of the Woman's Home and Overseas Missionary Society, A. M. E. Zion Church, 1880-1996," pp.51-53).

*The author is indebted to the WH&OM Society for its submission of "Historical Highlights of the Woman's Home and Overseas Missionary Society, A. M. E. Zion Church, 1880-1996," pp. 1-141. This account is based on that document.

African Methodist Episcopal Zion Church

The then second vice president, Dr. Adlise Ivey Porter, was charged with the responsibility of writing the initial department and operational guidelines, designing the program of Biblical studies and social concerns, and providing leadership in the formation, implementation, and operation of local units." This unit of the WH&OM has revitalized the participation of younger women in the organization. (pp. 51-53)

Another proposal in 1987 at the General Convention in Boston, Massachusetts for an elected official General Coordinator of the Young Adult Missionary Society was ratified by the General Conference in 1988 in Charlotte, North Carolina. Consequently, Mrs. JoAnn Bowens Holmes of Charlotte, North Carolina was elected the first General Coordinator of the Young Adult Missionary Society at the 1991 WH&OM Society Quadrennial Convention meeting in New Orleans, Louisiana. (p. 52)

The Motto of the YAMS is "With hearts and hand: We reach up to God for strength and direction, We reach out to love and touch others; We reach down to lift fallen humanity." Its theme song is "Promise, Praise and Petition." The official purpose of YAMS "is to unite women ages 22-40 of the A. M. E. Zion Church and communities for mission service in the church and community. (Among the prime objectives are social concerns such as child abuse, drug dependency, teenage pregnancy, world hunger, etc.); to provide an opportunity for Christian witness through the use of their time, talent, and treasure to support the mission cause; and to provide experiences that will enable young adult missionaries to perpetuate the existence and continued growth in the Woman's Home and Overseas Missionary Society, the African Methodist Episcopal Zion Church, and the Kingdom of God." (p. 52)

A new program instituted by the WH&OM Society during the period 1972-96 includes the Agape Luncheon as an official fund-raising project in support of Second Mile. Mary Gaither Meeks proposed this project during her first quadrennium as 1st vice president (1971-75). Funds raised from the Agape Luncheon and Second Mile are given, based on need, to an Episcopal District—one year to a home missions project and the following year to an overseas project. This idea was further extended in 1981 when the Executive Board, meeting in Tuscaloosa, Alabama, adopted the idea proposed by Mrs Theodora Smith, 1st vice president (1979-87) of celebrating Agape Sunday on the second Sunday in February. This initiative was intended " to enhance the Second Mile offering; to stimulate and motivate creative and sacrificial giving of our services and substances; and to involve all members of Zion in a loving, caring and sharing mission experience" (pp. 12, 96).

In 1981, General President Mrs. Alcestis Coleman (1979-87) proposed that the WH&OM Society participate in World Hunger Sunday, which was later changed to

Woman's Home and Overseas Missionary Society

December, as World Hunger Month. The Executive Board adopted her proposal. Thus, in 1982, the WH&OM Society presented a check for $20,000 to Church World Service in the fight against world hunger. This program is coordinated by the General Secretary of the Bureau of Overseas Supply who prepares an annual program that is circulated throughout the denomination. The response to this program has been very positive. Thousands of dollars have been contributed to various World Hunger projects since its inception. Funds are channeled through the ecumenical agency, Church World Service, which is based in the Interchurch Center at 475 Riverside Drive, N. Y., N. Y. (p. 99)

Two additional programs include the General Y-Retreat and the Walk-A-Mile for Second Mile fund-raising activity. Under the guidance of General Secretary Dorothy S. Johnson (1979-87), a retreat for Y's, Honorary Y's, and Y leaders was held at Livingstone College from June 20-27, 1985. Since then, the Society has continued to sponsor such Y-Retreats because they enhance leadership, fellowship, and personal and spiritual development of Y's. Mrs. Florena B. Johnson, the ninth general Y secretary, coordinated the third, fourth, and fifth Y-Retreats from June 29-July 1, 1991; June 30-July 2, 1993; and June 29-July 2, 1994. They were held at Livingstone College campus, Salisbury, North Carolina. In 1995, the 23rd Quadrennial Convention voted to name the annual retreats the Dorothy S. Johnson Annual Y Retreat in honor of the organizer of the first retreat for young women and men. (pp. 13, 59)

In 1979, in accordance with the General Conference's decision to rename the *Board of Foreign Missions*, the *Board of Overseas Missions*, the Society substituted the word *Overseas for Foreign* in its name. Thus, the Society took its current name—the Woman's Home and Overseas Missionary Society. (p. 13)

A milestone in the history of the Woman's Home and Overseas Missionary Society was its Centennial Celebration during August 1-3, 1980, at Old Ship A. M. E. Zion Church, the birthplace of the society, in Montgomery, Alabama. The Rev. Norman H. Hicklin was host pastor, Bishop John H. Miller, Sr. was host bishop, and Mrs. Alcestis Coleman was general president. Hundreds of Zionites participated in the celebration under the theme "Celebrating the Past—Charting the Future—Enlighten, Inspire, Empower Us, O Lord." The program included a banquet during which awards and citations were presented, a spiritual encounter worship program, and a colorful parade, all culminating in the special Celebration Service. (pp. 113-14)

The Old Ship A. M. E. Zion Church is located within the boundaries of the Central Alabama Conference. The presiding elders, ministers, and laity of this conference contributed much to the success of the Centennial Celebration. Other significant persons in the planning, promotion, and entertainment were: Pastor Sheffield

African Methodist Episcopal Zion Church

Henderson and members of Stone Chapel A. M. E. Zion Church; the presiding elders, ministers, and laity of the Central Alabama Conference; and the Woman's Home and Overseas Missionary Society ; District Presidents Mrs. Clara Ivery and Mrs. Princella Madison, of Montgomery and East Montgomery Districts, respectively. Mrs. Bernice Miller, missionary supervisor, and Mrs. Theodora Smith, 1st vice president, were general chairperson and co-chairperson, respectively of the celebration. During this observance, two former general presidents and the current general president were in attendance, namely, Dr. Abbie Clement Jackson, Dr. Willa Mae Rice, and Mrs. Alcestis M. Coleman. During the celebration, the Woman's Home and Missionary Society launched a Centennial Fund, which culminated in August, 1981. The goal was to raise funds over and above the regular budget askings in order to give Clinton Junior College, Rock Hill, South Carolina; Lomax-Hannon Junior College, Greenville, Alabama, and the Janie A. Speaks Hospital in Afrancho, Ghana, West Africa, money earmarked from the Centennial Fund. The total amount raised was $75,000.00, which was divided equally among the three designated beneficiary institutions. (pp. 114-16)

The general president, Mrs. Alcestis Coleman, the 2nd vice president, Mrs. Eliza Walker and the Episcopal district missionary supervisor, Mrs. Mary Marshall, made the presentation to Clinton Junior College of $25,000.00 for the purchase of equipment for the Business Education Department. Dr. Sallie V. Moreland and Bishop Arthur Marshall, Jr., president and chairperson of the Clinton Junior College Trustees Board, respectively, received the donation for the college from the Woman's Home and Missionary Society. (p. 116)

The general president, Mrs. Coleman, 1st vice president, Mrs. Theodora Smith, and the missionary supervisor, Mrs. Bernice Miller, made the presentation of $25,000.00 to Lomax-Hannon Junior College. This money was presented to Dr. James E. Cooke, interim president of Lomax-Hannon Junior College, and to Bishop John H. Miller, chairperson of the Lomax-Hannon Junior College Trustee Board. These funds were designated for use in restoring Zion Hall, which was registered in 1976 in the Distinguished Register of Alabama as an Historic Landmark Building. General President Alcestis Coleman made $25,000.00 gift presentation to the maternity unit of the Janie A. Speaks Hospital at Afrancho, Ghana, West Africa, at a session of the annual conference meeting in Cape Coast, Ghana. The money was placed in a special bank account to be drawn on by the bishop of the 12th Episcopal District for equipment for use in the hospital. The entire denomination participated in and benefited from the triumphal celebration of the Woman's Home and Missionary Society's Centenary Celebration because all the episcopal districts shared in the total funds that were raised. (pp. 114-16)

Woman's Home and Overseas Missionary Society

The Walk-A-Mile for Second Mile, which was proposed by 1st Vice President Dr. Vilma D. Leake (1987-95) and approved by the Executive Board to further support the Second Mile outreach, has become an effective and popular means for raising funds for Second Mile. The first Walk-A-Mile was in New Orleans, Louisiana, August 17-23, 1991, during the 22nd Quadrennial Convention. Thousands of dollars have been contributed from Walk-A-Mile activities held round the country. (p. 97)

At the Executive Board Meeting in Kansas City, Missouri, February 20-25, 1984, The Life Members' Council Department, under General Chairman Mrs. Margaret F. Willie (1983-91), proposed the establishment of a Scholarship Award Fund. This proposal was adopted by the Executive Board. In July 1989, Mrs. Willie and her husband, Earl Willie, donated eight thousand dollars ($8,000.00) solely for use in establishing the Scholarship Fund. The fund, to which Mrs. Willie had previously donated one thousand dollars ($1000.00), receives money annually from local and district Life Members' Councils throughout the denomination. Scholarship recipients can use the fund to attend one of the A. M. E. Zion centers of higher learning, namely, Livingstone College, Salisbury, North Carolina; Clinton Junior College, Rock Hill, South Carolina; and Zion Community College, Monrovia, Liberia. In 1991, the quadrennial convention voted to name the scholarship fund the "Margaret B. Willie Life Members' Scholarship Endowment Program." (pp. 73-74)

In 1987, delegates at the 21st WH&OM Society Quadrennial Convention meeting in Boston, Massachusetts voted to change the mission statement of the society from its 1931 statement: "to promote the cause of world evangelism, and by systematic means raise the funds for the promotion of the work" to a much expanded statement as follows:

> The purpose of the Woman's Home and Overseas Missionary Society of the African Methodist Episcopal Zion Church is to promote growth in the knowledge and understanding of God and His plan of redemption for the world, as revealed through Jesus Christ and the power of the Holy Spirit; to teach the concepts of Christian mission and provide experiences for participation in mission work and its ministries; to exemplify the principles of Christian living and to win others to Christ; to promote the cause of World Evangelism; and serve as a financial support system to undergird the world mission outreach of the African Methodist Episcopal Zion Church, at home and overseas, to the end that, through the power of the Holy Spirit, Christ is exalted and God is glorified. (p.14 [Matthew 25:31-46 and 28:18-20 provide the frame of reference for the mission purpose of the society.])

African Methodist Episcopal Zion Church

The women of the African Methodist Episcopal Zion Church have been involved in the overseas mission effort since Eliza Ann Gardener and others, as members of the Daughters of Conference of New England, a forerunner organization of the Woman's Home and Overseas Missionary Society, raised money to assist the Rev. Andrew Cartwright on his voyage to Africa on January 7, 1876. Through this effort, the first A. M. E. Zion Church on the African continent was established in Brewerville, Liberia, on February 7, 1878. (Walls, *African Methodist Episcopal Zion Church*, pp. 229-30)

Whether in the forefront as missionary supervisors for bishops or in the background raising money to assist overseas missions, the women of the A. M. E. Zion Church have contributed during 1972-96 to developments in the West Africa missions in Liberia, Ghana, Nigeria, and Cote d'Ivoire, and in South Africa. In 1972, Bishop Ruben L. Speaks and his wife and Missionary Supervisor Mrs. Janie A. Speaks were assigned to these annual conferences. In 1980, after two quadrennia, Bishop Speaks reported to the General Conference that there were 52 new congregations, 43 new churches, 37 new parsonages, a new hospital, two new health clinics, and 37 new schools. An episcopal residence had also been built in Accra, Ghana, in 1980, an amenity that would considerably facilitate the work of the presiding bishop in that district. Bishop Speaks also sought approval for establishment of the Rivers Conference from the 1980 General Conference meeting in Greensboro, North Carolina. This was approved on May 27, 1980. The Rev. Emmanuel Ekpo was made Bishop's Deputy of this conference in May 1980. During January 21-25, 1981, the first Rivers Annual Conference was held at A. M. E. Zion Obuama, Degema, Rivers State, Nigeria, with Bishop Cecil Bishop, Bishop Speaks's successor, presiding. Mrs. Wilhelma Bishop was the missionary supervisor. (p. 82)

During 1972-80, the Rev. and Mrs. Kermit DeGraffenreidt and their daughter, Keisha, enhanced Zion's missionary and educational effort in Monrovia, Liberia. The Rev. DeGraffenreidt served as pastor of the Bishop J. W. Brown Memorial A. M. E. Zion Church, Monrovia, and principal of the A. M. E. Zion Academy (grades 7- 12). He directed the rebuilding of the Brown Memorial Church and initially taught English and Social Studies, but his other duties forced him to relinquish this latter service. (p. 82)

In 1988, the newly elected Bishop Samuel Chukukanne Ekemam was assigned to the Nigeria, Central Nigeria, Rivers, and Liberia Conferences. He shared the African missionary work with the newly elected Bishop Milton A. Williams who was assigned to the Ivory Coast and to the three Ghana Conferences. In 1992, newly elected Bishop

Woman's Home and Overseas Missionary Society

Marshall H. Strickland was assigned to preside over the conferences in Ghana, Liberia, and Cote d'Ivoire, and Bishop Ekemam was assigned to the Nigeria, Central Nigeria, Rivers, Lagos-West Nigeria, and Mainland Nigeria Conferences. During this quadrennium, Bishop Ekemam continued the work begun in the Lagos-West Nigeria Conference by Bishop Alfred Dunston, Jr., who had established the William J. Walls A. M. E. Zion Church in Lagos in 1965, the first Zion church in the capital of Nigeria. The General Conference of 1992 received the Lagos-West Nigeria Conference, which was set apart from the Nigeria Conference in 1990, into the A. M. E. Zion Church. The Mainland Nigeria Conference was also set apart from the Nigeria Conference in 1992 under Bishop Ekemam's supervision. Mrs. Faustina Ekemam and Dr. Dorothy Brunson have served as the missionary supervisors to Bishop Ekemam and Bishop Strickland, respectively. From their respective efforts considerable progress was made. (p. 82)

Currently, the West Ghana Conference has over forty-six thousand members, with six presiding elder districts at Winneba, Akim Manso, Cape Coast, Akim Krosso, Assim Faso, and Sekondi Districts. Sister Elizabeth Hutchfield is the field worker for the West Ghana Conference. The East Ghana Conference has six presiding elder districts: Accra, Ho, Penyi, Tema, Agbozume, and Keta. Sister Theresa Acolaste is the field worker. (p. 82-83; "Report of the 11th Epis. Dist. to the 45th Quad. Sess. Gen. Conf.," pp. 30, 39)

The Mid-Ghana Conference also has six presiding elder districts: Kumasi, Tafo, Osenase, Twifo, Afrancho/Suyani, and Tamale/Togo. There are over fifty churches in the conference, the majority of which have organized missionary departments. Through various projects, the women in the conference support the churches, pastors, and students and assist in church building and renovation. (p. 83; "Report of 11th Epis. Dist. to 45th Quad. Sess. Gen. Conf.," p. 37)

The A. M. E. Zion Educational Unit operates in all ten regions of the Republic of Ghana and caters to all the A. M. E. Zion schools comprising 86 kindergarten schools, 212 primary schools, 68 junior secondary schools, and 4 senior secondary schools in Ghana. The numerical strength of the schools is as follows: day care, kindergarten, primary and junior secondary schools: boys: 27,834; girls: 21, 524; total: 49358. ("Report of 11th Epis. Dist. to 45th Gen. Conf.," p. 18)

The Ivory Coast Conference was admitted into the A. M. E. Zion Church under the leadership of Bishop Milton Alexander Williams during the 44th General Conference held in Atlanta, Georgia in 1992. Bishop Marshall Strickland was assigned

African Methodist Episcopal Zion Church

this conference in 1992. Unfortunately, the missionaries from Ghana who were working in the Ivory Coast to build this conference were attacked by local people, and many of them returned to Ghana, but some stayed despite the hardship, and continued to support the pastors and develop churches (p. 83).

The Liberia Conference comprises five presiding elder districts: Brewerville, Plahn, Greenville, Barfowin, and Rivercress. Despite tragic political upheavals in Liberia, the Transitional Legislative Assembly of the Republic of Liberia passed an act on February 8, 1996 establishing the former African Methodist Episcopal Zion Community College as a full-fledged university with the name *African Methodist Episcopal Zion University*. The institution will offer Bachelor of Arts and Science degrees. The former A. M. E. Zion Community College was founded in 1987 in Congotown, a suburb of Monrovia. Since its establishment, the college has awarded 712 associate degrees. (p. 83)

The A. M. E. Zion University has received funds annually from the Woman's Home and Overseas Missionary Society from its Life Members' Council funds. The A. M. E. Zion University has seven colleges on three campuses, which include Andrew J. Cartwright College of Business and Public Administration; Ruben L. Speaks College of Liberal Arts; Wilfred College of Criminal Justice and Law Enforcement Administration; John Cherry College of Science and Technology; Alfred E. White College of Allied Health Science; Alicia Smith-Lartey College of Education; and the Cecil Bishop College of Engineering. Over one thousand students are currently enrolled in the institution. This project is supervised by the Rev. Frederick Umoja, an American missionary serving in Liberia. (pp. 83-84)

In 1969, based on communications from the Rev. Maruping Samuel Macarvy Phasumane of South Africa to the Rev. Christopher W. B. Deane of Guyana, Bishop Stephen Gill Spottswood officially received a South African mission into the A. M. E. Zion Church during the Guyana Annual Conference. However, the liberation effort in South Africa during the 1970s and 1980s attenuated this connection. In 1972, the presiding bishop for South Africa, Bishop William A. Hilliard, went to South Africa to survey the work, but contact was not made. After four days, he returned to the United States. However, during Bishop Cecil Bishop's first quadrennium (1980-84), he and Secretary-Treasurer Rev. Kermit J. DeGraffenreidt, of the Overseas Missions Department, journeyed to South Africa and visited Seshego. They worshiped with the people and returned impressed with the prospects for a sustained connection. There was ongoing interest on both shores. In 1992, South African Rev. Phasumane wrote officials of the A. M. E. Zion Church to initiate a plan for action in South Africa. Bishops

Woman's Home and Overseas Missionary Society

Milton A. Williams and Enoch B. Rochester, together with the secretary-treasurer of Overseas Missions, Rev. Kermit DeGraffenreidt, visited South Africa. They were encouraged by the prospects. In 1993, the Board of Bishops, meeting in Knoxville, Tennessee, decided to assign Bishop Enoch Rochester to supervise the work in South Africa until the next General Conference in 1996. (p. 84)

When the Rev. Phasumane passed away on February 22, 1994, more than six hundred people gathered at the Spottswood Chapel A. M. E. Zion Church in Seshego, Northern Transvaal, for his funeral service on March 5, 1994. The WH&OM Society provided the necessary funds for Bishop Enoch Rochester and the Rev. James H. Dunlap, Sr., presiding elder of the Madisonville District of the Kentucky Conference, to represent the A. M. E. Zion Church at the funeral. (pp. 84-85)

Under the leadership of Bishop Rochester and Missionary Supervisor Dr. Mattilyn T. Rochester, the first South Africa Annual Conference was held in December 1993, twenty-five years after the initial relationship was established under presiding Bishop Stephen Gill Spottswood in 1969. (p. 85)

Besides overseas missions in West Africa and South Africa, the A. M. E. Zion Church has established conferences in Britain, India, and in South America and the Caribbean. These conferences include: the London-Birmingham, Manchester-Midland Conferences in Britain; the India Conference; and Jamaica Conferences, including Surrey, Cornwall, and Middlesex Conferences; the Bahama Islands Conference; the Virgin Islands Conference (now a Home Mission Conference); the Barbados Conference; Guyana Conference; and the Trinidad and Tobago Conference.

Recent developments during the period under review include the realization of a vision shared by Bishops Spottswood and Herbert Bell Shaw to see the A. M. E. Zion Church established in Barbados in memory of Bishops John B. Small and Cameron C. Alleyne, both of whom were born in Barbados. In 1980, Bishop and Mrs Hilliard reported Zion had a church in Barbados. The first Barbados Annual Conference was opened on May 6, 1981 at the Hilliard-Babb A. M. E. Zion Church with Bishop Charles Foggie as presiding bishop, Mrs. Madeline Foggie as missionary supervisor, and the Rev. George H. Grimes as host pastor. At the Barbados Annual Conference, the Rev. W. T. Kennedy of Philadelphia, Pennsylvania, was appointed presiding elder; the Rev. George Grimes, was appointed pastor of Hilliard-Babb A. M. E. Zion Church; and Brother Ralph King was asked to start a mission in Bridgetown, Barbados. There are now two congregations in Barbados. The Hoggard A. M. E. Zion Church was organized, built, and developed under the current pastorate of the Rev. Holligan with his wife serving as the missionary field worker for that area, while Bishop and Mrs. J. Clinton Hoggard served as bishop and missionary supervisor. (p. 86)

African Methodist Episcopal Zion Church

In Britain, Bishop and Mrs. Herbert Bell Shaw organized the London-Birmingham Conference in 1971 while Rev. (later Bishop) J. Clinton Hoggard served as the foreign missions secretary. Ransom A. M. E. Zion Church is the Mother Church in this country. In 1992, Bishop Milton Williams and the Rev. Lula Williams organized the Manchester-Midland Conference, which was received into the A. M. E. Zion Church at the 1992 General Conference.

During September 9-11 1994, the women of the London-Birmingham and Manchester-Midlands Conferences held a Retreat in East Sussex, England. Sixty-five "Women of Excellence" gathered for three days of praise, worship, and Bible study. Joining the Rev. Lula Williams as teachers were Missionary Supervisors Mrs. Dorothy Johnson and Mrs. Barbara Shaw, former executive secretary of WH&OM Society. The Mission Education and Retreat Coordinator was Ms. Dorothy McFarlane. (p. 87)

Bishop and the Rev. Mrs. Lula Williams and the Rev. Horace A. Gordon, the bishop's administrative assistant, led the London-Birmingham Conference in its 25th Anniversary celebration in November 1995. The celebration was attended by a large delegation from the United States that included the former presiding prelate of the London-Birmingham Conference—the Rt. Rev. J. Clinton Hoggard, who was retired in accordance with denominational rule from the active episcopacy of the church by the General Conference in 1992. Besides members of the episcopacy, others from the U. S. who attended the 25th anniversary celebration and participated in the November 12, 1995 Sunday evening service of worship were: the Revs. Kermit J. DeGraffenreidt, secretary of the Department of Overseas Missions, New York, N. Y.; Kevin McGill, pastor, Hood Temple, Richmond, Virginia; Gary W. Burns, pastor of Varick Memorial, Washington, D. C.; Doretha Hawkins, presiding elder, Bluefield District, East Tennessee-Virginia Conference; M. Luther Hill, pastor, Greater Faith, Richmond, Virginia; and Mr. Richard Hines, operational manager, North Carolina Bank; Mrs. Joyce Lamb, pastor's wife, Lomax A. M. E. Zion Church, Arlington, Virginia; and from England: the Rev. Wilbert Higgins, Presiding Elder L. B. Simpson, London District, London-Birmingham Conference, Mrs. Veronica Brown, Evangelist Murdell Haughton, the Revs. Eric Brown, pastor, New Testament Church of God, Noel Brown, New Testament Assembly, Lovell Bent, New Life Assembly, Hewie Andrew, Methodist Church in Britain, and Phillip Williams, presiding elder, Birmingham District, London-Birmingham Conference. The Rev. Assenath McKenzie gave the Welcome Address, and choirs from the Manchester District, Birmingham District, and London District provided appropriate music for the service, at which the Rev. Thomas E. Tucker, Jr., pastor of Greater Metropolitan, Norfolk, Virginia, preached the sermon. ("Program,

Woman's Home and Overseas Missionary Society

Sunday Evening Celebration, 25th Year Anniversary of the A. M. E. Zion Church in England, Nov. 12, 1995")

On Saturday, November 11, 1995, at 7:00 p.m. at the Mount Royal Hotel, Marble Arch, England, the 25th year Anniversary Banquet of the A. M. E. Zion Church in England was observed. This well-arranged program was participated in by members and friends of Zion from Birmingham, Wolverhampton, the Midlands, London, and its environs as well as from the United States. The banquet was a milestone in the historical development of the A. M. E. Zion Church in England. Bishop J. Clinton Hoggard, the former presiding prelate of the conference, was the keynote speaker for the observance. Bishop Hoggard was presented by Bishop Milton A. Williams, the presiding bishop. Other participants in this festive occasion included: Missionary Supervisor the Rev. Lula Williams; the Bishop's Administrative Assistant Rev. Horace A. Gordon; the Rev. Lurleen Gooden; Mrs. Ionie Anguin; Ms. Dorothy McFarlane; Mrs. Bernice Higgins; Ms. Joyce James; Ms. Paulette Simpson, representing the National Commercial Bank, Jamaica; the Rev. Carmel Jones, M. B. E., representing the Pentecostal Credit Union; the Rev. Kermit J. DeGraffenreidt, representing the Department of Overseas Missions, A. M. E. Zion Church; the Rev. Assenath McKenzie, who paid a respectful tribute to Bishop Herbert Bell Shaw, of sainted memory, who will be forever known as the organizer, on May 15-23, 1970, of the London-Birmingham Conference, A. M. E. Zion Church; the Rev. Medis Cheek, Gilmarton Star A. M. E. Zion Church, Chesapeake, Virginia; the Rev. Cameron Jackson, pastor of John Wesley, Washington, D. C.; Ms. Patricia Neil and Mrs. Audrey Gilkes, who made special unique presentations to the 25-year members of the conference. A dramatic presentation was given under the guidance and direction of Ms. June Higgins and Company , entitled "Still I Rise." The YAMS Choir of the London District provided music for the occasion. The Banquet Committee included chairperson Ms. Dorothy McFarlane; co-chairperson Mrs. Mavis Cameron; Mrs. Ionie Anguin; Ms. Patricia Neil; Ms. Joyce James; Mrs. Icyline Howell; Mrs. Gertrude Graham; Mrs. May Smith; and Mrs. Violet Allen. The major congregational songs sung during the banquet were "To God Be the Glory" and "We've Come This Far By Faith" ("Program of the 25th Year Anniversary Banquet of A. M. E. Zion Church in England")

The Woman's Home and Overseas Missionary Society has held twenty-three quadrennial conventions. Those within the confines of this study include the 17th to the 23rd quadrennial sessions. The Executive Board of the Society selects a theme to reflect the direction of the organization for the four-year period. The 17th Quadrennial Convention was held July 31- August 7, 1971, at Shaw Memorial A. M. E. Zion

African Methodist Episcopal Zion Church

Church, Buffalo, New York, with the theme "The New Age and the New Disciple." The 18th Quadrennial Convention met August 2-8 1975 at First Church A. M. E. Zion, Los Angeles, California, under the mission theme "Evangelism, Involvement, Social Action, Investment, Outreach, Celebration." The 19th Quadrennial Convention, with the theme "Celebrating the Past—Charting the Future," focused on the forthcoming Centennial Celebration of the WH&OM Society in 1980. The convention met from July 29- August 3, 1979 at Wactor Temple A. M. E. Zion Church, Miami, Florida. The 20th Quadrennial Convention was held at Petty Memorial, New Orleans, Louisiana, from July 21-August 5, 1983, with the theme "A New People: Called, Commissioned, Committed." "The Challenge of Missions: Preparation, Dedication, Service, Sacrifice" was the theme of the 21st Quadrennial Convention, which met in Boston, Massachusetts, during August 2-7, 1987. Petty Memorial A. M. E. Zion Church, New Orleans, Louisiana was again the site for the 22nd Quadrennial Convention, which met from August 17-23, 1991. The theme for the convention was "Empowered to Build a New Era Through Heritage, Faith, Responsibility, Implementation." The 23rd and most recent Quadrennial Convention, in anticipation of the Bicentennial Celebration of the A.M. E. Zion Church and the turn of the century, met under the theme: "Our Mission Mandate for the Twenty-first Century: Witnessing, Disciplining, Equipping, Reaching." The site of the convention was St. Paul A. M. E. Zion Church, Detroit, Michigan. (p. 18)

During the 21st convention, voting machines were introduced for elections. The innovation considerably reduced the time required for the election process. It also meant that other business could be conducted while voting was underway. The General Conference of 1988 followed the WH&OM Society by using voting machines. (p. 20)

The Executive Board of the Woman's Home and Overseas Missionary Society is composed of missionary supervisors who are each appointed at the discretion of a bishop and the officers elected by the General Convention, which meets every four years in the year preceding the General Conference. The Book of Discipline states that "at the discretion of the Bishop, a Supervisor of the Woman's Home and Overseas Missionary Society in each Episcopal District shall be appointed, whose duty it shall be to supervise the missionary work of each department in the Episcopal District. She shall see that all monies collected for missions have been forwarded immediately to the Executive Secretary. She shall keep in correspondence with the Executive Secretary and shall keep the program of the Episcopal District in harmony with that of the plans of the General Officers of the society. She shall hold conventions or convocations annually at which she presides, and for which she, in cooperation with the District Officers, plans the program. She shall confer frequently with the Chairman of Committees on Mission

Woman's Home and Overseas Missionary Society

Education and Literature that she may more effectively promote programs of Mission Education in the district. She shall attend the annual conference of the district at which time she shall receive reports from the District Missionary Officers. She shall require of each District Officer written reports and exhibits of official receipts for money sent during the year."

Many children and youth of the A. M. E. Zion Church were early challenged to give their lives in service for others in the name of Jesus the Christ, our Lord. The pledge of the Buds of Promise Society in its earlier days under the superintendency of Mrs. Marie L. Clinton was:

>By the cross of Christ My Savior
>Undismayed, I'll watch and pray.
>Dare to win the world for Jesus
>Serve and please Him day by day.

The Woman's Home and Overseas Missionary Society of the A. M. E. Zion Church has grown into an effective, totally committed, world-wide agency of the church that implements the goal of "winning them one by one" for Christ and His kingdom on earth. Beginning with the smallest of our local congregations and developing into intricate organizations in the largest congregations, districts, and conferences of our Zion, the society is perhaps the most closely organized unit in the entire church While the society in its personnel, function, and commitment is a long, long way from the days of its beginning in 1880, it does not rest on past achievements but is earnestly dedicated to the onward and upward growth of peoples of the world as they seek to bring the kingdom of God on earth in Africa, Asia, Europe, North America, South America, the isles of the sea, and in God's good time on the continent of Australia.

The General Officers and Missionary Supervisors of the Woman's Home and Overseas Missionary Society during the years 1972-2000 are as listed below:

GENERAL OFFICERS
1971-75

President	Willa Mae Rice, Pittsburgh, Pa.
1st Vice President	Mary Gaither Meeks, Chicago, Ill.
2nd Vice President	Elizabeth Arnold Michael, Phila., Pa.
Executive Secretary	Grace L. Holmes, Knoxville, Tenn.
Recording Secretary	Ida M. Francis, Sacramento, Calif.

African Methodist Episcopal Zion Church

Treasurer	Evelyn M. Harris, N. Y. , N. Y.
Secretary, Young Women's Society	Maggie K. Beard, Rockingham, N. C.
Superintendent, Buds of Promise	Willie Heath Bobo, Spartanburg, S. C.
Secretary, Bureau of Supplies	Josephine T. Morris, Charlotte, N. C.
Chairman, Life Members' Council	Ann Walker, Arlington, Va.
Editor, The Woman's Column, *Missionary Seer*	Frealy M. Garrison, Perry, Ia.
Secretary, Bureau of Supplies	Laura E. Small, Washington, D. C. (deceased)

MISSIONARY SUPERVISORS
1972-76

1st Episcopal District	M. Ardelle Shaw, Wilmington, N. C.
2nd Episcopal District	Ida M. Smith, Mobile, Ala.
3rd Episcopal District	Edra Mae Hilliard, Detroit, Mich.
4th Episcopal District	Armayne G. Dunston, Youngstown, Oh.
5th Episcopal District	Madeline Foggie, Pittsburgh, Pa.
6th Episcopal District	Eva S. Hoggard, Indianapolis, Ind.
7th Episcopal District	Hildred H. Wactor, Fayetteville, N. C.
8th Episcopal District	Ethel Coleman, Baltimore, Md.
9th Episcopal District	Mary Marshall, Atlanta, Ga.
10th Episcopal District	Bernice Miller, Dallas, Tex.
11th Episcopal District	Vilma Leake, Charlotte, N. C.
12th Episcopal District	Janie Speaks, Hempstead, N. Y.

GENERAL OFFICERS
1975-79

President	Willa Mae Rice, Pittsburgh, Pa.
1st Vice President	Mary G. Meeks, Chicago, Ill.
2nd Vice President	Eliza Walker, Heath Springs, S.C.
Executive Secretary	Lonia M. Gill, Whistler, Ala.
Recording Secretary	Ida M. Francis, Sacramento, Calif.
Treasurer	Farris A. Williams, Tuscaloosa, Ala.
Secretary , Young Women's Society	Maggie K. Beard, Rockingham, N. C.

Woman's Home and Overseas Missionary Society

Superintendent, Buds of Promise	Ellen Richmond, Jackson, Miss.
Secretary, Bureau of Supplies	Josephine T. Morris, Charlotte, N. C.
Chairman, Life Members' Council	Willie Byers, Salisbury, N. C.
Editor, The Woman's Column,	Frealy M. Garrison, Perry, Iowa
Missionary Seer	

MISSIONARY SUPERVISORS
1976-80

1st Episcopal District	M. Ardelle Shaw, Wilmington, N. C.
2nd Episcopal District	Ida M. Smith, Mobile, Ala.
3rd Episcopal District	Edra Mae Hilliard, Detroit, Mich.
4th Episcopal District	Armayne G. Dunston, N. C.
5th Episcopal District	Madeline S. Foggie, Pittsburgh, Pa.
6th Episcopal District	Eva S. Hoggard, Indianapolis, Ind.
7th Episcopal District	Hildred H. Wactor, Fayetteville, N. C.
8th Episcopal District	Ethel Coleman, Baltimore, Md.
9th Episcopal District	Mary A. Marshall, Atlanta, Ga.
10th Episcopal District	Bernice Miller, Dallas, Tex.
11th Episcopal District	Vilma D. Leake, Charlotte, N. C.
12th Episcopal District	Janie Speaks, Hempstead, N. Y.

GENERAL OFFICERS
1979-83

President	Alcestis M. Coleman, St. Albans, N.Y.
1st Vice President	Theodora S. Smith, Greenville, Ala.
2nd Vice President	Eliza E. Walker, Heath Springs, S. C.
Executive Secretary	Lonia M. Gill, Whistler, Ala.
Recording Secretary	Yyonette J. Rhodes, Baltimore, Md.
Treasurer	Farris A. Williams, Tuscaloosa, Ala.
Secretary, Young Women's Society	Dorothy S. Johnson, Salisbury, N. C.
Superintendent, Buds of Promise	Ellen M. Richmond, Tuskegee, Ala.
Secretary, Bureau of Supplies	Mildred S. Harvey, Concord, N. C.
Chairman, Life Members' Council	Willie G. Byers, Salisbury, N. C.
Editor, Woman's Column,	Clara V. Robertson, Hammond, La.
Missionary Seer	

African Methodist Episcopal Zion Church

MISSIONARY SUPERVISORS
1980-84

1st Episcopal District	Ida M. Smith, Mobile, Ala.
2nd Episcopal District	Armayne G. Dunston, New Orleans, La.
3rd Episcopal District	Madeline S. Foggie, Pittsburgh, Pa.
4th Episcopal District	Eva S. Hoggard, Indianapolis, Ind.
5th Episcopal District	Hildred H. Wactor, Fayetteville, N. C.
6th Episcopal District	Ethel G. Coleman, Baltimore, Md.
7th Episcopal District	Mary A. Marshall, Atlanta, Ga.
8th Episcopal District	Bernice F. Miller, Raleigh, N. C.
9th Episcopal District	Vilma D. Leake, Charlotte, N. C.
10th Episcopal District	Janie G. Speaks, Salisbury, N. C.
11th Episcopal District	Ruth Anderson, Charlotte, N. C.
12th Episcopal District	Wilhelma J. Bishop, Temple Hills, Md. (deceased)

GENERAL OFFICERS
1983-87

President	Alcestis M. Coleman, St. Albans, N. Y.
1st Vice President	Theodora S. Smith, Lancaster, S. C.
2nd Vice President	Adlise I. Porter, Detroit, Mich.
Executive Secretary	Alcenia Harps, Norfolk, Virginia
Recording Secretary	Yyonette J. Rhodes, Fayetteville, N. C.
Treasurer	Josephine Spaulding, Whiteville, N. C. (resigned 1986)
Interim Treasurer (1986-87)	Mildred Harvey, Concord, N. C.
Secretary of Young Women	Dorothy S. Johnson, Greensboro, N. C.
Superintendent, Buds of Promise	Charlottee N. Atkins, Wash., D. C.
Secretary, Bureau of Supplies	Mildred S. Harvey, Concord, N. C.
Chairman, Life Members' Council	Margaret S. Willie, Kannapolis, N. C.
Editor, Woman's Column, *Missionary Seer*	Clara V. Robertson, Hammond, La.

MISSIONARY SUPERVISORS
1984-88

1st Episcopal District	Ida M. Smith, Mobile, Ala.

Woman's Home and Overseas Missionary Society

2nd Episcopal District	Armayne G. Dunston, Philadelphia, Pa.
3rd Episcopal District	Madeline S. Foggie, Pittsburgh, Pa.
4th Episcopal District	Eva S. Hoggard, Indianapolis, Ind.
5th Episcopal District	Ethel G. Coleman, Baltimore, Md.
6th Episcopal District	Mary Ann Marshall, High Point, N. C.
7th Episcopal District	Bernice F. Miller, Raleigh, N. C.
8th Episcopal District	Janie A. Speaks, Salisbury, N. C.
9th Episcopal District	Ruth R. Anderson, Charlotte, N. C.
10th Episcopal District	Marlene Y. Bishop, Temple Hills, Md..
11th Episcopal District	Joan S. Fisher, St. Louis, Mo.
12th Episcopal District	Mamie W. White, Glastonbury, Conn.

GENERAL OFFICERS
1987-91

President	Grace L. Holmes, Knoxville, Tenn.
1st Vice President	Vilma D. Leake, Matthews, N. C.
2nd Vice President	Adlise I. Porter, Detroit, Mich.
Executive Secretary	Alcenia Harps, Norfolk, Va.
Recording Secretary	Clara B. Ivery, Montgomery, Ala.
Treasurer	Gwendolyn B. Johnson, L. A., Calif.
Secretary of Young Women	Florena B. Johnson, Greensburg, La.
Superintendent, Buds of Promise	Charlottee N. Umoja, Wash., D. C.
Secretary, Bureau of Supplies	Guytanna H. DeGraffenreidt, Mt. Vernon, N. Y.
Chairman, Life Members' Council	Margaret S. Willie, Kannapolis, N. C.
Editor, Woman's Column	Barbara Shaw, Baltimore, Md..
Missionary Seer	

MISSIONARY SUPERVISORS
1988-92

1st Episcopal District	Ida M. Smith, Mobile, Ala.
2nd Episcopal District	Armayne G. Dunston, Philadelphia, Pa.
3rd Episcopal District	Eva S. Hoggard, Chevy Chase, Md..
4th Episcopal District	Ethel G. Coleman, Baltimore, Md..
5th Episcopal District	Bernice F. Miller, Raleigh, N. C.

African Methodist Episcopal Zion Church

6th Episcopal District	Janie A. Speaks, Salisbury, N. C.
7th Episcopal District	Ruth R. Anderson, Charlotte, N. C.
8th Episcopal District	Marlene Y. Bishop, Temple Hills, Md..
9th Episcopal District	Joan S. Fisher, St. Louis, Mo.
10th Episcopal District	Mamie W. White, Glastonbury, Conn.
11th Episcopal District	Geraldine J. Walker, Flossmoor, Ill.
12th Episcopal District	Lula G. Williams, Jamestown, N. C.
13th Episcopal District	Faustina I. Ekemam, Owerri, Nigeria

GENERAL OFFICERS
1991-95

General President	Grace L. Holmes, Knoxville, Tenn.
1st Vice President	Vilma D. Leake, Matthews, N. C.
2nd Vice President	Essie Curnell, Houston, Tex.
Executive Secretary	Barbara Shaw, Baltimore, Md..
Recording Secretary	Betty V. Stith, New Rochelle, N. Y.
Treasurer	Gwendolyn B. Johnson Brumfield, Los Angeles, Calif.
Coordinator of YAMS	JoAnn Holmes, Charlotte, N. C.
Secretary of Young Women's Society	Florena B. Johnson, Greensburg, La.
Superintendent, Buds of Promise	Mary H. Jones, Rock Hill, S. C.
Secretary, Bureau of Supplies	Guytanna H. DeGraffenreidt, Mount Vernon, N. Y.
Chairman, Life Members' Council	Gladys M. Felton, Chicago, Ill.
Editor, Woman's Column, *Missionary Seer*	Mattie W. Taylor, Far Rockaway, N. Y.

MISSIONARY SUPERVISORS
1992-96

1st Episcopal District	Janie A. Speaks, Salisbury, N. C.
2nd Episcopal District	Ruth R. Anderson, Charlotte, N. C.
3rd Episcopal District	Marlene Y. Bishop, Charlotte, N. C.
4th Episcopal District	Geraldine J. Walker, Flossmoor, Ill.
5th Episcopal District	Lula G. Williams, Jamestown, N. C.
6th Episcopal District	Faustina I. Ekemam, Owerri, Nigeria

Woman's Home and Overseas Missionary Society

7th Episcopal District	Iris M. Battle, Charlotte, N. C.
8th Episcopal District	Dorothy S. Johnson, Little Rock, Ark.
9th Episcopal District	Georgia M. Thompson, Wash., D. C.
10th Episcopal District	Mattilyn T. Rochester, Willingboro, N. J.
11th Episcopal District	Dorothy E. Brunson, Baltimore, Md..
12th Episcopal District	Barbara S. Carr, Greendale, Mo.

GENERAL OFFICERS
1995-1999

President	Adlise Ivey Porter, Detroit, Michigan
1st Vice President	Lillian Turner Shelborne, Hickory Grove, S. C.
2nd Vice President	Essie Curnell, Houston, Texas
Executive Secretary	Alice Steele-Robinson, Concord, N. C.
Recording Secretary	Betty V. Stith, New Rochelle, N. Y.
Treasurer	Elease W. Johnson, Charlotte, N. C.
Coordinator of YAMS	JoAnn Holmes, Charlotte, N. C.
Secretary, Young Women's Society	Millicent D. Thomas, Jamestown, N.C.
Superintendent, Buds of Promise	Mary H. Jones, Rock Hill, S. C.
Secretary, Bureau of Supplies	Annette E. Whitted, Salisbury, N. C.
Chairman, Life Members' Council	Gladys M. Felton, Chicago, Ill.
Editor Woman's Column, *Missionary Seer*	Mattie W. Taylor, Far Rockaway, N. Y.

MISSIONARY SUPERVISORS
1996-2000

Piedmont Episcopal District	Marlene Y. Bishop, Charlotte, N. C.
Northeastern Region Episcopal District	Geraldine J. Walker, Flossmoor, Ill.
Mid-Atlantic Episcopal District	Rev. Lula G. Williams, Fort Wash., Md..
Eastern West Africa Episcopal District	Faustina I. Ekemam, Owerri, Nigeria
Eastern North Carolina Episcopal District	Iris M. Battle, Charlotte, N. C.
South Atlantic Episcopal District	Dorothy S. Johnson, Matthews, N. C.

African Methodist Episcopal Zion Church

Alabama -Florida Episcopal District

Georgia M. Thompson, Wash., D. C.

Mid-West Episcopal District

Mattilyn T. Rochester, Willingboro, N. J.

Mid-Atlantic I Episcopal District

Dorothy E. Brunson, Baltimore, Md.

Western Episcopal District

Barbara S. Carr, Greendale, Mo.

Southwestern Delta Episcopal District

Estella R. Jarrett, Chicago, Ill.

Western West Africa Episcopal District

Aurelia S. Brown, Randolph, Mass.

CONNECTIONAL LAY COUNCIL
1972-1996

On May 18, 1916, the organization of the Lay Members Council of the African Methodist Episcopal Zion Church was approved at the General Conference meeting in Louisville, Kentucky. Its main goals were: "To support the Bishops, general officers, pastors and all officers of the connection, and to cooperate with them in all their plans for the advancement of the kingdom of Jesus Christ. To work especially for the missionary cause. To give expression to the opinions of the laity on all matters relating to the ideals, principles, policies and servants of the Church, and to secure proper consideration of the wishes of the laity. To work for an increase in lay membership in the General Conferences and boards, to the end that equal lay representation may soon become an established fact. (This was achieved in 1928.) To promote progressive legislation in the councils of the Church, and to encourage only the best ideals, principles, policies, and people. To encourage the increased use of approved business methods of conducting the affairs of the Church; and to bring to the attention of the Church such laymen and others whose training and experience, especially qualify them to serve in elective or appointive positions. To keep the lay interest in connectional affairs, during the intervals between the various conferences, and to promote unity of action for the welfare of the church. To carry out the wishes of the lay electoral colleges, annual and general." Mr. J. H. Johnson was elected the first president of the organization. Equal lay and ministerial representation at General Conference was established in 1928 at St. Louis, Missouri, but the organization became dormant until 1948, when the Laymen's Association sought approval from General Conference, then meeting in Louisville, Kentucky, to create a Laymen's Association in each annual conference. The General Conference approved establishment of the Laymen's Council and directed that the organization present its constitution and by-laws to the next General Conference, which met at First A. M. E. Zion Church, in Brooklyn, New York, in 1952. Dr. Victor J. Tulane, who was elected president at the conference, presented the constitution and by-laws of the Laymen's Council to the General Conference. General Conference created a Board of Lay Activities, comprising a representative from each episcopal district, appointed by the bishop and confirmed by General Conference, to direct the Laymen's Council. In consequence, the Laymen's Council became a part of the constitutional structure of the church. Dr. Victor J. Tulane served as president until 1964. He was succeeded by Arthur E. Brooks who was elected in 1964 and reelected in 1968 and 1972 sessions of General Conference. (Walls, *African Methodist Episcopal Zion Church, pp. 450-52; The Doctrines and Discipline of the African Methodist Episcopal Zion Church*, 1976, p. 255)

African Methodist Episcopal Zion Church

Although the principle of equal lay representation had been accepted by the denomination, many of the administrative boards did not have an appointed lay representative. A resolution on Equal Lay Representation on the administrative boards passed in 1976 at the 40th General Conference, which was held in Chicago, Illinois. The resolution was affirmed by the 41st General Conference meeting in Greensboro, North Carolina following the recommendation of the Commission on Restructuring: "The committee agrees that Lay Persons on our administrative boards of the church is a worthy principle now practiced by church law. Every effort should be made to continue this practice thereby providing more opportunity for General Church participation of our Lay Persons." (*Official Journal, 41st Quad. Sess. Gen. Conf.*, p. 596)

During August 10-15, 1981, the Connectional Lay Council held its Second Quadrennial Convention in Birmingham, Alabama, at the Metropolitan A. M. E. Zion Church, with Rev. Dr. E. R. Faush, host pastor; Rev. Dr. M. C. Williams, host presiding elder; and the Rt. Rev. J. Clinton Hoggard, host bishop. The theme of the convention was "So Send I You." The convention established "A Laity Hall of Fame," financed the journey of Edwin E. Udechuku of Nigeria to attend a lay meeting in the U. S., and pre-pared a worship book with meditations. Officers elected for the 1981-85 quadrennium included Ms. Betty V. Stith, general president, Dr. C. DuPont Rippy, 1st vice president, Mr. James Hewitt, Jr., 2nd vice president; Ms. Lizzie M. Sykes, secretary; Mr. Robert H. Simms, treasurer, and Mr. Jasper J. McCormick, chaplain. Appointed officers included Ms. Alcenia Harps, assistant secretary; Mr. Albert Stout, Sr., parliamentarian; Mr. Gossie H. Hudson, Sr., public relations and editor of the "Laity Speaks" column. Appointed committee chairpersons included: Rosa Alexander, Special Projects; Mary E. Taylor, Legislation; James Lash, Social Concerns/Political Action; Coyal Cooper "We Care"; Alean Rush, Education; Willie Whitfield, Visual Aids; Theodore Shaw, History; Dennison D. Garrett, Sr., Bishop George J. Leake, III, Scholarship Fund; Margaret Willie, Junior College Library Fund; John H. Winston, M.D., Constitution Revision; Howard Crooms, Convention Site; Marlene McGhee and Bennie McCall, Music. Regional Directors (two from each of five regions of the denomination) were appointed and given the responsibility to plan the quarterly Lay Institute for their respective regions and a banquet to honor an outstanding lay person. (*Official Journal, 42nd Quad. Sess. Gen Conf.*, pp. 528-29)

The first time the Connectional Lay Council reported to General Conference was at the 42nd Quadrennial Session, in St. Louis, Missouri, in July-August, 1984, when President Betty V. Stith, who had succeeded Mr. Arthur E. Brooks as general president

Connectional Lay Council

in 1981, addressed the conference. Special activities during the 1981-85 quadrennium included the Memorial Service on November 12, 1983 in honor of the late Bishop George J. Leake, III, chairperson of the Board of Lay Activities, who passed away on June 15, 1981. Over three thousand dollars were collected for the scholarship fund in his name to benefit a student entering Hood Theological Seminary. A new handbook was prepared and distributed in 1982. Donations were made to benefit the libraries of Clinton and Lomax Hannon Junior Colleges. In each case, a contribution of one thousand dollars was given as initial payment toward $10,000.00 in monies and books for their respective libraries. Other special donations were made to Barnes Chapel A. M. E. Zion Church, in memory of the late Dr. Alexander Barnes, former director of Public Relations; the David H. Bradley Memorial Fund in memory of the late Rev. Dr. Bradley; former editor of the *A. M. E. Zion Quarterly Review*, and the Bishop Herbert Bell Shaw Caribbean Student Scholarship Fund at Livingstone College in memory of the late Bishop Shaw; the A. P. Morris (former secretary-treasurer of Home Missions, Brotherhood Pensions, and Ministerial Relief) Memorial Christmas Cheer Fund; and the Church Extension Fund. The Connectional Lay Council emphasized the observance of Lay Council Sunday. The Second Quadrennial Lay Convocation, held in High Point, North Carolina, March 23-24, 1981, with the theme "Preparation for Purposeful Action" was successful. Bishop Arthur Marshall, Jr., chairperson of the Board of Lay Activities, gave the sermon, and Bishop Alfred G. Dunston, Jr., host bishop, gave the luncheon speech. Workshops on tithing, pensions, contiguous districts, the General Conference, legislation, and the budget generated lively discussions. The Rev. Andrew Mackey, pastor of St. Stephens A. M. E. Zion Church, High Point, North Carolina, was host. Dr. C. D. Rippy contributed much to the effective organization of the convocation. (Ibid., pp. 528-31)

At the Connectional Lay Council Convention in Norfolk, Virginia, in 1985, Dr. C. D. Rippy was elected to succeed Dr. Betty V. Stith as general president. His report to the 43rd General Conference in 1988 showed evidence of the continuing work of the Connectional Lay Council. Dr. Rippy was assisted in leading the organization by James E. Hewitt, Jr., 1st vice president; Lizzie Sykes, 2nd vice president; Robert Simms, treasurer; Odessa Tyson, secretary, and Jasper McCormick, chaplain. Appointed officers included Rigna Askew, assistant secretary; Albert Stout, Sr., parliamentarian; and Theodore Shaw, editor of the "Laity Speaks" column. Committee chairpersons included Rosa Alexander, chairperson; Gilbert McRae, co-chairperson, Special Projects; Mary E. Taylor, Legislation; Atty. Adele Riley, Social Concerns/Political Action; Coyal Cooper, We Care; Alean Rush, Education; Phillip Hager, Visual Aids;

African Methodist Episcopal Zion Church

Dennison D. Garrett, Sr., Bishop George J. Leake, III, Scholarship Fund; Margaret Willie, Junior College Library Fund; John H. Winston, M. D., Constitution Revision; Margaret Meeks, Finance; Howard Crooms, Convention Site; Helen C. Scott, Membership; Joyce Zimmerman, Music. Co-directors of the five regions were: Marion Seay, Dorothy Maultsby, Samantha Wormley, assistant, Region I; William Orr and Carson Bethea, Region II; Bertha Howard and Willie King, Sr., Region III, Lynwood Howie and Raymond Richmond, Jr., Region IV; Henry and Tillman McClunie, Region V. (*Official Journal 43rd Quad. Sess., Gen. Conf.*, pp. 671-72)

The Third Quadrennial Lay Convocation, with the theme "Concerned Christians—Dedicated, Committed, and United for Service," was held March 17-19 1988, at Shaw Temple A. M. E. Zion Church and Westin Peachtree Plaza, Atlanta, Georgia. Bishop Cecil Bishop and Dr. J. W. Smith were host bishop and pastor, respectively. Chairperson of the Board of Lay Activities, Bishop Alfred G. Dunston, Jr., delivered the convocation sermon, and Bishop Cecil Bishop gave the banquet address. The Connectional Lay Council collected $3,020.00 for the Bishop George J. Leake, III, Memorial Scholarship Fund for the quadrennium and donated $2,000 and books valued at $4,000 to Clinton Junior College. (Ibid., pp. 672-73)

Because Dr. Rippy was elected to the Judicial Council at the General Conference in 1988, he had to resign as general president of the Connectional Lay Council. James E. Hewitt, Jr., who was serving as 1st vice president then assumed the presidency. Mr. Hewitt was elected general president at the Fourth Quadrennial Connectional Lay Convention held in Los Angeles, California in 1990. Other elected officers included Jasper J. McCormick, 1st vice president; William Orr, 2nd vice president; Odessa Tyson-Clapp, secretary, Robert H. Simms, treasurer; and Coyal C. Cooper, chaplain. Other appointments included Joyce P. Tillman, acting secretary; Lula K. Howard, Education chairperson; Samantha Wormley, co-director, Region I; and Lillian Williams, co-director, Region II. Shortly after the convention, Mr. Hewitt became ill and had to rely on the assistance of 1st Vice President Mr Jasper McCormick to lead the council until the convention in 1993. William Orr, the 2nd vice president, passed away, and Mrs. Odessa Tyson Clapp assumed the duties of 2nd vice president and membership chairperson. Mrs. Lizzie Sykes, secretary of the Connectional Lay Council, also passed away and was replaced by Mrs. Joyce Tillman who was appointed to serve as secretary during the interim by Bishop Alfred G. Dunston, Jr., chairperson of the Board of Lay Activities. (*Official Journal 44th Quad. Sess. Gen. Conf.*, pp. 682-83)

The following officers were elected to lead the Connectional Lay Council during the 1993-97 quadrennium: Mrs. Mary E. Taylor, general president; Mrs. Lula Howard,

Connectional Lay Council

1st vice president; Mrs. Frances J. Glenn, secretary; Mr. Ervin D. Reid, treasurer; Mr. Coyal Cooper, chaplain; Mr. Theodore Shaw, the "Laity Speaks" column; and Mr. Albert S. Stout, Sr., parliamentarian. Those appointed directors of the then twelve District Regions were, respectively, Mrs. Lillian P. Williams, 1st; Mr. Dennison D. Garrett, Sr., 2nd; Mrs. Cheryl Strong, 3rd; Mr. Carl Lovelady, 4th; Mrs. Samantha Wormley, 5th; Mrs. Annie Williams, 7th; Mrs. Mary Lynn Johnson 8th; Mrs. J. Fairbanks Leach, 9th; Mr. James Harper, 10th; Mr. Leon Henry, 12th. There were no appointees to the sixth and eleventh District Regions. Appointed committee chairpersons included: Ms. Mozzella Ritter, Evangelism; Dr. John H. Winston, M. D., Legislative; Judge Adele M. Riley and Dr. Betty V. Stith, Constitution; Mrs. Vivian Williams, Music; Mr. Dennison D. Garrett, Sr., Bishop George J. Leake Scholarship Fund; Mrs. Rosa Alexander, Special Projects; Mr. Phillip Hager and Mrs Alean Rush, Bicentennial Project; and Phillip Hagar, Photographer. (Letter, 9/4/96, from Albert S. Stout, Sr., to the author)

The Fifth Quadrennial Lay Convocation was held March 13-17, 1996, at Myrtle Beach, South Carolina. Approximately four hundred fifty people attended. Bishop Clarence Carr was the Opening speaker. He was followed by Bishop Richard Thompson, who was the Prayer Breakfast speaker. Dr. Andrew Best was the Challenge Luncheon speaker. Workshop leaders included Dr. Mattilyn Rochester, Mrs. Dorothy Johnson, Atty. Dorothy Maultsby, and Judge Adele Riley. Mrs. Lula K. Howard chaired the convocation, along with Mrs. Annie Williams as co-chair. ("Report of Connectional Lay Council, 1993-96, to 45th Quad. Sess. Gen. Conf.," pp. 1-5)

Highlights of the Connectional Lay Council's activities for the quadrennium include the Harriet Tubman Properties Grounds Beautification Bicentennial Project, to which $50,000 was pledged; the reinstitution of area meetings, the first of which was held at Blair Street A. M. E. Zion Church, Jackson, Mississippi, and the second, in February 1995, at Mt. Zion A. M. E. Zion Church, Montgomery, Alabama. The Connectional Lay Council organized its first Evangelistic Retreat, at Dinwiddie Institute, Dinwiddie, Virginia, 3-5 November 1995, with the theme "Empowered by Our Faith." It was hosted by the Fifth Episcopal District supervised by the Rt. Rev. Milton A. Williams and Mrs. Samantha Wormley, regional director. The Rev. Dr. Norman H. Hicklin, director of Evangelism, Rev. Lula Williams, missionary supervisor, Fifth Episcopal District, Rev. Cameron W. Jackson, pastor, John Wesley A. M. E. Zion Church, Rev. Rita Colbert, pastor, St. Mary's A. M. E. Zion Church, and Dr. Betty V. Stith, former president of the Connectional Lay Council, and eighty lay council leaders were in attendance. The Connectional Lay Council reported total membership of 16,672, which included 15,947 lay memberships, 439 ministerial memberships, and 286 life memberships. (Ibid., pp. 2-4)

African Methodist Episcopal Zion Church

The Sixth Quadrennial Convention of the Connectional Lay Council, met August 4th-8th, 1997, in Louisville, Kentucky, at the Executive West Hotel and at Stoner Memorial A. M. E. Zion Church, which was the host church. The convention was guided by the theme "Planning for Progress: God's Challenge and Our Response." The following members were elected to office: Mrs. Lula K. Howard, general president; Ms. Linda Fay Starnes, 1st vice president; Mr. Jasper McCormick, 2nd vice president; Ms Frances J. Glenn, secretary; Mr. Ervin D. Reid, treasurer; and Ms. Annie Williams, chaplain. The Revs. James C. Tutt and James H. Dunlap, Sr., Dr. Mattilyn Rochester, and Bishop Enoch B. Rochester were host pastor, presiding elder, missionary supervisor, and presiding prelate, respectively. ("Report of the Connectional Lay Council to the 45th Quad. Sess. Gen. Conf.," pp. 1-4)

BOARD OF LAY ACTIVITIES

1972-76
Bishop George J. Leake, III, chairperson
Bishop William M. Smith, vice chairperson
Members:

1. Mr. W. A. Foster	7. Mrs. Elizabeth Duffie
2. Mr. Albert Stout	8. Mrs. Grace L. Holmes
3. Mr. W. Mance Gilliam	9. Mr. J. W. Green
4. Dr. John H. Winston, Jr.	10. Mrs. Emma H. Strother
5. Mr. Arthur E. Brooks	11. Mr. Melvin Johnson
6. Mr. Oscar W. Adams, Esq.	12. Mr. Jasper J. McCormick

1976-80
Bishop George J. Leake, III, chairperson
Bishop W. M. Smith, 1st vice chairperson
Bishop Arthur Marshall, Jr., 2nd vice chairperson
Members:

1. Mrs. Betty V. Stith	7. Mr. W. F. Witherspoon
2. Rev. R. L. Perry	8. Mr. Amos Jackson
3. Mrs. Elizabeth J. Davis	9. Mr. J. W. Greene
4. Dr. John H. Winston, Jr.	10. Mrs. Mary B. Hicks
5. Mr. Arthur Brooks	11. Ms. Teresa Simmons
6. Ms. Georgia M. Farnsworth	12. Mrs. Helen L. DeBerry

Connectional Lay Council

1980-84

Bishop George J. Leake, III, chairperson
Bishop Arthur Marshall. Jr., first vice chairperson
Bishop A. G. Dunston, Jr., second vice chairperson
Members:

1. Mrs. Hattie Clark
2. Mr. H. W. Robinson
3. Mr. E. Myers Harvell
4. Mrs. Rosa Boyd
5. Mrs. Vernetta McIver
6. Dr. John A. Stringfield
7. Mr. J. W. Green
8. Mrs. Maple C. Williams
9. Dr. W. A. Best
10. Rev. S. M. Taylor
11. Mrs. Alcenia Harps
12. Ms. Helen DeBerry

1984-88

Bishop Arthur Marshall, Jr., chairperson
Bishop A. G. Dunston, Jr., 1st vice chairperson
Bishop William M. Smith, 2nd vice chairperson
Members:

1. Rev. Belvie Jackson
2. Mr. Clifford Johnson
3. Ms. Dorothy Maultsby, Esq.
4. Mr. Willie King
5. Mr. Lynwood Howie
6. Mr. J. W. Green
7. Rev. W. M. Freeman
8. Mrs. Odell Fleming
9. Mr. James Hewitt
10. Mrs. Mildred Cooke
11. Mr. Josh Curnell, Esq.
12. Mrs. Vilma D. Leake

1988-92

Bishop A. G. Dunston, Jr., chairperson
Bishop W. M. Smith, 1st vice chairperson
Bishop J. C. Hoggard, 2nd vice chairperson
Members:

1. Rev. J. A. Quick
2. Mr. Arthur L. Moultrie, Sr.
3. Ms. Mary Jones
4. Mr. Walter Johnson
5. Mr. Major Sanders
6. Mrs. Alice Spicer
7. Mrs. Joyce Booker
8. Mr. Willie King
9. Dr. J. W. Green
10. Mrs. Mildred Cooke
11. Mr. James Hewitt
12. Mrs. Helen Carroll-Scott
13. Rev. Seth Lartey

African Methodist Episcopal Zion Church

1992-96
Bishop Ruben L. Speaks, chairperson
Bishop Clarence Carr, 1st vice chairperson
Bishop Richard K. Thompson, 2nd vice chairperson
Members:

1. Dr. C. D. Rippy
2. Mrs. Alice Spicer
3. Mr. A. L. Moultrie, Sr.
4. Mr. Jasper J. McCormick
5. Mrs. Bennie McCall
6. Mr. S. I. Iheonunekwu
7. Mr. Charles Mackey
8. Mr. Raymond Richmond, Jr.
9. Rev. Eddie H. Hicklin, Jr.
10. Mrs. Harriet McElvaney
11. Ms. Mozella Ritter
12. Rev. Mary Helen Moore

1996-2000
Bishop Clarence Carr, chairperson
Bishop Richard K. Thompson, 1st vice chairperson
Bishop George E. Battle, Jr., 2nd vice chairperson
Members:

1. Mrs. Minnie McRae
2. Mr. David Aiken
3. Ms. Mozella B. Ritter
4. Mr. Sokari Sambo
5. Rev. Clyde Murphy
6. Mrs. Annie M. Williams
7. Mr. Sanford Davis
8. Mr. James Harper
9. Mr. A. L. Moultrie, Sr.
10. Rev. Joyce M. Smith
11. Mr. Raymond Richmond, Jr.
12. Mr. Clennie H. Murphy, Jr.

A. M. E. ZION CHURCH JUDICIAL COUNCIL
1988-1996

THE idea of a Judicial Council for the A. M. E. Zion Church dates back to the General Conference of 1956 when it was first proposed and then was again proposed at the General Conference of 1960. Both proposals were defeated. However, the 1960 General Conference agreed to forward to each annual conference the statutes passed by that General Conference for establishing a Judicial Council. The results of the voting in the annual conferences were twenty-three (23) conferences in favor and twenty-eight (28) against establishment of a Judicial Council. Thirty-five (35) affirmative votes were required to pass the resolution. (*Official Journal, 42nd Quad. Sess., Gen. Conf.*, p. 634)

At the 42nd General Conference, a resolution to institute a Judicial Council was again presented. The Resolutions Committee decided that the resolution "had merit" and referred it to the Executive and Judiciary Business Committee and the Revisions Committee. The Revisions Committee concurred with the Resolutions Committee, and the resolution was "adopted by the house." Following the 42nd General Conference, the Board of Bishops declared the resolution number thirty-five (35) "null and void." During the following quadrennium (1984-88), discussion was heard from both the Board of Bishops and the General Conference delegates concerning the legality of the procedure that had been followed. (Ibid., pp. 618, 622)

After thwarted attempts, much prayer, and deliberation, the Judicial Council of the A. M. E. Zion Church was finally established at the 43rd General Conference, which met July 27-August 5, 1988, in Charlotte, North Carolina. The duties of the Judicial Council were laid down as follows:

a. To study faithfully and earnestly the laws and rules governing the African Methodist Episcopal Zion Church.

b. To hear and make declaratory judgements when petitioned to do so when any law is subject to more than one interpretation or any paragraph in the Book of Discipline is of doubtful meaning. Any person in good and regular standing of the A. M. E. Zion Church can petition the Judicial Council for such a judgement. The Council's decision is final, unless modified or reversed by the General Conference.

c. To hear the appeal and determine any appeal from a Bishop's decision on a question or ruling made in an Annual Conference on some positive law which affects some substantial rights of the one(s) making the appeal.

d. The Judicial Council shall not have the right to interfere, in any way, with the right of a Bishop to appoint, transfer, or remove pastors as set forth in the Book of

African Methodist Episcopal Zion Church

Discipline, nor with the right of a Bishop to administer the Discipline of the A. M. E. Zion Church.

e. To hear and determine an appeal of a Bishop when taken from the decision of a trial court.

f. To hear and determine an appeal from an elder when taken from the decision of a trial court. (Book of Discipline, 1992, pp. 140-46; *Official Journal, 43rd Quad. Sess., Gen. Conf.*, p. 851)

According to the Constitution of the Judicial Council, it shall have appellate function and shall not have original jurisdiction. Members of the Judicial Council are nominated by a Nominating Committee, comprising the constituencies of Bishops, Laymen, and the Lay Council, which nominates fifteen (15) members and fifteen (15) alternates. The General Conference elects nine members (9) and nine (9) alternates, of whom five (5) are clergy and four (4) are lay persons. At least three (3) of the members shall be attorneys and/or judges who are members of the A. M. E. Zion Church. Nominations may be made from the floor of the General Conference. Members of the Judicial Council are elected for four years and may be reelected. They are not eligible for membership in the General Conference or the Connectional Council. They therefore cannot serve on any administrative board or hold any other elected or appointed position while they serve on the Judicial Council. (*Book of Discipline*,1992, pp. 141-42.)

At the 43rd General Conference, each General Conference delegate voted for five (5) clergy and four (4) lay persons to serve on the Judicial Council and five (5) clergy and four (4) lay persons to serve as alternates. Ms. Christine Triggs served as secretary. The following persons were successful in the election: Rev. James Crumlin, Esq., Rev. (later Bishop) Nathaniel Jarrett, Rev. Thaddeus Garrett, Rev. John E. Watts, and Rev. Leroy O. Perry. The clergy alternates were: Rev. Vernon A. Shannon, Rev. Gloria S. Moore, Rev. David Baker, Rev. G. Curtis Newby and Rev. Michael Ellis. The lay members were Judge Adele Riley, Dr. C. DuPont Rippy, Mrs. Alean Rush, and Mr. Albert Holland, Esq. The lay alternates were: Judge Oscar W. Adams, Mr. Albert Stout, Mrs. Mary Taylor, and Mr. Herbert Scott. (Ibid., p. 877)

At the 44th General Conference, held in Atlanta, Georgia in 1992, the following clergy were elected: Rev. Dr. James A. Crumlin, Esq., Rev. John E. Watts, Rev. Walter L. Leigh, Dr. Robert Clayton, Rev. Dr. Mozella G. Mitchell. Clergy alternates elected included Rev. Louis Richardson, and Rev. E. H. White. Lay persons elected included: Judge Adele M. Riley, Mr. Albert Holland, Esq., Mrs. Alean Rush, and Mr. Robert E. Richardson, Esq. Lay alternates elected were: Mr. J. R. Broughton, Mr. John Wesley Brooks, Esq., Mr. Neville Tucker, Esq., and Mr. Robert T. Perry, Esq., (*Official*

A. M. E. Zion Church Judicial Council

Journal, 44th Quad. Sess. Gen. Conf., pp. 838-39)

At the 45th General Conference held in Washington, D. C. and Temple Hills, Maryland, the following persons were elected to the Judicial Council for the years 1996-2000: Judge Adele M. Riley, president; Rev. Monica H. Roye, Esq., Mrs. Alean Rush, Dr. E. Alex Brower, Esq., Rev. Medis Cheek, Rev. Dr. George L. Blackwell, Rev. Dr. Mozella G. Mitchell, Mr. Robert E. Richardson, Esq., and Mr. Neville Tucker, Esq. (*Star of Zion*, Vol. 120, No. 37-38, p. 16)

Over the years since its inception, the Judicial Council has been regarded as a "safety valve" because its existence is a "caution" to all who participate in the administrative affairs of the church.

CONNECTIONAL TRUSTEES
1972-1996

THE *Book of Discipline of the African Methodist Episcopal Zion Church* includes a chapter entitled "Denominational Fund." This fund is under the supervision of the Board of Connectional Trustees. The following clauses from the *Book of Discipline*, 1996 (p. 161) set forth the composition of the Board of Connectional Trustees and its duties regarding this fund:

¶ 27. The General Conference shall appoint at each of its Quadrennial Sessions a Board of Connectional Trustees, consisting of one member from each Episcopal District, which shall be duly incorporated. [The incorporation is currently in Washington, D. C.]

¶ 28. The Connectional Trustees shall hold in trust for the benefit of the African Methodist Episcopal Zion Church any and all donations bequests, grants, and funds in trust, etc., that may be given or conveyed to said Board or to the African Methodist Episcopal Zion Church as such, for any benevolent object and to administer the said funds, and the proceeds of the same, in accordance with the directions of the donors and of the interest of the Church contemplated by said donors, under the direction of the General Conference.

¶ 429. When any such donation, bequests, grant or trust is made to this Board or to the Church, it shall be the duty of the Pastor within the bounds of whose Charge it occurs to give an early notice thereof to the Board, which shall proceed without delay to take possession of the same according to the provisions of its charter."

¶ 430. It shall be the duty of all our Ministers to obtain, as far as practicable, contributions to said fund by donations, bequests and otherwise.

¶ 431. The interest accumulating from said Fund shall be subject to the order of the General Conference for the following purposes: 1. To pay the expenses of the General Conference; 2. To pay the expenses of delegations appointed by the General Conference to corresponding bodies; 3. To make up any deficiencies in the salaries of the Bishops; 4. To relieve the necessities of the Superannuated Ministers, and the widows and children who have died in the work.

Connectional Trustees

¶ 432. The Board shall make a faithful report of its doings and of the funds and property on hand, to each Quadrennial Session of the General Conference of the African Methodist Episcopal Zion Church.

Currently the Board of the Connectional Trustees is responsible for the deposit of funds in the Industrial Bank of Washington accruing from the sale of the former denominational property located at 1326-28 U Street, N. W., Washington, D. C. in which the Department of Foreign Missions (now Overseas Missions) was located prior to its being moved in to the InterChurch Center office in New York City by action of the General Conference of 1960, meeting in Buffalo, New York. This building also housed the office of the General Secretary, which was moved to Charlotte, North Carolina in 1976, and the Department of Evangelism, which was moved to Luray, Virginia, in 1975.

These funds are held in trust by the Board of Connectional Trustees and are accounted for to each General Conference as required by law. The following persons served as Connectional Trustees during the period of our current review:

1972-76
Bishop Charles H. Foggie, chairperson
Bishop Stephen Gill Spottswood; 1st vice chairperson
Bishop J. Clinton Hoggard, 2nd vice chairperson
Members:

Rev. H. A. L. Clement	Rev. Jessie Williams
Rev. W. L. McDaniel	Rev. C. B. Howell
Rev. DeWitt Womack	Rev. R. E. Stephens, Jr.
Rev. George C. Buie	Mr. Josh Curnell
Rev. Richard A. Council	Rev. S. L. Hopkins
Rev. F. D. Mayweather	

1976-80
Bishop Charles H. Foggie, chairperson
Bishop Clinton R. Coleman, 1st vice chairperson
Bishop William A. Stewart, 2nd vice chairperson
Members

Rev. Calvin Marshall, III	Rev. Grady Riddle
Rev. R. L. Drew	Rev. A. F. Johnson
Rev. Tecumseh X. Graham	Rev. John Wesley Smith

309

African Methodist Episcopal Zion Church

Rev. W. C. Bankhead

Rev. H. H. Sink

Rev. J. T. Thomas

Rev. George F. Mills

Mr. Melvin Stevens

Rev. L. B. Perry

1980-84

Bishop Charles H. Foggie, chairperson

Bishop Cecil Bishop, 1st vice chairperson

Bishop William A. Stewart, 2nd vice chairperson

Members

Mr. M. L. Green

Rev. G. W. Beard

Mrs. Charlottee Atkins

Rev. R. M. Dickerson

Mr. W. C. Witherspoon

Rev. A. F. Johnson

Mr. C. H. Mackey

Rev. W. L. Burton

Rev. Osofo L. H. McDonald

Mr. R. C. Johnson

Mrs. Mary Moore

Rev. L. B. Perry

1984-88

Bishop Charles H. Foggie, chairperson

Bishop Cecil Bishop, 1st vice chairperson

Bishop Alfred G. Dunston, Jr., 2nd vice chairperson

Rev. Hera B. Lovell

Rev. W. Robert Johnson

Rev. J. D. McArthur

Rev. Erskine Wade

Rev. J. A. Stringfield

Rev. O. C. Dumas

Rev. S. L. Brown

Rev. S. M. Taylor

Rev. James H. Taylor

Rev. Lawrence Stevens

Rev. J. A. Vault

Rev. L. B. Perry

1988-92

Bishop J. Clinton Hoggard, chairperson

Bishop Cecil Bishop, 1st vice chairperson

Bishop Milton A. Williams, 2nd vice chairperson

Members

Mr. Jasper McCormick

Rev. G. Curtis Newby

Rev. Cameron W. Jackson

Rev. John A. Stringfield

Mrs. Darlene Bennett

Rev. O. C. Dumas

Mrs. Lois Parker

Rev. Lawrence Stevens

Connectional Trustees

ZION METHODISM AND ECUMENICITY

The churches working together provide a spiritual movement from the scandals of divisions and divisiveness toward wholeness as one people of God in the body of Christ. At the same time, the church as the temple of the Holy Spirit, promotes the ministry of healing those afflictions that cause alienation, but the church is the agent of God's power to transform the world.

In the one Gospel, the message and the mission, the mood and the mandate are clear. There is one Lord, one faith, one baptism, one birth, one Holy name, one vision in the labor of love and faith. Truly, it is the Kingdom of God that makes ultimate claim on the ecumenical movement toward the end of peace on earth among all people of goodwill. (*Official Journal, 41st Quad. Sess. Gen. Conf.* [1980], p. 88)

AT the core of the African Methodist Episcopal Zion Church's ecumenicity and practice is the conviction that a united Church would bring peace to a divided world. In *The African Methodist Episcopal Zion Church: Reality of the Black Church*, Bishop William J. Walls asserts, "Christian unity is the way to a peaceful world. . . . As long as the church is divided we will have a divided world, but the seed of uniting the church must be cultivated with indescribable and never ceasing faith and toil." The A. M. E. Zion Church also believes that true Christian unity cannot be realized without the Church becoming "inclusive," and although that ideal has not been realized, largely because of Western racism, the A. M. E. Zion Church has nevertheless actively embraced the principle of Christian ecumenical discourse and unity in interdenominational, national, and international settings. (Walls, p. 459; *Official Journal, 44th Quad. Sess. Gen. Conf.* [1992], p. 89)

The A. M. E. Zion Church has been an official participant in inter-denominational and interchurch ecumenical activities and agencies since the 1860s. Its ecumenicity has been shaped by its Christian world mission and its historical connections and experiences. As an African American Christian church, the A. M. E. Zion Church is mindful of Africa's ecumenical role in the development of early Christianity:

Zion recognizes a part of her ecumenical heritage in the movements of pre Protestant and pre-Catholic (Eastern and Western) history. From the early African centers of African Christian culture as the Ethiopian eunuch and Phillip in Acts of Apostles to the contemporary Ethiopian Orthodox churches; and St. Mark, at the first and oldest church in Alexandria, as in the Coptic Christian Church. The first four centuries of Christianity are chapters of African Christian

Zion Methodist and Ecumenicity

Ecumenism through the church fathers [such] as Tertullian; martyrs [such] as Perpetua; monks [such] as Anthony, and theologians [such] as Augustine. . . . African religious creativity in thought, spirit, and devotion early shaped the Christian faith in expansion across North and East Africa and laid the foundations for Christendom. The early councils would meet on African soil and in the midst of African culture. This ecumenical heritage is a part of the background of the African [Methodist Episcopal Zion Church]. (Official Journal, *41st Quad. Sess. Gen. Conf* [1980]., p. 88)

As a church organized in North America in response to the barbarisms of slavery and racism perpetrated by the white majority against African people, the A. M. E. Zion Church was founded to address the spiritual and social needs of an oppressed people. Thus, its ecumenism is informed by the heritage of the Black Church in its struggle for freedom:

Chafing under oppressive conditions, after the Black Diaspora (African peoples being brought to [the] America[s]), the African [Methodist Episcopal] Zion Church movement emerged from the black Christian experience with an affirmation of the humanity-heritage, as (African people: faith heritage, Christian Methodist, and a freedom-heritage of being called, covenanted and commissioned as a people of God). Their heritage of humanity, faith and freedom were incompatible with the spirit and practices of racism and exploitation in the body of Protest[ant] European churches in the American society. (Ibid.)

The A. M. E. Zion Church has historically pursued the ecumenical journey toward fellowship, ministry and mission as a church with a world view. Zion has prioritized the agenda of bringing healing and hope through the connectional identity and ecclesiastical unity committed to work among the scattered and victimized Black race often dispossessed . . . but always determined to struggle for freedom and justice, equality and peace. (Ibid.)

Thus, Zion's ecumenicity has embraced other black Christian denominations in the affirmation of Christian principles in the quest for social justice. The A. M. E. Zion Church was an organizing member of the National Fraternal Council of Churches in 1934. This was an interdenominational organization of the A. M. E., C. M. E., Church of God in Christ, the Central Jurisdiction of the Methodist Church, National Baptist Convention, the African Orthodox Church, Freewill Baptist, and Apostolic Churches.

African Methodist Episcopal Zion Church

These predominantly black institutions affirmed black Christianity in America in defense of the race and for the cause of Christ. The A. M. E. Zion Church is also a founding member of the Congress of National Black Churches, an agency comprising eight predominantly black national church bodies, with an all black executive leadership, that is organized to address social and economic issues peculiar to the needs of African Americans. The denominations include the A. M. E., A. M. E. Zion, C. M. E., Church of God in Christ, National Baptist Convention of America, Inc., the National Baptist Convention USA, Inc., the National Missionary Baptist Convention of America, and the Progressive National Baptist Convention, Inc. (*Official Journal, 43rd Quad. Sess. Gen. Conf* [1988]., p. 89; *44th Quad. Sess.* [1992],p. 89; "Bishops' Quad. Message, to 45th Quad. Sess. Gen. Conf. [1996]," p. 28)

Coupled with its Black Church heritage, the ecumenicity of the A. M. E. Zion Church has also been informed by the black Methodist Christian tradition in America:

> In the first reach for ecumenical fellowship with fraternal churches having common history, cause, and struggle, Zion, historically, has been in the vanguard with the sister churches, the A[frican]. M[ethodist]. E[piscopal]. and the C[hristian, formerly Colored], M[ethodist. E[piscopal]. From the General Conference in 1868, a platform for consolidation was confirmed between the A. M. E. and A. M. E. Zion [Churches]; again, a platform for consolidation was confirmed between the A. M. E., A. M. E. Zion, and C. M. E. via a joint commission in 1885. . . . (Ibid., p. 89)

Beyond the circle of its own historical heritage and the black Methodist tradition, the A. M. E. Zion Church has been involved in national and worldwide Methodist and Christian ecumenical bodies and agencies since September, 1881, when Zion sent Bishops J. W. Hood, W. H. Hillery, and Joseph P. T. Thompson, and the Revs. J. McH. Farley and J. C. Price as representatives to the Ecumenical Methodist Conference in London, England. (*41st Quad. Sess. Gen. Conf.* [1980], p. 89)

The A. M. E. Zion Church was an organizing member denomination of the World Council of Churches, a fellowship of more than three hundred churches of the Protestant, Anglican, Orthodox, and Old Catholic traditions coming together for study, witness, service, and the advancement of unity. Its membership includes churches in more than one hundred countries. It came into being on August 23, 1948, when the First Assembly was held in Amsterdam, Holland. "The World Council of Churches is a fellowship of Churches which confess the Lord Jesus Christ as God and Savior according to the Scriptures and therefore seek to fulfill together their common calling to the glory

Zion Methodist and Ecumenicity

of the one God, Father, Son, and Holy Spirit." Membership is open to churches that affirm this belief and satisfy other criteria of membership. This organization provides a venue for dialogue among the churches on matters concerning, creed, ministry, government, program, and missionary work. The reorganization of the World Council was approved at the meeting of the Central Committee in Addis Ababa, Ethiopia, in January, 1971. The changes took effect immediately although the complete restructuring was not completed until 1975. There are three units within the World Council that focus on Faith and Order, Missions and Evangelism, and Theological Education. Significant trends within the World Council are the acceptance of diversity and the encouragement of convergence. The former emphasizes participation with the intent to make the church whole by including women, youth, the disabled, and ordained women. Convergence emphasizes Baptism, the Eucharist, and Ministries, or BEM as it was formulated in a document of that name, whereby participating churches would recognize and agree on the doctrine of baptism, the Eucharist, and mutual recognition of ministers of the church (*41st Quad. Sess. Gen. Conf.* [1980], p. 89; *42nd Quad. Sess.* [1984], p. 630; "Bishops' *Quad. Address, 45th Quad. Sess. Gen. Conf.* [1996]," p. 29)

The A. M. E. Zion Church was also an organizing member of the National Council of Churches of Christ in the USA in 1950. This organization is the successor ecumenical agency to the Federal Council of Churches, which was established in 1905. "The National Council of the Churches of Christ in the United States of America is a community of Christian communions which, in response to the gospel revealed in the Scriptures, confess Jesus Christ, the incarnate Word of God, as Savior and Lord. These communions covenant with one another to manifest ever more fully the unity of the Church. Relying upon the transforming power of the Holy Spirit, the Council brings these communions into common mission, serving in all creation to the glory of God." (Ibid., p. 90)

Other agencies to which the A. M. E. Zion Church makes budgetary contributions and sends representatives include the Consultation on Church Union, which involves discourse among nine Protestant church bodies in the United States who convenant to fulfill the prayer of our Lord, "that they all may be one"; the World Methodist Council; the World Conference of Methodism; the International Society of Christian Endeavor; the U. S. Church Leaders' Conference; the Pan-Methodist Commission (U. S. A.); and the American Bible Society. The A. M. E. Zion Church also supports secular agencies, such as the National Association for the Advancement of Colored People; the National Urban League; and People United in Support of Humanity (PUSH), that are closely related to the mission of the A. M. E. Zion Church "to go into all the world and preach, teach, and practice the gospel of Jesus Christ." (*Official Journal, 42nd Quad. Sess. Gen. Conf.* [1984], p. 90)

Women of the A. M. E. Zion Church have taken active part in the ecumenical women's movements since 1956, when the women's movement asserted itself in the World Federation of Methodist Church Women. They have been continuing participants in the ecumenical movement of the World Methodist Council of Churches and Church Women United in the U. S. A., formerly called Church Women United. Zion women have been represented by Mrs. Ida Wallace, Mrs. Josephine H. Kyles, Mrs. Creola B. Cowan, Mrs. Abbie. C. Jackson, Mrs. Emma Watson, Mrs. Mabel Jones, and Mrs. Willa Mae Rice. (41st Quad. Sess. Gen. Conf.[1980], p. 89)

An outstanding ecumenical event during the period of this history was Bishop J. Clinton Hoggard's participation along with twenty-seven other Christian faith representatives in conversation with Pope John Paul II on September 11, 1987 at the University of South Carolina. The representatives spoke in private for an hour with His Holiness about the unity of the Church. The Pope presented each participant a medallion that had been struck in Rome and brought to the U. S. to commemorate the occasion. In addition, the President of the University of South Carolina sent each participant a chair embossed with the seal of the university and a plaque attached to the back of the chair that commemorates the visit of Pope John Paul II. (*Official Journal, 43rd Quad. Sess. Gen. Conf.* [1988], p. 198)

Organic Union: The Background

In *The African Methodist Episcopal Zion Church*, Bishop Walls recounts the various efforts to effect organic union among the African Methodist Episcopal Zion, the Methodist Episcopal, the African Methodist Episcopal, and the Colored (now *Christian*) Methodist Episcopal Churches in the period following Emancipation during the late 1860s. He examines the effort made by the A. M. E. Zion Church with each of these church bodies and the causes of failure in each instance. Conversations between the A. M. E. Zion and A. M. E. (Bethel) concerning organic union led to a formal proposition for union from the A. M. E. (Bethel) Church that was presented to the 12th Quadrennial Session of General Conference of the A. M. E. Zion Church, on May 26, 1864. During the next four years, the membership of both churches examined the plan for consolidation. However, A. M. E. (Bethel) Church membership failed to ratify the plan for consolidation in 1868 and then proposed a new platform for union. (Walls, p. 464)

In 1868, the A. M. E. Zion Church subsequently considered a plan of union

Zion Methodism and Ecumenicity

between itself and the Methodist Episcopal Church (northern division). Bishop Singleton T. Jones spearheaded the efforts for union with both the A. M. E. and the Methodist Episcopal Church. Bishop Jones's able representation of Zion on the terms of union with the Methodist Episcopal Church was historical. Bishop Jones insisted on perfect equality between the church bodies. Jones asserted that "a man is a man, and a Christian is a Christian, irrespective of the color of his skin." In 1870, the Board of Bishops of the A. M. E. Zion Church opposed union with the Methodist Episcopal Church. Walls contends that the plan of union in this instance failed because of the crisis the race and Black Church were going through during Reconstruction.

The efforts of both A. M. E. Zion and A. M. E. (Bethel) to proseltyze newly freed black Methodists in the South were somewhat frustrated by the Methodist Episcopal Church, South, which created the Colored Methodist Episcopal Church on a segregated basis under the leadership of local southern blacks. The establishment of the C. M. E. Church broke up denominational ties with the A. M. E. Zion and A. M. E. (Bethel) Churches that led to property loss by both bodies. The growth of the C. M. E. Church led to a second serious effort at church union between the A. M. E. (Bethel) and A. M. E. Zion Churches in 1884. The two denominations established committees to represent each church. The two committees worked out a plan for union. In 1885, union was prevented because the bishops failed to submit to the people the plan agreed on by the Joint Committees of the two churches. The 1888 General Conference affirmed the committee's report on union. In October 1891, at the Second Ecumenical Conference in Washington, D. C. , 23 of 24 commission members agreed on a basis of union, but the Board did not agree on a name. In 1892, the Commission of the A. M. E. Zion Church formulated a plan for union that was presented to the General Conference and adopted by that body. The plan was accepted by the A. M. E. General Conference. The commissioners met on May 20th, at Wesley Union Church in Harrisburg, Pennsylvania and agreed on total conditions of union to be submitted to their respective church bodies. The plan was presented to the members of the A. M. E. Zion Church and was approved at the church, quarterly conference, and annual conference levels. Walls reports that Bishop Hood placed responsibility for the failure of this union plan on the bishops of the A. M. E. Church because they divided on the subject. (Walls *The African Methodist Episcopal Zion Church*, pp. 466-69)

A similar earlier effort to effect union with the C. M. E. Church began in 1900 during the General Conference. Appointment of an A. M. E. Zion Commission of eighteen members occurred after receiving a suggestion from the Rev. M. T. Jamison, fraternal messenger to the General Conference from the C. M. E. Church. In May, 1902,

African Methodist Episcopal Zion Church

at the General Conference of the C. M. E. Church, in Nashville, Tennessee, a similar commission was appointed. A joint meeting of the two commissions took place at Israel C. M. E. Church, Washington, D. C., on October 7, 1902. The commissioners drew up Articles of Agreement for submission to the next general conferences of each church. In 1904, while this negotiation was in process, fraternal messengers of the African Methodist Episcopal and African Methodist Episcopal Zion Churches exchanged messages at their respective General Conferences. A proposal for a joint hymnal and catechism for Negro Methodists by the A. M. E. General Conference opened the door of Church Federation among all three families of black Methodists. (Ibid., p. 471)

During February 12-17, 1908, a joint meeting of all the Bishops of the A. M. E. Zion, A. M. E. (Bethel), and C. M. E. Churches was held at Metropolitan A. M. E. Church, Washington, D. C. This was the first meeting of the Tri-Federation Council of Bishops, as it was later called, representing the A. M. E., A. M. E. Zion, and C. M. E. Churches. The Tri-Federation held a second meeting at Big Zion A. M. E. Zion Church, Mobile, Alabama, February, 11-12, 1911, where a declaration favoring organic union was adopted. Progress was made, and when the third Tri-Federation Council met at Chestnut Street C. M. E. Church Louisville, Kentucky, February 16-17, 1918, a commission of three bishops, three elders, and three laymen from each church was appointed to formulate plans for effecting union and to set the next commission meeting in Birmingham, Alabama in April, 1918. The commission met and drew up plans, "The Birmingham Plan of Organic Union," which was approved by all and was to be voted on by the respective General Conference of the C. M. E. meeting in Chicago, May, 1918, and the General Conference of the A. M. E. and the A. M. E. Zion Churches in St. Louis and Knoxville, respectively in May, 1920. The A. M. E. General Conference adopted the plan for Organic Union without dissent. The A. M. E. Zion General Conference affirmed the plan by a vote of 378 for and 5 against. However, the C. M. E. General Conference defeated the plan in its vote. The A. M. E. Zion Church nevertheless pursued the union plan with the A. M. E. Church.

The Great Depression of 1929 slowed the pace of organic union between the A. M. E. and A. M. E. Zion Churches. The 1932 A. M. E. Zion General Conference affirmed its commitment to organic union, but the matter was left dormant by successive General Conferences until 1964, when the senior bishops of the three churches urged renewal of the union plan. On March 31-April 1, 1965, the Tri-Council of Bishops was revived at Lane Temple C. M. E. Church, St. Louis, Missouri. They approved a structure similar to that of 1908, empowered the senior bishops of the three denominations to organize meetings when necessary, and appointed a commission of twenty members from each church body. The principal object was to work for a plan of

Zion Methodism and Ecumenicity

union of the three churches by spring, 1972. Three subsequent meetings were held: December 14-15, 1965, at Big Bethel A. M. E., Atlanta, Georgia; December 5-6, 1967, at John Wesley A. M. E. Zion Church, Washington, D. C.; and January 28-19, 1969, at Carter Temple, C. M. E. Church, Chicago. (Walls, p. 476)

Thus, after laying the groundwork for organic union during the period from 1864 through 1969, the three black Methodist denominations failed to take the decisive step. In analyzing the search for organic union among the black Methodist Churches, Bishop Walls wonders if they were quite ready for the undertaking:

> Each church is on record with the majority strongly favoring organic union. On one word this entire subject hinges: Readiness. Are we ready to give and take, to sink ambitions, and to become Christian in spirit enough to bring these churches together so that they shall stay together?. . .
>
> Can we believe in each other firmly enough? Can we love each other deeply enough? . . . There is only one thing that can do it, and that will be to center our structures of experience [on] the Christian myth, which is love and f aith combined with God and His Son, Jesus in the midst, and the Holy Spirit giving the guidelines. (Ibid., pp. 476-77)

Consultation on Church Union

In May, 1966, the A. M. E. Zion Church became the ninth member of the fellowship of churches known as the *Consultation on Church Union*. This agency was the outgrowth of the National Council of Churches Triennial Assembly in 1960 in San Francisco, where a dialogue sermon preached from the pulpit of the Episcopal Cathedral by the Rev. Dr. Eugene Carson Blake, the stated clerk of the Presbyterian Church, U. S. A., and the Rt . Rev. James A. Pike, presiding bishop of the San Francisco Diocese of the Protestant Episcopal Church, proposed an organic merger of the Episcopalian, Presbyterian, and Congregational-Christian denominations. A later declaration stated that the restoration of the broken body of Christ as manifest in the denominational divisions could not be effected without the inclusion of church bodies that were led and populated by non-European persons. A study commission was appointed and the Consultation on Church Union (COCU) was officially constituted in 1962. This agency was authorized to "explore the formation of a united church truly catholic, truly evangelical, and truly reformed." The participating churches include the African Methodist Episcopal, African Methodist Episcopal Zion, the Christian Methodist Episcopal, the Christian Church (Disciples of Christ), International Council

African Methodist Episcopal Zion Church

of Community Churches, Presbyterian Church (U. S. A.), United Church of Christ, and the United Methodist Church. Bishop William J. Walls and the Rev. John H. Satterwhite of the A. M. E. Zion Church served on the Executive Committee through 1972. Bishops J. Clinton Hoggard and Arthur Marshall became the representatives in 1972. (Walls, *The African Methodist Episcopal Zion Church*, p. 495; *Official Journal, 39th Quad. Sess. Gen. Conf.* [1972], pp. 382-83; *44th Quad. Sess.* [1992], p. 90)

The General Organization of COCU has a "Plenary Assembly," comprising ten delegates and ten associate delegates, one each from the participating churches, that is proposed to meet every two to four years. An Executive Committee includes the president, two representatives from each of the participating churches, and the secreta-riat. The secretariat comprises the full-time executive staff of the Consultation, all of whom are based at the national office in Princeton, New Jersey. In September 26-30, 1971, the A. M. E. Zion Church participated in the 10th Plenary Session of COCU held in Denver, Colorado, where a "A Plan of Union" was circulated to the participating churches for further study, with June 1, 1972 indicated as the end of the first phase. At the 39th General Conference of the A. M. E. Zion Church, "A Plan of Union" was approved for further study. (*39th Quad. Sess. Gen. Conf.* [1972], p. 382)

As members of COCU, the black Methodist Churches are challenged by the ecumenical imperatives of the larger organization. In 1976, the three black Methodist bodies jointly published a booklet, *Lenten Meditations*. A joint hymnal, a unified order of worship, and joint publication of Church School literature were proposed for serious consideration and study by the three black Methodist denominations. The 40th General Conference of the A. M. E. Zion Church established a Committee on Church Union, comprising three bishops, three ministers, and three lay persons, to meet with a similar commission from "the black Methodist bodies concerned with union, to seek agreement on specific areas, levels, and stages of union; to attempt to reach consensus on a time schedule for each, and a proposed time, in terms of the year, for the possible consummation of the union; that the committee of Church Union be required to submit a written progress report at the 1978 Connectional Council." (*Official Journal, 40th Quad. Sess. Gen. Conf. [1976]*, p. 102)

The A. M. E. Zion Church has continued representation and conversation with the Consultation on Church Union (COCU). Plenary Sessions were held in 1984, in Baltimore, and in 1988, in New Orleans. The 1988 A. M. E. Zion General Conference endorsed the covenant document, which placed the denomination on record as moving toward endorsement of the baptismal, ministry, andi the proposal "Churches in Covenant Communion," or the Church of Christ Uniting. The Board of Bishops observed that racism throughout American church life is a constraint to each of the African American denominational bodies in COCU in deciding if it truly wants to be in a "body of Christ," with its disproportionate numerical representation based on "race." Despite these misgivings, the Bishops of the Church urged the General Conference to ratify the document on "Churches in Covenant Communion." The Rev. Lewis Anthony was appointed as "enabler" for the A. M. E. Zion Church in the discussion with other denominational facilitators. At the 45th General Conference of the A. M. E. Zion Church, the conference affirmed a resolution by the Board of Bishops for the A. M. E. Zion Church "to reaffirm its commitment to the Consultation on Church Union (COCU) and the process involved in the movement toward the Churches of Christ Uniting; and that the A. M. E. Zion Church will study, at the grassroots levels, relevant documents and materials; and that this General Conference vote affirmatively on the covenanting of church proposals that will be presented." (*Official Journal, 44th Quad. Sess. Gen. Conf* [1992]., p. 90; "Bishops' Quad. Message, 45th Quad. Sess. Gen. Conf. [1996], p. 37)

A. M. E. Zion and C. M. E. Church Merger

First-stage ecumenical unity is recognized as being fundamentally necessary between and among the sister Black Methodist Churches—A. M. E., C. M. E., and A. M. E. Zion. Under the leadership of the late Bishop Herbert Bell Shaw, senior bishop of the A. M. E. Zion Church, and his counterpart Bishop E. P. Murchison of the C. M. E. Church, another serious effort was made during the 1970s and 1980s to accomplish organic union between these two black Methodist denominations. Bishop Shaw's effort was continued by Bishop W. M. Smith, his successor as senior bishop. Bishop Chester A. Kirkendoll was the successor to Bishop Murchison as the senior bishop of the C. M. E. Church. In June, 1978, the College of Bishops of the C. M. E. Church unanimously voted its approval to seek union with the A. M. E. Zion Church. A resolution to this effect presented to the C. M. E. General Conference was unanimously passed. The Board of Bishops of the A. M. E. Zion Church recommended approval of union with the C. M. E. Church to the 41st General Conference meeting in Greensboro, North Carolina, in 1980. The A. M. E. Zion General Conference overwhelmingly approved the plan for merger with the C. M. E. Church. A joint steering committee was organized to coordinate the efforts toward union and create a commission for work on special areas of concern. (*Official Journal, 41st Quad. Sess. Gen. Conf* [1980]., pp. 77-78; *42nd Quad. Sess.*[1984], p. 76)

The meeting of the joint steering committee in Atlanta, Georgia, May 17-18,

African Methodist Episcopal Zion Church

1984, proved fruitful. The Joint Commission on Organic Union agreed that the Plan of Union would be ready for distribution by the end of August, 1984 and not later than September, 1984 to all Annual Conferences for discussion, review, and recommendation to each denominational body by September, 1985. The Board of Bishops of the A. M. E. Zion Church emphasized the advantages that would accrue from organic union of the two churches:

> There is some merit in working toward Organic Union because of the newness of life that will be engendered into the participating organizations through the Christian Education Departments, the Pension Programs, Missions Programs, Publishing House outreach and administrative efficiency. We recognize the practical value of sheer numbers being brought together under one leadership to enunciate economic, political, and social concerns in America and to the world. Can we remove the middle wall of partition which separates us and construct a united agency under God for the bringing forth of His Kingdom in our time? (Official Journal, 42nd Quad. Sess. Gen. Conf. [1984], p. 90)

At the 43rd General Conference of the A. M. E. Zion Church in May, 1988, which met in Charlotte, N. C., a document drawn up by the Joint Commissions of the C. M. E. and A. M. E. Zion Churches, "Principles of Union" (see Appendix B), outlining: A. Basic Affirmations; B. Reasons for Union; C. The Faith of the United Church; D. Structures of the Varick/Miles (V/M) Methodist Episcopal Church; E. The Ministry of the V/M Methodist Episcopal Church; F. Judicial Administration; G. Educational Institutions, was presented to the General Conference of the A. M. E. Zion Church and was adopted for continuing conversation and action by the respective commissions on Church Union of the African Methodist Episcopal Zion Church and the Christian Methodist Episcopal Church. Because the senior bishops of the two denominations were made responsible for calling meetings of joint commission meetings representing all of the subcommittees of each denomination, the failure by the leadership of the C. M. E. to call such meetings aborted the merger of the two church bodies. The leadership at that time of our sister communion did not favor, privately or publicly, the merging of the A. M. E. Zion Church and the C. M. E. Churches.

At the 45th General Conference of the A. M. E. Zion Church, the conference afffirmed a resolution from the Board of Bishops for the A. M. E. Zion Church "to reaffirm the commitment to a continuation of the process leading to merger with the Christian Methodist Episcopal Church," the reactivation and appointment of the commission, and the appropriation of necessary funds. As of March, 1998, the action to implement the resolution from either church body under review lies dormant. (*Official Journal, 43rd Quad. Sess. Gen. Conf.* [1988], p. 60; "Bishops' Quad. Message, 45th Quad. Sess. Gen. Conf. [1996] ," p. 37)

Commission on Pan-Methodist Cooperation

During the observances of the Bicentennial of American Methodism, leaders of four of the denominations, namely, the A. M. E., A. M. E. Zion, C. M. E., and the United Methodist (U. M.) Churches proposed establishment of a commission to foster interchurch cooperation. The General Conferences of the four churches each passed an enabling act to create a commission. Thus, the Commission on Pan-Methodist Cooperation was organized in Atlanta, Georgia, on May 27, 1985, as "an independent body . . . accountable to the individual General Conferences," with five representatives from each denomination: one bishop, one other clergy, one layman, one laywoman, and one youth or young adult." The first persons appointed to represent the A. M. E. Zion Church during 1985-88 were Bishop Herman L. Anderson, the Rev. Nathaniel Jarrett, Dr. C. DuPont Rippy, Mrs. Willa Mae Rice, and Ms. Mary A. Love. (*Official Journal, 43rd Quad. Sess. Gen. Conf.* [1988], p. 830)

The Pan-Methodist Commission was established to "study and help implement ways and means of developing a cooperative Christian witness among "People called Methodist" to a fragmented world in such areas but not limited to: higher education, national and world mission outreach, social witness, and evangelism." The task of the commission is to identify specific projects for cooperation among Methodists in the United States and to implement such projects. The work of the commission is effected through its Executive Committee and three committees: Curriculum/Publications; Evangelism/Mission Outreach/Social Witness; and Higher Education. Specific achievements reported during the first three years of the commission included:

1. A 20% discount extended to clergy by the respective publishing houses of the church bodies.

2. A conference was held on strategic marketing and planning to strengthen Methodist-related colleges, which established lines of communication among several institutions. The colleges participate in shared insurance and data analysis programs to their mutual advantage. (Ibid.)

At the National Conference of Methodist Bishops held in Arlington, Virginia, March 24-27, 1987, the bishops of the four denominations voted for "the responsibilities of the Steering Committee of the Consultation of Methodist Bishops be transferred to the Commission on Pan-Methodist Cooperation and that a consultation be held quadrennially for which the commission would create whatever structure is necessary to carry this out." The Commission on Pan-Methodist Cooperation voted to "accept the responsibilities as voted by the Consultation of Methodist Bishops and plan a Fifth Consultation." (Ibid.)

During the 1988-92 quadrennium, the Commission on Pan-Methodist Cooperation made significant strides within the commission and with external ecumenical bodies. The commission established a liaison relationship with the World Evangelism Institute; reported on the work of the commission at the World Methodist Council North American Section meeting; and affirmed and endorsed the Covenant of Action of the National Council of Churches of Christ and its resolutions on Gulf and Middle East crises and the conflict in Liberia. Dr. F. George Shipman served as chairperson of the committee on Ecumenical Sharing and Networking. In May, 1989, the Commission approved a resolution to wage a War on Substance Abuse and Violence. The Curriculum/Publications sub-committee made this issue part of its agenda and organized the Pan-Methodist Coalition on Substance Abuse, a project designed to raise awareness and enable action by local congregations against substance abuse. The Curriculum/Publications made a video, "A Revival of Hope," along with a user's guide, as part of a church kit to stimulate church involvement. Pan-ACTS, a series of events (Pan-Methodist Acts of Christian Witness, Training, and Serving) were planned to help train and empower local congregations. Pan-ACT I was held in December, 1991, in Forth Worth, Texas. Thirty members of the A. M. E. Zion Church attended the event. Regional coalitions against substance abuse are being organized to implement the program in churches and local communities. Members of the A. M. E. Zion Church actively participated in Charlotte and Rockingham, North Carolina, and in Jackson, Mississippi. The Commission worked with the Bishops' Initiative on Substance Abuse and Violence of the U. M. Church under the leadership of Bishop Felton E. May and affirmed the Pan-Methodist Youth Convocation on Drug Abuse and Violence held in Atlanta, Georgia, in September, 1991, at the Carter Presidential Center. Four A. M. E. Zion youth participated in this event. The Social Witness Committee prepared and distributed The *Pan-Methodist Social Witness Resource Book*, which lists congregations and agencies involved in outreach ministries. The Fifth Consultation of Methodist Bishops with the theme, "Methodism in the 21st Century: Fragmented or Divided," was held March 20-22, 1991, at Epworth-by-the-Sea in St. Simon's Island, Georgia. The Consultation created a Study Commission charged with responsibility to explore merger of the four denominations and draw up the agenda for the Sixth Consultation, under the theme, "Visioning from a Historical/Theological Perspective: Radical Implications

Zion Methodism and Ecumenicity

for Future Ministry." During the 1988-92 quadrennium, Ms. Mary Love, editor of Church School Literature, of the A. M. E. Zion Church was administrative secretary of the commission. Other A. M. E. Zion representatives included Bishops Herman L. Anderson and George W. C. Walker, Sr., the Rev. (now Bishop) Richard K. Thompson, Dr. F. George Shipman, and Mrs. Willa Mae Rice. (*Official Journal, 44th Quad. Sess. Gen. Conf.* [1992], pp. 818-20)

Representing the A. M. E., A. M. E. Zion, C. M. E., and U. M. Churches at the Sixth Consultation of Bishops, which was held April 26-28, 1995, in Austin, Texas, were Bishop Frederick H. Talbot, Bishop J. Clinton Hoggard, Bishop Othal H. Lakey, and Bishop James S. Thomas, respectively. Each addressed the theme "The Historical/Theological Basis for Unity." Bishop Hoggard supported programmatic unity but thought that organic unity was untenable in the light of past and present racism in the U. S. U. M. Bishops Thomas and David Lawson, however, contended that past historical experience should not preclude church union. Bishop Lawson urged a new vision: "Another perspective might be that the coming city of God might draw us out of that history toward the vision God seems to have for the flow of history, for the day when we are not separated from one another." CME Bishop Lakey expressed hope for union and predicted that "we will be united as sons and daughters of Wesley, but more importantly as sons and daughter of our Lord Jesus Christ." However, A. M. E. Bishop Talbot and C. M. E. Bishop Hoyt contended that it would be somewhat simplistic to think that the issues of ecumenical unity were merely social and not theological as well. Bishop Talbot read a paper written by historian Dennis C. Dickerson who argued that the conditions of oppression the A. M. E. Church was called on to address also affected its theological outlook. For members of the A. M. E. Church, "social activism is a theological imperative, rather than a social predilection," he argued. Reasoning in a similar vein, C. M. E. Bishop Hoyt asserted that in the black experience, issues such as housing and unemployment are "theological as well as ethical issues." During the deliberations, the participants examined their shared history and the reasons for separation from the mother Methodist Episcopal Church. They established a biblical rationale for reunion, discussed future possibilities, and instituted a Mission Statement:

MISSION STATEMENT

As members of the family of Methodism, we are called to redefine and strengthen our relationship by seeking more effective ways to acknowledge the sovereignty of God, to proclaim the reign of Jesus Christ as Lord and Savior, and to be receptive to the guidance of the Holy Spirit: by seeking signs of unity within the Body of Christ, and renewal of the human community;

- by recognizing the global nature of the connectional church;
- by witnessing to the Christian faith in a local and global context;
- by serving as instruments of God's liberating and reconciling grace throughout creation;
- by developing structures among the African Methodist Episcopal, African Methodist Episcopal Zion, Christian Methodist Episcopal, and United Methodist Churches;
- by fostering an inclusive, just, and caring fellowship among peoples; and
- by establishing and building up faith communities where persons are invited, formed, and sent as disciples whom God can use for the transformation of the whole world.

Building on our history and heritage, both common and unique; guided by our Wesleyan priorities and our similar polities; and challenged by our pursuit to establish a just society, we thus stand duty bound and reverently committed to this vocation of our shared faith. (*Star of Zion*, 18 May 1995, pp. 1,7; "Report of the Commission on Pan-Methodist Cooperation to the 45th General Conference of the A. M. E. Zion Church," [1996]pp. 1-2)

Following are achievements of the commission during the 1992-96 quadrennium: The commission sought to establish working relationships with other Wesleyan/American Methodist bodies and called for a disciplinary change that would promote inclusiveness; and shared resources concerning the issue of sexual harassment. The commission conducted three open worship sessions within local communities to foster discourse and sharing; provided opportunities for the presidents of historically black Methodist colleges and universities to explore joint ventures and for the Pan-Methodist Commission General Board of Higher Education and Ministry to share with such presidents avenues of possible cooperation; encouraged support and use of the "Revival of Hope" curriculum developed to assist the church's ministry to alcohol and substance abuse users; endorsed the "Urban Strategy" initiative of the National Council of Churches and the "Reclaiming the Cities" initiative of the United Methodist Church; and challenged Pan-Methodists to become "agents of good health" and work together in local churches and communities; and compared the social justice policies and resolutions of the four denominations. The Commission on Pan Methodist Cooperation sought approval from the four General Conferences for: a Committee of

Zion Methodism and Ecumenicity

Pan-Methodism to implement cooperative ventures at the local level; expansion of the Discipline of each church under the heading "Commission on Pan-Methodist Cooperation"; a Commission on Unity; the A. M. E. Zion share of $2,226.00 toward the annual budget of $100,000; incorporation of the Commission and/or groups specifically designed to address issues related to schools and colleges. Dr. F. George Shipman provided able leadership to the subgroup on Higher Education. ("Report of the Commission on Pan-Methodist Cooperation . . . " pp. 1-5)

In 1996, the Pan-Methodist Commission on Cooperation submitted to the 45th General Conference of the A. M. E. Zion Church "A Pan-Methodist Petition to the 1996 General Conferences Establishing A Commission on Union." Through this document the Commission sought a commitment to reunion from the respective General Conferences of the four Methodist denominations. The General Conferences were asked to establish a Commission on Union with six representatives from each denomination to prepare a Plan of Union for submission to the African Methodist Episcopal, African Methodist Episcopal Zion, and United Methodist Churches General Conferences in 2000 and the Christian Methodist Episcopal Church General Conference in 2002:

WHEREAS, we the followers of the Christ who prayed that all may be one; and

WHEREAS, historically, Methodism has had a commitment to unity and the ecumenical movement; and

WHEREAS, We acknowledge and repent that it was racism that separated American Methodism and fragmented ourselves and the world; and

WHEREAS, at the Fifth Consultation of Methodist Bishops in March 1991, it was requested that the episcopal bodies of the African Methodist Episcopal, African Methodist Episcopal Zion, Christian Methodist Episcopal and United Methodist Churches petition their respective General Conferences to authorize a Study Commission for the purpose of exploring possible merger; and

WHEREAS, in response to approval by the respective General Conferences, a Study Commission was established on March 9, 1994, in Birmingham, Alabama, and subsequently drew up a Mission Statement under the guidance of the Holy Spirit.

African Methodist Episcopal Zion Church

THEREFORE, this Study Commission now requests the respective General
Conferences to commit themselves in principle to a reunion of these denominations;
and

FURTHER, requests the four General Conferences to continue the Study Commission's
work by establishing a Commission on Union with six representatives from each
denomination with necessary funding; and

FURTHER, that this Commission on Union prepare a Plan of Union in order
that the wounds resulting from our past divisions may be healed, and that together we
may have a more effective witness in the global community as well as be good stewards of our God-given resources, and

FURTHER, that this Commission on Union submit the Plan of Union to the
African Methodist Episcopal, African Methodist Episcopal Zion, and United Methodist
Churches General Conference in 2000 and the Christian Methodist Episcopal Church
General Conference in 2002. (Ibid., p. 6)

A. M. E. Zion representatives to the Commission on Pan-Methodist Cooperation
during the 1992-96 quadrennium included Bishops Richard K. Thompson and Clarence
Carr; the Revs. (now Bishop) Nathaniel Jarrett, Donnell Williams; Drs. F. George
Shipman, Betty V. Stith, Gloria Moore; Ms. Mary A. Love and Mr. Raymond
Richmond. (Ibid., 4)

At the 45th General Conference, the A. M. E. Zion Church gave approval, in
accordance with the petition of the Pan-Methodist Commission on Cooperation, for
the four denominations of the commission to submit a plan of union to the next General
Conference. The Commission on Pan-Methodist Cooperation has moved in the direction of merger. This interdenominational agency offers some hope that the merger of
Methodist denominations may yet be realized through a more gradual approach of
shared projects and by stages. The following persons were appointed to represent the
A. M. E. Zion Church at the Commision on Pan-Methodist Cooperation during 1996-
2000: Bishop Richard K. Thompson, chairperson, Bishop Clarence Carr, 1st vice chairperson, Dr. F. George Shipman, Dr. Betty V. Stith, and the Rev. Donnel Williams.

Zion Methodism and Ecumenicity

A. M. E. ZION CHURCH ECUMENICAL MEMBERSHIPS AND APPOINTMENTS, 1976-2000

As earlier indicated, the A. M. E. Zion Church is affiliated with, and sends representatives to several ecumenical and interfaith agencies. Memberships and appointments to the various bodies during the period 1976-2000 are listed below.

1976-80
WORLD METHODIST COUNCIL

Bishop Clinton R. Coleman
Bishop Alfred G. Dunston, Jr.
Bishop Charles H. Foggie
Bishop William A. Hilliard
Bishop J. Clinton Hoggard
Bishop Arthur Marshall, Jr.
Bishop John H. Miller
Bishop Herbert Bell Shaw
Bishop William M. Smith
Bishop Ruben Lee Speaks
Bishop James W. Wactor
Rev. Herman L. Anderson
Rev. W. C. Ardrey
Rev. George Battle
Rev. Walter Beamon
Rev. Cecil Bishop
Rev. A. J. Blake
Rev. J. A. Brown
Rev. G. Ray Coleman
Rev. Kermit DeGraffenreidt
Rev. Edgar N. French
Rev. Richard L. Fisher
Rev. Raymond C. Hart
Rev. Belvie H. Jackson
Rev. C. J. Jenkins
Rev. Eulalia Jones
Rev. J. H. Jones

Rev. G. N. Spells
Rev. K. Melvin Taylor
Rev. C. C. Tyson
Rev. A. E. White
Rev. M. C. Williams
Ms. Agnes Brown
Ms. Gail Bundy
Ms. Katie Mae Goode
Mr. James E. Caldwell
Mr. David Crosby
Mr. Malachi Green
Mrs. Rose Marie Holmes
Mr. Arthur Jones
Mr. Kenith Jones
Mr. Lem Long
Mr. George Miller
Mr. Augustus Printz
Dr. F. George Shipman
Mr. Arthur C. Marshall
Mrs. Sallie V. Moreland
Mrs. Willa Mae Rice
Ms. Corean Stallworth
Ms. Betty V. Stith
Mr. Albert Stout
Mrs. Lula Williams
Mr. Spencer Williams
Mrs. Elizabeth Coleman

African Methodist Episcopal Zion Church

Rev. W. R. Jones
Rev. A. F. Johnson
Rev. G. W. Kendall
Rev. O. R. Lyons
Rev. A. W. Mapp
Rev. J. E. McKoy
Rev. L. A. Miller
Rev. B. W. Moncur
Rev. Maurice Pierre
Rev. Paree Porter
Rev. M. B. Robinson
Rev. J. Aggrey Smith

Dr. Armayne G. Dunston
Mrs. Madeline S. Foggie
Mrs. Edra Mae Hilliard
Mrs. Eva Stanton Hoggard
Mrs. Vilma D. Leake
Mrs. Mary Marshall
Mrs. Bernice Miller
Mrs. Ardell Shaw
Mrs. Janie Speaks
Mrs. Ida Mae Smith
Mrs. Hildred Wactor

NATIONAL COUNCIL OF CHURCHES OF CHRIST IN THE U.S.A.

MEMBERS

Bishop Clinton R. Coleman
Bishop Charles H. Foggie
Bishop George J. Leake
Bishop William M. Smith
Bishop Herbert Bell Shaw

ALTERNATES

Rev. D. L. Blakey
Mr. Raymond Hart
Ms. Lolita Davis
Rev. A. E. Whitted
Rev. V. Loma St. Clair
Ms. Willa Mae Rice

COMMISSION ON ORGANIC UNION

Bishop Herbert B. Shaw, chairperson
Bishop Clinton R. Coleman
Bishop George J. Leake

Bishop J. Clinton Hoggard
Bishop Charles H. Foggie
Bishop Arthur Marshall, Jr.

1980-84
NATIONAL COUNCIL OF CHURCHES OF CHRIST IN THE U.S.A.

MEMBERS

Bishop Clinton R. Coleman
Bishop John H. Miller
Bishop A. G. Dunston
Bishop George J. Leake
Rev. Bennie Malette
Mrs. Alcestis Coleman

ALTERNATES

Bishop Cecil Bishop
Bishop Herman Anderson
Bishop J. Clinton Hoggard
Bishop Ruben L. Speaks
Rev. J. C. White
Ms. Lonia Gill

Michael Wilson (Youth)
Rev. William T. Kennedy
Ms. Mary A. Love
Dr. C. D. Rippy

Ms. Carol Houston
Rev. W. M. Freeman
Mrs. Theodora Smith
Mr. D. V. Murrell, Jr.

COMMISSION ON ORGANIC UNION

Bishop William M. Smith
Bishop Clinton R. Coleman
Bishop John H. Miller
Bishop J. Clinton Hoggard
Bishop Arthur Marshall, Jr.
Bishop George J. Leake
Bishop Charles H. Foggie
Bishop Ruben L. Speaks
Bishop Herman L. Anderson

Rev. M. H. Williams
Mrs. Odessa Tyson
Rev. G. L. Blackwell
Rev. Petty D. McKinney
Rev. J. H. Satterwhite
Mr. Lem Long, Jr.
Rev. Kermit DeGraffendreidt
Rev. George Thomas
Dr. John H. Winston, M. D.

WORLD COUNCIL OF CHURCHES

MEMBERS
Bishop J. Clinton Hoggard
Bishop Charles H. Foggie

ALTERNATES
Bishop Arthur Marshall, Jr.
Bishop Cecil Bishop

RESTRUCTURING COMMISSION

Bishop Charles H. Foggie, chairperson
Bishop Ruben L. Speaks, 1st vice chairperson
Bishop George J. Leake, 2nd vice chairperson
Rev. Frank Jones
Mr. M. L. Greene
Rev. George Buie, Jr.
Mrs. Edgar N. French
Rev. Cameron Jackson
Mr. E. Myers Harvell
Mrs. Farris A. Williams
Rev. George C. Woodruff
Rev. Cajus Howell
Mrs. Sarah Pierre
Mr. M. M. Stitton

Rev. A. L. Wilson
Mrs. Bernice F. Miller
Rev. N. H. Hicklin
Rev. Bennie Malette
Rev. Harriet Hooks
Rev. Fred Shegog
Mrs. Janie Speaks
Rev. R. L. Clayton
Rev. E. L. Johnson
Rev. Fred Hubbard
Mrs. Rose Marie Holmes

African Methodist Episcopal Zion Church

1984-88
NATIONAL COUNCIL OF CHURCHES OF CHRIST IN THE U. S. A.

Bishop J. C. Hoggard
Bishop Richard L. Fisher
Ms. Mary A. Love

Rev. Kermit DeGraffenriedt
Rev. Nathaniel Jarrett
Mrs. Mattilyn Rochester

COMMISSION ON ORGANIC UNION
Bishop William M. Smith, chairperson

Rev. William White
Rev. Melvin L. Tate
Rev. John Satterwhite
Rev. T. X. Graham
Mrs. Lizzie Sykes
Rev. Jewett Walker

Rev. L. A. Miller
Rev. Staccato Powell
Rev. Milton Williams
Dr. John H. Winston
Mrs. Myrtle McKenzie
Rev. George Blackwell

RESTRUCTURING COMMISSION
Bishop William M. Smith, chairperson
Bishop R. L. Fisher, 1st vice chairperson

Rev. Elridge Gittens
Rev. Charlie O. Caldwell
Rev. Richard K. Thompson
Rev. Randy Brown
Rev. Arthur W. Walls
Rev. Andrew Mackey
Rev. Howard E. Haggler
Rev. Willie J. Johnson
Rev. Harriet Hooks
Rev. J. E. Fields
Rev. Silas Redd
Rev. Homer Jackson

Mrs. Mabel Jones
Mrs. Shirley Jackson
Mrs. Elnora Askey
Mrs. Lula K. Howard
Mr. Walter Johnson
Mrs. Frances J. Glenn
Mrs. Bernice Miller
Mrs. Janie Speaks
Mrs Eula Goode
Mrs. Clara Ivey
Mrs. Essie Curnell
Mrs. Ida Smith

WORLD COUNCIL OF CHURCHES
MEMBERS
Bishop J. Clinton Hoggard
Bishop Charles H. Foggie

ALTERNATES
Bishop Arthur Marshall, Jr.
Bishop Cecil Bishop

Zion Methodism and Ecumenicity

1988-92
CHURCH FEDERATION AND ORGANIC UNION

CLERGY	LAY
1. Rev. George McMurray	1. Dr. C. DuPont Rippy
2. Rev. Warren M. Brown	2. Mr. William M. Davis
3. Rev. W. W. Bowden	3. Mrs. Corrie Winston
4. Rev. T. X. Graham	4. Mrs. Mayfred Nall
5. Rev. Michael Ellis	5. Mrs. Lizzie M. Sykes
6. Rev. Ernest White	6. Mrs. Theodora Smith
7. Rev. Robert Dewitt Miller	7. Ms. Mary Roseburr
8. Rev. Dennis Proctor, Chpsn.	8. Mrs. Dororthy Addison
9. Rev. John C. Wyatt, Jr.	9. Mrs. Vivian Williams
10. Rev. Curtis T. Walker, Sr.	10. Mrs. Ruby Shambray
11. Rev. Silas Redd	11. Mrs. Minnie K. Harvey
12. Rev. Edwin M. Flowers	12. Mr. Benjamin O. Enyioko

NATIONAL COUNCIL OF CHURCHES OF CHRIST IN THE U. S. A.
Bishop J. Clinton Hoggard, chairperson and certifying officer
1. Bishop J. Clinton Hoggard
2. Bishop Ruben L. Speaks
3. Rev. Kermit DeGraffenreidt
4. Mrs. Mattilyn Rochester
5. Rev. George Blackwell
6. Ms. Mary A. Love
7. Rev. Eric Leak (Youth Representative)
Mrs. Christine E. Trigg, Alternate

RESTRUCTURING COMMISSION
Bishop Ruben L. Speaks, chairperson
Bishop R. L. Fisher, 1st vice chairperson
Bishop Herman L. Anderson, 2nd vice chairperson
1. Rev. Henry Hall
2. Rev. Leon W. Watts
3. Rev. J. David Armstrong
4. Ms. Juliette Smith
5. Mrs Elnora H. Askey
6. Rev. Joseph D. Kerr
7. Rev. Arthur W. Walls, Sr.
8. Rev. Earle E. Johnson
9. Rev. George F. Miller
10. Mr. Major Sanders
11. Rev. J. F. Willis
12. Ms. Anese Lee
13. Rev. Andrew Whitted
14. Mrs. Victoria Allen

15. Rev. Arizona Nicholson
16. Mrs. Maggie Beard
17. Rev. Willie J. Johnson
18. Ms. Frances Glenn
19. Rev. J. E. Fields
20. Mrs. Clara Ivey
21.
22. Rev. Frederick Hubbard
23. Rev. James H. Taylor
24. Mrs. Mary Taylor
25. Rev. O. A. Eyo
26. Chief O.E. Nyong

COMMISSION ON ORGANIC UNION

Bishop William M. Smith, chairperson
Bishop C. R. Coleman, 1st vice chairperson
Bishop Alfred G. Dunston, 2nd vice chairperson
Members:

1. Mrs. Geneva Holland
2. Rev. Melvin L. Tate
3. Rev. Richard K. Thompson
4. Mrs. Lizzie Sykes
5. Mrs. Ivia Dobbins
6. Rev. Willie Long, Jr.
7. Ms. Brenda Jackson
8. Mrs. Dorothy S. Johnson
9. Rev. C. O. Barnett
10. Dr. John H. Winston
11. Rev. Willie Smith
12. Rev. W. L. Burton, Jr.
13. Rev. E. J. Ekpo

WORLD COUNCIL OF CHURCHES

Bishop J. Clinton Hoggard, chairperson
Bishop Charles H. Foggie
Bishop Samuel C. Ekemam

ALTERNATES
Bishop Alfred E. White
Bishop Cecil Bishop

COMMISSION ON PAN-METHODIST COOPERATION

Bishop Herman L. Anderson, chairperson
Bishop Richard L. Fisher, 1st vice chairperson
Bishop George W. Walker, Sr., 2nd vice chairperson

1. Rev. Richard K. Thompson
2. Dr. Willa Mae Rice
3. Ms. Mary Love
4. Dr. George Shipman

CONSULTATION ON CHURCH UNION

Bishop J. Clinton Hoggard, chairperson
Bishop Cecil Bishop

Zion Methodism and Ecumenicity

1992-96
ECUMENICAL CONCERNS AND ORGANIC UNION

CLERGY

1. Rev. C. Guita McKinney
2. Rev. Warren M. Brown
3. Rev. Marshall H. Strickland
4. Rev. Nathaniel Jarrett
5. Rev. Ocie M. Brown
6. Rev. S. P. Patterson
7. Rev. Audie V. Simon
8. Rev. Joan Speaks
9. Rev. Windell Tucker
10. Rev. Vilirie Fifer
11. Rev. Harriet O. Hooks, Chpn.
12. Rev. Charles H. Mack
13. Rev. Thaddeus Garrett

LAY

Mr. Edward O. Tracey
Ms. Mary Mattock
Ms. June Slade Collins
Mrs. Grace L. Holmes
Mrs. Joyce Davis
Mrs. Freda Moss
Ms. Brenda Jackson
Mr. George Goodman
Ms. Dorothy D. Addison
Mrs. Marrie Chatmen
Dr. Betty J. Anderson
Mrs. Lorel Maude Walker
Mr. Edwin E. Udechuku

COMMISSION ON ORGANIC UNION
Bishop Milton A. Williams, chairperson
Bishop Herman L. Anderson, 1st vice chairperson
Bishop Enoch B. Rochester, 2nd vice chairperson
Members:

1. Rev. J. A. Quick
2. Ms. Mary Mattocks
3. Rev. John Wyatt
4. Mr. James E. Miller
5. Rev. E. M. Wilson
6. Rev. E. J. Ekpo
7. Rev. John Paul Ruth
8. Mrs. Imogene H.Williams
9. Mrs. Lonia Gill
10. Mrs. Ann Johnson
11. Ms. Rhandi Stith
12.

RESTRUCTURING COMMISSION
Bishop George W. Walker, Sr., chairperson
Bishop Enoch B. Rochester, 1st vice chairperson
Bishop J. Clinton Hoggard, 2nd vice chairperson

1. Rev. O. C. Dumas
2. Mrs. Ruth Thompson
3. Rev. Jermiah Asbury
4. Mrs. Josephine Spaulding
5. Rev. William Kelly
6. Mrs. Helena Zacharias

African Methodist Episcopal Zion Church

7. Rev. Darryl B. Starnes
8. Mrs. Evelyn Robinson
9. Rev. Fredrick B. Massey
10. Mrs. Ruth Scott Jackson
11. Rev. L. D. Udofa
12. Mrs. Marjorie Bonner
13. Mrs. Frances Glenn
14. Rev. Robert Christian
15. Rev. Fred Shegog

16. Mrs. Betty J. Anderson
17. Rev. Larry D. Robinson
18. Mrs. Bobbie Floyd
19. Rev. Earle E. Johnson
20. Mr. Leonard Wallace
21. Rev. Peter Sefogah
22. Mrs. Collette Bosworth
23. Rev. Sherman Dunmore
24. Mr. Coyle Cooper, Sr.

CONGRESS OF NATIONAL BLACK CHURCHES
Bishop Milton A. Williams, chairperson
Bishop Cecil Bishop, 1st vice chairperson
Bishop J. Clinton Hoggard
Dr. Thaddeus Garrett, Jr.

CONSULTATION ON CHURCH UNION
Bishop Cecil Bishop, chairperson
Bishop Marshall Strickland
Rev. Vincent Frosh (Alternate)

NATIONAL COUNCIL OF CHURCHES OF CHRIST IN THE U. S. A.
Bishop Ruben L. Speaks, chairperson
1. Bishop George Battle
2. Rev. Kermit DeGraffenreidt
3. Ms. Mary A. Love

4. Dr. Mattilyn Rochester
5. Rev. Ramon Hunt
6. Rev. George W. Walker, Jr.

COMMISSION ON PAN-METHODIST COOPERATION
Bishop Richard K. Thompson, chairperson
Bishop Clarence Carr, 1st vice chairperson
1. Dr. F. George Shipman
3. Rev. Alexander Jones

2. Dr. Betty V. Stith
4. Dr. Adlise Porter

WORLD COUNCIL OF CHURCHES
Bishop S. Chuka Ekemam
Bishop Cecil Bishop

Bishop Marshall Strickland
Rev. Stacatto Powell

Zion Methodism and Ecumenicity

1996-2000
COMMISSION ON ORGANIC UNION
Bishop Milton A. Williams, chairperson
Bishop Enoch B. Rochester, 1st vice chairperson
Bishop Warren M. Brown, 2nd vice chairperson
Members:

Rev. Jerry Quick	Mrs. Ida L. Bell
Rev. Errol E. Hunt	Mrs. Ann Johnson
Mrs. Melva Polk Wright	Rev. William Griffin (deceased)
Rev. A. O. Udo	Rev. Frederick D. Hubbard
Rev. R. P. McDougal	Ms. Imogene Williams
Rev. John P. Ruth	Rev. T. K. Venable

RESTRUCTURING COMMISSION
Bishop George W. Walker, Sr., chairperson
Bishop Enoch B. Rochester, 1st vice chairperson
Bishop Nathaniel Jarrett, 2nd vice chairperson
Members:

Rev. O. C. Dumas (deceased)	Mrs. Jessie Reddick
Mrs. Ruth Thompson	Mrs. Bobbie Floyd
Rev. Kenneth Q. James	Rev. Herolin Aiken
Rev. John A. Cherry	Rev. Stanley Dennison
Mrs. Olivia Cook	Mrs. Helen Zacharias
Mrs. Brenda Smith	Rev. Edwin Harris
Mrs. Elizabeth Wright Reid	Mrs. Olivia Tucker
Rev. Alexander Jones	Rev. Floyd Chambers
Mrs. Frances Glenn	Rev. Lewis Anthony
Rev. Robert Christian	Rev. Alton Hunnicut
Rev. Larry Robinson	

CONGRESS OF NATIONAL BLACK CHURCHES
Bishop Milton A. Williams, chairperson
Bishop Cecil Bishop, ist vice chairperson
Bishop J. Clinton Hoggard
Dr. Thaddeus Garrett

African Methodist Episcopal Zion Church

CONSULTATION ON CHURCH UNION
Bishop Marshall H. Strickland, chairperson
Bishop Cecil Bishop, 1st vice chairperson
Rev. Raymon Hunt (Alternate)

NATIONAL COUNCIL OF CHURCHES OF CHRIST IN THE U. S. A.
Bishop George W. Walker, Sr., chairperson and certifying officer

Bishop George E. Battle, Jr.	Dr. Mattilyn T. Rochester
Bishop Clarence Carr	Mrs. Dana Miggins-Rice
Rev. Kermit Degraffenreidt	Rev. W. Robert Johnson, III

PAN-METHODIST COMMISSION
Bishop Richard K. Thompson, chairperson
Bishop Clarence Carr, 1st vice chairperson
Dr. F. George Shipman
Dr. Betty V. Stith
Rev. Donnell Williams

WORLD COUNCIL OF CHURCHES
Bishop S. Chuka Ekemam
Bishop Cecil Bishop
Bishop Marshall S. Strickland
Rev. Staccato Powell

PART III: THE BISHOPS

OF THE

AFRICAN METHODIST EPISCOPAL ZION

CHURCH, 1822-1996

	CONSECRATED
1. James Varick (1750-1827)	1822
2. Christopher Rush (1777-1873)	1828
3. William Miller (1775-1845)	1840
4. George Galbraith [Galbreath] (1799-1853)	1848
5. William Haywood Bishop (1793-1873)	1852
6. George Alfred Spywood (1802-1875)	1853
7. John Tappan (1799-1870)	1853
8. James Simmons (1792-1874)	1856
9. Solomon Timothy Scott (1790-1862)	1856
10. Joseph Jackson Clinton (1823-1881)	1856
11. Peter Ross (1809-1890)	1860
12. John Delaware Brooks (1803-1874)	1864
13. Jermain Wesley Loguen (1813-1872)	1864, 1868*
14. Samson Dunbar Talbot (1819-1878)	1864
15. John Jamison Moore (c. 1804-1893)	1868
16. Singleton Thomas Webster Jones (1825-1891)	1868
17. James Walker Hood (1831-1918)	1872
18. Joseph Pascal Thompson (1818-1894)	1876
19. William Henry Hillery (1839-1893)	1876**
20. Thomas Henry Lomax (1832-1908)	1876
21. Charles Calvin Pettey (1849-1900)	1888
22. Cicero Richardson Harris (1844-1917)	1888
23. Isom Caleb Clinton (1830-1904)	1892

* elected and consecrated twice
** disrobed in 1884

African Methodist Episcopal Zion Church

	CONSECRATED
24. Alexander Walters (1858-1917)	1892
25. George Wylie Clinton (1859-1921)	1896
26. Jehu Holliday (1827-1899)	1896
27. John Bryan Small (1845-1905)	1896
28. John Wesley Alstork (1852-1920)	1900
29. John Wesley Smith (1862-1910)	1904
30. Josiah Samuel Caldwell (1862-1935)	1904
31. Martin Robert Franklin (1853-1909)	1908
32. George Lincoln Blackwell (1861-1926)	1908
33. Andrew Jackson Warner (1850-1920)	1908
34. Lynwood Westinghouse Kyles (1874-1941)	1916
35. Robert Blair Bruce (1861-1920)	1916
36. William Leonard Lee (1866-1927)	1916
37. George Clinton Clement (1871-1934)	1916
38. John Wesley Wood (1865-1940)	1920
39. Paris Arthur Wallace (1870-1952)	1920
40. Benjamin Garland Shaw (1878-1951)	1924
41. Edward Derusha Wilmot Jones (1871-1935)	1924
42. William Jacob Walls (1885-1975)	1924
43. John William Martin (1879-1955)	1924
44. Cameron Chesterfield Alleyne (1880-1955)	1924
45. William Walter Matthews (1871-1962)	1928*
46. Frederick Miller Jacobs (1865-1931)	1928
47. Elijah Lovette Madison (1876—1946)	1936
48. William Cornelius Brown (1877-1964)	1936
49. James Walter Brown (1872-1941)	1936
50. Walter William Slade (1875-1963)	1944
51. Buford Franklin Gordon (1893-1952)	1944
52. Frank Wesley Alstork (1885-1948)	1944
53. Edgar Benton Watson (1874-1951)	1944
54. James Clair Taylor (1893-1954)	1948
55. Raymond Luther Jones (1900-1972)	1948
56. Hampton Thomas Medford (1885-1964)	1948

* retired and divested of the episcopacy

Bishops of the A. M. E. Zion Church

57. Herbert Bell Shaw (1908-1980)	1952
58. Stephen Gill Spottswood (1897-1974)	1952
59. William Andrew Stewart (1890-1984)	1952
60. Daniel Carleton Pope (1887-1964)	1952
61. Charles Ewbank Tucker (1896-1975)	1956
62. Joseph Dixon Cauthen (1887-1974)	1956
63. Charles Cecil Coleman (1906-1958)	1956
64. Felix Sylvester Anderson (1893-1983)	1960
65. William Milton Smith (1915-1995)	1960
66. Solomon Dorme Lartey (1898-1969)	1960
67. William Alexander Hilliard (1904-)	1960
68. Alfred Gilbert Dunston, Jr. (1915-1995)	1964
69. Charles Herbert Foggie (1912-)	1968
70. James Clinton Hoggard, Sr. (1916-)	1972
71. James Wesley Wactor (1908-1985)	1972
72. Clinton Reuben Coleman, Sr. (1916-1996)	1972
73. Arthur Marshall, Jr. (1914-1987)	1972
74. John Henry Miller, Sr. (1917-)	1972
75. George Junius Leake, III (1929-1981)	1972
76. Ruben Lee Speaks (1920-)	1972
77. Herman Leroy Anderson (1923-1995)	1980
78. Cecil Bishop (1930-)	1980
79. Richard Laymon Fisher (1934-1991)	1984
80. Alfred Edward White (1921-1992)	1984
81. George Washington Carver Walker, Sr. (1940-)	1988
82. Milton Alexander Williams, Sr. (1938-)	1988
83. Samuel Chukukanne Ekemam, Sr. (1942-)	1988
84. George Edward Battle, Jr. (1947-)	1992
85. Joseph Johnson (1934-)	1992
86. Richard Keith Thompson (1943-)	1992
87. Enoch Benjamin Rochester (1937-)	1992
88. Marshall Hayward Strickland (1933-)	1992
89. Clarence Carr (1938-)	1992

African Methodist Episcopal Zion Church

	CONSECRATED
90. Nathaniel Jarrett (1937-)	1996
91. Warren M. Brown (1941-)	1996

THE BISHOPS OF THE A. M. E. ZION CHURCH

THE OFFICE AND FUNCTION

Because the first congregation of the connection was organized in October, 1796, in New York City, N. Y., the Bicentennial Year of the African Methodist Episcopal Zion Church was observed throughout the 1996 calendar year. It therefore seems appropriate to portray the persons who achieved the high office of General Superintendent or Bishop during two hundred years of growth in members, influence, and international activities as a Christian body. Known as "Bishops of the Church" since 1880, these men from varied backgrounds have risen to the heights of leadership. Beginning in 1822 until 1880, the early leaders of the African Methodist Episcopal Zion Church (often called the *Freedom Church*), whose roots were deeply sunk in the soil of both British and American Methodism, were men of unusual physical strength and intellectual acumen. This is attested to by the biographical sketches of the bishops. They each made immense contributions to a religious body that had only God as its inspiration. The rugged individualism of these pioneering men had as their support base the victims of a slave system that had denied them the resources of literacy and economic support.

In the tradition of the African Methodist Episcopal Zion Church, the office of Bishop has been regarded as the symbol of the episcopacy. The tradition follows the Wesleyan practice as described by Henry Wheeler in *One Thousand Questions and Answers* (pp. 21-25), which is quoted in *The African Methodist Episcopal Zion Church: The Reality of a Black Church* by William Jacob Walls (pp. 105-6):

> *Episcopacy*: "Wesley, after due deliberation and consultation, called Dr. Thomas Coke and Reverend James Creighton, presbyters of the Church of England to meet Richard Whatcoat, Thomas Vasey and himself at Bristol. There, on the first day of September, 1784, assisted by Coke and Creighton, Wesley ordained Vasey and Whatcoat deacons, and on the next day, elders. He also ordained Dr. Thomas Coke Superintendent or Bishop of the Methodist societies in America."

> The American Methodist societies, in a conference called December 24, 1784, subsequently agreed to organize themselves into a church with an episcopal form of government, thus resolving to have "superintendents, elders and deacons." They ratified Wesley's appointment and ordination of Dr. Coke by unanimously electing him superintendent. Francis Asbury was also unanimously elected superintendent on the second day of the conference, ordained deacon on

African Methodist Episcopal Zion Church

Sunday, the third day, and consecrated by Dr. Coke and presbyters, Vasey and Whatcoat, on the fourth day, with Otterbein of the German Reformed Church assisting in the service.

"Superintendent" is the word used by Wesley in the letter of instruction given by him to Dr. Coke: "I have accordingly appointed Dr. Coke and Mr. Francis Asbury to be joint superintendents over our brethren in North America." The words "superintendent" and "bishop" were used synonymously, as it appears in the Minutes of the Conference of 1785, where this sentence occurs: "We thought it best to become an episcopal church, making the episcopal office elective, and the elected superintendent or bishop, amenable to the body of ministers and preachers."

The A.M.E. Zion Church adopted this pattern in organizing their connection as a Methodist Episcopal Church. [The Church] also used the terms "superintendent" and "bishop" synonymously in [the] first Discipline. While defining the duties of the superintendent, the term "bishop" was used in ordaining elders and deacons. "We believe in two orders and three offices of the ministry" (*Doctrines and Discipline* . . ., Alexander Walters, Star of Zion, Sept. 4, 1897).

. . . In the Methodist system two orders are only regarded as the original movement of the Christian church. The bishop is an elder elected and consecrated to the office.

Walls observed that "two important changes have been made in the history of the A. M. E. Zion Church episcopacy. In 1868, the General Conference changed the title of . . . episcopal officers from "superintendent" to "bishop." Prior to 1880, a bishop was elected quadrennially. Upon adoption of a resolution presented by Rev. W. A. Foreman, the General Conference amended the law to elect and consecrate a bishop for life, so long as his conduct sustained it. After his consecration he is assigned a district. An episcopal district, which is the official territory of a bishop, is constituted of several annual conferences. It is here that he operates and enforces all the regulations of his area, subject to the general laws of the denomination, which only are enacted by the General Conference."(Walls 1974, pp. 105-6).

An understanding of the character of "the Bishopric," would better enable members, friends, and observers of the African Methodist Episcopal Zion Church to regard this office with deference. A holder of this office is regarded as a "holy man," called

Bishops of the A. M. E. Zion Church

by God, elected by the people, and consecrated to be a servant of the people for Christ and His Church. The following biographical sketches and pictures of the persons who have attained this high office by receiving at least two-thirds of the votes of the delegates at a General Conference and by being duly consecrated by at least three other bishops (or three elders in the event that all the bishops were deceased) are set forth in this publication. This is the first volume produced by the church that portrays all of the ninety-one bishops elected and consecrated by the African Methodist Episcopal Zion Church from 1822-1996.

1. BISHOP JAMES VARICK

JAMES VARICK along with thirty other blacks withdrew from the John Street Methodist Episcopal Church in New York City and organized their own congregation in 1796. They had suffered repeated insults, and it had become clear that they would not be permitted to worship as they pleased with one of their own in charge.

Varick, a shoemaker by trade, had been holding separate religious meetings in private in his home at 4 Orange (Now Baxter) Street since he was licensed to preach in 1780. In 1800 this group built its own church on property they purchased at the corner of Leonard and Church Streets in lower Manhattan. They named it *Zion*, and Varick preached the first sermon during the laying of the cornerstone on July 30, 1800.

Varick was born in Orange County near Newburgh, New York, in 1750. His mother was a slave or a former slave (whose name is not recorded) of the Varicks, a Dutch family. His father was Richard Varick. After giving birth, she returned to New York City with her son.

Varick was a scholar who availed himself of such schooling as African American children had at that time. He may have attended the Free School which opened for blacks on September 15, 1760. Varick married Aurelia Jones around 1790. They had seven children, four of whom (Daniel, Andrew, Emeline and Mary) survived (Wheeler, 1906, p. 17).

In 1806, Bishop Francis Asbury of the Methodist Episcopal Church ordained Varick, Abraham Thompson, and June Scott as deacons despite opposition from Southern delegates. By 1820, African American Methodists had formed several churches, but the Methodist Church still required white pastors to supervise their worship. So the ministers of several black churches, including Zion, met, with Rev. Varick presiding, to form their own denomination. On June 22, 1822, Revs. Varick, Abraham Thompson, and Leven Smith were ordained elders by three elders: Revs. James Covell, William M. Stilwell, and Sylvester Hutchinson, of the Methodist Church. In July 1822, the church known today as the African Methodist Episcopal Zion Church (Zion was added to the denomination's name in 1848) convened and elected Rev. Varick as its first Bishop or Superintendent as the office was then called.

Bishop Varick presided over the next five annual conferences of the New York Conference. He died on July 22, 1827. His ashes are buried in a crypt beneath the sanctuary of Mother A. M. E. Zion Church, now located at 146 W. 137th St. in New York City. A bust and tablet to his memory are on the wall of the sanctuary.

Bishop J. Varick
ELECTED 1822-DIED 1827

1. BISHOP JAMES VARICK

Born: In Orange County, near Newburgh, New York, probably in 1750, to Richard Varick and an unnamed slave or former slave who moved with her son to New York City. **Education:** Unknown, but was a scholar, so he probably took advantage of whatever education was available in New York City for African Americans at that time. As an adult he taught in his spare time in a school located in Zion Church. **Family:** Married Aurelia Jones in 1790. Seven children, four (Daniel, Andrew, Emeline and Mary) survived. **Died**: July 21, 1827. Ashes buried in a crypt beneath the sanctuary of Mother Zion Church, 146 W. 137th St., in New York City.

2. BISHOP CHRISTOPHER RUSH

CHRISTOPHER RUSH, a full-blooded African, was born a slave in Craven County, near New Bern, North Carolina, on February 4, 1777. The names of his parents are not known. He escaped to New York City in 1798 and joined Zion Church in 1803. Rush was licensed to preach in 1815. He was one of six preachers ordained deacon and elder on the same day, July 23, 1822, by Bishop Varick during the Second Annual Conference at Zion Church in New York City. Bishop Varick assigned Rev. Rush to Newark, New Jersey. Rev. Rush organized the first black church in that city, and on April 7, 1823, he laid the cornerstone of what is now the Clinton Memorial A. M. E. Zion Church, currently located at 151 Broadway, Newark, New Jersey.

Bishop Varick died in 1827. On May 18, 1828, Rev. Rush was elected by the Zion Connection for a four-year term as its second superintendent (Bishop) after Rev. Leven Smith, the senior elder, declined. Bishop Rush was reelected three times, in 1832, 1836, and 1840.

During his tenure, Bishop Rush was responsible for organizing several northern conferences, including the New England Conference, the Allegheny Conference, and the Genessee Conference (now called the Western New York Conference). Under his leadership the church expanded east, west, north and south within the United States. A. M. E. Zion churches were organized in Pittsburgh (1836); Washington, D.C. (1837) and Baltimore (1842). In addition, Zion spread into Canada in 1829 under his leadership.

Bishop Rush, who never married, was an avid abolitionist. He was president of the Phoenix Society, a center of antislavery activities in New York City. He also made major efforts to further education and secured property for a school in Essex County, New York. This project, unfortunately, did not succeed.

Bishop Rush published *A Short Account of the Rise and Progress of the African Methodist Episcopal (Zion) Church in America* in 1843. He went blind in the 1850s and remained in the background during and after the Civil War.

Bishop Rush died on July 16, 1873. He is buried beneath an imposing monument in Mother Zion's Cypress Hill Cemetery in Brooklyn, New York.

Bishop C. Rush
ELECTED 1827-DIED 1873

2. BISHOP CHRISTOPHER RUSH

Born: A slave in Craven County, near New Bern, North Carolina, Feb. 4, 1777. **Education:** Unknown but he was a scholar who wrote the first book about the A. M. E. Zion Church, and he made major efforts to further education among African Americans. **Major Publication:** *A Short Account of the Rise and Progress of the African Methodist Episcopal (Zion) Church in America.* **Family:** Was a full-blooded African, parents unknown. Never married. **Died:** July 16, 1873. Buried beneath an imposing monument in Mother Zion Church's Cypress Hill Cemetery, Brooklyn, New York.

3. BISHOP WILLIAM MILLER

WILLIAM MILLER was born on August 23, 1775, in Queen Anne's County, Maryland, a slave state. When or how he migrated to New York City is unknown, but he was a member of the group of African Americans who left John Street Methodist Episcopal Church in 1796. An exhorter at that time and a cabinetmaker, he occupied an old stable on Cross Street between Mulberry and Orange. This building was the group's first place of worship after they separated from the white Methodist Episcopal Church. (Moore 1884, pp. 16-17)

Miller's education is unknown, but he was literate and had an abiding interest in education. He turned part of his house at 36 Mulberry Street into a schoolroom, where the New York African Bible Society was established on January 17, 1817, and he was elected its president.

Miller was ordained a deacon, along with Daniel Coker, on April 27, 1808, by Bishop Francis Asbury of the Methodist Episcopal Church. Something of a wanderer, Rev. Miller took some of his followers out of the Zion congregation's first church and established Asbury Church, which was chartered by New York City in 1814. By 1819, however, Asbury was cooperating with Zion Church, and Rev. Miller was among those who voted themselves out of the Methodist Episcopal Church on July 26, 1820. He was one of the five appointed to a committee which met in his house to write Zion's first Discipline in 1820. He was one of the three persons (along with Abraham Thompson and James Varick) to sign the "Founders' Address." However, in 1823, Rev. Miller left the Zion Connection and joined Bishop Richard Allen's Bethel Connection. He was ordained an elder by that Connection.

In 1830, he applied for and was granted readmission to the Zion Connection and was appointed to a church in Philadelphia. Rev. Miller was elected assistant superintendent in 1840. He served with Bishop Rush for five years and died in Philadelphia on December 6, 1845. He was buried in Philadelphia after funeral services at Wesley Church, now located at 15th and Lombard Streets.

Bishop W. Miller
ELECTED 1840-DIED 1845

3. BISHOP WILLIAM MILLER

Born: August 23, 1775, in Queen Anne's County, Maryland. **Education:** Unknown but was literate and committed to education. Turned part of his house into a schoolroom and taught there. **Family:** Never married. **Died**: December 6, 1845, in Philadelphia. Buried in Philadelphia after funeral services at Wesley Church, now located at 15th and Lombard Streets.

4. BISHOP GEORGE GALBRAITH [GALBREATH]

GEORGE GALBRAITH [GALBREATH] was born March 4, 1799, in Lancaster County, Pennsylvania. His parents, who were named Adam and Eve, were slaves owned by a Dr. Galbraith. He was raised in the family of Moses Wilson (or Williams) of Hanover Township, Pennsylvania, who sent him to school with his own children. He learned the carpenter's trade and cabinetmaking in Middletown, Pennsylvania, where he embraced religion among the Winebrenarians in 1826. He was emancipated probably prior to 1830, but the exact date is not known.

Galbraith joined the A.M.E. Zion Church founded by Rev. J. D. Richardson in Middletown, Pennsylvania and the Philadelphia Annual Conference in June, 1830. He was ordained deacon and elder that year by Bishop C. Rush. Rev. Galbraith was responsible for organizing several churches in Washington, D.C., including Zion Wesley (now Metropolitan Wesley) in 1837 and Galbraith Church in 1843.

In 1848, following the death of Bishop W. Miller, he was elected assistant superintendent. He served in that position for four years. This was during the period when Bishop Rush was going blind. Rev. Galbraith has been credited with doing more than any other assistant superintendent before or after his time. He was one of three persons consecrated bishop by the 1852 General Conference. He died the following year in Philadelphia from an attack of asthma after a trip across the Allegheny mountains. His last rites were held at Wesley A.M.E. Zion Church in Philadelphia, now located at 15th and Lombard Streets.

Bishop Galbraith was a husband and a father, but the names of his wife and children are not recorded.

Bishop G. Galbreath
ELECTED 1848-DIED 1853

4. BISHOP GEORGE GALBRAITH [GALBREATH]

Born: In Lancaster County, Pennsylvania, March 4, 1799. Parents were slaves, named Adam and Eve, of a Dr. Galbraith. **Education:** Obtained a "common school" education by attending school with his master's children. **Family:** Was married and had children, but names are unknown. **Died:** In Philadelphia in 1853 from an attack of asthma after a trip across the Allegheny mountains. Buried in Philadelphia following last rites at Wesley A. M. E. Zion Church.

5. BISHOP WILLIAM HAYWOOD BISHOP

WILLIAM HAYWOOD BISHOP was born in 1793 in Maryland, a slave state at that time. His educational background is unknown. He joined Zion Church in New York City in September, 1825 and the New York Conference on May 18, 1826. He was ordained deacon on May 21, 1827 and elder on May 18, 1828 by Bishop James Varick.

Rev. Bishop was the host pastor in 1844 of the 7th General Conference held at Zion Church in New York City.

When Bishop Christopher Rush retired in 1852, Rev. Bishop was one of three elders who were elected superintendent "on equality"—Revs. George Galbraith and George A. Spywood—were the other two. However, Bishop Galbraith died in 1853, and Zion split into two factions. Bishop Bishop's faction, the "Southern Wing," was the larger of the two. It held a general conference in 1856 and elected Bishop Bishop the general superintendent and Rev. Joseph J. Clinton assistant superintendent. The courts, however, ruled against the Southern Wing and found it had acted illegally. (Bradley 1972, p. 144) This brought about overtures for reunion. At the 1860 General Conference the two factions reunited and elected three bishops "on equality" — William Haywood Bishop, Peter Ross, and Joseph J. Clinton.

Bishop Bishop served until 1868 and presided over every Northern conference of that day. He retired at his own request in 1868 and died in 1873. No family information is available. (Hood 1895, p. 184)

Bishop W.H. Bishop
ELECTED 1852-DIED 1873

5. BISHOP WILLIAM HAYWOOD BISHOP

Born: In 1793 in Maryland. Names of parents not known. **Education:** Unknown
Family: Unknown. **Died:** June, 1873.

6. BISHOP GEORGE ALFRED SPYWOOD

GEORGE ALFRED SPYWOOD was born in Mashpee, Maine, in 1802. The names of his parents are not known, but he was a mixture of African and Native American. He was converted in 1818, licensed to preach in Providence, Rhode Island in 1831, and ordained deacon in 1843 and elder in 1844.

The General Conference of 1852 elected him one of three superintendents "on equality" and placed him in charge of the newly formed Eastern District that included the New England, the Nova Scotia, and the British Guiana Conferences.

Following the death of Bishop Galbraith, the A.M.E. Zion Connection split, and Bishop Spywood was elected general superintendent in 1853 by the Eastern faction, the smaller of the two factions. However, the 1856 General Conference organized by the Eastern faction relieved Bishop Spywood of his office, made Rev. James Simmons the general superintendent, and made Rev. Solomon Scott the assistant superintendent. For the remainder of his life, Bishop Spywood was employed by the New England Conference Mission Board of the A.M.E. Zion Church as its agent. He died on January 15, 1875. No information is available on his family.

Bishop G.A. Spywood
ELECTED 1852-DIED 1875

6. BISHOP GEORGE ALFRED SPYWOOD

Born: In Mashpee, Maine, in 1802, a mixture of African and Native American. Names of parents unknown. **Education:** Unknown. **Family:** Unknown. **Died:** On January 15, 1875.

7. BISHOP JOHN TAPPAN

JOHN TAPPAN was born of slave parents in North Carolina on June 20, 1799. Their names are not recorded. He moved to New York and began preaching in 1832. He joined the New York Conference in 1833 and was ordained deacon on May 20, 1834 and elder on May 15, 1835.

On July 9, 1853, Rev. Tappan was elected assistant superintendent at a special convention called by the Eastern faction of the A.M.E. Zion Connection. However, at the 1856 General Conference, both he and Bishop Spywood failed to be reelected. Despite this disappointment, he continued to serve Zion as a minister and was the host pastor for the 13th General Conference, in May, 1868, at Wesley Zion (Metropolitan) Church in Washington, D.C., now located at North Capitol and R Streets., N.W.

Bishop Tappan died in 1870. No information is available on his family.

Bishop J. Tappan
ELECTED 1854-DIED 1870

7. BISHOP JOHN TAPPAN

Born: In North Carolina, June 20, 1799, of slave parents. **Education:** Unknown. **Family:** Unknown. **Died:** In 1870.

8. BISHOP JAMES SIMMONS

JAMES SIMMONS was born December 3, 1792, in Accomac County, Virginia, or on the Eastern Shore area in Maryland. No information is available on his parents, his family, or his early life. He migrated to New York City and joined the New York Conference in May, 1832. A year later, Rev. Simmons was ordained deacon and elder on the same date. On June 30, 1856, he was elected general superintendent by the faction opposed to Bishop W. H. Bishop during the split in the A. M. E. Zion Connection. Bishop Simmons replaced Bishop G. A. Spywood. Later in 1856, Bishop Simmons sent a missionary to establish a church in Friendship, East Coast, Demerara in the South American area now known as Guyana.

Bishop Simmons was ill and did not attend the 1860 reunification General Conference, where he was not reelected superintendent. However, he continued to give effective service to Zion in the New York and New England Conferences and was presiding over the New England Conference when he died in February, 1874.

Bishop J. Simmons
ELECTED 1854-DIED 1874

8. BISHOP JAMES SIMMONS

Born: On December 3, 1792, in Accomac County, Virginia, or on the Eastern Shore area in Maryland. Names of parents not known. **Education:** Unknown. **Family:** Unknown. **Died:** February, 1874. No other information available.

African Methodist Episcopal Zion Church
9. BISHOP SOLOMON TIMOTHY SCOTT

SOLOMON TIMOTHY SCOTT was born on August 20, 1790, in Smyrna, Delaware. The names of his parents are not known. He was converted there and licensed to preach in 1831. Rev. Scott joined the Philadelphia Annual Conference in June, 1833. He was ordained deacon on June 20, 1834 and elder on June 18, 1835.

During the 1852 General Conference Rev. Scott was nominated twice for the Connection's highest office, but he was not elected. On June 30, 1856, he was elected assistant superintendent by the General Conference held by the Eastern faction.

Bishop Scott did not take part in the 1860 General Conference of reconciliation, and he was not reelected. He died a year and a half later on January 4, 1862.

Bishop S.T. Scott
ELECTED 1856-DIED 1862

9. BISHOP SOLOMON TIMOTHY SCOTT

Born: August 20, 1790, in Smyrna, Delaware. Names of parents not known. **Education:** Unknown. **Family:** Unknown. **Died:** January 4, 1862.

African Methodist Episcopal Zion Church
10. BISHOP JOSEPH JACKSON CLINTON

JOSEPH JACKSON CLINTON, the youngest man ever elected a bishop by the A. M. E. Zion Church and the first bishop to organize A. M. E. Zion churches in the Deep South, was born in Philadelphia, Pennsylvania, on October 3, 1823.

As a youngster he studied in Mr. Bird's School in Philadelphia and then went to Allegheny Institute. He embraced religion in 1832, was licensed to preach in 1840 at the age of 17, and was admitted to Conference in 1843. Rev. Clinton was ordained a deacon on May 6, 1845, and an elder on June 30, 1846. On July 30, 1856, about three months shy of his 33rd birthday, the Southern faction of the Connection elected Rev. Clinton assistant superintendent. In 1860, he was one of three elected superintendents "on equality" by the reunited Connection at the 1860 General Conference.

In 1860 Bishop Clinton was given charge of the Southern and Philadelphia District. No Zion Bishop had gone south of Washington, D.C., at that time and Bishop Clinton was reluctant to go. The Civil War was still raging, and the outcome was in doubt. President Lincoln's Emancipation Proclamation went into effect January 1, 1863, but Gen. George G. Meade did not drive Gen. Robert E. Lee from Gettysburg, Pennsylvania, and Gen. U.S. Grant did not capture Vicksburg, Mississippi, until July, 1863. Bishop Clinton did not have the $300 he needed to transport his missionaries South. However, a dramatic 3 a.m. meeting in Washington, D. C., in the fall of 1863, with Melvina Fletcher, a prominent member of Zion Wesley (Metropolitan) Church, persuaded him to go. She promised to raise the funds and succeeded. In 1864 Bishop Clinton and five missionaries, including Rev. James Walker Hood and Rev. Wilbur Garrison Strong, went South. Rev. Hood was stationed in North Carolina. Rev. Strong did Zion's work in Louisiana, Florida, and Alabama. Bishop Clinton organized the North Carolina Conference on December 17, 1864, with 12 ministers and about 400 members. Afterwards he sailed to New Orleans, Louisiana and organized the Louisiana Conference on March. 13, 1865. There were 15,000 members when he left Louisiana. In all, Bishop Clinton organized thirteen annual conferences, took in more than seven hundred itinerant preachers, and added more than one hundred thousand Sunday School scholars to the church. Zion's youngest bishop and best organizer during this trying period died on May 24, 1881, in Atlantic City, New Jersey. He and his wife are buried in Mt. Olive Cemetery in Philadelphia, Pennsylvania.

Bishop Clinton married Letitia Sisco in Pittsburgh, Pennsylvania, on October 24, 1844. They had ten children, six of whom survived. One of their sons, Rev. Joseph N. Clinton, became a presiding elder in Florida.

Bishop J.J. Clinton
ELECTED 1856-DIED 1881

10. BISHOP JOSEPH JACKSON CLINTON

Born: On October 3, 1823, in Philadelphia, Pennsylvania. Names of parents not known **Education:** Studied at Mr. Bird's School in Philadelphia, then went to Allegheny Institute. **Family:** Married Letitia Sisco in Pittsburgh, Pennsylvania, on October 24, 1844. Ten children, six survived. One son, Rev. Joseph N. Clinton, became a presiding elder in Florida. A second son, Rev. Franklin A. Clinton, was also a minister. **Died:** May 24, 1881, in Atlantic City, New Jersey. Buried with his wife in Mt. Olive Cemetery, Philadelphia, Pennsylvania.

11. BISHOP PETER ROSS

PETER ROSS was born in New York City in 1809. The names of his parents are not known. He joined the New York Conference in May, 1834, and was sent as a missionary to Nova Scotia and New England. He was pastor for a short time at a little schoolhouse church known as *Zion on Second Street* in New Bedford, Massachusetts. Frederick Douglass was a leading member of the church at that time. Ross was a great pulpit orator and an abolitionist who stood for civil and religious liberty.

Rev. Ross was ordained a deacon by Bishop William Miller in New York City in December, 1840, and, an elder by Bishop Christopher Rush in Middletown in 1842. Rev. Ross, along with Bishops Bishop and Clinton, was elected a superintendent "on equality" by the reunited Connection in 1860. He, however, had great difficulty raising money. In May, 1864, Bishop Ross appeared before an A.M.E. Zion select committee and resigned his bishopric because, he said, he had no funds on which to live. The field had been so "gleaned," he said, by his fellow bishops that he barely secured $200 excluding travel expenses. Because it was impossible for him and his family to exist on that sum, he resigned, purchased a set of shoemaker's tools, and returned to his trade. He accepted an offer to serve as a chaplain for the 14th Rhode Island Heavy Artillery. (Bradley 1972, p. 152)

Bishop Ross's education background is unknown, but education was one of his interests. He was a member of an A.M.E. Zion committee charged in 1844 with drafting a constitution for a manual labor school. The names of his wife and children are unknown. He died July 25, 1890.

Bishop P. Ross
ELECTED 1860-DIED 1890

11. BISHOP PETER ROSS

Born: In New York City in 1809. Names of parents not known. **Education:** Unknown. **Family:** Unknown but was married and had children. **Died:** July 25, 1890.

12. BISHOP JOHN DELAWARE BROOKS

JOHN DELAWARE BROOKS was born in Baltimore, Maryland, on October 7, 1803. No information is available on his parents, their civic status, or on his educational training, but he was a well-prepared man.

Rev. Brooks was ordained a deacon on June 11, 1843 and an elder on May 4, 1845. In 1852, he was elected secretary of the General Conference held in Big Wesley A.M.E. Zion Church in Philadelphia, Pennsylvania. His character was above reproach, but it is said that he was extremely rigid and that he stressed the highest point of discipline and execution of laws. This, it is said, caused misunderstanding in his pastorates, with loss of some members, and a split at Zion Wesley (now Metropolitan Wesley) A.M.E. Zion Church in Washington, D.C. that led to the formation of St. Paul A.M.E. Church.

Rev. Brooks was one of six elders elected bishop by the 1864 General Conference. He did not agree with the idea of the rotation of bishops and tried to resign, but the Conference would not accept his resignation. The 1868 General Conference assigned Bishop Brooks and Bishop J. W. Loguen to the California Conference. They were to exchange places after two years, but Bishop Loguen died in 1872, and Bishop Brooks also passed away in 1874. Thus, Zion's work on the West Coast lagged.

Bishop Brooks was the host bishop for the 14th quadrennial General Conference held in June, 1872, at Clinton Chapel, Charlotte, North Carolina. In that same year he became president of the A.M.E. Zion Book Concern. In 1874, he associated with Bishop John J. Moore at the Philadelphia and Baltimore Annual Conference held in Carlisle, Pennsylvania. Before the year was gone he died in his home in York, Pennsylvania.

Bishop J.D. Brooks
ELECTED 1864-DIED 1874

12. BISHOP JOHN DELAWARE BROOKS

Born: In Baltimore, Maryland, on October 7, 1803. Names of parents not known. **Education:** Unknown, but a well-prepared man. **Family:** Unknown. **Died:** 1874 at his home in York, Pennsylvania.

13. BISHOP JERMAIN WESLEY LOGUEN (LOGAN)

JERMAIN WESLEY LOGUEN, the man who was to become known as the *Underground Railroad King* because of his efforts to help runaway slaves gain their freedom, was born a slave himself about 16 miles from Nashville, Tennessee, in 1813. His mother, Jane, had been born free in Ohio, but at the age of seven she was kidnaped, renamed *Cherry* and sold into slavery in Tennessee to David Logue who ran a whisky distillery with slave labor.

Logue fathered Jermain, but when hard times came, he sold the boy and his mother to a brutal master. Determined to be free and, if possible, to free his mother, Loguen ran away when he was twenty-one. He crossed the Ohio river and followed the North Star to Canada. There he became a farmer and a lumberjack. He learned to read and write in a Sabbath School in Hamilton, Canada, and graduated a Bible reader from a school in nearby Ancaster, Canada. While in Canada, he added the n to his name and adopted *Wesley* as a middle name. Loguen returned to the United States and married Caroline Storum in 1840 while he was a student at Oneida Institute, Whitesboro, New York. They had eight children. One of them, Helen Amelia, married a son of Frederick Douglass, the abolitionist, editor, and A. M. E. Zion member. A second daughter, Sarah Marinda, graduated from the Medical College of Syracuse in 1876 and practiced medicine for many years in Syracuse and Washington, D.C. (Hunter 1993, pp. 65-66)

Loguen started his ministry in 1841. He joined the New York Conference in May, 1842, and was ordained a deacon May 21, 1843 and an elder May 23, 1844. He built and stabilized nearly a half dozen churches in the western part of New York, including the first Zion church in Syracuse. He became a leader in the abolition movement in New York State and used his home as the underground railroad depot in Syracuse. He helped more than fifteen hundred slaves escape to freedom, including Harriet Tubman and Jerry. Jerry, a runaway, was arrested and jailed in Syracuse and scheduled to be sent back to his master. Rev. Loguen led a successful effort — with crowbars and battering rams — to free Jerry and send him to Canada.

Rev. Loguen was first elected a Bishop by the 1864 General Conference. He resigned because he was still a fugitive slave and did not want to go South while the 1850 Fugitive Slave Law was still in effect. After the end of the Civil War, he did go South and organized the first A. M. E. Zion church in Knoxville, now known as Loguen Temple. In 1868 he was again elected a bishop and assigned to the Fifth District (the Allegheny and Kentucky Conferences), to exchange after two years with Bishop S. T. W. Jones and go to the Second District, which included the Genesee (now Western New York) and the Philadelphia and Baltimore Conferences. In 1872 he was appointed to work on the Pacific Coast. He probably never got there, because he died September 30, 1872, in Saratoga Springs, New York.

Bishop J.W. Loquen

ELECTED 1864-DIED 1872

13. BISHOP JERMAIN WESLEY LOGUEN (LOGAN)

Born: A slave, in 1813, in Davidson County, Tennessee, near Nashville. His mother was a pure African who, though free, was kidnaped when seven, and sold into slavery. His father was his master, David Logue. **Education:** After escaping from slavery, learned to read and write in Sabbath School, Hamilton, Canada. Became a Bible reader at a school in nearby Ancaster. Studied at Oneida Institute, Whitesboro, New York. Major **Publication:** *The Rev. J. W. Loguen as a Slave and as a Freeman,* 1859. **Family:** Married Caroline Storum in 1840. They had eight children. A daughter, Helen Amelia, married Lewis Douglass, a son of Frederick Douglass. A second daughter, Sarah Marinda, graduated from the Medical College of Syracuse in 1876. **Died:** September 30, 1872, in Saratoga Springs, New York.

14. BISHOP SAMSON DUNBAR TALBOT

SAMSON DUNBAR TALBOT was born in West Bridgewater, Massachusetts, in 1819. His educational background is unknown. He joined the New York Conference in May, 1842. He was ordained deacon, May 21, 1843 and elder, May 23, 1844. He was regarded as one of the best preachers of his day. During his ministry, he had charge of churches in New York City and Boston.

Rev. Talbot served as secretary of the 1844 General Conference held in Zion Church, New York City. He was one of six elders elected bishop by the 1864 General Conference. Bishop Talbot was assigned to the First District, which included the New York, New England, and Genesee Conferences for two years and then rotated to the Fourth District, which included the Georgia, Alabama, and Louisiana Conferences. On June 6, 1866, he organized the Kentucky Conference at Center Street Church, Louisville, Kentucky. During Reconstruction, he helped establish the A. M. E. Zion Church in Georgia, where he lived until he died in 1878. No information is available on his family or his parents.

Bishop S.D. Talbot
ELECTED 1864-DIED 1878

14. BISHOP SAMSON DUNBAR TALBOT

Born: In 1819 in West Bridgewater, Massachusetts. **Education:** Unknown. **Family:** Married but no other details available. **Died:** In his home in Georgia in 1878.

15. BISHOP JOHN JAMISON MOORE

JOHN JAMISON MOORE was born in Berkeley County, West Virginia, about 1804, to slave parents. His mother, whose maiden name was *Riedoubt*, was born free but was kidnaped at the age of fifteen in Maryland and sold into slavery in West Virginia, where she married a man named *Hodge*. A change of owners caused the family to adopt the surname of *Moore*.

When he was six, his family attempted to escape but were recaptured. His four oldest siblings were sold farther south. A second attempt was successful, and the family reached Bedford County, Pennsylvania. He was taught to read and write and acquired a knowledge of farming. He bound himself to a white farmer who robbed him of two years or more and would have continued the robbery but for a friendly Quaker who told him his time was up and advised him to leave, which he did.

Moore embraced religion while in Harrisburg, Pennsylvania in 1833 and obtained an exhorter's license in 1834. He employed private tutors in 1836 and became proficient in English, Latin, Greek, and Hebrew.

After joining the Philadelphia Annual Conference in 1841, he was ordained a deacon on June 10, 1842 and an elder on June 12, 1843. Rev. Moore served as assistant secretary of the Conference in 1843 and was elected secretary in 1844. In 1848 he was elected secretary of the General Conference. In 1848 he was pastor of Big Wesley, Philadelphia, Pennsylvania. In 1852 he left for California where he established the first A. M. E. Zion Church in San Francisco. He became the first teacher of the first school established in California for black children. The school was set up in the basement of St. Cyprian A. M. E. Church in San Francisco. He also took an active part in the fight for funds to educate African American children.

He was consecrated a bishop on May 27, 1868. Bishop Moore wrote the catechisms for use in the A. M. E. Zion Sunday Schools that were adopted by the General Conference in a semi-annual session in September, 1888. He edited the *A. M. E. Zion Sunday School Banner for* several years and wrote a history of the church that was published in 1884.

The General Conference established a Western North Carolina Conference on November 25, 1891, and Bishop Moore organized it. He was married to Mrs. Frances Moore of Salisbury, North Carolina. Her maiden name is not known. The bishop died on December 9, 1893, on his way home after closing the Western North Carolina Conference. He was buried in Salisbury after services at Zion Chapel (Soldiers Memorial) Church in that city.

Bishop J.J. Moore
ELECTED 1868-DIED 1893

15. BISHOP JOHN JAMISON MOORE

Born: In Berkeley County, West Virginia, about 1804 of slave parents. His mother (maiden name Riedoubt) was born free in Maryland but at age fifteen she was kidnapped and sold into slavery in West Virginia. His father was a slave named Hodge. A change of owners caused the family to adopt the name of Moore. **Education:** Learned to read and write after family escaped to Pennsylvania. In 1836 he employed private tutors and became proficient in English, Latin, Greek, and Hebrew. **Major Publication:** *The History of the A. M. E. Zion Church of America*, 1884. **Family:** Married to Frances (maiden name unknown) Moore of Salisbury, North Carolina. Died: On December 9, 1893, on his way home after closing the Western North Carolina Conference. Buried in Salisbury, North Carolina, after services at Zion Chapel (Soldiers Memorial) Church in that city.

16. BISHOP SINGLETON THOMAS WEBSTER JONES

SINGLETON THOMAS WEBSTER JONES, an apostle of unity, champion debater, and major authority on ecclesiastical law, was born in Wrightsville, York County, Pennsylvania, on March 8, 1825. His parents, William H. And Catherine Jones, were from the Eastern Shore, Maryland. (Bradley 1972: p. 164) He worked as a hod carrier in Harrisburg, Pennsylvania and on a boat on the Ohio river when he was a young man.

Jones was licensed to preach in Allegheny, Pennsylvania, in September, 1846, by Rev. George Galbraith who became the church's fourth Bishop in 1848 . Two months later, Rev. Jones married Mary Jane Talbert, who was born in Brownsville, Pennsylvania, in 1831. They had twelve children, one of whom, Edward Derusha W. Jones, became Zion's 41st Bishop. In 1880, his wife became the founding president of Zion's Woman's Home and Foreign Missionary Society, a position she held until 1895. Their other children were George Galbreath, Chester Stevens, Ann Catherine, David Eddie, Elizabeth Jane, Mary Ann, Singleton Thomas, William Haywood Bishop, Alice Williamson, Joll Robinson, and Jennie Catherine. (Bradley 1972, p. 165)

Rev. Jones had only the bare rudiments of an education when he entered the ministry, but he prepared himself so well that he was able to speak French, converse in German, and use Latin. He also became an accomplished writer. He composed several poems, a number of addresses and papers, and a *Hand-Book of the Discipline*. Rev. Jones was a member of the Bishop faction during the schism in the A. M. E. Zion Church. He edited a Discipline for that faction in 1856. Ever an advocate of union, he wrote articles and letters to the *Weekly Anglo-American* pleading for and insisting upon reunification. He was the host pastor for the 1860 reunification General Conference that met in Wesley Church, Philadelphia, Pennsylvania, and wrote the Discipline for the reunited Connection. In 1864, while pastor of Mother Zion Church in New York City, Rev. Jones founded the *Zion Standard and Weekly Review*, a newspaper that lasted four years.

On May 31, 1868, Rev. Jones was consecrated a bishop and appointed to the Third Episcopal District (the Baltimore and Allegheny Conferences). This District gave new life to the Kentucky Conference that, in turn, carried the standard of Zion into Indiana and Missouri and organized the Arkansas and the Missouri Annual Conferences. Bishop Jones took charge of the Tennessee Conference (East Tennessee, Western North Carolina, Northern Georgia and Southwest Virginia) in the fall of 1872. This conference flourished under his leadership for the next ten years. Bishop Jones was assigned to the South Carolina Conference in 1888. He died three years later on April 18, 1891. Funeral services were held at John Wesley Church. He was buried in Harmony Cemetery, Washington, D.C. His wife died four years later at her home in Washington, D.C. She was also buried in Harmony Cemetery.

Bishop S.T.W. Jones
ELECTED 1868-DIED 1891

16. BISHOP SINGLETON THOMAS WEBSTER JONES

Born: March 8, 1825, in Wrightsville, York County, Pennsylvania. **Education:** Had only the bare rudiments of an education when he entered the ministry but prepared himself so well that he was able to speak French, converse in German, and use Latin. He wrote poems, addresses, and books. **Major Publications**: *Hand-Book of The Discipline of the African Methodist Episcopal Zion Church*, 1888. **Family**: Married November 29, 1846, Mary Jane Talbert, who was born in Brownsville, Pennsylvania, in 1831. Had twelve children, including Edward Derusha W. Jones, who became Zion's 41st Bishop. **Died:** On April 18, 1891. Buried in Harmony Cemetery, Washington, D.C., along with his wife who died four years later.

African Methodist Episcopal Zion Church
17. BISHOP JAMES WALKER HOOD

JAMES WALKER HOOD was born in Kennett Township, Chester County, Pennsylvania, to Levi and Harriett (Walker) Hood on May 30, 1831 (Marquis 1912, p. 1019). His father, two uncles, a brother, and two cousins were all ministers. He was educated in the public schools (Price 1916, p. 101). His mother taught him grammar and interested him in public speaking, and he had a tutor for Greek. Hood delivered his first abolitionist speech at the age of fifteen, during which he predicted the emancipation of the slaves — almost twenty years before it actually took place.

Hood was called to preach at the age of twenty-one but did not actively take up the ministry at that time. His first church was in New Haven, Connecticut. He also served in Nova Scotia, Canada. He was ordained deacon September 2, 1860 and elder on June 15, 1862. He was one of five ministers sent South by Bishop J. J. Clinton. He moved his family to Washington, D.C.,and on January 20th, he disembarked in New Bern, North Carolina, shortly after Union Forces had seized the territory. He organized congregations in New Bern, Wilmington, Fayetteville, and Charlotte, as the denomination spread in North Carolina from the sea to the mountains. In 1864 alone, he gathered almost three thousand members and nine ministers into Zion's Connection (Moore 1884, p. 374).

In 1867, Rev. Hood was elected to the North Carolina State Convention and took so prominent a part that the constitution they adopted was called the "Hood Constitution." In 1868, he was appointed assistant superintendent of public instruction in North Carolina. He wrote the state's public school laws and canvassed the state to get African American children into public schools.

On July 3, 1872, he was consecrated a bishop. He served for forty-four years and retired in 1916. He was responsible for launching the weekly newspaper, The Star of Zion. Bishop Hood was the first chair of the Livingstone College Board of Trustees. His writings include *The Negro in the Christian Pulpit, One Hundred Years of the A. M. E. Zion Church, and The Plan of the Apocalyps*e.

Bishop Hood was married three times: on October 4, 1852 to Hannah L. Ralph of Lancaster, Pennsylvania, who died April 5, 1855; on April 22, 1858 to Sophia J. Nugent of Washington, D.C., who died September 3, 1875; and to Mrs. Kizziah (Katie) P. McCoy of Wilmington, North Carolina, on June 6, 1877. His third wife served as corresponding secretary of A.M. E. Zion Woman's Home and Missionary Society and as the second president of that body from 1895-1912. He had ten children: Hattie, Aline, Josephine, Gertrude, Lillian, Joseph, and Maggie by his second wife, and Maude, James Walker, Jr. and Robert H. by his third wife (Price 1916, p. 101). Bishop Hood died on October 30, 1918, in his home town of Fayetteville, North Carolina. He was buried in that city after funeral services at Evans Chapel with the Grand Lodge, Masonic Order, of Prince Hall affiliation performing the last rites at the cemetery.

Bishop J.W. Hood
ELECTED 1872-DIED 1918

17. BISHOP JAMES WALKER HOOD

Born: May 30, 1831, in Kennett Township, Chester County, Pennsylvania, to Levi and Harriett (Walker) Hood. **Education:** Educated in the public schools. Mother taught him grammar and interested him in public speaking. Had a tutor for Greek. **Major Publications:** *The Negro in the Christian Pulpit: Twenty-One Practical Sermons, 1884; One Hundred Years of the A. M. E. Zion Church, 1895; The Plan of the Apocalypse, 1900; Sermons, Vol. II, 1908; History of the A. M. E. Zion Church, Vol. 2, 1914.* **Family:** Father, two uncles, a brother, and two cousins were ministers. Married three times: on October 4, 1852, to Hannah L. Ralph, Lancaster, Pennsylvania; on April 5, 1855, to Sophia J. Nugent, Washington, D.C.; on June 6, 1877, to Mrs. Kizziah (Katie) P. McCoy, Wilmington, North Carolina. Ten children: Hattie, Aline, Josephine, Gertrude, Lillian, Joseph, and Maggie by his second wife; and Maude and James Walker, Jr., and Robert by his third wife. **Died:** October 30, 1918, in Fayetteville, North Carolina. Buried there after funeral services at Evans Chapel in that city and last rites at the cemetery by the Grand Lodge of Prince Hall in affiliation with the Masonic Order.

18. BISHOP JOSEPH PASCAL THOMPSON, M.D.

JOSEPH PASCAL THOMPSON was born in slavery in Winchester, Virginia, on December 20, 1818. He ran away while still a youth and found a home in Pennsylvania. He acquired an education by attending night school and the district school. He also studied medicine with a physician who lived in what is now Matawan, New Jersey. When he decided to become a preacher, he studied theology with a Rev. Dr. Mills of Auburn Theological Seminary in Auburn, New York. Rev. Thompson also continued his medical studies and on April 1, 1858, graduated from the University of Medicine, Philadelphia, with a degree of Doctor of Medicine.

He was converted at the age of fifteen. He was licensed to preach in 1839 when he was twenty. He joined the New York Conference in May, 1844. He was ordained deacon on May 17, 1846 and elder on May 2, 1847. For the next twenty-nine years he served as pastor in most of Zion's churches along the Hudson. He was three times pastor of the Zion church in Newburgh, New York and was pastor of Mother Zion in New York City when its new building, then located at West 10th and Bleeker Streets, was dedicated on April 17, 1853.

On November 16, 1841, he married Catherine Gilchrist, the daughter of S. Gilchrist, an Underground Railroad conductor. They had one daughter who married Prof. D. B. Alsdorf of Newburg, New York (Hood 1895: p. 191). Rev. Thompson was also prominent in the Underground Railroad movement. He picked up runaways from the home of his father-in-law in Williamsport, Pennsylvania and took them to Harrisburg, Pennsylvania. He then walked with them 130 miles to the home of the Rev. (later Bishop) J. W. Loguen in Syracuse, New York.

He was consecrated bishop by the 1876 General Conference. He presided over a number of conferences, including the East Alabama, the Texas, and the Bahama Islands Conferences. When the A. M. E. Zion Book Concern reported a deficit to the 1888 General Conference, Bishop Thompson was appointed chair of a new oversight committee. He lent $1080 to the Book Concern so that the debt could be paid.

His wife was also active in Zion. In 1880, she was elected the first treasurer of the Woman's Home and Foreign Missionary Society. She held that position until her death in 1893. Bishop Thompson died the following year on December 21, 1894. Both he and his wife are buried in Newburgh, New York.

Bishop J.P. Thompson
ELECTED 1876-DIED 1894

18. BISHOP JOSEPH PASCAL THOMPSON, M.D.

Born: A slave in Winchester, Virginia, on December 20, 1818. Names of his parents are not known. **Education:** After running away, he attended school in Pennsylvania, studied medicine and theology, and on April 1, 1858, received a Doctor of Medicine degree from the University of Medicine, Philadelphia, Pennsylvania. **Family:** On November 16, 1841, married Catherine Gilchrist, the daughter of S. Gilchrist, of Williamsport, Pennsylvania, an Underground Railroad conductor. Wife became the first treasurer of A. M. E. Zion Woman's Home and Foreign Missionary Society in 1880 and served until she died in 1893. A daughter married Prof. D. B. Alsdorf of Newburg, New York. **Died:** December 21, 1894, buried in Newburgh, New York beside his wife.

19. BISHOP WILLIAM HENRY HILLERY

WILLIAM HENRY HILLERY was born in Virginia, May, 1839. The names of his parents are not known. He moved to Wilkes Barre, Pennsylvania, when very young. He started to preach when he was eighteen and joined the Genesee (Western New York) Conference on September 6, 1862. He was sent as a missionary to Tennessee and labored ardently in the Eastern Tennessee area from Strawberry Plains to Wheeling, West Virginia. He established several societies with hundreds of members during a reign of terror against blacks. He was afterwards transferred to Washington, North Carolina. He was ordained a deacon on November 10, 1864 and an elder on November 16, 1866.

In 1868, Rev. Hillery served as an assistant secretary of the General Conference. He transferred to the West Coast that same year and became presiding elder of the California Conference. He represented that conference at the next two General Conferences. In 1872, Rev. Hillery, then residing in San Francisco, was elected secretary of the General Conference. He was consecrated bishop on July 4, 1876. He was assigned to the California Conference. He went to England for fifteen months to solicit funds for the Zion church in San Francisco but did not make any report of the funds brought back from the trip to the 1880 General Conference. During his absence from his post many of his California members shifted to the A.M.E. Church.

Bishop Hillery developed a weakness that caused his failure. He was disrobed by the 1884 General Conference in New York City on charges of intemperance and immoral conduct. Final action on his case was taken by the Genesse Conference.

He died on July 22, 1893.

Bishop W.H. Hillery
ELECTED 1876-DIED 1908

19. BISHOP WILLIAM HENRY HILLERY

Born: May, 1839, in Virginia. Names of parents not known. **Education:** Not known. **Family:** Not known. **Died:** July 22, 1893.

African Methodist Episcopal Zion Church
20. BISHOP THOMAS HENRY LOMAX

THOMAS HENRY LOMAX, the son of Enoch and Rachel (Hammons or Hammonds) Lomax, was born free in Cumberland County, near Fayetteville, North Carolina, on January 15, 1832. His paternal grandfather, William Lomax, came to America from a French colony in Africa with General LaFayette and fought in the Revolutionary War. He was granted a pension and was buried when he died at age 105 with full military honors by the remnants of his regiment.

In 1850, Lomax learned to read and write in a night school. At the close of the Civil War, he and his brothers employed a Dr. Sanford to teach them privately.

At the age of fourteen he joined the Methodist Episcopal Church in Fayetteville, North Carolina. He converted to Zion in 1858 and was licensed to preach in 1864, before the end of the Civil War, by Bishop (then elder) J. W. Hood. Rev. Lomax was ordained a deacon on November 25, 1867 by Bishop J. J. Clinton and an elder on December 1, 1868 by Bishop J. J. Moore. He was the pastor of churches in various cities in North Carolina before he was consecrated bishop by the 1876 General Conference. He was immediately assigned to a missionary district in Michigan and Canada but without mission funds. Nevertheless, Bishop Lomax organized the Michigan and Canada Annual Conferences in September, 1879, with thirty-two preachers representing 499 members. In November, 1883, he organized the Texas Conference and ordained eighteen elders and deacons. Between 1888 and 1892 Bishop Lomax doubled the number of churches in Eastern Tennessee. He was second only to Bishop J. J. Clinton as an organizer.

Bishop Lomax was also involved in the founding of several Zion schools, including Zion Wesley Institute, a seminary that became Livingstone College in 1885; Lomax-Hannon Junior College, Greenville, Alabama, which was organized in 1893 as Greenville High School; and in 1887 a different Greenville High School in Greenville, Tennessee, which soon became Greenville College. Bishop Lomax influenced the decision to move the Publishing House from Livingstone College to its own quarters in Charlotte, North Carolina, in 1894. He chaired the committee that purchased the property for the Publishing House for six thousand dollars.

Bishop Lomax lived in Charlotte, North Carolina for thirty-six years with his wife, Elizabeth, who served as the Second Vice President of the Woman's Home and Foreign Missionary Society from 1904-12. Their daughter, Laura Etta Lomax, married the Rev. Frederick Miller Jacobs, who became Zion's 46th Bishop. Bishop Lomax died in Charlotte, N. C., on March 31, 1908. Funeral services were held at Clinton Chapel in Charlotte.

Bishop T.H. Lomax
ELECTED 1876-DIED 1908

20. BISHOP THOMAS HENRY LOMAX

Born: A free man in Cumberland County, near Fayetteville, North Carolina, on January 15, 1832. Son of Enoch and Rachel (Hammons or Hammonds) Lomax; grandson of William Lomax who fought in the Revolutionary War. **Education:** Learned to read and write at night school. At the close of the Civil War, he and his brothers employed a Dr. Sanford to teach them privately. **Family**: He was married to Elizabeth Lomax and had at least one child, a daughter, Laura Etta Lomax, who was married to Bishop Frederick Miller Jacobs, Zion's 46th bishop. **Died**: March 31, 1908, in Charlotte, North Carolina. Funeral services were held at Clinton Chapel in that city.

21. BISHOP CHARLES CALVIN PETTEY

CHARLES CALVIN PETTEY was born a slave in Wilkes County, near Wilkesboro, North Carolina, December 3, 1849. He was the son of Jordan and Fannie Pettey, both of whom were slaves (Hood 1895: p. 195). Pettey did not learn his alphabet until he was freed at age sixteen at the end of the Civil War. Before he died on December 8, 1900, he had become the first A. M. E. Zion bishop to receive a college degree and he had founded two connectional schools. After the Civil War ended, he went to common and night schools in his hometown. In 1872 he walked to Biddle Memorial Institute (now Johnson C. Smith University) and, probably, entered the institute's high school program. He graduated in June, 1878, second in his class with high honors.

Pettey was converted at age seventeen. He was licensed to exhort on August 4, 1868. Bishop J. W. Hood licensed him to preach on August 18, 1872 and ordained him deacon on December 17, 1872, shortly after Rev. Pettey entered Biddle. In 1878, following his graduation from Biddle, Bishop Hood ordained him an elder and placed him in charge of Zion's church in Lancaster Court House, South Carolina. Rev. Pettey soon founded Pettey High School with fifty students, including twenty boarders, on November 17, 1879. This school was accepted as a connectional school by the 1880 General Conference. In 1898, it became Lancaster Normal & Industrial Institute, which lasted until 1924. After becoming a bishop, he also founded Jones University in 1890, which was absorbed into what is now Lomax-Hannon Junior College, Greenville, Alabama.

Rev. Pettey served Zion faithfully as a preacher in North and South Carolina, Alabama, Tennessee, and California. He became General Secretary in 1884. On May 27, 1888, he was elected and consecrated a bishop and was assigned the Texas and California Conferences. When he moved to Texas, he found only one church with thirteen members in Stoneham, Texas. He traveled, preached, and lectured, and by 1896, he had organized churches in Dallas, Forth Worth, Waco, San Antonio, Dennison, and the Brazos. In the West, he established churches in Oregon and Washington state. In 1898, he ordained Zion's first woman elder, Rev. Mary J. Small, the wife of Bishop John B. Small. Rev. Mary Small had been ordained a deacon in 1895 by Bishop Alexander Walters.

Bishop Pettey married twice and had seven children, one of whom was named Sadie. (Star of Zion Dec. 20, 1900) His first wife was Lulu Pettey (maiden name not known). His second wife was the former Sarah E. C. Dudley of New Bern, North Carolina, who served Zion's Woman's Home and Foreign Missionary Society in various offices. She was treasurer from 1892-96 and general corresponding secretary from 1896-1900. She also wrote a weekly woman's column for the Star of Zion for a number of years. Bishop Pettey died December 8, 1900, in Clio, South Carolina, while presiding at a conference. (Star of Zion, March 8, 13, 1900)

Bishop C.C. Petty
ELECTED 1888-DIED 1900

21. BISHOP CHARLES CALVIN PETTEY

Born: A slave in Wilkes County, near Wilkesboro, North Carolina, on December 3, 1849, to Jordan and Fannie Pettey. **Education:** After the end of the Civil War, he learned his alphabet and went to common and night schools in his hometown. In 1872 he entered Biddle Memorial Institute (now Johnson C. Smith University). He graduated with high honors as the salutatorian of his class in 1878. **Family:** Married twice. Lulu Pettey (maiden name not known) was his first wife. Sarah E. C. Dudley of New Bern, North Carolina, was the second wife. He had seven children, including one named Sadie. **Died:** December 8, 1900, in Clio, South Carolina., while presiding at a conference.

22. BISHOP CICERO RICHARDSON HARRIS

CICERO RICHARDSON HARRIS was born August 20, 1844, in Fayetteville, North Carolina, to Jacob and Charlotte Harris (Marquis 1912: p. 920). His father died when he was three. When he was six, the family moved to Chillicothe, Ohio, where his education began. In 1857, the family moved to Cleveland. He finished Cleveland High School and took additional training before returning in 1866 to Fayetteville. He began teaching with his brother, Robert , under the commission of the American Missionary Society. He joined Zion in 1867. He was licensed to preach and joined the North Carolina Conference in 1872.

Rev. Harris married Meriah Elizabeth Gion of Lincolnton, North Carolina, in December, 1879, following her graduation with high honors from Atlanta University. In the same month, Rev. Harris opened Zion Wesley Institute in Concord, North Carolina, the predecessor to Livingstone College (now in Salisbury, North Carolina) with three students and four teachers: himself, his wife, his niece, Victoria Richardson, and his nephew, A.S. Richardson, who, in 1880, became the school's second principal. Rev. Harris' s wife served as the first matron of this school. She later was elected the first recording secretary of the Woman's Home and Foreign Missionary Society and made her first report to the 1884 General Conference. She served twelve years in that post and twenty years as treasurer of the Society. Rev. and Mrs. Harris had six children: Roberta, Harry, Charles, Lucile, Viola, and Mabel. (Price 1916, p. 89) Rev. Harris's niece, Victoria Richardson, was the founder of Zion's Young Women's Department. She continued that work until she died on August 1, 1928.

Rev. Harris and Bishop J. W. Hood guided the committee that produced Zion's first planned budget in 1880. Rev. Harris was elected secretary of the 1880 General Conference and was also elected Zion's first general steward. A highly competent mathematician and bookkeeper, he served in that dual capacity for four years until he was elevated to the episcopacy in 1888.

In 1891, Bishop Harris tried to found Arkansas High School in Parkdale, Arkansas but failed. However, in that same year he did succeed in founding Ashley County High School, Wilmot, Arkansas, out of which evolved Walters Institute. Bishop Harris was the first teacher of John Wesley Smith, who was to become Zion Methodism's 29th Bishop in 1904.

Bishop Harris presided with distinction over the South Florida, North and South Georgia, West Tennessee and Mississippi, and Arkansas Conferences. On October 15, 1910, he organized the Southwest Virginia Conference, which evolved into the East Tennessee-Virginia Conference. Bishop Harris died June 24, 1917. He was buried in Salisbury, North Carolina, after last rites at Soldiers Memorial Church.

Bishop C.R. Harris
ELECTED 1888-DIED 1917

22. BISHOP CICERO RICHARDSON HARRIS

Born: In Fayetteville, North Carolina, August 25, 1844, to Jacob and Charlotte Harris. **Education:** Graduated from Central High School, Cleveland, Ohio. Some advanced training. Received honorary A.M. degree from Livingstone College and an honorary doctorate from Howard University in 1891. **Major Publications**: *Doctrines and Disciplines of the A.M.E. Zion Church in America,* 1884; *Historical Catechism of the A.M.E. Zion Church,* 1898. **Family:** Married Meriah E. Gion of Lincolnton, North Carolina, December, 1879, the same month he opened Zion Wesley Institute, Concord, North Carolina, the predecessor to Livingstone College, Salisbury, North Carolina. His wife graduated from Atlanta University with high honors in 1879. They had six children: Roberta, Harry, Charles, Lucile, Viola, and Mabel. **Died:** June 24, 1917. Buried in Salisbury, North Carolina, after services at Soldiers Memorial A. M. E. Zion Church.

23. BISHOP ISOM CALEB CLINTON

ISOM CALEB CLINTON was born May 22, 1830, in Cedar Creek Township, Lancaster County, South Carolina. His mother, Camie Clinton, was a slave owned by Irwin Clinton, a prominent South Carolina lawyer. His father was a free man named Lewis McDonald. Irwin Clinton permitted his slaves to learn to read and write and cipher, and Isom Clinton did so before the end of the Civil War. He did so well that though a slave he became the trusted foreman and confidante of his master and continued in the management of his former master's business after Emancipation.

In 1866, Isom Clinton organized the Mount Carmel Church about eight miles from Lancaster and established a public school for former slaves in a private home on his former master's plantation. Here he taught his own and other children the first rudiments of a common school education. He also served as the treasurer for Lancaster County for eight years following the end of the Civil War.

On March 24, 1867, he was ordained deacon and elder by Bishop J. J. Clinton (no relation). He proceeded to help Bishop Clinton organize the South Carolina Conference. In 1872 this conference became the first in the Connection to organize a regular presiding elder system, and Rev. Clinton was one of four appointed to that office. He continued to serve as a presiding elder until he was elected bishop in 1892. Prior to becoming a bishop, he served on several important committees, including the 1884 committee on union with the African Methodist Episcopal Church. He was elected General Steward by the 1888 General Conference, a position he held until his consecration as bishop.

Clinton Institute (now Clinton Junior College), Rock Hill, South Carolina was named after him when it was organized. He was the presiding bishop of the South Carolina Conference at that time. Bishop Clinton served Zion with distinction for twelve years before he died in his home city of Lancaster, South Carolina, on October 18, 1904. He was buried in his beloved home town following funeral services in the Lancaster Courthouse.

Bishop Clinton was married twice. His first wife, Winnie Thompson Clinton, died in 1884, shortly after she was elected vice president of the South Carolina Conference Woman's Home and Foreign Missionary Society. His second wife, Mary Ivy Clinton, also served Zion with distinction.

Bishop I.C. Clinton
ELECTED 1892-DIED 1904

23. BISHOP ISOM CALEB CLINTON

Born: In Cedar Creek Township, Lancaster County, South Carolina, May 23, 1830. His Mother, Camie Clinton, was a slave owned by Irwin Clinton. His father, Lewis McDonald, was a free man, but the child was given the name of his master. **Education:** Learned to read, write, and cipher while still a slave. After the Civil War ended, he organized a school where he taught his own and other children. **Family:** Married twice. His first wife, Winnie Thompson Clinton, died in 1884. Second wife was Mary Ivy Clinton. Names and number of children not available. **Died**: October 18, 1904, in Lancaster, South Carolina. He was buried in his beloved home town following funeral services in the Lancaster Courthouse.

24. BISHOP ALEXANDER WALTERS

ALEXANDER WALTERS, a national and international leader, was born a slave August 1, 1858, in a room at the rear of the Donohue (Donahue) Hotel in Bardstown (Nelson County), Kentucky. His parents, Henry and Harriet (Mathers) Walters, were both slaves. (Logan and Winston 1982, p. 630) He was the sixth of eight children, four of whom died in infancy. In 1875, he graduated as valedictorian from a local primary school. In 1892, he earned an M.A. degree from Livingstone College (Price 1916, p. 233).

While working as a waiter in 1876, he began the study of theology with private tutors in Indianapolis, Indiana. In 1877, he was licensed to preach and assigned to a church, now known as Jones Tabernacle, in Indianapolis. He was ordained deacon on July 3, 1879 and elder on April 10, 1881. He held pastorates in Louisville, Kentucky, San Francisco, California, Portland, Oregon, and New York City, where he was the pastor of Mother Zion. The 1888 General Conference appointed him to its Board of Publications and, in 1889, the Board in turn appointed him its agent. He was consecrated a bishop on May 18, 1892.

Bishop Walters was active in the church and in the world. He headed the Missouri Conference from 1892-1900 and once traveled 1,900 miles in five days on behalf of the church. He sent missionaries from the Arkansas Conference to Oklahoma to establish the Oklahoma Conference in 1897. He was assigned to foreign work by the 1908 General Conference. He went to Africa, and in 1910, he organized the Liberia Conference, the East Gold Coast Conference, and the West Gold Coast Conference (now the Ghana Conferences). These mission stations had been established in Liberia in 1876 and in Ghana in 1896 by Bishop John Bryan Small. In 1911, Bishop Walters journeyed to the West Indies, to Demerara, Guiana, South America (now Guyana) to explore organizing a conference. Bishop Alstork succeeded Bishop Walters in 1912, and in 1919 he successfully organized the Demerara, Guiana, South American Conferences. Bishop Walters served on the International Christian Endeavor Society Board of Trustees from 1893 until his death. In 1888, he became president of the National Afro-American League, a civil rights group organized by editor T. Thomas Fortune. He was elected president of the first Pan-African Congress in London, England, in 1900. Bishop Walters was one of the organizers of the NAACP and was elected a vice president in 1910. In 1916, he was elected to the Howard University Board of Trustees. He was the presiding bishop of the New York Conference when he died.

Bishop Walters married three times and had six children, five by his first wife, Katie Knox of Louisville, Kentucky, whom he married on August 28, 1877 (Logan and Winston 1982, p. 631). She died in 1896. His second wife, Emeline Virginia Bird, who died in 1902, was secretary of Zion's Book Concern for many years. Lelia Coleman Brown of Bardstown, Kentucky, was his third wife and the mother of Hillis, his sixth child. (Price 1916, p. 233) He was buried in Mother Zion Cypress Hills Cemetery in Bklyn., N.Y.

Bishop A. Walters
ELECTED 1892-DIED 1917

24. BISHOP ALEXANDER WALTERS

Born: On August 1, 1858, in Bardstown, Nelson County, Kentucky, to slave parents, Henry and Harriet (Mathers) Walters, the sixth of eight children. **Education:** He attended public school and was the valedictorian of his primary school class in 1875. He earned a M.A. degree from Livingstone College in 1892. **Major Publications:** *Frederick Douglass and His Work,* 1904; *My Life and Work,* 1917. **Family:** Six children, five by his first wife, Katie Knox, whom he married August 28, 1877. She died December 22, 1896. His second wife, Emeline Virginia Bird, died February 27, 1902. His third wife was Lelia Coleman Brown of Bardstown, Kentucky. She was the mother of Hillis, the bishop's sixth child. **Died:** February 1, 1917. He is buried in the Mother A.M.E. Zion Cypress Hill Cemetery in Brooklyn, New York.

African Methodist Episcopal Zion Church
25. BISHOP GEORGE WYLIE CLINTON

GEORGE WYLIE CLINTON was born in Cedar Creek Township, Lancaster County, South Carolina, on March 28, 1859, to Jonathan and Rachel (Patterson) Clinton who was a slave. His father died when he was three, and he was raised by his mother in the home of his grandparents. After attending school in Lancaster, South Carolina, he won a $200 scholarship for four years to the University of South Carolina, then open to all residents of the state. He completed his sophomore year, but in 1876 the new governor, Wade Hampton, threw African American students out of USC. Clinton then began to read law with a local lawyer but became interested in the ministry. (Bradley 1970, p. 389)

He was licensed to preach on February 14, 1879 and joined the South Carolina Conference in November, 1880. While pastoring a church in Chester, South Carolina, Rev. Clinton completed his college work at Brainard Institute in Chester. He also studied theology at Livingstone College and received an A. M. degree in 1893. (Maser 1974, p. 525) Rev. Clinton preached and taught school until he was appointed by Bishop Singleton T. Jones to Old John Wesley in Pittsburgh. He was ordained a deacon November 5, 1882 and an elder November 8, 1885. While serving in Pittsburgh, he founded the *A. M. E. Zion Quarterly Review*, which he ran at his own expense for two years before turning it over to the General Conference. In 1892, Rev. Clinton was elected editor of the *Star of Zion*, a position he held until he was consecrated a bishop on May 21, 1896. The publication moved to Charlotte, North Carolina during his editorship. He was considered a "systematic editor" and "a lofty coiner of living phrases."

In 1897, Bishop Clinton journeyed West and established churches in Seattle and Spokane, Washington, and Kingman, Arizona. Through his efforts, by 1900, the California Conference (which then embraced California, Oregon, Washington and the Arizona Territory) grew from one church with eleven worshipers to thirteen well-established churches. Bishop Clinton was also one of those responsible for Zion's massive growth in North Carolina in the early 1900s.

Bishop Clinton married three times. One of his children, Willie Clinton, became a physician and practiced in Philadelphia, Pennsylvania. Bishop Clinton's first wife, Mrs. Eliza Clinton, served as vice president of the Woman's Home and Foreign Missionary Society before he was elected bishop. She died August 26, 1892. He married Mrs. Annie Kimball Clinton, on May 30, 1898 (Maser 1974, p. 525). She also served as a vice president during his early episcopacy. She died June 1, 1899. His third wife, Mrs. Marie Louise Clay Clinton, was born in Huntsville, Alabama, in 1871. She was an accomplished singer and a vice principal of a school in Huntsville when they married on February 6, 1901. In 1904, she was chosen to head Zion's Juvenile Missionary Society (renamed the Buds of Promise Department in 1908) and served in that capacity until her death on January 9, 1932. Bishop Clinton died May 12, 1921, in Charlotte, North Carolina. Last rites were held at Little Rock Church in Charlotte, where he once was pastor and member.

Bishop G.W. Clinton
ELECTED 1896-DIED 1921

25. BISHOP GEORGE WYLIE CLINTON

Born: A slave in Cedar Township, Lancaster County, South Carolina, on March 28, 1859, to Jonathan and Rachel (Patterson) Clinton. His father died when he was three. **Education:** Attended local schools. Won a $200 scholarship to the University of South Carolina. After finishing his sophomore year, a new governor expelled all of the black students. Studied law, theology. Graduated from Brainard Institute, Chester, South Carolina. **Family:** He had three wives. First wife, Eliza Clinton, died August 26, 1892. Second wife, Annie Kimball Clinton, died June 1, 1899. Married third wife, Marie Louise Clay of Huntsville, Alabama, February 6, 1901. One of his children, Willie Clinton, became a physician and practiced in Philadelphia, Pennsylvania. **Died:** May 12, 1921, at his home in Charlotte, North Carolina. Last rites were held at Little Rock Church where he once was pastor and member.

26. BISHOP JEHU HOLLIDAY

JEHU HOLLIDAY was born in Goshen Township, Columbia County, Ohio, Christmas Day, December 25, 1827.

He was converted in November, 1860. He joined the Allegheny Conference in 1861. On July 27, 1862, less than a year after he joined the conference, he was ordained a deacon in the morning and an elder in the afternoon. He founded churches in the Allegheny Conference faster than Bishop J. W. Hood could find men to fill them. His pastorates in the Allegheny, Ohio, and Kentucky Conferences included 15th Street Church (now Hughlett Temple), Louisville, Kentucky; Russellville, Kentucky; Bedford, Pennsylvania; Johnstown, Pennsylvania; and Avery Mission, Pittsburgh, Pennsylvania. In 1876, during his second pastorate of 15th Street church, he founded 12th Street Church (now Broadway Temple) in Louisville, Kentucky. He purchased the property, enlarged it, paid all the debt except for $1,000.00 and took in more than two hundred members before he was appointed in 1878 to Blackford Street (now Jones Tabernacle) Church in Indianapolis, Indiana. In 1880, he was appointed to John Wesley Chapel in Pittsburgh. He purchased a commodious church in which the 1892 General Conference convened.

In 1892, when Rev. Alexander Walters was elected bishop, he succeeded him as agent of Zion's Book Concern. In 1896, Rev. Holliday was consecrated bishop and assigned to the Southwest Conference. He went into the Arkansas-Oklahoma area and generated unusual growth in three short years. On March 2, 1899, Bishop Holliday died after having his ribs broken in an accident involving a runaway horse. Bishop Holliday was buried in Pittsburgh following funeral services at John Wesley Church in that city. His will provided for his wife, Mary, their six children, for Livingstone College, the 12th Street Church in Louisville, and the Dearborn Street Church (now Walters Memorial) in Chicago. The Holliday Memorial Church, Braddock, Pennsylvania, is named in his honor.

"As a preacher, he possessed simplicity of style and force of utterance, which frequently ended in eloquence of expression. His doctrine was practical, manner earnest, and appeals persuasive. His voice was musical and of extensive compass. He was a power in prayer, and, having unswerving confidence in his Maker, he fearlessly marched to his death. He was known and appreciated from the East to the West and from the North to the South. He erected his own monument in the hearts he gladdened, the churches he built, and the souls he pointed to the haven of eternal rest." (Quoted in Walls, p. 585 from *Minutes, 78th Sess.,* N.Y. Ann. Conf., pp. 73-74)

Bishop J. Holiday
ELECTED 1896-DIED 1899

26. BISHOP JEHU HOLLIDAY

Born: In Goshen Township, Columbia County, Ohio, on December 25, 1827. No information is available on his parents. **Education:** No information. **Major Publication:** *The Autobiography of Jehu Holliday,* 1892. **Family:** Married Mary Holliday. Six children. **Died:** March 2, 1899, following an accident involving a runway horse. Buried in Pittsburgh, Pennsylvania., following funeral services at John Wesley Church, where he once served as pastor.

27. BISHOP JOHN BRYAN SMALL

JOHN BRYAN SMALL was born on March 14, 1845, at Frazier, St. Joseph's Parish, Barbados, British West Indies, eleven years after England ended slavery in its colonies. The only child of John Bryan and Kittie Ann Small, he was taught at home by his half-sister (Bradley 1970, pp. 241, 388). He entered St. John Lodge and graduated at the head of his class. He then entered Codrington College in Barbados and graduated with first-class honors.

In 1862, Small traveled to several Caribbean islands before sailing to West Africa in 1863. He spent three years and three months in West Africa, where he learned to speak Fantee and traveled to Sierra Leone, Cape Coast, and the Gambia. After leaving Africa, he worked for five years in Belize, Honduras. While in Honduras he joined the Wesleyan Methodist Church and its ministry. In 1871, he came to the U.S. on his way to Europe. He preached at several Zion churches and so impressed Rev. R. H. G. Dyson and Bishop J. J. Clinton that they persuaded him to join Zion two weeks after his arrival. Rev. Small was ordained deacon May 26, 1872 and elder June 1, 1873. He served as pastor of several churches in the New England Conference and was elected secretary of that conference in 1873. He also served in the New York, Central North Carolina, and Philadelphia and Baltimore Conferences before he was consecrated a bishop in 1896.

At his own request, Bishop Small was assigned to Africa and the West Indies along with several U.S. conferences. He made his first episcopal visit to Africa in 1897 with funds raised by churches in Mobile, Alabama and Mother Zion in New York City. In 1899, he traveled to the West Indies with funds raised by his home conferences, and he made his second trip to Africa in 1902. Because he believed in raising up and training an indigenous leadership, he ordained Rev. Lewis B. Dudley a deacon and placed him in charge of the church in Brewerville, Liberia, a church founded by Rev. Andrew Cartwright, Zion's first missionary to Africa. Bishop Small also helped select a few young Africans (including James Emman Kwegyir Aggrey and Kobina Osam Pinanko [Frank Arthur] and West Indians for training at Livingstone College. Rev. Aggrey and Rev. Arthur both distinguished themselves in the service of the Church. Bishop Small's book *The Code of the Discipline of the African Methodist Episcopal Zion Church* was adopted by the 1896 General Conference and published in 1898. In 1901, he founded and served as the first editor of the *Missionary Seer*.

Bishop Small married Mary Julia Blair on October 23, 1873. Licensed to preach in 1892, she was ordained deacon on May 19, 1895, the second woman ordained deacon in the A. M. E. Zion Church, and the first ordained elder in 1898. She was the third president (1912-16) of the Woman's Home and Foreign Missionary Society. In November, 1904, Bishop Small was stricken while holding the West Alabama Annual Conference. He died January 5, 1905, in York, Pennsylvania, his home at that time.

Bishop J.B. Small
ELECTED 1895-DIED 1905

27. BISHOP JOHN BRYAN SMALL

Born: March 14, 1845 at Frazier, St. Joseph's Parish, Barbados, West Indies, to John Bryan and Kittie Ann Small. **Education:** Tutored by his half-sister; graduated St. John Lodge first in his class; graduated Codrington College, Barbados, with first-class honors. **Major Publications**: *Practical and Exegetical Pulpiteer, 1885; Code on the Discipline of the African Methodist Episcopal Zion Church, 1898; Predestination: Its Scriptural Import*, 1901. **Family**: Married Mary Julia Blair of Murfreesboro, Tennessee, on October 23, 1893. **Died:** January 5, 1905, in York, Pennsylvania, his home at that time. He took ill while presiding over the West Alabama Annual Conference.

28. BISHOP JOHN WESLEY ALSTORK

JOHN WESLEY ALSTORK was born in Talladega, Alabama, on September 1, 1852, to Rev. Frank and Mary Jane Alstork (Marquis 1912, p. 34). He was Zion's first bishop born in Alabama, a state second only to North Carolina in membership in the Connection. No information is available on his early life in what was a slave state at the time of his birth. He was educated at Logwood Institute and Talladega College in Alabama. (Bradley 1970, p. 390) Alstork was licensed to preach in 1878. He joined the Alabama Conference in 1879 and three years later was ordained a deacon. In 1884 Bishop J. W. Hood ordained him an elder.

Rev. Alstork was appointed to Opelika Station, Opelika, Alabama, in 1882. From 1884-88 he served as pastor of Old Ship Church in Montgomery, Alabama. He was elected presiding elder of the Alabama Conference in 1889. In 1892 the 19th General Conference elected Rev. Alstork as its General Steward, a position now called Financial Secretary. He served in that office until he was elected a bishop on May 20, 1900. His election as bishop was the first by acclamation in the church. He was also the National Grand Master of the A. A. York Masons of the U.S. His leadership in the church and among Masons stimulated the growth of Zion throughout Alabama.

Bishop Alstork organized two new conferences in Alabama — the South Alabama Conference on December 2, 1911 and the Cahaba Conference on November 12, 1912. Assigned to Georgia after the death of Bishop M. R. Franklin in 1908, Bishop Alstork labored arduously to put a metropolitan church in Atlanta, where Zion had only two small churches at the time. In 1916, Bishop Alstork was assigned to the South American and West Indies territories. He visited three years later and on July 10, 1919, he organized the British Guiana South American (now Guyana) Conference with seven preachers, including two women and Rev. W. A. Dean. Rev. Dean organized Zion's first church in the area and was a pivotal person in establishing the conference. A staunch friend of education, Bishop Alstork improved the financial status of Lomax-Hannon Junior College, Greenville, Alabama. He raised more money for the school than Zion had given prior to his administration as bishop of the area and as chairman of the board of trustees. When he died in 1920, he willed his home to the school.

Alstork married Mamie M. Lawson of Talladega, Alabama, on May 26, 1872. They had no children. Mrs. Alstork served Zion faithfully as a missionary supervisor. A nephew, Frank Wesley Alstork, became Zion's 54th Bishop in 1944. Bishop. Alstork died on July 23, 1920, while addressing a Sunday School Convention in Searcy, Alabama. He was buried in Montgomery, Alabama, following funeral services at Mt. Zion Church in that city.

Bishop J.W. Alstork
ELECTED 1900-DIED 1920

28. BISHOP JOHN WESLEY ALSTORK

Born: September 1, 1852, in Talladega, Alabama, to Rev. Frank and Mrs. Mary Jane Alstork. **Education:** Educated at Logwood Institute and Talladega College, Talladega, Alabama. He was acknowledged a brilliant scholar. **Family:** He married Mamie M. Lawson of Talladega, Alabama, on May 26, 1872. No children. A nephew, Frank Wesley Alstork, became Zion's 54th Bishop in 1944. **Died:** July 23, 1920, while addressing a Sunday School Convention in Searcy, Alabama. Buried in Montgomery, Alabama, following services at Mt. Zion Church, Montgomery, Alabama.

African Methodist Episcopal Zion Church
29. BISHOP JOHN WESLEY SMITH

JOHN WESLEY SMITH was born in Fayetteville, North Carolina, on January 27, 1862. He was raised by his grandmother after his mother's early death. (Bradley 1970, p. 390) His first teacher was Bishop (then Rev.) C. R. Harris. He attended the grade schools in Fayetteville and completed his studies at the state Normal School in Fayetteville (now Fayetteville State University). He also took a private course in higher studies.

In 1880, Smith and some three hundred others were converted by the Rev. J. W. Davis at a massive evangelical campaign. (Ibid.) He was licensed to preach October 4, 1880. The following year he was admitted on trial to the Central North Carolina Conference. He served as assistant secretary of the conference, passed the examination, and was ordained deacon before the end of the conference on November 21, 1881. The New Haven, Connecticut pulpit was vacant, and Bishop J. W. Hood was having difficulty finding a man for the church. He decided to try Rev. Smith. The church agreed to take him, young and inexperienced as he was, but only if he were ordained an elder. Bishop Hood consented and called a council of elders to meet him in Hartford to examine Rev. Smith who passed the examination and was ordained an elder September 4, 1882.

Rev. Smith was pastor of a number of churches including Little Rock, Arkansas; Fifteenth Street Church, Louisville, Kentucky; Baltimore, Maryland; John Wesley Church, Washington, D.C., Wesley Union, Harrisburg, and Carlisle, Pennsylvania. In 1896, while serving as pastor of the Zion church in Carlisle, Rev. Smith was elected editor of The *Star of Zion*. He served eight years until his election as bishop in 1904. He was also a member of the Board of Missions. Before Rev. Smith was elected to the episcopacy, he compiled and published some of the papers of Singleton T. W. Jones. (Walls 1972, p. 577)

After helping to build the South Florida Conference, he asked Bishop J. W. Hood in 1908 to help him organize the Albemarle Conference. However, Bishop Smith died at age forty-eight, a few months prior to the Virginia Conference meeting on November 30, 1910. Bishop Hood and Bishop G. W. Clinton nevertheless carried out his design.

Bishop Smith married twice. In 1888, he married Ms. Emma Thompson who died soon after their marriage. Later, he married Ms. Ida V. Thompson, who became the general treasurer of the Woman's Home & Foreign Missionary Society, an office she held for twenty-seven years (1912-39). The daughter of an affluent man, Mrs. Ida Smith assisted the connection many times because of her love for the church. In one instance, she placed a mortgage against her home for $6000.00 to lend Bishop J. S. Caldwell for the Mother Zion Church building program in New York City. The loan was repaid by the denomination with interest. She died in 1943.

After only six years in the episcopacy, Bishop Smith died on October 14, 1910. He is buried in Carlisle, Pennsylvania.

Bishop J.W. Smith
ELECTED 1904-DIED 1910

29. BISHOP JOHN WESLEY SMITH

Born: Fayetteville, North Carolina, on January 27, 1862. Names of parents not known. Raised by his grandmother after the early death of his mother. **Education:** Attended grade schools in Fayetteville and finished the state Normal School (now Fayetteville University). He also took a private course in higher education. **Major Publication:** *Sermons and Addresses of the Late Rev. Bishop S. T. W. Jones of the A. M. E. Zion Church.* **Family:** Married Emma Thompson in 1888, and after her death was married to Ida V. Thompson, who served as treasurer of the Woman's Home & Foreign Missionary Society for twenty-seven years. **Died**: October 14, 1910. Buried in Union Cemetery in Carlisle, Pennsylvania.

30. BISHOP JOSIAH SAMUEL CALDWELL

JOSIAH SAMUEL CALDWELL was born to Dice and Martha (Howie) Caldwell (Marquis 1912, p. 316) on August 2, 1862, in Charlotte, Mecklenburg County, North Carolina, a slave state at the time. After the Civil War ended in 1865, he was allowed to attend school but only for two to four months a year until he was sixteen. Converted at nineteen, he preached his trial sermon in Concord, North Carolina and was licensed as a local preacher. Rev. Caldwell entered Livingstone College in the fall of 1883, almost penniless and with the care of a wife and child entrusted to him. He studied at night, worked during the day on the family farm, and graduated in May, 1888 with high honors.

Rev. Caldwell joined the Central North Carolina Conference in 1884 while still a student. He was ordained a deacon by Bishop J. W. Hood on November 21, 1886 and an elder by Bishop C. R. Harris on November 9, 1888, shortly after he graduated from Livingstone College. He was pastor of several churches, including those located in Pineville, China Grove, Elizabeth City, North Carolina; and Oak Street, Petersburg, Virginia. For three months, he was pastor of Mother Zion, New York City and Big Wesley, Philadelphia, Pennsylvania., until the New York Conference met and released him from Mother Zion. While he was at Big Wesley, Philadelphia, the church had the largest membership in the Connection.

Rev. Caldwell was elected a member of the Bureau of Statistics in 1892 by the General Conference. In 1896, he served as co-editor of the *Varick Christian Endeavorer,* which promoted Christian education among youth. In 1900, he was elected General Steward. Rev. Caldwell was consecrated a bishop on May 19, 1904.

As bishop, he was assigned to the Pacific Coast, where he established a conference in the Philippines that did not survive. As a bishop, Caldwell supervised the Southern California and Arizona; Missouri; Oregon; Allegheny-Ohio; Kentucky; Philadelphia-Baltimore; and New York Conferences. He supervised the New York Conference from 1917 until his death in 1935. In July, 1923, excavation began for the current location of Mother Zion at 146 W. 137th Street in New York City. Mrs. Ida V. Thompson Smith, the widow of Bishop J. W. Smith, lent Bishop Caldwell six thousand dollars for the Mother Zion building program. The new building was dedicated on September 20, 1925. In 1925, a committee of the New York Conference headed by Bishop Caldwell had the ashes of Bishop Varick, the church's first bishop, brought from Newburgh, New York, in a crypt and placed beneath the sanctuary of the Mother A. M. E. Zion Church building, which had been constructed under the leadership and pastorate of Dr. James Walter Brown, who became a bishop in 1936.

The Rev. Caldwell married Ella J. Melcher of Concord, North Carolina in 1881. They had two children, Beulah and Daisy. Daisy served as a missionary supervisor for Bishop W. J. Walls Bishop Caldwell died April 7, 1935, at age seventy-two. Last rites were held at Big Wesley Church in Philadelphia. He was laid to rest in that city.

Bishop J.S. Caldwell
ELECTED 1904-DIED 1935

30. BISHOP JOSIAH SAMUEL CALDWELL

Born: August 2, 1862, in Charlotte, Mecklenburg County, North Carolina, to Dice and Martha (Howie) Caldwell. **Education:** Attended school two to four months a year until he was sixteen. Entered Livingstone College penniless in 1883, worked during the day, and graduated in 1888 with high honors. **Major Publication**: *Book of Sermons*, 1898. **Family:** In 1882 married Ella J. Melchor of Concord, North Carolina. Two children, Beulah and Daisy. Daisy served as missionary supervisor for Bishop W. J. Walls. **Died:** April 7, 1935. Buried following last rites at Big Wesley in Philadelphia, Pennsylvania.

31. BISHOP MARTIN ROBERT FRANKLIN

MARTIN ROBERT FRANKLIN was born in slavery on January 8, 1853, near Macon, Georgia. His parents were sold when he was an infant, and he never saw or heard from them again. When General William Tecumseh Sherman's march through Georgia reached Macon in 1864, Franklin followed the Union Army and left the South. In 1865, he was in Chicago. In 1879, he entered Wayland Seminary in Washington, D. C. and studied there for two years. While in Washington, he converted and joined the Asbury Methodist Episcopal Church.

He moved to Boston in 1881 and joined North Russell (Columbus Avenue) Street A. M. E. Zion Church. He was licensed to preach the same year. He was ordained a deacon by Bishop J. W. Hood in 1886 and an elder two years later by Bishop J. J. Moore. His first appointment was at Laurinburg, North Carolina, where he erected a church and gave new life to work that had been languishing for some years. He also served at Manley, Carthage, and Statesville in North Carolina. He transferred and served as pastor of Avery Mission (Allegheny City) and of Mother Zion in New York City. He was the host pastor for the 1896 Centennial Observance. On the national scene, he served as treasurer of the A. M. E. Zion Board of Missions from 1900 to 1904 and as the financial secretary from 1904-08.

Rev. Franklin was consecrated bishop May 20, 1908. He secured the highest vote of the three elected by that General Conference. He was assigned to the Eighth Episcopal District, which comprised Georgia, South Carolina, and the Palmetto Conferences. He and his family left their home in Brooklyn, New York and moved to Atlanta, Georgia. Everything he touched prospered, but he became ill and died May 13, 1909. His body was returned to New York, and he was buried in Cypress Hill, Brooklyn, New York, following funeral services at Mother Zion Church.

Bishop M.R. Franklin
ELECTED 1908-DIED 1909

31. BISHOP MARTIN ROBERT FRANKLIN

Born: In slavery, January 8, 1853, near Macon, Georgia. Parents sold when he was an infant, and he never saw or heard from them again. **Education**: Spent two years studying at Wayland Seminary, Washington, D. C. **Family:** Was married and had children. Names not recorded. **Died:** May 13, 1909 in Atlanta, Georgia. Buried in Cypress Hills, Brooklyn, New York, after services at Mother Zion Church.

32. BISHOP GEORGE LINCOLN BLACKWELL

GEORGE LINCOLN BLACKWELL, one of eleven children of Haley and Catharine (Wyche) Blackwell, was born July 3, 1861, in Henderson, North Carolina. (Marquis 1912-13, p. 183). Both parents died before he was ten, and he was reared in Granville County, near Oxford, where he also attended school.

He was converted in 1876 and joined the North Carolina Conference in 1881. He was appointed to the Morehead City Circuit. In the early 1880s he asked to be relieved of pastoral duties so that he could attend Livingstone College. Rev. Blackwell graduated from Livingstone with honors in 1888 and was assigned to the New England Conference. While there he attended and graduated from the Boston University School of Theology in 1892.

Rev. Blackwell returned to Livingstone College and became the first head of the Theology Department. In 1893, he was placed in charge of the Connection's Publishing House, then located at Livingstone. When the Book Concern was moved to Charlotte, North Carolina, the Board of Bishops elected Rev. Blackwell to be the Concern's first business manager. In 1896, he was elected manager of the Publishing House and editor of the Connection's Sunday School Literature, which in 1898 was printed on its own press for the first time. In 1901, on the death of Rev. William Howard Day, Rev. Blackwell was elected Zion's General Secretary. Reelected in 1904, he was also elected Secretary of the Missionary Department and Editor of the *Missionary Seer*. One of Zion's most creative men, Rev. Blackwell laid the foundation for Zion's present missionary department and served with distinction until he was elected bishop in 1908.

Bishop Blackwell presided over the Canada and Michigan; West Texas and Oklahoma; and Arkansas and North Arkansas Conferences. He gave new impetus to Zion's work in the Midwest and Southwest. In 1909, he organized the Michigan, Indiana, and Missouri Conferences and the Chicago district. Using his own salary to sustain his preachers, he established churches in many cities. Bishop Blackwell was recognized as the leading church expansionist since Reconstruction. Annie Walker Blackwell, his wife, served as corresponding secretary of the Woman's Home and Foreign Missionary Society from 1904 until her death in 1922. She did much to construct a connection wide society.

Blackwell married Annie E. Walker of Chester, South Carolina, on December 7, 1887. She was the oldest daughter of pioneer Presiding Elder Rev. D. I. Walker in South Carolina and was a graduate of Scotia Seminary, Concord, North Carolina. Mrs. Blackwell died December 7, 1922, on the thirty-fifth anniversary of their marriage. Bishop Blackwell died March 21, 1926. He was buried in Eden Cemetery, Philadelphia, Pennsylvania, after funeral services at Big Wesley Church in that city. Mrs. Blackwell is buried in the same cemetery.

Bishop G.L. Blackwell
ELECTED 1908-DIED 1926

32. BISHOP GEORGE LINCOLN BLACKWELL

Born: July 3, 1861, in Henderson, North Carolina, to Haley and Catharine (Wyche) Blackwell. Both parents died before he was ten. **Education:** Attended school in Granville County and graduated from Livingstone College in 1888 and from the Boston University School of Theology in 1892. **Major Publications**: *Cloaks of Sin,* 1904; *A Man Wanted,* 1907. **Family**: Married Annie E. Walker of Chester, South Carolina, December 7, 1887. **Died**: In Philadelphia, March 21, 1926. Buried in Eden Cemetery after funeral services at Big Wesley in that city.

33. BISHOP ANDREW JACKSON WARNER

ANDREW JACKSON WARNER was born a slave in Washington, Kentucky, March 4, 1850. He ran away in 1863 at the age of thirteen. He crossed the Ohio River at night, landing in Ripley, Ohio. A stranger and not knowing where to go, he went to the headquarters where African American soldiers were being enlisted. He too enlisted as a drummer boy. He served throughout the rest of the Civil War and was honorably discharged as a sergeant. His sympathy for his men and their loyalty to him earned him the name *Swamp Angel*. After the war, he returned to Kentucky, but, feeling the need for a better education than he could obtain in Kentucky, he went back to Ohio and attended high school in Cincinnati. From there he went to Wilberforce College in Xenia, Ohio. He also read law in the office of the Honorable W. H. Wordsworth of Marysville, Kentucky.

Warner joined the A. M. E. Zion Church while still in his teens and was called to the ministry before he was twenty. He was licensed to preach in 1874 and joined the Kentucky Conference under Bishop S. T. Jones. Bishop Jones ordained him a deacon in the morning and an elder in the evening of September 8, 1877. Bishop Jones sent him to Wesley Chapel, Greenville, Kentucky. He was there two and a half years and added more than one hundred new members. Transferred to Little Rock, he built the first Zion church in Arkansas. He lived to see that small beginning grow into two conferences. He also served as pastor in Russellville, Kentucky; and Washington Metropolitan, St. Louis, Missouri. He founded St. John in South St. Louis, Centralia, and DuQuoin and built Loguen Temple in Knoxville, Tennessee. He was pastor of Metropolitan, Birmingham, Alabama, and when he left after seven years, the church had more than a thousand members.

In 1896, he was made secretary of the reorganized A. M. E. Zion Missionary and Church Extension office. A magnetic speaker, in 1898, he traveled 12,000 miles and delivered 263 sermons and lectures in less than a year. He spent ten years as pastor of Clinton Chapel, Charlotte, North Carolina, where he added five hundred members and developed the church into one of the best stations in the Connection.

He was elected and consecrated a bishop on May 20, 1908. As a bishop he left his impress on the states of Kentucky, Mississippi, Louisiana, Tennessee, North Carolina, South Carolina, and Florida. His popularity as an able speaker brought him, unsought, nomination for Congress in the first Alabama District. He was twice chosen Presidential Elector and one time ran for governor of the state of Alabama. He died May 31, 1920 and was buried in Charlotte, North Carolina, following funeral services at Big Zion (Clinton Chapel) A.M.E. Zion Church.

He married three times: to Alice McNeil who died in 1891 (two children); to Mary Eliza Delmor who died in 1908 (four children); and to Annie Weddington of Charlotte who served as his missionary supervisor (one child).

Bishop A.J. Warner
ELECTED 1908-DIED 1920

33. BISHOP ANDREW JACKSON WARNER

Born: May 4, 1850, a slave, in Washington, Kentucky. No information on parents. Ran away at age thirteen and joined Union Army. **Education**: Attended high school in Cincinnati, Ohio and Wilberforce College, Xenia, Ohio. Also read law. **Family**: Married three times: to Alice McNeil (2 children) who died in 1891; to Mary Eliza Delmor (4 children) who died in 1908; and on July 10, 1910, to Annie Weddington of Charlotte (one child). **Died:** May 30, 1920. Buried after services at Big Zion (now Clinton Chapel) A.M.E. Zion Church, Charlotte, North Carolina.

34. BISHOP LYNWOOD WESTINGHOUSE KYLES

LYNWOOD WESTINGHOUSE KYLES was born May 3, 1874, to Burrell and Mary Kyles, in Ivy Depot, a small village located about seven miles from Charlottesville, Virginia, the county seat. He received his early education in a log cabin school house while he worked on a farm seven months a year for twenty-five cents a day. He used the money to buy shoes and clothing for the winter and supplies for school. In 1887 or 1888, he entered Hampton Institute and worked in the wheelwright and blacksmith shop until he finished his trade course. Kyles moved to the North, worked at his trade in various cities in New Jersey, and joined the A. M. E. Zion Church in Ridgewood, New Jersey. He entered the New Jersey Conference and was licensed as an exhorter and a local preacher in September, 1895.

Rev. Kyles' first pastoral charge was in Englewood, New Jersey, in 1896. Not content with his educational qualifications, he entered Lincoln University in Pennsylvania in 1897, remained for seven years and graduated from both the College and the Theological Department with honors (1901, A.B.; 1904, B.D.). He was ordained a deacon on May 2, 1897 and an elder on May 20, 1901. While attending Lincoln he was the pastor in Media, Pennsylvania. Afterwards, he served John Wesley Church, Washington, D.C.; Center Street Church, Statesville, North Carolina; Goler Memorial, Winston-Salem, North Carolina, and Big Zion, Mobile, Alabama. During his six years at Big Zion he built the largest parsonage owned by African Americans at that time.

On the national scene, he was elected editor of the homiletics section of the *Quarterly Review* in 1910. In 1912, he became editor of the entire publication. On the death of the Rev. John F. Moreland, Sr., he was appointed secretary-treasurer to the Ministerial Brotherhood Department. He held both offices until he was consecrated a bishop in 1916. Assigned work on the West Coast, Bishop Kyles and Rev. E. M. Clark, the presiding elder, bought or built nearly a dozen churches in the California-Arizona Conference. He had charge of the New York Conference for the six years prior to his death in 1941. His major accomplishment in that conference was salvaging Memorial Church (Institutional) in Yonkers, New York. Built during the Depression, Memorial had acquired a debt of ninety thousand dollars that Bishop Kyles, with the help of the church's pastor and parishioners, reduced to less than six thousand dollars by the time he died.

Rev. Kyles married Jenny (or Jennie) V. Smith in 1897. They had two sons and a daughter. She died in 1905, and he married Louella (or Luella) Marie Bryan (or Bryant) on December 18, 1908. They had four children: two boys and two girls. His second wife died in 1922, and he married Josephine Humbles in 1926. They had two children. (Bradley 1970, pp. 408-09). Bishop Kyles died July 8, 1941. He was buried in Winston-Salem, North Carolina, following last rites at Goler Memorial Church.

Bishop L.W. Kyles
ELECTED 1916-DIED 1941

34. BISHOP LYNWOOD WESTINGHOUSE KYLES

Born: May 3, 1874 at Ivy Depot, Albermarle County, Virginia, to Burrell and Mary Kyles. **Education:** His early education was in a log cabin school house. He completed the wheelwright and blacksmith trade program at Hampton. Later he spent seven years at Lincoln University, Pennsylvania and graduated in 1901 with an A.B. degree and in 1904 with a B.D. degree. **Family:** Married three times: in 1897 to Jenny (or Jennie) V. Smith who died in 1905; in 1908 to Louella (or Luella) M. Bryan who died in 1922; and to Josephine Humbles in 1926. Nine children: three by first wife; four by his second, and two by his third. **Died:** July 8, 1941. Buried in Winston-Salem, North Carolina, following services at Goler Memorial Church.

35. BISHOP ROBERT BLAIR BRUCE

ROBERT BLAIR BRUCE was born on June 26, 1861, at Charlie Hope, Brunswick County, Virginia. He grew up on a farm in his home town and was permitted to go to school on rainy days. He was raised by his grandmother and an uncle. Aspiring to a better education, he walked to and from the nearest school of importance, which was seven miles away in Lawrenceville, until he finished its course of study. Bruce was scarcely more than ten when he converted and joined Solomon's Temple in Charlie Hope, Virginia. He joined the Virginia Conference in 1884 and was ordained by Bishop J. W. Hood in Petersburg, Virginia while he was a student at Payne Divinity School in that city. After completing his studies at Payne, he transferred to the Western North Carolina Conference and was the pastor of the Zion church in Winston-Salem for two years. In 1894, he went to Grace Church, Charlotte, served for five years and began the building of its present edifice. He also was the pastor of Little Rock Church, Charlotte, for one year, and Soldiers Memorial, Salisbury, for two years.

When Rev. Robert R. Morris, the first general superintendent of A.M.E. Zion Sunday Schools, died in 1895, Rev. Bruce was appointed acting superintendent for the remainder of Rev. Morris's term. In 1900, Rev. Bruce was elected by the General Conference as editor of the Sunday School Literature office. While he was editor, he commuted to Livingstone College and taught part-time. In 1908, he reported to the General Conference that 96,000 picture lesson cards, 480,000 junior lesson quarterlies, 48,000 teacher's journals and 250,000 catechisms were sent out during the quadrennium. He held the editorship until he was consecrated bishop on May 19, 1916.

As bishop he did constructive work in South Carolina and Georgia and set the Pee Dee Conference aside from the South Carolina Conference in 1919.

He was married to the former Miss Henrietta Foster. Bishop Bruce died July 9, 1920. He was buried in Cedar Grove Cemetery, Charlotte, North Carolina following final rights at Grace Church in Charlotte.

Bishop R.B. Bruce
ELECTED 1916-DIED 1920

35. BISHOP ROBERT BLAIR BRUCE

Born: June 26, 1861, at Charlie Hope, Brunswick County, Virginia. Raised by his grandmother and uncle. **Education:** Initially only went to school on rainy days, then walked seven miles each way to attend school in Lawrenceville, Virginia. Graduated from Payne Divinity School, Petersburg, Virginia. **Family:** Married Henrietta Foster. **Died:** July 9, 1920. Buried in Cedar Grove Cemetery, Charlotte, North Carolina following last rites at Grace Church.

36. BISHOP WILLIAM LEONARD LEE

WILLIAM LEONARD LEE was born in Madison County, near Canton, Mississippi, on August 8, 1866. Lee took advantage of the common schools and then set himself to personal study, which he pursued assiduously. It is alleged that in his mature years Bishop Lee read a different set of encyclopedias every winter to enrich his mind.

He joined Middleton Grove Church in Madison County in 1888 and the West Tennessee and Mississippi Conference in 1889. Rev. Lee was ordained deacon November 12, 1893 and elder November 10, 1895 by Bishop Alexander Walters. He was widely respected as a leading pastor and missionary. He helped Bishop J. S. Caldwell and Bishop J. W. Hood to develop churches in Ohio and New York respectively. His pastorates included Batesville and Coffeeville, Mississippi.; Monroe and Wadesboro, North Carolina; Rock Hill, South Carolina; St. Luke, Wilmington, North Carolina; John Wesley, Pittsburgh, Pennsylvania; and Fleet Street Memorial (First Church), Brooklyn, New York.

Rev. Lee was consecrated bishop on May 19, 1916, along with the Reverends L. W. Kyles, R. B. Bruce, and G. C. Clement, after the General Conference retired Bishops J. W. Hood and C. R. Harris. Bishop Lee presided over several conferences, including the New England and Louisiana Conferences. He left his mark as a knowledgeable pulpiteer and a compassionate church administrator.

Rev. Lee married Amelia Aurilla Dunn of Grenada, Mississippi, in 1891. They had one son. Mrs. Lee soon passed away, and in September, 1900, he married Nettie Eleanor Tillman of Wadesboro, North Carolina. They had seven children: Dancy Hood, James Sumner, Joshua Wallace, Alice Tillman, Beatrice Eleanor, Julius Alexander, and Frederick Jacobs. (Lee 1997, telephone conversation)

He died October 3, 1927 and was buried in Brooklyn, New York after funeral services at Fleet Street Memorial Church, now known as First A. M. E. Zion Church.

Bishop W.L. Lee
ELECTED 1916-DIED 1927

36. BISHOP WILLIAM LEONARD LEE

Born: August 8, 1866, in Madison County, near Canton, Mississippi. Names of parents are not recorded. **Education:** Attended common schools in Mississippi, then pursued personal study. Largely self-taught. **Family:** Two wives. In 1891, married Amelia Aurilla Dunn of Grenada, Mississippi. They had one son. After she died, he married Nettie E. Tillman of Wadesboro, North Carolina in September, 1900. They had seven children: Dancy Hood, James Sumner, Joshua Wallace, Alice Tillman, Beatrice Eleanor, Julius Alexander, and Frederick Jacobs. **Died:** October 3, 1927. He was buried in Brooklyn, New York, following services at Fleet Street Memorial Church in that city.

37. BISHOP GEORGE CLINTON CLEMENT

GEORGE CLINTON CLEMENT was born in Mocksville, North Carolina, December 23, 1871, to the Rev. Albert Turner and Eleanor (Carter) Clement. He was educated primarily in the public schools of Mocksville, North Carolina. In 1898, he earned a B.A. degree with high honors from Livingstone College.

Clement entered the ministry September 18, 1888, at Mocksville, North Carolina and became a charter member of the Western North Carolina Conference. He was ordained deacon December 10, 1893 and elder December 9, 1895 by Bishop T. H. Lomax. He was a successful pastor of several churches in North Carolina before he transferred to Louisville, Kentucky, where he became pastor of Twelfth Street Church. While there he purchased valuable property upon which the Broadway Temple Church was later built.

In 1904, Rev. Clement succeeded the Rev. John W. Smith as editor of the Star of Zion when Rev. Smith was elected bishop. Highly respected as a widely informed editor, Rev. Clement served productively for twelve years. He extended the influence of the Star to every press association, national convention, and race institution of his time. On May 19, 1916, he was consecrated bishop.

Bishop Clement planted churches in the Oklahoma and the Ohio conferences. In 1917 he succeeded Bishop Walters as presiding bishop in Africa, but World War I prevented him from traveling there. In 1920 he headed the West Tennessee and Mississippi Conference when Johnson Rural High School was built in Batesville, Mississippi on five acres of land donated by Albert J. Johnson, a wealthy black farmer. Johnson, unfortunately, died before the school was finished but was buried from its chapel on the day the school was to open. Bishop Clement led a commission to investigate possibilities in Brazil in the 1920s but did not succeed. He was a towering figure in the Federal Council of Churches and served as the first chairman of its commission on race relations.

While a student at Livingstone, Rev. Clement married Emma C. Williams on May 25, 1898. They had eight children: Abbie, Rufus, Ruth, George, Emma, Fred, James, and John Clinton Clement (*J. Neg. Hist.* [1935], p. 118). Abbie Clement Jackson became the 10th president of the Woman's Home and Foreign Missionary Society and served from 1955 to 1963. A son, Dr. Rufus Clement, became president of Atlanta University and was an active member of Zion. A second son, the Rev. James Clement, taught at Livingstone College seminary and also served as a chaplain in the U.S. Army.

Bishop Clement died on October 23, 1934. He was buried in Louisville, Kentucky, following services at Broadway Temple Church. Some years after his death, his wife was named American Mother of the Year by the Golden Rule Foundation in 1945. Mrs. Clement was the first African American woman to be so honored.

Bishop G.C. Clement
ELECTED 1916-DIED 1935

37. BISHOP GEORGE CLINTON CLEMENT

Born: December 23, 1871, in Mocksville, North Carolina, to the Rev. Albert Turner and Eleanor (Carter) Clement. **Education:** Finished the public schools in Mocksville, North Carolina. Graduated from Livingstone College in 1898 with honors. **Family:** Married Emma C. Williams On May 25, 1898. Mrs Clement was named the 1945 American Mother of the Year by the Golden Rule Foundation. Eight children: Abbie (Clement Jackson) who became 10th president of WH&FMS, Rufus, who became president of Atlanta University; Ruth, George, Emma, Fred, John Clinton, and James who became a chaplain in the U.S. Army. **Died:** October 23, 1934. Buried in Louisville, Kentucky, after services at Broadway Temple Church, 13th Street and Broadway.

African Methodist Episcopal Zion Church
38. BISHOP JOHN WESLEY WOOD

JOHN WESLEY WOOD was born free in Tolbert County, Georgia, on May 10, 1865, to Isom B. and Amanda (Tignor) Wood. He attended the public schools of Troy County and LaGrange Academy in La Grange, Georgia, which he completed in 1882. He attended Morris Brown College, Atlanta, in 1896 and the Moody Bible Institute in Chicago, 1911-12. (Boris 1929, p. 481)

In 1888, he joined the West Tennessee and Mississippi Conference at Kosciusko, Mississippi. He was pastor of several churches in that conference before he transferred to the Virginia Conference and pastorates in Norfolk and Berkley, Virginia; Ahoskie and Edenton, North Carolina. He was pastor of Jones Tabernacle, Indianapolis, Indiana; and State Street Church, Mobile, Alabama. He visited Africa with great advantage to Zion while serving as the Secretary of Foreign (later, Overseas) Missions. During his early ministry he was president of Edenton High School in North Carolina and was a teacher in the public schools of Lincoln, Alabama and Marietta, Georgia.

In 1912, Rev. Wood was elected general secretary of the then Foreign Missions Department (now called the *Department of Overseas Missions*). The department was first incorporated in Indianapolis, Indiana by Dr. Wood with Senator Robert Lee Brokenburr serving as the legal representative. Wood was relentless in his appeals for help for foreign work. During his administration, training centers and day schools were opened in Africa and South America, and he established a good relationship with the workers on the field and the Woman's Home and Foreign Missionary Society. He held this position until he was consecrated bishop on May 20, 1920.

Bishop Wood served the episcopacy for almost twenty years. He was the host bishop for the 28th General Conference in May, 1928 at Washington Metropolitan Church, St. Louis, Missouri. He was married to M. Janice Edmond on February 10, 1891. They had five children: Jessie S., Ethel R., Inez A., Lillian D., and Charlesine R. Wood (Boris 1929, p. 481). On April 17, 1940, Bishop Wood died in Indianapolis and was buried there following final rites at Jones Tabernacle A. M. E. Zion Church then located at Blackford Street and now at 2510 E. 34th Street.

Bishop J.W. Wood
ELECTED 1920-DIED 1940

38. BISHOP JOHN WESLEY WOOD

Born: May 10, 1865, in Tolbert County, Georgia., to Isom B. and Amanda (Tignor) Wood. **Education:** Graduated from the public schools of Troy County, Georgia., and LaGrange Academy, La Grange, Georgia. Attended Morris Brown College, Atlanta, Georgia, 1896, and Moody Bible Institute, Chicago, Illinois, 1911-12. **Major Publications:** *Lyrics of Sunshine, 1922; Life and Travels of Bishop Wood.* **Family:** Married M. Janice Edmond on February 10, 1891. Five children: Jessie S., Ethel R., Inez A., Lillian D., and Charlesine R. Wood. **Died:** April 17, 1940, in Indianapolis, Indiana. Buried there after final rites at Jones Tabernacle A.M.E. Zion Church, then on Blackford Street, now at 2510 E. 34 Street.

African Methodist Episcopal Zion Church
39. BISHOP PARIS ARTHUR WALLACE

PARIS ARTHUR WALLACE was born in Blount County, Tennessee, near Maryville, on April 17, 1870. He was the third child of seven sons and two daughters born to Tobias and Amanda Wallace. He attended the three to four months County schools and worked on the farm until he was eighteen when he persuaded his parents to enroll him in the Freedmen's Normal Institute, a school founded by Quakers in Maryville.

He was converted in a school revival and joined the A. M. E. Zion Church in Maryville where he sang in the choir and taught in the Sunday School. He graduated from the Normal Institute in 1888, and three years later entered Maryville College, an interracial institution. In 1895 he graduated from Maryville and received a prize of $25 in gold for the best oration. Torn between his desire to become a teacher or a minister (he served as pastor of the Zion Church in Maryville during his senior year in college), Wallace became the principal of the colored school in Maryville but soon resigned to study theology at Lincoln University, Lincoln, Pennsylvania. He graduated in 1898 with the Bachelor of Sacred Theology and Master of Arts degrees.

He was licensed to preach in Maryville by the Rev. (later Bishop) Edward D. W. Jones in 1894. He joined the Tennessee Conference under Bishop Thomas H. Lomax in 1894 at Cleveland, Tennessee. He was ordained deacon September 20, 1896 and elder May 23, 1897 while still a student at Lincoln University. He was pastor of the A. M. E. Zion Church in Oxford, Pennsylvania; Thompkin's Chapel, Chattanooga, Tennessee; Jacob St. Tabernacle, Louisville, Kentucky; Metropolitan Wesley, Washington, D.C.; Gettysburg, Pennsylvania; and Fleet Street (First Church), Brooklyn, New York.

In 1920 he was elected and consecrated bishop at the General Conference held at Logan Temple, Knoxville, Tennessee. Bishop Wallace shared responsibility for creating Zion's budget system in 1924. He was host bishop for the 27th General Conference in 1924 at Jones Tabernacle, Indianapolis, Indiana and for the 29th General Conference in 1932 at Wesley Center Church, Pittsburgh. He retired in 1944. He died after a long illness on February 21, 1952. After funeral services at First A. M. E. Zion Church in Brooklyn, New York, at Tompkins and McDonough Streets, he was buried in Brooklyn.

While serving at Thompkin's Chapel, Chattanooga (1896-98), he met and married Ida L. Bannister, a public school teacher in that city. They had two daughters: Jean Wallace Edwards and Helen Wallace Smith.

Bishop P.A. Wallace
ELECTED 1920-DIED 1952

39. BISHOP PARIS ARTHUR WALLACE

Born: April 17, 1870, in Blount County, Tennessee, near Maryville, the third child of seven sons and two daughters, to Tobias and Amanda Wallace. **Education:** Attended County schools until he was eighteen. Graduated from the Freedmen's Normal Institute, Maryville, Tennessee in 1888 and from Lincoln University, Pennsylvania in 1898 with the Bachelor of Sacred Theology and Master of Arts degrees. **Family:** Married Ida L. Bannister, a public school teacher, while serving as pastor of Thompkin's Chapel, Chattanooga (1896-98). Two daughters, Jean Wallace Edwards and Helen Wallace Smith. **Died:** On February 21, 1952, after a long and trying illness, in Brooklyn, New York. Buried there after services at First Church, Tompkins and McDonough Sts.

40. BISHOP BENJAMIN GARLAND SHAW

BENJAMIN GARLAND SHAW was born in Pope, Mississippi, August 26, 1878, to Charles and Bridget (Jackson) Shaw. After attending public schools in Mississippi, he studied at Greenwood College, Greenwood, Mississippi, then transferred to and earned the B.A. degree from Philander-Smith College, Little Rock, Arkansas. He also took a correspondence course in theology from Oskaloosa, Iowa and completed the course of study at the Louisville Medical College in 1907.

Shaw started his ministry in the West Tennessee and Mississippi Conference in 1898. He was pastor of Greenwood Mission, Greenwood, and Charkey Circuit, Mississippi; Payne Chapel, Little Rock, Arkansas; St. John's Chapel, New Albany, and Hood Temple, Evansville, Indiana. He was ordained a deacon on November 13, 1898 and elder November 19, 1899. He served as presiding elder of the Chicago District and was pastor of Washington Metropolitan Church, St. Louis, Missouri., from 1910-20. He led that congregation in the purchase of its present mammoth structure in St. Louis, located on the corner of Garrison and Lucas Avenues, 613 Garrison Avenue, St. Louis, Missouri. In 1921, Rev. Shaw was elected the first director of the A. M. E. Zion Bureau of Evangelism. For four years he traveled across the country, filling churches. He and the evangelists associated with him gained over thirty-five thousand converts for Zion. He was elected to the episcopacy from this office. He was the first of the five bishops elected and consecrated on May 20, 1924 at the 27th General Conference held in Indianapolis, Indiana.

He presided over the North Alabama, South Alabama, Cahaba, Alabama, Central Alabama, Blue Ridge, Florida, South Georgia, Georgia, and Western North Carolina Conferences. In 1943-44, guided by Bishop Shaw, Goler Memorial Church of Winston-Salem, North Carolina was divided into two substantial congregations. Goler Metropolitan was established in a large edifice on 4th and Dunleith Streets, while Old Goler Memorial remained on its historic site. Bishop Shaw was treasurer of Zion's Sesquicentennial Committee in 1946. He was a delegate to the World Council of Churches in Amsterdam, Holland in 1948.

He married twice: to Garnett Wilkins Shaw (deceased) and Maybelle Leona Gunn Shaw. Both served admirably as missionary supervisors. He had three children: Benjamin Garland, Jr., Maxine Camille, and Charles M. Shaw (*Biographical Encyclopedia of the World* 1946, p. 817). Bishop Shaw died April 14, 1951, in Salisbury, North Carolina. He was buried in Birmingham, Alabama following funeral services at Livingstone College Auditorium in Salisbury and at Metropolitan Church in Birmingham, Alabama.

Bishop B.G. Shaw
ELECTED 1920-DIED 1951

40. BISHOP BENJAMIN GARLAND SHAW

Born: August 26, 1878, in Pope, Mississippi., to Charles and Bridget (Jackson) Shaw. **Education:** Studied at Greenwood College, Mississippi, earned B.A. degree in 1904 from Philander-Smith College, Little Rock, Arkansas. In 1907 graduated from the Louisville Medical College, Kentucky. **Family:** Married twice: to Garnett Wilkins (deceased) and to Maybelle Leona Gunn. Three children from his first marriage were Benjamin Garland, Jr., Maxine Camille, and Charles M. Shaw. **Died:** April 14, 1951, in Salisbury, North Carolina. Buried in Birmingham, Alabama following funeral services at the Livingstone College Auditorium, Salisbury, North Carolina, and at Metropolitan A. M. E. Zion, Birmingham, Alabama.

African Methodist Episcopal Zion Church

41. BISHOP EDWARD DERUSHA WILMOT JONES

EDWARD DERUSHA WILMOT JONES was born in Washington, D.C., on September 11, 1871, to Rev. Singleton T. W. Jones (who later became Zion's 16th Bishop) and missionary pioneer Mary Jane Talbert Jones. After attending public schools in Washington, D.C., he enrolled in Livingstone College and graduated with high honors. He was converted in 1887 while a student at Livingstone. He joined the John Wesley Church in Washington, D.C., and was licensed to preach in 1891. Later in the year he joined the Western North Carolina Conference at Hickory, North Carolina, and on October 6, 1891, he was ordained a deacon. On October 15, 1893, he was ordained an elder.

Rev. Jones was one of the ministers responsible for Zion's growth in eastern Tennessee and Missouri. He was a distinguished scholar, preacher, orator, pastor, and writer. He was pastor of Moore's Sanctuary, Charlotte, North Carolina; Maryville, Tennessee; Jacob Street Tabernacle, Louisville, Kentucky; Avery Church, Allegheny, Pennsylvania; Walters Memorial, Chicago, Illinois; Memorial Church, Rochester, New York; First Church, San Francisco, California; and Union Wesley Church, Washington, D.C., from which he was elected to the bishopric.

Rev. Jones was consecrated the 41st Bishop on May 20, 1924. On September 26, 1925, he was part of the delegation that responded to Bishop W. J. Walls's call after Bishop Walls and Mrs. Lucille Washington Alleyne, the wife of Bishop C.C. Alleyne, were refused service in the dining room of Union Station in Washington, D. C.

In 1934, Bishop Jones published *The Comprehensive Catechism of the A.M.E. Zion Church*. He was working on a history of the church when he died on June 16, 1935. He was laid to rest in Lincoln Memorial Cemetery, Washington, D. C., after funeral services at Union Wesley Church. Dr. Mordecai Johnson, the first black president of Howard University and a personal friend of Bishop Jones, paid tribute to him at the funeral.

Bishop Jones and his wife, Maggie E. Jones, had one son, Edward Dancy Jones.

Bishop E.D.W. Jones
ELECTED 1924-DIED 1935

41. BISHOP EDWARD DERUSHA WILMOT JONES

Born: September 11, 1871, in Washington, D.C., to Rev. (later Bishop) and Mrs. Singleton T. W. Jones. **Education**: Attended public schools in Washington, D.C. and graduated from Livingstone College with high honors. Major Publication: *The Comprehensive Catechism of the A. M. E. Zion Church*, 1934. **Family**: Was married to Maggie E. Jones. They had one son, Edward Dancy Jones. **Died:** June 16, 1935. Buried at Lincoln Memorial Cemetery on June 20, 1935 in Washington, D.C., the town of his birth, following services at Union Wesley Church.

42. BISHOP WILLIAM JACOB WALLS

WILLIAM JACOB WALLS, the "boy evangelist," was born May 8, 1885 to Edward and Harriet (Edgerton) Walls in Chimney Rock, Rutherford County, North Carolina. His grandparents were John and Patsey Edgerton (AMEZQR 59[1949]: p. 102). He was educated at the Allen Industrial School of the Methodist Episcopal Church, Asheville, North Carolina. He earned an A. B. degree from Livingstone College in 1908, a B. D. degree from Hood Theological Seminary in 1913, and an A. M. degree from the University of Chicago in 1939.

Walls began his public ministry at age fourteen. He was licensed to preach at Hopkins Chapel, Asheville, in September, 1899. He joined the Blue Ridge Conference on October 6, 1902. He was ordained a deacon October 20, 1903 by Bishop C. R. Harris and an elder,while he was still a college student, October 16, 1905, by Bishop J. W. Smith. He was pastor at Cleveland, North Carolina; Lincolnton, North Carolina; and Broadway Temple, Louisville, Kentucky, where he built the present church. Rev. Walls was elected editor of the *Star of Zion* in 1920. He served for four years and tripled its circulation. On May 20, 1924, he was elected to the episcopacy.

On September 26, 1925, Bishop Walls and Mrs. Annie Lucille Alleyne, wife of Bishop Alleyne, were refused service in the dining room of Union Station, Washington, D.C., because they had refused to sit in the rear. They refused to leave, and their highly publicized three hour sit-in led to the end of segregation in Union Station. Bishop Walls presided over the West Texas and Oklahoma; New York; Western New York; Alle-gheny; New England and Western North Carolina Conferences. He was made chair-person of the Board of Religious Education in 1924, a post he held for forty-four years until he retired in 1968. His accomplishments were many. In 1954 under his leadership, the First Episcopal District initiated the African Memorial Bank to raise money for work in Africa. Its first project was the restoration of the Cartwright Memorial Church in Brewerville, Liberia. During his tenure from 1941-64, pastoral appointments in the New York Conference increased from thirty-nine to seventy-four, and four new churches were established in the Bronx alone.

In 1956, at seventy-one, Bishop Walls, married his secretary, Dorothy L. Jordon, born March 18, 1932 in Chicago, Illinois and died November 15, 1977. They were benefactors of Livingstone College, Hood Theological Seminary, Camp Dorothy Walls in Black Mountain, North Carolina, and the Dorothy J. Walls School in Po River, Liberia. After his retirement, the General Conference appointed him Historiographer and commissioned him to write a comprehensive history. *The African Methodist Episcopal Zion Church: Reality of the Black Church* was published in 1974. (Douglas [Feb. 1975]: p. 108) Bishop Walls died in April, 1975. After lying in state at Institutional Church,Yonkers,N. Y. funeral services were held at Walters A. M. E. Zion Church, Chicago, Ill. followed by burial in Lincoln Cemetery of the same city.

Bishop W.J. Walls
ELECTED 1924-DIED 1975

42. BISHOP WILLIAM J. WALLS

Born: May 8, 1885, to Edward and Hattie (Edgerton) Walls, in Chimney Rock, Rutherford County, North Carolina. **Education:** Early education at the Methodist Episcopal Church Allen Industrial School, Asheville, North Carolina. Graduated in 1908 from Livingstone College (B.A.); from Hood Theological Seminary, 1913 (B.D.); and from the University of Chicago in 1941 (M.A.) in Christian Education. **Major Publications:** *Joseph Charles Price*, 1943; *The African Methodist Episcopal Zion Church: Reality of the Black Church*, 1974. **Family:** Married Dorothy L. Jordon in December 1956. **Died:** In April, 1975 in Yonkers, New York. After lying in state at Institutional A. M. E Zion Church, Yonkers, he was transported to Chicago for final services at Greater Walters A. M. E. Zion Church and burial in Lincoln Cemetary of that city.

43. BISHOP JOHN WILLIAM MARTIN

JOHN WILLIAM MARTIN was born June 30, 1879, in Russell County near Lebanon, Virginia, to Cornelius and Nancy Martin. His father was an industrious man who worked hard to take care of Martin's twelve brothers and sisters, three half-brothers, and one half-sister. His mother insisted upon the family moving from Virginia to Johnson City, Tennessee, where, she felt, "My children can get schooling." (*AMEZQR* 59[1949]: p. 104)

Martin graduated from Langston High School, Johnson City, Tennessee, and earned the A.B. and B.D. degrees from Lincoln University in Pennsylvania. Later, when he was a bishop, he spent two years in postgraduate study at the University of Southern California at Los Angeles. While attending Lincoln, Martin joined the Philadelphia and Baltimore Conference. He was pastor of Wooderville Circuit in the Washington District. After completing his education at Lincoln, he transferred to the Kentucky Conference and was appointed pastor of St. Mark Church, Indianapolis, Indiana. It was there that he met and married Ola M. Ecton. Their daughter, Ione LaVerne Martin, was also born there.

Bishop George W. Clinton insisted that Rev. Martin become head of Atkinson College, Madisonville, Kentucky, where he remained for the next ten years. Rev. Martin was ordained a deacon on May 21, 1905 and an elder on September 8, 1907. In 1916, he was elected Secretary of Education. He served in that capacity until he was elevated to the episcopacy on May 20, 1924.

His first assignments as a bishop were to the Pacific Coast and to Demerara (in Guyana), South America. In 1928, he was assigned the Missouri and Michigan Conferences, along with the Pacific Coast. He also supervised the Ohio, Cape Fear, and North Carolina Conferences during his more than thirty years as bishop. "He was a preacher of extraordinary ability, an administrator of great wisdom and courage, and a much beloved servant of the church."

Bishop Martin died October 16, 1955. After services at Greater Walters A. M. E. Zion Church, then located at 28th and Dearborn Streets, Chicago, Illinois, he was buried in Lincoln Cemetery, Chicago, Illinois.

Bishop J.W. Martin
ELECTED 1924-DIED 1955

43. BISHOP JOHN WILLIAM MARTIN

Born: June 30, 1879, in Russell County, near Lebanon, Virginia, to Cornelius and Nancy Martin. He had twelve full brothers and sisters, three half-sisters, and a half-brother. **Education:** Graduated from Langston High School, Johnson City, Tennessee, and the college and seminary program at Lincoln University, Pennsylvania. After becoming a bishop, he had two years of postgraduate study at the University of Southern California, Los Angeles. **Family:** Married the former Miss Ola M. Ecton of Indianapolis, Indiana. One child—Ione LaVerne Martin. **Died:** October 16, 1955. Funeral services were held at Greater Walters A. M. E. Zion Church in Chicago, and he was laid to rest in Lincoln Cemetery in Chicago.

44. BISHOP CAMERON CHESTERFIELD ALLEYNE

CAMERON CHESTERFIELD ALLEYNE was born in Bridgetown, Barbados, B. W. I., on September 3, 1880, to Robert Henry and Amelia (Clarke) Alleyne. (AMEZQR 59 [1949]: p. 106) He attended Naparima College, Port of Spain, Trinidad, from 1889 to 1903. He migrated to the U. S. in 1903 and attended Tuskegee Institute, Alabama, for a year. Rev. Alleyne was ordained a deacon in the A. M. E. Zion Church in 1904 and an elder in 1905.

Rev. Alleyne was the pastor of several of Zion's leading churches located in Anniston, Alabama, 1904-05; St. Elmo, Tennessee, 1905-08; John Wesley, Washington, D.C., 1908-12; People's First Church, now Hood Memorial, Providence, Rhode Island, 1912-16; Grace Church, Charlotte, North Carolina, 1916-17; and St. Catherine, New Rochelle, New York , 1917-24.

Rev. Alleyne became a naturalized citizen in 1911. He earned an A.M. degree from Livingstone College in 1915. He was elected editor of the *A. M. E. Zion Quarterly Review* in 1916 and served in that capacity until he was elected to the episcopacy on May 20, 1924.

Bishop Alleyne was Zion's first resident bishop to Africa. He and his wife left for Africa soon after the 1924 General Conference. The Annie Lucille Alleyne Girls' School in Ghana is named after his wife. Bishop Alleyne was successful in reviving Zion's work during his four years in Africa. He made vast improvements and left six churches under construction in Cape Coast.

After his return to the U.S. in 1928 he had great success with the conferences he supervised. They included the Philadelphia and Baltimore, New Jersey, Tennessee, South America,Western New York, and Virgin Islands Conferences.

Bishop Alleyne was married to Annie Lucille Washington of Charlotte, North Carolina on June 29, 1905. (*AMEZQR*, 59 [1949]: p. 106) They had one child, Mae. C. Latten. (Fleming and Burckell 1950: p. 8) In 1944, Mrs. Annie Lucille Alleyne died. His second wife, Bettye Lee Roberts, was the daughter of the Rev. and Mrs. F. Thomas Roberts of Fresno, California. In 1947, the Bishop and Mrs. Bettye Lee Alleyne visited South America and the Virgin Islands Conferences.

Bishop Alleyne died in Philadelphia on March 24, 1955. He was laid to rest in Beechwood Cemetery, New Rochelle, New York, following services at Big Wesley Church, at 15th and Lombard Streets, Philadelphia, Pennsylvania and St. Catherine A. M. E. Zion Church, New Rochelle, New York.

Bishop C.C. Alleyne
ELECTED 1924-DIED 1955

44. BISHOP CAMERON CHESTERFIELD ALLEYNE

Born: In Bridgetown, Barbados, B.W.I., September 3, 1880, to Robert Henry and Amelia (Clarke) Alleyne. **Education:** Early education at Naparima College, Port of Spain, Trinidad, 1889-1903. Attended Tuskegee Institute, Alabama, 1903-04 and received A.M. degree from Livingstone College, Salisbury, North Carolina, in 1915. **Major Publications:** *The Gold Coast at a Glance*, 1931; *Highways That Lead to God*, 1941; *The Negro Faces Christianity*, 1946; *Twenty-Five Years in the Episcopacy*, 1950. **Family:** Married Annie Lucille Washington of Charlotte, North Carolina on June 29, 1905. She died in 1944. His second wife was Bettye Lee Roberts, daughter of Rev. and Mrs. F. Thomas Roberts. He had one daughter, Mae C. Latten, by his first wife. **Died:** In Philadelphia, Pennsylvania, on March 24, 1955. Buried in Beechwood Cemetery, New Rochelle, New York, after last rites at Big Wesley Church, Philadelphia, and St. Catherine A. M. E. Zion Church, New Rochelle.

45. BISHOP WILLIAM WALTER MATTHEWS

WILLIAM WALTER MATTHEWS was born in Batesville, Mississippi, on October 28, 1871, to Thomas Augustus and Eliza Caroline (Bobo) Matthews (Fleming & Burckel 1950, pp. 359-60). Matthews attended Branch Normal College, Pine Bluff, Arkansas, 1890-1900 and New Orleans University, 1898-1901. He joined the Arkansas Conference in 1904 and was ordained a deacon that year and an elder in 1906.

He was the pastor of Cooper Church, Oakland, California; First Church, San Francisco (as pastor builder); Cherry Street Church, Pine Bluff, Arkansas; Zion Temple, McCloud, California; and The Old Ship, Montgomery, Alabama (as pastor builder).

Rev. Matthews was elected Secretary of the Foreign Missions Department in 1920. He executed this office skillfully and was elevated to the episcopacy from this office. Rev. Matthews was elected and consecrated bishop May 20, 1928 in St. Louis, Missouri. Bishop Matthews, accompanied by his wife the former Alice S. J. Johnson and his daughter Juanita Matthews, went to Africa for eight years as Bishop of Liberia and East and West Gold Coast. He organized the Nigeria Annual Conference in 1932. During his episcopacy in Africa, he erected four school buildings in Liberia, where he had eleven local pastors and twenty-four hundred members in the Liberia Annual Conference.

Rev. Matthews married Alice S. J. Johnson in 1908. They had six children — Nettie, James, Elmer, Julius, Willeta, and Juanita Matthews (Ibid.). Following the death of Alice S.J. Matthews, the bishop married Etoria Dryver who served a short while as his missionary supervisor. Bishop Matthews made notable contributions in the episcopacy. However, he grossly violated the rules of the Discipline governing the episcopacy. This led to his divesture through a judiciary action taken by the General Conference in 1948. He died March 15, 1962 in Washington, D.C. and was funeralized from the Metropolitan Wesley A. M. E. Zion Church.

Bishop W.W. Matthews
ELECTED 1928-DIED 1955

45. BISHOP WILLIAM WALTER MATTHEWS

Born: October 24, 1871, in Batesville, Mississippi, to Thomas Augustus and Eliza Caroline (Bobo) Matthews. **Education:** Went to school at Branch Normal College, Pine Bluff, Arkansas, 1890-1900, and New Orleans University, 1898-1901. **Family:** Married Alice S.J. Johnson in 1908. Six children: Nettie, James, Elmer, Julius, Willetta, and Juanita Matthews. **Died:** March 15, 1962, in Washington, D. C. Funeral services were held at Metropolitan Wesley A. M. E. Zion Church, Washington, D. C.

435

African Methodist Episcopal Zion Church
46. BISHOP FREDERICK MILLER JACOBS

FREDERICK MILLER JACOBS was born in Camden, South Carolina, on July 15, 1865. Jacobs was a highly educated man. He attended the normal schools in his home town, Jackson College and South Carolina University before that school was resegregated. After taking private tutoring in the Charleston Military College, he entered Howard University in 1884 and received the A.B. degree in 1888. He also attended Illinois Wesleyan College in 1896, received a M. D. degree from Long Island Medical College in 1901, and subsequently completed a thorough course in medicine and surgery at the New York Medical College. He practiced medicine in Brooklyn, New York and did well in real estate and business.

Jacobs joined the A. M. E. Zion Church in Charlotte, North Carolina in 1882. He was licensed to preach and joined the North Carolina Conference that fall. He transferred to the Philadelphia and Baltimore Conference where he was ordained a deacon on May 24, 1886, and an elder on May 20, 1888. He was one of the ministers responsible for Zion's growth in Eastern Tennessee and for the growth of Fleet St. Church (First Church) in Brooklyn, New York. He was the successful pastor of churches in Baltimore, Maryland; Harrisburg, Pennsylvania; Chattanooga, Tennessee; Hopkins Chapel, Asheville, North Carolina; and Loguen Temple, Knoxville, Tennessee. In 1895 he was professor of Latin, Greek, literature, and higher mathematics at Greenville College, Greenville, Tennessee.

Rev. Jacobs married Laura Etta Lomax on June 17, 1888. They had six children — Thomas Charles; Harold F.; Louis P.; Algenon M.; Gerald D.; and Henry P. (Boris 1929: p. 203)

A powerful preacher, excellent speaker, generous and model pastor, he was elected General Secretary of the connection in 1917 when the Rev. M. D. Lee left to become principal of Lancaster Normal and Industrial School, Lancaster, South Carolina. He served as General Secretary until he was elected to the episcopacy on May 20, 1928.

Bishop Jacobs was assigned to the West Tennessee-Mississippi, Arkansas, North Arkansas, Louisiana, Demerara, and Brazil Conferences, and the South Atlantic Insular work. He visited the South America area in 1930—the only bishop to do so from 1924 to 1940. He died December 31, 1931 in Brooklyn and was buried there following final rites at Fleet Street Memorial Church, now First Church, in Brooklyn, N.Y.

Bishop F.M. Jacobs
ELECTED 1928-DIED 1931

46. BISHOP FREDERICK MILLER JACOBS

Born: On July 15, 1865, in Camden, South Carolina. Parents names are not known.
Education: Attended normal schools, Jackson College, and South Carolina University and took private tutoring at Charleston Military College. He graduated with an A. B. degree in 1888 from Howard University and with an M. D. degree from Long Island Medical College in 1901. **Family:** Married Laura Etta Lomax on June 17, 1888. Six children — Thomas Charles; Harold F.; Louis P.; Algenon M.; Gerald D. and Henry P.
Died: Dec. 31, 1931 in Brooklyn, N.Y. Buried there following final rites at Fleet Street Memorial Church, now First A. M. E. Zion Church, at Tompkins and McDonough Streets, Brooklyn, N. Y.

47. BISHOP ELIJAH LOVETTE MADISON

ELIJAH LOVETTE MADISON was born in Madison Park, near Montgomery, Alabama, on May 20, 1876 to Eli and Frances Madison. He joined the Western North Carolina Conference at Lincolnton, North Carolina, in 1898. He entered Livingstone College and earned his A.B. degree. He was ordained a deacon on November 6, 1898 and an elder two years later on November 11, 1900.

He was pastor of Cedar Grove and Second Creek Circuit; Hopkins Chapel, Asheville; Clinton Chapel, Charlotte; St. Stephens, High Point; Trinity, Greensboro; St. Luke, Wilmington, all in North Carolina. He transferred to the Allegheny Conference and was pastor of John Wesley Church in 1920.

His first wife, Julia Moseley of New Bern, North Carolina, was the second woman to graduate from the college department of Livingstone College in 1902. She was the mother of eight of his nine children and died in childbirth while he was a pastor in Wilmington, North Carolina. He later married Lucy Coleman. That union produced one child.

In 1927, Rev. Madison led the Wesley Center Church, Pittsburgh in building a mammoth church at a cost of $250,000. At that time this was the largest black Methodist church building in Pittsburgh. In 1932 he was elected Financial Secretary, a position he held until he was elected to the bishopric. He was consecrated the 47th Bishop on May 20, 1936.

Bishop Madison was presiding over the Allegheny Conference of the Sixth Episcopal District when he was stricken ill. He lingered for some time before dying on June 26, 1946. He was buried in Pittsburgh following funeral services at Wesley Center Church.

Bishop E.L. Madison
ELECTED 1936-DIED 1946

47. BISHOP ELIJAH LOVETTE MADISON

Born: May 20, 1876, in Madison Park, near Montgomery, Alabama, to Eli and Frances Madison. **Education:** A. B. degree from Livingstone College, N.C., date not given **Family:** Married twice. Eight children by his first wife, Julia Moseley, and one by his second, Lucy Coleman. Names not given. First wife was the second woman to graduate (in 1902) from the college department of Livingstone College. **Died:** June 26, 1946. Buried in Pittsburgh following funeral services at Wesley Center Church.

African Methodist Episcopal Zion Church
48. BISHOP WILLIAM CORNELIUS BROWN

WILLIAM CORNELIUS BROWN, who was to become known as the *Father* of Zion's pension plan, was born in Chowan County, near Edenton, North Carolina, on June 24, 1877, to Whitman and Fannie Maria (Blount) Brown. (Yenser 1940, p. 89) He attended grade schools in his home county and later moved to Portland, Maine, where he attended Westbrook Seminary from 1900 to 1904. He completed the course of study while serving as pastor of the Portland Mission. Rev. Brown started as a lay preacher in Canaan Temple Church, Chowan County, North Carolina, and joined the New England Conference in 1901 at Providence, Rhode Island. He was ordained a deacon on May 5, 1901 and an elder on June 12, 1904, by Bishop J. W. Hood. Rev. Brown attended Yale University in 1912.

After leaving Portland, Rev. Brown was a successful pastor at Creswell Circuit in the Virginia Conference; Kadesh Chapel, Edenton, North Carolina; Walters Memorial, Bridgeport, Connecticut; Varick Memorial, New Haven, Connecticut; John Wesley Church, Washington, D. C., and Fleet Street Church, Brooklyn. Under his leadership, the congregation at John Wesley in Washington, D. C., the National Church of Zion Methodism, purchased its present edifice. He saved the situation in the only black church in Portland, Maine and built the Columbia Mission in Columbia, North Carolina.

Rev. Brown was consecrated the 48th Bishop on May 20, 1936. Bishop Brown presided over the Oregon, Washington, California, Southwest Rocky Mountain, Texas, Missouri, and Kentucky Conferences. (*Official Journal, 30th Quad. Sess. Gen. Conf. [1936]*, pp. 275-76; *35th Quad. Sess. Gen. Conf. [1956]*, pp. 133-37) In 1936, after he offered a resolution to study a pension plan for Zion ministers, he was appointed to head the pension plan commission. The plan was adopted by the 1944 General Conference, and he became known as the "Father of the Pension Fund." In 1948, he was the host bishop for the 33rd General Conference held at Broadway Temple, Louisville, Kentucky, and in 1954 he was the host bishop for the 9th Christian Education Convention, which was also held at Broadway Temple.

He married Gertrude Capehart in 1901. Bishop Brown retired in May, 1960. He died on January 2, 1964 in Brooklyn, where he then lived. He was buried in Edenton, North Carolina, after funeral services at First Church, Brooklyn, and Kadesh Chapel, Edenton.

Bishop W.C. Brown
ELECTED 1936-DIED 1964

48. BISHOP WILLIAM CORNELIUS BROWN

Born: In Chowan County, near Edenton, North Carolina, on June 24, 1877, to Whitman and Fannie Maria (Blount) Brown. **Education:** Attended grade schools in Chowan County; graduated from Westbrook Seminary in Portland, Maine, while serving as pastor of the Portland Mission. Also attended Yale University in 1912. **Family:** Married Ms. Gertrude Capehart in 1901. **Died:** Died Jan. 2, 1964, in Brooklyn, where he then lived. Buried in Edenton, North Carolina after funeral services at First Church, Brooklyn, and Kadesh Chapel, Edenton.

African Methodist Episcopal Zion Church
49. BISHOP JAMES WALTER BROWN

JAMES WALTER BROWN was born July 19, 1872, in Elizabeth City, North Carolina, to Jessie R. and Araminta (Griffin) Brown. (Yenser 1940, p. 89) He received his early training in Elizabeth City at the State Normal School. He graduated from Shaw University in 1893 with the A.B. degree. Brown taught at the State Normal School in Elizabeth City from 1893-99. He entered the ministry through the Philadelphia-Baltimore Conference and was ordained a deacon on May 17, 1903 and an elder on May 21, 1905.

He did further study at Lincoln University, Lincoln, Pennsylvania, where he earned S. T. B. and M. A. degrees in 1903. Rev. Brown was appointed pastor of St. Paul Church, Media and St. John Church, Bethlehem, both in Pennsylvania. In 1905, he transferred to the Western New York Conference and was assigned as pastor of Memorial Church, Rochester, N.Y. He built the church at Rochester with memorial windows to Susan B. Anthony and to such race pioneers as Frederick Douglass, Harriet Tubman, and Dr. Joseph Charles Price, all members of Zion.

Rev. Brown was married to Martha Hill in 1903. She served faithfully with him in his pastorates at Memorial, Rochester, New York, 1905-13 and at Mother Zion, New York City from 1913 to 1928 when she died. In 1930 he married Andrades Lindsay, a professional musician and organist.

In 1913, Rev. Brown was appointed by Bishop J. W. Hood to Mother Zion Church in New York City, then located on W. 89th Street. He arrived at a critical junction in Mother Zion's history. The church had lost its property. Rev. Brown led the congregation of a few hundred disorganized and dispirited members to nearly one thousand by 1915. In that year, they purchased an edifice at 157 W. 136th St. in Manhattan, and when the congregation outgrew that structure, he led them in the building of the current edifice at 146 W. 137th. St. Excavation for the new building, which cost $500,000, started in 1923. The building was dedicated in 1925. Rev. Brown started a weekday community program at Mother Zion; he was the first Zion minister to introduce this church activity. He served Mother Zion Church from 1913 to 1936 when he was elected and consecrated the 49th Bishop in succession.

Bishop Brown was assigned to the South American and Virgin Island territory, which he did not visit, and to Africa. In 1936, he became Zion's second resident bishop in Africa and had great success in organizing for the church. He organized a church in Monrovia, Liberia, with fifty members and erected a church building. He was reappointed in 1940 to the Africa Conferences, namely, Liberia, East Gold Coast, West Gold Coast, and Nigeria. He died in New York City, on February 27, 1941, at Harlem Hospital. He was struck by an automobile at 135th St. and Seventh Avenue. Bishop Brown was funeralized from the Mother A. M. E. Zion Church and buried at the Mother Zion Cemetery, Cypress Hills, Brooklyn, N. Y.

Bishop J. W. Brown
ELECTED 1936-DIED 1941

49. BISHOP JAMES WALTER BROWN

Born: July 19, 1872, in Elizabeth City, North Carolina, to Jessie R. and Araminta (Griffin) Brown. **Education:** Received early training in his hometown. Graduated from Shaw University with an A.B. degree in 1893 and from Lincoln University, Pennsylvania, with an M. A. and an S. T. B. degree in 1903. **Family:** Married in 1903 to Martha Hill who died in 1928; and in 1930 to Andrades Lindsay. **Died:** On Feb. 27, 1941, after being struck by a car while crossing a street near Mother Zion Church in New York City. Buried in the Mother Zion Cemetery, Cypress Hills, Brooklyn, N.Y., following services at the church.

50. BISHOP WALTER WILLIAM SLADE

WALTER WILLIAM SLADE was born in Newton, North Carolina, July 4, 1875, to the Rev. and Mrs. Mayfield Slade. His father was one of the outstanding pioneers in the Western North Carolina and Blue Ridge Conferences of the A. M. E. Zion Church. Slade joined the Blue Ridge Conference and was ordained a deacon at the age of twenty-one on November 10, 1896. He was ordained an elder two years later on November 13, 1898. Rev. Slade finished Livingstone College in 1901.

Between 1896 and 1900 this extraordinarily creative young preacher was responsible for building twelve churches in the Blue Ridge Conference. He was pastor of the Lebaum Circuit, Greenville, Tennessee, during the time that his father was the presiding elder of the Greenville District in the Blue Ridge Conference. He transferred to the Central and West Central North Carolina Conferences and was pastor of several churches. He also served as a presiding elder for almost twenty years.

In 1928, Rev. Slade was elected director of the Bureau of Evangelism. In 1932, Rev. Slade was sent to Wesley Center Church, Pittsburgh, Pennsylvania, where he served the pastorate and the Bureau until 1936. He was elected Financial Secretary of the denomination in 1940, and on May 14, 1944, he was consecrated the 50th Bishop of the church at the 32nd General Conference held in Detroit, Michigan.

Bishop Slade was an ardent evangelistic preacher, financier, and magnetic, congenial leader. His episcopal labors were confined principally to North and South Carolina. He also nurtured Clinton Junior College, Rock Hill, South Carolina. He retired at the 1960 General Conference and died on May 19, 1963. He was buried in Charlotte, North Carolina, after services at Grace Church in that city.

Rev. Slade married Ms. Mildred Burgen who died in 1927. They had several children, two of whom, Mayfield and Beatrice Slade, preceded him in death. In 1931, he married Mrs. Sallie Mae (Watson) Blake, a mother of three minor children, namely, Louella Mae, Cottrell and Caesar. Rev. and Mrs. Slade reared them with their own child, Jean Slade Riddick. ("Walter William Slade," *Star of Zion*, June 6, 1963, pp. 4-5)

Bishop W.W.Slade
ELECTED 1944-DIED 1963

50. BISHOP WALTER WILLIAM SLADE

Born: On July 4, 1875, in Newton, North Carolina, to Rev. and Mrs. Mayfield Slade. **Education:** Graduated from Livingstone College in 1901. **Family:** Married twice — to Ms. Mildred Burgen who died in 1927, and in 1931, to Mrs. Sallie Mae (Watson) Blake. He had several children by his first wife, two of whom, Mayfield and Beatrice Slade, preceded him in death. He had one child, Jean Slade Riddick, with his second wife. **Died:** May 19, 1963, in Charlotte, North Carolina. Buried there following services at Grace Church.

African Methodist Episcopal Zion Church
51. BISHOP BUFORD FRANKLIN GORDON

BUFORD FRANKLIN GORDON was born in Pulaski, Tennesee, on August 24, 1893, to Aaron Van and Matilda (Jackson) Gordon. He received his initial training at home then attended Fisk University where he earned the A.B. degree in 1917. He studied at Yale University from 1917-18, and in 1920, he received his B.D. degree from the University of Chicago. Gordon entered the ministry in 1917 and joined the Michigan Conference on June 24, 1920. He was ordained a deacon three days later on June 27, 1920 and an elder on June 18, 1922.

Rev. Gordon was pastor in Branford, Connecticut, 1917-18; First Church, South Bend, Indiana, 1920-24; and John Wesley, Akron, Ohio, 1925-31. He was responsible for building churches in South Bend and in Akron. He also attended Officers Training School during World War I, 1918-19. (Fleming & Burckel 1950, p. 218)

In 1931, Rev. Gordon was elected editor of Church School Literature, a position he held until he was consecrated a bishop on May 14, 1944.

Bishop Gordon directed an intensely constructive program for Lomax-Hannon Junior College, Greenville, Alabama. He was an author, educator, intellectual leader, and a noble family man. He died in Charlotte, North Carolina, on January 19, 1952. He was buried in that city, following services from Little Rock Church. His home church, Gethsemane, was too small for the service to be held there.

In 1920, Rev. Gordon married Thelma Ruth Pierce. They had five children — Buford, Jr.; Yvonne A.; Geraldine G.; Charles R., and Thelma R. Gordon (Fleming & Burckel 1950, p. 218).

Bishop B.F. Gordon
ELECTED 1944-DIED 1952

51. BISHOP BUFORD FRANKLIN GORDON

Born: August 24, 1893, in Pulaski, Tennessee, to Aaron Van and Matilda (Jackson) Gordon. **Education:** Received an A.B. degree from Fisk University in 1917; studied at Yale University, 1917-18; received B.D. degree from the University of Chicago, 1920. **Major Publications:** *The Pastor and People*, 1930; *Teaching for Abundant Living,* 1936. **Family:** Married Thelma Ruth Pierce in 1920. Five children—Buford, ,Jr.; Yvonne A.; Geraldine G.; Charles R.; and Thelma R. **Died:** January 19, 1951, in Charlotte, North Carolina. Buried there following services at Little Rock A. M. E. Zion Church, then located at 7th and Myers Street.

African Methodist Episcopal Zion Church
52. BISHOP FRANK WESLEY ALSTORK

FRANK WESLEY ALSTORK, one of seven children, was born in Coatopa, Alabama, June 16, 1885, to Rev. and Mrs. Alonzo Gary and Eliza Alstork (*J. Negro Hist.* [1948]: 502-3). His uncle, Rev. John Wesley Alstork, became Zion's 28th Bishop in 1900. Frank Alstork first joined Big Zion Church, Mobile, Alabama and then, Little Hope Chapel, Mobile, where he was licensed to preach at the age of twenty. He was ordained a deacon on December 1, 1907 and an elder on November 28, 1909.

He joined the West Alabama Conference and completed his studies at Talladega College, Alabama, while holding his first pastoral appointment at Talladega. He then became the pastor of Midland City, Hurtsboro, Alabama; St. Mark, St. Louis, Missouri; and Smith Memorial, DuQuoin, Illinois. After serving as presiding elder in the Missouri Conference, he became pastor of Metropolitan, Birmingham, Alabama; Union Wesley, Washington, D.C.; and Big Wesley, Philadelphia, Pennsylvania; from which pulpit he was elected to the episcopacy and consecrated a bishop on May 14, 1944. The General Conference assigned him to the 10th District in 1944 and to the 8th District in 1948.

Bishop Alstork was deeply committed to higher education. He was an indefatigable member of the Boards of Trustees of Lomax-Hannon Junior College, Greenville, Alabama; Dinwiddie Normal and Industrial School, Dinwiddie, Virginia; and of Livingstone College, Salisbury, North Carolina.

Rev. Alstork married Willie Gertrude Kemp of Tuskegee, Alabama in 1914. (*J. Negro Hist.* [1948], pp. 502-3). Mrs. Alstork served as missionary supervisor of the conferences over which the bishop presided. She later served as general treasurer of the Woman's Home and Foreign (later Overseas) Missionary Society from 1954-63. She was appointed by the Board of Bishops to complete the unexpired term of the general secretary, Rev. Dr. F. Claude Spurgeon, in August, 1959 until the General Conference in 1960. Mrs. Alstork was the first woman to head a general department in the A. M. E. Zion Church other than the WH&OM Society.

Bishop Alstork died on July 5, 1948 as a result of an auto accident that occurred in Virginia while he was performing episcopal duties there. Last rites were conducted at Galbraith A. M. E. Zion Church, located at 6th and L Streets, N.W., Washington, D. C., and burial was in Lincoln Cemetery.

Bishop F.W. Alstork
ELECTED 1944-DIED 1948

52. BISHOP FRANK WESLEY ALSTORK

Born: Coatopa, Alabama, June 16, 1885, to Rev. and Mrs. Alonzo Gary and Eliza Alstork. He was one of seven children and was the nephew of Rev. (later Bishop) John Wesley Alstork. **Education:** Graduated from Talledega College, Talledega, Alabama. **Family:** In 1914, he married Willie Gertrude Kemp of Tuskegee, Alabama. **Died:** July 4, 1948, in Washington, D. C., as a result of an auto accident in Virginia. Buried in Lincoln Cemetery in Washington, D. C., after services at Galbraith A. M. E. Zion Church.

53. BISHOP EDGAR BENTON WATSON

EDGAR BENTON WATSON was born in Chatham County, North Carolina., on February 7, 1874, to Louis and Nanie (Rieves) Watson (Yenser 1933, p. 447). Watson was admitted to the Central North Carolina Conference in 1905 and became a charter member of the West Central North Carolina Conference when it was organized in 1910. He was ordained a deacon on November 24, 1905 and an elder on November 21, 1909. He was the pastor of the following churches: Mt. Pleasant Circuit; Norwood Station; Zion Hill, Concord; Trinity, Greensboro; all in North Carolina; Metropolitan, Birmingham, Alabama; Oak Street, Petersburg; Hood Temple, Richmond; and Metropolitan, Norfolk; all in Virginia.

Rev. Watson married Margaret Morrow on June 22, 1911. They had one child, Edgar Morris Watson. After Mrs. Morrow's death, Rev. Watson married Mary Jane Hedgepath.

Rev. Watson graduated from Livingstone College in 1911 and earned the B.D. degree from Hood Theological Seminary in 1915.

Rev. Watson was consecrated a bishop on May 14, 1944 and was assigned to the Texas and Oklahoma home mission conferences and to the Liberia, East Ghana, West Ghana, and Nigeria Conferences in West Africa. He and his wife, Mary Jane (Hedgepath) Watson, spent four productive years in Africa. During his administration two schools were taken over by the church — Zion College of West Africa at Angola and Aggrey Memorial College of Cape Coast. Bishop Watson was the ninth bishop assigned by Zion to Africa and the third to reside there. In 1948 he was assigned to the Central North Carolina, Pee Dee, and East Tennessee and Virginia Conferences.

He died suddenly on January 17, 1951. He was buried in Greensboro, North Carolina, following last rites at Trinity A. M. E. Zion Church in that city.

Bishop E.B. Watson
ELECTED 1944-DIED 1951

53. BISHOP EDGAR BENTON WATSON

Born: In Chatham County, North Carolina, on February 7, 1874, to Louis and Nanie (Rieves) Watson. **Education:** Attended North Carolina A&T, Greensboro, North Carolina, graduated from Livingstone College in 1911. Earned B.D. degree from Hood Theological Seminary in 1915. **Family:** On June 22, 1911, married Margaret Morrow. One child — Edgar Morris. After his first wife died, he married Mary Jane Hedgepath. **Died:** January 17, 1951. Buried in Greensboro, North Carolina, after last rites at Trinity A. M. E. Zion Church in that city.

54. BISHOP JAMES CLAIR TAYLOR

JAMES CLAIR TAYLOR was born in Cambridge, Massachusetts, on May 3, 1893, to James Madison and Harriette Ann Taylor (Bradley 1970, pp. 436-37). He was the oldest of four children. His mother was a former school teacher. His father, a Baptist minister, died when Taylor was six. Taylor completed the elementary and high school programs in Cambridge and later studied at Bates College, Lewiston, Maine; Chicago Theological Seminary; and Union Theological Seminary, New York City.

Taylor was converted at fifteen and entered the ministry through his native New England Conference. His first pastorate was in Meriden, Connecticut. He also served churches in Goldsboro; Moore's Chapel, Salisbury; and St. John's, Rutherfordton, all in North Carolina; Memorial, Rochester, New York; Wesley Union, Harrisburg, Pennsylvania; and First Church, Paterson, New Jersey. He was ordained a deacon on June 16, 1918, and an elder on June 20, 1920.

Rev. Taylor married Alma Jackson in 1912. They had one son, Durward St. Clair Taylor. (Bradley 1970, p. 437) After the death of his first wife, he married Anne Pate of Goldsboro, North Carolina.

In 1936, Rev. Taylor was elected editor of the *A. M. E. Zion Quarterly Review*, a position he held for twelve years until he was elected to the bishopric. In 1940, Rev. Taylor was a member of the denomination's subcommittee on rituals and part of a group preparing a hymnal for the church. He was consecrated the 54th Bishop on May 16, 1948.

During his episcopacy he worked energetically to develop the church in Alabama and Mississippi and in the West Tennessee and Mississippi Conference. He died quite suddenly on July 23, 1954, in Birmingham, Alabama. He was buried in Montgomery, Alabama, following funeral services at Old Ship A. M. E. Zion Church in Montgomery.

Bishop J.C. Taylor
ELECTED 1948-DIED 1954

54. BISHOP JAMES CLAIR TAYLOR

Born: On May 3, 1893, in Cambridge, Massachusetts, to James Madison and Harriette Ann Taylor. **Education:** Graduated from the elementary and high school programs in Cambridge; studied at Bates College, Lewiston, Maine; Chicago Theological Seminary; and Union Theological Seminary, New York City. **Family:** Married Miss Alma Jackson of Boston in 1912. One son—Durward St. Clair Taylor. After death of first wife, married Miss Anne Pate of Goldsboro, North Carolina. **Died:** July 23, 1954, in Birmingham, Alabama. Buried in Montgomery, Alabama, following funeral services at Old Ship A. M. E. Zion Church.

55. BISHOP RAYMOND LUTHER JONES

RAYMOND LUTHER JONES was born in Chattanooga, Tennessee, on April 7, 1900, to Rev. B. James and Callie Victoria (Bradford) Jones (Bradley 1970, p. 437). He was Zion's first bishop born in the twentieth century. This son of a faithful A. M. E. Zion minister of the Tennessee Conference received his elementary and normal training in Knoxville, Tennessee. He earned the A.B. degree from Livingstone College and the B.D. degree from Hood Theological Seminary. He was converted in 1906 at Loguen Temple, Knoxville and began to think seriously of the ministry.

At the age of seventeen, he preached his trial sermon in Loguen Temple and joined the Tennessee Conference soon afterwards. He was a successful pastor at Second Creek Circuit near Salisbury; Marable Memorial, Kannapolis; and Grace Church, Charlotte, all in North Carolina; St. Paul, Johnson City, Tennessee; Hopkins Chapel, Asheville, North Carolina; and Broadway Temple, Louisville, Kentucky.

Rev. Jones married Carrie L. Smith in 1924. She died in 1955. A year later, he married Mabel L. Miller. He had four children: three by his first wife, Raymond Luther Jones who died in infancy; Suzette Victoria Jones; and Raymona L. Jones (who served for a time as his missionary supervisor). He had one daughter, Millicent Luthia Jones, by his second wife (*A. M. E. Zion Quart. Rev. 84* [1971]: 95).

Rev. Jones was consecrated the 55th Bishop of the A. M. E. Zion Church, May 16, 1948, while serving as the host pastor for the 33rd General Conference held at Broadway Temple A.M. E. Zion Church. Some of the conferences over which he presided as bishop were British Guiana (now called Guyana), the Virgin Islands, Texas, Oklahoma, East Tennessee-Virginia, Western North Carolina, Blue Ridge, and Philadelphia-Baltimore. During 1964-68, with the help of the Church Extension Department, he made a substantial reinforcement to Zion's presence in West Texas and Oklahoma by purchasing three major churches and building up a number of small ones. In 1962, Bishop Jones introduced to Zion the daily meditation booklet *The Strength of My Life*. In his last report to the General Conference, Bishop Jones presented five thousand dollars, which was raised by the Western North Carolina Conference, to Bishop W. A. Hilliard for a special project in Ghana, West Africa.

He died shortly after midnight of May 12, 1972 on the last day of the 1972 General Conference in Mobile, Alabama. Funeral services were held in the Varick Auditorium at Livingstone College, Salisbury, North Carolina, instead of his home church, Moore's Chapel A. M. E. Zion Church. He was buried in Salisbury, North Carolina.

Bishop R.L. Jones
ELECTED 1948-DIED 1972

55. BISHOP RAYMOND LUTHER JONES

Born: In Chattanooga, Tennessee, on April 7, 1900, to Rev. B. James and Callie Victoria (Bradford) Jones. **Education:** Received his elementary and normal training in Knoxville, Tennessee. Earned A.B. degree from Livingstone College and the B.D. degree from Hood Theological Seminary. **Family:** Married Carrie L. Smith in 1924. After she died, he married Mabel L. Miller. He had four children. Three by his first wife: Raymond Luther Jones who died in infancy; Suzette Victoria Jones; and Raymona L. Jones, who served for a time as his missionary supervisor. Millicent Luthia Jones was a daughter from his second marriage. **Died:** On May 12, 1972, on the final day of the 1972 General Conference. Buried in Salisbury, North Carolina, following funeral services at Varick Auditorium in Livingstone College.

56. BISHOP HAMPTON THOMAS MEDFORD

HAMPTON THOMAS MEDFORD was born January 29, 1885, in Marion, North Carolina, to Charles G. L. and Cecilia Medford. His public school education was delayed until he was 14 years old because of poverty (Bradley 1970, p. 438). He obtained his higher education at Livingstone College, where he earned his first degree in 1912. He obtained his B.D. degree from Hood Theological Seminary in 1915.

He joined the Western North Carolina Conference in 1906 and was ordained a deacon November 17, 1907. He was ordained an elder November 12, 1910. He was pastor of Cherryville Circuit; China Grove; and Cleveland Circuit; Moore's Chapel, Salisbury; and Grace Chapel, Charlotte; all in North Carolina; Jacob Street Tabernacle, Louisville, Kentucky; Loguen Temple, Knoxville, Tennessee; and John Wesley, Washington, D.C. In 1928, he was elected secretary-treasurer of the Department of Foreign Missions and editor of the *Missionary Seer*. He served in this capacity and as editor of the *Missionary Seer* for twenty years, from 1928-48, until he was elected a bishop. He was consecrated the 56th Bishop on May 16, 1948 in Louisville, Kentucky.

He was a resident bishop in Africa from 1948-52. His wife, Mary Elizabeth Camp Medford, was in failing health when the bishop was elected and assigned to West Africa. She requested the Foreign Mission Board to send their daughter, Mrs. Cordella Medford-Fauntleroy to Africa with the bishop when he visited the mission work in the Republic of Liberia, the former Gold Coast (now Ghana), and Nigeria. Mrs. Fauntleroy returned from this journey with her father an ill person. Within six weeks of her return she passed away. Soon afterwards, her mother, Mrs. Missouri Elizabeth Camp Medford also "folded her tent like the Arabs, and silently stole away," on September 30, 1951. (Medford, *This Is My Life: From Rags to Riches*, p. 34)

During his episcopacy, he presided over the Liberia, East and West Gold Coast, and the Nigeria Conferences of West Africa and the North Carolina, Tennessee, and Virginia Conferences in the United States.Bishop Medford served with distinction until his retirement in 1960. He was an active member of the World Methodist Conference, the National Council of Churches of Christ, U. S. A., and the World Council of Churches. He also served on the Commission for Publication of the A. M. E. Zion Hymnal.

Four children were born to his first marriage to Missouri Elizabeth Camp Medford, namely, Alma, Booker T., Cordella, and Thomas A. of Washington, D. C. who still survives. (Fleming & Burckel 1950, p. 370) Following the death of his first wife of forty years, the bishop married Mrs. Savannah Jones of Winston-Salem, North Carolina, on May 6, 1952, the evening before the opening of the 1952 session of General Conference at First A. M. E. Zion Church, Brooklyn, New York. Bishop Medford died on September 14, 1964, in Washington, D.C. Funeral services were held at his former pastorate, John Wesley A. M. E. Zion Church (the National Church of Zion Methodism), in Washington, D. C. He is buried in Lincoln Memorial Cemetery, Suitland, Maryland.

Bishop H.T. Medford
ELECTED 1948-DIED 1964

56. BISHOP HAMPTON THOMAS MEDFORD

Born: January 29, 1885, in Marion, North Carolina, to Charles G. L. and Cecilia Medford. Education: His public school education was delayed until he was fourteen, because of poverty. He received his first degree from Livingstone College in 1912 and his B. D. from Hood Theological Seminary in 1915. **Publications:** *The Negro's Part in Methodism*, 1931; *Zion Methodism Abroad*, 1937; *This Is My Life: From Rags to Riches*, 1960. **Family**: Married Missouri Elizabeth Camp in 1904. She died in 1951. They had four children—Alma, Booker T., Cordella, and Thomas A. Medford. Thomas A. of Washington, D. C., survives. On May 6, 1952, he married Mrs. Savannah Jones of Winston-Salem, North Carolina. **Died:** September 14, 1964. Funeral services were held at John Wesley, Washington, D. C., followed by burial in Lincoln Memorial Cemetery, in Suitland, Maryland.

57. BISHOP HERBERT BELL SHAW

HERBERT BELL SHAW was born in Wilmington, North Carolina, on February 9, 1908 to John Henry and Lummie V. Shaw (Bradley 1970, p. 442). He was named for the Rev. Herbert Bell, a pioneer Zion preacher in the Cape Fear Conference. He studied at Fisk University and the Howard University School of Religion.

He entered the ministry through the Cape Fear Conference in November, 1927. He afterwards transferred to the Philadelphia and Baltimore Conference, where he served as associate pastor of Union Wesley Church in Washington, D.C. He was ordained a deacon in April, 1928 and an elder on November 16, 1930.

Rev. Shaw returned to the Cape Fear Conference and served as pastor from 1929 to 1937 at Bowen's Chapel; St. Andrews; and Price Memorial, all in North Carolina. He was presiding elder of the Wilmington District from 1937-43. He served the denomination as Secretary-Treasurer of the Department of Home Missions, Pension and Ministerial Relief from 1943-52. In this capacity he helped to restructure the Brotherhood Pension Service. He was elected bishop from this office in May, 1952 at the 34th General Conference meeting in Brooklyn, New York.

Bishop Shaw organized the Jamaica, West Indies and England Conferences and reactivated the Bahama Islands Conference.

He was chairperson of the National Conference of Black Churchmen Board of Directors and was vice president of the World Methodist Conference. He was a member of the General Commission of the Army and Navy Chaplains; second vice president of the National Council of Churches of Christ in the U.S.A.; member of the Presidium of the World Methodist Council, 1971-76; the World Council of Churches; 4-H Club of America Board of Directors; Community Boys Club of America, Wilmington, North Carolina; Omega Psi Phi Fraternity; Chair of Curriculum Committee of Department of Education; Chair, Livingstone College Board of Trustees, Salisbury, North Carolina; Clinton Junior College Board of Trustees, Rock Hill, South Carolina; Lomax Hannon College Board of Trustees, Greenville, Alabama, among others. He was elected Grand Master of Prince Hall Masons of North Carolina in October, 1974.

He was married to M. Ardelle Stokes and was father of Rev. John Herbert Shaw and Marie Bell Barnhill and grandfather of five. Bishop Shaw died January 3, 1980 at the Board of Bishops meeting in Indianapolis, Indiana. Funeral services were held at Mother Zion Church, New York on January 7, 1980 and at St Luke Church, Wilmington, North Carolina, on January 9, 1980. He is entombed in a mausoleum in Wilmington.

Bishop H.B. Shaw
ELECTED 1952-DIED 1980

57. BISHOP HERBERT BELL SHAW

Born: February 9, 1908 in Wilmington, North Carolina, to John Henry and Lummie Virginia Hodges Shaw. **Education:** He attended the public schools of Wilmington and St. Emma's Preparatory School, Rock Castle, Virginia. He received his college education at Fisk University and a Masters degree from the Howard University School of Religion. **Family:** He married M. Ardelle Shaw in 1931. They were the parents of the Rev. John Herbert Shaw and Maria Shaw Barnhill and grandparents of five children. **Died:** On January 3, 1980 in Indianapolis, Indiana at the Board of Bishops Winter meeting. Funeral services were held at Mother A. M. E. Zion in New York and at St. Luke in Wilmington, North Carolina. Entombed in Wilmington, North Carolina.

African Methodist Episcopal Zion Church
58. BISHOP STEPHEN GILL SPOTTSWOOD

STEPHEN GILL SPOTTSWOOD was born July 18, 1897 in Boston, Massachusetts, the only child of Abraham Lincoln and Mary Elizabeth Gray Spottswood. He earned a B.A. degree in 1917 from Albright College and a Th.B. from Gordon Divinity School in 1919. He did graduate study at Yale University. Livingstone College awarded him an honorary D.D. in 1939.

He entered the traveling ministry through the New England Conference in 1919 and was appointed to West Newton and Lowell, Massachusetts. He was ordained a deacon by Bishop W. L. Lee on February 5, 1920 and an elder by Bishop George W. Clinton on June 20, 1920.

He was a pastor for thirty-four years, serving churches in Portland, Maine; West Newton and Lowell, Massachusetts; New Haven, Connecticut; Jones Tabernacle, Indianapolis, Indiana; Goler Memorial, Winston-Salem, North Carolina; St. Luke, Buffalo, New York; and John Wesley, Washington, D.C., from which he was elected and consecrated the 58th Bishop on May 18, 1952 at the General Conference in Brooklyn, New York.

As bishop he presided over the South Mississippi, West Tennessee and Mississippi, Oklahoma, Texas, Arkansas, and North Arkansas Conferences; the Ohio, Michigan, Allegheny, and Indiana Conferences; the Colorado, New England, Virgin Islands, and South American Conferences; and Philadelphia-Baltimore and Central North Carolina Conferences. He also served the Church as chairperson of the Board of Finance, now known as the Connectional Budget Board, and as a trustee of Livingstone College.

A civil rights activist, Spottswood joined the NAACP in 1919 and served successively on the branch executive committee of the organization in every city where he was a pastor. He was president of the District of Columbia NAACP, a member of the NAACP National Board of Directors from 1955 and its chairman from April 10, 1961 until his death in December, 1974.

Bishop Spottswood served twenty years in the episcopacy before he was retired in May, 1972. He was married to Viola Estelle Booker, who died October 24, 1953. They were the parents of Virginia Ruth Simon, the Rev. Stephen Paul Spottswood, Constance Booker Miller, Viola Stephanie Cabaniss, and Alleyne Hankerson Hall; grandparents of fourteen; and great grandparents of four. He later married Mrs. Mattie Brownita Johnson Elliott on December 15, 1969.

Bishop Spottswood died December 1, 1974 and was funeralized at the National Church of Zion Methodism, John Wesley, Washington, D.C., on December 6. He is buried in Lincoln Memorial Cemetery, Suitland, Maryland. Mrs. Mattie Spottswood died in September, 1995 and was funeralized at John Wesley Church, Washington, D. C., on October 2, 1995.

Bishop S.G. Spotswood
ELECTED 1952-DIED 1974

58. BISHOP STEPHEN GILL SPOTTSWOOD

Born: July 16, 1897, the only child of Abraham Lincoln and Mary Elizabeth Gray Spottswood, in Boston, Massachusetts. **Education:** He earned a B.A. degree from Albright College in 1917 and a Th. B. degree from Gordon Divinity School in 1919. He took postgraduate courses at Yale University. **Family:** He married Viola Estelle Booker, June 10, 1919. She died on October 24, 1953. They had five children: Virginia Ruth Simon, Rev. Stephen Paul Spottswood, Constance Booker Miller, Viola Stephanie Cabaniss, and Alleyne Hankerson Hall, and fourteen grandchildren. On December 15, 1969, he was married to Mrs. Mattie Brownita Johnson Elliott. **Died:** He died on December 1, 1974. Funeral services were held at John Wesley A. M. E. Zion Church, the National Church of Zion Methodism, in Washington, D. C. He is buried in Lincoln Memorial Cemetery, Suitland, Maryland.

59. BISHOP WILLIAM ANDREW STEWART

WILLIAM ANDREW STEWART was born August 20, 1890 to Eli and Allie Stewart (Bradley 1970, p. 442) in Burntcorn, Alabama. He was educated at Phelps Hall Training School and Tuskegee Institute. He earned his A.B. from Livingstone College and B.D. from Hood Theological Seminary. He also undertook studies at Howard University when he was a pastor in Washington, D. C. at the Union Wesley A. M. E. Zion Church.

He entered the ministry through the South Alabama Conference in 1915. He was ordained a deacon November 17, 1917 and later transferred to the Western North Carolina Conference. He was ordained an elder November 16, 1919. He taught school for several years after his completion of studies at Tuskegee and during his early years in the ministry.

He was pastor of Pineapple Circuit, River Falls, Alabama; People's Choice, Winston-Salem, Center Street, Statesville, and Hill Street (Varick) Chapel, Asheville, all in North Carolina; Loguen Temple, Knoxville, Tennessee; Old Ship, Montgomery, Alabama; and Union Wesley, Washington, D.C., where he built a large, impressive church, located at 23rd and L Streets, N.W. and from which he was elected to the episcopacy. He was consecrated the 59th Bishop on May 18, 1952, at the General Conference held in Brooklyn, New York at First A. M. E. Zion Church.

Bishop Stewart presided over the California, Oregon-Washington, the Southwest Rocky Mountain, and on the death of Bishop J. W. Martin, the Ohio, Cape Fear and Michigan Conferences in his first quadrennium; the Alabama, Cahaba, South Alabama, Central Alabama, and North Alabama Conferences; the Blue Ridge, North Carolina, Albemarle, Tennessee and Virginia Conferences; and the Central North Carolina Conferences. He was retired by the General Conference in 1972. (*Official Journal, 39th Quad. Sess. Gen. Conf.* [1972])

Bishop and Mrs. Stewart were hosts to the 13th Quadrennial Missionary Convention, August 6-12, 1955, at First Church, Los Angeles, California. He represented the A. M. E. Zion denomination at the independence ceremonies of Ghana on March 6, 1957. He served as chairperson of the Board of Publications from 1964-72, during the period when the new publishing house in Charlotte was built.

He was married to the former Sula Ruby Cunningham, a union that produced seven children. He passed away on August 5, 1984 and was funeralized from Union Wesley A. M. E. Zion Church, Washington, D. C., followed by burial at Lincoln Memorial Cemetery, Suitland, Maryland.

Bishop W.A. Stewart
ELECTED 1952-DIED 1984

59. BISHOP WILLIAM ANDREW STEWART

Born: August 20, 1890 in Burntcorn, Alabama, to Eli and Allie Stewart. **Education:** A graduate of Phelps Hall Training School and Tuskegee Institute. He earned his A. B. degree from Livingstone College and his B. D. degree from Hood Theological Seminary. **Family:** He was married to Sula Ruby Cunningham. They were the parents of Eli, Edward, William Andrew, Jr., Louise S. Carpenter, Raymond Calvin, Lynwood Eliott, and Ruby Clarice Romao. **Died:** He died on August 5, 1984. Funeral services were held at Union Wesley A. M. E. Zion Church followed by burial in Lincoln Memorial Cemetery, Suitland, Maryland.

60. BISHOP DANIEL CARLTON POPE

DANIEL CARLTON POPE was born to Mr. and Mrs. Americus Pope in Theodore, Mobile County, Alabama in 1887 . He was educated in the public schools of Mobile County and Tuskegee Institute. He earned his A.B. and B.D. degrees from Lincoln University in Pennsylvania.

He entered the traveling ministry through the Alabama Conference. He was ordained a deacon November 30, 1913 and an elder November 28, 1915. His first pastorate was Butler Chapel, Tuskegee, Alabama. Accompanied by his wife, Louise Hudson Pope, he served in Liberia from 1923-30. During this period, he worked with Bishop William Matthews in establishing the Annie Blackwell Memorial School at Mt. Coffee, Liberia, in West Africa, an ambitious undertaking comprising the erection of six buildings. During his stay in Liberia, he and his wife lost their first son. Rev. Pope returned to the U. S. in 1930 because of his wife's failing health. She died ten years later in November, 1940.

On his return to America, he was pastor of Wesley Union, Harrisburg, Pennsylvania; Galbraith, Washington, D.C.; Trinity, Southern Pines, North Carolina; and Evans Metropolitan, Fayetteville, North Carolina.

He was elected Secretary of Foreign Missions in 1948, a post he held until 1952, when he was elected to the episcopacy. He was consecrated the 60th Bishop on May 18, 1952 at the General Conference held in Brooklyn, New York. He was assigned as Resident Bishop of Africa and spent the next eight years in Liberia, Ghana, and Nigeria in West Africa. From 1960-64, he presided over the Georgia, South Georgia, South Carolina, and the East Tennessee-Virginia Conferences.

Bishop Pope passed away March 4, 1964, at the Bristol Memorial Hospital, Bristol, Tennessee. Funeral services were held on March 10, 1964, at Hood Memorial A. M. E. Zion Church, Bristol, Tennessee. He is buried in Warrenton, Georgia, beside his wife, Louise Hudson Pope. He was survived by a daughter, Mrs. Anna Mary Moore, and a son, Americus H. Pope. ("Funeral Service for the Late Bishop Daniel Carlton Pope, 1887-1964")

Bishop D.C. Pope
ELECTED 1952-DIED 1964

60. BISHOP DANIEL CARLTON POPE

Born: He was born in Theodore, Mobile County, Alabama, in 1887, to Mr. and Mrs. Americus Pope. **Education:** He was educated in the public schools of Mobile County and Tuskegee Institute. He earned his A. B. and B. D. degrees from Lincoln University in Pennsylvania. **Family:** He was married to Louisa Hudson Pope.They lost a son while serving as missionaries in Africa. His wife died in November, 1940. They had two other children: Anna Mary Moore and Americus H. Pope. **Died:** On March 4, 1964 in Bristol, Tennessee, where funeral services were held. He was buried in Warrenton, Georgia, beside his wife.

61. BISHOP CHARLES EWBANK TUCKER

CHARLES EWBANK TUCKER was born January 12, 1896 in Baltimore, Maryland to the Rev. William A. and Elivia Clark Tucker (Bradley 1970, p. 461). Reverend Tucker was a member of the English Baptist Union in Jamaica, W. I. Charles Tucker was educated at Beckford and Smith's College, Jamaica, West Indies, and was graduated in 1913. He then studied at Lincoln University, Pennsylvania, in 1917. He completed graduate work at Temple University in 1919 and then read law under the Hon. Charles Gogg at Point Pleasant, Virginia. He began practicing criminal law in Louisville, Kentucky in 1929.

Charles Tucker was received on credentials by the Philadelphia-Baltimore Conference in 1915. He was ordained an elder July 2, 1916. He was pastor of Middletown; Delta; and Salem, Williamsport, all in Pennsylvania; Hilliard Chapel, Montgomery, Alabama; Sharon Chapel, Sharon, Mississippi; Mt. Zion, Augusta, Georgia; Cornish Temple, Key West, Florida; and Stoner Memorial, Louisville, Kentucky.

He served as presiding elder of the Philadelphia-Baltimore, Kentucky, and Indiana Conferences. He was elected to the office of bishop from the presiding elder-ship of the Indianapolis District of the Indiana Conference. He was consecrated the 61st Bishop on May 13, 1956, in Pittsburgh, Pennsylvania, at the 35th General Conference, held at Wesley Center A. M. E. Zion Church.

Bishop Tucker presided over the Georgia, South Georgia, West Tennessee-Mississippi, and South Mississippi Conferences, and on the death of Bishop Cecil C. Coleman, he presided over the Louisiana, Oklahoma, Arkansas, and North Arkansas Conferences; and the Kentucky, West Alabama, Indiana, and the Blue Ridge Conferences. By garnering public support, Bishop and Mrs. Tucker distributed money, food, and clothing to alleviate the suffering of displaced black sharecroppers in the Mississippi Delta, many of whom were victims of agricultural mechanization and political backlash during the Civil Rights Movement in the late 1960s. (*Official Journals, 36th-39th Quad. Sess. Gen. Conf.*)

Bishop Tucker was married to the Rev. Amelia Moore Tucker. They had a daughter and a son: Bernice and Neville. Bishop Tucker spent sixteen active years in the episcopacy before he was retired at the 39th General Conference meeting in Mobile, Alabama, in 1972. He passed away December 25, 1975. Funeral rites were held at Broadway Temple A. M. E. Zion Church, Louisville, Kentucky. He was cremated and interred in Cave Hill, Louisville Cemetery, Kentucky.

Bishop C.E. Tucker
ELECTED 1956-DIED 1975

61. BISHOP CHARLES EWBANK TUCKER

Born: January 12, 1896 in Baltimore, Maryland, to the Rev. William and Elivia Clark Tucker. **Education:** He graduated from Beckford and Smith's College, Jamaica, W. I. in 1913. He completed Lincoln University, Pennsylvania in 1917. He read law under the Honorable Charles Goff in Pt. Pleasant, Virginia and started practicing law in Louisville, Kentucky in 1929. **Family:** He was married to the Rev. Amelia Moore Tucker. They had one daughter, Bernice, and one son, Neville. **Died:** He died December 25, 1975. After funeral services in Broadway Temple A. M. E. Zion Church, Louisville, Kentucky, Bishop Tucker was cremated and interred in Cave Hill, Louisville Cemetery, Louisville, Kentucky.

62. BISHOP JOSEPH DIXON CAUTHEN

JOSEPH DIXON CAUTHEN was born February 21, 1887 in Kershaw, South Carolina. He attended Lancaster Normal and Industrial School, Lancaster, South Carolina and Clinton Junior College, Rock Hill, South Carolina. He earned his A.B. degree from Livingstone College and B.D. from Hood Theological Seminary.

He entered the ministry through the South Carolina Conference in 1912. He was ordained a deacon November 26, 1916, in his home conference and was ordained an elder November 14, 1920, in the Western North Carolina Conference.

His pastorates included: Gethsemane, Charlotte, North Carolina; State Street, Mobile, Alabama; Varick Chapel, Philadelphia; and Metropolitan, Norfolk, Virginia. He was consecrated the 62nd Bishop on May 13, 1956 at the 35th Session of General Conference held in Wesley Center Church, Pittsburgh, Pennsylvania.

As bishop he presided over the Southwest Rocky Mountain, California, Oregon-Washington, South Carolina, Pee Dee, and Virginia Conferences.

Bishop and Mrs. Joseph D. Cauthen were hosts to the 15th Quadrennial Missionary Convention in August, 1963 at Washington-Metropolitan Church, St. Louis, Missouri. The bishop was a commissioner to the tri-council of bishops of the A. M. E., C. M. E., and A. M. E. Zion Churches meeting to discuss organic union of the three churches in 1965, 1967, and 1969.

In 1921, he married the former Ruth Smith from Concord, North Carolina, who passed away in 1929, shortly after the birth of their son, Joseph D., who would earn an M. D. from Howard University. In 1940, he married the former Georgia Little of Mobile, Alabama. This union produced one daughter, Muriel Little Cauthen. His wife passed away in January, 1964. ("Service of Triumph, Mrs. Georgia Little Cauthen," January 28, 1964) Bishop Cauthen died in July, 1974. Funeral services were held on July 8, 1974 at the Greater Metropolitan A. M. E. Zion Church, on Brambleton Avenue, in Norfolk, Virginia. He was buried in that city.

Bishop J. D. Cauthen
ELECTED 1956-DIED 1974

62. BISHOP JOSEPH DIXON CAUTHEN

Born: February 21, 1887 in Kershaw, South Carolina. **Education:** He studied at Lancaster Normal and Industrial School and Clinton Junior College. He earned his A.B. degree from Livingstone College and his B.D. from Hood Theological Seminary. **Family:** In 1921, he married the former Ruth Smith. His wife died in 1929 shortly after the birth of their son, Joseph. In 1940, he married the former Georgia Little. This union produced one daughter, Muriel. His second wife died in 1964. **Died:** He died in July , 1974. Funeral services were held on July 8, 1974 at the Greater Metropolitan A. M. E. Zion Church, Norfolk, Virginia.

African Methodist Episcopal Zion Church

63. BISHOP CHARLES CECIL COLEMAN

CHARLES CECIL COLEMAN was born in Key West, Florida on February 22, 1906. He enrolled at Livingstone College in 1925 and earned the A.B. degree with highest honors in 1929.

He entered the traveling ministry through the West Central North Carolina Conference before he began his higher education. He was ordained a deacon November 30, 1924 and an elder November 26, 1926.

He was pastor of Cedar Grove Circuit, Gold Hill, North Carolina; St. James, Southport, North Carolina; Clinton Chapel, New Bern, North Carolina; Metropolitan, Atlanta, Georgia; Monticello, Arkansas; St. Paul, Little Rock, Arkansas; Clinton Chapel, Union, South Carolina; Metropolitan, Clinton, South Carolina; and State Street, Mobile, Alabama, from which he was elected to the episcopacy. He was consecrated the 63rd Bishop on May 13, 1956 in Wesley Center Church at the 35th General Conference held in Pittsburgh, Pennsylvania.

As bishop he was assigned to the Southwest. He established an episcopal residence in Oklahoma City. Illness prevented him from realizing his vision. He died on July 17, 1958, just two years and two months after his election. Funeral services were held in First Church, Brooklyn. He is buried in Evergreen Cemetery, Brooklyn, New York.

He was married to the former Alcestis McCullough, who served as missionary supervisor of the episcopal district over which he presided. Later, following his death, Mrs. Coleman became General President of the Woman's Home and Overseas Missionary Society.

Bishop C.C. Coleman
ELECTED 1956-DIED 1958

63. BISHOP CHARLES CECIL COLEMAN

Born: February 22, 1906 in Key West, Florida. **Education:** He earned the A.B. degree from Livingstone College in 1919. Family: He was married to Alcestis McCullough Coleman. **Died:** He died July 17, 1958. Funeral services were held in First Church, Brooklyn, New York. He is buried at Evergreen Cemetery in Brooklyn, New York.

African Methodist Episcopal Zion Church
64. BISHOP FELIX SYLVESTER ANDERSON

FELIX SYLVESTER ANDERSON was born in Wilmington, North Carolina, to Charles and Betty Foye Anderson (Bradley 1970, p. 462), on October 3, 1893. He received his early education in Boston, Massachusetts at Rice and Dwight Elementary Schools and English High School. He earned his A.B. from Livingstone College in 1920. His religious studies were undertaken at Hood Theological Seminary in 1921 and at Western Theological Seminary in Pittsburgh, 1922-24.

He was called to preach in 1910 through the inspiration of Rev. Green W. Johnson at the Columbus Avenue Church in Boston. He was licensed in 1912 by the Rev. P. A. McCorkle. He was ordained a deacon November 15, 1915 and an elder November 17, 1917. He entered the traveling ministry through the Western North Carolina Conference. He was pastor of Rocky Creek Circuit, Maineville Circuit, and Cedar Grove, all in North Carolina; First Church, Providence, Rhode Island; Mt. Washington, Pittsburgh, Trimble Chapel, Oakdale, both in Pennsylvania; Mt. Lebanon, Elizabeth City, and Kadesh, Edenton, both in North Carolina; Hunter's Chapel, Tuscaloosa, Alabama; Shaw Metropolitan, Atlanta, and Union Chapel, Athens, both in Georgia; St. Peter's Southern Pines, North Carolina; Big Zion, Mobile, Alabama; and Broadway Temple, Louisville, Kentucky.

While pastor of Broadway Temple, Rev. Anderson represented the 42nd District in the Kentucky Legislature for three terms from 1954-60 and successfully sponsored desegregation legislation. He was elected to the episcopacy from Broadway Temple and was consecrated the 64th Bishop on May 15, 1960 at the 36th General Conference held in Buffalo, New York.

As bishop he presided over the Alabama, North Alabama, Cahaba, Central Alabama, and South Alabama; Kentucky and East Tennessee-Virginia Conferences. He served for twelve years in the episcopacy before he was retired by the General Conference in 1972.

On April 28, 1920, he married Bessie Bernice Bizzell. This union produced four sons and two daughters, namely, Felix S., Herman Leroy, Joseph D., Theodore M. and Vivian E. and Helena S., respectively. Herman Leroy Anderson, emulating his father's achievement, entered the ministry of the A. M. E. Zion Church and became the 77th Bishop of the A.M. E. Zion Church in 1980. Bishop Felix Anderson completed his earthy career in 1983. He was funeralized on May 11, 1983 from Broadway Temple Church, Louisville, Kentucky and is interred in that city. ("Funeral Service for Bishop Felix Sylvester Anderson," May 11, 1983)

Bishop F.S. Anderson
ELECTED 1960-DIED 1983

64. BISHOP FELIX SYLVESTER ANDERSON

Born: October 3, 1893, in Wilmington, North Carolina, to Charles and Betty Foye Anderson. **Education:** He was educated at Rice and Dwight Elementary Schools and English High School, Boston, Massachusetts. He earned his A.B. degree from Livingstone College in 1920. His religious studies were under-taken at Hood Theological Seminary and Western Theological Seminary, Pittsburgh, Pennsylvania. **Family:** On April 28, 1920, he was married to Bessie Bernice Bizzell. They had six children, one of whom, Herman Leroy Anderson, became a bishop in the A. M. E. Zion Church. **Died:** He died in 1983. He was funeralized from Broadway Temple A. M. E. Zion Church, Louisville, Kentucky and interred in Cave Hill Cemetery, Louisville, KY.

African Methodist Episcopal Zion Church
65. BISHOP WILLIAM MILTON SMITH

WILLIAM MILTON SMITH was born at Stockton, Baldwin County, Alabama on December 18, 1915 to George and Elizabeth Smith. He attended public schools and graduated from Lomax-Hannon High School. He earned a B.S. degree from Alabama State College, Montgomery, Alabama. He earned the A.M. degree from Tuskegee Institute and a B.D. from Hood Theological Seminary. He undertook advance religious study at the Perkins School of Theology, Southern Methodist University, Dallas, Texas. (Bradley 1970, p. 463)

He entered the ministry through the South Alabama Conference. He was ordained a deacon on November 14, 1937 and an elder November 12, 1939. He was pastor of St. Thomas, Perdita; Zion, Atmore; Zion Star and Zion Fountain, Brewton; Ebenezer, Montgomery; and Big Zion, Mobile, all in Alabama. He was elected to the episcopacy and was consecrated the 65th Bishop on May 15, 1960, at the 36th General Conference, held in Buffalo, New York.

As bishop he presided over the South American and Virgin Islands Conferences; the West Alabama, Western North Carolina, and New York Conferences. He was the host bishop to the 39th General Conference, which met in Big Zion A. M. E. Zion Church, Mobile, Alabama, in May, 1972.

Bishop Smith was active in civic and business affairs in Mobile County, Alabama. He served as a member of the Board of Directors of many organizations, including the Chamber of Commerce, the Red Cross, the General Hospital, the Mental Health Association, and the Gulf Federal Savings and Loan Bank.

An active participant in ecumenical affairs, he was a delegate to the World Methodist Conference in 1956 and 1966.

Bishop Smith was retired by the General Conference in 1992 after serving thirty-two years in the episcopacy. He died April 12, 1995, in Mobile, Alabama. Funeral rites were held at Big Zion A. M. E. Zion Church on April 19, 1995. He was buried in that city. He was married to the former Ida Mae Anderson. They had one daughter, Eula Goode.

Bishop W.M. Smith
ELECTED 1960 - DIED 1995

65. BISHOP WILLIAM MILTON SMITH

Born: December 18, 1915, in Baldwin County, Alabama, to George and Elizabeth Smith. **Education:** He completed Lomax-Hannon High School. He earned his B.S. degree from Alabama State College and his A.M. degree from Tuskegee. He received a B.D. from Hood Theological Seminary. **Family:** He married Ida M. Anderson. They had one daughter. **Died:** In 1995. Funeral services were conducted in Big Zion A. M. E. Zion Church, Mobile, Alabama, followed by entombment in the same city.

African Methodist Episcopal Zion Church
66. BISHOP SOLOMON DORME LARTEY

SOLOMON DORME LARTEY was born September 12, 1898 to Dorme and Amelia Arhuma Lartey at Christiansborg, Accra, Ghana and was educated at the Presbyterian Mission School in Accra, in the former Gold Coast. In 1928, he traveled to Liberia, where he settled and became a naturalized citizen. He was ordained a minister in the Presbyterian Church in 1933. In 1939, he joined the A. M. E. Zion Church. He was ordained an elder and appointed presiding elder in 1940 by Bishop James Walter Brown.

During World War II, Lartey was the chief representative of the A. M. E. Zion Church in Liberia and supervisor of the Mt. Coffee mission, at which time he extended the mission to Sinoe County from Montserrado County. He was appointed bishop's deputy by Bishop Edgar Benton Watson and served effectively in the absence of a presiding bishop. He organized the A.M. E. Zion Church in Monrovia, Liberia. He built the Brown Memorial Church and Zion Academy, of which he was pastor and general manager respectively. He was the first indigenous African consecrated bishop in the A. M. E. Zion Church on May 15, 1960 in Buffalo, New York at the 36th Session of General Conference.

As bishop he initially presided over the Liberia and West Ghana Conferences. His long-lasting contributions include the erection of Aggrey Memorial Church in Accra, and establishment of the first A. M. E. Zion Mission Hospital in Ghana in 1964, among many other schools and churches that he established with the assistance of dedicated ministers in Liberia and Ghana. He died on August 3, 1969.

He served Zion as trustee of Livingstone College; chairperson of the International Justice and Goodwill, and Worship and Ritual Committees of the Church; vice chairperson of Christian Education, Home and Church; and as chairperson of the Board of Bishops. He was a founding member of the Christian Ministers' Association of Liberia and was its first secretary.

His first marriage to Mrs. Caroline Lewis was dissolved. He later married Alecia Ethel Smith. He was father of eight children of his own and ten foster children, and grandfather of many children. He served the Liberia Public Service as Inspector of Internal Revenues, Treasurer Department, Accountant of the Bureau of Internal Revenues, and Postmaster of Monrovia Post Office. His funeral services were held at the Centennial Memorial Pavilion, Monrovia on August 10, 1969, with interment at the Po-River Station. The government of Liberia directed that the flag of the Republic be flown at half-mast throughout Monrovia on the day of his burial out of respect for his considerable contributions to Liberia. An American A.M. E. Zion delegation representing the Board of Bishops and the entire church, including Bishops W.A. Hilliard, A.G. Dunston, Jr., and the Rev. J. C. Hoggard, secretary of Foreign Missions, attended the memorial service for Bishop Lartey.

Bishop S.D. Lartey
ELECTED 1960-DIED 1969

66. BISHOP SOLOMON DORME LARTEY

Born: September 12, 1898, to Dorme and Amelia Arhuma Lartey, at Christiansborg, Accra, Ghana. Education: He was educated at the Presbyterian Mission School, Accra, in the former Gold Coast. **Family:** His first marriage to Mrs. Caroline Lewis was dissolved. On September 12, 1945, he married Alecia Ethel Smith. They had eight children, ten foster children, and many grandchildren. **Died:** He died August 3, 1969. Services were held at the Centennial Memorial Pavilion on August 10, 1969, with interment at Po-River Station, Liberia.

African Methodist Episcopal Zion Church
67. BISHOP WILLIAM ALEXANDER HILLIARD

WILLIAM ALEXANDER HILLIARD was born in Greenville, Texas on September 12, 1904 to John H. and Carrie Hicks Hilliard (Bradley 1970, p. 466). At an early age he moved with his parents to Kansas City, Kansas and then to Des Moines, Iowa, where he attended elementary school. He completed Western High School in Kansas City and then studied at both Western University in Quinders, Kansas and Wayne University in Detroit.

He entered the traveling ministry through the Missouri Conference in 1922. He was ordained a deacon July 8, 1924 and an elder on September 7, 1927. His pastorates included: St. Matthew, Kansas City; Mt. Zion, Argentine, Kansas; Metropolitan, Kansas City, Missouri; Metropolitan Church, Chester, South Carolina; St. John, Wilson, North Carolina; and St. Paul, Detroit, Michigan. He led the St. Paul congregation in purchasing a significant edifice at 11359 Dexter Avenue, in Detroit, Michigan and subsequently made two congregations from one. He was elected and consecrated the 67th Bishop on May 15, 1960 in Buffalo, New York at the 36th Session of General Conference.

He was a resident bishop in Africa where he was assigned to the East Ghana and West Ghana Conferences from 1960-64. Bishop and Mrs. Hilliard sponsored Skyne Uku of Owerri, Eastern Nigeria, at Livingstone College. She was the first female overseas student so sponsored at Livingstone. On Bishop Hilliard's return to the States, he presided over the Michigan, Ohio, Central North Carolina, Guyana, South America, and Virgin Island Conferences. At Bishop Shaw's death, the Board of Bishops assigned him to supervise the New York Conference. He was retired in accordance with church practice by the General Conference in 1980. (*Official Journal, 40th Quad. Sess.Gen. Conf.,* [1976])

He married the former Edra Mae Mael of Kansas City, Missouri in 1927. They currently reside in Detroit, Michigan.

Bishop W.A. Hillard
ELECTED 1960

67. BISHOP WILLIAM ALEXANDER HILLIARD

Born: September 12, 1904, in Greenville, Texas, to John H. and Carrie Hicks Hilliard. **Education:** He was educated in the public schools of Kansas City, Kansas and Des Moines, Iowa. He studied at Western University, Quinders, Kansas and Wayne University, Detroit, Michigan. **Family:** In 1927, he married Edra Mae Mael. They currently reside in Detroit, Michigan.

African Methodist Episcopal Zion Church
68. BISHOP ALFRED GILBERT DUNSTON, JR.

ALFRED GILBERT DUNSTON, JR.,was born in Coinjock, North Carolina to the Rev. Alfred G. and Cora Lee Charity Dunston, on June 25, 1915. He graduated from P. W. Moore High School in Elizabeth City, North Carolina. He graduated from Livingstone College in 1938 and completed the course work for an M. A. degree from Drew University in Madison, N. J. His M. A. degree was officially conferred, along with public recognition, on October 22, 1993.

He preached his trial sermon on September 4, 1935 at his home church, Mount Lebanon A. M. E. Zion Church, Elizabeth City, North Carolina. He joined the Western North Carolina Conference in November, 1936, at Moore's Chapel, Salisbury, North Carolina. He was ordained a deacon in July, 1937 in Salisbury, North Carolina and an elder in 1938 at Cornelius, North Carolina by Bishop L. W. Kyles, officiating. He was pastor of Smith Grove, Mocksville; Mt. Sinai at Vance; St. John, Thomasville, all in North Carolina; Wallace Temple, Bayonne, Price Memorial, Atlantic City; and Wallace Chapel, Summit, in New Jersey; Loguen Temple, Knoxville, Tennessee; Big Wesley, Philadelphia, Pennsylvania; and Mother Zion, New York City. He was elected to the episcopacy and consecrated the 68th Bishop in succession, on May 21, 1964.

During his episcopacy, he presided over the Nigeria, and Liberia, West Africa; the South Alabama, Central Alabama, Cahaba, West Tennessee-Mississippi, and Louisiana, North Carolina, West Central North Carolina, New Jersey, New England, the Virgin Islands, and Albemarle in North Carolina Conferences. Ms. E Loujean Lovett (deceased) and Dr. Armayne G. Dunston served as missionary supervisor during his episcopacy. Bishop Dunston was a Master Mason and the first member of Alpha Phi Alpha Fraternity to be elected a bishop in the A. M. E. Zion Church. He is author of *The Black Man in the Old Testament and Its World*. He was retired in July, 1992 by the 44th General Conference.

He served in the 92nd Infantry Artillery, (Buffalo Division) during World War II and was awarded two Battle Stars and a Citation for Meritorious Service from the Division. He established the 92nd Division's Illiteracy School. As a member of the Black Clergy Alliance of Philadelphia that used selective patronage to break down employment barriers, he was a founding member of the OIC and was appointed to the Philadelphia Human Rights Commission. He was celebrated by *Ebony* Magazine (1984) as one of America's "Fifteen Greatest Preachers." He is survived by three daughters: Mrs. Carol Dunston Goodrich, Tinton Falls, New Jersey; Dr. Aingred G. Dunston-Coleman, Lexington, Kentucky; and Dr. Armayne G. Dunston, New Orleans, Louisiana.

Bishop A.G. Dunston, Jr.
ELECTED 1964 - DIED 1995

68. BISHOP ALFRED GILBERT DUNSTON, JR.

Born: June 25, 1915, at Coinjock, North Carolina to the Rev. Alfred G. and Cora Lee Charity Dunston. **Education:** He completed P. W. Moore High School in Elizabeth City, North Carolina. He earned a B.A. degree from Livingstone College in 1938, and a B.D. from Hood Theological Seminary. His M. A. degree from Drew University was confer-red with public recognition on October 22, 1993. He is author of *The Black Man in the Old Testament and Its World*. **Family:** His marriage to Permilla Flack ended in divorce. They had three daughters: Aingred G., Carol, and Armayne Dunston. **Died:** On June 24, 1995. Funeral services were held on June 30, 1995, at Wesley A. M. E. Zion Church, Philadelphia, followed by interment in historic Mt. Lawn Cemetery, Philadelphia, Pennsylvania.

69. BISHOP CHARLES HERBERT FOGGIE

CHARLES HERBERT FOGGIE, one of eight children, was born in Sumter, South Carolina, August 4, 1912, to James and Mamie Foggie. He completed English High School in Boston, Massachusetts. He earned his A.B. degree from Livingstone College in 1936 and an A.M. degree from Boston University in 1938. He then went on to earn the S.T.B. and S.T.M. degrees from the Boston University School of Theology in May, 1939 and May, 1949, respectively.

He began preaching in 1931 at Columbus Avenue A. M. E. Zion Church, Boston, Massachusetts. In 1932, he was admitted to the New England Conference meeting at Hartford, Connecticut. He was ordained a deacon in 1934 at Bridgeport, Connecticut and an elder in 1936 at Waterbury, Connecticut by Bishop William J. Walls. He was pastor of the following A. M. E. Zion Churches: Wadsworth Street, Providence, Rhode Island; Rush Church, Cambridge, Massachusetts; and Wesley Center, Pittsburgh, Pennsylvania, from which pulpit he was elected and consecrated the 69th Bishop of the A. M. E. Zion Church, on May 15, 1968, at the 38th General Conference, held in St. Paul Church, Detroit, Michigan. He served as a bishop for twenty years and was retired in 1988.

Bishop Foggie presided over the Arkansas, Georgia, South Georgia, Oklahoma, Texas, Allegheny, Ohio, Philadelphia-Baltimore, Barbados, and Guyana Conferences. He was recalled from retirement in 1991 after the death of Bishop Richard Fisher to preside over the Pee Dee, South Carolina, Palmetto, Indiana, Louisiana, and Arizona Conferences until the General Conference in 1992. Mrs. Foggie served as missionary supervisor in the districts where her husband presided.

Bishop Foggie has contributed sermons and articles to the *A M E. Zion Quarterly Review* and the *Star of Zion*. His public activities include board member of the Pittsburgh Symphony, president of the Pittsburgh NAACP, and board chairman of the Pittsburgh City Housing Authority. He was also radio broadcaster of the Christian program "Music and Meditation" during his ministry in Pittsburgh. He is a member of the World Council of Churches, the World Methodist Council of Churches, and the Council of Methodist Bishops. On August 1, 1986, his contributions were cited in the Congressional Record and a flag was flown over the U.S. Capitol in recognition of his fifty years in the ministry. Bishop Foggie received the Reverend John Cherry into the Philadelphia-Baltimore Conference in 1981 and nurtured him during the early years of Cherry's mission at Full Gospel, Temple Hills, Maryland, now the largest congregation in the A. M. E. Zion Church.

Bishop Foggie married Madeline Sharpe and has two children: Charlene Barnett Foggie and Milton Lee Swan. They are the grandparents of seven and great grandparents of two children. Mrs. Foggie died on July 23, 1995. Bishop Foggie resides in Pittsburgh, Pennsylvania.

Bishop C.H. Foggie
ELECTED 1968

69. BISHOP CHARLES HERBERT FOGGIE

Born: August 4, 1912, one of eight children, to James and Mamie Foggie, in Sumter, South Carolina. **Education:** He completed English High School in Boston, Massachusetts. He earned his A.B. degree from Livingstone College; his A. M. degree from Boston University; and the S.T.B. and S.T.M. degrees from Boston University School of Theology. **Family:** He married Madeline Sharpe. He has a daughter—Charlene Barnett Foggie—and a stepson, Milton Lee Swan. Mrs. Foggie died on July 23, 1995. He resides in Pittsburgh, Pennsylvania.

African Methodist Episcopal Zion Church
70. BISHOP JAMES CLINTON HOGGARD, SR.
JAMES CLINTON HOGGARD, SR., was born in Jersey City, New Jersey, on August 9, 1916, to the Rev. Jeremiah Matthew and Symera Cherry Hoggard. He is one of seven children, five brothers and one sister. He attended public schools in New Jersey and earned his A. B. degree from Rutgers University in 1939 and an M. Div. degree in 1942 from Union Theological Seminary, New York City.

He was admitted to the traveling ministry in the New York Annual Conference, held at Fleet Street Memorial (First A. M. E. Zion) Brooklyn, N. Y., in June, 1939, Bishop L. W. Kyles, presiding bishop. In November, 1940, he was ordained a deacon by Bishop L. W. Kyles at Hood Memorial Church, located then on Lenox Avenue in New York City. He was ordained an elder by Bishop W. J. Walls in June, 1942, at the New York Annual Conference held in Troy, New York.

Rev. Hoggard pastored St. Francis A. M. E. Zion, Mount Kisco; Institutional A. M. E. Zion, Yonkers, both of New York; Little Rock A. M. E. Zion, Charlotte, North Carolina; Trinity A. M. E. Zion, Washington, D. C. (interim); and Greater Centennial A. M. E. Zion, Mount Vernon, New York (interim).

He was secretary-treasurer of the Department of Foreign Missions and editor of the *Missionary Seer*, from 1952-72. He was elected and consecrated the 70th Bishop on May 12, 1972 at the 39th General Conference held in Mobile, Alabama. As bishop he presided over the Indiana, Kentucky, North Alabama, East Tennessee-Virginia, Western New York, Philadelphia-Baltimore, Jamaica, West Indies, Barbados, Bahamas, Guyana, South America and London-Birmingham Conferences. He served two terms as president of the Board of Bishops.

Widely affiliated in ecumenical and civic affairs, Bishop Hoggard was a member of the executive committees of the World Council of Churches and the Consultation on Church Union. He was a member of the World Council of Churches Central Committee, the National Council of Churches of Christ in the U.S.A. Governing Board, and was president of the Interfaith Conference, Washington, D. C. He was a member of the the the Indiana and Kentucky State Council of Churches, the Religious Public Relations Council, the Congress of National Black Churches, and the Council of Churches of the Greater Washington, D. C. He is a member of the American Civil Liberties Union; a life member of the NAACP, the Urban League of Greater Washington, D.C., and of Alpha Phi Alpha Fraternity. He served on the spiritual aims committee of the Lawrence Club of Kiwanis. He is a member of Sigma Pi Phi Boule' Fraternity and a former member of the U. S. Conference of the World Council of Churches Executive Board.

Bishop Hoggard was married in 1949 to the former Eva W. Stanton, of Pittsburgh, Pennsylvania. Mrs. Hoggard died February 12, 1997. They had two sons: J. Clinton, Jr.,a professional vibraphonist and associate professor of music, Wesleyan University, and the Rev. Dr. Paul Stanton, an A.M. E. Zion minister; two grandchildren, Jamal and Kalila, and daughters-in-law Donna Dinkins-Hoggard and Dr. Debra Jeffries Hoggard.

Bishop J.C. Hoggard
ELECTED 1972

70. BISHOP JAMES CLINTON HOGGARD, SR.

Born: August 9, 1916, to the Rev. Jeremiah Matthew and Symera Cherry Hoggard, in Jersey City, New Jersey. **Education:** He attended public schools in Jersey City and Hackensack, N.J. He earned his A.B. degree from Rutgers University in 1939 and his M. Div. degree from Union Theological Seminary, New York City, in 1942. **Family:** He was married to the former Eva W. Stanton who died on Feb. 12, 1997. They had two sons: J. Clinton Hoggard, Jr., and the Rev. Dr. Paul Stanton Hoggard, and two grandchildren. He resides in Chevy Chase, Maryland.

African Methodist Episcopal Zion Church
71. BISHOP JAMES WESLEY WACTOR

JAMES WESLEY WACTOR was born September 13, 1908 at Hoke County, North Carolina to Henry Lee and Annie Bell Campbell Wactor (Williams, 1975: 514). He earned his A.B. from Livingstone College in 1935. He took theological courses at Hood Theological Seminary, Union Theological Seminary in New York, and Harvard University School for Chaplains.

He entered the ministry through his local church, Fair Promise, Sanford, North Carolina. He joined the Western North Carolina Conference in 1931, while he was a student at Livingstone. He was ordained a deacon July 30, 1933 and was ordained an elder November 17, 1935. During World War II, he served as a U.S. Chaplain, 1943-48. He was cited for erecting the first American chapel in Germany in 1946.

He was pastor of Maineville Circuit near Salisbury, White Rock, Granite Quarry and New Hope, Salisbury, all in North Carolina; Young's Chapel, Morristown, Tennessee; Kesler Temple, Henderson; Mattocks Memorial, Fayetteville; and St. James, Red Springs, all in North Carolina; Barry Avenue, Long Island, New York; Hood Memorial, New York City; Big Zion, Mobile Alabama; and Metropolitan, Birmingham, from which he was elected to the episcopacy. He was consecrated the 71st Bishop May 12, 1972 at the 39th Session of General Conference meeting in Mobile, Alabama.

As pastor at Hood Memorial, he led the congregation in the purchase of a large edifice that subsequently became Greater Hood Memorial Church in New York City. He served the denomination as dean, Ministers' and Laymen's Institute, Birmingham, Alabama; member, Lomax-Hannon Jr. College Board of Trustees; member, Church Extension Board. He was interested in youth development and was a member of A. G. Gaston Boys Club Board of Directors, Alabama; director, German Youth Activities, Mannheim, Germany. Other civic activities included member, Citizens Federal and Savings Loan Association, Alabama Board of Trustees.

As bishop he presided over the Blue Ridge, Albemarle, Florida, and South Florida; and Central North Carolina Conferences (*Discipline, A. M. E. Zion Church, 1976*, p. 341; *1980*, p. 340)

Bishop Wactor was married to the former Hildred Anita Henry. He passed away in 1985. Funeral services were held at Evans Metropolitan, Fayetteville, North Carolina. He is buried in Fayetteville, North Carolina. Mrs. Wactor died November 27, 1991.

Bishop J.W. Wactor
ELECTED 1972-DIED 1985

71. BISHOP JAMES WESLEY WACTOR

Born: September 13, 1908, in Hoke County, North Carolina, to Henry Lee and Annie Campbell Wactor. **Education:** He earned an A.B. degree from Livingstone College in 1935. He took theological courses at Hood Theological Seminary, Union Theological Seminary, and the Harvard University School for Chaplains. **Family:** He was married to the former Hildred Anita Henry. She died November 27, 1991. **Died:** In 1985. Funeral services were held at Evans Metropolitan A. M. E. Zion Church, Fayetteville, North Carolina, and he is buried in that city.

72. BISHOP CLINTON REUBEN COLEMAN, SR.

CLINTON REUBEN COLEMAN was born December 4, 1916, in Coden, Alabama. He earned a B. A. degree from Livingstone College in 1937 and then attended Hood Theological Seminary. He earned a M. Div. degree from the Howard University School of Religion in 1971. (Walls, p. 616)

He entered the traveling ministry through the West Central North Carolina Conference in 1935 ("Service of Triumphant Celebration"). He was ordained a deacon November 28, 1937. While attending school, he was pastor of Parker's Chapel Circuit, Concord, North Carolina. He was ordained an elder February 10, 1938. His other pastorates included Union Chapel, Albemarle; St. Stephen, Hamlet; Evans Metropolitan, Fayetteville; all in North Carolina; and Pennsylvania Avenue Church, Baltimore, Maryland, from which pastorate he was elected bishop. He was consecrated the 72nd Bishop of the church on May 12, 1972 at the 39th Session of the General Conference meeting in Mobile, Alabama, not very far from his birthplace. (Ibid.)

As bishop he presided over the Tennessee, West Tennessee and Mississippi, South Mississippi, Georgia, and South Georgia Conferences; the Michigan, Virginia, and Tennessee and Trinidad-Tobago Conferences. Bishop Coleman was active in the Civil Rights Movement in Baltimore during the 1960s. He was among the clergy who marched to integrate Gwynn Oak Park, and he sought improved race relations through a congregation-exchange program. He was retired after twenty years service in the episcopacy by the General Conference in 1992. Bishop Coleman died December 9, 1996. Funeral rites were held at Pennsylvania Avenue A. M. E. Zion, Baltimore, Maryland, on December 13, 1996, followed by interment at Arbutus Memorial Park, Baltimore. (*Official Journal, 40, 42, 43, 44th Quad. Sess. Gen. Conf.*;"Service of Triumphant Celebration for Bishop Clinton R. Coleman, Sr.," Dec. 13, 1996)

He was married to Ethel Gillis Coleman. They had two daughters and two sons: the Rev. Gordon Ray Coleman, a minister of the A. M. E. Zion Church, Frances C. Walford, Clinton R. Coleman, Jr., and Barbara C. Smith. They are the grandparents of eight children and one great grandchild, namely, Jocelyn, Trevor, Jr., Damion, JoAnn, LaMar, Kelly, Kenja, Clinton, III; and Breia, respectively.

Bishop C.R. Coleman
ELECTED 1972 - DIED 1996

72. BISHOP CLINTON REUBEN COLEMAN

Born: December 4, 1916, in Coden, Alabama. **Education:** He earned his B.A. degree in 1937 from Livingstone College and a M. Div. from the Howard University School of Religion in 1971. **Family:** He was married to the former Ethel Gillis. They are the parents of the Rev. Gordon Ray Coleman, an A.M. E. Zion minister, Frances C. Walford, Clinton R. Coleman, Jr., and Barbara C. Smith; grandparents of Jocelyn, Trevor, Jr., Damion, JoAnn, LaMar, Kelly, Kenja, Clinton, III; and great grandparents of Breia. **Died:** Dec. 9, 1996. The funeral service was held at Pennsylvania Avenue A. M. E. Zion, Baltimore, Md., with interment at Arbutus Memorial Park, Baltimore, on December 13, 1996.

African Methodist Episcopal Zion Church
73. BISHOP ARTHUR MARSHALL, JR.

ARTHUR MARSHALL, JR., was born in High Point, North Carolina, March 2, 1914, to Arthur, Sr., and Nellie Kendall Marshall (later Brown). He earned a B.A. degree from Livingstone College in 1937, a S.T. B. from Boston University in 1941, followed by a M. A. from that institution.

He began his ministry at his home church, St. Stephen A. M. E. Zion, High Point and joined the West Central North Carolina Conference in 1933. He was ordained a deacon on November 25, 1934 and an elder November 15, 1936. He was pastor of St. Philip Circuit in Greensboro, North Carolina. In 1938, he became dean of Walters-Southland Institute at Lexa, Arkansas and served as presiding elder of the Pine Bluff District, Arkansas Conference of the A. M. E. Zion Church.

While he was studying at Boston University, he served in the New England Conference as a pastor at Wadsworth Street A. M. E. Zion Church, Providence, Rhode Island. He was pastor of the following A. M. E. Zion Churches: Clinton, Ansonia, Connecticut; Peoples Church, Syracuse, New York; John Wesley, Pittsburgh; and Washington Metropolitan, St. Louis, from which pastorate he was elected bishop. He was consecrated the 73rd Bishop in succession on May 12, 1972 at the 39th General Conference held in Mobile, Alabama.

As bishop he presided over the Pee Dee, South Carolina, Alabama, Louisiana and Palmetto Conferences.

In August 1967, he was the host pastor to the 15th Quadrennial Missionary Convention held at Washington Metropolitan Church with Bishop and Mrs. Joseph D. Cauthen as hosts. He was a member of the Publications Board chaired by Bishop Stewart that directed erection of the Varick Memorial Publishing House. He was later appointed chairman of the Publications Board. He was a member of the Tri-Council of Bishops and Commissioners that considered organic unity of the black Methodist Churches during 1964-72. Bishop Marshall was a representative of the A. M. E. Zion Church at the Twelfth Methodist Conference in Denver, Colorado, 1971.

He was married to the former Mary Ann Stott of Pittsburgh, Pennsylvania. They are the parents of one son, Arthur, Jr. Bishop Marshall died in April, 1987. He was funeralized at St. Stephen's Church, High Point, his home church, on April 7, 1987, and is buried in that community.

Bishop A. Marshall, Jr.
ELECTED 1972-DIED 1987

73. BISHOP ARTHUR MARSHALL, JR.

Born: March 2, 1914, in High Point, North Carolina. **Education:** He earned a B.A. degree from Livingstone College in 1937 and the S.T.B. and M.A. degrees from Boston University. **Family:** He was married to the former Mary Ann Stott. They are parents of one son, Arthur, Jr. **Died:** In 1987. Funeral services were held at St. Stephen's A. M. E. Zion Church, High Point, North Carolina, and he is buried in that city.

African Methodist Episcopal Zion Church
74. BISHOP JOHN HENRY MILLER, SR.

JOHN HENRY MILLER was born December 3, 1917 in Ridgeway, Fairfield County, South Carolina to John H. Henderson and Frances Turner Miller. He completed James B. Dudley High School in Greensboro, North Carolina. Aspiring to the ministry, he attended Livingstone College and, while preparing himself for the ministry, he joined the West Central North Carolina Conference of the A. M. E. Zion Church. He received his A.B. from Livingstone College in 1941 and his B.D., later designated M. Div., from Hood Theological Seminary in 1945.

He began preaching at Trinity A. M. E. Zion Church, Greensboro, North Carolina in 1937. On November 27, 1938, he was admitted to the West Central North Carolina Conference and was ordained a deacon in November, 1938 and an elder the following year by Bishop William Walter Matthews. Rev. Miller was pastor of the following A. M. E. Zion Church congregations: Mt. Pleasant Circuit; Concord, Bennettesville, Norwood, and Union Church, Albemarle, all in North Carolina; Union Church, New Britain, Connecticut; Peoples Church, Syracuse, New York, and Fifth Avenue Church, Troy, New York; Mt. Olive, Waterbury, Connecticut; Goler Metropolitan, Winston Salem, North Carolina; and Broadway Temple, Louisville, Kentucky, from which pulpit he was elected and consecrated the 74th Bishop on May 12, 1972, at the 39th General Conference held in Mobile, Alabama.

As bishop he presided over the Oklahoma, Texas, North Arkansas, Arkansas and Cahaba Conferences; the Missouri, Colorado, Blue Ridge, Cahaba, South Alabama, and Central Alabama Conferences; the Central North Carolina Conference, and the Kentucky Conference. Following the death of Bishop Herbert Bell Shaw in 1980, Bishop Miller presided over the New England Conference until the General Conference met in May , 1980. Widely affiliated in ecumenical and civic organizations, Bishop Miller was a member of the World Council of Churches, the National Council of Churches; the Home and Church Division, Christian Education Department, A. M. E. Zion Church; a vice president of Connecticut Council of Churches, 1955-60; the Urban League Board of Trustees; the NAACP Executive Board of Trustees; a president of the Louisville area Council of Churches, 1969-71; chairman of the Board of Christian Education; and a member of Alpha Phi Alpha. He received the Livingstone College Outstanding Alumni Service Award, 1971 and was cited by the City of Winston-Salem for outstanding civic contributions (Williams 1975, p. 354). He was retired by the General Conference held in Atlanta, Georgia after twenty years service as a bishop in July 1992.

Bishop Miller nurtured twelve preachers into the ministry. He is author of *The Right Hand of Fellowship*, 1963; *Trustees and Stewards:The Continuing Power Struggle*, 1972, and *The Church Worker*, 1983. He is married to the former Bernice Frances Dillard. They have two sons: George Frederick, a presiding elder in the A. M. E. Zion Church, and John Henry, Jr., a deputy commissioner of education in New York.

Bishop J. H. Miller
ELECTED 1972

74. BISHOP JOHN HENRY MILLER, SR.

Born: December 3, 1917, in Ridgeway, Fairfield County, South Carolina, to John H. Henderson and Frances Turner Miller. **Education:** He graduated from James B. Dudley High School. He received his B.A. degree from Livingstone College in 1941, and his B.D. and M. Div. degrees from Hood Theological Seminary in 1945 and 1954, respectively. **Family:** He is married to the former Bernice Frances Dillard. They are the parents of George Frederick, a presiding elder in the A. M. E. Zion Church, and John Henry, Jr., a deputy commissioner in the New York State Department of Education.

75. BISHOP GEORGE JUNIUS LEAKE, III

GEORGE JUNIUS LEAKE, III, was born in Wilson, North Carolina, November 21, 1929. He completed his first degree at Livingstone College in 1957 and earned a B.D. from Hood Theological Seminary in 1960.

He entered the traveling ministry in 1950 before he enrolled in Livingstone College. He was ordained a deacon in November 1951 and an elder November 15, 1953. He was pastor of the following A. M. E. Zion Churches: Shelby and Pleasant Ridge, Gastonia, both in North Carolina; Durham Memorial, Buffalo, New York; and Little Rock, Charlotte, North Carolina, from which he was elected and consecrated the 75th Bishop on May 12, 1972 at the 39th General Conference meeting in Mobile, Alabama.

As bishop he presided over the California, Colorado, Missouri, Oregon-Washington, Southwest Rocky Mountain, and Alaska Conferences of the A. M. E. Zion Church. (*Official Journal, 40th Quad. Sess. Gen. Conf.*) and the Cape Fear Conference following the death of Bishop H. B. Shaw in 1980.

He served the denomination as a member of the Budget and Apportionment Committee that proposed a new budget to the 1964 General Conference. He was a member of the Board of Publications led by Bishop Stewart that was responsible for oversight of the new Varick Memorial Publishing House erected in Charlotte, North Carolina. He directed the effort to establish the Little Rock A. M. E. Zion Church Apartments in Charlotte, North Carolina that were part of government and church efforts to meet low and middle-income housing needs.

He was a freedom rider during the Civil Rights Movement in the 1960s. Bishop Leake died June 15, 1981. He was married to Vilma Louise Dew Leake. They had two daughters: Dierdra J. (deceased) and Yolanda Georgetta Leake.

Bishop G.J. Leake
ELECTED 1972-DIED 1981

75. BISHOP GEORGE JUNIUS LEAKE, III

Born: November 21, 1929, in Wilson, North Carolina, son of the late Mr. George J. Leake, II and the late Mrs. Elsie Stevenson, he was reared by a grandmother, the late Mrs. Barnes of Wilson, N.C. **Education:** He earned a B.A. degree from Livingstone College in 1957 and a B. D. degree from Hood Theological Seminary in 1960. **Family:** He was married to the former Vilma Louise Dew. They had two children, Dierdra J. and Yolanda G. Leake. **Died:** He died June 15, 1981. Funeral services were held in Little Rock, A. M. E. Zion Church, Charlotte, North Carolina. He was buried in that city at the Forest Lawn Cemetery, Freedom Drive.

African Methodist Episcopal Zion Church
76. BISHOP RUBEN LEE SPEAKS

RUBEN LEE SPEAKS was born on January 8, 1920 at Lake Providence, Louisiana to Benjamin and Jessie Bell Speaks. He was educated in public schools and graduated from G. W. Griffin High School. He earned an A.B. from Drake University, Iowa in 1946; a B.D. from Drew Theological Seminary in 1949, a S. T. M. from Temple University in 1952, and a M. Div. from Duke University Divinity School.

He was ordained a deacon in 1940 by the Reverend William Fox at the Southern Christian Institute in Edwards, Mississippi and was received on Credentials, May 12, 1946 at the A. M. E. Zion New Jersey Conference, where he was ordained an elder by Bishop Cameron Chesterfield Alleyne.

He was pastor of the following A. M. E. Zion Churches: St. Thomas, Somerville and Wallace Chapel, Summit in New Jersey; Varick Memorial, Philadelphia, Pennsylvania; St. Mark, Durham, North Carolina; and First Church, Brooklyn, New York City. He served Hood Theological Seminary as a teacher while he was pastor at St. Mark A. M. E. Zion Church in Durham, North Carolina.

He was consecrated the 76th Bishop of the A. M. E. Zion Church, on May 12, 1972 at the 39th General Conference held in Mobile, Alabama.As bishop he presided over the East Ghana, West Ghana, Liberia, Nigeria, Rivers and Central Nigeria Conferences in West Africa from 1972-80. For the remainder of his active episcopacy from 1980-96, Bishop Speaks presided over the Arkansas, North Arkansas, West Tennessee-Mississippi, South Mississippi, Cape Fear, Louisiana, East tennessee-Virginia, Misouri-Colorado, Blue Ridge, Western North Carolina, and the West Central North Carolina Conferences in the United States. He also presided over the Cornwall, Middlesex and Surrey Conferences of Jamaica, West Indies.

Bishop Speaks is author of *Handbook for Ministers and Lay Readers* (1963); *The Minister and His Task* (1969; *The Church and Black Liberation* (1972); *God in an Age of Scarcity* (1988); and *Prelude to Pentecost* (1988). The late President William Tolbert of Liberia dubbed him "Knight of African Redemption" when he presided over the Liberia Conference. He received the Chancellor's Award from the University of North Carolina at Wilmington and the Distinguished Citizen Award from the Brooklyn Advisory Committee of the New York Urban League. *Ebony Magazine* named him one of the "100 most influential black leaders in America." He became Senior Bishop of the A. M. E. Zion Church at the 44th General Conference.

Bishop Speaks is married to the former Janie Angeline Griffin and has two daughters: the Rev. Joan C. Speaks and Dr. Faith Speaks Sims, and an adopted son, Robert B. Speaks. Bishop Speaks currently resides in Salisbury, North Carolina.

Bishop R.L. Speaks
ELECTED 1972

76. BISHOP RUBEN LEE SPEAKS

Born: January 1, 1920, at Lake Providence, Louisiana, to Benjamin and Jessie Bell Speaks. **Education:** He graduated from G.W. Griffith High School. He earned an A.B. degree from Drake University; a B.D. from Drew Theological Seminary; a S.T.M. from Temple University; and a M. Div. from Duke University Divinity School. **Family:** He is married to the former Janie Angeline Griffin. They are the parents of two daughters, Joan and Faith, and an adopted son, Robert. Bishop Speaks lives in Salisbury, North Carolina.

77. BISHOP HERMAN LEROY ANDERSON

HERMAN LEROY ANDERSON, one of six children, was born February 23, 1923 in Wilmington, New Hanover, North Carolina to Rev., later Bishop, Felix S. And Bessie B. Anderson. He graduated from Williston High School and then earned a B.S. degree from Tuskegee Institute in 1943 and a B.D. from Hood Theological Seminary in 1959.

He began preaching in 1956 at St. Luke A. M. E. Zion Church, Wilmington, North Carolina. He was admitted to annual conference in 1956 at Gastonia, North Carolina. He was ordained deacon November 17, 1957 at Winston Salem, North Carolina and elder July 3, 1959 at Hood Theological Seminary by Bishop William J. Walls in both instances.

He was pastor of the following A. M. E. Zion Churches: Hood Memorial, Belmont, North Carolina; St. James, Ithaca, New York; Soldiers Memorial, Salisbury, North Carolina; Broadway Temple, Louisville, Kentucky; and Mount Pleasant, Statesville, North Carolina. He was elected General Secretary-Auditor of the denomination in 1976 at the General Conference held in Chicago, Illinois. He served in this office from 1976-80. He was elected to the episcopacy and was consecrated the 77th Bishop on May 16, 1980 at Greensboro, North Carolina, during the 41st General Conference.

As bishop he presided over the Texas, Georgia, South Georgia, Oklahoma, Oregon-Washington, Alaska, California, Southwest Rocky Mountain, the West Alabama, Florida, South Florida, Ohio, Jamaica, the Central North Carolina, North Carolina, Cape Fear, Albemarle, and Virgin Islands Conferences during his episcopacy. He died on January 26, 1995. Funeral rites were held in Livingstone College Auditorium on January 31, 1995. He is buried in the National Cemetery, Salisbury, North Carolina.

Bishop Anderson was married to the former Ruth Rogers. They had a daughter and two sons, Nurse Deborah R. Kareem, Dr. Herman Anderson, Jr., and the Rev. Derrick Anderson, a pastor in the A. M. E. Zion Church ministry.

Bishop H. Anderson

ELECTED 1980-DIED 1995

77. BISHOP HERMAN LEROY ANDERSON

Born: February 23, 1923 in Wilmington, New Hanover, North Carolina, to the Rev. Felix S. and Bessie B. Anderson. **Education:** He graduated from Williston High School and received a B.S. degree from Tuskegee Institute in 1943. He earned a B.D. from Hood Theological Seminary in 1959. **Family:** He was married to the former Ruth Rogers. They had a daughter and two sons: Deborah, Herman, Jr., and Derrick Anderson. **Died:** He died in January, 1995. Funeral rites were held in Livingstone College Auditorium, on January 31, 1995, and he is buried at National Cemetery, Salisbury, North Carolina.

78. BISHOP CECIL BISHOP

CECIL BISHOP was born on May 12, 1930 in Beaver, Pennsylvania to Ross Mance and Diana Bishop. He graduated from Fifth Avenue High School and then earned his A.B. degree from Knoxville College in 1954; his M. Div. from Howard University School of Divinity in 1958; and a S.T.M. from Wesley Theological Seminary in 1960.

He began preaching at Loguen Temple A. M. E. Zion Church, Knoxville, Tennessee in 1953 and was admitted to the Western North Carolina Conference in 1954. He was ordained a deacon by Bishop William J. Walls in 1954, at Little Rock A. M. E. Zion Church, Charlotte, North Carolina, and an elder by Bishop Raymond Luther Jones in 1957, at Galbraith A. M. E. Zion Church in Washington, D. C.

He was pastor of the following A. M. E. Zion Churches: Center Grove, Tobaccoville, North Carolina; assistant pastor of John Wesley, Washington, D. C.; pastor of Clinton, Rockville, Maryland; Trinity, Greensboro, North Carolina; and John Wesley, Washington, D.C., from which he was elected bishop. He was consecrated the 78th Bishop in succession in 1980 in Greensboro, North Carolina, at the 41st General Conference. As a pastor, he directed the building of the new Trinity A. M. E. Zion Church and Trinity Garden Apartments comprising 152 units, which are located at 631 E. Florida Street, Greensboro, North Carolina. He also guided the remodeling and restoration of John Wesley, the National Church of Zion Methodism, located at 14th and Corcoran Streets, N. W. Washington, D.C.

As bishop he presided over the East Ghana, West Ghana, Liberia, Nigeria, Central Nigeria, Rivers, Alabama, Central Alabama, Cahaba, South Alabama, North Alabama, Georgia, South Georgia, West Central North Carolina, the Allegheny, Ohio, New Jersey, Barbados, Guyana, and Trinidad-Tobago Conferences from 1980-1996. In 1996, he was assigned to the Piedmont Episcopal District comprising Blue Ridge, West Central North Carolina, Western North Carolina, and Jamaica, which includes all the divisions, Cornwall, Middlesex, and Surrey.

In 1981, Bishop Bishop delivered papers on "Sermon and Prayer Preparation" to the New Jersey Conference and on "Merging for Missions" to bishops of the Christian Methodist Episcopal and African Methodist Episcopal Zion Churches. He is a past president of the North Carolina Council of Churches. In 1986, he was invited to preach at the World Methodist Conference in Nairobi, Kenya.

His first wife, Wilhelma Jones Bishop, died April 29, 1982. He is now married to Marlene Yvette Bishop. They are the parents of Jason Ryan and Elizabeth Ryan Bishop. They reside in Charlotte, North Carolina.

Bishop C. Bishop
ELECTED 1980

78. BISHOP CECIL BISHOP

Born: May 12, 1930, one of two children, to Ross Mance and Diana Bishop, in Beaver, Pennsylvania. **Education:** He graduated from Fifth Avenue High School and then earned an A. B. degree from Knoxville College, Tennessee, in 1954. He received a M. Div. degree from Howard University School of Religion in 1958 and a S. T. M. from Wesley Theological seminary in 1960. **Family:** His first wife, Wilhelma Jones Bishop, died. He is now married to Marlene Yvette Bishop. They are the parents of Jason Ryan and Elizabeth Ryan Bishop. They reside in Charlotte, North Carolina.

501

79. BISHOP RICHARD LAYMON FISHER

RICHARD LAYMON FISHER was born to the Rev. William Frederick and Julia E. Fisher September 28, 1934 in Evanston, Illinois. He graduated from Evanston Township High School and then attended Boston University. He earned a B.S. in Education in 1956 and a B. S. T. from the Boston University School of Sacred Theology in 1959. He did advanced studies in theology at Butler University, Christian Theological Seminary, Indianapolis, Indiana, and the University of Chicago Theological Seminary.

He began preaching in 1954 while a student at Boston University. He was admitted to annual conference in 1955 in Chicago, Illinois, at the Michigan Annual Conference, where he was ordained a deacon by Bishop Stephen Gill Spottswood, who also ordained him an elder in 1956 in Chicago at the Michigan Annual Conference.

He was pastor of Campbell Chapel A.M. E. Zion Church, Indianapolis, Indiana, 1959-61; Martin Temple, Chicago, Illinois, 1961-72; and Washington Metropolitan, St. Louis, Missouri, 1972-84, from which pastorate he was elected and consecrated the 79th Bishop of the A. M. E. Zion Church, on August 3, 1984, at the 42nd General Conference held in St. Louis, Missouri.

As bishop he presided over the Texas, Oklahoma, Arkansas, North Arkansas, Florida, and South Florida Conferences, 1984-88; and the Indiana, Louisiana, Palmetto, Pee Dee, Arizona, and South Carolina Conferences, 1988-91. Bishop Fisher died suddenly October 25, 1991, while holding a special meeting of the Palmetto Conference in Rock Hill, South Carolina.

Bishop Fisher was a former public school teacher and a member of the St. Louis Inter-Faith Clergy, the St. Louis Dialogue Group, the St. Louis Police Clergy Council, the Missouri Council of Churches, the Board of Home Missions, and the Board of Schools and Colleges of the A. M. E. Zion Church. He was chairman of the St. Louis Urban League Board and Executive Committee and of the Ministers Support Group for School Tax Levy, Metropolitan Ministerial Alliance. He was chaplain of the St. Louis Fire Department and a vice president of the Lucas Heights Redevelopment Corporation. He was an occasional guest lecturer at Eden Seminary, Webster College, the University of Missouri, Fisk University, and Livingstone College.

He was married to the former Joan Marie Spratley and had two children: Susan Elizabeth and Richard Laymon, Jr. Funeral services for Bishop Fisher were held in the Washington Metropolitan A. M. E. Zion Church, St. Louis, Missouri, followed by entombment in the Valhalla Mausoleum, Missouri.

Bishop R.L. Fisher
ELECTED 1984-DIED 1991

79. BISHOP RICHARD LAYMON FISHER

Born: September 28, 1934, one of six children, in Evanston, Illinois to the Rev. William Frederick and Julia E. Fisher. **Education:** He graduated from Evanston Township High School. He earned a B. S. degree from Boston University and a S. T. B. in 1959 from Boston University School of Sacred Theology. **Family:** He was married to the former Joan Marie Spratley. They had two childred: Susan Elizabeth and Richard Laymon, Jr. **Died:** He died suddenly on October 25, 1991. Funeral rites were held at Washington Metropolitan A. M. E. Zion Church, and he is entombed in the Valhalla Mausoleum, Missouri.

African Methodist Episcopal Zion Church
80. BISHOP ALFRED EDWARD WHITE

ALFRED EDWARD WHITE was born to John and Laura Lewis White on April 29, 1921 in Pittsburgh, Pennsylvania. He graduated from Schenley High School in Pittsburgh and then attended Livingstone College and Hood Theological Seminary, where he earned the B.A. and M. Div. degrees respectively. He did further postgraduate work at Hartford Seminary and earned a D.Min. degree in 1956. He was ordained deacon on October 24, 1944 at Johnstown, Pennsylvania by Bishop Elijah Lovett Madison and elder on February 11, 1946 at Hood Seminary Chapel by Bishop Benjamin Garland Shaw.

He was pastor of the following A. M. E. Zion Churches: Rockwell Church, Derita, 1945-48, St. Peter's Gastonia, 1948-52, East Stonewall, Charlotte, 1952-56, and Soldiers Memorial, Salisbury, 1956-62, all in North Carolina; and Metropolitan, Hartford, Connecticut, 1962-84, from which pulpit he was elected the 80th Bishop and consecrated on August 3, 1984, at the 42nd Session of General Conference held in St. Louis, Missouri..

Bishop White presided over the Liberia, Central Nigeria, Rivers, East Ghana, and West Ghana Conferences, 1984-88; and the Alabama, Central Alabama, Cahaba, South Alabama, South Mississippi, West Tennessee-Mississippi Conferences, 1988-92. He died July 21, 1992, on the eve of the 44th General Conference, which met in Atlanta, Georgia.

Bishop White served the denomination as second vice chairman of the Board of International Justice and Goodwill; member of the Livingstone College and Clinton Junior College Board of Trustees; the Commission on Organic Union; the Commission on Family Life; the A. M. E. Zion Church School and College Division Board of Christian Education; and as secretary of the Western North Carolina Conference. He was a presiding elder of the Hartford District for eight years.

Active in civic affairs, he was a board member of St. Francis Hospital, Hartford, Connecticut; Horace Bushnell Memorial Auditorium, Hartford, Connecticut; Connecticut Council of Churches; YMCA, Hartford; secretary of the Connecticut State Conference of Churches; Hartford Conservatory of Music; the Urban League of Hartford; Church Coordinator for NAACP, Charlotte, North Carolina; and president of the Greater Hartford Inter-denominational Ministerial Alliance. He was a thirty-second degree Prince Hall Mason. He served thirteen years as chairman of the Human Relations Commission, Hartford, Connecticut.

He was married to Mamie Williams White and was father of Gwendolyn White Moore. Bishop White's funeral was held in the Metropolitan A. M. E. Zion Church, Hartford, Connecticut. A General Conference church delegation in attendance at the last rites was headed by Bishop Alfred G. Dunston, Jr., presiding bishop of the New England Conference in which Bishop White held conference membership.

Bishop A.E. White
ELECTED 1984-DIED 1992

80. BISHOP ALFRED EDWARD WHITE

Born: April 29, 1921, an only child of John and Laura Lewis White, in Pittsburgh, Pennsylvania. **Education:** He graduated from high school in Pittsburgh. He earned a B.A. degree from Livingstone College in 1948, a M. Div. from Hood Theological Seminary in 1951, and a D.M. degree from Hartford Seminary in 1986. **Family:** He was married to the former Mamie Williams. They had one daughter, Gwendolyn White, and three grandchildren. **Died:** He died July 21, 1992. Last rites were held at Metropolitan A. M. E. Zion Church, Hartford, Connecticut. He is interred at Green Cemetery in Gastonbury, Connecticut.

African Methodist Episcopal Zion Church
81. BISHOP GEORGE WASHINGTON CARVER WALKER, SR.

GEORGE WASHINGTON CARVER WALKER, SR., was born October 11, 1940 to the Rev. Roosevelt Leon and Lemon Louise Pace Walker in Montgomery , Alabama. He attended public schools in Fair Hope, Greenville and Luverne, Alabama. He received an A.A. degree from Clinton Jr. College, Rock Hill, South Carolina and then attended Benedict College, Columbia, South Carolina, and Hood Theological Seminary, Salisbury, North Carolina, from which he earned his A.B. in 1970 and M. Div. in 1971, respectively. He was admitted to the traveling ministry in 1959. In November, 1960, he was ordained a deacon by Bishop Daniel C. Pope and was admitted to the Pee Dee Annual Conference. He was ordained an elder in April, 1961 at Clinton Jr. College by Bishop Daniel Carlton Pope.

He was pastor of the following A. M. E. Zion Churches: Rock Hill and Piney Grove, Pageland, South Carolina; St. James and Mt. Airy, Chesterfield, South Carolina; Foundation and Tabernacle, Rock Hill, South Carolina; Jones Memorial, Columbia, South Carolina; and Greater Walters, Chicago, Illinois. In 1994, he led this congregation in purchasing the property at 8400-22 S. Damen Ave. and completed payment for it seven years in advance. He was elected to the episcopacy from this pastorate on August 5, 1988, at Little Rock A. M. E. Zion Church, Charlotte, North Carolina, where the 43rd General Conference was held.

Bishop Walker has presided over the Arkansas, North Arkansas, Oklahoma, Texas, Oregon-Washington, Alaska, Southwest Rocky Mountain and California Conferences. He presides over the New York, Western, New York, New England, and Bahama Islands Conferences since 1992. After the Bicentennial observance in 1996, Bishop Walker led the North Eastern Region Episcopal District, comprising the New York, Western New York, New England, and Bahama Islands Conferences in the purchase of a stately episcopal residence located in Farmington, Connecticut. The edifice was dedicated at a celebration on Saturday, October 11, 1997.

He has served the denomination as chairperson of the Publishing House Board; Harriet Tubman Foundation; the Restructuring Commission; and as first vice-chairperson and chairperson, on the resignation of Bishop Speaks, of the Bicentennial Commission; treasurer of the Michigan Annual Conference; and a member of the Connectional Budget Board. He was host pastor to the 40th General Conference held in Greater Walters A. M. E. Zion Church, Chicago, Illinois, in May, 1976.

He is a former president of the Chicago District Ministerium and was a member of the Ministerial Relief Board and the Episcopal Committee.

He is married to the former Geraldine Jackson. They are the parents of two daughters and two sons: Cynthia Lelita, Dwayne Anthony, Deborah Olivia, and George W. C. Walker, Jr., and grandparents of seven. Both of their sons are active pastors in the ministry of the A. M. E. Zion Church.

Bishop G. Walker. Sr.
ELECTED 1988

81. BISHOP GEORGE WASHINGTON CARVER WALKER, SR.

Born: October 11, 1940, one of three children to Roosevelt Leon and Lemon Louise Pace Walker in Montgomery, Alabama. **Education:** He graduated from Clinton Junior College High School Department. He earned an A.B. degree from Benedict College in 1970 and a M. Div. from Hood Theological Seminary in 1971. **Family:** He is married to the former Geraldine Jackson. They have two sons and two daughters: Cynthia Lelita, Rev. Dwayne Anthony, Deborah Olivia, Rev. George W. C. Walker, Jr., and seven grandchildren. Bishop Walker resides in Farmington, Connecticut.

African Methodist Episcopal Zion Church
82. BISHOP MILTON ALEXANDER WILLIAMS, SR.

MILTON ALEXANDER WILLIAMS was born to Booker T. and Lillian Gaither Williams, on June 28, 1938, at Monksville, Davie County, North Carolina. He attended Central Davie High School and then earned a B.A. degree in 1960 from Livingstone College and a M. Div. in 1963 from Hood Theological Seminary. His preaching career began in 1956 at his home church, St. John A. M. E. Zion Church, Mocksville, North Carolina. He was admitted to the Western North Carolina Annual Conference in 1958 at Little Rock Church, Charlotte, North Carolina. He was ordained a deacon in 1960 at Salisbury, North Carolina and an elder in 1962 at Charlotte, North Carolina, by Bishop William J. Walls.

He was pastor of Steward Chapel and Hayden Grove Circuit, North Carolina, 1958-63; Snow Hill, Newton, North Carolina, 1963-64; Wardell Chapel, Shelby, North Carolina, 1964-65; Durham Memorial, 1965-70 and Shaw Memorial, 1971-81, both in Buffalo, New York; and Big Zion, Mobile, Alabama, 1981-88, from which he was elected and consecrated the 82nd Bishop on August 5, 1988 at the 43rd session of General Conference meeting in Charlotte, N. C.

Rev. Williams was presiding elder of the Rochester, Syracuse, Buffalo District of the Western New York Conference, 1970-81 and was executive secretary of the Ministers and Laymen's Association 1974-82. He contributed "100 Years of Zion Methodism," to the volume *Black Methodism* (1963).

Bishop Williams presided over the East Ghana and West Ghana Conferences, 1988-92; London-Birmingham Conference, 1988 to the present. He organized three new conferences that were admitted to the A. M. E. Zion Church Connection at the 1992 General Conference: Mid-Ghana Conference (organized in 1990), 1990-92; Ivory Coast Conference (organized in 1991), 1991-92; Manchester Midland (organized in 1990), 1990-96. He currently presides over the Philadelphia-Baltimore, East Tennessee-Virginia, and Virginia Conferences in the United States, and the India, London-Birmingham, and Manchester-Midland Conferences overseas.

Bishop Williams led his Mid-Atlantic II Episcopal District in the renovation and refurbishing of Dinwiddie Institute buildings and the erection of a Wellness and Health Facility at Dinwiddie, Virginia. He was the first bishop to implement the 1992 General Conference directive to acquire episcopal residences. The spacious and well situated residence in Fort Washington, Maryland was opened July, 1996, with a dedication service and celebration that were widely attended. Bishop Williams was the host bishop of the 1996 General Conference, held in Washington, D. C. and Maryland.

He is married to the Rev. Lula G. Williams. They have three daughters, and a son: Angela, a lawyer; Cynthia, wife of an A. M. E. Zion pastor, Millicent, general secretary of the Young Women, Woman's Home and Overseas Missionary Society, and Milton, Jr., a student at Loyola University, Baltimore, Maryland.

Bishop M.A. Williams, Sr.
ELECTED 1988

82. BISHOP MILTON ALEXANDER WILLIAMS, SR.

Born: June 28, 1938, one of three sons and two daughters, to Booker T. And Lillian Gaither Williams, at Monksville Davie County, North Carolina. **Education:** He graduated from Central Davie High School. He earned a B.A. degree from Livingstone College in 1960 and a M. Div. from Hood Theological Seminary in 1963. **Family:** He is married to Rev. Lula G. Williams. They have three daughters and a son: Angela, Cynthia, Milicent, and Milton, Jr.

African Methodist Episcopal Zion Church
83. BISHOP SAMUEL CHUKAKANNE EKEMAM, SR.

SAMUEL CHUKAKANNE EKEMAM, one of eight children, was born June 27, 1942 in Owerri, Eastern Nigeria to Chief J. A. and Catherine Ogoma Ekemam. One of four Nigerian youths brought from Nigeria by Bishop Alfred Gilbert Dunston, Jr., through A. M. E. Zion Church missionary effort, he was educated at the A. M. E. Zion Teachers College, Ndon Ebom, Uyo, Nigeria. He earned an A. A. from Clinton Junior College; B. A. from Livingstone College; M. Div. from Yale University Divinity School; a M. A. (Ed.), from Teachers College, Columbia University; and an Ed. D. from Columbia University., New York City.

He was admitted to the traveling ministry of the A. M. E. Zion Church in 1963. He was assistant pastor of Okporowo, Rivers, 1964-69; assistant pastor, Doggetts Grove, Harris Circuit, Lincolnton, North Carolina, 1969-70; assistant pastor, Varick Memorial, New Haven, Connecticut, 1970-71; assistant pastor, Evers Memorial, New Haven, Connecticut, 1971-73; assistant pastor, Mother Zion, New York, New York, 1973-75; pastor-moderator, Sound View United Presbyterian, Bronx, New York, 1976-80.

He served as the presiding elder of the Aba District, Central Nigeria Conference and as the bishop's deputy-field superintendent from 1980-88. From this office, he was elected and consecrated the 83rd Bishop on August 5, 1988 at Little Rock, A. M. E. Zion Church, Charlotte, North Carolina where the 43rd General Conference was held. Bishop Ekemam is the second African-born bishop to serve as an episcopate in the A. M. E. Zion Church. He is the first African-born bishop to have received his collegiate and theological training in A. M. E. Zion Church schools in America in addition to graduate study in American colleges and universities.

As bishop he has presided over the Nigeria, Central Nigeria, and Liberia Conference, 1988-92, and the Eastern West Africa Episcopal District, including the Nigeria, Central Nigeria, and Rivers Nigeria, Lagos-West Nigeria, and Mainland Nigeria Conferences during 1992-96. In 1991, Bishop Ekemam started and helped build the Hood-Speaks Theological Seminary in Nigeria. Bishop Ekemam organized the Lagos-West Nigeria Conference in 1991 and the Mainland Nigeria Conference in 1992. He now presides over the six existing Nigeria Conferences, including a new Northern Nigeria Conference.

Bishop Ekemam married the former Fautina Ifechukwa Akubuiro in 1970.They are parents of seven children: Kathy Adaoha, Rosalind Ubuamudo, Earnestina Chimaobie, Christina Ahuruole, Mabel-May Aggi, Stella Amauchechi, and Samuel Chuka, Jr.

Bishop S.C. Ekemann, Sr.
ELECTED 1988

83. BISHOP SAMUEL CHUKUKANNE EKEMAM, SR.

Born:. June 27, 1942, one of eight children, to Chief J. A. and Catherine Ogoma Ekemam, in Owerri, Eastern Nigeria. **Education:** He completed A. M. E. Zion Teachers College, Uyo, Nigeria, and Clinton Junior College, Rock Hill, South Carolina. He earned a B.A. degree from Livingstone College; an M. Div. from Yale Divinity School; an M. Ed. from Teachers College, Columbia University; and an Ed. D. from Columbia University. **Family:** He is married to the former Fautina Ifechukwa Akubuiro. They have seven children: Kathy Adaoha, Rosalind Ubuamudo, Earnestina Chimaobie, Christina Ahurole, Mabel-May Aggi, Stella Amauchechi, and Samuel Chuka, Jr.

84. BISHOP GEORGE EDWARD BATTLE, JR.

GEORGE EDWARD BATTLE, JR., one of eight children, was born on May 14, 1947 at Edgecombe County, North Carolina to George and Mary I. Battle. He attended George Washington Carver High School and Clinton Junior College, from which he was graduated in 1967. He earned a B.A. degree from Livingstone College in 1969, a M. Div. degree from Hood Theological Seminary in 1972, and a D. Min. from Howard University School of Divinity in 1990.

He began preaching in 1966 at St. Matthews A. M. E. Zion Church, Rock Hill, South Carolina and was admitted to the South Carolina Annual Conference in 1967. He was ordained a deacon in 1967 and an elder in 1968 by Bishop Joseph Dixon Cauthen.

His pastorates included Center Grove Circuit, Tobaccoville, North Carolina, November 1966; Mt. Vernon Circuit, Statesville, North Carolina, December 1966; Foundation Tabernacle Circuit, 1968-72; Mt. Zion, Lancaster, South Carolina, 1972-74; and Gethsemane, Charlotte, North Carolina, 1974-92, from which pulpit he was elected bishop. He was consecrated the 84th Bishop in succession at Shaw Memorial A. M. E. Zion Church, Atlanta, Georgia, during the 44th General Conference, on July 31, 1992.

As bishop he has presided over the Palmetto, Pee Dee, Georgia, South Georgia, and South Carolina Conferences, 1992-96; and the Central North Carolina and North Carolina, and Virgin Islands Conferences after the death of Bishop Herman Leroy Anderson in 1995. In 1996, he was assigned the Eastern North Carolina Episcopal District comprising the Albemarle, Cape Fear, Central North Carolina, Virgin Islands, and North Carolina. He manifests unusual administrative ability. He served as president of the Charlotte-Mecklenberg Board of Education. He was elected a school board member in 1978 and became the chairperson in 1990. He served until 1995 when he resigned because of his duties as bishop.

Bishop Battle is married to the former Iris Miller. They are the parents of George, E. Jr., a college student at the University of North Carolina, and LaChandra N. Battle, a student at Livingstone College.

Bishop G.E. Battle
ELECTED 1992

84. BISHOP GEORGE EDWARD BATTLE, JR.

Born: May 14, 1947, one of eight children, to George and Mary I. Battle, at Edgecombe Co., North Carolina. **Education:** He graduated from George Washington Carver High School and Clinton Junior College. He earned a B.A. from Livingstone College in 1969 and a M. Div. from Hood Theological Seminary in 1972. He earned a D. Min. from Howard University School of Divinity. **Family:** He is married to the former Iris Miller. They have a son and a daughter: George E. and LaChandra Battle, and a daughter-in-law. Bishop Battle resides in Davidson, North Carolina.

African Methodist Episcopal Zion Church
85. BISHOP JOSEPH JOHNSON

JOSEPH JOHNSON, one of four children, was born on May 28, 1934, in Jacksonville, Florida to James and Vietta Johnson. He completed Booker T. Washington High School in Tampa, Florida. He graduated from North Carolina State University, Raleigh in 1971 with a B.A. degree. He earned a M. Div. degree from Duke University, Durham, North Carolina in 1975 and a D. Min. degree from Emory University in 1981.

He began preaching in 1964 at Evans Metropolitan A. M. E. Zion Church, Fayetteville, North Carolina. He was admitted to annual conference in 1965. He was ordained a deacon and an elder by Bishop William A. Stewart in 1966 at Fair Promise, Sanford, North Carolina, and in 1968 at St. Mark, Durham, North Carolina, respectively.

He was pastor of St. John, Fayetteville, North Carolina, 1966-68; Trinity, Southern Pines, North Carolina, 1968-75; Soldiers Memorial, Salisbury, North Carolina, 1975-82; and Trinity, Greensboro, North Carolina, 1982-92. He was elected and consecrated the 85th Bishop July 31, 1992, at the 44th General Conference held in Atlanta, Georgia.

As bishop he has presided over the Arkansas, Oklahoma, Texas, Louisiana, South Mississippi, West Tennessee-Mississippi Conferences during 1992-96; and the Cape Fear Conference following the death of Bishop Herman L. Anderson in 1995. In 1996, he was assigned the South Atlantic Episcopal District comprising the Palmetto, Pee Dee, Georgia, South Georgia, and South Carolina Conferences.

He was assistant professor of practical ministry at Hood Theological Seminary from 1981-91. He is the author of *A Manual for Ministerial Course of Study*, 1988; "Developing an Intergenerational and Intentional Model of Ministry with the Elderly in the Black Church" (1988) D. Min. diss., Emory University; "The Moral and Spiritual Requisites of the Black Preacher," *A. M. E. Zion Quarterly Review* (1994); and "Christian Stewardship," *Church School Herald Journal* (1980).

Bishop Johnson is married to the former Dorothy M. Sharpe. They are the parents of Timothy Johnson and the Rev. Anthony Johnson, an A. M. E. Zion pastor.

Bishop J. Johnson
ELECTED 1992

85. BISHOP JOSEPH JOHNSON

Born: May 28, 1934, to James and Vietta Johnson, in Jacksonville, Florida. **Education:** He graduated from Booker T. Washington High School in Tampa, Florida. He earned a B.A. degree from North Carolina State University in 1971, a M. Div. from Duke University Divinity School in 1975, and a D. Min. from Emory University in 1981. **Family:** He is married to the former Dorothy M. Sharpe. They have two sons: Timothy Johnson and the Rev. Anthony Johnson.

African Methodist Episcopal Zion Church
86. BISHOP RICHARD KEITH THOMPSON

RICHARD KEITH THOMPSON, one of three sons and four daughters, was born July 7, 1943, to Ernest Thompson and Willie Ree Thompson, at Kannapolis, North Carolina. He graduated from George Washington Carver High School and then attended Livingstone College, from which he earned an A.B. degree in 1965. He earned the M. Div. degree from Hood Theological Seminary in 1968.

He began his ministry in 1964 at Marable Memorial A. M. E. Zion Church, Kannapolis, North Carolina. He was admitted to annual conference in November 1965. He was ordained a deacon in 1967 at Hood Theological Seminary and an elder at Goler Metropolitan Church, Winston-Salem, North Carolina, in November 1967, by Bishop William Jacob Walls in both instances.

He was pastor of Poplar Springs, Lincolnton, North Carolina (Circuit); Smyre's Chapel, Catawba, North Carolina (Circuit); Walls Chapel, Oklahoma City, Oklahoma; and Trinity, Washington, D.C. At Trinity A. M. E. Zion Church, he led the congregation in purchasing the new Trinity Church located at 3505 16th Street, N. W. and in paying off the mortgage. He was elected to the episcopacy from this pastorate. He was consecrated the 86th Bishop on July 31, 1992, at Shaw Temple, Atlanta, Georgia, where the 44th Session of General Conference was held.

As bishop he has presided over what is now called the Alabama-Florida Episcopal District, namely, the Alabama, Central Alabama, Cahaba, South Alabama, North Alabama, West Alabama, South Florida, and Florida Conferences. Bishop Thompson led this district in acquiring the Episcopal Headquarters for the Alabama-Florida Episcopal District on March 17, 1993. In June, 1993 he led his district in structuring the Varick Bookstore housed in the Episcopal Headquarters located at 808 Lawrence Street, Mongomery, Alabama. Bishop Thompson also led this district in the purchase of an impressive episcopal residence located at 2159 Vaughn Lane, Montgomery, Alabama. The dedication on January 24, 1998 was a glorious experience for this uniquely unified episcopal district.

He is author of "The Pastor's Voice" (1992).

Bishop Thompson married the former Georgia McNair. They are the parents of two children: Kerri Elaine, a practicing attorney, and Richard Keith, II, a recent graduate of Virginia State College, Petersburg, Virginia.

Bishop R. Thompson
ELECTED 1992

86. BISHOP RICHARD KEITH THOMPSON

Born: July 7, 1943, one of seven children to Ernest and Willie Ree Thompson, at Kannapolis, North Carolina. **Education:** He graduated from George Washington Carver High School and then earned a B.A. degree from Livingstone College in 1965. In 1968, he received the M. Div. from Hood Theological Seminary. **Family:** He is married to the former Georgia McNair. They have two children: Kerri Elaine, a practicing attorney, and Richard Keith, II, a recent graduate of Virginia State College, Petersburg, Virginia. Bishop Thompson resides in Montgomery, Alabama.

87. BISHOP ENOCH BENJAMIN ROCHESTER

ENOCH BENJAMIN ROCHESTER, one of ten children, was born to Frederick and Henrietta Rochester on June 27, 1937 in Hackensack, New Jersey. He was educated in the public schools and graduated from Hackensack High School. He earned his BA degree from Livingstone College. During 1962-63, he studied at Wesley Theological Seminary.

He began preaching in his home church, Varick Memorial A. M. E. Zion Church, New Jersey, in 1955. He was admitted to the traveling ministry May 17, 1959. He was ordained an elder April 18, 1964 by Bishop Herbert Bell Shaw. He was pastor of Greater Fair Plains, McCoy, South Carolina and Wesley, Burlington, New Jersey. He was presiding elder of the Jersey City District, New Jersey Conference from 1978-92. He was elevated to the episcopacy from this office and was consecrated the 87th Bishop on July 31, 1992, at the 44th Session of General Conference held in Atlanta, Georgia.

As bishop he has presided over the Mid-West Episcopal District comprising the Indiana, Kentucky, Michigan, Missouri, and Tennessee Conferences. Since 1993, he has also had responsibility for the South Africa Conference. He reorganized this conference and led in the construction of Spottswood Memorial A. M. E. Zion Church in Seshego, South Africa. He also organized a conference in Malawi with ninety-six pastoral appointments.

He served the church as director of Christian Education for Youth; administrative assistant to the secretary-treasurer of the Department of Christian Education; executive secretary of the Presiding Elders Council; and executive secretary of the Ministers' and Laymen's Association.

Bishop Rochester, in compliance with the 1992 mandate of General Conference to Episcopal Districts has led the Mid West Episcopal District in the acquisition of an episcopal residence located at 129 Sagebush Drive, Belleville, Illinois. The residence was dedicated on Saturday, July 11, 1998. Beautiful for situation.

Bishop Rochester is married to Dr. Mattilyn Talford Rochester. They are parents of Enoch B. Rochester, II, and Mattilyn C. Rochester.

Bishop E. Rochester
ELECTED 1992

87. BISHOP ENOCH BENJAMIN ROCHESTER

Born: One of ten children born to Frederick and Henrietta Rochester on June 17, 1937, in Hackensack, New Jersey. **Education:** He earned a B.A. degree from Livingstone College and did graduate study at Wesley Theological Seminary. **Family:** He is married to Dr. Mattilyn Talford Rochester. They have a son and a daughter: Enoch B. and Mattilyn C. Rochester. Bishop Rochester resides in Belleville, Ill.

African Methodist Episcopal Zion Church
88. BISHOP MARSHALL HAYWARD STRICKLAND

MARSHALL HAYWARD STRICKLAND, one of three children, was born October 8, 1933 in Floyd County, Georgia to Allen A. and Elzie Grier Strickland. He completed Booker T. Washington High School and then graduated from Livingstone College in 1955. He earned a B.D. degree from Hood Theological Seminary; a M.A. from Vanderbilt University; Nashville, Tennessee, a D. Min. from St. Mary's Ecumenical Institute, and a Ph. D. from St. Mary's University, Baltimore, Maryland in 1984.

He began preaching in 1945 at Patton Memorial A. M. E. Zion Church, Chattanooga, Tennessee. He was admitted to annual conference in November 1948 at Thompkins Chapel, Chattanooga, Tennessee. He was ordained deacon October 9, 1951 at Loguen Temple and an elder in February 1953 at the Tennessee Annual Conference by Bishop Cameron Chesterfield Alleyne.

His pastorates included Patton Memorial, Chattanooga, Tennessee; David Stand, Lancaster, South Carolina; Hood Memorial, Bristol, Tennessee; Big Zion, Mobile Alabama; and Pennsylvania Avenue Church, Baltimore, Maryland. He also led the congregation in the construction of a new Pennsylvania Avenue A. M. E. Zion Church edifice and in paying off the mortgage in eleven years. He also led the congregation in purchasing a parsonage and the construction of Zion Towers, a 216-unit apartment complex. He was elected a bishop from the pastorate of Pennsylvania Avenue congregation. He was consecrated the 88th Bishop on July 31, 1992, at the 44th General Conference, which was held in Atlanta, Georgia.

Bishop Strickland was assigned to the Liberia, West Ghana, East Ghana, Mid-Ghana, and Ivory Coast Conferences during the 1992-96 quadrennium. In 1996, he was assigned to the Mid-Atlantic I Episcopal District comprising the Ohio, Allegheny, New Jersey, Guyana, Trinidad-Tobago, and Barbados Conferences.

He is author of *Kennedy: The Dreamer* (1967); and "How Big Is Your God?" *Pulpit Digest* (1959), among other publications.

Bishop Strickland is secretary of the Board of Bishops; chair of the Brotherhood Pension Service Board; 1st vice chair, School and College Division of the Board of Christian Education; 2nd vice chair of the Bicentennial Commission; 2nd vice chair, Connectional Trustees; 1st vice chair, Theological Seminary; chair, Consultation on Church Union, appointee, The World Council of Churches; 2nd vice chairman, The Year 2000 General Conference Committee, chair, Compilation Committee.

He is the father of Marshall H. Strickland, II, and grandfather of three children: Marshee, Marshall, III, and Mara.

Bishop M. Strickland
ELECTED 1992

88. BISHOP MARSHALL HAYWARD STRICKLAND

Born: October 8, 1933, one of three children, to Allen A. and Elzie Grier Strickland, in Floyd County, Georgia. **Education:** He graduated from Booker T. Washington High School and then earned a B. A. degree from Livingstone College in 1955. He has a B. D. from Hood Theological Seminary; M.A. from Vanderbilt University; D. Min. from St. Mary's Ecumenical Institute; and a Ph. D. from St. Mary's University. He is author of *Kennedy: The Dreamer* and journal articles. **Family:**He has one son and three grand-children. Bishop Strickland resides in Baltimore, Maryland.

African Methodist Episcopal Zion Church
89. BISHOP CLARENCE CARR

CLARENCE CARR, one of four children, was born February 7, 1938, in Orangeburg, South Carolina to Joseph and Willie Mae Carr. He graduated from Woodrow Wilson High School and then earned his B.A. degree from Livingstone College in 1970 and a M. Div. from Hood Theological Seminary in 1972.

He began his ministry in 1961 at Rush Temple A. M. E. Zion Church, Jamaica, New York. He was admitted to annual conference in 1963 at Jackson Memorial, Hempstead, New York. He was ordained a deacon in June 1964 at Centennial, Mt. Vernon, New York by Bishop Herbert Bell Shaw and was ordained an elder February 4, 1966 at Walls Center, Hood Theological Seminary, Salisbury, North Carolina by Bishop William Jacob Walls.

He was pastor of Roosevelt Mission, Roosevelt, Long Island, New York; Grace, Patchogue, Long Island, New York; Moore's Chapel, Lincolnton, North Carolina; Southern City, East Spencer, North Carolina; Jackson Memorial, Hempstead, Long Island, New York; and Washington Metropolitan, St. Louis, Missouri. While he was at Jackson Memorial, he led the congregation in purchasing a parsonage and pre-paid the mortgage on the church several years early. He was elected to the episcopacy from the pastorate of Washington Metropolitan A. M. E. Zion Church and was conse-crated the 89th Bishop on July 28, 1992, at the 44th General Conference meeting in Atlanta, Georgia.

Bishop Carr was assigned to the Alaska, Oregon-Washington, Southwest Rocky Mountain, California, Arizona, and Colorado Conferences during 1992-96 and 1996-2000. He also presided over the Albemarle Conference after Bishop Anderson's death in 1995 until the General Conference in 1996. He is the chairperson of the Bicentennial Historical Commission publication and Assistant Secretary of the Board of Bishops.

His extensive civic activities include member, Board of Aldermen, East Spencer, North Carolina; Mayor-protem, East Spencer, North Carolina; member, Village of Hempstead Board of Trustees Senior Citizen Nutritional and Recreational Program, Nassau County, New York; leadership role in the integration of public schools, Rowan County, North Carolina; establishment of a Group Home for Juvenile Boys and Girls in Hempstead, New York; completion of phase III of Lucas Heights Housing Development, St. Louis, Missouri; participation in organizing the Airport Chaplaincy, St. Louis, Missouri; and chairperson of Tower Village Nursing Home Board, St. Louis, Missouri.

Bishop Carr is married to the former Barbara Shuemake. They are the parents of Leslie Denise Carr and Mark Anson Carr.

Bishop Clarence Carr
ELECTED 1992

89. BISHOP CLARENCE CARR

Born: February 7, 1938, one of four children, to Joseph and Willie Mae Carr, in Orangeburg, South Carolina. **Education:** He graduated from Woodrow Wilson High School. He earned a B.A. degree from Livingstone College in 1970 and a M. Div. from Hood Theological Seminary in 1972. **Family:** He is married to the former Barbara Shuemake. They have two children: Leslie Denise and Mark Anson Carr. Bishop Carr resides in Greendale, Missouri.

African Methodist Episcopal Zion Church
90. BISHOP NATHANIEL JARRETT, JR.

NATHANIEL JARRETT, Jr., was born May 9, 1937 to Nathaniel and Rose Jarrett in Montgomery, AL. He attended public schools in Montgomery, Alabama and Detroit, Michigan. He earned the B.S. and M. Ed. degrees from Wayne State University, Detroit, Michigan in 1960 and 1967, respectively. He received his theological training at Yale Divinity School and the Chicago Theological Seminary, from which he graduated with a M. Div. in 1969 and a D. Min. in 1982, respectively.

He was admitted to the traveling ministry on June 20, 1965 and was ordained the same day at St. Paul A. M. E. Zion Church, Detroit, Michigan, by Bishop Stephen Gill Spottswood. He was ordained an elder in May 1967, at Mt. Pleasant A. M. E. Zion Church in Danbury, Connecticut. His first pastorates were in Connecticut at Workman Memorial in Torrington and Clinton A. M. E. Zion, in Ansonia. He was assistant pastor at St. Paul A. M. E. Zion from 1970-72 and pastor-builder of Martin Temple A. M. E. Zion Church, 7158 South Indiana Ave., Chicago, Illinois, from 1972-96. He was elected a bishop from this pastorate.

He was consecrated the 90th Bishop on August 2, 1996 during the 45th General Conference, which was held at Full Gospel A. M. E. Zion Church, Temple Hills, Maryland and the Renaissance Hotel in Washington, D. C. He was assigned to the Southwestern Delta Episcopal District, which comprises the Arkansas, West Tennessee-Mississippi, South Mississippi, Louisiana, Texas, and Oklahoma Conferences.

He served the A. M. E. Zion Church as a member of the Judicial Council, director of Youth Ministries of the Christian Education Department; delegate to the General Conference; member of the Christian Education Board, Home and Church Division; delegate to the World Council of Churches, and as a member of the following ecumenical organizations: Commission on Pan Methodist Cooperation, Pan Methodist Study Commission, and Faith and Order Commission of the National Council of Churches of Christ in the U.S.A.

He is married to the former Estella Rudisel. They have three children: Craig, Todd, and Tonya Jarrett, and one grandson.

Nathaniel Jarrett
ELECTED 1996

90. BISHOP NATHANIEL JARRETT, JR.

Born: One of two sons, on May 9, 1937, in Montgomery, Alabama, to Nathaniel and Rose Jarrett. **Education:** He was educated in the public schools of Montgomery, Alabama and Detroit, Michigan. He earned his B.S. and M. Ed. degrees from Wayne State University in 1960 and 1967. He earned a M. Div. from Yale Divinity School in 1969 and a D. Min. from Chicago Theological Seminary in 1982. **Family:** He is married to the former Estella Rudisel. They are the parents of Craig, Todd, and Tonya Jarrett. They have one grandson. Bishop Jarrett resides in Chicago, Illinois.

91. BISHOP WARREN MATTHEW BROWN

WARREN MATTHEW BROWN, one of three sons, was born August 14, 1941 in Knoxville, Tennessee to the Rev. William Matthew and Edith McGinns Brown. He was educated in public schools and graduated from Austin High School, Knoxville, Tennessee. In 1962, he graduated from Knoxville College with a B.S. degree. He later attended the Interdenominational Theological Center in Atlanta, Georgia.

He began preaching at his local church, First A. M. E. Zion, Knoxville, Tennessee, in January 1959 and was admitted to the Tennessee Annual Conference in October 1959. On October 18, 1959, Bishop H. T. Medford ordained him a deacon at Clinton Chapel, Knoxville, Tennessee. He was ordained an elder by Bishop William Andrew Stewart on January 13, 1962, at Varick Chapel, Asheville, North Carolina.

He was pastor of Oak Grove, Knoxville, Tennessee from 1959-61; Youngs Temple, Morristown, Tennessee, 1961-62; Jones Temple, Waynesville, North Carolina, 1962-65; Walls Temple, Albany, New York, 1965-73; Columbus Avenue, Boston, 1973-92; and Trinity, Washington, D.C., from 1992-96, from which pastorate he was elected to the episcopacy.

He was a presiding elder, Boston District, New England Conference from 1973-92. During his tenure, he expanded the number of churches in the district from thirteen to twenty-seven. He was an associate presiding elder in the Virgin Islands Conference from 1980-92 and supervised the rebuilding of Beulah and Medford A. M. E. Zion churches after the destruction of Hurricane Hugo. He was elected treasurer of the Presiding Elders Council in 1980 and served for eleven years. He was the pastor-builder of Walls Temple, Albany, New York and was a member of the Board of Overseas Missions from 1968-92. He was a three-term member of the Boston University Seminary Board of Visitors.

He was elected and consecrated the 91st Bishop on August 2, 1996 at Full Gospel A. M. E. Zion Church, Temple Hills, Maryland, during the 45th General Conference meeting in Washington, D. C. He was assigned to the Western West Africa Episcopal District, comprising Liberia, Cote d'Ivoire, East Ghana, West Ghana, and Mid-Ghana Conferences.

Bishop Brown is married to Aurelia Sanders Brown. They are the parents of two daughters: Angelyne E. and Anita E. Brown.

Warren M. Brown
ELECTED 1996

91. BISHOP WARREN MATTHEW BROWN

Born: August 14, 1941, one of three sons, to the Rev. William Matthew and Edith McGinns Brown, in Knoxville, Tennessee. **Education:** He graduated from Austin High School, Knoxville, Tennessee. He earned a B. S. degree from Knoxville College, Tennessee in 1959. He later attended Interdenominational Theological Center. **Family:** He is married to the former Aurelia Sanders. They have two daughters: Angelyne E. and Anita E. Brown. Bishop Brown currently resides in Randolph, Massachusetts.

REFERENCES

More than twenty-five sources were consulted to provide as complete a picture as possible of the bishops, their service to the A. M. E. Zion Church, and of their families. Unless otherwise indicated, the information on bishops 1-76 (Varick to Speaks) came from Walls, *The African Methodist Episcopal Zion Church: The Reality of the Black Church*. Walls, in turn, noted that the record of birth, ordination and consecration of bishops 1-24 came from J. Harvey Anderson, *A. M. E. Zion Handbook, 1895*, p. 35 and that other information on bishops 1-49 came from Samuel Madison Dudley, *Handbook of the A. M. E. Zion Church, 1944*, p. 14. Again, unless otherwise indicated, information on bishops 77-to 91 came from responses by the respective person or a family member to a questionnaire prepared and circulated by the Bicentennial Commission Publication Office.

A. M. E. Zion Publishing House. 1972-1992. *Official Journals, 39th-44th Quadrennial Sessions of General Conference.*

A. M. E. Zion Quarterly Review. "Bishop Cameron Chesterfield Alleyne." 59 (3) 1949: 106-07; "Bishop John William Martin." 104-05; "Frank Wesley Alstork." 102-03.
_____. "Raymond Luther Jones." 82 (4) 1972: 94-96.

Biographical Encyclopedia of the World. 1946. New York: Institute for Research in Biography.

Boris, Joseph J., ed. 1929. *Who's Who in Colored America*, 1928-1929, 2d ed. New York: Who's Who in Colored America Corp.

Bradley, Sr., David Henry. 1972. *A History of the A.M.E. Zion Church, Part I, 1796-1872.* Nashville, Tenn: Parthenon Press.

———. 1970. *A History of the A. M. E. Zion Church, Part II, 1872-1968.* Nashville, Tenn: Parthenon Press.

Clement, Rufus E. 1936. "Alexander Walters." Pp. 398-99 in *Dictionary of American Biography* 19, ed. Dumas Malone. New York: Charles Scribner's Sons.

Douglas, Carlyle C. 1975. "50 Years a Bishop." Ebony (February): 104-09.

Hood, James Walker. 1895. *One Hundred Years of the A.M.E. Zion Church.* New York: A. M. E. Zion Book Concern.

Hunter, Carol. 1993. To Set the Captives Free. New York: Garland Press.

Journal of Negro History. "George Clinton Clement." 20 (1) 1935: pp. 117-18.
_____. "Frank Wesley Alstork." 33(4) 1948: pp. 502-3.

Logan, Rayford W., and Michael R. Winston, eds. 1982. *Dictionary of American*

References

Negro Biography. New York: W. W. Norton.

Lovell, Walter, R. "Walter William Slade." Pp. 4-5 in *Star of Zion*, June 6, 1963.

Marquis, Albert Nelson, ed. 1912. *Who's Who in America*, 1912-13; 1916-17; 1926-27. Chicago: A. N. Marquis and Co.

_____. 1916. *Who's Who in America*, 1916-17

Maser, Frederick E. 1974. "Clinton, George Wylie." P. 525 in *Encyclopedia of World Methodism* I, ed. Noland B. Harmon et al. Nashville: United Methodist Publishing House.

Medford, Hampton Thomas. 1960. *This is My Life, An Autobiography: From Rags to Riches*, 2d ed. Washington, D. C.

Moore, John Jamison. 1884. *History of the A.M.E. Zion Church*. York, Pa.: Teachers Journal Office.

Price, Carl F., comp. and ed. 1916. *Who's Who in American Methodism*. New York: E. B. Treat.

Roundtree, Louise M. 1963. *An Index to Biographical Sketches and Publications of the Bishops of the A. M. E. Zion Church*. Salisbury, North Carolina: Livingstone College.

Walls, William J. 1974. *The African Methodist Episcopal Zion Church. Reality of the Black Church*. Charlotte, N.C.: A. M. E. Zion Publishing Co.

Wheeler, Rev. B. F. 1936. *The Varick Family*. Mobile, Ala.: B. F. Wheeler.

Yenser, Thomas, ed. *Who's Who in Colored America, 1933-1937*, 4th ed.; *1938-1940*, 5th ed.; 1950, 7th ed. New York: Thomas Yenser.

Who's Who in America, 1912-13; 1916-17; 1926-27. Chicago: A. N. Marquis and Co.

Who's Who in Colored America, 1930-1932, 3rd ed.; 1933-1937, 4th ed.; 1938-1940, 5th ed.; New York: Thomas Yenser.

Who's Who in Colored America, 1950, 7th ed. Yonkers-on-Hudson, N.Y.: Christian E. Burckel and Associates.

Who Was Who In America I, 1897-1942. 1942. Chicago: A. N. Marquis.

Who Was Who In America: Historical Volume, 1607-1896, Revised. 1967. Chicago: A. N. Marquis.

GALLERY
OF
PHOTOGRAPHS

GENERAL OFFICERS
OF THE A. M. E. ZION CHURCH, 1996

Rev. Dr. W. Robert Johnson, III
General Secretary-Auditor, 1988-

Dr. Madie L. Simpsom
Chief Financial Officer, 1976-

Rev. Dr. David Miller
Secretary-Treasurer
Brotherhood Pensions and Ministerial
Relief, 1992-
and
General Manager (Interim)
A. M. E. Zion Publishing House, 1996-

Rev. Dr. Morgan W. Tann
Editor, *Star of Zion*,
1980-

GENERAL OFFICERS, 1996

Rev. James David Armstrong
Editor, *A. M. E. Zion Quarterly Review*
and Secretary
A. M. E. Zion Historical Society, 1989-

Rev. Dr. Kermit J. DeGraffenreidt
Secretary-Treasurer
Dept. of Overseas Missions
and Editor, *The Missionary Seer*, 1980-

Rev. Raymon E. Hunt
Secretary-Treasurer
Dept. of Christian Education
1992-

Dr. Mary A. Love
Editor
Church School Literature
1980-

GENERAL OFFICERS, 1996

Dr. Lem Long, Jr.
  Secretary
Dept. of Church Extension
  1968-1992
  Secretary
Dept. of Home Missions and
  Church Extension, 1992-

Rev. Darryl B. Starnes, Sr.
  Director
Bureau of Evangelism
  1996

Rev. George E. McKain
  Director
Public Affairs and Convention
  Manager, 1996-

Rev. Dr. Bernard Sullivan
  Director
Dept. of Health and Social
  Concerns, 1996-

GENERAL OFFICERS, 1948-1996

General Officers of the A. M. E. Zion Church, 1976-1980

L-R: Rev. Harold A. L. Clement, Sec'y-Treasurer, Dept. of Overseas Missions, 1972-80; Rev. Dr. David H. Bradley, Sr., Editor, A. M. E. Zion Quarterly Review, 1948-79; Rev. Dr. M. B. Robinson, Editor, Star of Zion, 1970-80; Rev. Herman L. Anderson, General Secretary-Auditor, 1976-80; Ms. Madie L. Simpson, Secretary, Department of Finance, 1976- ; Rev. Dr. Jewett L. Walker, Secretary-Treasurer, Department of Home Missions, Brotherhood Pensions and Ministerial Relief, 1974-92; Mr. Lem Long, Jr., Secretary, Department of Church Extension, 1968-1992; Secretary, Home Missions and Church Extension, 1992- ; Rev. Dr. George Lincoln Blackwell, Secretary, Department of Christian Education, 1967-92

GENERAL OFFICERS, 1972-1996

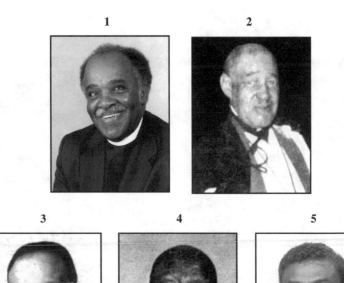

Clockwise: Rev. Dr. Earle E. Johnson, General Secretary-Auditor, 1980-88; Dr. R. H. Collins Lee, General Secretary-Auditor, 1967-76; Dr. John H. Satterwhite, Editor, A. M. E. Zion Quarterly Review and Secretary, A. M. E. Zion Historical Society, 1980-89; Rev. Dr. Austin Paul Morris, Secretary-Treasurer, Department of Home Missions, Brotherhood Pensions and Ministerial Relief, 1956-73; Rev. Dr. Norman H. Hicklin, Director, Bureau of Evangelism, 1988-96

GENERAL OFFICERS, 1972-1996

Clockwise:
1. Rev. Dr. Louis J. Baptiste, Editor, Church School Literature, 1962-80
2. Rev. Dr. J. Dallas Jenkins, Director, Bureau of Evangelism, 1968-88
3. Rev. Dr. Thaddeus Garrett, Jr., Director, Department of Public Relations and Convention Manager, 1988-92; Member, Howard University Board of Trustees, 1984-97; Chairperson, Howard University Board of Trustees, 1995-97
4. Rev. Gregory Robeson Smith, Director, Department of Public Relations and Convention Manager, 1976-88
5. Dr. Samuel Coleman, Founder and Director, Department of Health, 1956-1984.. Died, April 6, 1984 at age 106 years.

A. M. E. ZION EDUCATIONAL INSTITUTIONS

LIVINGSTONE COLLEGE

Dr. Burnett Joiner
Tenth President
Livingstone College
Salisbury, North Carolina
July 1, 1996-

A. M. E. ZION EDUCATIONAL INSTITUTIONS

LIVINGSTONE COLLEGE
Former Presidents - 1972-1996

1

Dr. F. George Shipman
1969 - 1982

2

Dr. William H. Greene
1984- 1988

3

Dr. Roy D. Hudson
Interim President - Feb.
9, 1995 - March 1, 1995
President - Mar. 1, 1995-
June 1996

4

Dr. Ozell K. Beatty
Interim President - Jan.
1988- July 1988
President - July 1988-
July 1989

5

Dr. Bernard W. Franklin
1989 - 1995

HOOD THEOLOGICAL SEMINARY

Dr. Albert J. D. Aymer
Dean, Hood Theological Seminary
Salisbury, North Carolina
1994

FORMER DEANS
Hood Theological Seminary
L-R: Rev. Dr. John H. Satterwhite, 1938 - 1958
Dr. Frank R. Brown - acting 1953-55; Dean 1955-1970
Rev. Dr. Walter L. Yates, 1970-84

540

HOOD THEOLOGICAL SEMINARY

Dr. William Lawrence
Dean, 1981-90

Dr. James R. Samuel
Interim Dean, 1990-93

CLINTON JUNIOR COLLEGE
ROCK HILL, SOUTH CAROLINA

Dr. Cynthia McCullough Russell
President, 1994-

Dr. Sallie V. Moreland
President, 1946-94

LOMAX-HANNON JUNIOR COLLEGE

Rev. David Knight, Interim President, 1996-Current

Rev. James E. Cook, Interim President, 1977-1996

LOMAX-HANNON JUNIOR COLLEGE

Rev. C. Mifflin Smith, President, 1972-77

Dr. B. M. Montgomery, President, 1968-72

544

A. M. E. ZION UNIVERSITY, MONROVIA
LIBERIA

Rev. Frederick Umoja
President
A. M. E. Zion College
Monrovia, Liberia

WOMAN'S HOME AND OVERSEAS
MISSIONARY SOCIETY

Dr. Adlise Ivey Porter
General President, WH&OM Society, 1995-

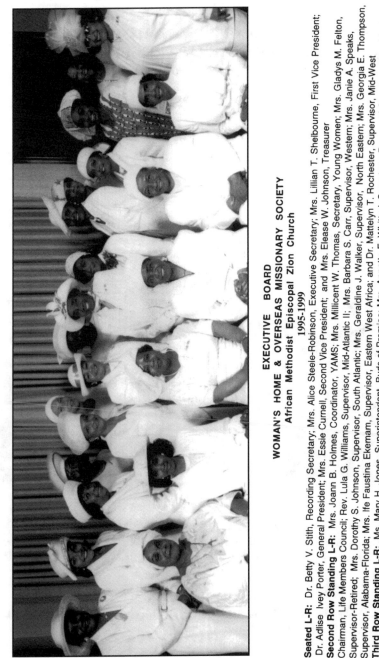

EXECUTIVE BOARD
WOMAN'S HOME & OVERSEAS MISSIONARY SOCIETY
African Methodist Episcopal Zion Church
1995-1999

Seated L-R: Dr. Betty V. Stith, Recording Secretary; Mrs. Alice Steele-Robinson, Executive Secretary; Mrs. Lillian T. Shelbourne, First Vice President; Dr. Adlise Ivey Porter, General President; Mrs. Essie Curnell, Second Vice President; and Mrs. Elease W. Johnson, Treasurer

Second Row Standing L-R: Mrs. Joann B. Holmes, Coordinator, YAMS; Mrs. Millicent W. Thomas, Secretary, Young Women; Mrs. Gladys M. Felton, Chairman, Life Members Council; Rev. Lula G. Williams, Supervisor, Mid-Atlantic II; Mrs. Barbara S. Carr, Supervisor, Western; Mrs. Janie A. Speaks, Supervisor-Retired; Mrs. Dorothy S. Johnson, Supervisor, South Atlantic; Mrs. Geraldine J. Walker, Supervisor, North Eastern; Mrs. Georgia E. Thompson, Supervisor, Alabama-Florida; Mrs. Ife Faustina Ekemam, Supervisor, Eastern West Africa; and Dr. Mattelyn T. Rochester, Supervisor, Mid-West

Third Row Standing L-R: Ms. Mary H. Jones, Superintendent, Buds of Promise; Mrs. Annette E. Whitted, Secretary, Bureau of Supplies; Mrs. Mattie W. Taylor, Editor, Woman's Section, SEER; Mrs. Ruth R. Anderson, Supervisor-Retired; and Mrs. Marlene Y. Bishop, Supervisor, Piedmont;

Not Shown: Mrs. Iris M. Battle, Supervisor, Eastern North Carolina; Dr. Dorothy E. Brunson, Supervisor, Mid-Atlantic I; Mrs. Estelle Jarrett, Supervisor, Southwestern Delta; Mrs. Aurelia Brown, Supervisor, Western West Africa.

WOMAN'S HOME AND OVERSEAS MISSIONARY SOCIETY
FORMER GENERAL PRESIDENTS

L-R: Dr. Willa Mae Rice, 1971-79; Mrs. Alcestis McCullough Coleman, 1979-87; Mrs. Grace L. Holmes, 1987-95

CONNECTIONAL LAY COUNCIL

Mrs. Lula K. Howard
President, 1997-

Connectional Lay Council, 1973-97

L-R: Mrs. Frances J. Glenn, Secretary; Mrs. Odess Tyson-Clapp (deceased), 2nd
Vice President; Mrs. Lula K. Howard, 1st Vice President; Mrs. Mary E. Taylor,
President; Mr. Ervin D. Reid, Treasurer; and Mr. Coyal Cooper, Chaplain

A. M. E. ZION CHURCH JUDICIAL COUNCIL

Hon. Adele M. Riley
President, 1992-

EPISCOPAL RESIDENCES

North Eastern Episcopal District
137 Talcott Notch Road
Farmington, Connecticut 06032
(Bishop George W. C. Walker, Sr.)

Mid-Atlantic Episcopal District
12904 Canoe Court
Fort Washington, Maryland 20744
(Bishop Milton A. Williams, Sr.)

EPISCOPAL RESIDENCES

Alabama-Florida Episcopal District
2159 Vaughn Lane
Montgomery, Alabama 36106
(Bishop Richard K. Thompson)

Western West Africa Episcopal District
Accra, Ghana
(Bishop Warren Matthew Brown)

A. M. E. ZION CHURCH
RELIGIOUS, CIVIC, AND PUBLIC LEADERS

Rev. Dr. Alvin T. Durant
Pastor, Mother Zion
A. M. E. Zion Church, NYC
1993-

The Hon. Louis Stokes, Ohio
Congressman
U. S. House of
Representatives
1968-1999

Dr. Bernard E. Anderson,
Philadelphia, PA
Assistant Secretary,
U. S. Department of Labor
Employment Standards
Administration, 19—-19-

Mr. Andra' R. Ward, Ohio
Executive Director,
1994-1996
A. M. E. Zion Church
Bicentennial Commission

A. M. E. ZION CHURCH
RELIGIOUS, CIVIC, AND PUBLIC LEADERS, Cont'd.

Dr. Abbie Clement Jackson

Former Executive Secretary, Woman's Home and Overseas Missionary Society,1943-51; Former President, Woman's Home and Missionary Society, 1955-63; 1st Vice President, National Council of Churches in the U. S. A., 1950; Delegateto the First Assembly of the World Council of Churches, Amsterdam, Holland,1948; Officer, Church Women United; and Officer, North American Section ofWorld Methodist Women. She died on April 8, 1986 and is buried in Louisville, Kentucky

Rev. Dr. William James Lord Wallace
President, West Virginia State College 1953-73 and presiding Elder of the West Virginia District of the Allegheny Conference of the A. M. E. Zion Church

Rev. Dr. Clarence G. Newsome,
Washington, DC
Dean, Howard University School of Divinity, 1992-

Rev. Dr. Bernard Richardson
Dean, Howard University Andrew Rankin Memorial Chapel, 1963-
A. M. E. Zion Minister

APPENDIX A

THE GENERAL CONFERENCES

The lawmaking body of Zion Methodism meets every four years. The bishops preside in rotation, and the delegates elect bishops and general officers of the denomination and promote the necessary legislation for the progress of the church. The African Methodist Episcopal Zion Church has held forty-five general conferences in its 200 years history:

General Conference	Date	Days in Session
1st: ZION CHURCH, NEW YORK CITY Presiding Officer: James Varick Host Pastor: Abraham Thompson	July 10, 1820	6
2ND: ZION CHURCH NEW YORK CITY Host Bishop: James Varick Host Pastor: Leven Smith	July 15, 1824	6
3RD: ZION CHURCH NEW YORK CITY Presiding Officer: Christopher Rush Host Pastor: James Smith	May 15, 1828	6
4TH: ZION CHURCH NEW YORK CITY Host Bishop: Christopher Rush Host Pastor: Peter Vanhas	May 19, 1832	6
5TH: ZION CHURCH NEW YORK CITY Host Bishop: Christopher Rush Host Pastor: Peter Vanhas	May 14, 1836	6
6TH: ASBURY CHURCH NEW YORK CITY Host Bishop: Christopher Rush Host Pastor: Thomas Eato	May 28, 1840	3

Appendix A

General Conference	Date	Days in Session
7th: ZION CHURCH, NEW YORK CITY Host Bishop: Christopher Rush Host Pastor: William H. Bishop	May 18, 1844	6
8TH: ZION CHURCH NEW YORK CITY Host Bishop: Christopher Rush Host Pastor: John P. Thompson	May 29, 1848	6
9TH: WESLEY CHURCH PHILADELPHIA Host Bishop: Christopher Rush Host Pastor: Jacob Trusty	May 26, 1852	20
10TH: ZION CHURCH NEW YORK CITY Host Bishop: James Simmons Host Pastor: Dempsey Kennedy	June 26, 1856	15
11TH: WESLEY CHURCH PHILADELPHIA Host Bishop: William H. Bishop Host Pastor: Singleton T. Jones	May 30, 1860	12
12TH: WESLEY CHURCH PHILADELPHIA Host Bishop: William H. Bishop Host Pastor: John A. Williams	May 25, 1864	25
13TH: WESLEY ZION (METRO- POLITAN) WASH., D. C. Host Bishop: Simon D. Talbot Host Pastor: John Tappan	May 6, 1868	20

Appendix A

General Conference	Date	Days in Session
14TH: CLINTON CHAPEL CHARLOTTE, N. C. Host Bishop: John D. Brooks Host Pastor: William J. Moore	June 19, 1872	14
15TH: FIFTEENTH STREET CHURCH (HUGHLETT TEMPLE), LOUISVILLE, KENTUCKY Host Bishop: Singleton T. Jones Presiding Elder: E. H. Curry Host Pastor: Jehu Holliday	June 1, 1876	17
16TH: CLINTON CHAPEL (THE OLD SHIP) MONTGOMERY, ALA. Host Bishop: Joseph P. Thompson Presiding Elder: Wilbur G. Strong Host Pastor: Allen Hannon	May 5, 1880	18
17TH: MOTHER ZION CHURCH NEW YORK CITY Host Bishop: Singleton T. Jones Presiding Elder: Abram Anderson Host Pastor: R. H. G. Dyson	May 7, 1884	25
18TH: ST. PETER'S NEW BERN, N. C Host Bishop: Joseph P. Thompson Presiding Elder: Abram W. Allison Host Pastor: C. H. Smith	May 2, 1888	18
19TH: JOHN WESLEY CHURCH PITTSBURGH Host Bishop: Singleton T. Jones Presiding Elder: Jehu Holliday Host Pastor: George W. Clinton	May 4, 1892	21

Appendix A

General Conference	Date	Days in Session
20TH: STATE STREET CHURCH MOBILE, ALA. Host Bishop: Charles C. Pettey Presiding Elder: Wilbur C. Strong Host Pastor: P. J. McEntosh	May 6, 1896	20
21ST: METROPOLITAN WESLEY CHURCH, WASH., D. C. Host Bishop: Charles C. Pettey Presiding Elder: W. H. Snowden Host Pastor: P. J. McEntosh	May 2, 1900	23
22ND: WASHINGTON MEMORIAL CHURCH, ST. LOUIS Host Bishop: Alexander Walters Presiding Elder: Jesse B. Colbert Host Pastor: E. D. W. Jones	May 4, 1904	15
23RD: BIG WESLEY PHILADELPHIA Host Bishop: George W. Clinton Presiding Elder: E. H. Curry Host Pastor: R. A. Morrisey	May 6, 1908	16
24TH: CLINTON CHAPEL CHARLOTTE, N. C. Host Bishop: George W. Clinton Presiding Elder: S. D. Watkins Host Pastor: P. A. McCorkle	May 1, 1912	22
25TH: BROADWAY TEMPLE, LOUISVILLE, KY. Host Bishop: Josiah S. Caldwell Presiding Elder: R. B. Hendricks Host Pastor: William J. Walls	May 3, 1916	15

Appendix A

General Conference	Date	Days in Session
26TH: LOGUEN TEMPLE KNOXVILLE, TENN. Host Bishop: George C. Clement Presiding Elder: W. H. Mitchell Host Pastor: J. L. Black	May 5, 1920	15
27TH: JONES TABERNACLE INDIANAPOLIS, INDIANA Host Bishop: Paris A. Wallace Presiding Elder: L. D. Davis Host Pastor: S. D. Davis	May 5, 1924	23
28TH: WASHINGTON METROPOLITAN CHURCH, ST. LOUIS Host Bishop: John W. Wood Presiding Elder: S. D. Davis Host Pastor: H. H. Jackson	May 2, 1928	20
29TH: WESLEY CENTER CHURCH PITTSBURGH Host Bishop: W. W. Matthews Presiding Elder: D. H. Thomas Host Pastor: Elijah L. Madison	May 4, 1932	14
30TH: TRINITY CHURCH, GREENSBORO N. C. Host Bishop: W. W. Matthews Presiding Elder: T. J. Houston Host Pastor: W. F. Witherspoon	May 6, 1936	15
31ST: JOHN WESLEY WASHINGTON, D. C. Host Bishop: C. C. Alleyne Presiding Elder: A. A. Crooke Pastor: Stephen G. Spottswood	May 1, 1940	16

Appendix A

General Conference	Date	Days in Session

32ND:ST. PAUL CHURCH   May 3, 1944   13
DETROIT, MICH.
Host Bishop: John W. Martin
Presiding Elder: Fred D. Porter
Host Pastor: Lott P. Powell

33RD:BROADWAY TEMPLE   May 5, 1948   16
LOUISVILLE, KY.
Host Bishop: William C. Brown
Presiding Elder: B.N. Henningham
Host Pastor: Raymond L. Jones

34TH: FIRST CHURCH   May 7, 1952   15
BROOKLYN, N. Y.
Host Bishop: Willliam J. Walls
Presiding Elder: J. H. Tucker
Host Pastor: W. O. Carrington

35TH: WESLEY CENTER CHURCH   May 2, 1956   15
PITTSBURGH
Host Bishop: William C. Brown
Presiding Elder: Alexander L. Pierce
Host Pastor: Charles H. Foggie

36TH: ST. LUKE CHURCH   May 4, 1960   15
BUFFALO, N. Y.
Host Bishop: William J. Walls
Presiding Elder: Arthur E. May
Host Pastor: Hunter B. Bess

37TH: JONES TABERNACLE,   May 6, 1964   15
INDIANAPOLIS, INDIANA
Host Bishop: Stephen G. Spottswood
Presiding Elder: J. Humphrey Lee
Host Pastor: I. Benjamin Pierce

Appendix A

General Conference	Date	Days in Session
38TH: ST. PAUL CHURCH DETROIT, MICH Host Bishop: Stephen G. Spottswood Presiding Elder: William M. Poe Host Pastor: William C. Ardrey	May 1, 1968	15
39TH: BIG ZION CHURCH MOBILE. ALA. Host Bishop: William M. Smith Presiding Elder: Leon W. Watts, Sr. Host Pastor: Marshall H. Strickland	May 3, 1972	10
40TH: GREATER WALTERS AND MCCORMICK INN, CHICAGO Host Bishop: William A. Hilliard Presiding Elder: Norsie L. Meeks Host Pastor: G. W. C. Walker, Sr.	May 5, 1976	10
41ST: TRINITY AND COLISEUM GREENSBORO, N. C. Host Bishop: A. G. Dunston Presiding Elder: S. A. Speight Host Pastor: Vaughn T. Eason	May 7, 1980	10
42ND:WASHINGTON METROPOLITAN AND SHERATON ST. LOUIS CONVENTION CENTER Host Bishop: J. H. Miller, Sr. Presiding Elder: Joseph H. Jones Host Pastor: Richard L. Fisher	July 25, 1984	10

Appendix A

General Conference	Date	Days in Session
43RD:LITTLE ROCK AND ADAMS MARK CONVENTION CENTER, CHARLOTTE, N. C. Host Bishop: William M. Smith Presiding Elder: Horace C. Walser Host Pastor: William M. White	July 27, 1988	10
44TH: SHAW TEMPLE, ATLANTA HILTON AND TOWERS HOTEL, ATLANTA, GA. Host Bishop: Cecil Bishop Presiding Elder: J. W. Smith Host Pastor: J. W. Smith	July 22, 1992	10
45TH: FULL GOSPEL, RENAISSANCE HOTEL, AND WASHINGTON D. C. CONVENTION CENTER Host Bishop: Milton A. Williams, Sr. Presiding Elder: Joseph A. Davis Host Pastor: John A. Cherry	July 24, 1996	10

APPENDIX B

PRINCIPLES OF UNION-BETWEEN A. M. E. ZION AND C. M. E. CHURCHES

A. Basic Affirmations

1. We affirm our common belief in God, who is Sovereign, Infinite, and Eternal; the creator and Sustainor of all that is and all that is to come, the Source of all wisdom and truth.

2. We affirm the common Christian witness that Jesus Christ is the Supreme Revelation of this Sovereign God and is Lord and Savior of the world, the Church and the individual.

3. We affirm our common belief in the Holy Spirit as the full presence of God in the Church, world, and persons; teaching, guiding and fulfilling the purpose of God in all life.

4. We affirm the catholicity of the Christian Faith in which no particular culture, race, generation, or gender can make an exclusive claim or priority of the Faith.

5. We affirm our belief in the Church as the Body of Christ, the visible congregation of the faithful, where the Word of God is preached and the sacraments of Baptism and Communion are administered, that the Holy Church was chosen by God to become God's agent of reconciliation in the world, open to all who have a desire to flee from the wrath to come.

6. We affirm the common Christian witness through the heritage of Methodism, emphasizing the teachings of John Wesley and the movement known as Methodism, but showing clearly, and without apology, that the founders of the African Methodist Episcopal Zion and the CME Churches developed in respose to the social and cultural patterns in which the founders of these two churches were excluded from full participation in American Methodism.

7. We affirm the divergent historical developments of African Methodist Episcopal Zion and Christian Methodist Episcopal traditions, recognizing clearly, and without apology, that the two Churches developed along different historical paths with different histories, traditions, and loyalties.

8. We affirm the common Christian witness engendered by our founding fore-parents' response to God's call to liberation since the social, cultural, and religious practices excluded them from full participation in the total American society, secular and sacred.

Appendix B

9. We affirm the common Black heritage which emphasized our unique understanding of the faith and mission to Black people, the world, and to others as integral to the historical and spiritual understanding of the A. M. E. Zion and C. M. E. Churches.

B. Reasons for Union

1. The A. M. E. Zion and the C. M. E. Churches, two historic black denominations, proposed to come together in organic union in response to a clearer understanding of the call of God in Jesus Christ and a conviction that this period of history calls for a witness of the Christian Faith in a peculiar and unique way that such union would provide.

2. The empowerment for service and mission that has been integral to the history of the A. M. E. Zion and the C. M. E. Churches would be greatly enhanced were the two denominations united.

3. Greater opportunities for theological awareness and understanding for our existence as Churches and our being as persons would be afforded were the African Methodist Episcopal Zion and the Christian Methodist Episcopal Churches to come together as one.

4. The union of these two historically and predominantly Black Churches would greatly enhance the efforts to bring unity to the Body of Christ, now broken and divided. (p. 103)

5. The courageous history and arduous efforts on the part of our foreparents in generations past as early as 1874, then in 1902, 1910, and again in 1918, in bringing together these two Churches encumbers us to culminate in our time their dream of union.

C. The Faith of the United Church

1. The Varick/Miles Methodist Episcopal Church will hold fast to the tradition of the Christian Faith as found in the New Testament, the Protestant Reformation, and the Wesley heritage.

2. The V/M Methodist Episcopal Church will hold fast to the Articles of Religion as set forth by John Wesley and common to the two (2) uniting Churches.

3. The V/M Methodist Episcopal Church will hold fast to the Old and New Testaments of the Hebrew and Christian Scriptures as containing all things necessary to salvation and that which cannot be found therein or proved thereby cannot be required of any persons as requisites to their salvation.

Appendix B

4. The V/M Methodist Episcopal Church will hold fast to the principles, precepts, faith experiences, and theological postulates of the founders who made these two (2) Churches possible, and will always be open to God's continuing revelation through Jesus Christ.

5. The V/M Methodist Episcopal Church will hold fast to the conviction that subscription to any particular creedal formulation shall not be a condition of membership in the Church; it will hold fast that the historic creed usually referred to as "The Apostles' creed" and "The Nicene Creed" affirm the essence of the Christian Faith. The V/M Methodist Episcopal Church would desire the formulation of another creed expressing its understanding of the particular histories of the two (2) uniting Churches, but such a creedal formulation would not be a precondition of union.

D. Structure of the (V/M)Methodist Episcopal Church

1. The General Conference

The governing body of the V/M Methodist Episcopal Church will be the General Conference in accordance with its adopted constitution.

A. It will be composed of an equal number of clerical and lay persons elected by the several Annual Conferences.

B. It will have full authority to make rules and regulations for the operation of the V/M Methodist Episcopal Church.

C. It will establish general or connectional departments and/or agencies to carry forth the ministry and mission of the Denomination.

2. The Annual Conferences

The basic organizational unit of the V/M Methodist Episcopal Church will be the Annual Conference with the following composition and authority:

A. It will be composed of ministers who are travelling members of it and lay persons as will be determined by the DISCIPLINE.

B. It will elect delegates to the General Conference.

C. It will elect persons to orders, discipline, and examine the character of its clerical members.

D. It will oversee the operation of the Denomination within its bounds.

3. The District Conference

There will be a District Conference composed of local congregations of a given geographical area over which a Presiding Elder will preside. The purpose of the District Conference will be to carry forth the mission of the Denomination in that area through worship, fellowship, education, and other related activities. (p. 104)

4. The Quarterly Conference

The Quarterly Conference will be the ruling authority of the local congregation. It will be composed of designated leaders of the congregation, along with the ministers appointed to it. It will be presided over by the Presiding Elder appointed in the manner prescribed by the United Church. It will have authority to confirm officers of the local congregation, approve applications to exhort and preach, recommend local preachers for admission on trial in the appropriate conferences, and will have authority, in accordance with the DISCIPLINE, to approve the purchase, sale, rental, or any disposition or transaction related to the real property and bonded indebtedness of the local congregation. It shall have such legislative authority as prescribed in accordance with the DISCIPLINE of the New Church.

5. The Church Conference

The Church Conference will be composed of all members of a local congregation as described by the DISCIPLINE of the New Church. It shall meet periodically at the call of the Pastor-in-Charge, who shall have the exclusive right to preside. It shall have the authority to set forth the spiritual, temporal, and special ministries of the local congregation.

6. Church Membership

The V/M Methodist Episcopal Church will recognize as members in full and good standing all persons who are members in full and good standing in the African Methodist Episcopal Zion and Christian Methodist Episcopal Churches at the time the two (2) Churches unite, in accordance with their respective DISCIPLINES.

The V/M Methodist Episcopal Church will accept into membership those persons who:

A. Have been baptized with water in the name of the Father, Son, and Holy Ghost, and

B. Are willing to take a vow to abide by the rules and regulations of the Church and to support its institutions with their means and services.

Baptized children are members of the Church and share in the privileges and obligations of membership as far as they are capable of doing.

Appendix B

E. The Ministry of the V/M Methodist Episcopal Church

In the V/M Methodist Episcopal Church, the ordained ministry is to bring sinners to repentance and to lead God's people in worship, prayer, and praise through the preaching of the Gospel, pastoral ministrations, and the administration of the Sacraments; to assist persons to receive the saving and sanctifying benefits of Jesus Christ, and to fit them for service in the world of His name. The V/M Methodist Episcopal Church views ordination as the means through which God bestows on and assures to those whom He has called and His Church has accepted for ministry, the commission for such ministry, and the grace appropriate to it. There will be two (2) orders of ministry in the V/M Methodist Episcopal Church: Deacon and Elder.

Deacon

The Deacon is the initial and lesser of the ministerial orders. The function of the Deacon will include assisting the Elder in the administration of the Holy Communion; administering the Sacrament of Baptism, giving succor to the poor, the needy, and the sick; instructing children in the faith; preaching, burying the dead; and generally giving assistance in pastoral and evangelistic work. Deacons will be set apart for their ministry upon their election by the Annual Conference and the laying on of hands by a Bishop, assisted by an Elder.

Elder

The Elder is the higher of the two (2) ministerial orders. The Elder will have the authority to preach and expound the Word of God, administer the Sacraments, bury the dead, perform the rite of matrimony, and assist in the laying on of hands in the ordination of Deacon and Elder. The Elder will receive the order upon election by the clerical members of the Annual Conference and the laying on of hands by other Elders. (p. 105)

Bishops

The general oversight of the people of God in the V/M Methodist Episcopal Church, as well as the Church itself, will be vested in the office of Bishops. Bishops shall be Elders in the Church who have been set aside for special service to the Church through election by the General Conference and consecrated in the historic manner of American Methodism.

The Bishop will have authority to appoint pastors to their respective charges, commission Annual Conference and District officers in accordance with the laws of the United Church, preside over Annual Conferences, and ordain Deacons and Elders.

Appendix B

F. Judicial Administration

The Judicial Administration of the V/M Methodist Episcopal Church will be vested in a Judicial Council, which will not be empowered with original jurisdiction. (An item for further study and understanding by both Denominations.)

G. Educational Institutions

Support of Institutions of Learning for our people has been an essential element of the historic mission of the African Methodist Episcopal Zion and Christian Methodist Episcopal Churches. The V/M Methodist Episcopal Church affirms that historic mission as of significance beyond estimation, and, in accordance with the legal and moral obligations obtaining therefrom, affirms that those educational and theological institutions which will be operative under the auspices of either of the two (2) Churches at the time of union at home and overseas will have the same relationship to the V/M Methodist Episcopal Church as they had with either of the two (2) Churches, and will have no less level of financial and moral support in and by the V/M Methodist Episcopal Church as they had in the two (2) Churches. (*Official Journal, 43rd Quad. Sess. Gen. Conf.*, pp. 103-6)

APPENDIX C

MEMBERS OF THE A. M. E. ZION CHURCH
HOLDING KNOWN ELECTED OR APPOINTED STATE OR FEDERAL
GOVERNMENT OFFICE, 1972-1996

Joanne M. Collins, former president, City Council, Kansas City, Missouri; currently executive director, Community Leaders Network for Uran Energy and Transportation Corporation. She is a member of the A. M. E. Zion Church, Kansas, Missouri.

Congressman Louis Stokes, U. S. House of Representatives, 11th District, Ohio. He is a member of St. Paul A. M. E. Zion Church, Cleveland, Ohio.

Dr. Bernard Anderson, assistant secretary, U. S. Department of Labor, Washington, D. C. He is a member of Big Wesley A. M. E. Zion Church, Philadelphia, Pennsylvania.

The Rev. Dr. Bernard Richardson, dean, Andrew Rankin Memorial Chapel, Howard University; He is a member of the New England Conference of the A. M. E. Zion Church and former pastor of Archer Memorial A. M. E. Zion Church, Windsor, Connecticut.

The Hon. Oscar William Adams, Jr., was an Associate Justice of the Alabama State Supreme Court. He was raised and became a member of Metropolitan A. M. E. Zion Church, Birmingham, Alabama. Succeeding his father, he was chairperson of the A. M. E. Zion Board of Trustees for several years. His father also served as secretary, Department of Church Extension of the A. M. E. Zion Church. His mother was a retired school teacher and was active in the district and conference Missionary Society.

The Hon. Adele M. Riley, judge, Montgomery County Court of Common Pleas, Dayton, Ohio. She is a member of St. Paul A. M. E. Zion Church, Dayton, Ohio.

The Hon. Paul Armstrong, assemblyman, Tennessee State Legislature. He is a member of First A. M. E. Zion Church, Knoxville, Tennessee.

Dr. William James Lord Wallace, distinguished president, West Virginia State College from 1953-73. Governor Arch Moore awarded him the Distinguished Service Award; and Gov. Jay Rockefeller awarded him the Distinguished West Virginian Certificate. Dr. Wallace was a graduate of Livingstone College. He was a son of a minister, pastor,

Appendix C

teacher, and General Officer of the A. M. E. Zion Church—Dr. Thomas W. Wallace. His mother was Mrs. Loretta J. Wallace. Dr. Wallace died April 26, 1997. Funeral services were held at Ferrell Hall Institute, West Virginia State Coll ege, West Virginia. He was eulogized by Bishop Marshall H. Strickland, presiding bishop of the Allegheny Conference, A. M. E. Zion Chuch.

The Hon. John Bonner Duncan, Esq., Recorder of Deeds, District of Columbia, 1952-61; appointed commissioner, District of Columbia, by President John F. Kennedy, July, 1961; appointed assistant to the secretary, U. S. Department of the Interior for Urban Relations, 1967. He was a member and trustee of John Wesley A. M. E. Zion Church, Washington, D. C. He was funeralized from the same church June 25, 1994. He was a life-long member of the A. M. E. Zion Church, son of the late Lena Jordan and Samuel E. Duncan, who was born in Springfield, Kentucky, February 6, 1910. He was a brother of the late Dr. Samuel E. Duncan, former president, Livingstone College, and Mrs. Elizabet Duncan Koontz.

Mrs. Elizabeth Duncan Koontz, former director, U. S. Department of Labor, Women's Bureau, in the Nixon adminstration; and president, National Education Association, 1965.

The Rev. William L. Wainwright, elected member from Havelock, North Carolina to the House of Delegates, State of North Carolina. He resides in Havelock, North Carolina. He also is presiding elder, New Bern District, North Carolina Conference.

The Rev. John R. Kinard (deceased), director, Anacostia Museum, Smithsonian Institution, 1967-89; and first assistant pastor, John Wesley A. M. E. Zion Church, Washington, D. C.. He was a graduate of Livingstone College and Hood Theological Seminary.

Mr. John H. White, a Pulitzer Prize winning photojournalist. A member of Blackwell Memorial A. M. E. Zion Church, Chicago, Illinois, Mr. White wone the prize for his photgraph "Before the Blessing." He was elected to the Chicago Journalism Hall of Fame in 1993.

APPENDIX D

A. M. E. ZION CHURCH MEMBERS ELECTED TO THE HOWARD UNI-VERSITY BOARD OF TRUSTEES

The Hon. Frederick Douglass, member of the New Bedford A. M. E. Zion Church (now Douglass Memorial), Second Street, New Bedford, Massachusetts, in 1838; recorder of deeds, District of Columbia, 1881-86; served on the Howard University Board of Trustees from 1870-1895. (Moorland-Spingarn Research Center)

Bishop Alexander Walters, 24th Bishop of the A. M. E. Zion Church, served on the Howard University Board of Trustees from 1916-1917. He was a founding member and first president of the Pan-African Association; a founding member of the National Association for the Advancement of Colored People (NAACP); president of the National Colored Democratic League; and assisted in the election of Woodrow Wilson as president of the U. S. In 1912, and in 1915, President Willson offered Bishop Walters the post of Minister to Liberia, which Walters declined. He was administrative council member of the Federal (now National) Council of Churches; and a trustee of the International Society of Christian Endeavor. In 1916, he succeeded Bishop James Hood as senior bishop of the denomination.

The Rev. Dr. Thaddeus Garrett, presidential advisor to Presidents Gerald R. Ford, Ronald Reagan, and George Bush; elected member of the Ohio State Board of Education, 1972-1980; and chairperson emeritus, Howard University Board of Trustees, 1984-97 as a member and from 1995-97 as chairperson; currently visiting professor, Harvard University Kennedy School of Political Affairs, Cambridge, Massachusetts; A. M. E. Zion minister; member, Ohio Annual Conference and assistant pastor, Wesley Temple A. M. E. Zion Church, Akron, Ohio.

APPENDIX E

THE NATIONAL A. M. E. ZION CHURCH BICENTENNIAL OBSERVANCES
OCTOBER 10-13, 1996

The following facsimile pages highlight the activities of the A. M. E. Zion Church during the national bicentennial ovservances in New York City, October 10-13, 1996. The pages are reproduced from the specially prepared brochure, *A. M. E. Zion Church, 1796-1996 Bicentennial, October 10-13, 1996, New York, New York: Celebrating a Legacy of Liberation, The Program & Souvenir Journal.*

PROFILE OF MOTHER A. M. E. ZION CHURCH:
GIVING BIRTH TO A VISION

The history of the Mother African Methodist Episcopal Zion Church, its growth and development, is one of the remarkable stories of American history. In 1776, a group of free and enslaved black men - along with James Varick, walked out of the John Street. Methodist Church to establish a separate Black church called Zion.

From its humble beginnings in a stable, on Cross Street, the growing congregation worshipped until 1800, when the construction of the first church built by and expressly for persons of African descent was completed. From that point forward, Zion Church played a critical role in every aspect of African-American life in early New York City.

Many societies and organizations, founded to assist and improve the condition of the Negro and Mother Zion, played a key role in that process. In 1808, William Miller, one of Mother Zion's trustees, was the first President of The New York African Society for Mutual Relief. In 1817, New York African Bible Society would also be established in his home.

On July 22, 1820, Zion Church withdrew from the Methodist Episcopal Church at John Street. The following year, the first Annual Conference was held at Mother Zion. James Varick was elected Zion's first Bishop and is thereby considered its founder. Leven Smith was appointed the first pastor of Mother Zion.

Mother Zion was one of the earliest and most vocal opponents of slavery and championed the Abolitionist Movement. "Freedom's Journal" the first Negro newspaper was published and operated from the basement of Mother Zion from May 1827 through May 1828.

The nurturing of great men and women is another of Mother Zion's legacies:

Sojourner Truth transferred her membership from the John Street Methodist Episcopal Church to Zion Church in 1827. It was at the altar of Mother Zion that she changed her name from Isabella Brumfree and was reunited with her sisters who had been separated during slavery. She would become one of the country's leading voices for women's rights, equal rights, and the abolition of slavery.

Christopher Rush, Zion's second Bishop, was founder and first president of the Phoenix

Giving Birth to a Vision

Society in 1833. This society was considered the most progressive and democratic organization in the country at that time. It was inter-racial, pro-women's rights, provided for adult education, established a high school for boys and girls, a library, and a work training and placement center.

Many of the early bishops, including Varick, Rush, William Haywood Bishop, and J. J. Clinton, were noted for their social action. They promoted organizations and societies within the church to provide literacy and educational training for its members during the preemancipation era.

The African Wilbeforce Benevolent Society of New York and the African Clarkson Associations were formed to fight for justice, equality, and dignity for all men. These organizations were forerunners of the Urban League and the National Association for the Advancement of Colored People. Here again, Zion played a significant leadership role.

Throughout history, each of Mother Zion's early churches had a school attached.

The large numbers of slaves, who escaped north to New York City, knew they could find refuge and assistance at Zion Church, which later became known as "Freedom's Church." At the West Tenth and Bleecker Street location, the African Dorcas Society was founded expressly to provide aid to the escaped slave. Mother Zion proved to be an important station on the Underground Railroad, conducted by Harriet Tubman.

In 1864, under the editorial leadership of Rev. Singleton Jones and William Howard Day, Mother Zion established the "Zion Standard and Weekly," which was purchased from the church by the General Conference in 1868. After many name changes, the paper became known as the "Star of Zion" in 1876.

During 1870 the first split occurred in the church following the dissatisfaction between some of the church leaders and the pastor. Rev. William Frederick Butler established the St. Marks Methodist Episcopal Church located at W. 137th Street and St. Nicholas Avenue.

The nineteenth century for Mother Zion had been one of exciting and explosive growth. Many of our well known twentieth century institutions had their beginnings in the previous century.

African Methodist Episcopal Zion Church

Rev. Joseph Sulla Cooper moved the Church to 127 West 89th Street; the church's last downtown location. In 1896, the Centennial Celebration for the denomination was held at that address. Noted Black activists, political and religious leaders of the day were all present. Zionite Frederick Douglass, a licensed, local preacher, gave many fiery speeches and sermons from Zion's pulpits.

The city's continual northward expansion made it necessary for the church to move again. The move to West 136th Street came at an exciting time in the history of Black residents in New York City. The Harlem Renaissance was on the horizon and Mother Zion would soon play an important role in a new Black community, not only as a religious institution, but as a cultural and civic institution (that community, of course, is the Village of Harlem).

In 1913 a second split occurred in the church when the pastor was charged with insubordination and approximately 200 to 300 members left the church. The church was heavily in debt and almost lost all of its property. Rev. James Walter Brown was appointed pastor and moved the church to the Church of the Redeemer at 151-153 West 136th Street. The church again experienced rapid growth. By 1919 the church had completely outgrown those facilities and Mr. George W. Foster Jr., a Black architect, designed an impressive neogothic cathedral house of worship. In 1925 the congregation moved into its present location at West 137th Street.

Under Pastors (Bishop) James Walter Brown, Dr. B. C. Robeson, and (Bishop) Alfred G. Dunston, Jr., the church membership grew in excess of 6,000 members. During the recent pastorate of Rev. Dr. George W. McMurray, the church continued with a social agenda in the building of the James Varick Community Center.

Currently, Rev. Dr. Alvin T. Durant is pastor and the church is once again on the move. This year (1996), along with Zion congregations around the world, we are celebrating 200 years of Christian service as Zion Methodists.

INTERNATIONAL WELCOME RECEPTION
THURSDAY OCTOBER 10, 1996
RYE TOWN HILTON HOTEL
RYE BROOK, NEW YORK
2:00 P.M.

The Call to Order

Bishop George W. C. Walker, Sr.
Host Bishop and General Chairman
A.M.E. Zion Bicentennial Commission

The Invocation

Rev. Dr. Patricia A. Tyson, Pastor,
St. Frances A. M. E. Zion Church
Port Chester, New York

The Greetings

Rev. Dr. Alvin T. Durant, Host Pastor,
Mother A. M. E. Zion Church

Bishop Richard K. Thompson,
President, Board of Bishops
A. M. E. Zion Church

Bishiop Cecil Bishop,
Senior Bishop,
A. M. E. Zion Church

The Acknowledgments/Announcements

Mr. Andra' R. Ward,
Executive Director
A.M.E. Zion Bicentennial Commission, Inc.

The Entertainment

Imani African Dancers
Greater Centennial A. M. E. Zion Church,
Mount Vernon, New York

The Reception Hors d'oeuvers
Courtesy of Kraft Foods, Inc.

PROFILE: BISHOP MCKINLEY YOUNG

Bishop McKinley Young is the President of the Council of Bishops, 1996-1997, and is also the Ecumenical and Urban Affairs Officer for the A.M.E. Church.

Bishop Young was born and raised in Atlanta, Georgia. He received his Bachelor of Arts degree from Morris Brown College. He then attended the Andover Newton Theological School where he received his Master of Divinity Degree. He has also received a Master of Arts degree from the University of Chicago Divinity School.

Bishop Young has been a pastor in the A.M.E. Church for over 30 years where he first was a minister at the Fountain Memorial A.M.E. Church. He then was a Minister at Bethel A.M.E. Church in Providence, RI from 1968-1969. His ministry then moved to Chicago where he was an Assistant Minister at the Coppin A.M.E. Church (1969-1971), a Minister at the Greater St. Paul A.M.E. Church (1971-1972), Senior Minister at the Carey Tercentenary A.M.E. Church (1972-1977), and Senior Minister at the Ebenezer A.M.E. Church in Evanston, IL from 1977-1980. He then continued his ministry as Senior Minister at the Big Bethel A.M.E. Church in Atlanta, Georgia from 1980-1992. He was elected the 109th Bishop of the A.M.E. Church in 1992 and has served as Presiding Bishop, 15th Episcopal District, Chair, The Commission on Women in Ministry from 1992-1996. He is presently serving as Ecumenical and Urban Affairs Officer and the Endorsing Agent for all Chaplains in the A.M.E. Church.

His special ministries include President, Council of Bishops, June 1996-1997, and Chair, Commission on Missions, A.M.E. Church, 1992-1996. He is also one of the founders and second President of Concerned Black Clergy (CBC) - an Interracial, Interdenominational, Interfaith and Ecumenical fellowship of more than 65 Atlanta Congregations.

Bishop Young has served as President of Evanston Ecumenical Action Council (EEAC) and the Christian Council of Metropolitan Atlanta. He is also a member, Board of Trustees, Turner Theological Seminary at I.T.C. Atlanta and R.R. Wright Theological Seminary, Evaton, Republic of South Africa.

He is also Co-Chair/Chair, Atlanta Police Civilian Review Board, a member of the Georgia Housing Trust Fund for the Homeless and has led members of the 15th District in the Centennial Celebration of The African Methodist Episccopal Church in Southern Africa. As Secretary of the Council of Bishops and Presiding Bishop of the 15th District, Bishop Young has traveled to Luanda, Angola where a reported 12,000 members of the Angolan Independent Methodist Church joined the A.M.E. Church and

Profile: Bishop McKinley Young

became the Angola Annual Conference of the 15th District A.M.E. Church.

A lively and vibrant faith propelled McKinley Young from the pulpit of historic Big Bethel A.M.E. Church, Atlanta to the Episcopacy. As a Pastor and Bishop in the African Methodist Episcopal Church, McKinley Young has encouraged the church to underwrite its dreams and support its mission and community commitments without excuses. The 45th Quadrennial Session of the General Conference of the A.M.E. Church appointed Bishop Young as the Ecumenical and Urban Affairs Officer of the African Methodist Episcopal Church thereby giving Bishop Young a National and International platform to represent the Global Witness and Minstries of the A.M.E. Church in the Ecumenical, Interfaith, Urban and Institutional context.

Bishop Young is married and is the father of three daughters and one granddaughter.

African Methodist Episcopal Zion Church

ECUMINICAL WORSHIP SERVICE
THURSDAY OCTOBER 10, 1996
MOTHER AME ZION CHURCH
HARLEM, NEW YORK
7:30 PM

Bishop Marshall H. Strickland,I Presiding

THE ORDER OF SERVICE

THE PRELUDE   Dr. Joseph L. Knight

*THE PROCESSIONAL *"GOD OF OUR FATHERS, WHOSE ALMIGHTY HAND"*
Daniel Roberts
Verse 1. God of our fathers, whose almighty hand, leads forth in beauty all the starry band. Of shining worlds in splendor through the skies, Our grateful songs before Thy throne arise.

Verse 2. Thy love divine hath lead us in the past in this free land, by Thee our lot is cast; Be Thou our ruler, Guardian, Guide, and stay; Thy word our law, Thy paths our chosen way.

Verse 3. From war's alarms, from deadly pestilence, Be Thy strong arm our ever sure defense; Thy true religion in our hearts increase, Thy bounteous goodness nourish us in peace.

Verse 4. Refresh Thy people on their toil-some way; Lead us from night to never ending day; Fill all our lives with love and grace divine, And glory, laud, and praise be ever Thine. AMEN.

*THE CALL TO WORSHIP   Bishop Marshall H. Strickland,I

M: This is the day which the Lord has made: let us rejoice and be glad in it

P: THIS IS NONE OTHER THAN THE HOUSE OF GOD AND THIS IS THE GATE OF HEAVEN

Ecumenical Worship Service

M: The hour is coming and now is when the true worshipers will worship the Father in spirit and truth, for such the Father seeks to worship Him

P: ENTER HIS GATES WITH THANKSGIVING, AND HIS COURTS WITH PRAISE! GIVE THANKS TO HIM, BLESS HIS NAME. AMEN.

*THE INTROIT

THE INVOCATION   Bishop John H. Miller
Lord of life and love, help us to worship thee in the holiness of beauty, that some beauty of holiness may appear in us. Quiet our souls in thy presence with the stillness of a wise trust. Lift us above dark moods, and the shadow of sin, that we may find thy will for our lives, through Jesus Christ our Lord. AMEN.

THE CHORAL RESPONSE   *"THE LORDS PRAYER"*
New York Conference Mass Choir

THE OCCASION/GREETING   Bishop J. Clinton Hoggard

* THE HYMN OF PRAISE   *"O GOD, OUR ROCK AND OUR SALVATION"*
Bishop Joseph Johnson

(Lyrics by Mrs. Dorothy S. Johnson to the tune of God of Grace and God of Glory)

Verse 1. O God, Our Rock and our Salvation Two hundred years you've heard our cries. Without your love, We would have faltered; Thou art ever by our side. gracious Master, Zion doth praise thee, For Thy great and steadfast love, For Thy great and steadfast love.

Verse 2. Lift our minds to lofty places, Give us visions of will. Lead us in Thy righteous pathways, Till our hearts with rapture thrill. Blessed Saviour, Zion doth praise Thee For Thy great and saving grace, For Thy great and saving grace.

Verse 3. Guard our life 'gainst evil forces, Arm us with Thy power divine. Spark our zeal to fight for freedom, Till sin's wars all be confined. Strong Deliverer, Zion doth praise thee For Thy mighty, sure defense, For Thy might, sure defense

Verse 4. O God, Our Rock and Our Salvation, Grant that Zion may ever be true. Till her march on earth is ended, Safe on high, in Zion with you. King Eternal Zion doth praise Thee For Thine Everlasting love, For Thine everlasting love. AMEN.

African Methodist Episcopal Zion Church

*THE RESPONSIVE READING   Bishop Ruben L. Speaks

"NATION" Deut 6:4-9,11-13

L: Hear, O Israel: The Lord our God is one Lord:

P: And thou shalt love the lord the God, with all thine heart, and with all thy soul, and with all thy might

L: And these words, which I command thee this day, shall be in thine heart

P: And thou shalt teach them diligently unto thy children, and shalt talk of them when thou sitteth in thine house, and when thou liest down, and when thou risest up.

L: And thou shalt bind them for a sign upon thine hand, and they shall be as frontlets between thine eyes.

P: And thou shalt write them upon the posts of thy houses, and on thy gates

L: And houses full of good things, which thou fillest not, and wells digged, which thou diggest not, and vineyards and olive trees which thou plantest not; when thou shalt have eaten and be full;

P: Then beware lest thou forget the Lord, which brought thee forth out of the land of Egypt, from the house of bondage.

All: Thou shalt fear the Lord thy God, and serve Him, and Shalt swear by his name.

*THE GLORIA PATRI:
Glory be to the Father, and to the Son, and to the Holy Ghost, As it was in the beginning, is now and ever shalt be, world without end. AMEN. AMEN.

THE ANTHEM   *"LET MOUNT ZION REJOICE"*   J. B. Herbert
                                          The New York Conference Choir

582

African Methodist Episcopal Zion Church

THE AFFIRMATION OF FAITH: The Apostles Creed

Bishop Nathaniel Jarrett, Jr.

WHERE THE SPIRIT OF THE LORD IS, THE ONE TRUE CHURCH, APOSTOLIC AND UNIVERSAL, IN WHOSE HOLY FAITH LET US NOW REVERENTLY AND SINCERELY DECLARE:

I believe in God the Father Almighty, maker of heaven and earth; And in Jesus Christ, His only Son, our Lord; Who was conceived by the Holy Ghost, Born of the Virgin Mary, suffered under Pontius Pilate; Was crucified dead and buried; The third day He arose from the dead; He ascended into heaven, And sitteth on the right hand of God, the Father Almighty; From thence He shall come to judge the quick and the dead. I believe in the Holy Ghost, The Holy Catholic Church, the Communion of Saints, the Forgiveness of sins, the Resurrection of the body; And the life everlasting. AMEN.

THE DOXOLOGY   PRAISE GOD FROM WHOM ALL BLESSINGS FLOW

THE OLD TESTAMENT LESSON Psalm 33   Bishop S. Chuka Ekemam, Sr.

THE EPISTLE   I Corinthians 12:12-27   Bishop Enoch B. Rochester

THE GOSPEL   Matthew 16:13-20   Bishop Clarence Carr

THE CHORAL RESPONSE   New York Conference Choir

God be merciful unto us and bless us, And cause His face to shine upon us.
That Thy way maybe known upon earth. Thy saving health among all nations. AMEN.

THE PRAYER HYMN   "GUIDE ME O THOU GREAT JEHOVAH"

THE EVENING PRAYER   Bishop Milton A. Williams, Sr.

ECUMENICAL GREETINGS (PLEASE LIMIT TO TWO MINUTES)

Rev. Clifton Kirkpatrick, Stated Clerk, Presbyterian Church, USA

Bishop Earnest S. Lyght, Resident Bishop, New York, United Methodist Church

Dr. Norman Dansfield, President of New Brunswick Theological Seminary

The Right Reverend R. O. Bass Presiding Prelate,

Christian Methodist Episcopal Church

THE OFFERING APPEAL   Bishop George E. Battle, Jr.

African Methodist Episcopal Zion Church

*THE OFFERTORY   *"ALL THINGS COME OF THEE"*

THE CHORAL SELECTION   The New York Conference Choir

ECUMENICAL GREETINGS (continued) (PLEASE LIMIT TO TWO MINUTES)

Rev. Dr. Calvin O. Butts, Pastor, Abyssinian Baptist Church

Rev. Michael Lemmon, Executive Director, Congress of National Black Churches

Rev. Dr. Joan B. Campbell, General Secretary, National Council of Churches

Dr. Charles Yrigoyen, General Secretary, World Methodist Historical Society

THE RESPONSE TO THE ECUMENICAL GREETINGS
Dr. Adlise I. Porter, General President
A.M.E. Zion Woman's Home And
Overseas Missionary Society

THE CHORAL SELECTION   The New York Conference Choir

THE INTRODUCTION OF THE PREACHER   Bishop George W. C. Walker, Sr.

THE HYMN OF MEDITATION   "O THOU IN WHOSE PRESENCE"
Verse 1. O Thou in whose presence my soul takes delight, On whom in affliction I call
My comfort by day, and song in the night, My hope, my salvation, my all!

Verse 2. Where dost Thou dear Shepherd, resort with Thy sheep, To feed them in pastures of love? Say why in the valley of death should I weep, Or alone in this wilderness rove?

Verse 3. O why should I wander an alien from Thee, Or cry in the desert for bread? Thy foes will rejoice when my sorrows they see, And smile at the tears I have shed.

Verse 4. Restore, my dear Saviour, the light of Thy face; Thy soul-cheering comfort impart; And let the sweet tokens of pardoning grace Bring joy to my desolate heart.

Verse 5. He looks! and ten thousands of angels rejoice, And myriads wait for his word; He speaks and eternity, filled with His voice, Re-echoes the praise of the Lord. AMEN.

Ecumenical Worship Service

THE BICENTENNIAL ECUMENICAL SERMON

The Right Reverend McKinley Young
President and Ecumenical Officer
African Methodist Episcopal Church -
Council of Bishops

THE INVITATION TO CHRISTIAN DISCIPLESHIP   Bishop Cecil Bishop

THE INVITATIONAL HYMN   "JUST AS I AM"   Charlotte Elliott

REMARKS/ ANNOUNCEMENTS

THE BENEDICTION   Bishop Richard K. Thompson

THE RECESSIONAL HYMN "MINE EYES HAVE SEEN THE GLORY OF THE LORD"

Julia Ward Howe

Verse 1. Mine eyes have seen the glory of the coming of the Lord; He is trampling out the vintage where the grapes of wrath are stored; He hath loosed the fateful lighting of His terrible swift sword; His truth is marching on.

Verse 2. I have seen Him in the watch-fires of a hundred circling camps; They have built Him an alter in the evening dews and damps; I can read His righteous sentence by the dim and flaring lamps; His day is marching on.

Verse 3. He has sounded forth the trumpet that shall never call retreat; He is sifting out the hearts of men before the judgment seat; O be swift my soul to answer Him; be jubilant my feet, While God is marching on.

Verse 4. In the beauty of the lilies Christ was born across the sea, With a glory in His bosom that transfigures you and me; As He died to make men holy, let us die to make men free, Our God is marching on.

Refrain — Glory! Glory! Hallelujah! Glory! Glory! Hallelujah! Glory! Glory! Hallelujah! His truth is marching on. AMEN.

THE BICENTENNIAL FORUM & PANEL DISCUSSION
FRIDAY OCTOBER 11, 1996
THE RYE TOWN HILTON, RYE BROOK, NEW YORK
9:00 AM

This forum will attempt to examine some issues and concerns of our church and society which have historically affected our church and which will determine our framework for ministry as we approach the Twenty-First Century.
The following topics will be presented for discussion:

"The Freeman's Church For Today"
Presenter: Rev. Dr. Bernard Sullivan
Pastor, St. Stephens A. M. E. Zion Church
Gastonia, North Carolina
Director of Health and Social Concerns -
A. M. E. Zion Church

"God Gave Me A Song" - Womanist Theology and Voice"
Presenter: Rev. Natalie Wimberly Pastor,
Wesley Chapel A. M. E. Zion Church
Greenville, Kentucky

"The Thrust for Theological Education"
Presenter: Rev. Reginald Broadnax
Pastor, St. Mark A.M.E., Zion Church
Chicago, Illinois

**"Normality Considerations for a Structuring Ministry
on the Brink of the Twenty-First Century"**
Presenter: Rev. Dr. Richard Chappel
Pastor, Big Zion A. M. E. Church
Mobile, Alabama

"A Holistic View of Missions" Presenter: Dr. Niama A. Quarles
International Coordinator
Mission Advocate Program Department
of Overseas Missions of the A. M. E. Zion Church

"The Church's Approach to Health Issues and Our Social Environment"
Presenter: Dr. Vergel Lattimore, III
Chair of Pastoral Care
Director, M. A. Alcoholism and Drug Abuse
Ministry Methodist Theology School in Ohio

PROFILE: KWEISI MFUME
PRESIDENT & CEO OF THE NAACP

Kweisi Mfume (pronounced Kwah-EE-see Oom-FOO-may) became President and Chief Executive Officer of the National Association for the Advancement of Colored People (NAACP) on February 15, 1996. After being elected to the post by the NAACP Board of Directors in December of 1995, Kweisi Mfume gave up his Congressional seat in the United States Congress where he had, for ten years, represented Maryland's 7th Congressional District. He was born, raised and educated in the Baltimore area, and it was there that he followed his dreams to impact society and shape a more human public policy.

Kweisi Mfume, whose African name means "conquering son of kings", became politically active as a freshman in college. He graduated magna cum laude from Morgan State University in 1976 and later returned as Adjunct Professor, teaching courses in political science and communications. He earned an advanced degree in liberal arts, with a concentration in International Studies, from John Hopkins University.

As Mfume's community involvement grew; so did his popularity. He translated that approval into a grassroots election victory when he won a seat on the Baltimore City Council in 1979. He was later elected to the Congressional seat he held for a decade in 1986.

As a member of Congress, Mfume was active with broad committee obligations. He served on the Banking and Financial Services Committee and held the ranking democratic seat on the General Oversight and Investigations subcommittee. He also served as a member of the Financial Institutions and Consumer Credit subcommittee, the Small Business Committee and the subcommittee on Governmental Programs. During his tenure as a member of the House of Representatives, he was able to focus congressional attention on a broad range of minority business development concerns in the United States. Those efforts included minority business development in federal government contracting, the Personal Communications System (PCS) Spectrum Auction and health care reform. He also served a brief term as Chairman of the Joint Economic Committee.

While in the House of Representatives, Congressman Mfume consistently advocated landmark minority business and civil rights legislation. He successfully co-sponsored the Americans with Disabilities Act and authorized the minority contracting and employment amendments to the Financial Institutions Reform and Recovery Act. He strengthened the Equal Credit Opportunity Act and amended the Community Reinvestment Act in the interest of minority financial institutions. He co-authored and

African Methodist Episcopal Zion Church

amended the Civil Rights Act of 1991 to apply the act to U.S. citizens working for companies abroad. He also sponsored legislative initiatives banning assault weapons and establishing stalking as a federal crime.

Kweise Mfume served two successful years as chairman of the Congressional Black Caucus and later served as the Caucus' Chair of the Task Force to Provide Affirmative Action. During his last term in Congress, he was appointed to a leadership position within the House Democratic Caucus as the Vice Chairman for Communications. He presently serves on the Morgan State University Board of Regents, the Board of Visitors for the United States Naval Academy and on the Advisory Board of the Schomburg Commission for the Preservation of Black Culture. Kweise Mfume is a Life Member of the NAACP. He is Honorary Chair of the Theater for a New Generation Advocacy at Baltimore's Center Stage and is also a member of Big Brothers and Big Sisters of Central Maryland and Parents Anonymous of Maryland. His background in broadcasting includes 13 years in radio; for the last three years, he has hosted local and national television shows.

PROFILE: JYLLA MOORE FOSTER

Jylla Moore Foster is Vice President for Northeastern Area Marketing Operations of the IBM Corporation.

Mrs. Foster's responsibilities include Customer Relationship Management, Customer Responsiveness, International Marketing, Opportunity Management, Recruiting/ Training, External Programs, Communications/Media Relations and Business Partner Alliances. The territory services more than 6,500 colleagues who market IBM solutions to customers in New York, New Jersey, most of Pennsylvania, New England states, Delaware and Puerto Rico.

An 18-year veteran, she has held numerous marketing positions including Branch Manager in both Cincinnati, OH and Los Angeles where she established a very successful business marketing office. Recognized as a key contributor, she has achieved six hundred percent clubs, two Systems Engineering Symposiums and three Golden Circles, IBM's highest marketing award. In 1988, she was recognized with the U.S. Field Marketing Excellence Award and in 1992, the IBM U.S. Leadership Award. She led an IBM Task Force on Women Customers in 1995 resulting in a national marketing segment focused on women customers.

She received a B.S. in Mathematics (magna cum laude) from Livingstone College in Salisbury, NC (1976) and an MBA in Marketing from Indiana University (1978) where she was awarded a Consortium for Graduate Study in Business Fellowship. She was recognized by Livingstone College in 1993 with the "Distinguished Service Medallion" and by Bennett College, Greensboro, NC as a "Belle Ringer" in 1995.

Mrs. Foster is the immediate past International President of Zeta Phi Beta Sorority, Inc. serving from July 1992 until July 1996. This service organization, headquartered in Washington, DC has more than 70,000 members. She established a challenging yet visionary direction for the Sorority with the theme of "World Class Service." During her tenure, she developed partnerships with the American Lung Association's "Open Airways" asthma program, Black Enterprise Magazine, Center for the Caucus on the Aged and the National Council of Negro Women (NCNW) Centers for African American Women. She sustained the "Storks Nest" program founded in 1970 with the National Foundation, March of Dimes, and she established the "Challenge Kids" program with NASA's U.S. Space Camp where more than 75 kids were afforded this educational experience.

Mrs. Foster, a golden life member of the Sorority, participated in the Fourth United Nations World Conference on Women in Beijing, China in 1995 and established a chap-

African Methodist Episcopal Zion Church

ter in Seoul, Korea. She also established a new youth organization for young girls aged 4-8, Pearlettes, and a Male Network affiliate.

Affilations with community service organizations include Life Membership in the Urban League; National Black MBA Association; Corporate Advisory Board of NCNW; Boy's Choir of Harlem Board of Directors; and Corporate Liaison to the Dance Theater of Harlem and the Association to Preserve Eatonville, FL. Previously, she was a member of the Board of the National Pan Hellenic Council, member of the Rotary Clubs of Santa Monica, CA and Cincinnati; Beverly Hills West Chapter of the Links, Inc.; City of Hope, Professions and Finance Associates, Los Angeles; Cincinnati Bicentennial Sponsor of the John Roebling Statue; Big Brothers and Big Sisters Board, Cincinnati; and the University of Cincinnati's ADVANCE Program Board of Directors.

She has been featured in Jet Magazine; Ebony as one of the "100 Most Influential African Americans"; Cincinnati "United Way People"; NIP Magazine; and Minority Business News USA. Her community work has been profiled in news stories across the country. In 1994, she was recognized by Phi Beta Sigma Fraternity with their National Award to a Distinguished African American Woman. She has received keys to more than 25 cities and numerous citations for her contributions.

Mrs. Foster is married and the mother of a six-year-old daughter. A recent resident of Bethel, CT, she maintains her church membership with the New Prospect Baptist Church family in Cincinnati, OH.

FREEDOM HERITAGE GALA DINNER
FRIDAY, OCTOBER 11, 1996
NEW YORK HILTON & TOWERS
NEW YORK, NEW YORK
6:30 PM

Incidental Music

Introduction of the Toastmaster/MC   Rev. Dr. Dennis V. Proctor, I
                                                      General Program Committee Chairman

Toastmaster/Mistress of Ceremonies   Mrs. Jylla Moore Foster,
                                                      Vice President - IBM, Corp.

"Lift Every Voice"

Greetings and Welcome   Rev. Dr. Alvin T. Durant
                                       Chairman, Freedom Heritage Gala Committee

The Invocation   Bishop Milton A. Williams, Sr.
                                                      1st Vice Chairman, A.M.E. Zion
                                                      Bicentennial Commission

Vocal Solo   Mrs. Marva M. Robinson
                                                      Mezzo Soprano
                                                      Wilmington, North Carolina

DINNER SERVED

Presentations & Awards   Mr. Andra' R. Ward, Executive Director
                                        A.M.E. Zion Bicentennial Commission, Inc.

Musical Selection   Jay Hoggard & Ensemble

Greetings   Mr. Robert J. Brown

                                       Freedom Heritage Gala, Honorary Co-Chair
                                       The Honorable Rudolph Guilani Mayor,
                                       The City of New York, NY

African Methodist Episcopal Zion Church

Dr. Bernard Anderson Assistant Secretary,
U.S. Department of Labor

Bishop Richard K. Thompson President,
Board of Bishops A. M. E. Zion Church

Bishop Cecil Bishop
Senior Bishop, The A. M. E. Zion Church

Introduction of the Keynote Speaker   Bishop George W. C. Walker, Sr
Host Bishop & General Chairman
A.M.E. Zion Bicentennial Commission

The Bicentennial Address   Mr. Kweisi Mfume
President/CEO NAACP

Vocal Solo   Ms. Karen Kneger, Soprano
Brooklyn, New York

Acknowledgments

Benediction

TWILIGHT GOSPEL CONCERT
FRIDAY, OCTOBER 11, 1996
MOTHER AME ZION CHURCH
HARLEM, NEW YORK
10:00 PM

CECE WINANS

She has performed on "The Tonight Show", counted with Big Bird on "Sesame Street", guest-starred on Fox's sitcom "Martin" and even appeared in television commercials for Crest and McDonald's. CeCe Winans - one of contemporary music's most acclaimed vocalists - just keeps popping up in unexpected places. As one half of the award-winning duo, BeBe & CeCe, she has garnered unprecedented acceptance in R&B and Christian circles alike.

Since their debut, BeBe & CeCe have earned one platinum record and two gold records, seven Grammy Awards, seven Christian music Dove Awards, five Stellar Awards, and three NAACP Image Awards. Now with the release of her much anticipated debut solo project, *Alone in His Presence*, CeCe embarks on a new chapter in her acclaimed musical career. Cece hopes *Alone in His Presence* will have a universal appeal, crossing the lines of race, color, and denomination. "I just hope that everybody will be reached," she says. "There shouldn't be any boundaries, because worship is worship."

When asked what she would like to do next, what unrealized goal she may have over the horizon, she smiles and shakes her head. "It's nothing new. It's just to do more. To reach more. To encourage others to fall in love with Christ."

WILLIAM E. BECTON, JR.

William Becton, a 27-year old Washington, DC native, began singing in the church, where his musical talents were nurtured and developed through his participation in the Young and Young Adult Choirs of the New Samaritan Baptist Church. In the Fall of 1991, Becton established himself as a songwriter and producer with *He's in the Midst of It All* and *Bye and Bye* sung by the Washington Fellowship Mass Choir and the Columbia Union College Mass Choir, respectively. His position as Minister of Music at

African Methodist Episcopal Zion Church

his local fellowship, Uberty Temple A.M.E. Zion Church, led him to continue sharing his gift of song with the public.

A major turning point in Becton's career occurred in 1994 when he founded WEB Records to produce *Broken*, his first contemporary gospel album. The smash single, *Be Encouraged*, has remained at the top of the charts ever since, and its success as a best-selling album is due to its widespread acceptance on both gospel and R&B radio stations.

At the 1996 Gospel Stellar Awards, he ascended the stage to receive awards for Best New Artist of the Year and Best Urban Gospel Artist. He is also a nominee for a 1996 Dove Awards for Best New Artist and a 1996 Alpha Award for Best Performance by a Group or Duo.

Hezekiah Walker

Hezekiah Walker has made a life out of beating the odds. Born and raised in the harsh environment of Brooklyn's projects, he has risen in his 33 years to found, build, and lead one of the premier Gospel choirs. Ever since Hezekiah and he choir's 1992 debut, FOCUS ON GLORY, and their hit follow up project, LIVE IN TORONTO, the group has established permanent residence at the top of the Gospel charts.

It's only fitting that fresh on the heels of his Grammy Award-winning album, LIVE IN ATLANTA AT MOREHOUSE COLLEGE, Hezekiah and the Love Fellowship Crusade Choir decided to bring their music where it all began with their latest release, LIVE IN NEW YORK...BY ANY MEANS.

My vision is for the choir, the church, and the ministry to reach thousands of souls for the Lord, and just give out what the Lord has given to us," he concluded. "As for myself, I would just hope it could be said that I've lived a life where people could see Jesus in me, and were won to Him through my music, my ministry, and my life.

Also Appearing: Men of Standard

YOUTH & YOUNG ADULTS ESSAY & ORATORICAL EXPOSITION

SATURDAY, OCTOBER 12, 1996
MOTHER AME ZION CHURCH
HARLEM NEW YORK
10.00 AM

The Prelude

Flag Ceremony

Presentation of Colors   The A. M. E. Zion Scouts

Call to Worship

Opening Hymn   *Lift Every Voice and Sing*

Pledge(s) of Allegiance   * Varick's Children and Ms. Nora K. McNeil

The Pledge To The Christian Flag

I pledge allegiance to the Christian Flag and to the Redeemer for whose kingdom it stands. One Savior, crucified, risen, and coming again, with life everlasting for all who believe.

The Pledge To The Bible

I pledge allegiance to the Bible, Gods holy word. I will make it a lamp unto my feet, and a light unto my path. And I will hide its words in my heart, that I might not sin against God.

The Christian Endeavor Pledge

Trusting in the Lord Jesus Christ for strength, I promise Him that I will strive to do whatever He would like to have me do; that I will make it the rule of my life to pray and to read the Bible every day, and to support the work of my own church in every way possible;

The Pledge of Allegiance To The American Flag

I Pledge allegiance to the Flag of the United States of America and to the Republic for which it stands one Nation, under God, Indivisible, with Liberty and Justice for All.

African Methodist Episcopal Zion Church

Scripture Lessons

Old Testament   Rev. Clifford D. Barnett, Sr.
New Testament   Rev. Kathryn Brown

Prayer of Celebration

Musical Selection

Statement of Occasion   Mrs. Autry K. Richmond

A.M.E. Zion Bicentennial Hymn   Mrs. Dorothy S. Johnson

Presentation of Bicentennial Commission & CED Staff   Rev. Raymon E. Hunt
Secretary-Treasurer
Dept. of Christian Education, A.M.E. Zion Church

Reflections and Projections of Contributions   Mrs. Brenda Smith
from Zion to the Arts and Cultural World

Musical Selections   Western New York, Y. P. C. Mass Choir

Recognition of Essay Entries and Presentation for Archives
Rev. George E. McKain, II

Essays & Oratorical Presentations

Recognition of Corporate Sponsor,
Program Participants & Special Guests   Mr. Andra R. Ward
Executive Director
A.M.E. Zion Bicentennial Commission, Inc.

Award Presentation for Essays and Oratorical Presentations
Dr. Helen Scott-Carter

Remarks   Rev. Raymon E. Hunt
Secretary-Treasurer
Dept. of Christian Education, A.M.E. Zion Church
A.M.E. Zion Board Church of Bishops

Closing Song   *"They'll Know We Are Christians By Our Love"*

"The Continuing Goal"

Benediction

LITANY OF CELEBRATION!

LEADER: The African Methodist Episcopal Zion Church stands as a denomination with a firm commitment to God. Born in the midst of struggle, racism, and injustice, it has served for 200 years as the spiritual home for thousands of people of color who needed independence, self-expression and ecclesiastical freedom. We now look back, rejoicing and reflect on the work of God's hand within this denomination.

PEOPLE: O God, we are thankful for your grace, mercy and guidance of a people through the maze of existing in a topsy-turvy world.

LEADER: Mother A.M.E. Zion Church in New York City is the first congregation of the denomination called "The Freedom Church." Now, the A.M.E. Zion Church stands as a monument to God and the result of the labors of persons committed to sharing the gospel without restrictions as they explored uncharted waters. Proudly, we stand today giving thanks and praise for the founders of the A.M.E. Zion Church who began with meager resources and little property.

PEOPLE: We affirm that with God all things are possible. We are witnesses that God has blessed, continues to bless, and provides for the needs of the people. God is a good God. God is a loving God. God is a caring God.

LEADER: This denomination began with one congregation and has grown to 2,145 congregations in 67 conferences in twelve countries.

PEOPLE: O God, we give thanks for the determination of those early members of the Mother Church who persevered in spite of the obstacles.

LEADER: James Varick and others were committed to meeting the needs of the people and led the denomination in by teaching, providing leadership speaking out for justice for people of color.

PEOPLE: O God, let us continue to keep the needs of persons before us as we minister, both as clergy and laity. Enable us to provide meaningful leadership, fellowship and ministry for the furtherance of the Church Universal.

LEADER: A firm foundation is necessary for anything or anyone to stand. For Christians, that foundation is in Christ Jesus, the solid rock, the anchor of our souls. To insure that we remain anchored on a firm foundation requires consistency in studying and obeying the Word, learning the tenets of the faith, understanding Methodism and the doctrines of the A.M.E. Zion Church.

African Methodist Episcopal Zion Church

PEOPLE: We commit ourselves to be faithful stewards of what has been entrusted to us and we pledge to pass it on. We will be disciples, making and teaching other disciples.

ALL: Today, we stand before God, giving praise and thanksgiving. As we celebrate our rich history, we also accept the responsibility to add worthy contributions to this rich legacy. We will also look to Jesus as our example and work for the cause of Christ as long as we have breath. To God Be the Glory!! AMEN. AMEN. AMEN.

Written by Dr. Mary A. Love, Editor, A.M.E. Zion Dept. of Church School Literature

African Methodist Episcopal Zion Church
BICENTENNIAL HOMECOMING
WORSHIP SERVICE
SATURDAY, OCTOBER 12, 1996
OLD JOHN STREET UNITED METHODIST CHURCH
NEW YORK, NEW YORK
1:00 PM
Reverend James McGraw, Pastor

ORDER OF WORSHIP   The Prelude

THE PROCESSIONAL HYMN   *The Church's One Foundation*
Verse 1. The Church's one foundation is Jesus Christ her Lord; She is His new creation by water And the word: From heaven He came and sought Her to be His holy bride; With His own blood He bought Her, And for Her life He died.

Verse 2. Elect from every nation, Yet one o'er all The earth, Her charter of Salvation, One Lord, one faith, one birth; one Holy Name She blesses. Partakes one holy food, And to one hope She presses, With every grace endured.

Verse 3. Mid toil and tribulation, And tumult of her war She waits the consummation of Peace for evermore; Till, with the vision Glorious, Her longing eyes are blest And the great Church victorious shall be the Church at rest

Verse 4. Yet She on earth hath union With God, The Three in One, And mystic sweet communion, With those whose rest is won: O happy One and holy! Lord, give us grace that we, like them, the meek and lowly, On high may dwell with Thee.

THE CALL TO WORSHIP *"Litany of Homecoming Remembrance"*
                                              Rev. Dr. Alvin T. Durant
                                       Pastor, Mother A.M.E. Zion Church
Minister: God has gifted us with memory; exalted and inspiring memory and humbling memory; memories which should make us proud of our faith witness and memories which should make us ashamed of our infidelity.

Congregation: With us in this Holy space is the remembered presence of many others who have gone before us.

599

African Methodist Episcopal Zion Church

Minister: We gratefully celebrate the memory of the saints and believers who have preceded us in worship, praise, and witness upon this holy ground; some whose names are written in the annals of our recorded history, most whose names are no longer remembered on earth but are indelibly inscribed upon the rolls of heaven: such as Peter Williams and Phillip Embury, James Varick and Francis Asbury, Barbara Heck, and a slave known only by the name of Betty; and countless others who lived and loved by faith, and in faith endured to the end.

Congregation: We bless and praise thee, O God for the bold, courageous, and passionate witness of those who have gone before us. Make us worthy of their memory.

Minister: We remember in shame and sorrow the racist attitudes and practices which have emanated from this very place and which still linger and persist to stain the soil of this holy ground and taint our sacred memory; which make separation an essential condition for the exercise of true discipleship; which divide the congregation those who claim a common kinship as children of God; and which both mock and dismember the body of Christ.

Congregation: Stir and inspire us with renewed memory this very hour, O God. Make us remember that by thy grace we are joined one to another; and only by allegiance and obedience to thy word and will, can we be protected against the infectious plague of racism. Compel us to reject hatred in all forms, and drive us to accept, embrace, reflect, and share your love.

THE INVOCATION
Rev. Dr. Carol M. Cox
Superintendent: Metropolitan North District
The United Methodist Church

THE OPENING HYMN *O Zion Haste, Thy Mission High Fulfilling*
Verse 1. O Zion, haste, thy mission high fulfilling, to tell to all the world that God is Light, That He who made all nations is not willing One should perish, lost in shades of night

Verse 2. Behold how many thousands still are lying bound in the dark prison house of sin, With none to tell them of the savior's dying, Or of the life He died for them to win.

Bicentennial Homecoming Worship Service

Verse 3. Proclaim to every people, tongue, and Nation that God, in whom they live and move, is Love: Tell how He stooped to save His lost creation, And died on earth that man might live above.

Verse 4. Give of thy sons to bear the message glorious; Give of thy wealth to speed them on their way, Pour out thy soul for them in prayer victorious; O Zion, haste to bring the brighter day.

Refrain: Publish glad tidings; Tidings of Peace; Tidings of Jesus, redemption and release...

THE SCRIPTURE LESSON
Old Testament: Isaiah 2:3-5
New Testament: Ephesians 4:1-6

WELCOME AND CALL TO CONFESSION   Rev. James McGraw
Pastor, John Street United Methodist Church

THE PRAYER OF CONFESSION (In Unison)
We are people divided, O God of Oneness; and we confess that our divisions are of our own making. We remain silent in our comfort, raising our voices only when we are threatened. We blame others, not ourselves. Even though you have created us in your image, we live divided, creating barriers to wholeness. We are uncaring to the young and old, handicapped and hurt, sick and dying, and any who are of a color or composition different than our own. We confess to you, O God, that we allow ourselves to become instruments of a sick and broken society. Hear us, God. Lead us to be instruments of healing and mending. Hear us, O God, as we cry to you from the depths of our division. In your mercy, grant us forgiveness, lifting us from our sin to a new spirit of hope. Heal our wounded souls, mend our broken lives, give us courage to be your instruments of reconciliation. Make us weavers, O creator God, and Keep us from being one who tears apart. We pray in the name of Christ Jesus, the One whose body was broken so that we might be made whole, your Son and our Savior. AMEN.

THE PRAYER OF THANKSGIVING   Bishop George W. C. Walker, Sr.
Host Bishop & General Chairman
A.M.E. Zion Church Bicentennial Commission

African Methodist Episcopal Zion Church

WORDS OF REMEMBRANCE AND REFLECTION
The Right Rev. Ernest S. Lyght
Resident Bishop, New York
United Methodist Church

Bishop Richard K. Thompson,
President Board of Bishops
A. M. E. Zion Church

Bishop Cecil Bishop,
Senior Bishop A.M.E. Zion Church

THE HYMN OF PREPARATION   *"O For A Thousand Tongues to Sing"*
Verse 1. O for a thousand tongue to sing my great Redeemer's praise, The glories of my God and King. The triumphs of His grace.
Verse 2. My gracious Master and my God, Assist me to proclaim, to spread through all the earth abroad the honors of thy name.
Verse 3. Jesus! The name that charms our fears, That bids our sorrows cease; Tis music in the sinner's ears, Tis life, and health, And peace.
Verse 4. He speaks, and listening to His voice. New Life the dead receive, the mournful broken hearts rejoice, the humble poor believe.
Verse 5. He breaks the power of canceled sin, He sets the prisoner free; HIS blood can make the foulest clean, His blood availed for me.
Verse 6. See all your sins on Jesus laid: the Lamb of God was slain, His soul was once as offering made for every soul of man.

THE BICENTENNIAL RE-ENACTMENT   *"Upon This Rock"*
By Mrs. Jean Bligen
The Cast - Jackson Memorial
A. M. E. Zion Church Hempstead,
Long Island, NY

THE BICENTENNIAL COMMEMORATIONAL HYMN   *"Amazing Grace"*
Verse 1. Amazing Grace! How sweet the sound, that saved a wretch like me! I once was

602

Bicentennial Homecoming Worship Service

lost, but now I am found, was blind, but now I see.

Verse 2. Twas grace that taught my heart to fear And grace my fears relieved; How precious did that grace appear the hour I first believed!

Verse 3. Thro many dangers, toils, and snares, I have already come; Tis grace hath brought me safe thus far, And grace will lead me home.

Verse 4. The Lord has promised good to me, His word my Hope secures; He will my shield and portion be as long as life endures.

Verse 5. Yes, when this flesh and heart shall fail, And mortal life shall cease, I shall possess within the veil, A life of joy and peace.

Verse 6. The earth shall soon dissolve like snow the sun forbear to shine; but God, who called me here below, will be forever mine.

THE DEDICATION SERVICE OF A MEMORIAL PLAQUE

Bishop George W. C. Walker, Sr.

In the name of the Father, Son, and Holy Spirit, we dedicate this memorial to the glory of Almighty God and for permanent commemoration in this church, in loving memory of all the saints of Zion. The memory of the righteous is ever blessed. Give to the Lord the glory due to God's name.

Bishop Ernest S. Lyght

We accept this gift as a sacred trust and shall guard it reverently, in honor of the faithful and devoted lives in whose memory and honor it has been erected.

LET US PRAY

Almighty God our heavenly Father, without whom no words or works of ours have meaning, but who dost accept the gifts of our hands as the tokens of our devotion: Grant thy blessing upon us as we dedicate these gifts to thy glory. May this memorial which we now dedicate, be an enduring witness before all thy people of the faithful service of thy servants. May our lives, being consecrated unto thy service, be joined with thy faithful ones into that building which groweth unto a holy temple in the Lord. AMEN.

THE BENEDICTION

THE RECESSIONAL *Come We That Love The Lord* Issac Watts, 1674-1748

Verse 1. Come we that love the Lord, and let Our Joys be known, join in a song with sweet accord, join in a song with sweet accord, and thus surround the Throne, and thus

African Methodist Episcopal Zion Church

surround the Throne.

Verse 2. Let those refuse to sing who never knew our God; but children of the heavenly King, but Children of the heavenly King, May speak Their Joys abroad, May speak Their Joys abroad.

Verse 3. The hill of Zion yields A thousand sacred sweets before we reach the heavenly fields, before we reach the heavenly fields, or walk the golden streets, Or walk the golden streets.

Verse 4. Then let our songs abound, and every tear be dry; We're marching through Immanuel's ground, to fairer worlds on high, To fairer Worlds on high.

Refrain - We're marching to Zion, Beautiful, beautiful Zion; We're marching upward to Zion, the beautiful city of God.

BICENTENNIAL MASS CHOIR CONCERT
SATURDAY, OCTOBER 12, 1996
MOTHER AME ZION CHURCH
HARLEM, NEW YORK
7:00 PM

Welcome

Processional

PART I

Allelula, We Adore You	Ruby Mann Pool
The Omnipotence	F. Schubert
Praise Ye The Lord	A. Randegger
Lord, I'm Out Here On Your Word	John Work
Ride Up In The Chariot	H. Alvin Green
Great Is Thy Faithfulness	Nathan M. Carter

INTERMISSION

PART II

Lift Up Your Heads	E. L. Ashford
Let Mt. Zion Rejoice	J. B. Herbert
I Will Give Thanks	G. Rossini
Thank You	Richard Smallwood
He's Never Failed Me Yet	Robert Ray
Two Prayers	Arthur Cunningham
Lord Look Down	
We Gonna Make It	

Notation: Special selections from the A.M.E. Zion South Carolina Hymn Choir.

MUSICIANS

Dr. Charlotte Alston	Rev. George Maize, IV
Mr. Milas Armor	Rev. Brian Moore
Dr. Solomon Heriott, Jr.	Ms. Ingrid Faniel
Mr. William Pearson	Ms. Joyce Zimmerman
Rev. Jimmy Allen Thomas	

Acknowledgements & Remarks

Benediction

BICENTENNIAL MORNING WORSHIP SERVICE
SUNDAY OCTOBER 13, 1996
MOTHER AME ZION CHURCH
HARLEM, NEW YORK
11:00 A.M.

LITURGICAL COLOR GREEN: The color of growth is used in the seasons of ordinary time after Epiphany.

Bishop George W. C. Walker, Sr., Presiding

THE ORDER OF SERVICE

Before the service speak to the Lord.
During the service let the Lord speak to you.
After the service speak to one another.

THE ORGAN PRELUDE
"Joyful, Joyful, We Adore Thee"   *Beethoven*   Dr. Solomon Heriott, Jr.

Verse 1. Joyful, joyful we adore Thee, God of glory, Lord of love; Hearts unfold. Like flow'rs before Thee, opening to the sun above. Melt the clouds sin and sadness; Drive the dark doubt away; Giver of immortal gladness, Fill us with the light of day!

Verse 2. All Thy work with joy surround Thee, Earth. And heaven reflect Thy rays Stars and angels sing around Thee, Center of unbroken praise; Field and forest, vale and mountain, flowery meadow, flashing sea, Chanting bird and flowing fountain, Call us to rejoice in Thee.

Verse 3. Thou art giving and forgiving, ever Blessing, ever blest, well-spring of the joy of living ocean depth of happy rest! Thou our Father Christ our Brother all who live in love are thine; Teach us how to love each other lift Us to the Joy Divine.

Verse 4. Mortals, join the mighty chorus which the Morning stars began; Father love is reigning over us brother love binds man to man to man. Ever singing, march we onward, Victors in the midst of strife; Joyful music leads us sunward in the triumph song of life.

Bicentennial Morning Worship Service

THE PROCESSIONAL HYMN: Zion Church Goes Marching Onward

Verse 1. Zion Church goes marching onward, As it serves both God and man; We have come two hundred years now, Facing trials on every hand. God has blessed us Through His grace and power divine.

Verse 2. Sons of Varick, we have struggled, through the years of toils and tears; Men and women of endurance kept the faith two hundred years, Nothing earthly can keep us from serving God. Nothing earthly can keep us from serving God.

Verse 3. May our future still be brighter as we travel on our way. May our youth be ever stronger in their faith from day to day. Happy Zion bound for Canaan's peaceful shore; Happy Zion bound for Canaan's peaceful shore.

* THE CALL TO WORSHIP   Bishop Clarence Carr

Minister: Give thanks unto the Lord, for he is good; for his love endures forever.

Congregation: Let the people of Zion with rejoicing say: His steadfast love endures forever.

Minister: The Lord is our strength and salvation. He has afforded us the opportunity to pass through a time of reflecting, reclaiming, and renewing; And now we can rejoice.

Congregation: Let the people of Zion with rejoicing declare: His grace and mercy has brought us through.

Minister: Worship the Lord and give Him the praise and glory.

Congregation: That we may be drawn to our Savior, Jesus the Christ in intimate fellowship with Him and each other.

All: Let the people of Zion rejoice and affirm our love for Almighty God, And the great things he has done.

African Methodist Episcopal Zion Church

THE CHORAL INTROIT *"The Lord Is In His Holy Temple; let all the earth keep Silence before Him."*

* *THE INVOCATION   Bishop Richard K. Thompson
Do something mighty in us today, Lord. We grow complacent and reticent. We are prone to become overly familiar with holy things, leaving behind awe and reverence and the majesty due Thy Name. Hide great hopes in our souls; Stir mighty visions in our minds; Fan noble desires in our hearts. That more perfectly we may worship thee, and more receptively we may be filled by Thee. Do something mighty in us today, Lord Do it for Thy Name's sake
AMEN.

* THE DOXOLOGY "Praise God From Whom All Blessings Flow"
Old One Hundredth

THE OCCASION/GREETING   Bishop J. Clinton Hoggard

THE MORNING HYMN "O Zion Lift A Mighty Voice" Bishop Nathaniel Jarrett, Jr.

Verse 1. Through Zion's wars we have triumphant come through rough valleys and streams. We've crossed the mountains tall and high and some fell away from their dreams. But all the saints with power prevailed in His strength we have not failed. O Zion lift a mighty voice we have cause to rejoice.

Verse 2. Now we are here through blood sweat and tears we have come thru the night Jesus Himself has cast away our fears and remains in the fight. So plant your feet, stand your ground, His perfect love and grace abound. O Zion lift a mighty voice, we have cause to rejoice.

Verse 3. Joy evermore we serve a risen king who is the brightest And best. Lift holy hands give praise to Him and sing in His name we are blest. Soon things of life shall be past, Zion's goal is met at last. O Zion lift a mighty voice we have cause to rejoice.

* * THE RESPONSIVE READING   Bishop S. Chuka Ekemam, Sr.
A Call To Solemn Worship (Psalm 95)

Minister: O come, Let's sing unto the Lord: Let us make a joyful noise to the rock

608

Bicentennial Morning Worship Service

of our salvation.

Congregation: Let us come before His presence with thanksgiving, and a joyful noise unto Him with psalm.

Minister: For the Lord is a great God, and a great King above all gods.

Congregation: In his hands are the deep places of the earth: The strength of the Hills is His also.

Minister: The sea is His, and He made it: and with His hands formed the dry land.

Congregation: O come, let us worship and bow down: Let us kneel before the Lord our maker.

Minister: For He is our God; and we are the people of His pasture, and the sheep of His hand. Today, if ye will hear His voice.

Congregation: "Harden not your heart, as in the provocation, and as in the day of temptation in the wilderness.

Minister: When your fathers tempted me, proved me, and saw my wilderness.

Congregation: Forty years long WAS I grieved with this generation, and said, it is a people that do err in their heart, and they have not know My ways:

All: Unto whom I swear in my wrath that they should not enter into my rest."

THE GLORIA PATRI
* *THE SCRIPTURE LESSONS

The Old Testament:	Psalms 19	Bishop Joseph Johnson
The Choral Response:	*"Thy Word Is A Lamp Unto My Feet"*	
The New Testament:	Mark 10:17-30	Bishop George E. Battle, Jr.
The Choral Response:	*"Hosanna The Highest"*	

THE PRAYER   Bishop Milton A. Williams, Sr.
THE CHORAL RESPONSE

African Methodist Episcopal Zion Church

THE ANTHEM   Cathedral Choir

* THE AFFIRMATION OF FAITH   The Apostle's Creed
                                                    Bishop Enoch B. Rochester

THE CHORAL SELECTION   Odell Ricks Combined Gospel Chorus
                                                    Mrs. Gracie Hyman, Director

** *THE ANNOUNCEMENTS/REMARKS   Bishop Marshall H. Strickland, I

THE MINISTRY OF KINDNESS OFFERING   Bishop Warren M. Brown

THE CHORAL SELECTION   Living In Faith Ensemble (LIFE) &
                                                    Inspirational Choirs,
                                                    Brother Kevin Allen, Director

THE PRESENTATION OF THE SPEAKER   Bishop George W. C. Walker, Sr.

* *THE MEDITATION HYMN   *"O God, Our Rock and Our Salvation"*
                                                    Bishop Ruben L. Speaks
                                                    Dorothy S. Johnson

Verse 1. O God, Our Rock and our Salvation, Two Hundred years you've heard our cries. Without your love, we would have faltered; Thou art ever by our side. Gracious Master Zion doth praise Thee, For Thy great and steadfast love.

Verse 2. Lift our minds to lofty place, give us visions of Thy will lead us in Thy righteous pathways, till our hearts with rapture thrill Blessed Savior Zion doth Praise Thee for Thy great and saving grace, for Thy great and saving grace.

Verse 3. Guard our lives against evil forces, Arm us with power divine. Spark our zeal to fight for freedom, Till sin's wars all be confined. Strong Deliverer Zion doth praise Thee For Thy mighty, sure defense, For Thy sure defense.

Verse 4. O God, Our Rock and Our Salvation, Grant that Zion may ever be true. Till her march on earth is ended, Safe on high, in Zion with You. King Eternal Zion doth praise Thee For Thine everlasting love, For Thine everlasting love. AMEN.

610

Bicentennial Morning Worship Service

THE BICENTENNIAL SERMON Bishop Cecil Bishop
Senior Bishop, A. M. E. Zion Church

*THE INVITATION TO CHRISTIAN DISCIPLESHIP
Bishop J. Clinton Hoggard

* *THE HYMN OF INVITATION *Just As I Am, Without One Plea*
Verse 1. Just as I am, without one plea, But that Thy Blood was shed for me, And that Thou bidd'st me come to Thee, O Lamb of God, I come, I come.

Verse 2. Just as I am and waiting not to rid my soul of one dark blot; to Thee whose blood can cleanse each spot, O Lamb of God, I come, I come!

Verse 3. Just as I am, though tossed about with many a conflict; many a doubt; fightings and fears Within, without; O Lamb of God, I come, I come.

Verse 4. Just as I am, poor, wretched, blind; Sight, riches healing of the mind-Yea, all/need, in Thee to find, O Lamb of God, I come, I come!

Verse 5. Just as I am! thou wilt receive, wilt welcome, pardon cleanse, relieve; because Thy promise/believe, Thy promise I believe, O Lamb of God, I come!

Verse 6. Just as I am! thy love unknown Hath broken every barrier down; Now, to be Thine, yea, Thine alone, O Lamb of God, I come!

*THE OFFERING Bishop George E. Battle, Jr.

THE OFFERTORY

THE CHORAL ANTHEM *"Hallelujah Chorus: (Messiah)"* George F. Handel

THE RETIRING PROCESSION *"Blessed Assurance, Jesus Is Mine"* Fannie, J. Crosby (1820-1915)

Verse 1. Blessed assurance, Jesus is mine! O what a fore-taste of glory divine! Heir of salvation, purchase of God, Born of His Spirit washed in His blood.

611

African Methodist Episcopal Zion Church

Verse 2. Perfect submission, perfect delight; Visions of rapture now burst on my sight Angels descending, bring from above, Echoes of mercy whispers of love.

Verse 3. Perfect submission, all is rest, I in my Savior am happy and blest, Watching and waiting, looking above, Filled with His goodness, lost in His love.

Refrain - This is mystory, this is my song, Praising my Savior all the day long, This is mystory, this is my song, Praising my Savior all the day long. AMEN.

* *THE BENEDICTION   Bishop Cecil Bishop

THE CHORAL RESPONSE   *"Go Ye Now In Peace & Twofold Amen"*
                                                                           Eilers & Lutkin

THE MOMENT OF REVERENT REFLECTION (Organ Played Softly)

THE ORGAN POSTLUDE   *"Grand Choeur"*   George F. Handel

(*Congregation Standing   * *Seated   * * *Late worshippers may enter)

612

NOTABLE ZIONITES

FREDERICK DOUGLASS

Frederick Douglas was a local preacher, Sunday School Superintendent, Steward, class leader, clerk, exhorter, and sexton in the New Bedford A.M. E. Zion Church before he became a major abolitionist, associating Garrison Sumner, and John Brown.

Frederick Douglass' accomplishments included: Advisor to Presidents Abraham Lincoln and Ulysses S. Grant; Minister to Haiti, U. S. Chief Marshal, and was orator of the day for the dedication of the first Abraham Lincoln Monument in Washington with the President, Cabinet, houses of Congress, the Diplomatic Corp., governors, other distinguished Americans present.

Frederick Douglass was also one of the pioneers of the Underground Railroad. His house on Alexander Street in Rochester, New York, became an important station. He was made the leader of the Underground Railroad in Rochester, superintending all activities, and having contact with agents of the rest of the country.

SOJOURNER TRUTH

Sojourner Truth was an abolitionist and lecturer in the anti-slavery movement. She was born a slave in Ulster county, New York, and named Isabella, Baumfree.

Upon moving into New York City, Isabella attended the class for Negroes in John Street Methodist Church and later transferred to the A. M. E. Zion Church located on Church and Leonard Street (later called Mother Zion). It was at this church that her name was written into fame.

During a religious meeting one night, Isabella rose and announced herself to be no longer Isabella Brumfree but 'Sojourner Truth.' She informed the meeting that the Lord had commanded her to travel throughout the land to declare Truth! She became one of the most effective anti-slavery speakers.

Sojourner Truth was one of the great inspirations to her race as she preached freedom and pleaded the cause of justice for all. After a life well spent in the service of mankind, she died at Battle Creek, Michigan on November 26, 1883.

African Methodist Episcopal Zion Church
HARRIET TUBMAN

Harriet Tubman was the heroine of the Underground Railroad who ferried 316 slaves to freedom. "The Moses of her People" is the title accorded to this woman. In 1821 she was born a slave on the Eastern Shore of Maryland, in Dorchester County, as Harriet Ross.

Harriet joined the A. M. E. Zion Church in Auburn, New York, and devoutly worshipped there until the end of her days. She took an active part in the growth of the Western New York Conference of the A. M. E. Zion Church. One of the final acts of Harriet's life was the purchase of twenty-five acres adjacent to her home. This property was deeded to the A. M. E. Zion Church for a home for the aged.

Today, as homage to Harriet Tubman, an annual pilgrimage is made to her home. People from all walks of life gather together in Auburn, New York to pay tribute to this great Woman of Zion.

BISHOP JAMES WALKER HOOD (M.A., D.D., LL.D)

Born in Kennett Township, Chester County, Pa., May 30,1831; Ordained Deacon, September 2, 1860; Elder, June 15, 1862; Consecrated Bishop, July 3,1872; Died, October 30, 1918.

He was principally self-educated. "His mother taught him grammar, and interested him in the act of public speaking. He delivered his first Abolitionist speech at the age of fifteen years. In this speech he predicted the emancipation of the slaves, and this in the face of Judge Taney's unjust decision (Dred Scott), the Fugitive Slave Law and the Missouri Compromise."

Hood was distinguished for his coolness and deliberation in excitement. He was a great projector of measures in council; a conciliator, a deep reasoner, and a self-sacrificer for the cause to which he was devoted... His Christian integrity stood unimpeached. He was a tireless worker, and of an invulnerable spirit, very discerning, genial and affable in his personal bearing, and kind to friend and foe, aged and young.

"After forty-six years of the highest quality of service in the office of bishop, he yielded up the ghost... His very busy life, his untold sacrifices for his church, rich contribution to the uplift of his race, and his long tenure of service, entitled him to the foremost place among his peers in the advancement of the church of his choice." Hood

Notable Zionites

served 44 active years, being retired by the General Conference of 1916. He died in his home town of Fayetteville, N.C., and was buried in that city after funeral at Evans Chapel.

BISHOP ALEXANDER WALTERS (M.A., D.D.)

Born at Bardstown (Nelson County), Ky. August 1, 1858; Ordained Deacon, July 3, 1879; Elder, April 10, 1881; Consecrated Bishop, May 18,1892; Died, February 1, 1917.

The second youngest bishop elected in the history of our church was a man of extraordinary ability. "At an early age he manifested deep concern about spiritual things. At the age of eight he became a pupil under Mr. Brown of Wickliffe, and at twelve years of age he joined the church." He busied himself in Louisville in early life, removed to Indianapolis, Indiana, and began the study of theology under private tutors. " His wonderful pastoral career embraced Corydon, Ky., Clovesport, Ky., Fifteenth Street (Hughlett Temple, Louisville, Ky., and was made secretary of the conference, and of Zion's Banner, a popular journal of the conference and episcopal district. In 1883 he took charge of the leading Negro Church on the Pacific Coast-Stockton Street (First) A.M.E. Zion church, San Francisco, Calif; then Chattanooga, Tenn., Knoxville, Tenn, Mother Zion Church, New York City, where, as general agent he resuscitated and fully developed the Book Concern, and was the leading factor in local affairs of the city concerning his race....He traveled extensively through European countries, Egypt and the Holy Land," and also Africa.

As a man, Walters was "sympathetic, liberal, conscientious, industrious, affable, painstaking and thorough. As a preacher - scholarly, brilliant, logical, eloquent, enthusiastic, fiery. As an orator - popular, captivating, pleasing and forceful. As an executive - strong, persuasive, parliamentarian, graceful, easy." Participating in all popular movements of the race, he was the best known of the younger black bishops of his day, "a real race leader." As a contemporary leader and social activist, Bishop Walters is credited as being one of the Founding Members of the NAACP movement. Walters was laid to rest at Mother Zion's Cypress Hill Cemetery in Brooklyn.

DR. JOSEPH CHARLES PRICE

Joseph C. Price was born February 10,1854 in New Bern, North Carolina. As a youth, Price exhibited extraordinary talent in the Sunday School of St. Peter's A.M.E. Zion Church of that city. He was first discovered by the Sunday School Superintendent,

African Methodist Episcopal Zion Church

Thomas Battle and later by Bishop W.J. Hood who provided aid for his education at Shaw and Lincoln Universities. Price accepted an urgent appeal of Bishop Hood to become the agent of Zion Wesley School which he and Bishop C.R. Harris were attempting to develop at Concord, North Carolina. While attending The Ecumenical Council in London, it was Price's original intention to spend several months in Europe. However, he returned from England after one year lecture trip with $10,000 above his expenses. The additional funds raised by Dr. Price were used to remove the school to Salisbury, N.C. and the present property was purchased.

The immortal J.C. Price planted the school on a firm foundation, toiling the remaining 11 years of his life to build a creditable race institution. At the suggestion of Dr. Price the name of the institution was changed to Livingstone College in 1885, in memory of the great explorer and missionary to Africa, David Livingstone. Thus, the adeptness of Price, his resonant skill, resolute and sacrificial determination, afford him the place in history as founder and first president of Livingstone College. One historian wrote:

It is doubtful if the nineteenth century produced a superior or more popular orator of the type that enlists the sympathies, entertains and compels conviction than Joseph C. Price. In little more than a brief decade he was known in Great Britain and the United States, both on the Pacific and the Atlantic, as a peerless orator. In 1881 he first rose to eminence as a platform speaker; in 1893 his star sank below the horizon. Yet he was more than orator; he was a recognized race leader, a most potential force in politics, though not a politician, a builder of a great school - a most conspicuous object lesson of "Negro Capabilities." His fame rests not alone upon his popularity within his own church or his own race, for the evidence is conclusive that though unmistakably identified with the Negro, Democratic whites and whole communities recognized his worth, highly esteemed him, honored him in life and mourned him in death.

Livingstone College was growing like a mushroom under Price's leadership. W.E.B. Dubois said that: "The star of achievement which Joseph C. Price, a black boy of those days, hitched his wagon to was the founding of a school for colored youth, a sort of black Harvard. . .
Bishop W.J. Walls states:
During these days, "what the Black Community needed most of all was a wise and unselfish leadership, not only politically but in every walk of life - in education, in religion and in industry. It had developed some of these leaders, but its need was still obvious and most acute when Joseph C. Price grew to manhood...It was as a public speaker that he won distinction and was able to find the means to carry on constructive work along other lines."

HOOD THEOLOGICAL SEMINARY

In his History of the A. M. E. Zion Church, Rev. Dr. David H. Bradley wrote that as early as 1820, Zion Methodism cherished a profound interest in education for the training of Negro preachers. "Unprepared ministers were not welcome even among the Africans of Zion Church, themselves, for they were quite well aware of the standards of preaching." In the early days of Zion Methodism, according to Bishop J. W. Hood, such training was a main activity in the early conferences.

With the founding of Zion Wesley Institute in Concord, N. C. which later became Livingstone College, Hood Theological Seminary emerged as Zion's proud divinity school for the preparing of our ministers. Named after the bishop whose inspiration and dream were vital factors in Zion's venture into higher education, the Seminary received an identity of its own with the erection of its first building on the campus of Livingstone College in 1906. Approximately sixty years later, the Seminary outgrew that building and has since been housed in a new edifice erected on lands adjacent to the college, donated by the late Bishop W. J. Walls.

Hood Theological Seminary has and continues to serve these ninety years as the cradle of Zion Methodism. It is the divinity school where the majority of the seminary trained ministers of Zion received their ministerial education. Hood is not simply a graduate school of religion, but a community of faith in which intellectual discourse and ministerial preparation occur in tandem.

In its beliefs, the seminary affirms the sovereignty of God, salvation through Christ, and the empowerment of the Holy Spirit as the only basis for meaningful engagement with the world. In its objectives, the Seminary adheres to the highest Christian principles, and encourages the members of its community to embody those prindples in their lives; and in its activities, the Seminary advocates excellence as the only acceptable standard worthy of Christian worship, life, and work.

In its attempt to serve Zion effectively, as we move into the next century of church's witness and mission, Hood now offers five programs; three degrees; one certificate, and continuing education. The following are the programs:

A **Master of Theological Studies** (M.T.S.) program designed to offer theological education for purposes other than the ordained ministry;

African Methodist Episcopal Zion Church

A **Master of Divinity** (M. DIV.) program designed to prepare persons for the ordained ministry of word, sacrament, and order;

A joint **Doctor of Ministry** (D. MIN.) program with United Theological Seminary in Dayton, Ohio, designed to offer advanced ministerial preparation for persons in the ministry.

A **Certificate in Christian Ministry** (C. MIN.) program designed to offer substantive theological education to persons in any type of ministry, who may or may not have a baccalaureate degree; and

Continuing Education (CON. ED.) opportunities for persons who are seminary educated but desire to continue their education in order to remain current and relevant in their theological knowledge and ministerial practice.

In conjunction with Livingstone College, Hood, is fully accredited by the Southern Association of Colleges and Schools (SACS), and is a Candidate for Accreditation in the Association of Theological Schools (ATS) in the United States and Canada. It is presently in the second year if its comprehensive self-study in preparation for a full accreditation visit next September. Full accreditation in the ATS will standardize our curricula, give universal acceptance to our degrees, and enable us to participate fully in the arena of theological educators.

Hood Theological Seminary looks forward with excitement to the new century of Zion's witness and mission, and is preparing itself to play a vital role in that future.

Dr. Albert J. D. Aymer
Vice President/Dean
Hood Theological Seminary
Salisbury, North Carolina

EDUCATIONAL INSTITUTIONS Of THE AFRICAN METHODIST EPISCOPAL ZION CHURCH

UNIVERSITIES/COLLEGES

UNITED STATES OF AMERICA

Hood Theological Seminary	Salisbury, North Carolina
Livingstone College	Salisbury, North Carolina
Clinton Junior College	Rock Hill, South Carolina
Lomax-Hannon Junior College	Greenville, Alabama

OVERSEAS

AME Zion University	Monrovia, Liberia, WestAfrica
Hood-Speaks Theological Seminary	Ndon Ebom, Akwa Ibom, Nigeria, West Africa

SECONDARY SCHOOLS AND HIGH SCHOOLS

AME Zion Secondary School	Ndon, Ebom, Nigeria, WestAfrica
AME Zion Secondary School	Mbuko, Oduobo, Nigeria, WestAfrica
AME Zion Secondary School	Ikot Obio, Ekpong, Nigeria, WestAfrica
AME Zion Academy	Monrovia, Liberia, WestAfrica
Zion Secondary School	Angola, Ghana, WestAfrica
Aggrey Memorial School	Cape Coast, Ghana, WestAfrica

SUCCESSION OF BISHOPS
AFRICAN METHODIST EPISCOPAL ZION CHURCH
1821-PRESENT

Bishop James Varick
Bishop Christopher Rush
Bishop William Miller
Bishop George Galbraith
Bishop W. H. Bishop
Bishop G. A. Spywood
Bishop John Tappan
Bishop James Simmons
Bishop S. T. Scott
Bishop Peter Ross
Bishop J. J. Clinton
Bishop John D. Brooks
Bishop S.D. Talbor
Bishop J. J. Moore
Bishop S. T. W. Jones
Bishop J. P. Thompson
Bishop J. W. Hood
Bishop J. W. Loguen
Bishop W. H. Hilliery
Bishop V. H. Lomax
Bishop C. C. Petty
Bishop C. R. Harris
Bishop I. C. Clinton
Bishop A. Walters
Bishop G. W. Clinton
Bishop J. J. Holliday
Bishop J. B. Small
Bishop J. W. Alstork
Bishop J. W. Smith
Bishop J. S. Caldwell
Bishop M. R. Franklin
Bishop G. L. Blackwell
Bishop A. J. Warner
Bishop L. W. Kyles

Bishop R. B. Bruce
Bishop W. L. Lee
Bishop G. C. Clement
Bishop J. W. Wood
Bishop P. A. Wallace
Bishop B. G. Shaw
Bishop E. D. W. Jones
Bishop W. J. Walls
Bishop J. W. Martin
Bishop C. C. Alleyne
Bishop W. W. Matthews
Bishop F. M. Jacobs
Bishop E. L. Madison
Bishop W. C. Brown
Bishop W. J. Brown
Bishop W. W. Slade
Bishop B. F. Gordon
Bishop F. W. Aistork
Bishop E. B. Watson
Bishbp J. C. Taylor
Bishop R. L Jones
Bishop H. T. Medford
Bishop Herbert Bell Shaw
Bishop S. G. Spottswood
Bishop W. A. Stewart
Bishop D. C. Pope
Bishop C. E. Tucker
Bishop J. D. Cauthen
Bishop C. C. Coleman
Bishop F. S. Anderson
Bishop W. M. Smith
Bishop S. Dorme Lartey
Bishop W. A. Hilliard
Bishop A. G. Dunston, Jr.

Bishop C. H. Foggie
Bishop J. Clinton Hoggard
Bishop James Wesley Wactor
Bishop Clinton R. Coleman
Bishop Arthur Marshall, Jr.
Bishop John Henry Miller, Sr.
Bishop George J. Leake, III
Bishop Ruben Lee Speaks
Bishop Herman L Anderson
Bishop Cecil Bishop
Bishop Richard L Rsher
Bishop Alfred Edward White
Bishop George W. C. Walker, Sr.
Bishop Milton A. Williams, Sr.
Bishop Samuel Chuka Ekemam, Sr.
Bishop George E. Battle, Jr.
Bishop Joseph Johnson
Bishop Richard K. Thompson
Bishop Enoch B. Rochester
Bishop Marshall H. Strickland, I
Bishop Clarence Carr
Bishop Nathaniel Jarrett, Jr.
Bishop Warren M. Brown

THE BICENTENNIAL COMMISSION OF THE A.M E. ZION CHURCH, INC

Bishop George W. C. Walker, Sr. - *General Chairman*
Bishop Milton A. Williams, Sr. - *1st Vice Chairman*
Bishop Marshall H. Strickland, I - *2nd Vice Chairman*
Bishop Cecil Bishop - *Chairman of Budget & Finance*

Mr. Andra' R. Ward - *Executive Director*
Mrs. Colleen Y. Butler - *Administrative Assistant*
Mrs. Amelia Montgomery - *Administrative Assistant*
Mrs. Ullian T. Shelborne- *Commission Secretary*

Board of Bishops of the A.M.E. Zion Church

Bishop Cecil Bishop, Senior Bishop
Bishop George W. C. Walker, Sr.
Bishop Milton A. Williams, Sr.
Bishop S. Chuka Ekemam, Sr.
Bishop George E. Battle, Jr.
Bishop Joseph Johnson
Bishop Richard K. Thompson
Bishop Enoch B. Rochester
Bishop Marshall H. Strickland, I

Bishop Clarence Carr
Bishop Nathaniel Jarrett
Bishop Warren M. Brown
Bishop William Hillard*
Bishop Charles H. Foggie*
Bishop J. Clinton Hoggard
Bishop Clinton R. Coleman*
Bishop John H. Miller, Sr.*
Bishop Ruben L. Speaks*

Committee Chairpersons

Rev. Dr. James D. Armstrong
Rev. Dr. Kermit Degraffenreidt
Rev. Dr. Alvin T. Durant
Rev. Dr. Norman H. Hickrin
Mrs. Lula K. Howard
Rev. Raymond Hunt
Rev. Frank E. Jones
Rev. Dr. Calvin B. Marshall, III

Rev. Dr. James E. McCoy
Rev. W. Darin Moore
Rev. Dr. Dennis V. Proctor, Sr.
Mrs. Mary Hopkins-Runyon **
Rev. Dr. Vernon Shannon
Rev. Joan C. Speaks
Rev. Dr. Morgan W. Tann
Rev. Jimmy A. Thomas

The Commission

Piedmont Episcopal District
Rev. Johnson K. Asibuo
Rev. Joan C. Speaks

Alabama-Florida Episcopal District
Mrs. Chiquita V. Lee
Rev. James H. Taylor, Jr.

North Eastern Region Episcopal District
Mr. Marion Seay
Rev. Dr. Vernon Shannon

Midwest Episcopal District
Mr. Edgar E. Atkins
Rev. Gwendol Faye McCaskil

Mid-Atlantic II Episcopal District
Mrs. June Slade Collins
Rev. Kevin W. McGill, Sr.

Mid-Atlantic I Episcopal District
Mrs. Corrie Winston
Rev. John G. Wyatt, Jr.

African Methodist Episcopal Zion Church

Eastern West Africa Episcopal District
Dr. O. N. Ekeman, Atty.
Rev. Dr. Calvin B. Marshall, III

Eastern North Carolina Episcopal District
Mr. D. D. Garrett
Rev. Franklin L. Rush

South Atlantic Episcopal District
Rev. George E. McKain, II
Mrs. Ullian T. Shelborne

Western Episcopal District
Mr. Howard Croom
Rev. Dr. Percy Smith, Jr.

Southwestern Delta Episcopal District
Rev. William C. Bailey
Mrs. Dorothy S. Johnson

Western West Africa Episcopal District
Rev. Bernard G. Crawford
Mrs. Dema S. Nappier

* Deceased
** Retired

THE BICENTENNIAL JOURNAL COMMITTEE

It is a single honor to have been assigned the responsibility of serving our Zion as the Bicentennial Journal Committee for the Bicentennial Celebration of the African Methodist Episcopal Zion Church. We are tremendously happy to greet the "World" upon this historic and momentous occasion.

We feel more than ordinarily indebted to all contributors, who through their sacrificial thought-full and noble efforts, have made this unique presentation possible. We deeply appreciate the greetings and felicitations of Zion's many friends on our 200th Anniversary observance.

Pictured left to right, top row- Mrs. Mildred Ray, Mrs. Delma Marshali, Mrs. Brenda Durant, Ms. Marcella Shelton, Ms. Fay Fagan, and Rev. Seth M. Moulton;

Bottom Row - Dr. E. Alex Brower, Dr. Betty V. Stith, Rev. Vernon A. Shannon, Mrs. Mildred Shannon, and Ms. Eloise Homer.

African Methodist Episcopal Zion Church

INDEX

Rev. Joseph Sulla Cooper moved the Church to 127 West 89th Street; the church's last downtown location. In 1896, the Centennial Celebration for the denomination was held at that address. Noted Black activists, political and religious leaders of the day were all present. Zionite Frederick Douglass, a licensed, local preacher, gave many fiery speeches and sermons from Zion's pulpits.

The city's continual northward expansion made it necessary for the church to move again. The move to West 136th Street came at an exciting time in the history of Black residents in New York City. The Harlem Renaissance was on the horizon and Mother Zion would soon play an important role in a new Black community, not only as a religious institution, but as a cultural and civic institution (that community, of course, is the Village of Harlem).

In 1913 a second split occurred in the church when the pastor was charged with insubordination and approximately 200 to 300 members left the church. The church was heavily in debt and almost lost all of its property. Rev. James Walter Brown was appointed pastor and moved the church to the Church of the Redeemer at 151-153 West 136th Street. The church again experienced rapid growth. By 1919 the church had completely outgrown those facilities and Mr. George W. Foster Jr., a Black architect, designed an impressive neogothic cathedral house of wor-

ship. In 1925 the congregation moved into its present location at West 137th Street.

Under Pastors (Bishop) James Walter Brown, Dr. B. C. Robeson, and (Bishop) Alfred G. Dunston, Jr., the church membership grew in excess of 6,000 members. During the recent pastorate of Rev. Dr. George W. McMurray, the church continued with a social agenda in the building of the James Varick Community Center.

Currently, Rev. Dr. Alvin T. Durant is pastor and the church is once again on the move. This year (1996), along with Zion congregations around the world, we are celebrating 200 years of Christian service as Zion Methodists.

Index

African Methodist Episcopal Zion Church

Index

Black Church, the, xvi, 175, 178, 207, 241, 244, 254, 255, 260, 261; ecumenical and historical heritage, 313-14

"Black Church and Evangelism, The", 255

Black Collegian Magazine, 239

Black Executives in Denominations, Related Organizations and Communions (BEDROC), 175

"Black Experience and Religious Education, The", 246

Black Family Conference, 246

Black Families Ministries Conference, 207

Black Methodist Christian Tradition, 314

Blackman Chapel, Norton, Va., 44, 47

Blackwell, George Lincoln, I, 408-409

Blackwell, George Lincoln, II, 139, 195-98, 200-3, 205-6, 208, 209, 210, 216, 222, 244, 261, 307

Blackwell, Geraldine, 196-98, 203, 245, 246

Blackwell Memorial Church, Chicago, Ill., 202

Blair, Leroy, 258

Blair Street Church, Jackson, Miss., 301

Blake, Eugene Carson, 319

Blake, R. L., 153

Blakey, Durocher L., 133

Blalock, W. E., 257

Blanton, Martha, 68

Blay, Joseph, 91, 92

Block, Joyce, 63

Blue Ridge Conference, 25, 101, 104, 109, 113, 117, 121, 127

Blunt, Howard, 81

Blunt, Kay, 74

Blunt, Pat, 75

Board, Public Affairs and Convention Manager Board, 271-73

Board of Bishops, ii, xi, xiii, xv, 26, 86, 92, 133, 138, 142, 152, 154, 163, 165, 173, 177, 184, 195, 197, 198, 218, 244, 245, 248, 249, 253, 260, 262, 268-70, 274, 285, 305, 321, 322

Board of Brotherhood Pension Service, 184, 188-90, 249

Board of Christian Education, 200, 215, 218

Board of Christian Education Home and Church Division, 199, 218-21, 244

Board of Christian Education School and College Division, 198, 199, 235-37

Board of Church Extension, 249-51

Board of Church Extension and Home Missions, 251-52

Board of the Historical Society, 143

Board of Foreign Missions, 279

Board of the Historical Society, 143

Board of Home Missions, 193-194

Board of Lay Activities, 297, 299, 300, 302-4

Board of Ministerial Relief, 191-93

Board of Overseas (Foreign) Missions, 177, 178, 180-82, 279

Board of Publications, 86

Board on Statistics and Records, 93-95

Boger, James E. 197, 198, 216

Bolton, H. Dwight, 76

Bonner, Harrison D., 35, 36, 255

Bonwell, Rodney (Rev.), 74

Booker, James, 37, 39

Bostic, Alvin L., 60

Boston University School of Theology, 37

Boulware, Marcus Hanna, 59

Bowers, Norma, 45

Boy Scouts of America, (BSA) 199, 240; of South Africa, 217; Membership of

629

African Methodist Episcopal Zion Church

Index

Commission on Audio-Visual Education, 214

Commission on Boy Scouting, 198, 199, 216-17

Commission on Children's Ministry, 197-99, 214-15

Commission on Family Ministries, 199

Commission on Family Ministries and Human Sexuality, 207

Commission on Girl Scouting, 197-98, 217-18

Commission on Pan-Methodist Cooperation, 4, 246, 251, 323-28

Commission on Leadership Education, 197, 209

Commission on Restructuring, 249

Commission on Social Education, 198

Commission on Social Education and Action, 198, 210-12

Commission on Youth Ministry, 197, 198, 203, 213-14

Committee on Church Union, (A. M. E. Zion Church), 320

Committee on Ecumenical Sharing and Networking, 324

Committee on Evangelism (A. M. E. Zion Church), 256

Committee on Uniform Series, 246, 251

Committee on Mission Education, 289

Committee on Literature, 289

Community Church, Vancouver, Wash., 76, 204

Comprehensive Employment Training Act (CETA), 234

Comprehensive Community Services Complex, 224

Concerned Clergy and Laity About Viet Nam, 177

Congress of National Black Churches, 4, 260, 314

Conly's Chapel, W. Va., 258

Connectional Budget Board, 96, 97-98, 128-32

Connectional Congress on Evangelism, 262

Connectional Council, 86, 91, 98, 134, 143, 185, 230, 247, 248, 263, 308-11

Connectional Lay Council, xiv, 2, 124, 159, 230, 261, 262, 297-304, 306; Conventions of, 299; Lay Council Sunday, 299; Lay Institute, 298, Lay Members Council, 287, Board of Lay Activities, 297, 302-4

Connectional Trustees, xiv, 308-11

Consultation of Methodist Bishops, 324; Sixth, 325-28, *See Commision on Pan-Methodist Cooperation*

Consultation on Church Union (COCU), 4, 86, 139, 208, 210, 212, 315, 319, 320

Contee Memorial A. M. E. Zion (Wash. D. C.), 215

Cook, James E., 150, 224, 225

Cook, James E., 150, 224, 225

Cooke, Leonard, 14

Cooper, Coyal C., 298, 299, 300, 301

Cooper, Tom, 233

Cornwall Conference, Jamaica, W. I., 121, 127, 151

Cote d'Ivoire Conference, 161, 162

Council, Mary , 32

Cousin, Philip, 175

Cowan, Creola B. , 316

Cox, Pedro, 155

Craig, Annie , 24, 25

Cratic, Linda, 14, 61

Crawford, G. Bernard, 16

Crawford, Vickie, 47

Crawley, Ola W., 201, 212

Crenshaw, George D., 55

Crittenden House, 239, 240

Crockett, Nero A. , 227

Index

African Methodist Episcopal Zion Church

309; Evangelistic Clinic, 254; First Evangelistic Retreat, 301; First Quadrennial Connectional Congress on Evangelism, 262; Fourth General Evangelistic Convocation, 259; Fourth Quadrennial Evangelistic Convocation, 264; Fifth General Evagelistic Convocation, 261

Evans, Carrie B., 62

Evers-Williams, Myrlie

Ewing, Charles H., 23

Exploring and Your Youth Ministry, 216

Eze, Ipeghan S., 49

Fagan, Vincent G. , 152

Falkerson, Martha, 43

Family Ministries, 199

Families 2000 Conference, 207

Fanuiel, Ingrid, 37

Farley, J. McH., 314

Farrar, C. T., 33

Farrar, Leonia, 27, 28, 33

Faush, Erskine R., 64, 65, 67, 298

Federal Council of Churches, 278, 281

Felder, Cain Hope, 36

Felton, Carroll M, 177, 203

Fentress-Williams, Judy , 36

Ferguson, Francina, 245

Ferguson, Gerald, 224

Ferguson, Rosetta, 24

Ferry, Henry, xv

Fiawoo, E. G., 258

Fields, J. E., 65

Fields, Symanski, 65

Fifth General Evangelistic Convocation, 261; Finance, Dept. of, xiv, 96-132, 133, 185, 186, 187, 234 ; budget allocations: 99-100, 102-4, 106-8, 110-11, 115-17, 119-21, 121-23; con-

ference assessments: 100-102, 104-6, 108-9, 112- 14, 117-18, 121-23,

Findley, J. W., 268

Fine-Country, B. A., 231

First Baptist Church, W. Va., 258

First Church, Bklyn. N. Y.,81, 209, 258, 297

First Church, Los Angeles, Calif., 73, 76, 288

First Church, San Francisco, Calif., x

First Church, San Jose, Calif., x

First Evangelistic Retreat, 301

First Quadrennial Connectional Congress on Evangelism, 262

Fisher Church, Phoenix, Arizona, 76

Fisher, Richard Laymon, 14, 204, 225, 228, 238, 261, 502-503

Flack, C. V., 254

Flame, The, 259

Florida Conference, 109, 117, 122, 127

Flournoy, Diana, 245

Flowers, Sr., Edwin M., 164, 167

Floyd, Bobby D., 205

Foggie, Charles Herbert, 13, 14, 15, 78, 154, 157, 166, 177, 185, 203, 205, 228, 234, 255, 285, 482-83

Foggie, Madeline, 285

Fomby, John, 73

Fonville, P. K., 141

Ford Foundation, 234

Ford, Harriette, 25

Foreign Missions, dept of, 309, *see Overseas Missions*

Foreign Missions Board, 156, 174, *see also Overseas Missions Board*

Forrester, Lester, 23

Foster, Emmett D., 34

Foster, Jylla Moore, 589

Founders' Address, A. M. E. Zion Church, 7-9

Index

African Methodist Episcopal Zion Church

Goler Memorial Church, Winston-Salem, N. C., 179
Goler, William Harvey, 240
Gomoa Akwamu Church, 161
Goode Temple (Lynch, Ky.), 43, 47
Gooden, Lurleen, 43, 47
Goodloe, C. C., 233
Gordon, Buford Franklin, 244, 446-447
Gordon, Horace A., 152, 286, 287
Gordon, Larry, 30
Gordon, Mamie E., 214
Govan, Vertell, 207
Grace (Growing Roots Academically in Christian Education) Project, 204
Graham, Gertrude, 287
Graham, Robert L., 14, 39, 204
Graham, Tecumseh X., 225, 261
Graves, Ollie, 256
Gray, J. C. (Rev.), 33
Greater Centennial Church, Mt. Vernon, N. Y., 38
Greater Faith Church, Richmond, Va.,286
Greater Metropolitan Church, Norfolk, Va.,287
Greater Walters Church, Chicago, Ill., 184
Greater Warner Tabernacle, Knoxville, Tenn., 67, 68, 69, 263
Green, Bertram, 154
Greene, James W., 14, 23, 240
Green, William, 258
Greene, William H. , 239
Greenfield, Wilbert, 239
Greenville High School, 222
Gregory, Coleen H., 31, 32
Gregory, Henry A., 27
Grieg, Edvard, 82
Griffin, Mary, 24
Grimes, George H. , 154, 285

Gulley, Lyrtee B., 73
Gunter, Vivien, 23
Guyana Conference, 102, 105, 108, 112, 122, 127, 156-58, 284, 285
Gwinn, Andrew O., 91, 92

Hackett, David E., 253
Hackney, Carrie, xv
Hagar, Phillip, 301
Hagler, Sr., Howard E., 74, 256
Haigler, Barbara A., 68
Hairston, S. H., 257
Hall, Henry L., 23
Hall, James, 83
Hamilton, Lillian, C. H., 30
Hamilton, William, 11
Hamlett, Lesa (Ms.), 62
Handbook for the Local Historical Society of the African Methodist Episcopal Zion Church, 143
Hannon, Allen, 222
Hannum House (Livingston College), 139, 239
Hardge, Sr., Elias S., 253
Hardy, Dawn, 81
Hargis, James W. 234
Harper, James H., 68, 69, 301
Harper's Dictionary on Christian Education, 246
Harps, Alcenia, 298
Harriet Tubman Home, 104, 107, 111, 120, 125, 183, 259, 614; Annual pilgrimage, 22; Association, 183 Grounds Beautification Bicentennial Project, 301;
Harris, Cicero Richardson, 9, 388-89
Harris, Edwin, 73
Harris, Evelyn, 150
Harris, Jerome, 224

Index

Harris, Keith I. , 73, 75
Harris, Michelle, 75
Harrison, John A., 73
Hart, Edward, 91
Hart, Jacqui, 69
Hart, Raymond C., 91, 92
Hartford, Raymond C., 91, 92
Hartford Seminary Black Ministries
  Certificate Program, 36
Harvey, Eugene, 74, 76
Haughton, Murdell, 286
Hawkins, Doretha, 286
Hawkins, Joyce, 28
Haynes, John W., 91
Health and Social Concerns, Dept. of,
  xiv, 99, 119, 124, 274-76
Height, Dorothy I., 79
Helms, Raymond, 91
Hemphill, Jacqueland, 224
Henderson, Johnnie, 91, 92
Henderson, Michael, 74
Henderson, Sheffield, 279
Hendrix, James E., 65
Henry, Leon, 301
Hensfiled, John, 151
Henson, Daisy, 68
Herald Journal, 245
Herbert Bell Shaw Student Union
  Building, 227
Herbert Bell Shaw Caribbean Student
  Scholarship Fund, 299
Herbert, P. James and Mrs., 172, 173
Heritage Hall, (Livingstone College), xv,
  142, 143, 215
Heriott, Jr., Solomon, 37, 38, 80, 81, 82,
  84
Hewitt, Jr., James E., 299, 300
Heymann, Jimmy, 72
Hicklin, Norman H., 16, 64, 261, 262,
  263, 279. 301

Higgins, Bernice, 287
Higgins, Wilbert, 286
Hill, M. Luther, 42, 286
Hillery, William Henry, 314, 392-93
Hilliard Church, 157
Hilliard, William Alexander, 149, 150,
  154, 156, 157, 158, 163, 164, 166,
  177, 197, 256, 258, 284, 285 478-
  79
Hilliard-Babb Church, Barbados, W. I.,
  285
Hines, Harry, 245
Hinson, Carlos, 24
Historical Society (A. M. E. Zion), 143
*History of the A. M. E. Zion Church in
  America*, xiii
*History of the A. M. E. Zion Church in
  America, A*, xiii
Hitch, Kevan (Rev.), 36
HIV/AIDS, 275
Hoard, Pam, 45
Hodge, Evelyn, 218
Hoggard Church, Barbados, W. I., 154,
  155, 285
Hoggard, Eva Stanton, xvi, 69, 285
Hoggard, Sr., J.[ames] Clinton, xi, xvi, 1,
  5, 13, 14, 15, 37, 38, 67, 72, 78, 81,
  149, 150, 151, 152, 154, 156, 163,
  164, 184, 204, 205, 207, 208, 232,
  258, 261, 285, 286, 287, 298, 316,
  320, 325, 484-85
Hoggard, James [Jay] Clinton, Jr., xvi,
  78, 83
Hoggard, Paul Stanton, xvi, 91
Holden, Evelyn, 207
Holland, Albert, 306
Holliday, Jehu, 396-97
Holligan, Izalene, 154, 286
Holligan, Martin L., 154, 155, 285,286
Holmes, Grace L., 68, 156, 165

Index

Index

Index

Index

African Methodist Episcopal Zion Church

Index

African Methodist Episcopal Zion Church

Index

African Methodist Episcopal Zion Church

Index

African Methodist Episcopal Zion Church

Index

Index

657

African Methodist Episcopal Zion Church

Wesley Center Church, Pitts., Pa., 203, 213

Wesley, John, 46

Wesley Temple, Akron, Oh., 34, 35

Wesley Theological Seminary, 245

West Alabama Conference, 102, 105, 108, 113, 118, 123, 128, 261

West Central North Carolina Conference, 25, 92, 102, 105, 108, 113, 118, 123, 128, 215

West, Cornel, 22

West Africa missions, 282

West Ghana Conference, 102, 105, 109, 114, 118, 123, 128, 149, 158, 159, 160, 163, 164, 170, 202, 283

West-Tennessee and Mississippi Conference, 102, 109, 113, 118, 123, 128, 159

Westerfield, Samuel Z., 163

Western New York Conference, 92, 105, 108, 112, 118, 123, 128, 159

Western North Carolina Conference, 25, 92, 105, 108, 112, 118, 123, 128, 140, 215. 257

Western (Twelfth) Episcopal District, 73-77, 159

Western West Africa (Eleventh) Episcopal District, 71-73

Weston, Kevin, 92

Weston, Perry, W., 91

White, Alfred Edward, 14, 16, 159, 160, 167, 225, 233, 238, 261, 262, 504-05

White, Jr., Ernest H., 92, 306

White House Conference on Aging, 211

White House Task Force for Welfare Reform and Health Care Reform, 275

White, Jerry T., 23

White, Lula B. , 31, 32

White, Mabel M., 28

White Memorial Church (Middlesboro, Ky.), 44, 47

White, Jr., Reid R., 92

White Rock and Soldiers Memorial Church, 255

White, Sr., William M., 225

Whiteurs, Paul, 178

Whitfield, Alphonso, 39

Whitfield, Willie, 298

Whitley, Catherine, 42

Whitley, Edmond H., 42

Whitted, Andrew E. and Mrs., 23, 152, 157, 178

Wilberforce, Wirecko, 72

Wilcher, Evelyn, 196

Wilfred College of Criminal Justice and Law Enforcement Administration, 284

Wilhema Bishop Clinic, Ghana, 175

William J. Walls Church, Lagos, Nigeria, 283

Williams, A, 285

Williams, Annie, 301, 302

Williams, Armonia F. , 75, 76

Williams, B. R., 164

Williams Chapel, Big Stone Gap, Va., 44, 47

Williams, Cynthia, 14

Williams, Donnell , 64, 67, 328

Williams, Farris A., 67

Williams, Leola, 28

Williams, Lillian P., 300, 301

Williams, Lula, xiii, 286, 287

Williams, Lynnard, 80

Williams, Merchuria Chase, 61, 298

Williams, Sr., Milton Alexander, xiii, 13, 14, 15, 41, 78, 160, 162, 173, 199, 204, 264, 285-87, 508- 09

Williams, Milton H., 27, 28

Williams, Nora, 164

Index

Williams, Peter, 11, 48
Williams, Philip, 154, 286
Williams, Samuel Hart, 151
Williams, Sandra, 25
Williams, Spencer, 98
Williams, Vivian, 301
Williamson, Frederick , 62
Williamson, Rosemary , 62
Williamson, William B., 246
Willie, III, C. E., 28, 30
Willie, Earl, 281
Willie, Margaret F., 281, 298, 299
Willis, Cynthia. *See* Cynthia Willis
  Stewart
Wilson, A. L. , 65
Wilson, E. M., 42
Wilson, Marion, R., 91
Wimberly, Doris, 62
Winans, Cece, 592, 593
Winston, Corrie, 16
Winston, Jr., John H., 226, 298, 300, 301
Winston, John H., 226, 298, 300, 301
Winston, Michael, xv
Woman's Home and Overseas
  Missionary, Society, dept. of, 4, 22,
  71, 78,, 149, 150, 156, 159, 160,
  161, 164, 165, 183, 184, 185, 186,
  277-96, 289; Quadrennial
  Conventions and themes, 278, 281,
  287-88; General Officers and
  Missionary Supervisors of, 289-96;
  Life Members' Council Dept., 281,
  284; Mission Statement, 281-82;
  Supply Dept., 155, 245; YAMS
  Dept., 278
"Women of Excellence" Retreat, 286
Wood, John Wesley, 420-21
Woods, Frederick K, 27, 28
Woods, Larry, 68
Woodyard Memorial Building, 231

Woodyard W. E., 231
World Christian Endeavor Union, 213
World Conference of Methodism, 4, 140,
  254
World Consultation and Convocation on
  Evangelism, 254
World Council of Churches, 4, 86, 175,
  177, 178, 205, 314
World Evangelism Institute, 324
World Federation of Methodist Church
  Women, 316
World Future Society, 211
World Hunger Month, 279
World Hunger Sunday, 278
World Methodist Council on Churches,
  4, 86, 205, 207, 254, 268, 270, 315;
  Evangelism and Youth Committees,
  257; Evangelism Committee, 254,
  256, 260
World Methodist Council North
  American Section, 324
World Methodist Evangelism Youth
  Conference, 270
World Mission in Evangelism London,
  U. K., 256
Wormley, Samantha, 300, 301
Wright, Arnold DeCosta, 151
Wright, Edna Earl Jones , 164
Wright, H. T. , 164
Wyatt, Jr., John G., 16
Wynn, Asa, 59

YWCA (Young Women's Christian
  Association), 210, 212
Yale University Divinity School, 37
Yancy, Roberta, xv
Yates, Walter L., 239-41, 254, 257
Yearbook of American and Canadian
  Churches, 86

659